Welcome to Scandinavia

Scandinavia technically refers to the kingdoms of Norway, Sweden, and Denmark, but it more commonly refers to the Nordic region that also encompasses Finland and Iceland. From Norway's breathtaking fjords and Sweden's pristine lakes, to Denmark's castle-dotted countryside, Finland's bear-filled forests, and Iceland's steaming geysers, the region offers endless dramatic scenery and outdoor adventures. Stockholm, Copenhagen, Oslo, Helsinki, and Reykjavík are filled with museums, shopping, nightlife, and award-winning restaurants. Beyond the Arctic Circle you'll find Sami villages, reindeer farms, ice and tree hotels, and the aurora borealis.

TOP REASONS TO GO

★ **Norway:** Explore picturesque harbors, spectacular fjords, and design-forward cities.

★ **Sweden:** Find pristine lakes and forests and a crystal-filled kingdom.

★ **Denmark:** Visit the world's oldest amusement park and wow at viking boats, castles, and odes to Hans Christian Andersen.

★ **Finland:** Shop Helsinki's Design District; cruise the Åland Islands; sweat in a sauna; meet Santa Claus; ski, sled, and sleep in snow.

★ **Iceland:** Swim between tectonic plates; climb glaciers; horseback ride to waterfalls, and relax in the world-famous Blue Lagoon.

Contents

Contents

MAPS

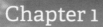

Chapter 1

EXPERIENCE
SCANDINAVIA

30 ULTIMATE EXPERIENCES

Scandinavia offers terrific experiences that should be on every traveler's list. Here are Fodor's top picks for a memorable trip.

1 Bryggen, Bergen, Norway

The colorful wooden buildings of the old Hanseatic wharf in Bergen are a UNESCO Heritage Site, with a history that makes them much more than popular postcard motifs. (Ch. 3)

2 Northern Lights, Finland

In northern Finland, the aurora borealis bathes the sky in mystical hues as many as 200 days a year. Glamp in a glass igloo for the ultimate viewing experience. (Ch. 6)

3 Silfra, Iceland

Snorkeling in the crystal-clear waters of Silfra, a fissure between the North American and Eurasian tectonic plates, is an incredible experience. (Ch. 7)

4 Downtown Reykjavík, Iceland

Home to nearly half of Iceland's population, Reykjavík is the political, cultural, and culinary hub of the country, with events that will delight every kind of visitor. (Ch. 7)

5 Swedish Lapland

With its incredible natural beauty, Lapland offers the opportunity to enjoy a full-on outdoor adventure complete with hunting, fishing, and reindeer sledding. (Ch. 4)

6 Art in North Zealand, Denmark

Home to artists for centuries, North Zealand is also home to some of the country's most spectacular museums, including Louisiana and the Rudolph Tegner Museum and Statue Park. (Ch. 5)

7 The Golden Circle, Iceland

This loop of essential Iceland sites includes Gullfoss waterfall, the Geysir hot spring area, and Þingvellir National Park. (Ch. 7)

8 Hurtigruten Cruise, Norway

The former post and freight boats of the Hurtigruten line have been transformed into modern cruise vessels that take you on amazing voyages. (Ch. 3)

9 Dining in Malmö, Sweden

Enjoy fine dining opulence at the likes of superb two-Michelin-starred Vollmers to a huge selection of delicious, unpretentious street food from all around the world. (Ch. 4)

10 Møns Klint, Denmark

Hike some of Denmark's most dramatic coastline with milky-white chalk cliffs plunging into the emerald sea. Look for 70-million-year-old fossils and a geological museum on site. (Ch. 5)

11 The Snæfellsnes Peninsula, Iceland

This stunning peninsula is sprinkled with waterfalls, golden- and pink-sand beaches, and lava fields, as well as the ice-capped volcano from *Journey to the Center of the Earth*. (Ch. 7)

12 Bornholm, Denmark

Denmark's version of Nantucket lures summer crowds with its foodie scene, rugged cliffs, dramatic landscape, and beautiful beaches. (Ch. 5)

13 Opera House in Oslo, Norway

Oslo has plenty of popular hangouts, but few have the fantastic views afforded by the rooftop of the Opera House. (Ch. 3)

14 Lakeland, Finland

Finnish Lakeland is Europe's largest lake district. Winding canals and other bodies of water are ripe for exploring by kayak or steamboat. (Ch. 6)

15 Flåmsbanen, Norway

The thrilling train ride between the mountain communities of Flåm and Myrdal boasts some particularly scenic views. (Ch. 3)

16 Vatnajökull Glacier, Iceland

Europe's largest glacier (after the Severny Island ice cap) isn't on the mainland but in Iceland. Hike or go dog sledding. (Ch. 7)

17 Suomenlinna, Finland

This epic medieval fortress has several museums, bunkers, the last Finnish World War II submarine, and walls spread over a network of car-free islands connected by bridges. (Ch. 6)

18 Ærø, Denmark

This small island looks like the setting of a Hans Christian Andersen fairy tale with its cobblestoned streets full of hollyhocks and timber-framed houses with thatched roofs. (Ch. 5)

19 Gamla Stan, Sweden

Stockholm's stunning Old Town is a delightful maze of cobbled streets and winding alleyways, and one of the best-preserved medieval city centers in Europe (Ch. 4)

20 Design District, Helsinki, Finland

Helsinki's downtown Design District is a hub of Finnish style, packed with boutiques, ateliers, vintage shops, and galleries. Look for labels like Marimekko, Artek, and Iittala. (Ch. 6)

21 Svansele, Sweden

King of the forest, the moose is one of Sweden's most renowned national symbols. Take a moose safari in northern Sweden to see these majestic beasts safely. (Ch. 4)

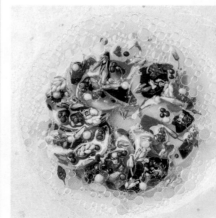

22 The Lofoten Islands, Norway

With mountains, fjords, rugged coastlines, sandy beaches, and lots of farmland, the landscapes of this Arctic archipelago seem the embodiment of Norway. (Ch. 3)

23 Fine Dining in Copenhagen, Denmark

The New Nordic Food revolution started 15 years ago and it's still reshaping Denmark. Noma alumni have opened eateries all over Copenhagen, from taco trucks to Michelin-starred restaurants. (Ch. 5)

24 Sweden's National Parks

Sweden is a hiker's paradise with a massive 730,000 hectares of national parkland spread across 30 different parks, with breathtaking landscapes. (Ch. 4)

25 Visit Santa Claus in Finland

It's Christmas all year long at the big guy's HQ in Rovaniemi where you'll find elves in pointy hats, workshop tours, and the world's cheeriest post office. (Ch. 6)

26 Sauna, Finland

Finns are crazy about their most famous invention. Many have saunas at home and work, and there are also wild versions like a sauna gondola and a sauna Ferris wheel. (Ch. 6)

27 Geirangerfjord, Norway

Geiranger is Norway's most famous fjord, a UNESCO World Heritage Site, and the inspiration for the fictional Arendelle in Disney's *Frozen*. (Ch. 3)

28 Swedish Design

Swedish design is famous around the world for being practical, minimalist, sustainable, and aesthetically pleasing. (Ch. 4)

29 The Blue Lagoon, Iceland

No Iceland attraction is more iconic than the dazzling Blue Lagoon, a naturally heated seawater pool and spa between Rekyjavík and Iceland's Keflavík airport. (Ch. 7)

30 Royal Castles, Denmark

There are more than 100 castles and palaces in Denmark, some of them still in use by the royal family. Frederiksborg and Kronborg are an easy day-trip from Copenhagen. (Ch. 5)

WHAT'S WHERE

1 Norway. Norway, roughly 400,000 square km (155,000 square miles), is about the same size as California. Western Norway is the land of the fjords, with storybook Bergen as the region's capital. Less mountainous eastern Norway is home to the country's real capital, Oslo. The Sørlandet region, to Oslo's south, is known for its long, unspoiled stretches of beach and cute white wooden towns.

2 Sweden. In Sweden, ultramodern cities give way to lush forests. With 450,295 square km (173,860 square miles) for only 9 million residents, almost all have room to live as they choose. Stockholm, one of Europe's most beautiful capitals, is built on 14 small islands.

3 Denmark. The Kingdom of Denmark dapples the Baltic Sea with some 450 islands and the arc of one peninsula. Copenhagen is Scandinavia's largest city (population 1.5 million). North of Copenhagen are royal castles (including Helsingør's Kronborg of *Hamlet* fame), ritzy beach towns, and top-notch museums. Funen, the smaller of

the country's two main islands, is the birthplace of Hans Christian Andersen. Jutland, Denmark's western peninsula, shares its southern border with Germany.

4 Finland. Finland is one of the world's northernmost countries, with its entire Lapland region above the Arctic Circle. Helsinki, the capital since 1812, is built on peninsulas and islands along the Baltic coast. Stunning architecture abounds, from 19th-century neoclassical buildings to sleek, modern high-rises.

5 Iceland. Forged in the middle of the Atlantic Ocean by geothermal activity, Iceland offers epic, unspoiled landscapes filled with volcanoes, black sand beaches, sparkling fjords, milky-blue geothermal pools, and spouting geysers. The capital, Reykjavík, is home to island's famously vibrant cultural life. West Iceland and the Snæfellsnes Peninsula are often referred to as Iceland in a nutshell with its glacier-topped volcano, wild landscapes, historic villages, and teeming wildlife. Reykjanes Peninsula and the South Coast are home to the country's most famous attraction, the Blue Lagoon, as well as the Golden Circle loop.

What to Eat in Scandinavia

SKOLEBOLLER
"School buns," which feature a custard filling and grated coconut, are so called as they were once a common lunch for schoolchildren. Today, they're a must for anyone with a sweet tooth, so it's a good thing that you can find them in pretty much any café.

REINDEER
Many of Norway's indigenous Sami people still herd reindeer, and you simply can't visit northern Norway without trying reindeer meat. It's traditionally served with mashed potatoes and cranberry or lingonberry sauce, though on special occasions such as Sami People's Day (February 6) or during Tromsø's street food festival, SMAK (third week of September), you can also find it dried or prepared as kebabs and sausages.

RAGGMUNK
These Swedish thick potato pancakes, fried in butter and served with lingonberries or pork, will fuel your sightseeing all day. One for the winter days where you need plenty of calories and carbs.

MEATBALLS
Meatballs are a popular dish throughout the nordic region. In Sweden they are called *köttbullar* and are usually a mix of beef and pork. Finland's meatballs, *lihapullat*, can sometimes incorporate reindeer meat. Danish meatballs, *frikadeller*, are often boiled, minced pork. Norwegian meatballs, *Kjøttkaker* are thicker and less round than their Swedish counterparts. Most versions are served with creamy mashed potatoes, thick gravy, and lingonberry jam.

RØDGRØD MED FLØDE
This classic Danish dessert, a porridge with Danish summer berries topped with heavy cream, isn't just an old-school way to end a meal, it's also a test of outsiders' linguistic skills; if you manage to pronounce the mix of Danish letters correctly, you're basically guaranteed citizenship.

ÆBLESKIVER
A holiday classic, these perfectly round baked balls made out of vanilla-flavored pancake dough, are a perennial favorite among Danish kids and grown-ups. The fluffy, light balls of goodness are fried in a special pan and eaten with the fingers, dipped in jam and powdered sugar.

HERRING
Herring is about as Scandinavian as it gets. You'll find it smoked and fried across the Nordic region, but you have to try fermented herring, *surströmming*, in Sweden and pickled herring in Denmark.

SMØRREBRØD
Open-faced sandwiches, *smørrebrød*, are a must in Denmark. Rye bread is piled high with Danish delicacies such as pickled herring, cold cuts, meatballs, fried fish, and cheese. Typically washed down with beer and aquavit.

LOBSTER
In Iceland it is technically called a langoustine, but it's very similar in appearance and flavor to its southerly cousin. There is an annual lobster festival in Höfn.

FISH SOUP
You'll find a version of creamy fish soup made with hunks of cod and lots of vegetables across the Nordic region. In Finland, it's made with salmon, potatoes, cream, and onion and served in harbor-side stalls and traditional restaurants all over the country.

FRIED VENDACE
In the summertime Finland's harbors are usually packed with stalls selling fishy delicacies. One of the most popular snacks is vendace, a small fish, covered in rye flour and fried until it's golden, crispy, and fatty. Squeeze lemon over the dish and dip it in garlicky mayonnaise to look like a local.

JANSSON'S TEMPTATION
A holiday classic, this creamy dish is the stuff of childhood dreams for many Swedes. The creamy casserole of potato and anchovy is named after the opera singer Pelle Janzon, and though Swedes will usually only indulge in it during the holidays, visitors can dig in at traditional restaurants all over the country all through the year.

KARELIAN PASTIES
Finland's traditional pierogi-like pasties, *karjalanpiirakkat*, are a crust of rye filled with rice porridge and topped with egg butter.

KNÄCKEBRÖD
Forget bread, it's all about crackers for breakfast or lunch in Sweden. The hard, crackly bread, crispbread, is often topped with butter, cheese, and cold cuts and makes for an excellent picnic lunch.

KOLDSKÅL MED KAMMERJUNKERE
The taste of Danish summers and many a childhood, *koldskål med kammerjunkere*—a kind of buttermilk topped with vanilla-flavored crispy cookies—should be enjoyed on summer days, preferably in a garden. The buttermilk is mixed with eggs, sugar, vanilla, and often lemon and topped with crushed pieces of crispy cookies and, if you're feeling extra Danish, chopped strawberries.

RISTET HOT DOG
Denmark can't claim to have invented the hot dog, but the country has developed a creative take on it, now a classic Danish fastfood dish. *Pølsevogne* (hot dog carts) are strategically positioned in Danish cities, dishing up grilled sausages in hot dog buns, topped with mustard, ketchup, and sometimes remoulade as well as roasted onion, raw onion, and pickled cucumber.

STEGT FLÆSK MED PERSILLESOVS
One of the most beloved classics in Danish cuisine, this dish consists of crispy fried pork, boiled potatoes, and creamy parsley sauce.

SALTY LICORICE
It might be an acquired taste to outsiders, but Scandinavians love *salmiakki*, a salty licorice from

Lobster

Finland. It's usually eaten alone as a candy, but some creative bartenders and chefs incorporate in their menus, too.

LAPSKAUS
A stew with beef or pork, vegetables, and potatoes, *lapskaus* originated in northern Germany before being adopted by Scandinavian kitchens. This staple of Norwegian home cooking goes well with any of the local craft beers.

LEIPÄJUUSTO
Known as Finnish squeaky cheese or bread cheese, this fresh cheese made from cow's milk is traditionally eaten as a dessert topped with cloudberry jam or as a snack on rye crackers or rye bread.

LEFSE
Lefse is a very thin and versatile potato flatbread. To eat, spread butter, sugar, and cinnamon over it, roll it up, and cut it into pieces.

SKYR
Ever since the first explorers arrived in Iceland 1,000 years ago, yogurt-like skyr has been a staple of the local diet. It's often served with bilberries or lingonberries mixed in.

Family-Friendly Experiences in Scandinavia

TROLLSTIGEN, NORWAY
Known as the Trolls Road, this 62-mile stretch is one of Norway's best known National Tourist Routes. Surrounded by amazing views, cascading waterfalls, and mountains with names like Dronningen ("The Queen") and Trollveggen ("The Trolls Wall"), this is family-bonding at its best and can be explored by car or bike.

BLUE LAGOON, ICELAND
The Blue Lagoon is an amazing experience to share with the whole family, and your kids will freak out over the blue water and stinky smell. Children under the age of 13 are free with parents; kids under the age of 2 aren't permitted. Bathing suits can be rented.

SANTA CLAUS VILLAGE, FINLAND
In the heart of Lapland, within the Arctic Circle, you'll find Santa Claus Village. Known as the home of Santa, you can meet the jolly fellow (one-on-one) all year long, as well as meet (and feed) Santa's reindeer. Stop by the Santa Claus Main Post Office to arrange to have a letter sent to a loved one from Santa.

SKANSEN, SWEDEN
The world's first open-air museum, Skansen includes farmhouses, windmills, and barns, as well as a zoo, aquarium, theater, and cafés. It also provides insight into the life and culture of Sweden's various regions, so there are lots of teachable moments.

LEGOLAND BILLUND RESORT, DENMARK
Opened in 1968, this original LEGOLAND Resort is the blueprint for all other LEGO amusement parks. Located next to the original Lego factory, there are 50 rides, including those in the brand new LEGO MOVIE World. You can stay at Hotel LEGOLAND and visit the nearby LEGO House.

VASA MUSEUM, SWEDEN

What could be cooler than visiting a real life Viking warship that's more than 300 years old? Unearthed from the seas, the ship is the centerpiece of the Vasa Museum. Daily tours in English are available year-round and there are activities for kids like the Sail the Ship game.

PERLAN, ICELAND

The science-focused, disco ball-looking Perlan is a monument to Iceland's invaluable geothermal water supplies. There's also a planetarium show about the Northern Lights (great if you don't get to see them on your visit) and a 328-foot long Ice Cave that's made from more than 350 tons of Icelandic mountain snow.

TIVOLI GARDENS, DENMARK

The world's second-oldest amusement park, Tivoli Gardens has a pantomime theater, an open-air stage, and a number of restaurants and rides including the park's wooden Roller Coaster built in 1914. As an added bonus, visit at night to see the Chinese pagoda and the main fountain illuminated by 100,000 colored lights.

NOBEL PEACE CENTER, NORWAY

While the Nobel Peace Center may be a bit of a reach for children under 10, it's perfect for families with teenagers, and kids under 16 are free. There are daily kid-centric activities for would-be peace activists and free guided tours during the summer.

MOOMINWORLD, FINLAND

Based on the beloved novels by Tove Jansson and subsequent TV show, Moominworld is a recreation of the world of the Moomin family. You can visit their home and workshop, and meet all of the characters. There are no rides, but kids will get wrapped up in the simple joy of it all.

Fairy-Tale Castles in Scandinavia

FREDERIKSBORG CASTLE, DENMARK

A great day-trip from Copenhagen, Frederiksborg Castle is one of the largest Renaissance-era castles in Scandinavia. The castle is set on three islands and surrounded by a lake and expansive, formal gardens. Frederiksborg Castle was originally built as the royal residence for King Christian IV but has been home to Denmark's Museum of Natural History since 1878.

ÖREBRO CASTLE, SWEDEN

This former royal castle, parts of which date to the mid-14th century, is located on an island in the Svartån River, west of Stockholm. You'll find a variety of themed historical tours and activities here, including ghost tours, coin-stamping, and witches and thieves in the dungeons.

AKERSHUS CASTLE, NORWAY

Norway doesn't contain many fairy-tale castles due to its largely Viking heritage, but the best example of a traditional castle is Akershus Castle, located in Oslo's Sentrum neighborhood. This medieval castle was completed in the 14th century and has since served as a fortress, military base, and museum. Today, Akershus is home to the Royal Mausoleum, a historic church, government reception rooms, and Norway's Resistance Museum, which focuses on the Norwegian resistance to Nazi occupation from 1940 to 1945.

TURKU CASTLE, FINLAND

Set on the banks of the Aura River since the 13th century, Turku Castle has had a long and interesting history. It served as a home to the royal court, a prison, and a military fortress, and today is a museum for several rotating exhibitions.

LÄCKÖ CASTLE, SWEDEN

Set on a lake in western Sweden, this baroque castle has foundations that date back to the Middle Ages. Beyond tours of the baroque interiors, there's also a restaurant, seasonal activities, and extensive gardens. There's also a hugely popular opera concert in the castle's courtyard each summer.

KRONBORG CASTLE, DENMARK

Kronborg Castle in Helsingør is considered Denmark's most famous castle because it was forever immortalized in Shakespeare's Hamlet as the inspiration and model for Hamlet's Elsinore Castle. This UNESCO World Heritage Site dates back to the 16th century and offers daily tours.

Egeskov Castle, Denmark

HÄME CASTLE, FINLAND

Built toward the end of the 13th century, Häme Castle is an impressive, medieval castle located on Lake Vanajavesi. It has also transformed over the centuries to serve several important roles—from fortress and residential castle to a prison and now a museum. It's considered a highlight of southern Finland and the centerpiece of the city of Hämeenlinna.

ROSENBORG CASTLE, DENMARK

Located in the heart of Copenhagen, those interested in Denmark's royal heritage will adore Rosenborg Castle. Dating back to the early 17th century, the interiors contain 400 years of Danish royal history. Highlights include the Danish crown jewels, coronation thrones, tapestries, and various other historical collections.

EGESKOV CASTLE, DENMARK

Located in southern Funen, Denmark's Egeskov Castle dates back 460 years and is considered the best-preserved moat castle in Europe. It's classified as a Renaissance-style water castle, and the ground and first floors are open to visitors. Perhaps equally as well known are the extensive grounds and gardens. Egeskov Castle is not only a feast for the eyes but fun for the whole family, as kids are encouraged to explore the forest. There are also many on-site exhibitions, like the world's largest dollhouse.

OLAVINLINNA CASTLE, FINLAND

Originally built in the 15th century to repel potential attacks from Russia, this medieval stone fortress has a dramatic island setting on Lake Saimaa. It's a popular spot year-round as host to various festivals and rotating exhibitions.

Picture-Perfect Scandinavian Towns

GEIRANGER, NORWAY
This tiny village at the head of the Geirangerfjord, a UNESCO World Heritage Site, is a photographer's dream, with steep mountains surrounding the village, blue waters unfolding into the fjord, and epic waterfalls. Arrive by boat or by the Trollstigen and Nibbevegen scenic drives.

BERGEN, NORWAY
Known as the "gateway to the fjords," this UNESCO World Heritage site is surrounded by seven mountains and is notable for its cobbled alleyways lined with traditional wooden houses and its historic wharf. Bryggen, the Hanseatic wharf, has been the commercial and cultural center of Bergen for centuries.

SKAGEN, DENMARK
The northernmost point of Denmark, Skagen is located on the island of North Jutland and is best known for its beautiful beaches and lighthouses. Coastal oddities and scenic treasures include Råbjerg Mile, Scandinavia's largest shifting dunes, and Tilsandede Kirke (the Sand-Buried Church).

VISBY, SWEDEN
Set on the island of Gotland in the Baltic Sea off the southeastern coast of Sweden, Visby is best known for its medieval wall, centuries-old churches, and cobblestone streets. In August, the Medieval Week festival draws crowds for its jousting tournaments, street theater, and medieval markets.

REINE, NORWAY
A tiny fishing village on the island of Moskenesøya, Reine is nestled between the Norwegian Sea and dramatic mountain peaks. Traditional, colorful wooden houses provide a cozy contrast to the soaring surroundings. Stay in a traditional *rorbuer* (fisherman's cottage) along the coast to soak in the scenery. Enjoy the midnight sun in summer and the aurora borealis in winter.

GUDHJEM, DENMARK
Located on Denmark's "sunshine island," Bornholm, Gudhjem is a small fishing village that's notable for its dramatic hills and sweeping Baltic views. A hike to the top of Bokul will gift amazing photos, and the Kaffeslottet (Coffee Castle) also overlooks the town.

PORVOO, FINLAND
Founded nearly 800 years ago, medieval Porvoo is one of the most picturesque places in Finland, with cobblestone streets, charming cafes, an early 15th-century cathedral, and its famous red shore houses that were originally painted red in honor of the arrival of Gustav III, the king of Sweden.

MARSTRAND, SWEDEN
Founded in the 13th century, this scenic seaside town is known as the "sailing capital of Sweden." Marstrand is spread across two islands (it's a two-minute ferry ride between islands) in the northeastern Kattegat Sea.

VIK, ICELAND
Iceland's southernmost village is known for its dramatic black-sand beaches and basalt stacks. Vik is located within a UNESCO Global Geopark, Katla Geopark, named after the nearby volcano. Look for puffins on the cliffs of Reynisfjall Mountain and a large rock arch off the Dyrhólaey Peninsula.

HÚSAVÍK, ICELAND
Located on Iceland's northern coast, Húsavík is known as the whale capital of Iceland and is also the oldest settlement on the island. The town claims that, in recent years, 98% of whale-watching trips have resulted in sightings. Up to 23 whale species can be spotted off-shore, including blue whale. Fans of smaller wildlife can enjoy puffins, which can also be found in Shaky Bay.

Natural Wonders to Experience in Norway

SOGNEFJORD

As Norway's deepest (almost 4,300 feet) and longest (127 miles) fjord, Sognefjord is a must see. Equally impressive is the fact that 12 other fjords branch off from it, including the well-known Nærøyfjord, a UNESCO World Heritage Site, and Aurlandsfjord, home to the scenic Flåm Railway.

DOVREFJELL NATIONAL PARK

Together Dovre and Dovrefjell-Sunndalsfjella national parks cover some 770 square miles in south-eastern Norway. The region is home to wild reindeer, as well as Norway's only population of wild musk ox, which were imported from Greenland in the first half of the 20th century. Today, safaris take you to see these giants up close.

SVARTISEN

Although Svartisen is at the Arctic Circle, Norway's second-largest glacier is very accessible thanks to its lower elevations. What was once a single large formation has separated into two parts, one to the west and the other to the east. The glacier is almost 5,300 feet above sea level at its highest point.

MARMORSLOTTET

Not many visitors know about Marmorslottet (Marble Castle), but if you're heading to Svartisen glacier, you should also check out this formation less than an hour from Mo i Rana. The water is a deep, icy blue—appropriate given its glacial origins.

GLOPPEDALSURA

In the lunar-like landscape of Gloppedalsura, some of the boulders are as big as cars; others are the size of buildings. They're all remnants of an ancient rockslide that's thought to have been the largest in northern Europe. Because this granite was originally formed from magma, Gloppedalsura is also part of the Magma Geopark.

SALTSTRAUMEN

Saltstraumen, close to the city of Bodø, has the world's strongest tidal current. Each day, during high and low tides, vast amounts of seawater are forced through the tiny, 492-foot-wide, roughly 2-mile-long strait separating mainland Norway from the island of Straumøya.

VETTISFOSSEN

The 900-foot Vettisfossen is Europe's highest free-falling, unregulated waterfall. Situated in Jotunheimen National Park, Vettisfossen has been protected since the 1920s and is only accessible from Utladalen via a steep (it rises roughly 1,000 feet), 7.5-mile round-trip hike.

JOTUNHEIMEN NATIONAL PARK

Jotunheimen National Park is a haven for hikers, climbers, and skiers. Its roughly 1,300 square miles encompass northern Europe's greatest concentration of peaks over 6,500 feet, including 8,100-foot Galdhøppingen, Norway's highest mountain.

HARDANGERVIDDA

At an average height of 3,600 feet, Hardangervidda is Europe's largest (almost 3,300 square miles) high-altitude plateau. It's also part of the biggest national park in the Nordic countries, stretching from western to eastern Norway across the three counties of Hordaland, Buskerud, and Telemark.

JOSTEDALSBREEN

Jostedalsbreen is the biggest glacier not only in Norway, but also in continental Europe. It stretches across almost 200 square miles and has dozens of branches. One of the most popular is Briksdalsbreen, which is near Olden and is accessible on guided tours in "troll cars" (aka buggies).

Unmissable Icelandic Museums

PERLAN, REYKJAVÍK
This glass-domed museum is hard to miss. It includes a real ice cave that stretches more than 100 meters, as well as Áróra, the world's first 8K resolution planetarium show to focus on the northern lights.

THE LAVA CENTRE, HVOLSVÖLLUR
Another of Iceland's most immersive museums takes visitors inside of the country's famous volcanoes at the Lava Centre. Strategic red lighting immediately creates the illusion of being surrounded by hot magma, while exhibits showcase the powerful systems in place to track earthquakes, lava flow, and all the other geologic activity.

THE NATIONAL MUSEUM OF ICELAND, REYKJAVÍK
This museum presents the evolution of Iceland over the past 1,000 years—from the original ship that brought settlers here to the airport that Icelanders use today for travel abroad.

SKÓGAR MUSEUM, SKÓGAR
Skógar presents the architectural and technological history of the country, from turf houses to modern transportation. There's also a folk museum on-site dedicated to the collection and preservation of more than 15,000 individual items reflective of Iceland's cultural heritage.

THE ICELANDIC SEA MONSTER MUSEUM, BÍLDUDALUR
Located in Bíldudalur, a coastal village in the Westfjords, this highly interactive museum takes visitors through the stories, sightings, and various monsters from Iceland's nautical lore.

THE VIKING SAGA MUSEUM, REYKJAVÍK
Iceland's history was recorded since the first settlers arrived to find a barren land of ice and fire. With lifelike animatronics, the Viking Saga Museum takes visitors through 17 stories from different eras that have helped shape it into the country we know and love today.

The Lava Centre

THE GHOST CENTRE, STOKKSEYRI

Although it's open only during the summer, this museum is a must-see for visitors who want to experience Icelandic ghost stories and mythologies, which are pervasive in this country. Visitors walk through a ghost maze while listening to the tales on headsets in a number of languages.

THE MUSEUM OF ICELANDIC WITCHCRAFT AND SORCERY, HÓLMAVÍK

The town's main attraction, this museum takes visitors back to a time when witches were still deeply feared, detailing the kinds of spells and staves these (typically male) witches would use.

Aurora Borealis 101

Seeing the otherworldly aurora borealis, or northern lights, dance across the sky is one of nature's most spectacular displays. It is also at the top of most travel bucket lists but not necessarily the easiest to check off, thanks, Mother Nature. What exactly is it? Why does it happen? And how can you increase your chances of seeing it? While it's impossible to perfectly predict solar activity, there are some basic tips and tricks to enhance your chances. It also doesn't hurt to keep your mittens crossed.

WHAT IS IT?

Auroras are caused by collisions between charged particles from the sun's atmosphere and gas particles like oxygen and nitrogen in the earth's atmosphere. More specifically, these charged particles from the sun become trapped in the earth's magnetic field—hence why auroras, or polar lights, are most prevalent near the earth's north and south magnetic poles. It's solar wind that blows these charged particles from the sun and toward earth's magnetic field. In short, a mighty celestial scene.

WHY DOES IT HAPPEN?

When most people picture the northern lights, they think of green waves, but the aurora borealis can actually take many shapes and colors. The color of aurora borealis is determined by the type of gas particles that are colliding and how much charged energy is being produced. The most common color is a greenish light that is emitted by oxygen, and the second-most-common is a blueish-purple light that is emitted by nitrogen. Red and yellow auroras are also possible but much more rare. What gives the aurora borealis its shape is actually a bit of a mystery. Scientists are still trying to figure this part out but believe the shape depends on exactly where in the earth's magnetic field the charged particles

are interacting. Aside from the most common rippling wave shape, other possible shapes include patches of light, streamers, arcs, and shooting rays.

While "aurora borealis" refers to the occurrence around earth's northern pole, the same phenomenon also occurs at earth's southern pole. This is called the aurora australis, or southern lights. These occur in the Southern Hemisphere in Antarctica, but limited geographical access means the northern lights get all the attention.

WHEN?

Winter in the north is the best season to view the lights in part because of the long periods of darkness and the frequency of clear nights. Dramatic sightings are more likely when there is a significant event on the sun and it is earth facing, i.e., more charged particles closer to the earth's magnetic field. There is also a correlation between a significant aurora borealis and the earth's equinoxes. This is due to the position and angle of the Earth in relation to the sun at these times. The autumn equinox in September is your best bet.

WHERE?

While visibility depends on the weather and other conditions, location is key. The aurora borealis is generally seen in high-latitude regions (higher than 55 degrees) around the Arctic. With that said, strong solar storms can sometimes increase the auroras and blow them farther south than is typical.

Norway: The best areas to see the aurora borealis in Norway are Tromsø, the Lofoten Islands, Alta, Nordkapp, Svalbard, and Kirkenes.

Sweden: The best areas to see the aurora borealis in Sweden are Kiruna and Abisko National Park.

Denmark: The best place to see the northern lights are Denmark's Faroe Islands archipelago located between the Norwegian Sea and the North Atlantic. Greenland's Kangerlussuaq is one of Scandinavia's best spots to catch the lights. This is especially true between the months of October and April. Its combination of location, clear skies, and low population makes it an optimal spot for witnessing this incredible phenomenon.

Finland: The best areas to see the aurora borealis in Finland are spots in the Lapland region like Rovaniemi. In Finland, the aurora can appear as frequently as 200 nights a year.

Iceland: While the latitude and longitude are good for viewing the aurora borealis in Iceland, the weather is unpredictable. You need a clear night with no cloud cover and it's best to avoid light pollution.

HOW?

Getting as close as possible to the Northern Hemisphere's magnetic pole will increase the likelihood of seeing the lights. The best time of night is between 10 pm and 2 am, and since darkness is paramount, a moonless night is also best. Light pollution can be a real hindrance, so it's best to get out of town to avoid any modern light obstruction. If far enough north, the lights will appear overhead, but for lower-latitude locations, high ground is best. The farther away you are from the north pole, the lower on the horizon the aurora will appear.

TOURS

Lapland Safaris. In winter, you can hunt for the northern lights on snowmobiles, with reindeer, or on snowshoes. In summer and autumn, Lapland Safaris offers aurora experiences by foot and boat. ⊕ *www.laplandsaafaris.com*

Off The Map Travel. Suit up in a high-quality thermal suit and take in the northern lights from the comfort of freezing Arctic waters in Rovaniemi with Off the Map Travel. This tour company also offers a six-night itinerary that takes you to Finnish Lapland and Northern Norway for some cross-border lights-viewing. Travel by snowmobile, sleep in a glass cabin, and chase aurora from a cozy bubble sled. ⊕ *www.offthemap.travel*

Kiruna. Kiruna in Swedish Lapland offers multiple experiences that include a snowshoe hike to an isolated hut to see and learn about the lights by an open fire, to an overnight stay in Aurora Village, to a special Nordic dinner at Aurora Sky Station. ⊕ *www.kirunalapland.se*

Arctic Explorers. One of the most reputable whale-watching excursions in Tromsø and northern Norway offers speedy boats with small groups and opportunities to see humpback whales, orcas, and other species under the northern lights (if you're lucky). ⊕ *articholidays.org*

Chasing Lights. One of the main draws to northern Norway is the magical northern lights, and Chasing Lights is a Tromsø-based tour company that offers diverse packages to help you witness this amazing natural phenomenon. As the name suggests, the company will chase the lights with you rather than standing still in one spot and allowing them to come—or not come—to you. The company also has other activities such as snowmobile adventures and trips to the fjords. ⊕ *www.chasinglights.com*

What to Watch and Read Before Visiting

Movies

THE MILLENNIUM TRILOGY

Swedish author Stieg Larsson's Milennium Trilogy, a trio of novels that teams up a disgraced journalist with a punk hacker, sold millions in translations across the globe and was first brought to the screen in Sweden in a six-part TV series, followed by three theatrically released films in 2009: *The Girl with the Dragon Tattoo*, *The Girl Who Played with Fire*, and *The Girl Who Kicked the Hornet's Nest*. Skip the later, polished U.S. adaptations and watch the original Swedish versions (with English subtitles) of Stieg Larsson's best-sellers.

THE BRIDGE

A woman's dead body is discovered on the Öresund Bridge that links Sweden and Denmark—half of her in Sweden, the other half in Denmark. The Danish and Swedish police forces have to share jurisdiction and work together to solve the case, led by the reluctant pairing of Danish inspector Martin Rohde and the Swedish Saga Norén. It doesn't take long for the investigation to escalate and for the partners to discover that they are dealing with a callous serial killer. This 10-part series is binge-worthy Nordic noir at its gritty best.

THE KILLING

If you thought the U.S. crime series *The Killing* was an original story, think again. The tale of the events following the gruesome murder of 17-year-old Rosie Larsen that premiered in the United States in 2011 was based on the 2007 Danish series *Forbrydelsen* about the murder of 19-year-old Nanna Birk Larsen. The Danish series was such a resounding success that it resulted in a U.S. spin-off that ended up running for four seasons. Needless to say, the original is better.

BORGEN

Nordic noir may be the dominant genre coming out of Scandinavia, but there's more to Scandinavian pop culture than grisly murders and peculiar police detectives. Danish political blockbuster and drama-thriller *Borgen* is the gripping story of Birgitte Nyborg (convincingly portrayed by Sidse Babett Knudsen, better known to international audiences as Theresa Cullen from *Westworld*), an obscure politician who becomes the first-ever female prime minister of Denmark. The series was also a springboard for Pilou Asbæk, who went from his role as eccentric spin doctor Kasper Juul to snatch the part of treacherous villain Euron Greyjoy in *Game of Thrones*.

MAMMON

Not wanting to be outdone by their Nordic neighbors, the Norwegians have created an award-winning detective drama of their own. Not entirely dissimilar from Stieg Larsson's Milennium series, *Mammon* centers on Peter Veras, an uncompromising journalist, and his female computer-whiz sidekick Vibeke Haglund. A must for conspiracy theorists everywhere, this is the story of two investigators who uncover a dark secret that Norway's elite would prefer to keep quiet.

THE SEVENTH SEAL

Swedish film director Ingmar Bergman may not be everyone's cup of tea, but you can't visit Sweden without watching at least one of his movies. Bergman's films are notoriously long, and while his fans consider them ingenious, others argue that they are pretentious at best and anxiety provoking at worst. Make up your own mind by watching the most classic of Bergman's movies, *The Seventh Seal*, known for the famous scene in which the main character plays a fateful game of chess on a beach. His opponent? Death.

THE UNKNOWN SOLDIER

Finland may not be best known for producing great cinema, but the country has a rich and complex backstory that history enthusiasts will want to explore before visiting. Based on the best-selling classic novel by the same name, *The Unknown Soldier* follows a fictional Finnish army machine-gun company on the Karelian front during World War II, featuring realistic portrayals of a diverse group of men with varying backgrounds.

WHAT WILL PEOPLE SAY?

This powerful drama from 2017 depicts the struggles faced by a Norwegian teenage girl born to Pakistani parents as she seeks to reconcile her two cultures. The film provides an important insight into the difficulties faced by the significant immigrant communities that have moved to Scandinavia in recent years.

LET THE RIGHT ONE IN

A shy 12-year-old boy gets relentlessly bullied at school. He befriends a pale young girl who only comes out at night. Then, suddenly, a string of disappearances and murders start shaking things up in a sleepy Swedish town. This 2008 film adaptation of the best-selling book by the same name is a horror-cum-romance-cum-vampire movie that provides a unique insight into the dreariness of life in suburban Sweden.

BORDERTOWN

The best-known Finnish contribution to the gritty world of Nordic thrillers is *Bordertown*, a two-series crime drama about a quirky police detective who takes a job in a small Finnish town, featuring some excellent acting and stunning Finnish countryside scenery.

Books

BLOOD ON SNOW, BY JO NESBØ

Our protagonist stands over the body of man he has just shot in the chest and neck, as his blood stains the snow red. This is the opening scene of *Blood on Snow*, an unputdownable page-turner by Norwegian author Jo Nesbø that stands out as one of the darkest and most brilliant of all the Nordic noir novels on the market.

BLACKWATER, BY KERSTIN EKMAN

Set in an eerie, isolated village in the remote Arctic landscape in the northernmost part of Sweden, Kerstin Ekman's *Blackwater* is packed with the kind of creeping tension that most crime writers can only dream of. Published in 1993, more than a decade before anyone had ever heard of Stieg Larsson, Mikael Blomkvist, or Lisbeth Salander, Blackwater is one of the great forerunners of the Nordic noir megatrend.

THE ICE PRINCESS, BY CAMILLA LÄCKBERG

Among the best of a growing number of Swedish female thriller writers who have emerged in recent years, Läckberg's writing is grim, violent, and incredibly compelling. Like most of her stories, her debut novel *The Ice Princess* is set in the dreamy summer tourist resort of Fjällbacka, but needless to say, things are not as peaceful as they seem. A young woman's dead body is found frozen in a bathtub. A police detective is brought in to investigate. You know the drill.

SMILLA'S SENSE OF SNOW, BY PETER HØEG

What could be more fundamentally Scandinavian than a book about snow? Peter Høeg's international best-seller also examines important cultural issues relating to Denmark's modern history and its relationship with former colony Greenland. And it's a chilling detective story too—in fact, this is Denmark's most famous contribution to the Nordic noir literature genre. It tells the story of Smilla, who sets off on a dangerous mission to solve a murder, following a path of clues as clear to her as her footsteps in the snow.

FACELESS KILLERS, BY HENNING MANKELL

The first book in the Wallander series by Henning Mankell, the so-called godfather of Swedish crime writing, takes us to the southern Swedish region of Skåne. But if you think the seaside town of Ystad, with its charming medieval center filled with cobblestoned streets and half-timbered houses, is far too idyllic to play host to a series of gruesome murders, think again. Ystad is the setting for 10 of Mankell's most-read detective novels, all starring Inspector Kurt Wallander (later played by Sir Kenneth Branagh in the excellent British TV adaptation).

PIPPI LONGSTOCKING, BY ASTRID LINDGREN

Sweden gave the world Astrid Lindgren, the most beloved Swedish children's writer of all time. Her rare ability to connect with her readers—and her child readers in particular—in a way that makes them feel truly understood, remains unprecedented. Lindgren's masterpieces include the stories about fearless red-haired superhuman Pippi Longstocking, resourceful prankster Emil of Lönneberga, and the heart-wrenchingly tragic *Brothers Lionheart*. Translated into more than 100 languages, her work is guaranteed to delight children and adults of all ages.

FINN FAMILY MOOMINTROLL, BY TOVE JANSSON

Tove Jansson is to Finland what Astrid Lindgren is to Sweden. Although her 13 books about the troll family Moomin have "only" been translated into just over 40 languages, these lovable, hippo-like fairy-tale characters with their large snouts have become a worldwide phenomenon.

THE EMIGRANTS, BY VILHELM MOBERG

This Swedish classic is required reading in Swedish high schools. The Emigrants is a realistic portrayal of the Swedish pioneers who left their impoverished existence in rural Sweden behind to build a new life in Minnesota in the 19th century.

OUT STEALING HORSES, PER PETTERSON

An unexpected meeting causes Trond, a retired 67-year-old man, to recall a summer he spent in the countryside at the age of 15, when he went out stealing horses. The memory conjures up a story he would prefer to have forgotten. An account of the way Norway was before and after World War II, *Out Stealing Horses* is a beautifully written, multi-award-winning description of rural life in Scandinavia.

MERCY, JUSSI ADLER-OLSEN

Jussi Adler-Olsen is one of the new it boys of Nordic noir. *Mercy* is the first novel in his immensely popular Department Q series, a dark, disturbing story about the deeply flawed, disastrously burned-out chief detective Carl Mørck. Fully expecting to get fired, he is instead put in charge of newly created Department Q, tasked with solving "cases of special focus." What could possibly go wrong?

Chapter 2

TRAVEL SMART

Updated by
Barbara Woolsey

Know Before You Go

From Greenland to the Faroe Islands, the rest of Denmark's kingdom, and up the Arctic Circle, Scandinavia and the Nordics cover a lot of ground and their regions are incredibly eclectic. Still, there are some rules of thumb to remember no matter where you are.

SCANDINAVIA ITSELF IS AMBIGUOUS

Which countries are Scandinavian? The answer is different depending on the northerner you ask. The name "Scandinavia" originated in the early 18th century as part of a cultural movement promoting cooperation and a shared heritage between Norway, Sweden, and Denmark. But don't forget: Viking rampages left diverse ancestry all over the north. Iceland might be considered Scandinavian because of its Norse roots; some disagree. Finland often gets lumped into this general category (as we did here for convenience), but it should be noted that it has quite a different language and history, and it's not on the Scandinavian Peninsula. There is an argument that Scandinavia is defined by a similar way of life, but "the Nordic Region" is probably a more accurate categorization when referring to these countries. Just try to avoid sweeping generalizations and be sensitive to how distinct the different regions are.

CASH ISN'T KING

Sweden is on its way to becoming the world's first cashless society—and across Scandinavia, card systems get a better workout than chump change. This is good news for country hoppers, considering Denmark and Finland take euros, while Sweden, Norway, and Iceland all have their own currency. Call your credit card provider to inform them of your travel dates and destinations; otherwise, your plastic may get blocked for unusual activity.

NO CHATTY CATHYS HERE

Some say Scandinavians are cold on the outside, warm on the inside. While people can be polite, they're generally reserved or even shy at first. Those from farther north fancy themselves to be more open and laid-back than southern city dwellers who prefer to keep to themselves rather than engage in small talk. Don't take the aloofness personally.

IT'S SUNNY AT MIDNIGHT

For several weeks during the Arctic or Antarctic summer, the earth's axis tilts toward the sun—meaning the sun is above the horizon at midnight. While the so-called midnight sun can be a blessing, making late-night hikes and lake dips possible, it can be annoying when it comes to getting shut-eye. Sleep masks help a lot but you may want to scout out accommodation options with basement rooms and thick curtains.

THE NORTHERN LIGHTS ARE NOT GUARANTEED

The aurora borealis, which is caused by electrical particles traveling from the sun to the earth, dazzles when the skies are clear and there's lots of solar activity. It happens between autumn and early spring, especially up north in areas with minimal light pollution. It's always a lucky strike—you may just get a couple of green streaks or a full dance of red and purple on the most active side of the spectrum. Inquire at your hotel, as some offer a wake-up-call service if the northern lights appear. Otherwise, shelling out for an expensive glass igloo or aurora hotel can always be a risk without reward.

DRINK TAP WATER

Some of the world's purest water is found in this pocket of the world. Don't waste money on plastic water bottles. Bring a reusable bottle and fill up from the spout or even rivers and lakes accordingly.

LET IT ALL HANG OUT IN THE SAUNA

No need to be prudish. Saunas and thermal baths are a big part of the culture, and it's a communal activity—meaning mom, dad, and grandma all sweat it out in the buff together. Be aware that saunas are mostly mixed-sex. Proper etiquette includes showering or swimming before entering, putting a towel down, and making sure your body touches only your towel. You can also wrap a towel around you. No one will bother you if you do choose to wear a swimsuit—just don't be shocked by the birthday suits.

DON'T TIP (UNLESS YOU WANT TO)

Tipping isn't very common in Scandinavia due to higher wages. Despite this, a tip is still appreciated in acknowledgment of good service by rounding up to a max of 10%. If you do want to tip in a restaurant, just make sure to say it at the time the server makes your payment by simply naming the total amount; servers will often type the amount in themselves and hand the card back to you. Be sure to check the bill first for a service charge, as some establishments already tack one on.

HYGGE HOW-TO

You've probably heard that you should "get" yourself some hygge while in this part of the world, but there are two things you need to know: 1. It's pronounced hyoo·guh, and 2. It is not something you can necessarily buy, eat, see, or do. It's much deeper than that. Hygge is a quality of coziness and comfort that creates a deep feeling of contentment and well-being. You may find your cozy, zen state while hiking Sweden's National Parks or when soaking in that perfect light that has for centuries drawn artists to North Zealand ... or just while appreciating a hot cinnamon bun at the start of your day. Hey, this region is consistently said to have the world's most content people, so it's worth trying to be present when you visit.

KNOW YOUR "EVERY-MAN'S RIGHTS"

The "everyman's rights" are unique outdoor laws that make it easy to camp and explore nature. In Norway, you may put up a tent or sleep under the stars anywhere in the countryside as long as you keep 150 meters away from the nearest inhabited house or cabin. If you want to stay more than two nights in a row, though, you need to ask the landowner. In Sweden, only one night is allowed. Similarly, in Finland, you can fish, forage, and wander on privately owned land and rivers for recreation and exercise. Authorities also provide wood at campfire sites, so no need to bring your own.

IT'S A WONDERLAND IN WINTER

Don't let the sub-zero temperatures scare you off—there is something magical about winters in Scandinavia, whether it's the snow blankets outdoors or the cozy wooly ones inside. If you dress warmly, you'll be able to sustain the cold and, who knows, maybe even begin to relish it. Some of the best experiences happen in the winter months: the northern lights, snowmobiling, skiing, and ice fishing, to name a few—not to mention Santa, reindeer, and cozy lodges and glass igloos to stay in.

BE WARY OF WILDLIFE EXPERIENCES

There is an unbelievable opportunity to get up close and personal with animals here—whether it's whale-watching, sledding with huskies, or visiting reindeer parks. These brushes with wildlife can be enriching and unforgettable, but only if you are doing so in a way that respects the animals and their livelihood. In 2019, Finland and Sweden were named the top two countries for wildlife viewing in the Global Wildlife Travel Index. Categories such as conservation and environmental sustainability are taken into account. But that doesn't mean every establishment operates with the utmost responsibility. Fodor's only recommends experiences and tour operators that we know to be truly ethical. If you are unsure, use your best judgment by talking to locals, reading online reviews, and asking plenty of questions before you go.

Getting Here and Around

Air

Low-cost airline carrier Norwegian offers direct flights from New York and Los Angeles to Stockholm Arlanda, Oslo Gardermoen, and Copenhagen, while Scandinavian Airlines System (SAS) flies direct from New York to Oslo Gardermoen, Copenhagen, Stockholm Arlanda, and Helsinki, and from Los Angeles to Stockholm. Finnair flies direct to Helsinki, while Icelandair goes to Reykjavík's Keflavík airport. All Scandinavian carriers offer a large selection of domestic flights, connecting harder-to-reach areas. Taking a plane up north can be a truly unique experience—they are small, often without assigned seating, and make several stops en route. A good regional airline to know is Widerøe, which offers the Explore Norway ticket allowing an unlimited number of flights within Norway over a two-week period in July and August. Some restrictions apply, such as flying more than four times between the same two cities.

AIRPORTS

Copenhagen is one of Europe's oldest airports and Scandinavia's busiest airport, having welcomed 30 million passengers in 2018. Oslo Gardermoen is the region's second most frequented airport, taking in 28 million passengers, followed by Stockholm Arlanda at 26 million, Helsinki at 20 million, and Reykjavík's Keflavík airport at 9 million.

Bicycle

Scandinavia is fantastic for cycling tours, offering long hours of summer daylight and an abundance of beautiful countryside. Camping laws tend to be more relaxed, and safety generally isn't an issue. The only caveat is that Mother Nature's wrath can bring bad road conditions at a moment's notice. Denmark is the most bike-friendly country of the lot, with excellent infrastructure in both urban areas and the sticks, including the well-known Danish National Cycle Routes. Copenhagen is also considered by some to be the most bike-friendly city in the world, with the majority of citizens commuting on two wheels.

Boat

Car and passenger ferries are an essential means of transportation all over the region, making communities large and small accessible, especially on the islands. Smyril Line, a Faroese company, runs ferry service between Hirtshals, Demark, and Seyðisfjörður, Iceland, every Saturday (except during Christmastime). They allow vehicles, including campers and motorcycles, and sometimes stop in the Faroe Islands. There are several companies operating connections in the region, like Stena Line operating between Norway, Sweden, and Denmark and Viking Line between Finland, the Åland Islands, Sweden, and Estonia. Journeys reveal a lot of scenery but can take several hours compared to a short plane ride. In Sweden, the five-day Båtluffarkortet, also known as the "island-hopping pass," makes it easy to see lots of the little islands on the Stockholm archipelago. A popular day-trip for Helsinki folks is across the Baltic Sea to Tallinn, Estonia. As many as 10 boats leave every day, and the ride takes just two hours.

Bus

Denmark, as well as the lower parts of Sweden and Norway, are serviced by FlixBus, which also offers the InterFlex deal: travel to five European cities for €99 within a three-month period. In Norway, there are also Nettbuss and Nor-Way Bussekspress, a chain of 50 Norwegian bus companies serving 500 destinations. In Iceland, there is an excellent bus system called Strætó, which offers regular service in Reykjavík and long-distance buses that go outside of the city. The Strætó website is an exceptional tool for route planning and general information, and paying for bus fare is easy with the app.

🚗 Car

You can drive in Scandinavia with a valid U.S., Canadian, European Union, Australian, or U.K. driver's license. High-quality, well-marked roads make driving a great way to explore the landscape. That's especially true in Iceland, where driving offers the most ease, and the Ring Road is where a lot of popular sights are located. Denmark and the southern parts of Sweden, Norway, and Finland are fairly compact, but the distances are felt much more on the way north as communities become scarcer. In Norway, ferry tickets and toll roads can be costly, while in Finland and Sweden they are usually free with the exception of the Øresundsbroen (Øresund Bridge) between Denmark and Sweden, where toll prices start at €14 per vehicle.

Be aware that there are relatively low legal blood-alcohol limits and tough penalties for driving while intoxicated in Scandinavia; Sweden, Iceland, and Finland have zero-tolerance laws. Penalties include license suspension and fines or imprisonment, and the laws are sometimes enforced by random police roadblocks in urban areas on weekends. An accident involving a driver who has an illegal blood-alcohol level usually voids all insurance agreements, making the driver responsible for all medical and car-repair bills.

CAR RENTALS
Before you rent—and purchase collision or theft coverage—see what coverage you already have under your own auto insurance policy and credit cards. The minimum age for renting is usually 21, but some companies require that drivers under 25 pay a surcharge. Picking up a car in one country and leaving it in another is usually no problem, but ask about drop-off charges or one-way service fees, which can be substantial. Also inquire about early-return policies; some rental agencies charge extra if you return the car before the time specified in your contract, while others give you a refund for the days not used. Be aware that collision policies that car rental companies sell for European rentals typically do not cover stolen vehicles.

GASOLINE
In Scandinavia, fuel is expensive and heavily taxed. Gas stations get scarcer in Iceland outside of Reykjavík and in northern parts of Norway, Sweden, and Finland, so don't wait until you're running on empty to fill up. Unleaded gas and diesel fuel are sold everywhere. Often, there are self-service pumps that take credit card payment.

PARKING
Parking in major cities can be costly and scarce. Some hotels offer free parking, while others charge an additional fee. Underground parking is your best option in the winter.

ROAD CONDITIONS
Road conditions can be unpredictable, particularly in northern, remote areas, where some roads close as early as September due to snow and do not open

Getting Here and Around

again until June. Be aware of speed cameras, as tickets can be wildly expensive, and in Denmark, watch for cyclists, who usually have the right of way. In Iceland, don't pull off to the side of the road. Even the Ring Road is mostly just two narrow lanes going in opposite directions, so there is no room for half of the vehicle. This problem has led to tourist deaths. Particularly here, you'll find that most other cars on the road are manned by travelers, some of whom may not have a lot of experience driving in blustering snow. Always drive cautiously.

RULES OF THE ROAD

Speeding is punished severely. Many roads are monitored by radar and cameras in metal boxes. Always keep your headlights on and wear a seat belt.

🛳 Cruise

Cruises keep becoming more popular around Scandinavia. The mother of all slow travel in Scandinavia, though, is the coastal steamer route Hurtigruten; ships have been sailing along Norway's coast on the route since 1893. The full route, which the company calls "the world's most beautiful sea voyage," departs daily from Bergen in the southwest and heads north to Kirkenes, close to the Finnish and Russian borders, and back to Bergen, along a total of 34 ports. The entire trip clocks in at 2,500 nautical miles and takes 12 days, revealing tiny fishing villages along the way. There are cabins, a restaurant, a cafeteria, and shops on board. You can purchase tickets for the entire stretch or individual legs directly from the Hurtigruten company.

🚗 Ride-Sharing

Uber operates in Oslo, Sweden, and in Finland's capital region (including Helsinki, Vantaa, Espoo, and Kauniainen). Due to struggles with local governments, the ride-sharing app's budget service, UberPOP, is not available. You can book premium rides, but the rates won't be less expensive than local taxis, if at all.

🚕 Taxi

Taxis in Scandinavia cost a pretty penny. Fares vary a lot between companies, and in cities they tend to be pricier on weekends, evenings, and public holidays. Beware of taxis in Sweden, where deregulation has made scamming common. Your best bet is to ask locals for the most trusted taxi company where you are. If you know how much the trip should cost, arrange a flat rate with the driver beforehand. Meanwhile, in Iceland, taxis aren't hailed but called. Taxis run on a meter unless they're taking you to the airport or out of the city, for which a high set price is given. Consider public transport when the opportunity presents itself!

🚆 Train

Trains in Scandinavia are comfortable and efficient. Booking ahead can help you get discounts as well as secure spots on overnight and long-distance trains, which operate on a first-come, first-serve basis. Eurail offers a Scandinavia Pass for Denmark, Norway, Sweden, and Finland with options of three to eight days of travel in a month for a set price. Iceland does not have a public railway system.

Essentials

🏃 Activities

Experiencing Scandinavia is all about the outdoors, soaking up the fresh air and amazing landscapes. There are many ways to do this, but it all depends on the season. During winter, activities require braving the elements: skiing, dogsledding, ice fishing, and chasing the northern lights. In summer, the midnight sun makes hiking, boating, and cycling possible from early morning to evening. Whale-watching excursions, reindeer parks, and other brushes with wildlife are also unique to the region—but only recommended when provided by reputable, ethical tour operators. In 2019, Finland and Sweden were named the top two countries in the world for wildlife travel, including conservation and environmental sustainability, by the Global Wildlife Travel Index.

Iceland's purebred ponies are a major draw for tourists, but a ride means leaving Reykjavík. Plenty of tour operators provide shuttle service from the downtown area to horse farms, or you can just drive right up. Many outfitters are geared towards multiday rides and include an on-site hotel and restaurant for serious riders. Eldhestar has the largest variety of riding options in South Iceland, which is where most tourists spend their time, offering rides as short as a half day or as long as eight days. In winter there's a particularly lovely ride where guests go on horseback to witness the northern lights. Eldhestar's happy horses make magnificent companions for a of tour the Icelandic countryside, and the staff are knowledgeable and helpful. Those who choose to stay at the hotel will find comfortable rooms and a deep bath for soothing aching muscles after a long ride.

🍴 Restaurants

New Nordic cuisine, pioneered by the famous Copenhagen restaurant Noma, has had an immense impact on global dining trends over the last 15 years. While the hype has now died down a bit, you should try it while you're here. The philosophy is "back to basics"—local, seasonal ingredients, fermentation, and foraging are a few of the main concepts trailblazed and still explored by Scandinavian chefs. Reindeer, fresh fish and seafood, and forest-picked mushrooms and berries are some delicacies you can look forward to. High prices are a factor in eating your heart out, though, and alcohol is also highly taxed. But it may just be worth an incredible meal.

PAYING

Most restaurants these days take credit cards. You may even encounter some restaurants which are cash-free, especially in Sweden.

MEALS AND MEALTIMES

Kitchens usually open around noon and close by 11 or midnight. Many restaurants are closed on Sunday. Some upscale restaurants only do specific seating times, so reservations are crucial. The options dwindle when it comes to late-night grub, but there will usually be at least a kebab or pizza shop open even in smaller towns.

🛏 Hotels

You'll find a wide variety of accommodation throughout Scandinavia. In cities, there are regional and international chains at the upper end of the scale. In remote areas, most lodging is family run or independent, offering much more personal service. Guesthouses, pensions, and bed-and-breakfasts tend to be most

Essentials

active on websites like Booking.com and Airbnb. Budget-minded hostels are a mainstay. Ice hotels and glass igloos are luxury options for sleeping under the northern lights in season. Camping laws also tend to be quite lax, though it's best to consult with local tourism offices for up-to-date information. ■TIP➔ **Reservations are highly recommended in the summer high season as well as in winter due to the harsh weather conditions. Ask for a room without windows if you wish to escape the midnight sun.**

Norwegian hotels have high standards in cleanliness and comfort—and often sky-high prices to match. Even the simplest youth hostels provide good mattresses with fluffy down comforters and clean showers or baths. Breakfast, usually served buffet style, is often included in the room price at hotels. Bellhops are not the norm, so expect to carry your own bags, even in high end hotels.

FACILITIES
Most hotels serve continental breakfast, though independently run guesthouses may not. Lodgings like guesthouses and hostels will usually have a selection of rooms with shared and private bathrooms. Facilities tend to be quite standard, although you may find some rooms have heated bathroom flooring.

PRICES
Lodging prices vary greatly depending on the destination and whether summer or winter is the high season. Prices are also typically higher on the weekends.

💲 Money

Cash is not king in Scandinavia, and most establishments prefer that you pay with card. Particularly in Sweden, there is a big movement toward becoming the world's first cashless society, so you may even be able to use a credit card the whole time. ATMs are widespread in case you do need to make a withdrawal.

💼 Packing

Pack layers. The weather can change swiftly, and you might be surprised at the chills as early as September. A rain jacket is essential—you'll never see an Icelander using an umbrella—as are a beanie, gloves, scarf, warm socks, thermal underwear, and sturdy shoes that can withstand wet or icy ground. If you're hiking, pack long-sleeved shirts and trousers to fend off ticks. The sun can be harsh, so sunscreen and a hat are must-haves. A swimsuit is essential for both planned and unplanned pool and hot spring visits.

💰 Tipping

Tipping is not expected but appreciated. Giving a 10% tip is enough; 20% is far too much. Always check your restaurant bill first to make sure a service charge has not already been added. The exception is Denmark, where service charges are already included in your bill by law, so tipping isn't necessary. Taxi drivers also won't expect a tip, but rounding up slightly to acknowledge good service is appreciated.

Which City Should I Stay In?

CITY	CITY VIBE	PROS	CONS
Oslo, Norway	A scenic capital between mountains and sea, also serving up eclectic architecture.	A wealth of culture, including art galleries, museums, and nightclubs, that you probably didn't bargain for.	High prices on everything from parking to accommodation and hefty taxes on alcohol.
Stockholm, Sweden	A city made up of islands! Lakeside scenery and greenery abound.	Easy to get around by public transport and walking. Friendly people and an overall buzzy, edgy vibe.	The city gets quiet during summer. Alcohol is sold at government-run establishments with limited opening hours.
Copenhagen, Denmark	Iconic architecture along charming canals, and the birthplace of New Nordic cuisine.	Diverse neighborhoods like the commune of freetown Christiania and more attractions than you'll be able to visit.	English is not as widespread as in other major Scandinavian cities.
Helsinki, Finland	Sleek architecture and design everywhere you turn.	Great shopping in the Design District, historic food markets, and the Suomenlinna fortress.	Coffee you may not be used to and long lines at nightclubs.
Reykjavík, Iceland	More of a town than a city, a place that's surprisingly youthful and warm.	Lots to do including live music gigs, festivals, and geothermal swimming pools. Easy to explore on foot.	Compact city center makes it feel very touristy; not a big highlight of Iceland.

Tours

Active

Fjord Tours

WALKING TOURS | This Bergen-based tour company specializing in hiking offers day- and week-long hiking tours in Norway's remote fjords. ⊠ *Bergen* ☎ *55/55–76–60* ⊕ *fjordtours.com* 🖃 *From $191.*

Kajak and Uteliv

ADVENTURE TOURS | Whether you'd like to kayak through the Swedish archipelago for a few hours or go on a five-day long kayaking adventure among the thousands of islands, this tour company has got you covered. ⊠ *Gräddö Brygga* ☎ *0176/403–15* ⊕ *kajak-uteliv.com/en* 🖃 *From $68.*

Nordic Footprints

ADVENTURE TOURS | This company, based in Sweden's Dalarna, focuses on sustainable travel in Sweden's wild nature, with a special emphasis on hunting and fishing. ⊠ *Husvallsgölen 28* ☎ *070/374–9074* ⊕ *nordicfootprints.se* 🖃 *From €270.*

Norsk Rejsebureau

ADVENTURE TOURS | This tour company is specialized in tours to the Norwegian fjords, whether it's mountain biking or boating in the summer or ski holidays in the winter months. ☎ *33/12–45–65* ⊕ *norskrejsebureau.dk.*

Cruise

Hurtigruten

BOAT TOURS | Hurtigruten is known for its cruises along Norway's dramatic coast, exploring the green fjords and northern lights and even heading all the way up to Antarctica and Greenland. ☎ *020/3553–0663* ⊕ *global.hurtigruten.com* 🖃 *From $1,200.*

Nyhavn Rejser

BOAT TOURS | Based in Copenhagen, this upscale travel agency organizes cruises to the other Scandinavian countries, with a focus on Norway, starting in Copenhagen. ☎ *78/73–60–90* ⊕ *nyhavn.dk* 🖃 *From $1,030.*

Scandinavia-wide

Authentic Scandinavia

BUS TOURS | Offering trips in single Scandinavian countries as well as longer tours to several of them, this company is specialized in travel in Scandinavia. ☎ *22/94–13–70* ⊕ *authentic-scandinavia.com* 🖃 *From $296.*

Baltic Travel Company

SPECIAL-INTEREST | This tour operator focuses on upscale, tailormade travels through the Nordic countries. ☎ *020/8233–2875* ⊕ *baltictravelcompany.com* 🖃 *From $2,500.*

Intrepid Travel

BUS TOURS | This tour company offers a 15-day trip through Norway, Sweden, and Finland, focusing on the stylish capitals as well as on the Norwegian fjords and Swedish lakes. ☎ *020/3308–9757* ⊕ *intrepidtravel.com/eu* 🖃 *From €4,220.*

Nordic Visitor

SPECIAL-INTEREST | Offering 10-day tours through Sweden, Denmark, and Norway as well as other itineraries to single or multiple Scandinavian countries. ☎ *578–2080* ⊕ *nordicvisitor.com* 🖃 *From $4,200 for 10-day tour.*

Contacts

✈ Air

AIRPORTS

DENMARK Copenhagen Airport (CPH). ✉ *Lufthavnsboulevarden 6, Kastrup* ☎ *32/31–32–31* ⊕ *www.cph.dk.*

FINLAND Helsinki Airport. (*HEL*). ☎ *0200/14636* ⊕ *www.finavia.fi.*

ICELAND Reiykjavík Keflavík Airport (KEF). ✉ *Keflavíkurflugvöllur, 235 Keflavík, Reykjavík* ☎ *354/424–4000 general info on Icelandic airports* ⊕ *www.isavia.is/en/keflavik-airport.*

NORWAY Oslo Airport (ARN). ✉ *Edvard Munchs veg* ☎ *67/03–00–00* ⊕ *www.oslo-airport.com.*

SWEDEN Stockholm Arlanda Airport. ☎ *010/1091000* ⊕ *www.swedavia.com/arlanda.*

AIRLINES

CONTACTS Finnair. ☎ *810–01–100 in Norway* ⊕ *www.finnair.com.* **Icelandair.** ☎ *22–03–40–50 in Norway* ⊕ *www.icelandair.com.* **Norwegian.** ☎ *815–21–815* ⊕ *www.norwegian.com.* **SAS.** ☎ *800/221–2350 in U.S. and Canada, 05400 in Norway* ⊕ *www.flysas.com.*

⛴ Boat

CONTACTS DFDS Seaways. ✉ *Sundkrogsgade 11, Copenhagen* ⊕ *www.dfdsseaways.dk.* **Molslinjen.** ⊕ *www.molslinjen.dk .* **Stena Line.** ☎ *0770/575700* ⊕ *www.stenaline.se.* **Viking Line.** ✉ *Katajanokka Terminal, South Harbour* ☎ *09/123–574 in Helsinki* ⊕ *www.vikingline.fi.*

🚌 Bus

DENMARK FlixBus. ☎ *32/72–93–86* ⊕ *www.flixbus.dk.*

FINLAND Matkahuolto. ☎ *0200/4000 €1.99/min + local network charge* ⊕ *www.matkahuolto.com.* **OnniBus.** ☎ *0600/02010 €0.99/minute* ⊕ *www.onnibus.com.*

ICELAND Strætó. ✉ *Hestháls 14, 110 Rekyjavík, Reykjavík* ☎ *354/540–2700* ⊕ *www.straeto.is.*

NORWAY NOR-WAY Bussekspress. ☎ *815–44–444* ⊕ *www.nor-way.no.*

SWEDEN FlixBus. ☎ *08/50513750* ⊕ *www.flixbus.se.*

🚆 Train

EURAIL Rail Europe. ☎ *888/382–7245, 800/622–8600 in the*

United States ⊕ *www.raileurope.com.*

DENMARK Arriva. ☎ *70/27–74–82* ⊕ *www.arriva.dk.* **DSB.** ☎ *70/13–14–15* ⊕ *www.dsb.dk.*

FINLAND Finnish State Railways. (*VR*). ☎ *0600/41900 €1.99 plus local network charge* ⊕ *www.vr.fi.*

NORWAY NSB (Norwegian State Railways). ☎ *815–00–888* ⊕ *www.nsb.no.*

SWEDEN SJ. (*State Railway Company*). ☎ *0771/757575* ⊕ *www.sj.se.*

🇺🇸 U.S. Embassy/Consulate

Denmark. ✉ *Dag Hammarskjölds Allé 24* ☎ *45/3–341–7100* ⊕ *dk.usembassy.gov*

Finland. ✉ *Itäinen Puistotie 14 B* ☎ *35/8–961–6250* ⊕ *fi.usembassy.gov*

Iceland. ✉ *Laufásvegur 21* ☎ *354/595–2200* ⊕ *is.usembassy.gov*

Norway. ✉ *Morgedalsvegen 36* ☎ *47/2–130–8540* ⊕ *no.usembassy.gov*

Sweden. ✉ *Dag Hammarskjölds Väg 31* ☎ *46/8–783–5300* ⊕ *se.usembassy.gov*

Great Itineraries

6 Days in Norway

This extremely popular trip from Oslo to Bergen—or vice versa—was created the 1960s by officials at the national rail service and is still growing in popularity today. While this train-and-ferry journey is totally doable in a single day, it pays to take more time to enjoy the scenery along the route. The five-hour trip across Norway's interior is considered one of the most spectacular train rides in the world. You can join an organized tour following this route, but there's no part of the trip that can't easily be done on your own.

DAY 1 & 2: OSLO

Chances are you'll fly into Oslo Airport on an international flight, which makes the city a great starting point for your Norway in a Nutshell adventure. While the city is quite compact and you could, in theory, see all main sights in a day, don't rush but rather take it all in, especially if this is your first time in Norway. Spend your first day in the Sentrum exploring the rooftop of the gleaming white **Opera House,** then stop at some of the newly unveiled museums, including the **Nasjonalmuseet** (set to open in 2021) and the **Munchmuseet.** In the afternoon you can wander along the waterfront to the neighborhoods of Aker Brygge and Tjuvholmen, where you'll find dozens of options for dinner. On your second day, explore the fortress of **Akershus Festning** and the opulent castle of **Slottet** before visiting the peninsula of Bygdøy with its many museums, including the **Norsk Folkemuseum** and the **Viking Ship Museum.** For dinner consider the neighborhood of Grünerløkka, which is a favorite destination for locals.

Logistics: The city center of Oslo is very walkable. You can reach the peninsula of Bygdøy by ferry or bus.

DAY 3: OSLO TO FLÅM

On your third day, start early and take the Bergen train line to the mountain village **Myrdal.** When you reach the station, transfer to the **Flåmsbana** railway, a tiny train that winds its way down the mountain between towering cliffs and cascading waterfalls. The trip from Myrdal to **Flåm** covers 12 miles and takes a little under an hour. You should reach Flåm by late afternoon, giving you enough time to relax in an outdoor café, do a little souvenir shopping, and perhaps visit the **Flåmsbanemuseet,** which gives you a look at how the railway was constructed. Stay overnight in Flåm or one of the nearby villages

Logistics: You can easily explore Flåm on foot.

DAY 4: FLÅM TO VOSS

This leg of your journey begins with a boat trip from Flåm through Aurlandsfjord and into the UNESCO World Heritage Site of Nærøyfjord, the narrowest fjord in Europe. Both inlets are part of the larger Sognefjord, one of Norway's most famous fjords and, at 127 miles from end to end, its longest. The ride lasts two hours and ends at Gudvangen, at which point you board a bus for the one-hour trip to Voss along the old Stalheimskleivane Road with its dramatic hairpin bends. If you can, try to book your stay at the 18th-century Stalheim Hotel, about 22 miles outside Voss.

Logistics: You can easily explore Voss on foot.

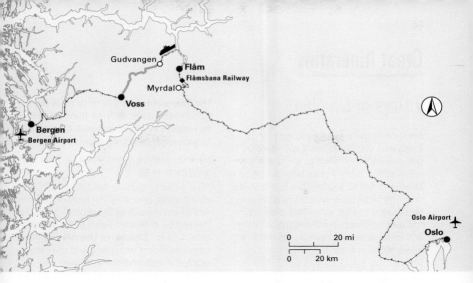

DAY 5 & 6: BERGEN

From Voss, the train to Bergen takes one hour. When you get to Bergen, check into your hotel and head to **Bryggen** to explore the old wharf where some of the city's oldest and best-preserved buildings are found, followed by some souvenir shopping and dinner down by the fish market. Spend your sixth day exploring more of Bergen, starting with a ride on the **Fløibanen** funicular and a walk at the top of **Mt. Fløyen,** where you have a magnificent view of the town from above. If you still have time afterwards, visit the **Edvard Greig Museum** south of the city. Head back to Oslo by train or plane, or see if you can find an outbound flight home that departs from Bergen.

Logistics: The city center of Bergen can easily be explored on foot.

Tips

Especially during peak season in summer, booking your own train and ferry tickets can be significantly cheaper than opting for a tour package.

Train tickets between Oslo and Bergen are usually cheapest about three months in advance.

When traveling in winter, remember that you're only going to get six or seven hours of daylight.

Great Itineraries

7 Days in Sweden

Sweden is quite a large country by European standards, so if you've only got a week you'll want to choose a few areas to focus on. Public transportation is excellent, but to explore the countryside properly, especially with limited time, you'll want to rent a car. This itinerary focuses on Sweden's three major cities and other areas that can be visited in a week without a car.

DAYS 1–2: STOCKHOLM

Stockholm is the arrival point for most international travelers to Sweden, and you'll want to linger in the national capital for at least a couple of days. Start with a tour of **Stadshuset** (City Hall), where Nobel Prize banquets and balls are held. If you're visiting between May and September, don't miss the chance to admire the view from the top of the tower—get your timed tickets first thing in the morning to avoid disappointment. Next, head to **Gamla Stan**, the beautifully preserved Old Town, which has narrow cobblestoned streets lined with shops and restaurants. Stop into two of the city's oldest churches, **Storkyrkan** and **Riddarholmskyrkan**, both of which date to the 13th century, or explore the past and present of Swedish royalty at the **Kungliga Slottet** (Royal Palace), the **Tre Kronor Museum**, and **Livrustkammaren** (the Royal Armory). Wrap up the day's sightseeing with a look at Stockholm from the water on a guided boat tour (you'll find several at the quay by the Grand Hôtel). On day 2, head to the island of **Djurgården**, home to several of Stockholm's best museums, including the must-see **Vasamuseet** and the world's oldest open-air museum, **Skansen**. It's well worth walking at least one way along the splendid waterfront boulevard **Strandvägen**. The surrounding streets of the **Östermalm** neighborhood have many good restaurants. ■ TIP→ **Djurgården can be reached by streetcar from T-Centralen or by passenger ferry from Slussen.**

DAY 3: DAY-TRIP FROM STOCKHOLM

Take a day to explore the beautiful countryside or one of the historic towns within easy reach of Stockholm. If you're interested in history, head to Sweden's oldest town, **Sigtuna**, or **Uppsala**, home to both the oldest university and the tallest cathedral in Scandinavia, as well as ancient burial mounds from pre-Christian times. If you love castles and palaces, **Drottningholm**, **Skokloster**, and **Mariefred** are all great options. For stunning coastal scenery and pretty small towns, travel an hour south of Stockholm to **Nynäshamn** or **Trosa**, or catch an archipelago boat to **Vaxholm** or **Sandhamn**. ■ TIP→ **Uppsala, Trosa, and Nynäshamn are easily reachable by train or bus. Sigtuna, Skokloster, and Mariefred can be visited on boat excursions from Stockholm or by bus or train. Boats to the Vaxholm, Sandhamn, and other islands in the Stockholm archipelago depart from Strömkajen or Nybrokajen.**

DAYS 4–5: GÖTEBORG

Catch a morning train for the three- to four-hour journey from Stockholm to Sweden's second city, arriving midday. Head to Göteborg's **Stadsmuseum** to learn about the city's past, then take a boat tour from Kungsportsplatsen along the old moat and into the harbor for a good overview of central **Göteborg**. You'll find many shops and restaurants around **Kungsportsplatsen** and the surrounding downtown streets. On your second day, take a walk through the pretty **Trädgårdsföreningen Park**, then continue west to the Haga neighborhood. Stroll along **Haga Nygata**, once one of Göteborg's poorest neighborhoods but now one of the city's most delightful

shopping streets. Continue through the leafy **Vasastaden** neighborhood, home to Göteborg University. Eventually you'll arrive at **Kungsportsavenyn**, the city's main thoroughfare. At its southeastern end, you'll find **Götaplatsen**, surrounded by several of the city's top cultural institutions, including **Göteborgs Konstmuseum**, one of Sweden's best art museums. Many outstanding restaurants are located in this neighborhood, making it a great place for dinner. ■ TIP→ **Göteborg is a very walkable city, and also has an efficient network of streetcars and buses.**

DAYS 6–7: SKÅNE

In the morning, catch the train for the three-hour journey to **Malmö**, Sweden's third-largest city, located in Sweden's southernmost province, **Skåne**. This region was a part of Denmark for centuries and retains its distinct character. Spend the afternoon exploring Malmö's compact city center with its many squares and delightful mix of old and new. As in Göteborg, a good way to get an overview and learn about the city's history is by taking a guided boat tour on the canals; boats depart from opposite the train station. **Malmöhus**, the city's 16th-century castle, is also worth a visit. On your second day in Skåne, take the train to historic **Lund**, home to Sweden's

Tips

Boat trips on Lake Mälaren and to the Stockholm archipelago generally operate only in summer.

Swedish summers have been getting hotter, but air conditioning is still relatively uncommon in hotels. Choose your accommodations carefully if this is an issue for you. Also, note that most Swedes take vacation from around late June to early August, so hotels in popular destinations may be crowded during this time.

To avoid backtracking to Stockholm, look for a return flight departing from Copenhagen Airport. It's only 20 minutes from Malmö by train, or 33 minutes from Lund.

second-oldest university, a magnificent 12th-century cathedral, several interesting museums, and an appealing maze of streets reflecting the city's medieval origins. ■ TIP→ **Logistics: Both Malmö and Lund are easily explored on foot. Trains run very frequently and take less than 15 minutes.**

Great Itineraries

10 Days in Denmark

Denmark is the smallest of the Scandinavian countries—it only takes five hours to drive from Copenhagen to Skagen, the northernmost part of the country. Given its small size and its many public roads, ferries, trains, and buses, it's easy to see most of the country in a week. Though well linked to the rest of the country, the many beautiful islands beckon you to stay longer. If you truly want to enjoy the Danish way of life—biking rather than driving, cooking with local produce from roadside stands, exploring its forests and beaches on foot, lazing at the many harbor baths in the big cities, picnicking in royal parks, and having plenty of time for *hygge* (coziness) at cute cafés—it's a good idea to stay longer and travel more slowly. For a whirlwind tour of the top attractions, you can get by with a bit over a week.

DAYS 1–2: COPENHAGEN

Copenhagen is the arrival point for most international travelers and the gateway to the rest of Scandinavia. The cosmopolitan capital is a pleasant place to get your bearings, and you could easily spend a week here exploring the royal castles, historical attractions, contemporary architecture, and the restaurants, amusement parks, public harbor baths, and design stores. Biking is the best way to get around, though the public transport is great too. Start off in the center, **Indre By**, where most of the castles and historical attractions are located. Explore those by bike or boat—the canal tours are a great way of checking off the top attractions while also seeing local life unfold by the sides of the canals—before heading off into the bridge quarters, pretty **Christianshavn** (and the nearby freetown Christiania), and the island of **Refshaleøen**. The latter is a former shipyard that's now

an urban paradise with harbor baths and saunas, an artificial ski slope, and some of the country's best restaurants.

DAY 3: NORTH OF COPENHAGEN AND DENMARK'S RIVIERA

The area north of Copenhagen is home to many of Denmark's most affluent suburbs, Renaissance castles, and art museums, while the northern coast of **Zealand** is dotted by a string of small, coastal villages that once were home to fishermen but now attract well-off vacationers. Head to Dyrehaven, the Deer Park, for a stroll through the lush forest, cruise up the coast to the modern art museum Louisiana, make a stop at the Renaissance castle **Kronborg**, and end the day by checking into a storied beach hotel such as Helenekilde. The coastal towns hugging the northern coast are home to sandy beaches, traditional fish restaurants, and upscale dining options.

DAYS 4–5: ODENSE, SVENDBORG, AND ÆRØ

Denmark's most famous person might be Hans Christian Andersen, who spun fairy tales such as "The Little Mermaid," "The Nightingale," and "The Emperor's New Clothes." He was born in **Odense**, Funen's biggest city, where you'll find several museums and gardens dedicated to him. The museums are located in a quaint part of town with cobblestoned streets and traditional restaurants, though the city is also home to some of Denmark's best contemporary dining and wine bars. Spend the day exploring Odense, and then head south to **Svendborg**, stopping at the Renaissance castle **Egeskov** on the way. Svendborg is a charming town with a strong maritime history and the gateway to the southern isles of Denmark. Spend the night here before getting on a ferry to the islands, leaving from Svendborg's atmospheric marina. With its cobblestone streets, half-timber houses, coastal bike paths, and colorful beach shacks, **Ærø** might be the prettiest of the many islands dotting the waters south of Funen.

DAYS 6–7: AARHUS

Take the ferry from Ærø to **Jutland** and drive through pretty **Sønderborg** and storied **Ribe**, Denmark's oldest town, on your way up to **Aarhus**. Denmark's second city is home to a pretty Latin Quarter bursting with cute cafés, stylish shops, and great restaurants, a popular harbor bath, and ARoS, one of northern Europe's largest and most popular art museums. The city is located on the coast, and to the south of it you'll find a royal castle, beautiful beaches, a circular bridge over the sea, and the **Moesgaard Museum**. The museum focuses on archaeology and ethnography, but with its stunning design and interactive elements, it is anything but dusty.

DAY 8: SAMSØ

With its rolling hills, roadside stands selling organic strawberries, beautiful sandy beaches, endless bike paths, and stunning sunsets, **Samsø** is the perfect place to spend a Danish summer day. Accommodation ranges from traditional beach hotels to beachside camping, and the restaurants—traditional as well as contemporary—serve fresh fish, vegetables, and meat from local farmers. There are ferry connections—1 to 1½ hours—to both Zealand and Jutland, making it possible to stay just for a day, though it's tempting to stay much longer.

DAYS 9–10: SKAGEN OR BORNHOLM

For your last few days, head either to **Skagen**, famed for its natural light and the artists that have flocked to it, or to **Bornholm**, an island of rugged beauty and culinary renown. At the former you

can stroll along the beaches the Skagen School painters depicted and stay at the hotels they frequented. In July, Skagen is a popular vacation spot of the moneyed classes as well as those who like to party hard. On Bornholm you can hike Denmark's most dramatic coast, dine at a Michelin-starred restaurant surrounded by sand dunes and pine forest, and go on a day trip to tiny **Christiansø**. The island is hillier than the rest of Denmark, and the rugged cliffs and medieval ruins offer excellent hiking. From Skagen it's easy to take the ferry onward to Norway. Bornholm is located closer to Sweden than the Danish mainland, and there are direct ferry connections to Sweden's southern coast.

Great Itineraries

7 Days in Finland

Crisp winter days are thrilling and bracing in Helsinki, with the inlets of the Baltic Sea frozen so thick you can walk on them, the trees sugared with frost, and the many cafés and bars offering cozy replenishments. The vivid colors of autumn and the sudden explosion of spring offer their own seasonal rewards in the capital and across the country, but if you want to plan your visit for the optimal time, it has to be summer.

DAYS 1–3: HELSINKI

Whether you arrive in **Helsinki** at the airy and expanding international airport or disembark by ferry from Sweden or Estonia, you'll be able to bask in the magical northern light and general sense of breezy contentment among the citizenry from around mid-May until the end of August. Check in to one of the many comfortable and modern downtown hotels before spending your first full day exploring the islands. Shop for ingredients for a picnic lunch at the quayside **Kauppatori** (Market Square) or **Old Market Hall**, before jumping on the ferry to the **Suomenlinna** sea fortress, with its romantic sea views, 18th-century fortifications, museums, and cafés. On your return trip take a ferry that stops at thickly wooded **Vallisaari island**, with more breathtaking sea and city views. Save time for a swim at the heated **Allas Sea Pool** in Eteläsatama (South Harbour), where you'll also have the perfect opportunity to sample that most Finnish of traditions: the sauna. Complete the day with a seafood meal at the offshore island summer restaurant **Saari**.

The Finnish capital is a great outdoor summer city, but it's well supplied with absorbing cultural attractions, most of them within comfortable strolling distance of each other. Spend your second day exploring them. Start by dropping into Helsinki's new pride and joy, the new central library known as **Oodi** near the **Central Railway Station**. Head up to the third-floor open balcony, admiring the bright, open-plan architecture on the way, and soak up the view of the somewhat solemn but impressive parliament. Next stop could be **Museum of Contemporary Art Kiasma**, another strikingly modern landmark housing always thought-provoking exhibits, followed by **Amos Rex**, nestling under the **Lasipalatsi** (Glass Palace) across Mannerheimintie street and another magnet for modern art enthusiasts. The church-like spire of the **National Museum**, guarded by an impressive stone bear, is a nearby landmark. Secure tickets for an evening concert at the **Music Center** or **Finlandia Hall** or for a performance at the **Opera House**.

Rent a bike in the morning from one of the many City Bike stands around town and head out into the suburbs and along the leafy tracks that trace the shorelines, out toward the islands of **Lauttasaari** to the west or **Kulosaari** in the east. For a more leisurely ride, head off into the Central Park or follow the former rail track, known as Baana, before following the coast to **Kaivopuisto Park**; have lunch at the seaside Café Ursula before heading back downtown via the South Harbour. In the afternoon, park your bike and indulge in some quality souvenir and gift shopping in the boutiques and brand showrooms of the Design District.

DAY 4: PORVOO OR TURKU

Option 1: Hang on to your Helsinki lodgings and take the old coastal steamer, the *J. L. Runeberg,* to the charming old town of **Porvoo**, and drink in the restful archipelago scenery—along with a beer, perhaps—during the voyage. Spend the day wandering the cobbled lanes, riverside warehouse cafés, and handsome

stone cathedral, calling in to some of the quaint cafés and bars. Don't miss the Brunberg chocolate shop! Take the 50-minute bus back to Helsinki in the evening.

Option 2: Take the two-hour train trip to **Turku**, Finland's former capital, in the morning. Head down to the banks of the Aura River and explore the historical sites clustered along its banks. Start with the dominant originally 12th-century cathedral, now the center of the Lutheran Church in Finland. Follow up with the **Aboa Vetus** and **Ars Nova** Museums, continue to the **Forum Marinum maritime museum** and the magnificent *Suomen Joutsen* sailing barque, and finish up with a visit to the 700-year-old castle. There are cafés, bars, and restaurants along the way where you can enjoy a riverside lunch or early dinner. Take a taxi or bus from the castle back to the station to catch the train back to Helsinki.

DAYS 5–6: LAKELAND

Take the train to **Lakeland**. You could head off to **Savonlinna** and catch an opera if you are there for the opera festival in the courtyard of its splendid castle, or just take a lunch cruise on one of the beautifully preserved Lakeland steamers docked in the harbor. Spend the night in the town or at the **Hotel Punkaharju** on the spectacular lake-splitting ridge of the same name, which you can reach by leisurely steamer in summer or by a 30-minute train ride. Dine at the hotel or seek out a menu of tiny, crisp fried vendace in town. And don't forget to sample a fresh *lörtsy*, a sumptuous doughnut, at the marketplace in Savonlinna.

Spend a quiet day enjoying the classic Lakeland scenery with walks in and around Savonlinna. Visit the **Lusto Museum of the Forest** at Punkaharju. If you are a guest at the Hotel Punkaharju or if you have arranged a lakeside cabin stay, this is your chance to sample the essence of Finnish summer, reading or rowing and relaxing in a wood-fired sauna interspersed with the occasional swim.

DAY 7: HELSINKI

Take the train back to Helsinki for last-minute shopping before a final night in the capital. Spend part of it having an aperitif in one of the trendy bars in the bohemian **Kallio** district to the east of the city, before heading back to the downtown area to splurge on a gourmet meal at one of Helsinki's six Michelin-starred restaurants.

Great Itineraries

Iceland in 3 Days

Make the most of a stopover by seeing everything Reykjavík has to offer, which is quite doable thanks to the capital's small size.

Start with a dip in the **Blue Lagoon** on your way in from the airport—it's the perfect cure for jet lag. While you're here, you can relax, get a massage, eat lunch—and grab that essential photo of being surrounded by otherworldly blue water.

Give yourself a day to explore the must-sees of downtown Reykjavík. Stick to the water's edge for views of the **Harpa Concert Hall,** with its beguiling windows, then walk along the shore to the **Sun Voyager** sculpture proudly displayed against a backdrop of mountains. Heading into the downtown area, explore everything the main shopping street, **Laugavegur,** has to offer, plus its neighbors **Austurstræti, Bankastræti,** and **Lækjargata.** Climb the hill to enjoy the intense architecture and serene interior of **Hallgrímskirkja church,** which can be seen from almost anywhere in the city (making it an excellent wayfinder).

Spend your third day diving more deeply into the city by taking in a concert at **Harpa,** buying a *lopapeysa* (traditional Icelandic sweater) at the **Kolaportið** flea market, or reserving dinner at **Dill,** the finest restaurant in the city. Keep an eye out for public art works like giant murals or tiny sculptures: Reykjavík is full of them.

GOLDEN CIRCLE

Almost every trip to Iceland includes a tour of the Golden Circle, a trifecta of unmissable sights in southwest Iceland, about an hour's drive from Reykjavík.

The Golden Circle includes **Þingvellir National Park,** the **Geysir Geothermal Area,** and **Gullfoss waterfall,** each of which is remarkable in its own way. This particular itinerary covering these three iconic sights is roughly 155 miles, and a full day should be enough time to enjoy each sight thoroughly. Þingvellir National Park, which is where most begin their tour, is a place of great historical significance, as it was the site of Iceland's first parliamentary meeting in AD 930. These days, it's beloved for its beautiful geologic features, as this is where the North American and Eurasian tectonic plates are moving apart, creating a rift visible only in Iceland. About 50 minutes away is the Geysir Geothermal Area, where the geyser Strokkur reliably shoots 140°F water into the air every 10 minutes or so. Finish at the remarkable Gullfoss waterfall, just 10 minutes from Geysir. This powerful work of nature is exciting to see any time of year, but it's especially fun when the sun is out, creating rainbows.

THE RING ROAD

This 828-mile-long stretch, known as the Ring Road (Route 1), is one of Iceland's top attractions. Most major sights can be found along this road, and although it can be driven in as little as 14 hours (nobody does this), some take a full month to enjoy everything it has to offer. Weather and road conditions will play a factor in your pace, which is especially

important for those planning a winter visit. The speed limit is almost always 55 mph, but a snowstorm can cut that down quite a bit—sometimes to zero, when you have to stop and wait out the storm. In summer, a week is a good amount of time for the Ring Road, and at least two weeks in winter. In the south, waterfalls like **Seljalandsfoss** and **Skógafoss** are must-sees, and the black-sand beach of **Reynisfjara** is also very popular. In North Iceland, **Mývatn** is the best stop that doesn't entail a detour from the Ring Road, and fortunately it has a lot to offer: **Lake Mývatn** is a natural wonder, where plant and animal life flourish, while hot springs and caves delight visitors. Some of these caves are part of the **Dimmuborgir** lava field (sometimes called "the Gateway to Hell"), which is right next to Mývatn. Finally, no Ring Road trip is complete without witnessing the beauty of the **Jökulsárlón glacial lake** and the nearby beach covered in little icebergs.

WESTERN ICELAND

The Westfjords are an underappreciated region of the country, making them an ideal destination for those wishing to ditch the crowds. There's a lot to see in this quirky system of fjords, from the **Látrabjarg bird cliffs,** which is one of the best places in the country to spot Atlantic puffins, to the random collection of accordions at the **Westfjord Heritage Museum** in Ísafjörður. The **Dynjandi** waterfall is perhaps the best of the Westfjords waterfalls and also a great place to camp. The road out here can be rocky and full of potholes, so be sure to get car insurance if you're headed this way. Other highlights include the **Sea Monster Museum** in Bíldudalur and the Belgian waffles at **Simbahöllin Cafe** in Þingeyri. Animal lovers should check out the **Arctic Fox Centre** in Súðavík, where guests can sometimes catch a glimpse of a live fox under care.

Great Itineraries

2 Weeks in Scandinavia

Scandinavia is defined by water. Glaciers, rivers, and tides determine the geography; oceans shape history and culture. What better way, then, to see the land of the Vikings than by water?

DENMARK: 3 DAYS

Fly to Copenhagen. Explore the city and its waterways: Nyhavn's tall ships and myriad restaurants; Christianshavn, with its moat and canals reflecting colorful old buildings; and the canal-ringed palace of Christiansborg, where you can visit the Danish parliament and the royal reception rooms. Enjoy the twinkling lights and happy atmosphere of Tivoli from mid-April through mid-September and its Christmas market from mid-November to early January. Take a harbor cruise, passing Den Lille Havfrue (The Little Mermaid) perched on her rock. Sun on the beaches north of town or sail the Øresund along the Danish-Swedish border. You'll love the castle of Frederiksborg, set in its lake a little less than an hour north of Copenhagen, and the Karen Blixen Museum at Rungstedlund. Continue by air to Stockholm.

SWEDEN: 6 DAYS

Stockholm is made up of 14 islands surrounded by sparkling water, clean enough for fishing and swimming even in the city center. You can take ferries all around town and out to the enchanting archipelago of 24,000 islands. Don't miss the picturesque Old Town; the museum for the salvaged 17th-century warship *Vasa*; or Skansen, the world's oldest open-air museum. From Stockholm, take the train across Sweden to Göteborg, where you can explore the west-coast beaches warmed by the Gulf Stream. Try sea fishing or windsurfing, and visit the 17th-century fortress of Elfsborg, which guards the harbor entrance. Take a ferry to Oslo.

NORWAY: 5 DAYS

In Oslo, visit the Viking Ship and Kon-Tiki museums and the fabulous Vigeland sculpture park. The Bergen Railway will carry you across Norway in about seven hours. If you have an extra day, stop in Myrdal for a side trip on the Flåm Railway and a short cruise on Aurlandsfjord before continuing to Bergen. Here you can explore Bryggen, a collection of reconstructed houses dating from the 14th century, the famous fish market, and the funicular. View the magnificent, ever-changing Norwegian coastline aboard a Hurtigruten coastal express ship to Trondheim, where you can fly to Oslo or Copenhagen, then home.

ALTERNATES: BORNHOLM AND GOTLAND

If you already know Copenhagen and Stockholm, consider visiting the island of Bornholm in Denmark or Sweden's Gotland. Bornholm is graced by beaches perfect for surfing and sailing; excellent golf courses; one of the largest castle ruins in Scandinavia; and some memorable architecture, including the famous round churches from the 12th and 13th centuries. You can reach it by ferry from Copenhagen or Ystad, in southern Sweden, bringing your car if you like. Or you can fly to Rønne, the capital of Bornholm, directly from Copenhagen in about 30 minutes. Gotland is the largest island in the Baltic, with peaceful towns and fishing villages and a striking capital, Visby, with medieval flavor and a well-preserved city wall dating from the 14th and 15th centuries. Medieval Week in early August is celebrated with knights, tournaments, and other special attractions. Ferries sail from Stockholm and several other Swedish ports.

On the Calendar

January

Tromsø International Film Festival. The world's northernmost film festival screens national and international films on an outdoor screen during the third week of January. ⊕ *https://tiff.no/en*

Northern Lights Festival. This classical music festival in Tromsø also features jazz, opera, and chamber music. ⊕ *https://www.nordlysfestivalen.no/en/*

Thorrablot. Also known as Iceland's "ugly food festival," Thorrablot is celebrated from mid-January to mid-February with mixed platters of Icelandic traditional foods like boiled sheep's head, fermented shark, and blood sausage showing up on restaurant menus.

February

Finlandia Ski Marathon. Over 4,000 skiers take part in daring freestyle and classic races in Lahti. ⊕ *www.finlandiahiihto.fi*

Ice Music Festival. All the instruments at this annual celebration are made of ice, including ice cellos and ice drums. ⊕ *https://www.icemusicfestivalnorway.no*

Jokkmokk Winter Market. The annual Sami winter market in Swedish Lapland is a mainstay over hundreds of years. Discover the indigenous culture via traditional meals, art, and clothing. ⊕ *www.swedishlapland.com/stories/jokkmokk-winter-market-with-a-taste-of-history-and-nature*

Røros Winter Fair. Held since 1854, this massive outdoor market welcomes 80 horse-drawn sleighs from around the region. ⊕ *https://www.roros.no/en/roros-winter-fair/*

March

Borealis. Bergen's experimental music festival includes everything from art exhibitions to film screenings. ⊕ *https://www.borealisfestival.no/en/*

Finnmarksløpet. This dogsled race travels across Norway's northernmost region. ⊕ *https://www.finnmarkslopet.no/home/*

Inari Reindeer Championships. Hundreds of reindeer pull racers on skis in this Lapland competition. It takes place over several heats, with a grand finale showdown to finish. ⊕ *www.inarisaariselka.fi/events/reindeer-championships-in-inari*

Iceland Winter Games. Dogsledding, skiing, and snowboarding off Icelandic volcano jumps, snowmobiling races, and more take place during this three-day winter sports extravaganza. ⊕ *www.icelandwintergames.com*

Vasaloppet. On the first Sunday, cross-country skiers enter into an exhilarating long-distance race where stamina and the elements are put to the test. ⊕ *www.vasaloppet.se*

April

Friday Rock in Tivoli. From mid-April to September, catch an open-air concert in Copenhagen's Tivoli Gardens every Friday night. ⊕ *www.fredagsrock.dk*

Sami Easter Festival. A cultural gathering in Karasjok where the Sami people enjoy ice-fishing competitions and reindeer races. ⊕ *http://www.samieasterfestival.com/home.html*

Walpurgis Night. This ancient Christian feast day is celebrated on April 30. In Helsinki, crowds gather around a nude female statue while in Sweden, giant bonfires are lit to ward away evil spirits.

On the Calendar

May

Aalborg Carnival. This Danish carnival, the largest in northern Europe, has fun and games for all the family.

Norwegian National Day. On May 17, Norwegians celebrate their country with parades, hot dogs, and ice cream. ⊕ *https://www.visitnorway.com/typically-norwegian/norways-national-day/*

June

Arctic Open. Golf under the midnight sun, anyone? During this 36-hole tournament in northern Iceland, players tee off into the evening against a breathtaking green landscape. ⊕ *www.arcticopen.is*

A Taste of Stockholm. The food festival boasts food trucks and stands from local restaurants and artisans. ⊕ *www.smakapastockholm.se*

Fanø International Kite Fliers Meeting. Thousands of kites fill the sky on the Danish island of Fanø over two weeks. ⊕ *www.visitdenmark.com/danmark/explore/fano-internationale-dragefestival-gdk975870*

Midnight Sun Marathon. The Arctic city of Tromsø sponsors this run on a night when the sun doesn't set. ⊕ *https://www.msm.no/en/arrangement/midnight-sun-marathon/*

Roskilde Festival. An annual nonprofit music festival held in the Danish city of Roskilde since 1971. Big-name acts have included Bob Marley, Metallica, and Nirvana over the years. ⊕ *www.roskilde-festival.dk*

Sankthansaften. On Saint John's Eve on June 23, Norwegians celebrate with bonfires all around the country but with the most gusto in Ålesund. ⊕ *www.visitnorway.com/media/news-from-norway/sankthans-finds-norway-at-its-brightest-and-most-summery*

Ystad Sweden Jazz Festival. Five days of cool beats in the beautiful century-old Ystad Theater. Tickets tend to sell out by April. ⊕ *www.ystadjazz.se*

July

Copenhagen Jazz Festival. Copenhagen's biggest festival takes place in early July with a wave of Danish and international talent. A sister event, Vinterjazz, is held in February. ⊕ *www.jazz.dk*

Moldejazz. The biggest jazz festival in Norway, Moldejazz takes place in the western fjords. ⊕ *https://www.moldejazz.no/en/*

Riddu Riddu. Riddu Riddu is an indigenous culture and music festival hosted in the Lyngen Alps near Tromsø in mid-July. ⊕ *https://riddu.no/en*

Savonlinna Opera Festival. Opera singers show off their pipes in this world-renowned festival taking place in the medieval Olavinlinna fortress. ⊕ *www.operafestival.fi*

National Festival. Iceland's largest outdoor annual festival is all about bonfire flames, fireworks, music, and a lot of alcohol in Vestmannaeyjar off the coast. ⊕ *www.dalurinn.is*

August

Copenhagen Cooking and Food Festival.
Discover trendy New Nordic cuisine in its
birthplace with food stands, dinners, and
workshops on everything from sustainability to pickling. ⊕ www.copenhagen-
cooking.com

Malmö Festival. With over a million visitors
every year, the Swedish city's festival is
a whirlwind of band and orchestra performances and art installations. ⊕ www.
malmofestivalen.se

Norwegian International Film Festival. Held
in Haugesund, this festival gives out the
prestigious Amanda Award. ⊕ https://
filmfestivalen.no/en/

September

Helsinki Design Week. Style gurus
brandish the best of Finnish design and
aesthetic with plenty of parties and pop-
ups over 10 days. ⊕ www.helsinkidesign-
week.com

SMAK. This salute to northern Norwegian cuisine is held annually in Tromsø.
⊕ https://www.smakfest.no/en/

October

Helsinki Baltic Herring Market. Taking place
since 1743, this fair in Helsinki's Market
Square is the place to try the salty,
marinated specialty. ⊕ www.silakkamark-
kinat.fi

Dark Season Blues Festival. The sun
doesn't rise in Svalbard for four months,
and locals like to say goodbye to the light
with a bang. ⊕ https://www.svalbard-
blues.com

November

Iceland Airwaves. Reykjavík reinforces
itself as an awesome live-music destination with this downtown festival spread
across several clubs and bars. ⊕ www.
icelandairwaves.is

Pepperkakebyen Bergen. Norway's biggest
gingerbread village opens in Bergen.
⊕ http://www.pepperkakebyen.org

Stockholm Film Festival. In the second
half of November, catch screenings from
around the globe—and perhaps even
sightings of big-name actors and direc-
tors. ⊕ www.stockholmfilmfestival.se

December

Christmas Market Røros. This UNESCO
World Heritage Site becomes a winter
wonderland. ⊕ https://julemarkedroros.no

Tivoli Christmas Market. From mid-November to early January, experience true
hygge with mulled wine and a winter
wonderland of fairy lights. ⊕ www.tivoli-
gardens.com/en/saesoner/jul

Helpful Icleandic Phrases

BASICS

Hello	Halló	hahl-lo
Yes/No	Já / Nei	yow / nay
Thank you	Takk fyrir	tak fear-ir
You're welcome	Verði þér að góðu	Vare-thee thear ahh goh-thu
I'm Sorry (apology)	Ég biðst afsökunar	Yehg bithst af-seh-kunar
Sorry (Excuse me)	Afsakið	af-sah-kith
Good morning	Góðan daginn	goh-thahn dahg-in
Good day	Góðan daginn	goh-thahn dahg-in
Good evening	Gott kvöld	goht kvuhld
Goodbye	Bless	bless
Mr. (Sir)	Herra	her rah
Mrs.	Frú	froo
Miss	Fröken	fruh-ken
Pleased to meet you	Gaman að kynnast þér	gam-an ath kin-nast thear
How are you?	Hvað segirðu gott?	kvahth seg-ir-thu goht

NUMBERS

one-half	hálfur	howl-ver
one	einn	ehnn
two	tveir	tvere
three	þrír	threer
four	fjórir	fyohr-eer
five	fimm	fim
six	sex	sex
seven	Sjö	syuh
eight	átta	owt-ta
nine	níu	nee-uh
ten	tíu	tee-uh
eleven	ellefu	elh-leh-vu
twelve	tólf	tulv
thirteen	Þrettán	Thret-town
fourteen	fjórtán	fyor-town
fifteen	fimmtán	fim-town
sixteen	sextán	sex-town
seventeen	sautján	soy-tyown
eighteen	átján	owt-yown
nineteen	nítján	nee-tyown
twenty	tuttugu	too-too-goo
twenty-one	tuttugu og einn	too-too-goo og ehnn
thirty	þrjátíu	thryow-tee-uh
fifty	fimmtíu	fim-tee-uh
sixty	sextíu	sex-tee-uh
seventy	sjötíu	syuh-tee-uh
eighty	áttatíu	owt-ta-tee-uh
ninety	nítíu	nee-tee-uh
one hundred	eitt hundrað	eht-hundrath
one thousand	eitt þúsund	eht- thoo-sund
one million	ein milljón	ehn-mill-yohn

COLORS

black	svartur	svar-ter
blue	blár	blaowr
brown	brúnn	broon
green	grænn	grine
orange	appelsínugulur	apple-see-nuh-guh-lur
red	rauður	roy-therr
white	hvítur	hvee-tur
yellow	gulur	goo-lur

DAYS OF THE WEEK

Sunday	sunnudagur	soon-new-dah-g
Monday	mánudagur	mow-new-dah-g
Tuesday	þriðjudagur	thrith-hue-dah-g
Wednesday	miðvikudagur	mith-vik-oo-dah-
Thursday	Fimmtudagur	fim-too-dah-gur
Friday	föstudagur	fuhst-oo-dah-gu
Saturday	laugardagur	loy-gahr-dah-gu

MONTHS

January	Janúar	yah-new-ahr
February	Febrúar	feb-roo-ahr
March	Mars	mars
April	Apríl	ahh-preel
May	Mai	my
June	Júní	yoon-ee
July	Júlí	yoo-lee
August	Ágúst	ow-goost
September	September	sef-tem-ber
October	Október	og-toh-beer
November	Nóvember	noh-vem-beer
December	Desember	deh-sem-beer

USEFUL WORDS AND PHRASES

Do you speak English?	Talar þú ensku	tah-lahr thoo ehn-skuh
I don't speak [Language].	Ég tala ekki tungumálið	yehg tah-lah eh-kee toon-guh-mow-li
I don't understand.	Ég skil ekki	yehg skill eh-kee
I don't know.	Éég veit það ekki	yehg veht thahth eh-kee
I understand.	Ég skil	yehg skill
I'm American.	Ég er ameríkani	yehg ehr ah-meh ee-kahn-ee
I'm British.	Ég er breti	yehg ehr breht-e
What's your name.	Hvað heitirðu?	kvahth hate-er-th
My name is ...	Ég heiti	yehg hate-ee
What time is it?	Hvað er klukkan?	kvahth ehr kluh-kahn
How?	Hvernig?	kvehr-nig
When?	Hvenær	kveh-nuyr
Yesterday	Í gær	ee guy-r
Today	Í dag	ee dahg

Tomorrow	Á morgunn	ow mor-guhn
This morning	Þennan morgunn	then-nahn mor-guhn
This afternoon	Þennan eftirmiðdag	then-nahn eftir-mith-dahg
Tonight	Í kvöld	ee-kvuhld
What?	Hvað?	kvahth
What is it?	Hvað er það?	kvahth ehr thahth
Why?	Af hverju?	ahf kvair-yoo
Who?	Hver?	kvair
Where is ...	Hvar er...	kvahr ehr
... the bus stop?	strætó stoppistöðin?	strie-toe stop-pi-stuh-thin
... the airport?	flugvöllurinn?	floog-vuhllh-uh-rinn
... the post office?	pósthúsið?	post-hoosith
... the bank?	bankinn?	bank-inn
... the hotel?	hótelið?	hotel-ith
... the museum?	safnið?	sabn-ith
... the hospital?	spítalinn?	speet-ahl-in
... the elevator?	lyfturnar?	lift-ur-nar
Where are the restrooms?	klósettin?	cloe-set-in
Here/there	hér / þar	here/thar
Left/right	vinstri / hægri	vin-stree/high-gree
Is it near/far?	Er það nálægt/ langt í burtu?	ehr thahth now-legt
I'd like ...	Ég myndi vilja	yehg mind-ee vil-yah
... a room	herbergi	hair-behr-gee
... the key	lykill	lih-kilh
... a newspaper	fréttablað	Fretta-blahth
... a stamp	stimpill	Stim-pilh
I'd like to buy ...	Ég myndi vilja kaupa	yehg mind-ee vil-yah koy-pah....
... a city map	kort af borginni	kort ahf borg-in-nee
... a road map	kort af vegunum	kort ahf veg-oo-num
... a magaine	tímarit	teem ar-it
... envelopes	umslög	um-sluhgh
... writing paper	blöð til að skrifa á	bluhth til ahth skriva ow
... a postcard	póstkort	post-kort
... a ticket	miða	mi-tha
How much is it?	Hvað kostar það mikið?	kvath koe-star thahth mikith
It's expensive/ cheap	það er dýrt / ódýrt	thath ehr deert / oh-deert
A little/a lot	Smá / mikið	smow / mi-kith
More/less	meira / minna	mare-ah / min-na
Enough/too (much)	þetta er nóg / þetta er of mikið	thetta ehr noeg / thetta ehr oh-fv mikith
I am ill/sick	Ég er veik / veikur	yehg ehr vake / vake-ur
Call a doctor.	Hringdu í lækni	hring-doo ee like-nee

Help!	Hjálp	hyowlp
Stop!	Stopp	stop

A bottle of ...	flösku af....	fluhs-ku ahf
A cup of ...	bolla af....	bollah ahf
A glass of ...	glas af....	glass ahf
Beer	bjór	byore
Bill/check	reikninginn	rake-ning-in
Bread	brauð	broyth
Breakfast	morgunnmatur	morg-un-mat-ur
Butter	smjör	smyoore
Cocktail/aperatif	kokteill / fordrykkur	cock-tale for-dring-kur
Coffee	kaffi	kahf-fee
Dinner	kvöldmatur	kvuhld-mat-ur
Fixed-price menu	matseðill	mahts-ehthilh
Fork	gaffall	gahf-falh
I am a vegetarian/I don't eat meat	Ég er grænmetisæta	yehg ehr grine-meh-tih-sight-ah
I cannot eat ...	Ég get ekki borðað	yehg get ehk-kee bor-thahth
I'd like to order ...	Ég myndi vilja panta	yehg mind-ee vil-yah pan-tah
Is service included?	Er þjónustan innifalinn?	ehrr thyohn-uh-stahn in-nih-fahl-in
I'm hungry/ thirsty	Ég er svangur/ svöng // þyrstur/ þyrst	yehg air svahn-gur / svuhng. // thirst-ur / thirst
It's good/bad	Það er gott / slæmt	thahth air goht / sly-mt
It's hot/cold	Það er heitt / kalt	thahth ehrr hayt / kahlt
Knife	hnífur	hnee-vur
Lunch	hádegismatur	how-dehg-is-maht-ur
Menu	matseðill	maht-seh-thilh
Napkin	þurrka	thur-kah
Pepper	pipar	pay-pahr
Plate	diskur	Disk-ur
Please give me ...	vinsamlegast gefðu mér	vin-sahm-leh-gahst geb-thu mare
Salt	salt	sahlt
Spoon	skeið	skathe
Tea	te	teh
Water	vatn	vaht
Wine	vín	veen

Helpful Norwegian Phrases

BASICS

Hello	Hei	Hi
Yes/No	Ja/Nei	yah/nay
Please	Vær så snill	vehr soh snihl
Thank you	Takk	tahk
You're welcome	Vær så god	vehr soh goh
I'm sorry (apology)	Unnskyld	ewn-shewl
Sorry (Excuse Me)	Unnskyld meg	ewn-shewl may
Good morning	God morgen	goo mohr-ghen
Good day	God dag	goo dahg
Good evening	God kveld	goo kvehl
Goodbye	Ha det	ha day
Mr. (Sir)	Herr	heh-r
Mrs.	Fru	frooh
Miss	Frøken	freh-kehn
Pleased to meet you	Hyggelig å møte deg	higg-eh-leeg oh mehte day
How are you?	Hvordan går det?	voor-dahn gohr deh

NUMBERS

one-half	halv	hahlv
one	en	ehn
two	to	too
three	tre	treh
four	fire	feer-eh
five	fem	fehm
six	seks	sehks
seven	sju	shew
eight	åtte	oh-teh
nine	ni	nee
ten	ti	tee
eleven	elleve	ehl-veh
twelve	tolv	toll
thirteen	tretten	treh-tehn
fourteen	fjorten	fjor-tehn
fifteen	femten	fehm-tehn
sixteen	seksten	sex-tehn
seventeen	sytten	soh-tehn
eighteen	atten	ah-tehn
nineteen	nitten	nee-tehn
twenty	tjue	sho-eh
twenty-one	tjue-en	sho-eh-ehn
thirty	tretti	treh-tee
fifty	femti	fehm-tee
sixty	seksti	sex-tee
seventy	sytti	soh-tee
eighty	åtti	oh-tee
ninety	nitti	nee-tee
one hundred	hundre	hoon-dreh
one thousand	tusen	too-sehn
one million	en million	ehn million

COLORS

black	svart	svahrt
blue	blå	bloh
brown	brun	broon
green	grønn	groehn
orange	oransje	o-ranch
red	rød	roehd
white	hvit	veet
yellow	gul	ghool

DAYS OF THE WEEK

Sunday	søndag	suhn-dahg
Monday	mandag	mahn-dahg
Tuesday	tirsdag	teesh-dahg
Wednesday	onsdag	ohns-dahg
Thursday	torsdag	toosh-dahg
Friday	fredag	freh-dahg
Saturday	lørdag	loor-dahg

MONTHS

January	januar	jah-noo-ahr
February	februar	feh-broo-ahr
March	mars	mars
April	april	ahp-reel
May	mai	mah-ee
June	juni	joon-ee
July	juli	jool-ee
August	august	auh-goost
September	september	sehpt-ehm-behr
October	oktober	octo-behr
November	november	no-vehm-behr
December	desember	deh-sehm-behr

USEFUL WORDS AND PHRASES

Do you speak English?	Snakker du engelsk?	snahk-kerr doo ehng-ehlsk
I don't speak [Language].	Jeg snakker ikke norsk	yay snahk-kerr ik-keh nohrshk
I don't understand.	Jeg forstår ikke	yay fosh-tawr ik-keh
I don't know.	Jeg vet ikke	yay veht ik-keh
I understand.	Jeg forstår	yay fosh-tawr
I'm American.	Jeg er amerikansk	Yay ahr ah-mehr-ee-kahnsk
I'm British.	Jeg er britisk	yay ahr bree-teesk
What's your name?	Hva heter du	vah heh-tehr doh
My name is …	Jeg heter …	yay heh-tehr …
What time is it?	Hva er klokken?	vah ehr klohk-kehn
How?	Hvordan?	voor-dahn
When?	Når?	nohr
Yesterday	I går	ee gohr
Today	I dag	ee dahg

Tomorrow	I morgen	ee mohr-gehn
This morning	I dag tidlig	ee dahg teed-leeg
Afternoon	I ettermiddag	ee eh-tehr-medd-ahg
Tonight	I kveld	ee kveh-ld
What?	Hva?	vah
What is it?	Hva er det?	vah ehr deht
Why?	Hvorfor?	vor-fohr
Who?	Hvem?	vehm
Where is ...	Hvor er ...	voor ahr
... the train station?	... togstasjonen	toog-sta-shoon-ern
... the subway station?	... t-bane-stasjonen	teh-bahneh-sta-shoon-ern
... the bus stop?	... busstoppet	boos-stahp-eht
... the airport?	... flyplassen	fleeh-plahs-sehn
... the post office?	... postkontoret	pohsst-kohn-tohr-eht
... the bank?	... banken	bahnk-ehn
... the hotel?	... hotellet	ho-tehl-eht
... the museum?	... museet	muse-eht
... the hospital?	... sykehuset	seek-eh-hoos-eht
... the elevator?	... heisen	hi-sehn
Where are the restrooms?	Hvor er toalettet?	voor ahr too-ah-leht-eht
Here/there	Her / Der	hahr / dahr
Left/right	Venstre / Høyre	vehn-strej / hooy-reh
Is it near/far?	Er det langt?	ahr deht lah-nt
I'd like ...	Jeg vil ha ..	yay veel hah
... a room	... et rom	eht rohm
... the key	.. nøkkelen	nooh-kehl-ehn
... a newspaper	.. en avis	ehn ah-vees
... a stamp	.. et frimerke	eht free-mehr-keh
I'd like to buy ...	Jeg vil kjøpe ..	yay veel chohpe
... a city map	.. et bykart	eht bee-kahrt
... a road map	.. et veikart	eht vay-kahrt
... a magaine	.. et blad	eht blah-d
... envelopes	.. konvolutter	con-voh-loot-ehr
... writing paper	.. papir	pah-peer
... a postcard	.. et postkort	eht post-kohrt
... a ticket	.. en billett	ehn beel-lehtt
How much is it?	Hva koster det?	vah koss-terr deh
It's expensive/cheap	Er det dyrt/billig?	ahr deht deert / beeh-leeh
A little/a lot	Litt / Mye	leet / mee-eh
More/less	Mer / Mindre	mehr / meen-dreh
Enough/too (much)	Nok / for mye	nohk / fohr mee-eh
I am ill/sick	Jeg er syk	yay ehr seehk
Call a doctor	Ring en lege	ring ehn lay-geh
Help!	Hjelp!	yehlp
Stop!	Stopp!	stop

DINING OUT

A bottle of ...	En flaske med ..	ehn flah-skah meh
A cup of ...	En kopp med ..	ehn cuhp meh
A glass of ...	Et glass med ..	eht glass meh
Beer	Øl	ohl
Bill/check	Regning	rehg-neeng
Bread	Brød	brur
Breakfast	Frokost	frooh-kohst
Butter	Smør	smurr
Cocktail/aperitif	Cocktail	cocktail
Coffee	Kaffe	kah-feh
Dinner	Middag	meed-dahg
Fixed-price menu	Meny med fast pris	meh-new mehd fahst prees
Fork	Gaffel	gahff-erl
I am vegetarian/ I don't eat meat	Jeg er vegetarianer	yay ahr vegh-eh-tahr-ee-ah-nehr
I cannot eat ...	Jeg kan ikke spise ..	yay kahn eeh-keh speeh-seh
I'd like to order...	Jeg vil bestille ..	yay veel beh-steel-leh
Is service included?	Er tips inkludert?	ahr tips ink-loo-dehrt
I'm hungry/thirsty	Jeg er sulten /tørst	yay ahr sool-tehn / tohrst
It's good/bad	Det er godt / ikke godt	deht ahr goh-t / eek-keh goh-t
It's hot/cold	Det er varmt / kaldt	deht ahr vahr-mt / kahl-t
Knife	Kniv	kneev
Lunch	Lunsj	lunch
Menu	Meny	meh-new
Napkin	Serviett	ssehr-vy-eht
Pepper	Pepper	pehp-pehr
Plate	Tallerken	tahl-ehr-kehn
Please give me ...	Kan jeg få ..	kahn yay foh
Salt	Salt	sahlt
Spoon	Skje	shay
Tea	Te	teh
Water	Vann	cahn
Wine	Vin	veen

Helpful Finnish Phrases

BASICS

Hello	Hei	hay
Yes/No	Kyllä/ei	kew-la/ay
Please	Oolkaa hyvää	ohl-kah hew-va
Thank you	Kiitos	kii-tos
You're welcome	Eipa kestä	ay-pah kes-ta
I'm Sorry (apology)	Anteeksi	ahn-tayk-si
Sorry (Excuse me)	Anteeksi	ahn-tayk-si
Good morning	Hyvää huomenta	hew-va hu-oh-men-ta
Good day	Hyvää päivää	hew-va peh-y va
Good evening	Hyvää iltaa	hew-va il-tah
Goodbye	Näkemiin	na-ke-meen
Mr. (Sir)	Herra	hehrah
Mrs.	Rouva	roh-vah
Miss	Neiti	neh-ee-ti
Pleased to meet you	Hauska tavata	how-skah tuh-vah-tah
How are you?	Mitä kuuluu?	mi-tah koo-looh

NUMBERS

one-half	puoli	poo-oh-lih
one	yksi	ewk-sih
two	kaksi	kahk-sih
three	kolme	kohl-mih
four	neljä	nel-yah
five	viisi	vee-sih
six	kuusi	koo-sih
seven	seitsemän	sayt-seh-man
eight	kahdeksan	kah-dek-san
nine	yhdeksän	ew-dek-san
ten	kymmenen	kewm-meh-nen
eleven	yksitoista	ewk-sih-tois-tah
twelve	kaksitoista	kahk-sih-tois-tah
thirteen	kolmetoista	kohl-meh-tois-tah
fourteen	neljätoista	nel-yah-tois-tah
fifteen	viisitoista	vee-sih-tois-tah
sixteen	kuusitoista	koo-si-tois-tah
seventeen	seitsemäntoista	sayt-seh-man-tois-tah
eighteen	kahdeksantoista	kah-dek-san-tois-tah
nineteen	yhdeksäntoista	ew-dek-san-tois-tah
twenty	kaksikymmentä	kahk-sih-kewm-men-tah
twenty-one	kaksikymmentäyksi	kahk-sih-kewm-men-tah-ewk-sih
thirty	kolmekymmentä	kohl-meh-kewm-men-tah
fifty	viisikymmentä	vee-sih-kewm-men-tah
sixty	kuusikymmentä	koo-sih-kewm-men-tah
seventy	seitsemänkymmentä	sayt-seh-man-kewm-men-tah
eighty	kahdeksankymmentä	kah-dek-san-kewm-men-tah
ninety	yhdeksänkymmentä	ew-dek-san-kewm-men-tah
one hundred	yksi sata	ewk-sih sah-tah
one thousand	tuhat	too-hat
one million	miljoona	mil-yoh-nah

COLORS

black	musta	moo-stah
blue	sininen	sin-ih-nen
brown	ruskea	roos-keh-ah
green	vihreä	vih-reh-ah
orange	oranssi	oh-rans-sih
red	punainen	poo-neye-nen
white	valkoinen	vahl-koi-nen
yellow	keltainen	kel-teye-nen

DAYS OF THE WEEK

Sunday	Sunnuntai	soon-noon-teye
Monday	Maanantai	mah-nahn-teye
Tuesday	Tiistai	tihs-teye
Wednesday	Keskiviikko	kes-kih-vee-koh
Thursday	Torstai	tohrs-teye
Friday	Perjantai	pehr-yan-teye
Saturday	Lauantai	lou-ahn-teye

MONTHS

January	Tammikuu	tam-mih-koo
February	Helmikuu	hel-mih-koo
March	Maaliskuu	mah-lis-koo
April	Huhtikuu	hooh-tee-koo
May	Toukokuu	toh-koh-koo
June	Kesäkuu	kes-ah-koo
July	Heinäkuu	hay-nah-koo
August	Elokuu	el-oh-koo
September	Syyskuu	sews-koo
October	Lokakuu	lok-ah-koo
November	Maaliskuu	mah-lis-koo
December	Joulukuu	yoh-loo-koo

USEFUL WORDS AND PHRASES

Do you understand English?	Puhutko englantia?	poo-hoot-koh en-glahn-tee-ah
I don't speak [Language].	En puhuu englanti	en poo-hoo en-glahn-tee-ah
I don't understand.	En ymmärää	en ewm-mah-rah
I don't know.	En tiedä	en tee-eh-dah
I understand.	Ymmärrän	ewm-mah-rah
I'm American.	Olen amerikkalainen	oh-lehn ah-meh-rik-ah-leye-nen
I'm British.	Olen brittilainen	oh-len brit-tee-leye-len
What's your name?	Mikä on sinun nimesi?	mik-ah ohn sin-uhn nim-eh-si
My name is ...	Nimeni on...	ni-meh-ni on

What time is it?	Paljonko kello on?	pahl-yon-koh kehl-loh
How?	Kuinka?	koo-in-kah
When?	Milloin?	mil-loin
Yesterday	Eilen	eh-ih-len
Today	Tänään	tah-naahn
Tomorrow	Huomenna	hoo-oh-mehn-nah
This morning	Tänä aamuna	tahnah ah-moo-nah
This afternoon	Tänä iltapäivänä	tahnah il-tah-peye-vah-nah
Tonight	Tänä yöllä	tahnah ewe-uh-lah
What?	Mitä?	mit-ah
What is it?	Mikä se on?	mik-ah seh on
Why?	Miksi?	mik-sih
Who?	Kuka?	koo-kah
Where is ...	Missä on...	mis-sah ohn
... the train station?	...rautatieasema?	row-tah-tee-ah-seh-mah
... the subway station?	...metroasema?	meh-troh-ah-seh-mah
... the bus stop?	...bussi pysäkki?	boos-sih pewe-sahk-kih
... the airport?	...lentoasema?	len-toh-ah-seh-mah
... the post office?	...posti?	pos-tih
... the bank?	...pankki?	pahnk-kih
... the hotel?	...hotelli?	hoh-tel-lih
... the museum?	...museo?	moo-seh-oh
... the hospital?	...sairaala?	seye-rah-lah
... the elevator?	...hissi?	his-sih
Where are the restrooms?	...missä on WC?	mis-sah ohn ves-sah
Here/there	Täällä/tuolla?	taahla/too-oh-lah
Left/right	Vasea/oikea	vah-seh-ah/ oy-keh-ah
Is it near/far?	Onko lähellä/ kaukana?	on-koh lh-hel-lah/ kou-kah-nah
I'd like ...	Haluaisin saada	hahl-oo-eye-sin sah-dah
... a room	...huone	hoo-oh-neh
... the key	...avain	ahv-eyen
... a newspaper	...päivänlehti	pah-eye-vahn-leh-tih
... a stamp	...postimerkki	pos-tih mehr-kih
I'd like to buy ...	haluaisin ostaa...	hal-oo-eye-sin os-tah
... a city map	...kaupungin karta	kou-poon-gin kahr-tah
... a road map	...tien kartta	tih-en kahr-tah
... a magaine	...kuvalehti	koo-vah-leh-tih
... envelopes	...kirjekuoret	kirh-yeh-kuu-oh-ret
... writing paper	...kirjoituspaperi	kirh-oi-toos-pah-peh-rih
... a postcard	...postikortti	pos-tih-korh-tih
... a ticket	...lippu	lip-poo
How much is it?	Paljonko maksaa?	pahl-yonkoh mak-sah

It's expensive/ cheap	On kallis/halpa	ohn kahl-lis/hal-pah
A little/a lot	Vähän/paljon	vah-han/pal-yon
More/less	Lisää/vähemmän	lih-sah/ vah-hem-mahn
Enough/too (much)	Tarpeeksi/liian Paljon	tahr-payk-sih/lih-ahn pal-yon
I am ill/sick	Olen sairas	oh-len seye-rahs
Call a doctor	Soita lääkärille	soi-tah laah-kah-ril-leh
Help!	Apua!	ah-poo-ah
Stop!	Lopettaa!	lop-et-tah

DINING OUT

A bottle of ...	pullo	poo-loh
A cup of ...	kuppi	koop-pih
A glass of ...	lasi	lah-sih
Beer	Olut	oh-loot
Bill/check	Lasku	lahs-koo
Bread	Leipä	lay-pah
Breakfast	Samiainen	ah-mih-eye-nen
Butter	Voi	voh-ih
Cocktail/aperatif	Cocktail/aperitif	
Coffee	Kahvi	kah-vih
Dinner	Päivällinen	peye-vahl-linen
Fixed-price menu	Ruokalista	roo-oh-kah-listah
Fork	Haarukka	haah-rook-kah
I am a vegetarian/I don't eat meat	Olen kasvissyöjä	oh-len kahs-vihs-sew-uh-yah
I cannot eat ...	En voi syödä	en voi su-uh-dah
I'd like to order ...	Haluaisin tilata	hah-loo-eye-sin til-ah-tah
Is service included?	Sisältyykö palvelu?	sis-ahl-tew-kuh pahl-vehl-oo
I'm hungry/ thirsty	Minulla on nälkä/ jano	min-uhl-lah ohn nahl-kah/yah-noh
It's good/bad	On hyvä/huono	ohn hu-vah/ hoo-oh-nah
It's hot/cold	On lämmin/kylmä	ohn lahm-min/ kul-mah
Knife	Veitsi	vayt-sih
Lunch	Lounas	loh-nahs
Menu	Ruokalista	roo-oh-kah-listah
Napkin	Lautasliina	lou-tas-lih-nah
Pepper	Pippuri	pip-puh-rih
Plate	Lauttanen	lout-tah-nen
Please give me ...	Voisitko antaa...	voi-siht-koh ahn-tah
Salt	Suola	soo-oh-lah
Spoon	Lusikka	loo-sik-kah
Tea	Tee	tay
Water	Vesi	veh-sih
Wine	Viini	vih-nih

Helpful Danish Phrases

BASICS

Hello/Good Day	Hej	hai
Yes/no	Ja/nej	ya/nai
Please	Vær så venlig	ver saw venlee
Thank you (very much)	Tak	taak
You're welcome.	Selv tak	sell taak
I'm sorry (apology)	Undskyld	ownskewl
Sorry. (Excuse me.)	Undskyld mig	ownskewl mai
Good morning	Godmorgen	got mornen
Good Day	Goddag	got daa
Good evening	Godaften	got awften
Goodbye	Farvel	faarvel
Mr. (Sir)	Hr.	haer
Mrs.	Fru	fruu
Miss	Frøken	freuken
Pleased to meet you.	Hyggeligt at møde dig	
How are you?	Hvordan har du det?	vordan gawr dey

NUMBERS

half	halvanden	halaanden
one	en	in
two	to	toh
three	tre	trey
four	fire	feer
five	fem	femh
six	seks	seks
seven	syv	sew
eight	otte	awte
nine	ni	nee
ten	ti	tee
eleven	elleve	aelveh
twelve	tolv	towl
thirteen	tretten	treyten
fourteen	fjorten	fjohrten
fifteen	femten	femhten
sixteen	seksten	seksten
seventeen	sytten	sewten
eighteen	atten	awten
nineteen	nitten	neeten
twenty	tyve	tewhe
twenty-one	enogtyve	inoktewhe
thirty	tredive	traadhve
fifty	halvtreds	haltres
sixty	treds	tres
seventy	halvfjers	halfyers
eighty	firs	feers
ninety	halvfems	halfems
one hundred	hundrede	houndredhe
one thousand	tusinde	toosen
one million	million	millijon

COLORS

black	sort	sohrt
blue	blå	blaw
brown	brun	broon
green	grøn	groyn
orange	orange	ohranje
red	rød	reudh
white	hvid	vihd
yellow	gul	gool

DAYS OF THE WEEK

Sunday	Søndag	seunda
Monday	Mandag	manda
Tuesday	Tirsdag	teersda
Wednesday	Onsdag	awnsda
Thursday	Torsdag	torsda
Friday	Fredag	frehda
Saturday	Lørdag	leurda

MONTHS

January	Januar	yanooar
February	Februar	febrooar
March	Marts	maarts
April	April	apreel
May	Maj	mai
June	Juni	yoonee
July	Juli	yoolee
August	August	awgowst
September	September	siptember
October	Oktober	ohktohba
November	November	nohvemba
December	December	deysemba

USEFUL WORDS AND PHRASES

Do you understand English?	Taler du engelsk?	talee doo engelsk?
I don't speak [Language]..	Jeg snakker ikke (sprog)	yai taler ike
I don't understand.	Jeg forstår ikke	yai forstawrh ike
I don't know.	Det ved jeg ikke	dey vet yai ike
I understand.	Jeg forstår	yai forstawrh
I'm American.	Jeg er amerikaner	yai ir aamerikaaner
I'm British.	Jeg er britisk	yai ir breeteesh
What's your name?	Hvad hedder du?	va heter doo
My name is ...	Jeg hedder...	yai heter
What time is it?	Hvad er klokken?	va ir kloken
How?	Hvordan?	vordan
When?	Hvornår?	vornowr
Yesterday	I går	eegawr
Today	I dag	eeda
Tomorrow	I morgen	eemornen
This morning	I morges	eemores
This afternoon	I eftermiddags	ee aeftermeedas

Tonight	I aften	eeaften
What?	Hvad?	va
What is it?	Hvad er det?	va ir dey
Why?	Hvorfor?	vorfor
Who?	Hvem?	vem
Where is ...	Hvor er...	vor ir...
... the train station?	...togstationen?	tawkstasohn
... the subway station?	...metrostationen?	metrowstasohn
... the bus stop?	...busstoppet?	boosstopet
... the airport?	...lufthavnen?	lawfthawvnen
... the post office?	...postkontoret?	powstkorntohret
... the bank?	...banken?	bawnken
... the hotel?	...hotellet?	hohtelhet
... the museum?	...museet?	moosehet
... the hospital?	...hospitalet?	hohspeetahlet
... the elevator?	...elevatoren?	ehlehvartor
Where are the restrooms?	Hvor er badeværelserne?	vor ir toyletet
Here / there	Her/der	hir/dir
Left / right	Højre/venstre	hoyre/venstre
Is it near / far?	Er det tæt på/langt væk?	ir dey teet paw/laangt vek
I'd like ...	Jeg vil gerne bede om...	yai vil girne ha
... a room	... et værelse	it verlse
... the key	... nøglen	neyklen
... a newspaper	... avisen	awwisen
... a stamp	... et frimærke	it freemerge
I'd like to buy ...	Jeg vil gerne købe...	yai vil girne keupe
... a city map	... et bykort	it beekohrt
... a road map	... et vejkort	it vaikohrt
... a magaine	... et magasin	it mahgaseen
... envelopes	... konvolutter	kohnveluter
... writing paper	... brevpapir	brehvpahpeer
... a postcard	... et postkort	it pohstkohrt
... a ticket	... en billet	ayn beelet
How much is it?	Hvad koster det?	va kohster dey
It's expensive/ cheap	Det er dyrt/billig	dey ir deert/beeleet
A little/a lot	Lidt/meget	litt/mahket
More/less	Meget/mindre	maayet/mindrer
Enough/too (much)	Nok/for meget	nohk/fohr maayet
I am ill/sick	Jeg er syg/jeg har det dårligt	yai ir sew/yai hahr owndt heyr
Call a doctor	Ring efter en læge	ring efta in leye
Help!	Hjælp!	yelp
Stop!	Stop!	stawp

DINING OUT

A bottle of ...	En flaske...	in flawske
A cup of ...	En kop...	in kohp
A glass of ...	Et glas...	it glahs
Beer	Øl	eul
Bill/check	Regningen	rainingen
Bread	Brød	breudh
Breakfast	Morgenmad	mornenmat
Butter	Smør	smeur
Cocktail/aperatif	Cocktail/aperitif	cocktail/aperitif
Coffee	Kaffe	kafe
Dinner	Middag	meeta
Fixed-price menu	Tasting menu	tasting menu
Fork	Gaffel	gahfel
I am a vegetarian/I don't eat meat..	Jeg er vegetar/jeg spiser ikke kød	yai ir vejetahr/yai speeser ike keut
I cannot eat ...	Jeg kan ikke spise...	yai kan ike speese...
I'd like to order ...	Jeg vil gerne bestille...	yai vil gehrne behsteele
Is service included?	Er betjening inkluderet?	ir behtjaening ihnkluuderet
I'm hungry/ thirsty.	Jeg er sulten/ tørstig	yai ir sooltewn/ teursti
It's good/bad	Det er godt/dårligt	dey ir got/dohrlit
It's hot/cold	Det er varmt/koldt	dey ir vahrmt/kohlt
Knife	Kniv	kneevh
Lunch	Frokost	frohkohst
Menu	Menu	menu
Napkin	Serviet	serviette
Pepper	Peber	pehpehr
Plate	Tallerken	tahlirken
Please give me ...	Vil du venligst række mig...	vil dooh
Salt	Salt	sahlt
Spoon	Ske	skeh
Tea	Te	teh
Water	Vand	vann
Wine	Vin	veen

Helpful Swedish Phrases

BASICS

Hello	Hej	hey
Yes/No	Ja/nej	yah/nay
Please	Är du snäll	air doo snell
Thank you	Tack	tahk
You're welcome	Varsågod	vahr-so-good
I'm Sorry (apology)	Förlåt	fur-lowt
Sorry (Excuse me)	Ursäkta	oor-shek-ta
Good morning	God morgon	goo mohr-rohn
Good day	Goddag	goo-dahg
Good night	God natt	goo nut
Goodbye	Hej då	hay doh
Mr. (Sir)	Herr	hair
Mrs.	Fru	froo
Miss	Fröken	fruh-ken
Pleased to meet you	Trevligt att träffas	trev-ligt aht tref-fahs
How are you?	Hur mår du	hoor mor doo

NUMBERS

one-half	en halv/ett halvt	en holv/et holvt
one	en/ett	en/et
two	två	tvoh
three	tre	treh
four	fyra	fee-rah
five	fem	fem
six	sex	sex
seven	sju	hwoo
eight	åtta	oht-ta
nine	nio	nee-yoo
ten	tio	tee-yoo
eleven	elva	el-vah
twelve	tolv	tohlv
thirteen	tretton	tret-tohn
fourteen	fjorton	fyoor-tohn
fifteen	femton	fem-tohn
sixteen	sexton	sex-tohn
seventeen	sjutton	hwoo-tohn
eighteen	arton	ahr-tohn
nineteen	nitton	neet-tohn
twenty	tjugo	shoo-goo
twenty-one	tjugoen/tjugoett	shoo-goo-en/ shoo-goo-et
forty	trettio	tret-tee-oo
thirty	fyrtio	fur-tee-oo
fifty	femtio	fem-tee-oo
sixty	sextio	sex-tee-oo
seventy	sjuttio	hwoo-tee-oo
eighty	åttio	oht-tee-oo
ninety	nittio	neet-tee-oo
one hundred	ett hundra	ett hoon-drah
one thousand	ett tusen	en/ett too-sen
one million	en miljon	en mil-yoon

COLORS

black	svart	svahrt
blue	blå	bloa
brown	brun	broon
green	grön	grun
orange	orange/brandgul	oo-rahnj/ brahnd-gool
red	röd	rud
white	vit	veet
yellow	gul	gool

DAYS OF THE WEEK

Sunday	Söndag	sun-dahg
Monday	Måndag	moan-dahg
Tuesday	Tisdag	tees-dahg
Wednesday	Onsdag	oons-dahg
Thursday	Torsdag	toorsh-dahg
Friday	Fredag	freh-dahg
Saturday	Lördag	lur-dahg

MONTHS

January	Januari	yahn-war-ee
February	Februari	feb-rawr-ee
March	Mars	mahrsh
April	April	ah-preel
May	Maj	my
June	Juni	yoo-nee
July	Juli	yoo-lee
August	Augusti	ao-goo-stee
September	September	sep-tem-bear
October	Oktober	ohk-too-bear
November	November	noo-vem-bear
December	December	deh-sem-bear

USEFUL WORDS AND PHRASES

Do you understand English?	Talar du engelska?	tah-lar doo eng-el-skah
I don't speak [Language].	Jag talar inte svenska.	yahg tah-lar een-teh sven-skah
I don't understand.	Jag förstår inte.	yahg fur-stor een-teh
I don't know.	Jag vet inte.	yahg vet een-teh
I understand.	Jag förstår.	yahg fur-stor
I'm American.	Jag är amerikansk.	yahg air ah-meh-ree-kahnsk
I'm British.	Jag är brittisk.	yahg air britt-isk
What's your name?	Vad heter du?	vahd heh-ter doo
My name is ...	Jag heter...	yahg heh-ter...
What time is it?	Vad är klockan?	vahd air kloh-kan?
How?	Hur?	hoor
When?	När?	nair
Yesterday	I går	ee gor
Today	vb dag	ee dahg
Tomorrow	i morgon	ee mor-ron
This morning	I morse	ee mor-sheh

This afternoon	I eftermiddag	ee ef-ter-mee-dahg
Tonight	I kväll	ee kvell
What?	Vad?	vahd
What is it?	Vad är det?	vahd air deh
Why?	Varför?	vahr-fur
Who?	Vem?	vem
Where is ...	Var är...?	vahr air
... the train station?	tågstationen	towg-sta-hwo-nen
... the subway station?	tunnelbane-stationen	too-nel-bah-ne-sta-hwo-nen
... the bus stop?	busshållplatsen	boos-hol-plaht-sen
... the airport?	flygplatsen	fleeg-plaht-sen
... the post office?	posten	pow-sten
... the bank?	banken	bahn-ken
... the hotel?	hotellet	hoo-tel-let
... the museum?	museet	moo-seh-et
... the hospital?	sjukhuset	hwuk-hu-set
... the elevator?	hissen	hee-sen
Where are the restrooms?	Var är toaletten?	vahr air too-ah-let-ten
Here/there	Här/där	hair/dair
Left/right	Vänster/höger	ven-ster/huh-ger
Is it near/far?	Är det nära/långt?	air deh nair-ra/lowngt
I'd like ...	Haluaisin saada	yahg skoo-leh veel-yah hah
... a room	...huone	ett room
... the key	...avain	en nee-kel
... a newspaper	...päivänlehti	en teed-ning
... a stamp	...postimerkki	ett free-mair-keh
I'd like to buy ...	Haluaisin ostaa...	yahg skoo-leh veel-yah shuh-pa
... a city map	...kaupungin karta	en studs-kar-tah
... a road map	...tien kartta	en trah-feek-kar-tah
... a magazine	...kuvalehti	en teed-ning
... envelopes	...kirjekuoret	koo-vair
... writing paper	...kirjoituspaperi	skreev pah-per
... a postcard	...postikortti	ett vee-koort
... a ticket	...lippu	en beel-yett
How much is it?	Vad kostar det?	vahd kos-tar deh
It's expensive/cheap	Det är dyrt/billigt	deh air deert/beel-ligt
A little/a lot	Lite/mycket	lee-teh/mick-eh
More/less	Mer/mindre	mair/meen-dreh
Enough/too (much)	Nog/för mycket	noog/fur mick-eh
I am ill/sick	Jag är sjuk	yahg air hwuk
Call a doctor	Ring en doktor	reeng en dock-toor
Help!	Hjälp	yelp
Stop!	Stanna/sluta	stah-nah/sloo-tah

DINING OUT

A bottle of ...	En flaska	en flah-skah
A cup of ...	En kopp	en kohp
A glass of ...	Ett glas	ett glahs
Beer	Öl	uhl
Bill/check	Notan	noo-tahn
Bread	Bröd	bruhd
Breakfast	Frukost	froo-kowst
Butter	Smör	smuhr
Cocktail/aperatif	Drink	dreenk
Coffee	Kaffe	kah-feh
Dinner	Middag	mee-dahg
Fixed-price menu	Fast meny	fahst men-ee
Fork	Gaffel	gah-fell
I am a vegetarian/I don't eat meat	Jag är vegetarian/ äter inte kött	yahg air ve-geh-tar-ee-ahn/yahg ay-ter een-teh shutt
I cannot eat ...	Jag kan inte äta...	yahg kahn een-teh ay-ta
I'd like to order ...	Jag skulle vilja beställa	yahg skoo-leh veel-yah beh-stel-la
Is service included?	Är dricks inkluderat?	air dreeks in-kloo-dair-aht
I'm hungry/thirsty	Jag är hungrig/törstig	yahg air hoong-reeg/turst-eeg
It's good/bad	Det är bra/dåligt	deh air bra/dow-leet
It's hot/cold	Det är varmt/kallt	deh air vahrmt/kahlt
Knife	Kniv	kneev
Lunch	Lunch	lunsh
Menu	Meny	meh-nee
Napkin	Servett	sair-vett
Pepper	Peppar	pep-pahr
Plate	Tallrik	tahl-reek
Please give me ...	Skulle jag kunna få	Skoo-leh yahg koo-nah fau
Salt	Salt	sahlt
Spoon	Sked	hwed
Tea	Te	teh
Water	Vatten	vah-ten
Wine	Vin	veen

Did You Know?

Central Norway's Jostedalsbreen National Park is home to the Jostedal Glacier, the largest in Europe.

Chapter 3

NORWAY

Updated by Cecilie Hauge Eggen,
Alexandra Pereira, Anne-Sophie Redisch,
Megan Starr, Lisa Stentvedt,
and Aram Vardanyan

◉ Sights	🍴 Restaurants	🛏 Hotels	🛍 Shopping	🍸 Nightlife
★★★★★	★★★★☆	★★★★☆	★★★☆☆	★★☆☆☆

WELCOME TO NORWAY

TOP REASONS TO GO

★ **Explore Norway's Fjords.** The Norwegian fjords are known for their majestic beauty, and should top your agenda. Geirangerfjord, the most photographed, and Sognefjord, the longest and deepest, are the most popular, but some of the smaller fjords are just as stunning.

★ **Enjoy the Great Outdoors.** Get close to nature. Whether you fancy hiking, skiing in some of northern Europe's best resorts, sailing along the southern coast or fishing in some of the world's best salmon rivers, the choice is yours. Wildlife is plentiful, too, so if you can't see the elusive moose, you're guaranteed to spot other mammals and birds.

★ **Catch the Midnight Sun.** Seeking 24-hour sunlight? Travel north of the Arctic Circle in summer, where the sun never drops below the horizon, to experience this unique phenomenon, and make the most of the longest days of the year. Or go between November and February to witness the awe-inspiring spectacle of the northern lights.

Norway is long and narrow, with a jagged coastline carved by deep fjords. The southern coast is filled with wide beaches and seaside communities. Bergen is considered the gateway to fjord country.

1 **Oslo**

2 **Kristiansand**

3 **Stavanger**

4 **Haugesund**

5 **Lillehammer**

6 **Dombås**

7 **Beitostølen**

8 **Bergen**

9 **Odda**

10 **Voss**

11 **Gudvangen**

12 **Flåm**

13 **Myrdal**

14 **Fjærland**

15 **Loen**

16 **Geiranger**

17 **Åndalsnes**

18 **Ålesund**

19 **Kristiansund**

20 **Trondheim**

21 **Bodø**

22 **The Lofoten Islands**

23 **Tromsø**

24 **Hammerfest**

25 **Nordkapp**

ST. OLAV WAYS

St. Olav Ways offers silent landscapes and serenity

Unlike the cramped, crowded Camino and other famous trails, only 22,000 travelers trek this lesser-known pilgrimage each year, navigating rural farmland, villages, and misty mountain passes across Norway for one-on-one time with Mother Nature, a digital detox, or religious connection.

St. Olav Ways consists of seven main paths, spanning Norway, Sweden, and Denmark. Norway contains most of the official paths, and more than 5,000 km (3,100 miles) of the route have been mapped and marked. The most popular St. Olav Ways route, the Gudbrandsdalen Path, covers 643 km (400 miles) from Oslo to Trondheim and takes approximately 32 days to trek on foot. Norway's St. Olav Ways contain six regional Pilgrim Centers, where pilgrims get information and often find overnight accommodations and historic religious landmarks nearby. Each center is run by local volunteers.

WHO WAS ST. OLAV?

Olav II Haraldsson, born in 995, was the son of Viking King Harald Grenske; he was elected as the first King of Norway in 1015 and introduced the country's first Christian legislation. He was forced into exile in 1028, but returned to Norway in 1030, following a dream urging the king to retake his homeland. He arrived in Stiklestad with a small army, but was quickly defeated and killed. Legend has it that miracles began to occur surrounding the battle site following his death in 1030. Olav II was officially canonized and declared a martyr to the Christian cause. Once named St. Olav, pilgrimages to Nidaros (known as Trondheim today) and Olav's grave began. Nidaros Cathedral was later built over the grave and all of St. Olav Ways' paths lead here. Olav remains the patron saint of Norway.

THE PILGRIMAGE EXPERIENCE

Pilgrims can walk St. Olav Ways along one or multiple paths, with many breaking down the popular 643 km (400 miles) Gudbrandsdalen Path into multiple visits. While some still complete the pilgrimage for religious purposes, most trekkers are in search of a cultural experience or just peace and quiet among scenic landscapes. What the trail lacks in fellow pilgrims, it makes up for with friendly locals. Portions of path pass through family farms where pilgrims might be invited in for a cup of coffee or even offered overnight accommodations. Pilgrims stay on track with trail markers in the form of St. Olav's Cross.

A TYPICAL DAY

On average, pilgrims cover 20–25 km (12½–15½ miles) a day. Beyond meals and a place to overnight, pilgrims focus on getting their Pilgrim Passports stamped daily; these can be purchased at regional Pilgrim Centers for 50 NOK (US$5) and represent the credentials pilgrims carried in the Middle Ages

Olaf II Haraldsson, patron saint of Norway

Gala Hogfjellshotell is located in the heart of Gudbrandsdalen

for safe passage. The Pilgrim Centers, pilgrim hotels and hostels, and religious landmarks along St. Olav Ways all have unique stamps to help you track a pilgrim's progress. It's best to pace each day's trek according to landmarks along the trail.

THE FINISH LINE

The final 100 km (62 miles) into Trondheim to Nidaros Cathedral is the most special portion. Pilgrims who complete this section receive the coveted St. Olav Letter, *Olavsbrevet*, upon arrival at the Nidaros Pilgrim Center. This certificate of completion can only be collected by presenting a passport with stamps from stops along the last 100 km. Upon arrival at Nidaros Cathedral, religious pilgrims usually attend a service that takes place daily at 6 p.m. Another tradition is to drink from St. Olav's Well in Hadrians Place, near the cathedral. Legend has it that a magical spring emerged from the ground after St. Olav was buried at Nidaros. Remnants of the original spring can still be seen inside the cathedral.

The busiest time in Trondheim is July 29, the day of the St. Olav Festival and a special mass honoring Norway's patron saint. Find trip planners, maps, recommended walks, and tips at ⊕ *pilegrimsleden.no/en*.

NORWAY SNAPSHOT

AT A GLANCE

Capital: Oslo

Population: 5,223,300

Currency: Norwegian krone

Money: ATMs are common; credit cards widely accepted

Language: Norwegian

Country Code: 47

Emergencies: 110 for fire, 112 for police, 113 for ambulance

Driving: On the right

Electricity: 230v/50 cycles; plugs have two round prongs

Time: Six hours ahead of New York

Documents: Up to 90 days with valid passport; Schengen rules apply

Mobile Phones: GSM (900 and 1800 bands), UMTS (900 and 2100 bands), LTE (800, 1800, and 2600 bands)

Major Mobile Companies: Telenor, Telia, Tele2

WHEN TO GO

High Season: June, July, and August mark Norway's high tourist season. This is the best time for exploring the magical fjords, and the only time to experience the midnight sun.

Low Season: November to April are the low months for Norway travel, when days are short and snow and cold are common. It's a great time for skiers, and the best time to see Norway's incredible northern lights.

Value Season: May and September through October are excellent times to visit Norway, when the weather is still pleasant and crowds are well off their summer peaks. The weather is generally not too cold, and the ski season and its higher prices haven't yet begun.

BIG EVENTS

■ **January:** Tromsø's Northern Lights Festival brings together top classical and contemporary music from Norway and beyond. ⊕ www.nordlysfestivalen.no

■ **March:** Oslo's Holmenkollen Ski Festival is one of Europe's largest ski events, including several World Cup competitions. ⊕ www.holmenkollen.com

■ **May:** Music, theater, dance, opera, and visual art come together for the Bergen International Festival. ⊕ www.fib.no

■ **June:** The little coastal town of Karmøy hosts one of Norway's largest Viking festivals at a reconstructed Viking settlement. ⊕ www.vikingfestivalen.no

One of the world's most beautiful countries, Norway has long been a popular cruising destination, famed for its stunning fjords. Formed during the last ice age's meltdown when the inland valleys carved by huge glaciers filled with seawater, fjords are undoubtedly Norway's top attractions—they shape the country's unique landscape and never fail to take your breath away.

Although the fjords are Norway's most striking and dramatic scenic features, there is much else to see, from the vast expanses of rugged tundra in the north to the huge evergreen forests along the Swedish border, from fertile coastal plains in the southwest to the snow-covered peaks and glaciers of the center.

One of the least densely populated countries in Europe, Norway is also one of the richest (thanks to the discovery of oil and gas in the North Sea in the late 1960s), and this wealth has changed the country significantly in the past decades, transforming cities like Stavanger into global players and boosting both the economy and the self-confidence of the Norwegian people.

Norway also regularly tops surveys as the country with the highest quality of life in the world, owing a great deal to the well-developed welfare system. The country's social democratic political system is to a large extent based on compromise, cooperation, and tolerance. These qualities are also at the heart of the country's reputation as a diplomatic mediator in world affairs.

It wasn't always like this. In the Middle Ages, the Vikings, accomplished seamen, crossed over to continental Europe and the British Isles on their famed long-ships (you can see a few well-preserved examples at the Viking Ship Museum in Oslo). In their attempt to establish new trade links and settlements, they waged a campaign of violence that lasted for 200 years. The Vikings' tough nature, coupled with their excellent skills as navigators, live on in their descendants, and it's no coincidence that some of the foremost explorers of modern times (Fridtjof Nansen, Thor Heyerdahl, and Roald Amundsen among them) hail from Norway.

So do many professional skiers and ice skaters; Norwegians have always excelled at winter sports, as they proved during the Lillehammer Winter Olympics in 1994, and keep reminding the rest of the world at every major international competition.

From 1537 to 1814, Norway was under Danish rule. In 1814, the country was forced into a union with Sweden until 1905, during which time the rise of the Norwegian romantic nationalism cultural movement took root. The composer Edvard Grieg, the playwright Henrik Ibsen, and the artist Edvard Munch were among those who put Norway on the international cultural map. Today Oslo, Bergen, and Stavanger are all vibrant cities with rich culture, including many festivals and world-class artists (homegrown and imported) performing regularly to discerning audiences.

But it's nature tourists come to see, and the Norwegians themselves have a strong attachment to the natural beauty of their homeland. In almost any kind of weather, blasting or balmy, large numbers of Norwegians are outdoors, fishing, biking, skiing, hiking, or sailing. Everybody—from cherubic children to hardy, knapsack-toting seniors—bundles up for just one more ski trip or hike in the mountains.

When discussing the size of their country, Norwegians like to say that if Oslo remained fixed and the northern part of the country were swung south, it would reach all the way to Rome. Perched at the very top of the globe, this northern land is long and rangy, stretching 2,750 km (1,705 miles) from north to south with vast expanses of unspoiled terrain—a fantastic playground for nature lovers, wildlife enthusiasts, and sporty types.

MAJOR REGIONS

Oslo. The Norwegian capital is home to just more than 650,000 inhabitants, and boasts great museums, top restaurants, and a stunning opera house. Check out the Royal Palace, at the end of Karl Johans gate (Oslo's main thoroughfare) before heading to Aker Brygge, the trendy area by the harbor. Then visit Vigeland's statue park or Holmenkollen ski jump, before ending your day in one of Grünerløkka's many buzzing restaurants.

Southern Norway. In summer, many of Oslo's residents migrate to the beautiful and sunny southern coast. Southern Norway is an ideal getaway for those who want to get close to nature, with a mild summer climate and terrain varying from inland mountains and forests to coastal flatland. Nicknamed Norway's Riviera, the coast stretching around the southern tip of the country is dotted with resort towns such as **Kristiansand**, Sandefjord, and **Lillesand**. But you'll also want to be on the lookout for picturesque coastal villages, busy harbors full of fishing boats, and the clusters of colorful, 18th- and 19th-century wooden houses that dot the countryside.

Central Norway. Have no doubt, Central Norway boasts some of the country's finest scenery. Yes, the fjords are fantastic, but there are good reasons why the Norwegians call this area the heart of Norway; Nature is a big one. Northwards from Oslo, the landscape turns to rolling hills that become steeper and sharper the further you go. The lush valleys of Valdres and Gudbrandsdalen charm you with picturesque farming villages huddled around impressive wooden stave churches.

Maybe you'll stop and pause here, breathing in the history and traditions of Norway, or maybe you'll head towards the pride and joy of most Norwegians, the vast wilderness of three impressive national parks: Rondane, Jotunheimen and Dovrefjell-Sunndalsfjella. You'll discover emerald lakes, gushing rivers, vast plateaus, and steep massifs literally reaching sky high.

The Western Fjords. The intricate outline of the fjords makes Norway's coastline of 21,347 km (13,264 miles) longer than the distance between the north and south poles. Majestic and magical, the fjords can take any traveler's breath away in a moment. In spectacular inlets like Nærøyfjord and the Geirangerfjord—both UNESCO World Heritage Sites—walls of water shoot up the mountainsides, jagged snowcapped peaks blot out the sky, and water tumbles down the mountains in an endless variety of colors.

The farther north you travel, the more rugged and wild the landscape. The still, peaceful Sognefjord is the longest inlet, snaking 190 km (110 mi) inland. At the top of Sogn og Fjordane county is a group of fjords referred to as Nordfjord, with the massive Jostedalsbreen, mainland Europe's largest glacier, to the south. In the county of Møre og Romsdal, you'll see mountains that would seem more natural on the moon—all gray rock—as well as cliffs hanging over the water below.

Trondheim to the Lofoten Islands. The mind-blowing scenery and the feeling that you're discovering something for the time makes the area of Norway directly above and below the Arctic Circle the perfect gateway to the magical north. From the vibrance of **Trondheim** to the dramatic landscapes of **the Lofoten Islands**, the popularity of this Norwegian region is beginning to skyrocket, and it's not difficult to see why. Often overlooked by travelers, it's your best bet for world-class dining, undiscovered beaches, unparalleled views, and villages that echo the old ways of life.

A narrow but immensley long strip of land stretches between Trondheim and Kirkenes in northern Norway. In this vast territory you'll encounter the sawtooth, glacier-carved peaks of the Lofoten Islands and the world's strongest tidal current, in **Bodø**. Thousands of islands and skerries hug the coast of northern Norway, and the provinces of Nordland, Troms, and Finnmark, up to the North Cape. Along this wild, unpredictable coast, the weather is as dramatic as the scenery: in summer you can see the midnight sun, and in winter experience aurora borealis, the northern lights.

Northern Norway. Despite its rugged landscapes and unapologetic weather, Northern Norway draws a constant stream of intrepid travelers during both the summer and winter months. From July's glistening midnight sun to colorful auroras dancing across the sky in December, it's one of the world's most mysterious and captivating destinations. If the Arctic Circle is on your bucket list, this is the best place to experience all that it has to offer.

Northern Norwegians still make their living in the fishing villages of the Lofoten Islands, in small, provincial towns, and in modern cities like **Tromsø**. Tourism plays an important role in the region, especially with those seeking wild landscapes, outdoor activities, and adventure, whether it's mountaineering, dogsledding, skiing, caving, or wreck-diving. Basking in the midnight sun is one of Norway's most popular attractions; every year, thousands of people flock to **Nordkapp** (the North Cape) for it.

Planning

Getting Here and Around

AIR

Gardermoen Airport (OSL), about 45 km (28 miles) north of Oslo, is the major entry point for most visitors. Most flights from North America have at least one connection, though Scandinavian Airlines (SAS), United Airlines (UA), and the budget airline Norwegian have direct flights from New York. Various European airlines fly through their hubs, including Icelandair via Reykjavík, British Airways via London, Lufthansa via Frankfurt, KLM via Amsterdam, and Air France via Paris. A flight from New York to Oslo takes about eight hours.

Within Norway, Norwegian, SAS and Widerøe connect many of the cities by regular flights. SAS and the low-cost airline Norwegian also serve many destinations in Europe, while Widerøe also has flights to a handful of destinations in Sweden, Denmark, and the United Kingdom. Emirates has direct flights from Oslo to Dubai, and Thai Airways and Norwegian fly directly to Bangkok.

AIRPORT Oslo Airport (ARN). ⊠ *Edvard Munchs veg* ☎ *67/03–00–00* ⊕ *www. oslo-airport.com.*

AIRLINES Finnair. ☎ *810–01–100 in Norway* ⊕ *www.finnair.com.* **Icelandair.** ☎ *22–03–40–50 in Norway* ⊕ *www.icelandair. com.* **Norwegian.** ☎ *815–21–815* ⊕ *www. norwegian.com.* **SAS.** ☎ *800/221–2350 in U.S. and Canada, 05400 in Norway* ⊕ *www.flysas.com.* **Widerøe.** ☎ *810–01– 200 in Norway* ⊕ *www.wideroe.no.*

BOAT AND FERRY
Taking a ferry isn't only fun, it's often necessary in Norway, as they remain an important means of transportation along the west coast. More specialized boat service includes hydrofoil (catamaran) trips between Stavanger, Haugesund, and Bergen. There are also fjord cruises out of these cities and others in the north. Fjord1 and Norled are the main ferry companies.

Norway's most renowned boat service is Hurtigruten, which literally means "Rapid Route." Also known as the Coastal Express, the boat departs from Bergen and stops at 34 ports along the coast in six days, ending with Kirkenes, near the Russian border, before turning back. Tickets can be purchased for the entire journey or for individual legs.

FERRY CONTACTS Norled. ☎ *51–86–87– 00 Press 9 for English.* ⊕ *www.norled. no.* **Fjord1.** ☎ *57–75–70–00* ⊕ *www.fjord1. no.* **Ruteinformasjonen (Route information).* ⊕ *www.ruteinfo.no.*

BUS
Bus tours can be effective for smaller regions within Norway, but the train system is excellent and offers much greater coverage in less time. Buses do, however, tend to be less expensive.

Every end station of the railroad is supported by a number of bus routes, some of which are operated by the Norwegian State Railways (NSB), others by local companies. Long-distance buses usually take longer than rail. Virtually every settlement on the mainland is served by bus, and for anyone with a desire to get off the beaten track, a pay-as-you-go, open-ended bus trip is the best way to see Norway.

Most long-distance buses leave from Bussterminalen close to Oslo Central Station. NOR-WAY Bussekspress, a chain of about 30 Norwegian bus companies serving 500 destinations in south and central Norway, can arrange almost any journey.

CONTACTS Ruteinformasjonen (Route information). ☎ *177* ⊕ *www.ruteinfo.no.* **Bussterminalen Oslo (Main bus terminal).** ⊠ *Galleri Oslo, Schweigaardsgt. 10, Oslo.* **NOR-WAY Bussekspress.** ☎ *815–44–444* ⊕ *www.nor-way.no.* **NSB.** (*Norwegian State Railways*) ☎ *815–00–888* ⊕ *www. nsb.no.*

CAR
You can drive in Norway with your valid U.S. driver's license. Excellent, well-marked roads make driving a great way to explore Norway, but it can be an expensive choice. Ferry costs can be steep, and you should turn up early in peak season for the most popular crossings. Tolls on some major roads and to enter the larger cities add to the expense, as do the high fees for city parking. Tickets for illegal parking are painfully costly.

Eighteen roads around the country are designated as national tourist routes, so designated for picturesque scenery and tourist-friendly infrastructure, including parts of Route 7 across the Hardangervidda plateau, the Geiranger-Trollstigen road and the Atlantic Ocean Road. If you're planning to drive around Norway, call or check the website of the Statens Vegvesen (Norwegian Public Roads Administration), which monitors and provides information about roads, conditions, tolls, distances, and ferry timetables. Phones are open 24 hours a day.

Four-lane highways are found only around major cities. Elsewhere, roads tend to be narrow and twisting, with only token guardrails. The southern part of Norway is compact—all major cities are about a day's drive from each other. Along the west coast, waits for ferries and passage through tunnels can be significant. Don't expect to cover more than 240 km (150 miles) in a day, especially in fjord country.

In a few remote areas, especially in northern Norway, road conditions can be unpredictable in autumn, winter, or spring. Some high mountain roads are closed as early as October due to snow, and do not open again until June. When driving in remote areas, especially in winter, let someone know your travel plans, use a four-wheel-drive vehicle, and travel with at least one other car.

CONTACTS Statens Vegvesen. (*Norwegian Public Roads Administration*) ☎ *02030* ⊕ *www.vegvesen.no.*

GASOLINE

Gas is expensive and costs approximately NKr 15 per liter (that's around US$10.50 per gallon). Stations are only self-serve, and hours vary greatly. Those marked kort are 24-hour pumps, which take credit or debit cards, inserted directly into the pump.

RULES OF THE ROAD

Driving is on the right. The maximum speed limit is 100 kph (62 mph) on major highways. On other highways the limit is 80 kph (50 mph) or 70 kph (43 mph). The speed limit in cities and towns is 50

kph (30 mph), and 30 kph (18 mph) in residential areas. Speeding is punished severely.

By law, you must keep your headlights on at all times, and everyone must wear seat belts. Children under four years of age must ride in a car seat, and children over four years must ride in the back. Norway has strict drinking-and-driving laws, and there are routine roadside checks. The legal limit is a blood-alcohol level of 0.02%, which effectively means that you should not drink any alcohol before driving. If you are stopped, you may be required to take a breath test. If it is positive, you must submit to a blood test. No exceptions are made for foreigners, who can lose their licenses on the spot. Other penalties include fines and imprisonment. An accident involving a driver with an illegal blood-alcohol level usually voids all insurance agreements, so the driver becomes responsible for his own medical bills and damage to the cars.

PARKING

You can usually park on the side of the road, though not on main roads and highways. Signs reading "*parkering forbudt*" or "*stans forbudt*" mean no parking or no stopping, respectively. For most downtown parking you must either buy a ticket from an automatic vending machine and display it on the dash, or use a public car park. The latter is more expensive (from NKr 250 a day in Oslo, and NKr 100–NKr 150 in other major cities).

TAXI

Even the smallest villages have some form of taxi service. Towns on the railroad normally have taxi stands just outside the station. All city taxis are connected with a central dispatching office, so there is only one main telephone number for calling a cab. Never use an unmarked, or pirate, taxi, since their drivers are unlicensed and in some cases may be dangerous.

3

Norway PLANNING

TRAIN

NSB, Norwegian State Railways, has five main lines originating from Oslo S (Oslo Central Station). Its 4,000 km (2,500 miles) of track connect all main cities as far north as Bodø and Fauske. Train tickets can be purchased in railway stations. Many travelers assume rail passes guarantee seats on the trains they wish to ride. Not so. You need to book seats ahead even if you are using a rail pass.

NSB trains are clean, comfortable, and punctual. Most have special compartments for travelers with disabilities and for families with children younger than age two. First- and second-class tickets are available. Most trains offer free Wi-Fi.

Norway's longest rail route runs north across the Arctic Circle. The southern line hugs the coast to Stavanger, while the stunning western line crosses Hardangervidda, the scenic plateau between Oslo and Bergen. An eastern line to Stockholm links Norway with Sweden, while another southern line through Göteborg, Sweden, is the main connection with continental Europe. Narvik, north of Bodø, is the last stop on Sweden's Ofot line, the world's northernmost rail system, which runs from Stockholm via Kiruna.

CONTACT NSB (Norwegian State Railways).
☎ 815–00–888 ⊕ www.nsb.no.

Restaurants

Although major cities like Oslo, Bergen, and Stavanger have many options, there's less variety in more rural areas. Pizza restaurants are very popular, particularly in the south, and often offer the best value for money. Chains like Peppes and Dolly Dimples have outlets throughout the country. Norwegians usually eat their dinner, or middag, as soon as they get home from work (4 pm is not unusual). Reservations are required for the most sought-after restaurants in major cities,

and during the extremely busy period between mid-November and Christmas, but are not usually necessary otherwise. It is generally much cheaper to eat out at lunchtime than in the evening, as many establishments have good value lunch menus. That said, most restaurants outside of major cities are not open for lunch.

Although not widely known abroad, Norwegian food is surprisingly tasty and varied. Fish, as one would expect from a country with such a long coastline, is a strong component of the Norwegian diet, with cod a particular favorite. The latter appears in many dishes, including lutefisk, a traditional Christmas dish (usually eaten with a dash of aquavit, or schnapps). Shellfish is also excellent— from prawns to lobster, the choice is ample, and the *kongekrabbe*, or giant crab, is a much-prized local specialty. Game is another specialty in season; make sure you try moose or reindeer if you get the chance. And do seek out the Lofoten lamb (free-range lamb reared on the Lofoten archipelago in the north). Last but not least, leave room for dessert—the pastries, from *boller* to *skolebrød*, are delicious, as are the many different breads.

Hotels

Norwegian hotels have high standards in cleanliness and comfort—and often sky-high prices to match. Even the simplest youth hostels provide good mattresses with fluffy down comforters and clean showers or baths. Breakfast, usually served buffet style, is often included in the room price at hotels. Bellhops are not the norm, so expect to carry your own bags, even in high-end hotels.

Quintessentially Scandinavian "*hytter,*" rentals that range from small wooden cabins to bigger chalet-type houses, are as ubiquitous on the coast as they are in mountainous areas. Ideally suited to families and small groups, they offer good value for money, and allow you to be close to nature while still enjoying some degree of comfort. Local and regional tourist offices can help you book accommodation in a hytter, as well as the company Norgesbooking.

CONTACT Norgesbooking. ☎ 32–08–57–10 ⊕ www.norgesbooking.com.

HOTEL AND RESTAURANT PRICES
Hotel prices in the reviews are the lowest cost of a standard double room in high season. Restaurant prices in the reviews are the average cost of a main course at dinner, or if dinner is not served, at lunch.

WHAT IT COSTS in Norwegian Krone

$	$$	$$$	$$$$
RESTAURANTS			
Under NKr 125	NKr 125– NKr 250	NKr 251– NKr 350	over NKr 350
HOTELS			
Under NKr 750	NKr 750– NKr 1250	NKr 1251– NKr 1900	over NKr 1900

Visitor Info

CONTACTS VisitNorway. ⊕ www.visit-norway.com. Scandinavian Tourist Board. ☎ 212/885–9700 in New York ⊕ www.goscandinavia.com.

Oslo

What sets Oslo apart from other European cities is not so much its cultural traditions or its internationally renowned museums as its simply stunning natural beauty. How many world capitals have subway service to the forest, or lakes and hiking trails within city limits? But Norwegians will be quick to remind you

that Oslo is a cosmopolitan metropolis with world-renowned cultural attractions, a foodie scene that draws people from around the world, and a thriving nightlife comparable to Scandinavia's other capital cities.

Once overlooked by travelers to Norway, Oslo is now a destination in its own right and the gateway to what many believe is Scandinavia's most scenic land. That's just one more change for this town of 670,000—a place that has become good at survival and rebirth throughout its 1,000-year history. In 1348 a plague wiped out half the city's population. In 1624 a fire burned almost the whole of Oslo to the ground. It was redesigned and renamed Christiania by Denmark's royal builder, King Christian IV. After that it slowly gained prominence as the largest and most economically significant city in Norway.

During the mid-19th century, Norway and Sweden were ruled as one kingdom, under Karl Johan. It was then that his namesake grand main street was built, and Karl Johans Gate has been at the center of city life ever since. In 1905 the country separated from Sweden, and in 1925 an act of Parliament finally changed the city's name back to Oslo. Today, Oslo is Norway's political, economic, industrial, and cultural capital. It's also one of the continent's most eco-friendly cities, having earned the title of European Eco Capital in 2019.

WHEN TO GO
You can visit Oslo throughout the year, with locals heading out of doors no matter what the season. Think there's not much to do in a Scandinavian city in the winter? An urban sauna culture has taken the capital by storm, with locals taking dips in the icy waters of the fjord followed by sweats in floating pods. Others take advantage of more traditional winter activities, from ice skating in the city center to tobogganing down the nearby

hills. Temperatures can dip to -15°C (5°F), and daylight hours are scarce, so dress warmly and get an early start. And while this most northern of Europe's capitals is geared toward outdoors activities, it caters to indoors types, too.

May through September are most pleasant months, with the warmest weather coming in a short burst between June and August. Temperatures can sometimes rise to 30°C (86°F), and when this rarity occurs locals embrace it, flocking fjordside to the beaches. Many also escape to their summer houses further down the fjord or in the mountains. Those who stay take advantage of summertime celebrations like August's five-day music festival Øyafestivalen.

GETTING HERE AND AROUND
AIR
About 45 km (28 miles) north of the city, Oslo Airport is most likely your first impression of Norway. Luckily it has huge windows with excellent views of the landscape and a state-of-the-art weather system that has drastically decreased the number of delayed flights.

Oslo Airport is a 50-minute drive to the city center along the E6. There is a taxi queue at the front of the airport if you have a lot of luggage or are nervous about negotiating public transport. If you're traveling light, Flybussen buses depart every 30 minutes, one route headed to the center of the city and the other following the ring roads. A quicker way to get downtown is the Flytoget express train, which has departures every 10 minutes to Oslo Central Station. Uber is currently not available in Oslo.

If you're flying RyanAir, you'll touch down in Torp Airport in Sandefjord, about 110 km (68 miles) south of Oslo. Torp Express Buss departs approximately 35 minutes after every arrival. They take almost two hours to reach the city center.

BOAT
Several ferry lines connect Oslo with ports in the United Kingdom, Denmark, Sweden, and Germany. Color Line sails to Kiel, Germany, and to Hirtshals, Denmark. DFDS Scandinavian Seaways sails to Copenhagen via Helsingborg, Sweden; and Stena Line to Frederikshavn, Denmark.

Small boats and ferries are common in the capital's waters, predominantly as a tourist activity. A ferry to Hovedøya and other islands in the harbor leaves from Aker Brygge. These are great spots for picnics and short hikes. From April through September, ferries run between Aker Brygge and the peninsula of Bygdøy, where many of Oslo's major museums are located.

BUS
There are some handy buses, trams, and trains traversing the city. About 50 bus lines, including 16 night buses that run on weekends, serve the city. Most stop at Jernbanetorget opposite Oslo Central Station. The most convenient way to use the system is buying an Oslo Pass (from NKr 445), which makes all your trips free.

SUBWAY
The Oslo subway system—which you'll see marked with a Blue letter T within a circle and hear refered to as the Oslo Tunnelbane, Oslo T-bane, or just T-banen—has five lines covering 101 stations. In Sentrum, all five lines converge, so you can take any train to downtown stations like Nationaltheatret, Stortinget, Jernbanetorget, and Grønland. All trains also head to Majorstuen, where you can walk to the sculpture garden at Vigeland Park. Line 1 is popular with travelers because it goes to Holmenkollen ski jump. Other than these destinations, the Metro bypasses most neighborhoods popular with tourists. Buses and trams, or your own two feet, are a better option.

TAXI

Taxis tend to be extortionately priced in Oslo, but are easy to call or hail on the street.

CONTACTS OsloTaxi. ☎ 02323 ⊕ www.oslotaxi.no.

TRAIN

Norway's state railway, newly rechristened Vy, has two train stations downtown: one at Oslo Sentralstasjon and one at Nationaltheatret. Long distance domestic and international trains use Sentralstasjon, while commuter trains use Nationaltheatret. Cars reserved for monthly-pass holders are marked with a large black "M" on a yellow circle. Trains marked "C," or InterCity, offer such upgraded services as breakfast and business-class seats for an added fee.

RESTAURANTS

With the rise of ecologically conscious eating habits and an increasingly diverse population, Oslo has a dining scene that's rapidly expanding beyond classic dishes using seafood and game. A few years after New Nordic cuisine emerged on the world stage, the embrace of local meats and cheeses and organic produce remains strong. In fact, there's a good chance that your chef is using ingredients that came from a neighborhood farm or even a greenhouse perched on the roof of the restaurant. But all this doesn't mean that restaurants are limited to regionally focused fare. There's an unusually wide range of European, African, Asian, and Middle Eastern eateries popping up around the city. If you can't decide which sounds the best, try a little bit of everything at one of the city's many multicultural food halls. Vegetarians and vegans find lots of options here, with a significant number of high-end establishments offering meat-free tasting menus. As the city strives to be one of the most proudly sustainable in the world, there are even restaurants serving entire menus made up of food that otherwise would have gone into the waste bin. *Restaurant reviews have been shortened. For full information, visit Fodors.com.*

HOTELS

An impressive number of boutique and design hotels have given the Oslo hotel scene a much-needed facelift in recent years. More and more are focusing on sustainability, so they have found ingenious ways to save electricity and reduce waste without impacting your comfort one bit. Many of the city's old favorites are located in the Sentrum, a stone's throw from Oslo Central Station. For a quieter stay, you might choose a hotel in Frogner or Majorstuen, elegant residential neighborhoods, or for views of the city you can head up the mountain to Holmenkollen. Newer neighborhoods like Tjuvholmen have fewer options, but they are likey to be very modern and have the latest amenities like TVs that take your room service order. Most hotels in Oslo include at least a continental breakfast in their rates, and some offer huge buffets that you have to see to believe. *Hotel reviews have been shortened. For full information, visit Fodors.com.*

NIGHTLIFE

This is a fun-loving city after dark. Into the early evening, locals often head to Sentrum to the bars on or around the main street of Karl Johans Gate. There's a number of cool wine and cocktails bars tucked among the more rowdy pubs and crowded tourist spots. Aker Brygge and Tjuvholmen, the more glamorous neighborhoods along the old wharf, have many bars and clubs, attracting mostly people willing to spend a little extra for the waterfront location. Grünerløkka has small bars, pubs, cafés, and art spaces catering to a younger clientele. A free-spending crowd also heads to the neighborhoods of Frogner and Bygdøy, where more and more trendy bars are springing up.

Bartending here is a serious profession, which means in cocktail bars ranging from dingy dives to cavernous clubs you're likely to be served creative concoctions with unusual garnishes. Sustainability is a factor here as well, with many bars growing their own botanicals. To find out what's going on around town, pick up a copy of the free monthly paper *Natt og Dag* or Friday's edition of *Avis 1.*

SHOPPING

Oslo is the best place in the country for buying anything Norwegian. The country is famous for its colorful hand-knitted wool sweaters, and even mass-produced models are of top quality. Prices are regulated, and they are always lower than buying them back home. You'll find designer brands located in Sentrum, where you'll find high-end boutiques and department stores showcasing the very best Norwegian fashion houses like Holzweiler. There's a wide range of antiques in Grünerløkka and Frogner.

Prices in Norway, as in all of Scandinavia, are generally much higher than in other European countries. Prices of handmade articles like knitwear are tightly controlled, making comparison shopping pointless. Otherwise, shops have both sales and specials—look for the words "salg" and "tilbud." Almost all shops are closed Sunday.

TOURS

Walking and biking tours are a great way to see Oslo. Various "official" and "unofficial" free walking tours start from Sentrum, but if you want to book ahead, Oslo City and Nature Walks offers hikes along rivers and tours that take you to the city's spookiest haunts. Our Way Tours takes you to spots on and off the beaten path by foot, bike, or Segway. Oslo Guideservice offers very good private group tours focusing on everything from architecture to Vikings. Specialized tours have popped up in recent years, including visits to hipster neighborhood with Our Way Tours.

There are many hop-on/hop-off bus and boat routes run by Stromma, and theme cruises by Båtservice Sightseeing.

CONTACTS Båtservice Sightseeing. ⊕ *nyc. no/boatservice-sightseeing.* **Oslo Guideservice.** ⊕ *guideservice.no.* **Oslo City and Nature Walks.** ⊕ *oslowalks.no.* **Our Way Tours.** ⊕ *ourwaytours.com/our-tours/ location/oslo.* **Stromma.** ⊕ *stromma.com/ en-no/oslo.*

VISITOR INFORMATION
CONTACTS Visit Oslo. ✉ *Oslo Central Station, Østbanehallen, Oslo* ☎ *23–10–62–00* ⊕ *www.visitoslo.com* Ⓜ *Jernbanetorget.*

Sentrum

Although the city region is huge (454 square km [175 square miles]), downtown Oslo is compact, with shops, museums, historic buildings, restaurants, and clubs concentrated in a small, walkable center that's brightly illuminated at night. The rapidly diversifying population means some streets maintain a certain quiet charm, while others are a bit more noisy and bustling. Here you'll find the lion's share of historic buildings, such as the Royal Palace and the Parliament Building. This area is also chock full of museums, including the gleaming new National Museum complex.

⊙ Sights

★ **Nasjonalmuseet** (*National Museum*)
MUSEUM | Set to open its doors in 2021, the newly constructed National Museum now stands as the largest art museum in the Nordic region. The eye-catching modern structure not far from the waterfront includes a rooftop hall longer than the Royal Palace and has views of Oslo City Hall, Akershus Fortress, and the Oslofjord. The Edvard Munch section holds such major paintings as *The Dance of Life,* one of two existing oil versions of *The Scream,* and several

self-portraits. Classic landscapes by Hans Gude and Adolph Tidemand—including *Bridal Voyage on the Hardangerfjord*— share space with other works by major Norwegian artists. The museum also has works by Monet, Renoir, Van Gogh, and Gauguin, as well as contemporary works by 20th-century Nordic artists. Enjoy the landscaped garden seating areas and special events throughout the year. ⊠ *Sentrum* ☎ *21–98–20–00* ⊕ *www. nasjonalmuseet.no* Ⓜ *Nationaltheatret.*

Nationaltheatret (*National Theater*)
ARTS VENUE | In front of this neoclassical theater, built in 1899, are statues of Norway's great playwrights, Henrik Ibsen and Bjørnstjerne Bjørnson, who also composed the national anthem. Most performances are in Norwegian, so you may just want to take an English-language guided tour of the interior, which costs NKr 90 and can be arranged in advance. ⊠ *Johanne Dybwads pl. 1, Sentrum* ☎ *22–00–14–00* ⊕ *www.nation-altheatret.no.*

Nobels Fredssenter (*Nobel Peace Center*)
MUSEUM | FAMILY | Every year the Nobel Peace Prize is awarded in Oslo—at this high-tech attraction by the harbor, you can learn about past and present laureates and their work through an original installation featuring 1,000 fiber-optic lights; read about Alfred Nobel's inventions and travels in a huge interactive book; and see a documentary on the current laureate in the Passage of Honor room. There are wonderful activities for young would-be peace activists, and changing exhibitions throughout the year. Next to the lobby is a fantastic shop selling unusual designs from around the world. ⊠ *Brynjulf Bulls pl. 1, Sentrum* ☎ *483–01–000* ⊕ *www.nobelpeacecenter.org* 🖾 *NKr 120* ☉ *Closed Mon. Oct.–Apr.* Ⓜ *Nationaltheatret.*

Oslo Domkirke (*Oslo Cathedral*)
RELIGIOUS SITE | Consecrated in 1697 as Oslo's third cathedral, this dark-brown

brick structure has since been Oslo's main church. The original pulpit, altarpiece, and organ front with acanthus carvings still stand. Take a look at the ceiling murals painted between 1936 and 1950 by artist Hugo Louis Mohr, and stained-glass windows by Emanuel Vigeland. In the 19th century the fire department operated a lookout from the bell tower, which you can visit. ⊠ *Karl Johans gt. 11, Sentrum* ☎ *23–62–90–10* ⊕ *kirken.no* 🖾 *Free* Ⓜ *Stortinget.*

Rådhuset (*City Hall*)
GOVERNMENT BUILDING | This boxy brick building is best known today for the awarding of the Nobel Peace Prize, which takes place here every December 10. Inside, many museum-quality masterpieces grace the walls. After viewing the frescoes in the Main Hall, walk upstairs to the Banquet Hall to see the royal portraits. In June and July, free 45-minute guided tours are available and meet in the main hall. To visit the City Hall Gallery, enter harborside. Special exhibits are hung throughout the year. On festive occasions, the Central Hall is illuminated from outside by 60 large spotlights. ⊠ *Rådhusplassen 1, Sentrum* ☎ *23–46–16–30* ⊕ *www.oslo.kommune. no/politics-and-administration/oslo-city-hall* 🖾 *Free* Ⓜ *Nationaltheatret.*

Slottet (*The Royal Palace*)
CASTLE/PALACE | At one end of Karl Johans Gate, the vanilla-and-cream-color neoclassical palace was completed in 1848. The equestrian statue out in front is of Karl Johan, King of Sweden and Norway from 1818 to 1844. The palace is open to the public only in summer, when there are highly sought after guided tours in English that should be booked in advance. Don't miss the 11 am Sunday Service in the Palace Chapel. ■ TIP→ **Kids of all ages will love the Royal Palace's changing of the guard ceremony, accompanied by the Norwegian Military Band, that takes place daily, rain or shine, at 1:30.** ⊠ *Slottsplassen 1, Sentrum* ☎ *81–53–31–33* ⊕ *www.*

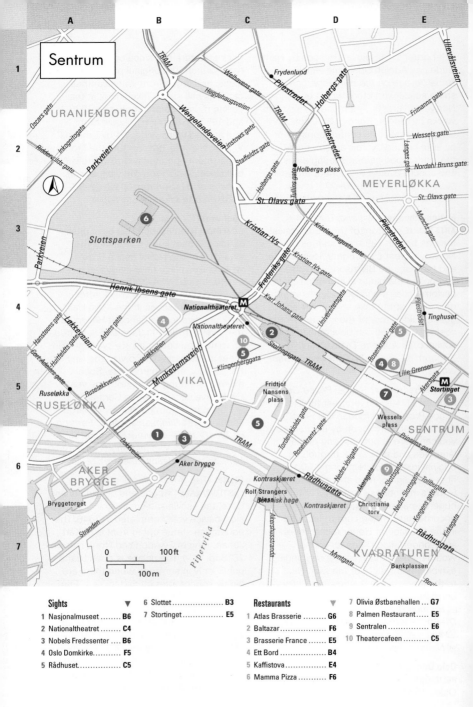

Sentrum

Sights	▼	6 Slottet **B3**	**Restaurants**	▼	7 Olivia Østbanehallen ... **G7**
1 Nasjonalmuseet **B6**		7 Stortinget **E5**	1 Atlas Brasserie **G6**		8 Palmen Restaurant **E5**
2 Nationaltheatret **C4**			2 Baltazar **F6**		9 Sentralen **E6**
3 Nobels Fredssenter **B6**			3 Brasserie France **E5**		10 Theatercafeen **C5**
4 Oslo Domkirke **F5**			4 Ett Bord **B4**		
5 Rådhuset **C5**			5 Kaffistova **E4**		
			6 Mamma Pizza **F6**		

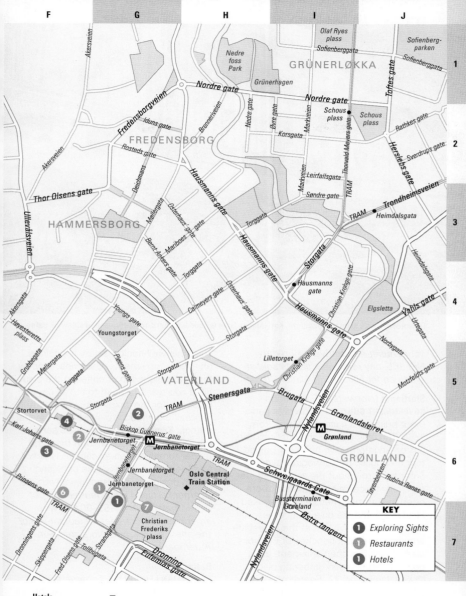

Hotels ▼

Downtown Oslo's main thoroughfare, Karl Johans Gate is lined with bars, restaurants, and sidewalk cafés.

kongehuset.no ✉ Advance tickets NKr 165, any remaining tickets sold at entrance for NKr 125. Ⓜ Nationaltheatret.

Stortinget (Norwegian Parliament)
GOVERNMENT BUILDING | Norway's parliament building is a classic dating from 1866. The only way for the public to see it is on an informative one-hour guided tour (in English or Norwegian) every Saturday throughout the year; tours are generally twice-daily but are run more often in summer. They can't be booked in advance and are on a first-come, first-served basis. Meet at the Akersgata entrance. The park benches of Eidsvolls plass, in front of the Parliament, are a popular meeting and gathering place. ✉ Karl Johans gt. 22, Sentrum ☎ 23–31–30–50 ⊕ www.stortinget.no ✉ Free. Ⓜ Stortinget.

 Restaurants

Atlas Brasserie
$$ | **BRASSERIE** | In the former headquarters of the Norwegian America cruise ship, this well-heeled eatery capitalizes on a New York–meets–Oslo vibe. Stop by for an excellent cup of coffee in the plant-filled courtyard, or head to the all-day brasserie for the dazzling seafood platter or steak big enough to share with several friends. **Known for:** blue mussels served in a Roquefort reduction with fries; the tender tomahawk steak can easily serve four; decor is a cheeky take on Scandinavian design. $ Average main: NKr 250 ✉ Amerikalinjen Hotel, Jernbanetorget 2, Sentrum ☎ 21–40–59–00 ⊕ www.amerikalinjen.com/best-restaurant-i-oslo/the-atlas-restaurant ☉ No dinner Sun. Ⓜ Jernbanetorget.

Baltazar
$$ | **ITALIAN** | **FAMILY** | A longtime favorite, this restaurant tucked away under the graceful arcades behind the cathedral does an impressive job of re-creating the sort of trattoria you'd only find in Italy. With wood beams and exposed brick, the casual dining room spreads over three floors. **Known for:** an epic sharing menu for the whole table;

classic meat-and-potatoes dishes; reliably good fish soup. $ *Average main: NKr 250* ✉ *Domkirkeparken, Dronningensgt. 27, Sentrum* ☎ *23–35–70–60* ⊕ *www.baltazar.no* ⊗ *Closed Sun.* Ⓜ *Jernbanetorget.*

★ Brasserie France

$$$ | FRENCH | As its name suggests, this wine bar is straight out of Paris: the long white aprons on the waiters, the art nouveau flourishes in the dining room, the old French posters on the walls, and the closely packed tables all add to the illusion. The sumptuous menu includes the classics: steak tartare, entrecôte, duck confit. **Known for:** an indulgent "bouillabaisse a la maison"; an impressive vegetarian set menu; perfect location near Parliament. $ *Average main: NKr 300* ✉ *Øvre Slottsgt. 16, Sentrum* ☎ *23–10–01–65* ⊕ *www.brasseriefrance. no* ⊗ *Closed July and Sun. No lunch weekdays* Ⓜ *Stortinget.*

Ett Bord

$$ | SCANDINAVIAN | Nordic-style tapas are served here with a maximum of style and sustenance, alongside a dedication to sustainability. The usual open-faced shrimp sandwich is done extremely well, as are the steamed mussels, fried peppers, and other small plates. **Known for:** freshest local ingredients; marketlike atmosphere; sunny dining room. $ *Average main: NKr 150* ✉ *Ruseløkkveien 3, Sentrum* ☎ *22–83–83–03* ⊕ *www.ettbord.no* ⊗ *Closed Sun.* Ⓜ *Nationaltheatret.*

Kaffistova

$$ | NORWEGIAN | Norwegian home cooking is served at this casual eatery on the ground floor of the Hotell Bondeheimen. Classic such as *raspeballer* (potato dumplings), *boknafisk* (dried and salted cod), and *rømmegrøt* (sour cream porridge) are always available. **Known for:** homemade meatballs are famous; open-faced shrimp sandwiches; anything from the dessert display. $ *Average main: NKr 180* ✉ *Hotell Bondeheimen, Rosenkrantz gt. 8, Sentrum* ☎ *23–21–41–00* ⊕ *www. kaffistova.com* Ⓜ *Stortinget.*

Mamma Pizza

$$ | ITALIAN | FAMILY | Featuring famous sourdough pizzas, this tiny osteria has the traditional checkered tablecloths and striped awning that call to mind the Emilia-Romagna region of Italy. Serving the city's most authentic pie—head and shoulders above its overpriced competitors—the eatery takes things one step further with refreshing yet strong cocktails or classic aperitifs served while you wait. **Known for:** short stroll from the central train station; don't miss the dessert of the day; gluten-free dough available. $ *Average main: NKr 180* ✉ *Dronningens gt. 22, Sentrum* ☎ *915–11–841* ⊕ *www. mammapizza.no* Ⓜ *Jernbanetorget.*

Olivia Østbanehallen

$$ | ITALIAN | FAMILY | With high ceilings, stained-glass windows, and lots of foliage, the dining room of this long-running Italian eatery is comfortable and cozy—although if the weather cooperates, you'll probably opt for an alfresco meal in the square outside. The food is inexpensive, but very generous in terms of portions. **Known for:** a grand dining room; free focaccia with every meal; central location. $ *Average main: NKr 200* ✉ *Jernbanetorget 1, Sentrum* ☎ *23–11–54–70* ⊕ *www.oliviarestauranter.no* Ⓜ *Jernbanetorget.*

Palmen Restaurant

$$$ | BISTRO | The Grand Cafe gets all the attention, but The Grand Hotel's more casual—but still quite beautiful—lobby restaurant is what Bohemian dreams are made of, with marble, gold, crystal, and velvet adding a luxurious touch. Underneath a spectacular glass ceiling, the dining room is a place where locals come to see and be seen. **Known for:** afternoon tea is a tradition here; dry martinis at the bar; a more relaxed affair. $ *Average main: NKr 265* ✉ *The Grand Hotel, Karl Johans gt. 31, Sentrum* ☎ *23–21–20–00* ⊕ *www.grand.no* Ⓜ *Stortinget.*

Sentralen

$$$$ | SCANDINAVIAN | This debonair dining room—a relatively new kid on the block—focuses on organic ingredients prepared with continental flair. Many dishes are presented in unusual new combinations, such as the whole-baked cauliflower in miso and red curry. **Known for:** freshly baked croissants and great coffee in the attached café; the atmosphere is casual; the king crab is amazing. $ Average main: NKr 655 ⊠ Upper Slottsgate 3, Sentrum ☎ 22–33–33–22 ⊕ www.sentralenrestaurant.no ⊗ Closed Sun. Ⓜ Stortinget.

★ Theatercafeen

$$$ | NORWEGIAN | An Oslo institution, Theatercafeen has been a meeting place for artists and intellectuals for more than a century. Today it still attracts Oslo's beau monde, and as it's right across the street from the National Theater, it's a good bet for celebrity spotting. **Known for:** traditional dishes like spicy moules frites; desserts like wild strawberry sorbet; sublime fish cakes. $ Average main: NKr 300 ⊠ Continental Hotel, Stortingsgt. 24–26, Sentrum ☎ 22–82–40–50 ⊕ www.theatercafeen.no ⊗ Closed July Ⓜ Nationaltheatret.

🏨 Hotels

★ Amerikalinjen Hotel

$$$$ | HOTEL | The handsome headquarters of the Norwegian America Line opened its doors in 1919, and 100 years later it was transformed into this boutique hotel appealing to the design-conscious explorer. **Pros:** sophisticated design throughout; wonderful gym and sauna; room-service cocktails. **Cons:** extremely steep rates; can be a bit of a scene; no space for extra beds. $ Rooms from: NKr 2092 ⊠ Jernbanetorget 2, Oslo ☎ 21–40–59–00 ⊕ www.amerikalinjen.com ⤴ 122 rooms ⦿ No meals Ⓜ Jernbanetorget.

Clarion Hotel The Hub

$$ | HOTEL | This slick business hotel has all the features of a design hotel: great restaurants and bar, contemporary interiors, and elegantly appointed rooms. **Pros:** location near the central station; sustainability is their mantra; atmosphere. **Cons:** filled with corporate clients; labyrinthine corridors; expensive drinks. $ Rooms from: NKr 1200 ⊠ Biskop Gunnerusgt. 3, Sentrum ☎ 23–10–80–00 ⊕ www.nordicchoicehotels.com/hotels/norway/oslo/clarion-hotel-the-hub ⤴ 810 rooms ⦿ Free breakfast Ⓜ Jernbanetorget.

Comfort Hotel Karl Johan

$$ | HOTEL | FAMILY | Along the historic main street of Karl Johan—but tucked away in its own courtyard away from the hustle and bustle—this handy hotel has nicely sized rooms and an eco-friendly vibe. **Pros:** sought-after location; attractive courtyard; delicious bistro. **Cons:** some rooms are extremely small; snacks at the reception area; can be a little noisy. $ Rooms from: NKr 1200 ⊠ Karl Johans gt. 12, Sentrum ☎ 23–01–03–52 ⊕ www.nordicchoicehotels.com ⤴ 181 rooms ⦿ Free breakfast Ⓜ Jernbanetorget.

★ Grand Hotel

$$$$ | HOTEL | Looking like it would be at home on any street in Paris, this grand dame with a mansard roof and Beaux-Arts entrance is the choice of visiting heads of state, rock musicians, and Nobel Peace Prize winners. **Pros:** period touches have been preserved throughout; step-out balconies overlooking the town square; beautiful pool and spa facilities. **Cons:** gets busy during any of the city's festivals; spa and pool are short walk away from hotel; occasionally overrun by conference attendees. $ Rooms from: NKr 2000 ⊠ Karl Johans gt. 31, Sentrum ☎ 23–21–20–00 ⊕ www.grand.no ⤴ 283 rooms ⦿ No meals Ⓜ Stortinget.

★ **Hotel Continental**
$$$ | **HOTEL** | History meets modernity at this landmark—it's a sophisticated stay with stylish guest rooms and posh common areas. **Pros:** exemplary service; eco-friendly ethos; great fitness area. **Cons:** restaurants are often booked in advance; nondescript exterior; business hotel feel. [$] *Rooms from: NKr 1800* ✉ *Stortingsgt. 24–26, Sentrum* ☎ *22–82–40–00* 🌐 *www.hotelcontinental.no* 🛏 *151 rooms* 🍴 *Free breakfast* [M] *Nationaltheatret.*

Nightlife

BARS AND LOUNGES

Andre til Høyre
BARS/PUBS | The name means "Second to the Right," and that's basically a roadmap to finding this bar up the stairs at Håndslag. It's a sumptuously decorated space, designed like an elegant, living room fit for entertaining glamorous guests at all hours. Lavish seating and heavy curtains make for a wonderful setting to explore Burgundy and sparkling wines. ✉ *Youngs gt. 19, Sentrum* 🌐 *andretilhoyre.no* 🕒 *Closed Sun.* [M] *Jernbanetorget.*

Crowbar and Bryggeri
BREWPUBS/BEER GARDENS | Spread across two floors, Oslo's largest microbrewery offers tasty beers and hearty pub fare like whole suckling pig. The menu changes weekly, and there's always a friendly bearded face to talk you through all the options. ✉ *Torggata 32, Sentrum* ☎ *21–38–67–57* 🌐 *crowbryggeri.com* [M] *Jernbanetorget.*

Einbar
WINE BARS—NIGHTLIFE | Where Sentrum meets Kvadvraturen, this former potato cellar is the perfect winter hideaway. There's an impressively long list of wines (which complements a small but very good dinner menu) and a Moroccan vibe complete with arched ceilings, squishy seats, and lavish rugs. ✉ *Prinsens gt. 18, Sentrum* ☎ *22–41–55–55* 🌐 *www.restauranteiner.no/einbar* [M] *Stortinget.*

Himkok
BARS/PUBS | Draped in stark white lab coats, the city's most mysterious and skilled mixologists whip up their concoctions in a bar so well hidden that you might miss it if you don't search carefully for the tiny door. The name translates as "Moonshine," and this secretive locale doubles as a distillery. In the summer there's an herb-filled garden with a cider bar. ✉ *Storgata 27, Sentrum* ☎ *22–42–22–02* 🌐 *himkok.squarespace.com* [M] *Jernbanetorget.*

Lardo
WINE BARS—NIGHTLIFE | If natural wines are your thing, slip into this small and low-key bar with a robust selection from around the world. It's a great place to talk grapes with the knowledgeable staff over some salty charcuterie, creamy cheeses, and an ever-changing selection of bar snacks. ✉ *Møllergata 38, Sentrum* ☎ *979–17–477* 🌐 *www.barlardo.no* [M] *Stortinget.*

Lorry
BARS/PUBS | Behind the Royal Palace, this funky spot has stuffed wildlife and century-old sketches of famous Norwegians adorning the walls. It advertises 180 different types of beer, and the mountain trout and other dishes are surprisingly good. It's a local institution that's hugely popular during the *julebord* season (mid-November to Christmas). ✉ *Parkvn. 12, Sentrum* ☎ *22–69–69–04* 🌐 *www.lorry.no* [M] *Storinget.*

★ **Pier 42**
BARS/PUBS | When early-20th-century Osloites decided to set sail for the United States, they embarked on the Amerikalinjen ships at Oslo Harbor. The cruise line's former HQ is now home to a gorgeous cocktail bar named for their first landing point in New York. This fun locale serves tipples from the

Oslo's Nonstop Festival

It's an audacious idea, to say the least. Instead of the usual cultural festival taking place every other year, Norway's capital city decided to host a five-year-long celebration that began in 2019 and won't wind up until 2024. Then it plans to start the whole thing all over again in 2025. The Oslo Biennalen (⊕ www.oslobiennalen. no) aims to make art more accessible, more dynamic, and, most of all, more out in the open.

"The City of Oslo has a long-standing tradition of supporting art in public space," said Ole G. Slyngstadli, the biennial's executive director. "It is one of our priorities to find new ways of connecting the arts and the general public." So performances are scheduled to take place on the rooftop of the Oslo Opera House, the hallways of City Hall, the waiting area of Oslo Central Station, and dozens of other locations. Buildings will be transformed into huge canvases, and parks will be filled with works of art.

Among the provocative works being presented is "Seven Works for Seven Locations," by Hlynur Hallsson, which will include the words of ordinary residents sprayed on city walls. "Oslo Collected Works," by Jan Freuchen, Jonas Høgli Major, and Sigurd Tenningen, is a sculpture park taking over a empty lot near a subway station. And "Migrant Car" is a three-dimensional photo of a wrecked car reproduced at full size and rolled around the city.

boat's heyday, carefully assembled by the shipping line's former bar manager. ⊠ *Amerikalinjen Hotel, Jernbanetorget 2, Sentrum* ☎ *21–40–59–00* ⊕ *amerikalinjen.com* Ⓜ *Jernbanetorget.*

★ Torggata Botaniske

BARS/PUBS | Vines and other botanical wonders grow across the ceiling at this bar known for its creative cocktail selection. The nature-centric vibe is a welcome breath of fresh air as you step inside from one of the busiest downtown streets. The ingredients come from the bar's own greenhouse. ⊠ *Torggata 17B, Oslo* Ⓜ *Jernbanetorget.*

MUSIC CLUBS

★ Gustav

MUSIC CLUBS | With a free-spirited vibe, this intimate jazz club is named for Gustav Henriksen, founder of the Amerikalinjen cruise ship company. The club in the basement of the Amerikalinjen Hotel boasts an excellent sound system, atmospheric lighting, and a cool crowd that hangs around until the wee hours of the morning. ⊠ *Amerikalinjen Hotel, Jernbanetorget 2, Sentrum* ☎ *21–40–59–00* ⊕ *amerikalinjen.com* Ⓜ *Jernbanetorget.*

Rockefeller Music Hall

MUSIC CLUBS | Commonly referred to as Torggata Bad because the building used to be a public bathing facility, this club has a lineup that includes internationally known hard-rock, alternative, and hip-hop acts—Nick Cave, Blondie, and Fetty Wap have all appeared. Drink prices are steep. ⊠ *Torggt. 16, Sentrum* ☎ *22–20–32–32* ⊕ *www.rockefeller.no* Ⓜ *Jernbanetorget.*

🎭 Performing Arts

Oslo Konserthus

ARTS CENTERS | Officially the home of the Oslo Philharmonic, Oslo Konserthus is a leading venue for classical musicians, along with jazz and pop performers and ballet dancers. ⊠ *Munkedamsveien 14, Sentrum* ☎ *23–11–31–11* ⊕ *www.oslokonserthus.no* Ⓜ *Nationaltheatret.*

⚓ Shopping

ART GALLERIES

Kunstnernes Hus (*The Artists' House*)
ART GALLERIES | This gallery exhibits contemporary art and hosts the annual Autumn Exhibition. It also has a bar-restaurant that's a weekend hot spot for artists and local celebrities and the bookstore Nordic Art Press. ⊠ *Wergelandsvn. 17, Sentrum* ☎ *22–85–34–10* ⊕ *www.kunstnerneshus.no* ⊗ *Closed Mon.* Ⓜ *Nationaltheatret.*

CLOTHING

FWSS
CLOTHING | This Norwegian brand is characterized by its no-fuss approach to fashion. The chic, natural stone interior of the store in Oslo's Promenaden Fashion District reflects its dedication to simple pieces that build a timeless wardrobe. ⊠ *Prinsens gt. 22, Sentrum* ☎ *45–85–10–21* ⊕ *fallwinterspringsummer.com/eu* Ⓜ *Stortinget.*

Mette Møller
CLOTHING | This Norwegian women's fashion brand has an ultra-feminine style and an emphasis on sustainable practices. It's designed to be both stylish and durable. ⊠ *Prinsens gt. 10, Sentrum* ☎ *942–50–011* ⊕ *www.mettemoller.no* Ⓜ *Jernbanetorget.*

Oleana
CLOTHING | Designer Solveig Hisdal, behind Oleana's success, has won many awards for her collections, which she now exports as far as Australia. ⊠ *Stortingsgt. 8, Sentrum* ☎ *22–33–31–63* ⊕ *www.oleana.no* Ⓜ *Stortinget.*

JEWELRY

Hasla
JEWELRY/ACCESSORIES | Norway's natural wonders are the inspiration behind these modern yet timeless pieces. A family business since 1980, it creates jewelry in its own studio deep in the Setesdal Valley. ⊠ *Markveien 54, Grünerløkka* ☎ *922–78–777* ⊕ *haslajewelry.com.*

Sugar Shop Smykkestudio
LOCAL SPECIALTIES | On the edge of Sentrum, this shop, workshop, and gallery focuses on Norwegian design and craftmanship. Many of the pieces in the relaxed showroom are one of a kind. ⊠ *Briskebyveien 30, Sentrum* ☎ *22–44–52–79* ⊕ *sugarshop.no.*

Kvadraturen, Aker Brygge, Tjuvholmen, and Bjørvika

Kvadraturen is the oldest part of Oslo. In 1624, after the town burned down for the 14th time, King Christian IV renamed the city Christiania and moved it to the more easily defendable area adjacent to Akershus Fortress. In order to prevent future fires, the king decreed that houses were to be built of stone or brick instead of wood. Kvadraturen translates roughly as "square township," which refers to the area's geometrically ordered streets.

For more than a century this waterfront district was the home of a massive commercial shipyard called Akers Mekaniske Verksted. Postmodern steel-and-glass structures now dominate the skyline. The promenade along the water's edge is crowded with families whenever the weather is sunny. Facing the water are dozens of high-end eateries, upmarket boutiques, and art galleries. Bridges connect it to the quieter Tjuvholmen neighborhood.

◉ Sights

★ **Akershus Festning** (*Akershus Fortress*)
CASTLE/PALACE | Dating to 1299, this stone medieval castle and royal residence was developed into a fortress armed with cannons by 1592. After that time, it withstood a number of sieges and then fell into decay. It was finally restored in 1899. Summer tours take you through its magnificent halls, the castle church, the royal mausoleum, reception rooms, and

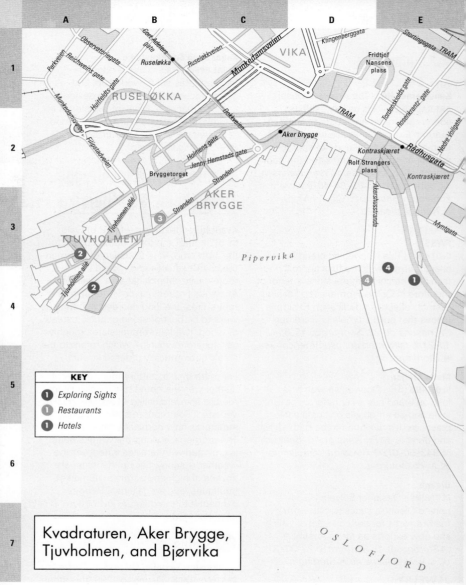

Tilting downward toward the fjord, Oslo's Opera House has one of the best views of the ever-expanding waterfront.

banquet halls. Explore Akershus Fortress and its resplendent green gardens on your own with the Fortress Trail Map, which you can pick up at the visitor center or download from the website. ⚠ **The castle (or at least selected sections) may be closed to the public on short notice due to functions. Dates are always listed on the website.** ✉ *Akershus festning, Sentrum* ☎ *23–09–39–17* ⊕ *akershusfestning. no* ✉ *Free, NKr 100 for Akershus Slott.*

★ **Astrup Fearnley Museet** (*Astrup Fearnley Museum of Modern Art*)
MUSEUM | Across the pedestrian bridge from Aker Brygge, the privately funded Astrup Fearnley Museum of Modern Art is one of the city's architectural gems. The waterfront structure was designed by architect Renzo Piano, who placed three separate pavilions under one massive glass roof that—appropriate enough for this former shipbuilding center—resembles a billowing sail. The collection has earned a stellar reputation for its contemporary art from around the world. ✉ *Strandpromenaden 2, Tjuvholmen* ☎ *22–93–60–60* ⊕ *www.afmuseet.no* ✉ *NKr 130* ☾ *Closed Mon.*

Munchmuseet (*Munch Museum*)
MUSEUM | Edvard Munch, Norway's most famous artist, bequeathed his enormous collection of works (about 1,100 paintings, 3,000 drawings, and 18,000 graphic works) to the city when he died in 1944. This newly built museum—moved here from a rather dowdy location in a residential neighborhood—is a monument to his artistic genius, housing the largest collection of his works and also mounting changing exhibitions. Munch actually painted four different versions of *The Scream,* the image for which he's best known, and one of them is on display here. While most of the Munch legend focuses on the artist as a troubled, angst-ridden man, he moved away from that pessimistic and dark approach to more optimistic themes later in his career. ✉ *Operagata, Sentrum* ☎ *23–49–35–00* ⊕ *www.munchmuseet.no* ✉ *NKr 120* Ⓜ *Jernbanetorget.*

Norges Hjemmefront Museum (*Norway's Resistance Museum*)

MUSEUM | Striped prison uniforms, underground news sheets, and homemade weapons tell the history of the resistance movement that arose before and during Norway's occupation by Nazi Germany. A gray, winding path leads to two underground stone vaults in which models, pictures, writings, and recordings trace the times between Germany's first attack in 1940 to Norway's liberation on May 8, 1945. Every year, on the anniversaries of these dates, Norwegian resistance veterans gather here to commemorate Norway's dark days and honor those who lost their lives. The former ammunitions depot and the memorial lie at the exact spot where Norwegian patriots were executed by the Germans. ✉ *Bygning 21, Kvadraturen* ☎ *23–09–31–38* 🌐 *www.forsvaretsmuseer.no/Hjemmefrontmuseet/Information-in-English* 🎫 *NKr 60.*

★ **Operahuset** (*Opera House*)

ARTS VENUE | One of the crown jewels of Scandinavian architecture, the Oslo Opera House is a stunning addition to the city's waterfront. When its first opened its doors, the gala ceremony attracted Denmark's royal family, the leaders of several countries, and a host of celebrities. Designed by the renowned Norwegian architect firm Snøhetta, the white marble and glass building slopes downward toward the water's edge, giving visitors spectacular views of the fjord, the surrounding mountains, and the city skyline. And it doesn't just look good; the acoustics inside the 1,364-seat auditorium are excellent, as are those in the two smaller performance spaces. The space is the permanent home of the Norwegian National Opera and Ballet, and also hosts a full calendar of music, theater, and dance. The Oslo Biennale will be staging performances on the rooftop through 2023. ✉ *Kirsten Flagstads pl. 1, Sentrum* ☎ *21–42–21–21* 🌐 *www.operaen.no* 🎫 *Free; guided tours NKr 120* [M] *Jernbanetorget.*

🍴 Restaurants

★ **Gamle Rådhus**

$$$ | **NORWEGIAN** | If you're in Oslo for just one night and want an authentic dining experience, head to the city's oldest restaurant—housed in Oslo's first town hall, a building that dates from 1641. It is known for its traditional fish and game dishes that take full advantage of the city's access to the best seasonal produce. **Known for:** reliably robust and salty catch prepared to perfection; elegant paneled surroundings lit by candles; the unparalleled delicacy is lutefisk. [$] *Average main: NKr 320* ✉ *Nedre Slottsgt. 1, Sentrum* ☎ *22–42–01–07* 🌐 *www.gamleraadhus.no* 🕒 *Closed Sun.* [M] *Stortinget.*

★ **Hakkaiza**

$$ | **ASIAN FUSION** | Just a 10-minute stroll from the opera house, this Asian eatery on the edge of the Sørenga Marina hits you with the aromatic smells of Peking duck and Korean wings as soon as you walk in the door. The restaurant's dark slate and glass decor is softened a bit with cherry blossoms and twinkling candles. **Known for:** a little bit of every Asian cuisine; lovely location by the waterfront; cutting-edge design. [$] *Average main: NKr 240* ✉ *Sørengkaia 146, Sentrum* ☎ *40–08–91–82* 🌐 *www.hakkaiza.no.*

Lofoten Fiskerestaurant

$$$ | **SEAFOOD** | Named for the remote Lofoten Islands, this Aker Brygge mainstay is considered one of Oslo's best destinations for seafood, from Maine lobster to Greenland shrimp. It has a bright, minimalistic interior with harbor views and a sunny patio. **Known for:** platters of seafood big enough to share; traditional fish soup; outdoor seating. [$] *Average main: NKr 350* ✉ *Stranden 75, Aker Brygge* ☎ *22–83–08–08* 🌐 *www.lofoten-fiskerestaurant.no.*

★ **Solsiden**

$$$ | **SEAFOOD** | With its high ceiling and huge windows facing the sunny side of the capital, this summer-only seafood

restaurant is housed in a former warehouse right by the harbor. Follow the lead of the many locals who call this their favorite spot and indulge yourself with a *plateau de fruits de mer* (seafood platter, the house specialty) or opt for one of the other longtime favorites like the turbot with horseradish puree, the king crab au gratin, or the vegetarian-friendly salt-baked celeriac with walnuts. **Known for:** celebrity sightings are common; good list of wines by the glass; desserts are decadent. [$] *Average main: NKr 330* ✉ *Akershusstranda 13, Aker Brygge* ☎ *22–33–36–30* 🌐 *www.solsiden.no* 🕑 *Closed Sept.–mid-May.*

Statholdergaarden
$$$$ | **SCANDINAVIAN** | More than 400 years old, the elegant rococo dining room at Statholdergaarden is one of the oldest and most impressive in Norway. Award-winning celebrity chef Bent Stiansen's Asian-inspired French dishes have long been popular with locals. **Known for:** resplendent furnishings; Norwegian delicacies; excellent wine list. [$] *Average main: NKr 470* ✉ *Rådhusgate 11, Kvadraturen* ☎ *22–41–88–00* 🌐 *statholdergaarden.no* 🕑 *Closed Mon.* [M] *Stortinget.*

Hotels

First Hotel Grims Grenka
$$ | **HOTEL** | In a handsome brick building, Oslo's first design hotel has smart lighting, a striking color scheme, and contemporary touches like a clever use of mirrors and glassed-in bathrooms. **Pros:** central location; spacious rooms; comfortable beds. **Cons:** can sometimes feel overdesigned; hallways can be a bit gloomy; can be a bit pricey. [$] *Rooms from: NKr 1196* ✉ *Kongensgt. 5, Kvadraturen* ☎ *23–10–72–00* 🌐 *www.firsthotels.com* 🛏 *65 rooms* 🍴 *Free breakfast* [M] *Stortinget.*

★ **The Thief**
$$$$ | **HOTEL** | Oslo's most tongue-in-cheek boutique hotel is located on Tjuvholmen, meaning Thief Islet, hence the unusual name. **Pros:** free admission to museum next door; a sumptuous breakfast spread; excellent location by the water. **Cons:** expensive rates; small swimming pool; isolated location. [$] *Rooms from: NKr 3000* ✉ *Landgangen 1, Tjuvholmen* ☎ *24–00–40–00* 🌐 *thethief.com* 🛏 *118 rooms* 🍴 *Free breakfast.*

Nightlife

BARS

BA3
BARS/PUBS | The unusual name refers to the address of this stylish spot with four different bars that cater to your every mood. The Terrassebaren has a light, breezy feel, while the scarlet stools of Inkognito make it feel a bit clandestine. ✉ *Bygdøy Allé 3, Frogner* ☎ *22–55–11–86* 🌐 *www.ba3.no.*

Bygdøy

Southwest of the city center is the Bygdøy Peninsula, where several of the best-known historic sights are concentrated. This is where you'll find the Vikingskipshuset, one of Norway's most popular attractions. The pink castle nestled in the trees is Oscarshall Slott Åd, once a royal summer palace. The royal family's current summer residence—actually just a big white house—is also here.

The subway completely bypasses this sprawling peninsula. The most pleasant way to get to Bygdøy—available from May to September—is to catch the ferry from Pier 3 at the rear of City Hall. Year-round, Bus No. 30 will take you there in 10 to 20 minutes.

Sights

Bygdø Kongsgård (*Bygdøy Royal Estate*)
FARM/RANCH | **FAMILY** | Part of the Norwegian Folk Museum, this manor house and farm of almost 500 acres actually belongs to, and has been occupied by,

Norway's royal family. It's a fully operational organic farm offering activities like horseback riding lessons and a chance for kids to pet barnyard animals. The manor house, the king's official summer residence, was built in 1733 by Count Christian Rantzau. Hours are erratic when the royal family is here. ⊠ *Dronning Biancas vei, Bygdøy* ☎ *22–12–37–00* ⊕ *bygdokongsgard.no* ⊗ *Closed summer and winter.*

★ Frammuseet (*Fram Museum*)
MUSEUM | FAMILY | The *Fram* was used by the legendary Polar explorer Roald Amundsen when he became the first man to reach the South Pole in December 1911. Once known as the strongest vessel in the world, this enormous Norwegian polar ship has advanced farther north and south than any other surface vessel. Built in 1892, the *Fram* made three voyages to the Arctic (they were conducted by Fridtjof Nansen and Otto Sverdrup, in addition to Amundsen). Climb on board and peer inside the captain's quarters, which has explorers' sealskin jackets and other relics on display. Surrounding the ship are many artifacts from expeditions. ⊠ *Bygdøynesvn. 36, Bygdøy* ☎ *22–13–52–80* ⊕ *www.frammuseum.no* ⊠ *NKr 120.*

Kon-Tiki Museet (*Kon-Tiki Museum*)
MUSEUM | FAMILY | The museum celebrates Norway's most famous 20th-century explorer. Thor Heyerdahl made a voyage in 1947 from Peru to Polynesia on the *Kon-Tiki,* a balsa raft, to lend weight to his theory that the first Polynesians came from the Americas. His second craft, the *Ra II,* was used to test his theory that a reed boat could have reached the West Indies before Columbus. The museum also has a film room and artifacts from Peru, Polynesia, and Easter Island. ⊠ *Bygdøynesvn. 36, Bygdøy* ☎ *23–08–67–67* ⊕ *www.kon-tiki.no* ⊠ *NKr 120.*

★ Norsk Folkemuseum (*Norwegian Museum of Cultural History*)
MUSEUM VILLAGE | FAMILY | One of the largest open-air museums in Europe offers the perfect way to see Norway in a day. From the stoic stave church (built in 1200) to farmers' houses made of sod, the old buildings here span Norway's regions and most of its recorded history. Indoors, fascinating displays of richly embroidered, colorful *bunader* (national costumes) from every region includes one set at a Telemark country wedding. The museum also has stunning dragon-style wood carvings from 1550 and some beautiful *rosemaling,* or decorative painted floral patterns. The traditional costumes of the Sami (Lapp) people of northern Norway are exhibited around one of their tents. If you're visiting in summer, ask about Norwegian Evening, a summer program of folk dancing, guided tours, and food tastings. ⊠ *Museumsvn. 10, Bygdøy* ☎ *22–12–37–00* ⊕ *www.norskfolkemuseum.no* ⊠ *NKr 160.*

Norsk Maritimt Museum (*Norwegian Maritime Museum*)
MUSEUM | FAMILY | Norwegian fishing boats, paintings of fishermen braving rough seas, and intricate ship models are all on display here. The arctic vessel *Gjøa* is docked outside. The breathtaking movie *The Ocean: A Way of Life* delves into Norway's unique coastal and maritime past. Also on display is the model of the Kvaldor boat (AD 600), a 19th-century armed wooden warship, and a modern-day tanker. ⊠ *Bygdøynesvn. 37, Bygdøy* ☎ *22–12–37–00* ⊕ *marmuseum.no* ⊠ *NKr 120.*

★ Vikingskipshuset (*Viking Ship Museum*)
MUSEUM | FAMILY | The Viking legacy in all its glory lives on at this classic Oslo museum. Chances are you'll come away fascinated by the *Gokstad, Oseberg,* and *Tune,* three blackened wooden Viking ships that date to AD 800. Discovered

The best-preserved Viking ships ever discovered are in Oslo's dazzling Vikingskipshuset.

in Viking tombs around the Oslo fjords between 1860 and 1904, the boats are the best-preserved Viking ships ever found; they have been on display since the museum's 1957 opening. In Viking times, it was customary to bury the dead with food, drink, useful and decorative objects, and even their horses and dogs. Many of the well-preserved tapestries, household utensils, dragon-style wood carvings, and sledges were found aboard ships. The museum's rounded white walls give the feeling of a burial mound. Avoid summertime crowds by visiting at lunchtime. ✉ *Huk Aveny 35, Bygdøy* ☎ *22–13–52–80* 🌐 *www.khm.uio.no* 🎟 *NKr 100.*

🍴 Restaurants

Lanternen

$$ | **SCANDINAVIAN** | Located on a dock extending into the fjord, this eatery is tucked inside a 1920s building that once served as waiting room for ferry passengers. Today it's a popular summertime destination for locals who love the picture-perfect terrace. **Known for:** towering shellfish platters; views of the city; perfect pizzas. [$] *Average main: NKr 180* ✉ *Huk Aveny 2, Bygdøy* ☎ *22–43–78–38* 🌐 *www.restaurantlanternen.no* 🕒 *Closed weekends and no dinner in winter.*

★ Lille Herbern

$$ | **SCANDINAVIAN** | **FAMILY** | Family-run since 1929, this eatery sits on a tiny island of its own just off the Bygdøy Peninsula and is reached by boat. The prime seating is on the breezy terrace, which is shaded from the summer sun by oversized umbrellas and heated to keep out the chill the rest of the year. **Known for:** towering platters of shellfish for sharing; views of the fjord and another leafy islet; historic atmosphere. [$] *Average main: NKr 200* ✉ *Herbernveien 1, Bygdøy* ☎ *22–44–97–00* 🌐 *www.lilleherbern.no.*

Frogner and Majorstuen

Also known as Oslo West, Frogner and Majorstuen combine classic Scandinavian elegance with contemporary European chic. Hip boutiques, excellent restaurants, and esteemed galleries coexist with embassies and ambassadors' residences on the streets near and around Bygdøy Allé.

The trams and buses are very well connected to the Sentrum. The major subway lines bypass much of this neighborhood.

Sights

Nationalbibliotek (*National Library*)
LIBRARY | Complete with elaborate facades, classical statues, and painted dome ceilings, this large, peaceful library has a collection containing the entire cultural and knowledge heritage of Norway. Though mostly in Norwegian, the library regularly hosts exhibits, concerts, lectures, and guided tours (call ahead for English) that detail the vast collections. There's a very good café open all day serving open-faced sandwiches and pastries. ✉ *Henrik Ibsens gt. 110, Frogner* ☎ *81–00–13–00* 🌐 *www.nb.no* 🕒 *Closed Sun.*

Oslo Bymuseum (*Oslo City Museum*)
MUSEUM | **FAMILY** | One of Scandinavia's largest cities, Oslo has changed and evolved greatly over its thousand years. A two-floor, meandering exhibition covers Oslo's prominence in 1050, the Black Death that came in 1348, the great fire of 1624 and subsequent rebuilding, and the urban development of the 20th century. Among the more interesting relics are the red coats that the first Oslo police officers wore in 1700 and the town's first fire wagon, which appeared in 1765. ✉ *Frognervn. 67, Frogner* ☎ *23–28–41–70* 🌐 *www.oslomuseum.no* 🎫 *NKr 90* 🕒 *Closed Mon.*

★ **Vigelandsparken** (*Vigeland Sculpture Park*)
NATIONAL/STATE PARK | **FAMILY** | A favorite hangout for locals, Vigeland Sculpture Park has 212 bronze, granite, and wrought-iron sculptures by Gustav Vigeland (1869–1943). The 56-foot-high granite *Monolith* is a column of 121 upward-striving nudes surrounded by 36 groups on circular stairs. The *Angry Boy*, a bronze of an enraged cherubic child stamping his foot, draws legions of visitors and has been filmed, parodied, painted red, and even stolen. Kids love to climb on the statues. There's an on-site museum for those wishing to delve deeper into the artist's work. ✉ *Frognerparken, Frogner* ☎ *23–49–37–00 for museum* 🌐 *www.vigeland.museum.no* 🎫 *Free.*

Restaurants

Á L'aise
$$$$ | **FRENCH** | This is the restaurant to visit on a dark, starry night when you need warming up with a candlelit dining room, five-star service, and fine French cuisine. Draped with heavy curtains, elegant linens, and buttery soft seating, it's a very fancy affair. **Known for:** resplendent sparkling wine trolley; meals finished with a flourish; vast cheese selection. [$] *Average main: NKr 500* ✉ *Essendrops gt. 6, Frogner* ☎ *21–05–57–00* 🌐 *www.alaise.no* 🕒 *Closed Sun. and Mon.* [M] *Majorstuen.*

Feinschmecker
$$$$ | **FUSION** | The name is German, but the food at this warm and stylish eatery spans the globe. Owners Lars Erik Underthun, one of Oslo's foremost chefs, and Bengt Wilson, a leading food stylist, make sure each dish looks as good as it tastes. **Known for:** if you like the food you can buy the cookbook; particularly interesting wine list; elegant dining room. [$] *Average main: NKr 400* ✉ *Balchens gt. 5, Frogner* ☎ *22–12–93–80* 🌐 *www.feinschmecker.no* 🕒 *Closed Sun.*

Goat
$$$ | **SCANDINAVIAN** | In the stylish Guldsmeden Hotel, this eatery looks like a place you'd come across in a small village, with brick walls, beamed ceilings,

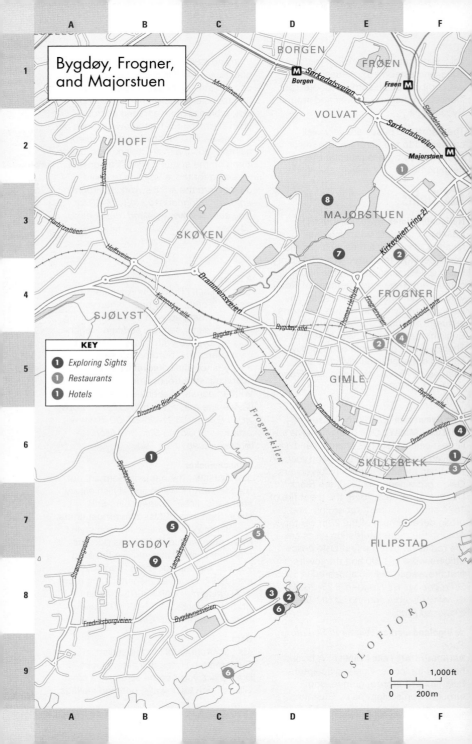

Bygdøy, Frogner, and Majorstuen

BORGEN

FRØEN

M Sørkedalsveien
Borgen

Frøen **M**

Mongthveien

VOLVAT

Sørkedalsveien

Majorstuen **M**

HOFF

❶

MAJORSTUEN

❽

Harbitztoppen

SKØYEN

Hoffsveien

Kirkeveien (ring 2)

❼

❷

Drammensveien

FROGNER

Karenslyst allé

SJØLYST

Bygdøy allé

Bygdøy allé

Løvenskiolds gate

Thomas Heftyes

Frognerveien

❷

❹

KEY

❶ Exploring Sights

❶ Restaurants

❶ Hotels

GIMLE

Dronning Blancas vei

Frognerkilen

Drammensveien

Bygdøy allé

Drammensveien

❹

❶

❸

SKILLEBEKK

Bygdøyveien

FILIPSTAD

❺

❺

BYGDØY

Langviksveien

❾

❸ ❷

❻

Fredriksborgveien

Bygdøynesveien

O S L O F J O R D

❻

0   1,000ft

0   200m

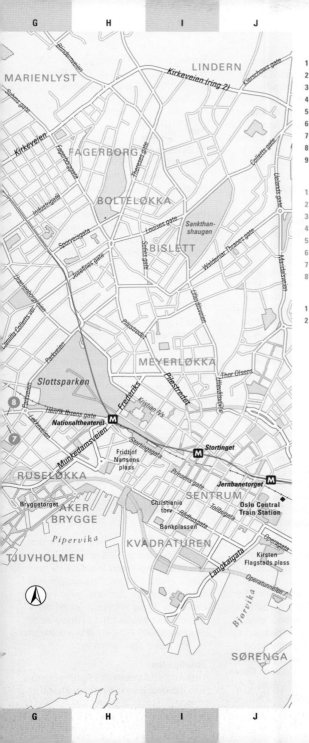

3

Norway OSLO

and arched windows. The chef here made waves with the signature pulled goat burger, and continues to serve innovative food made with organic ingredients from around the country. **Known for:** creative dishes like black sesame ice cream; wonderful wine pairings; relaxed atmosphere. [$] *Average main: NKr 325* ✉ *Guldsmeden Hotel, Parkveien 78, Frogner* ☎ *455–03–729* 🌐 *guldsmedenhotels.com/goat-organic-restaurant.*

★ Kolonihagen Frogner

$$$ | **FUSION** | With a resident chef who authored an exquisitely illustrated book on foraging, this leafy courtyard restaurant offers an ever-changing menu of unpretentious comfort food with a Nordic twist. It also has plenty of indoor seating for cozy evenings dining by candlelight. **Known for:** extensive wine list; botanical cocktails; vegan-friendly options. [$] *Average main: NKr 295* ✉ *Frognerveien 33, Frogner* ☎ *993–16–810* 🌐 *kolonihagenfrogner.no* 🕒 *Closed Sun. and Mon.*

★ Palace Grill

$$$ | **FRENCH FUSION** | An eight-table restaurant near the Royal Palace, this is one of the most fashionable spots in Oslo. Don't let the "grill" in the name fool you—the atmosphere may be relaxed, but the French-inspired cuisine is taken very seriously. **Known for:** late-night camaraderie; so many wonderful courses; not far from the Sentrum. [$] *Average main: NKr 300* ✉ *Solligaten 2, Frogner* ☎ *23–13–11–40* 🌐 *palacegrill.no.*

Topphem

$$$$ | **SCANDINAVIAN** | On the edge of Frogner, this eatery not far from the Sentrum proudly names itself an everyday restaurant while maintaining the caliber of a fine-dining establishment. The Mediterranean-meets-Nordic interior design carries through to the food: There's an abundance of freshly caught seafood served with sauces and reductions that avoid any hint of pretentiousness. **Known for:** New Nordic cuisine without all the fuss; cozy leather banquettes; great tasting menus. [$] *Average main: NKr 590* ✉ *Henrik ibsens gt. 60c, Frogner* ☎ *930–70–872* 🌐 *www.topphem.no* 🕒 *Closed Sun. and Mon.*

Hotels

★ Guldsmeden Hotel

$$$ | **HOTEL** | The inviting reception area with soft leather couches, a crackling fireplace, and charm to spare let you know you're in the ultimate Oslo escape. **Pros:** close to the neighborhood's top attractions; on-site hammam big enough for two; rooms are selfie-ready. **Cons:** 20-minute walk to Oslo Central Station; no fitness center; no room service. [$] *Rooms from: NKr 1300* ✉ *Parkveien 78, Frogner* ☎ *23–27–40–00* 🌐 *guldsmedenhotels.com* 🛏 *50 rooms* 🍴 *No meals.*

Villa Frogner

$ | **B&B/INN** | In a 19th-century villa close to Vigelandparken, this elegant bed-and-breakfast will appeal to anyone who appreciates individually decorated rooms and homemade breakfasts. **Pros:** close to the sculpture park and other attractions; outdoor swimming pool; traditional decor. **Cons:** 15 minute walk to subway; no room service; parking is tricky. [$] *Rooms from: NKr 700* ✉ *Nordraaks gt. 26, Frogner* ☎ *22–56–07–42* 🛏 *14 rooms* 🍴 *Free breakfast* [M] *Majorstuen.*

Nightlife

BarOtto

BARS/PUBS | You'll find wines from Burgundy, Bordeaux, Champagne, Tuscany, and Piedmont, many available by the glass, in this slick bar. The mixologists focus on gin concoctions, which you can enjoy along with your grilled ham-and-cheese sandwich. ✉ *Parkveien 80, Frogner* ☎ *909–37–961* 🌐 *www.barotto.no* 🕒 *Closed Sun. and Mon.*

Josefine Inn

THEMED ENTERTAINMENT | A 19th-century villa hides one of the neighborhood's most pleasant places for aperitifs or digestifs. ✉ *Josefines gt. 16, Majorstuen* ☎ *22–69–34–99* ⊕ *www.josefine.no.*

🛍 Shopping

ANTIQUES

Damms Antikvariat

ANTIQUES/COLLECTIBLES | Antiquarian man-uscripts, books, and maps are available from this bookstore, which first opened in 1843. ✉ *Frederik Stangs gt. 41, Frogner* ☎ *22–41–04–02* ⊕ *www.damms.no* ⊗ *Closed Sun.*

Kristiansand

319 km (198 miles) southwest of Oslo, 28 km (17 miles) southwest of Lillesand.

Nicknamed *Sommerbyen* ("Summer City"), Norway's fifth-largest city draws visitors for its sun-soaked beaches and beautiful harbor. According to legend, in 1641 King Christian IV marked the four corners of Kristiansand with his walking stick, and within that framework the grid of wide streets was laid down. The center of town, called Kvadraturen ("The Quad"), still retains the grid, even after numerous fires. In the northeast corner is Posebyen, one of northern Europe's largest collections of low, connected wooden houses. There's a market here every Saturday in summer. The fish mar-ket is near the south corner of the town's grid, right on the sea.

GETTING HERE AND AROUND

From Oslo take the E18, from Stavanger the E39.

AIR

Kristiansand is served by Scandinavian Airlines, with nonstop flights from Oslo, Bergen, and Trondheim. Widerøe and Norwegian also link Kristiansand with other cities within Norway. Kjevik Airport is about 16 km (10 miles) northeast of the town center. The Flybussen airport bus heads downtown, stopping at several

hotels along the way. The journey takes 25 minutes.

BUS

Several bus companies have daily departures for the 5-hour journey to Oslo and the 4-hour trip to Stavanger. All leave from Kristiansand Bus Terminal. Buses are much slower than trains, taking roughly an hour longer to reach their destination.

CAR

From Oslo it's a 326-km (202-mile) drive to Kristiansand along route E18.

TRAIN

There are regular train departures for Kristiansand from Oslo (4½–5 hours) and Stavanger (3 hours). Kristiansand's train station is at Vestre Strandgata.

VISITOR INFORMATION

CONTACTS Kristiansand Turistinformas-jon. (*Kristiansand Tourist Information*) ✉ *Rådhusgt. 18, Kristiansand* ☎ *38–07–50–00* ⊕ *visitnorway.com/places-to-go/southern-norway/kristiansand.*

👁 Sights

Agder Naturmuseum og Botanisk Hage (*Agder Natural History Museum and Botanical Garden*)

MUSEUM | The area's natural history from the Ice Age to the present is on display at this museum, starting with the coast and moving on to the mountains. There's a rainbow of minerals on display, as well as a rose garden with varieties from 1850. There's even the country's largest collection of cacti. ✉ *Gimle gård, Gim-leveien 23, Kristiansand* ☎ *38–05–86–20* ⊕ *naturmuseum.no* ➷ *NKr 80* ⊗ *Closed Mon. and Sat. in mid-Aug.–mid-June.*

Christiansholm Festning (*Christiansholm Fortress*)

HISTORIC SITE | This circular fortress with 16-foot-thick walls, on a promontory opposite Festningsgata, was completed in 1672. Its role has been much more decorative than defensive; it was used once, in 1807, during the Napoleonic Wars, to defend the city against British invasion. Now it contains art exhibits. However, the best part is walking around the grounds. ⊠ *Kristiansand* ☎ *38–00–74–60* ⊘ *Closed Jan. and Feb.*

★ **Dyreparken i Kristiansand** (*Kristiansand Zoo and Amusement Park*)
ZOO | FAMILY | One of Norway's most popular attractions, Dyreparken Kristiansand is actually five separate parks, including a water park (bring bathing suits and towels), a forested park, an entertainment park, a theme park, and a zoo, which contains an enclosure for Scandinavian animals such as wolves, snow foxes, lynxes, and elks. The theme park, Kardemomme By (Cardamom Town), is named for a book by the Norwegian illustrator and writer Thorbjørn Egner. In the zoo, the "My Africa" exhibition allows you to move along a bridge observing native savanna animals such as giraffes and zebras. The park is 11 km (6 miles) east of town. ⊠ *Kristiansand Dyrepark, Kristiansand* ☎ *97–05–97–00* ⊕ *dyreparken. no* 🎫 *NKr 479.*

★ **Gimle Gård** (*Gimle Manor*)
MUSEUM | A wealthy merchant-shipowner built handsome Gimle Manor around 1800 in the Empire style. Inside are furnishings from that period, along with moody portraits, glittering chandeliers, and hand-printed wallpaper. It is said to be the most beautiful manor house in the region, and if you enjoy picturesque buildings with a history, you'll enjoy visiting Gimle. ⊠ *Gimleveien 23, Lillesand* ☎ *38–12–03–50* ⊕ *vestagdermuseet.no/ gimlegard* ⊘ *Closed Sept.–May.*

Kristiansand Kanonmuseum (*Kristiansand Cannon Museum*)
MUSEUM | FAMILY | At the Kristiansand Cannon Museum you can see the cannon that the occupying Germans rigged up during World War II. With a caliber of 15 inches, the cannon was said to be capable of shooting a projectile halfway to Denmark. In the bunkers, related military materials are on display. Kids love running around the grounds, but keep an eye on them, since there aren't railings everywhere. ⊠ *Kroodden, Kristiansand* ☎ *38–08–50–90* ⊕ *vestagdermuseet. no/kanonmuseum/* ⊘ *Closed Mon.–Sat. Sept.–Nov and Feb.–May. Closed Dec. and Jan.*

Kristiansand Museum (*Vest-Agder County Museum Kristiansand*)
MUSEUM VILLAGE | FAMILY | The region's largest cultural museum has more than 40 old buildings on display. The structures, transported from other locations in the area, include two *tun* farm buildings traditionally set in clusters around a common area, which were intended for extended families. If you have children with you, check out the old-fashioned toys, which can still be played with. The museum is 4 km (2½ miles) east of Kristiansand on E18. ⊠ *Vigeveien 22B, Kongsgård, Kristiansand* ☎ *38–12–03–50* ⊕ *vestagdermuseet.no/kristiansand* 🎫 *NKr 100* ⊘ *Closed Sept.–May (except Sun. in Sept.).*

Oddernes Kirke (*Oddernes Church*)
RELIGIOUS SITE | The striking rune stone in the cemetery of Oddernes kirke says that Øyvind, godson of Saint Olav, built this church in 1040 on property he inherited from his father. One of the oldest churches in Norway, it has a baroque pulpit from 1704 and is dedicated to Saint Olav. ⊠ *Jegersbergvn. 6, Kristiansand* ⊕ *oddernes.no* 🎫 *Free.*

Ravnedalen (*Ravnedalen Valley Nature Park*)
NATIONAL/STATE PARK | A favorite with hikers and strolling nannies, Ravnedalen is a lush park that's filled with flowers in springtime. Wear comfortable shoes to hike the narrow, winding paths up the hills and climb the 200 steps up to a 304-foot lookout. There is a café on-site, and open-air concerts in summer. ⊠ *Kristiansand.*

Restaurants

Bølgen & Moi

$$$ | **NORWEGIAN** | Toralf Bølgen and Trond
Moi, two of Norway's most celebrated
restaurateurs, run what's the southernmost addition to their chain of high-pro-
file restaurants. Near the old fishing pier,
the scene is more chic than rustic, with
artwork and dinnerware designed by
local artist Kjell Nupen. **Known for:** great
seafood; refined atmosphere; smooth
service. $ *Average main: NKr 335 ⊠ No-
deviga 2, Kristiansand* ☎ *38–17–83–00*
⊕ *bolgenogmoi.no/restauranter/kris-
tiansand* ⊗ *No lunch weekdays.*

Sjøhuset Restaurant

$$$ | **SEAFOOD** | Considered one of the
city's best restaurants, this white-
trimmed red building was built in 1892
as a salt warehouse. The specialty is
seafood. **Known for:** fresh seafood; local
ingredients; traditional dishes. $ *Average
main: NKr 345 ⊠ Østre Strandgt. 12A,
Kristiansand* ☎ *38–02–62–60* ⊕ *sjohu-
set.no* ⊗ *Closed Sun. No lunch except
summer.*

Hotels

Clarion Hotel Ernst

$$$ | **HOTEL** | This traditional city hotel
opened in 1858 and is still considered
among Kristiansand's best. **Pros:** lots of
contemporary artworks; breakfast gets
rave reviews; pleasant and helpful staff.
Cons: some rooms get noise from nearby
nightlife; parking in the city center is
often difficult; standard rooms are on
the small side. $ *Rooms from: NKr 1400
⊠ Rådhusgt. 2, Kristiansand* ☎ *38–12–
86–00* ⊕ *nordicchoicehotels.no/hotell/
norge/kristiansand/clarion-hotel-ernst*
⤴ *200 rooms* ⦿ *Free breakfast.*

Dyreparken Hotell

$$$ | **HOTEL** | **FAMILY** | Built like Noah's Ark,
this modern hotel is designed to appeal
to children of all ages: inspired by the
nearby zoo, many of the rooms go a little
wild, with tiger-stripe chairs and paw
prints on walls. **Pros:** fun design; next
to the zoo; easy parking. **Cons:** children
everywhere, especially holidays and
weekends; some rooms are a bit small;
so-so breakfast. $ *Rooms from: NKr
1300 ⊠ Dyreparkveien 2, Kristiansand*
☎ *97–05–97–00* ⊕ *dyreparken.no/over-
natting/dyreparken-hotell* ⤴ *160 rooms*
⦿ *Free breakfast.*

Stavanger

*206 km (128 miles) northwest of Man-
dal, 211 km (131 miles) south of Bergen
via car and ferry, 540 km (336 miles)
west of Oslo.*

Stavanger has always prospered from the
riches of the sea. During the 19th century, huge harvests of brisling (also called
sprat) and herring helped put it on the
map as the sardine capital of the world.
Some people claim the locals are called
Siddis, from S(tavanger) plus iddis, which
means "sardine label," although some
linguists argue it's actually a mispronunci-
ation of the English word "citizen."

During the past three decades a different
product from the sea has been Stavanger's lifeblood—oil. Since its discovery in
the late 1960s, North Sea oil hasn't just
transformed the economy; Stavanger has
emerged as cosmopolitan and vibrant,
more bustling than other cities with a
population of only 130,000. Norway's
most international city, it has attracted
residents from more than 90 nations.
Roam its cobblestone streets or wander
the harbor front and you're likely to see
many cafés, fine restaurants, and lively
pubs, as well as many museums, galleries, and other venues that are part of its
rich, dynamic art scene.

Stavanger has earned the title "Festi-
valbyen" (festival city) for its year-round
celebrations. More than 20 official festivals are held throughout the year—comedy, food, chamber music, jazz, organ,

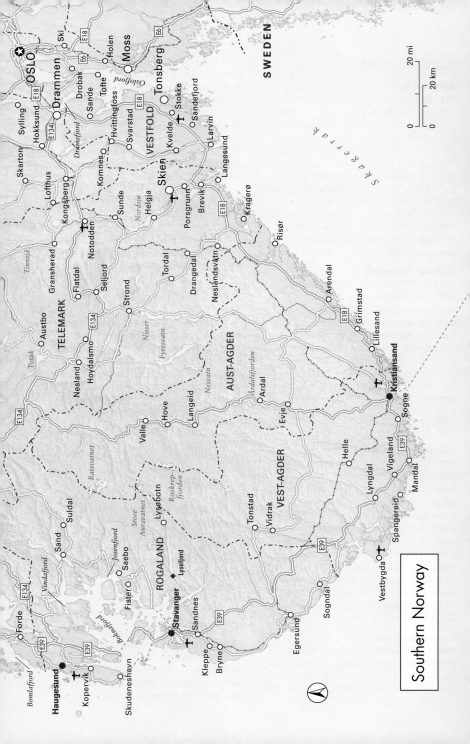

Southern Norway

literature, beach volleyball, biathlon, wine, and more. There are probably just as many unofficial events, since locals love any reason to have a party.

GETTING HERE AND AROUND

AIR

Stavanger's Sola Airport, 14 km (11 miles) south of downtown, is served by SAS, with nonstop flights from Oslo, Bergen, and Kristiansand, as well as some European cities. The low-cost airline Norwegian also has flights from Oslo to Stavanger.

The Flybussen (airport bus) leaves the airport every 15 minutes. It stops at hotels and outside the train station in Stavanger before heading back to the airport.

NOR-WAY Bussekspress and Vy runs regularly between Stavanger and Oslo (nine hours), Bergen (five hours), and Kristiansand (four hours).

BUS

Public transport within Stavanger is operated by the bus company Kolumbus. It's more than adequate for getting you to the major sites and then some. There's reason to consider not bothering with the bus, though; the center of town is pedestrians-only in places, and if you're of average fitness you could easily rely on your own two feet all day.

CAR

Driving from Bergen to Stavanger along the jagged western coastline is difficult and requires a detour of 150 km (93 miles), or many ferry crossings. Some areas in Stavanger's city center are closed to car traffic, and one-way traffic is the norm in the rest of the downtown area.

TRAIN

Sørlandsbanen leaves Oslo Central Station several times daily for the eight-hour journey to Stavanger. Trains travel the three-hour Kristiansand–Stavanger route throughout the day.

VISITOR INFORMATION
CONTACTS Region Stavanger og Ryfylke. (*Stavanger tourist information*) ☎ 51–85–92–00 ⊕ regionstavanger-ryfylke.com.

Sights

Breidablikk

HISTORIC SITE | FAMILY | With a perfectly preserved interior, this 19th-century manor house feels as if the owner has only momentarily slipped away. The building is an outstanding example of what the Norwegians call "Swiss-style" architecture, and also has some elements of the Norwegian National Romantic style. It was built in 1882 by the Norwegian merchant and shipowner Lars Berentsen. ⊠ *Eiganesveien 40A, Stavanger* ☎ *51–84–27–00* ⊕ *breidablikkmuseum.no* 🖬 *NKr 95* ☉ *Closed Sept.–May.*

★ Gamle Stavanger (*Old Stavanger*)

HISTORIC SITE | The charm of the city's past is on view in Old Stavanger, northern Europe's largest and best-preserved wooden house settlement. The 150 houses here were built in the late 1700s and early 1800s. Wind down the narrow cobblestone streets past small white houses and craft shops with many-paned windows and terra-cotta roof tiles. ⊠ *Stavanger.*

★ Lysefjord

SCENIC DRIVE | A very popular attraction in Stavanger, the breathtaking Lysefjord is best seen by boat. Along the way you can take in famous sights, like the sheer cliffs of Pulpit's Rock and the balancing act of the Kjerag Boulder. Most travelers drive to Lauvvik and take a round-trip cruise from there.

Norsk Hermetikkmuseum (*Norwegian Canning Museum*)

MUSEUM | From the 1890s to the 1960s, canning sardines and other fish products was Stavanger's main industry. This fascinating museum, in a former canning factory, recounts what it was like to live here during that period. Occasionally the public can take part in the production process, sometimes tasting newly smoked brisling. The museum is slated to reopen in late 2020 after extensive renovations. ✉ *Øvre Strandgate 88, Stavanger* ☎ *51–84–27–00* 🌐 *norskhermetikkmuseum.no* 🎟 *NKr 95* 🕒 *Closed mid-Aug.–mid-May.*

★ **Norsk Oljemuseum** (*Norwegian Petroleum Museum*)
MUSEUM | FAMILY | Resembling a shiny offshore oil platform, the dynamic Norsk Oljemuseum is an absolute must-see. In 1969 oil was discovered off the coast of Norway. The museum explains how oil forms, how it's found and produced, its many uses, and its impact on Norway. Interactive multimedia exhibits accompany original artifacts, models, and films. A reconstructed offshore platform includes oil workers' living quarters—as well as the sound of drilling and the smell of oil. The highly recommended museum café, by restaurateurs Bølgen og Moi, serves dinners as well as lighter fare. ✉ *Kjeringholmen, Stavanger Havn, Stavanger* ☎ *51–93–93–00* 🌐 *norskolje.museum.no* 🎟 *NKr 120.*

★ **Preikestolen** (*Pulpit Rock*)
VIEWPOINT | A huge cube with a vertical drop of 2,000 feet, Pulpit Rock is not a good destination if you suffer from vertigo—it has a heart-stopping view. The clifflike rock sits on the banks of the finger-shape Lysefjord. You can join a boat tour from Stavanger to see the rock from below, or you can hike two hours to the top on a marked trail. The track goes from Preikestolhytta, where there is a big parking lot.

Stavanger Maritime Museum
MUSEUM | Housed in the only two shipping merchants' houses that remain completely intact is Stavanger Maritime Museum. Built between 1770 and 1840, the restored buildings trace the past 200 years of trade, sea traffic, and shipbuilding. Visit a turn-of-the-20th-century general store, merchant's apartment, and a sailmaker's loft. A reconstruction of a shipowner's office and a memorial are also here, as are two 19th-century ships, the sloop *Anna af Sand,* and the Colin Archer yacht *Wyvern,* moored at the pier. ✉ *Strandkaien 22, Stavanger* ☎ *51–84–27–00* 🌐 *stavangermaritimemuseum.no* 🎟 *NKr 95* 🕒 *Closed Mon. mid-Sept.–mid-May.*

🍴 Restaurants

★ **N. B. Sørensens Dampskibsexpedition**
$$$ | NORWEGIAN | Norwegian emigrants waited here before boarding steamships crossing the ocean to North America 150 years ago. The historic wharf house is now a popular waterfront restaurant and bar. **Known for:** creative cocktails at the bar; a well-thought-out theme; sizzling steaks. [$] *Average main: NKr 275* ✉ *Skagen 26, Stavanger* ☎ *81–55–28–81* 🌐 *nbsorensen.no.*

Sjøhuset Skagen
$$ | NORWEGIAN | A sort of museum, this former boathouse from 1770 is filled with wooden beams, ship models, lobster traps, and other sea relics. The Norwegian and international menu may offer such fare as baked lime- and chili–marinated halibut, trout, whale steak, and reindeer and baked fennel, or, in fall and winter, turkey served with cabbage, prunes, Waldorf salad, and boiled potatoes. **Known for:** the best ingredients from the countryside; authentic atmosphere; lots of history. [$] *Average main: NKr 250* ✉ *Skagenkaien 13, Stavanger* ☎ *90–41–73–27* 🌐 *skagenrestaurant.no* 🕒 *Closed Sun.*

XO Steakhouse
$$$ | NORWEGIAN | This pub-style restaurant's interior is in keeping with the traditional Norwegian dishes that emerge from the kitchen. Enjoy local favorites such as lutefisk and *pinnekjøtt* (lamb cooked on birch twigs) during the months leading up to Christmas, or the grilled steaks and other meats that are available the rest of the year. **Known for:** a

longtime favorite; live music on weekends; casual atmosphere. $ *Average main: NKr 300* ✉ *Skagen 10, Stavanger* ☎ *91–00–03–07* ⊕ *xosteakhouse.no* ⊘ *Closed Sun.*

🛏 Hotels

Clarion Collection Hotel Skagen Brygge

$$ | **HOTEL** | A symbol of Stavanger, this classic hotel's white wooden wharf houses are common subjects for city postcards and photographs, and it has a well-deserved reputation for superb service. **Pros:** central location; good views of the harbor; complimentary afternoon tea and evening meal. **Cons:** some rooms are small; noise from nearby nightlife; added charge for pets. $ *Rooms from: NKr 1100* ✉ *Skagenkaien 28–30, Stavanger* ☎ *51–85–00–00* ⊕ *nordicchoicehotels. no/hotell/norge/stavanger/clarion-collection-hotel-skagen-brygge* ⤴ *118 rooms* ⊙⊙ *Some meals.*

Victoria Hotel

$$$ | **HOTEL** | Built in 1900, Stavanger's oldest hotel retains a clubby Victorian style, with elegant carved furniture and floral patterns. **Pros:** great location; stylish restaurant; good breakfast. **Cons:** some rooms are small; can be a bit noisy on weekends; old-fashioned wallpaper. $ *Rooms from: NKr 1300* ✉ *Skansegt. 1, Stavanger* ☎ *51–86–70–00* ⊕ *victoria-hotel.no* ⤴ *107 rooms* ⊙⊙ *Free breakfast.*

🏃 Activities

HIKING

Stavanger Turistforening (*Stavanger Trekking Association*)

HIKING/WALKING | Specialized books and maps are available through Stavanger Turistforening, the local trekking association. The office can help you plan a hike through the area, particularly in the rolling Setesdalsveiene Hills and the thousands of islands and skerries of the Ryfylke Archipelago. The association has 44 cabins for members (you can join on the spot) for sleeping along the way. ✉ *Olav Vs gt. 18, Stavanger* ☎ *51–84–02–00* ⊕ *stf.no.*

Haugesund

82 km (51 miles) north of Stavanger, 138 km (86 miles) south of Bergen via car and ferry, 443 km (275 miles) west of Oslo.

The small port town of Haugesund prides itself on its historical importance as the seat of the Viking kings and birthplace of Norway (the country was unified in the 9th century by King Harald Fairhair, who ruled from Avaldsnes, a short distance from Haugesund). The town's origins lie in its position near an important straight, where ships could avoid stormy open seas. It was also a major source of herring. Nowadays Haugesund is best known as one of Norway's principal cultural centers. The city hosts the Norwegian International Film Festival and an important citywide jazz festival held every August.

GETTING HERE AND AROUND

The Haugesund Airport, located on the island of Karmøy, connects the city with Oslo, Bergen, London, Copenhagen, and other major international cities, serviced by SAS, Ryanair, Norway, and Widerøe airlines. Haugesund connects by bus to Bergen and Oslo.

Car and passenger ferries link Haugesund with Utsira, and passenger ferries connect to Røvaer and Feøy.

👁 Sights

★ **Nordvegen Historiesenter** (*Nordvegen History Center*)

MUSEUM VILLAGE | **FAMILY** | Outside of Haugesund, Avaldnes is the seat of Norway's first kings and thus considered the "birthplace of Norway," an important status for the city. For a rich overview—from the Bronze Age to the Middle Ages—of this historically significant region, the Norwegian History Center is a must. In the center, Norway's story is laid out through timelines, life-size costumed figures, and multimedia exhibits. The grounds include a fascinating outdoor Viking farm re-creating life in the 7th and 8th centuries, and 13th-century St. Olav's church, the last vestige of the kings' royal manor. ✉ *Kong Augvalds veg 103, Avaldsnes* ☎ *52–81–24–00* 🌐 *viking-garden.no* 🎟 *NKr 110* ⏲ *Closed Mon., Tues., and Thurs.–Sat. Oct.–Apr.*

🍴 Restaurants

Il Forno

$$ | ITALIAN | FAMILY | Italy meets Norway at this cozy dockside eatery, a standout among the other casual restaurants on this popular restaurant row, specializing in a large selection of fresh pasta (many dishes capitalize on the local seafood), crostini, and a superb oven-fired pizza. The restaurant takes reservations, but walk-ins are welcome and food can be taken out. **Known for:** stone-oven pizzas; friendly atmosphere; quick service. [$] *Average main: NKr 170* ✉ *Smedasundet 91, Haugesund* ☎ *47–77–92–77* 🌐 *inventum.no/il-forno.*

★ Lothes Restaurant

$$$$ | EUROPEAN | This waterfront restaurant, café, and bar in a pretty white clapboard house is a good bet for consistently well-prepared, high-quality dining. The cozy restaurant focuses on a more sophisticated cuisine, and the offerings may include crayfish gazpacho and veal entrecôte on its prix-fixe menu. **Known for:** views of Smedasundet; interesting set menu; two different dining rooms. [$] *Average main: NKr 585* ✉ *Skippergt 4, Haugesund* ☎ *52–71–22–01* 🌐 *lothesmat.no* ⏲ *Closed Sun. and Mon.*

🛏 Hotels

★ Clarion Collection Hotel Amanda

$$$ | HOTEL | Scenic views over the waterfront and marina are just one advantage of this centrally located hotel, named for the Norwegian International Film Festival (held in Haugesund), hence the film-named rooms. **Pros:** free Wi-Fi and other amenities; casual atmosphere; meals included in rates. **Cons:** rooms facing harbor can be noisy; not all rooms have views; slightly expensive rates. [$] *Rooms from: NKr 1500* ✉ *Smedasundet 93, Haugesund* ☎ *52–80–82–00* 🌐 *nordic-choicehotels.no/hotell/norge/haugesund/clarion-collection-hotel-amanda/* 🛏 *133 rooms* 🍽 *Some meals.*

Lillehammer

168 km (104 miles) north of Oslo, 62 km (39 miles) northwst of Hamar.

Overlooking Lake Mjøsa, Lillehammer enjoys an idyllic location and is the main gateway to the Gudbrandsdalen Valley. The city is not very large, but is rich in museums and features some of the most beautifully preserved late-19th-century wooden houses, many of them along the main pedestian street of Storgata. Many Norwegians have great affection for Lillehammer, the winter sports resort town that hosted the 1994 Winter Olympics. Many of the Olympic venues are still in use and open to visitors, making the region a popular destination for winter sports enthusiasts. In winter, several ski resorts offer a vast network of groomed cross-country trails. The same mountains make the region excellent for hikes and bicyling during the summer months.

GETTING HERE AND AROUND

Travelling from Oslo Airport to Lillehammer takes less than two hours by car (via Route E6), bus, or train. From there you can get to most resorts in the area in less than 90 minutes.

TOURS

Lillehammer Guide Union leads free 60- to 90-minute walks through Lillehammer to help you get to know the city and the people who live there.

CONTACTS Lillehammer Guide Union.
✉ *Jernbanetorget 2, Lillehammer*
☎ *90–86–45–53* ⊕ *www.facebook.com/
LillehammerGuideforening.*

**CONTACTS Lillehammer and Gudbrands-
dalen Tourism Office.** ✉ *Jernbanetorget 2,
Lillehammer* ☎ *61–28–98–00* ⊕ *www.lil-
lehammer.com.* **Lillehammer Taxi.** ✉ *Oskar
Skoglys vei 2* ☎ *06565* ⊕ *www.06565.no.*

◎ Sights

Lillehammer Kunstmuseum (*Lillehammer
Museum of Art*)
MUSEUM | One of the most important art
collections in Norway is housed at the
Lillehammer Kunstmuseum, a venerable
institution that first opened its doors in
1927. The 1,400 works include pieces by
Edvard Munch and Adolph Tidemand. The
original building has been remodeled and
joined by a newer building designed by
Snøhetta. Sculptor Bård Breivik created
a sculpture garden that sits between
the two buildings. ✉ *Stortorget 2,
Lillehammer* ☎ *61–05–44–60* ⊕ *www.
lillehammerartmuseum.com* ⌚ *Nkr 135*
⊘ *Closed Mon. Sept.–May.*

Norges Olympiske Museum (*Norwegian
Olympic Museum*)
MUSEUM | This popular museum is a
tribute to the Olympic ideal and covers
the history of the games from their
start in ancient Greece in 776 BC to the
present day. Multimedia presentations,
interactive installations, and artifacts
like sailboats and skis illustrate Norwegian sporting history in the Gallery
of Honor. Some of the captions are in
English. ✉ *Maihaugvegen 1, Lillehammer*
☎ *61–28–89–00* ⊕ *ol.museum.no* ⌚ *Nkr
135* ⊘ *Closed Mon. Sept.–Apr.*

Olympiaparken (*Olympic Park*)
SPORTS—SIGHT | **FAMILY** | This park might
be the closest thing to actually competing in the Olympics. You can visit
the ski-jump tower, ride the chairlift, or
step inside the bobsled simulator at the

Lysgårdsbakkene Ski Jump Arena, where
the 1994 Winter Olympics opening and
closing ceremonies were held. You can
go tobogganing at the Kanthaugen Freestyle Arena or bobsled—or "wheelbob"
in the summer—at the Olympic Bob-
sleigh and Luge Track. ✉ *Birkebeinerve-
gen 122, Lillehammer* ☎ *61–05–42–00*
⊕ *www.olympiaparken.no.*

🍴 Restaurants

Bryggerikjelleren
$$$$ | **NORWEGIAN** | Located in the cellar
of an old brewery dating from 1855,
Bryggerikjelleren has been serving Lillehammer's best steaks for at least three
decades. The interiors are dark, intimate,
and cozy, consisting of three rooms
with vaulted ceilings centered around a
stylish bar. **Known for:** bartenders pour a
perfect gin and tonic; excellent wine list;
attentive staff. $ *Average main: NKr 400*
✉ *Elvegata 19, Lillehammer* ☎ *61–27–06–
60* ⊕ *www.bblillehammer.no* ⊘ *No lunch.*

Heim Gastropub
$$ | **BURGER** | A cozy, rustic restaurant
with a casual atmosphere focusing on
home-made burgers and fish-and-chips,
but also offering some Norwegian
specialties such as cured meat salad and
local cheeses in addition to an impressive range of beers. Gets extra lively on
the weekends. **Known for:** great chili fries;
self-tap system gives you the opportunity
to tap the beer yourself; charming interiors. $ *Average main: NKr 200* ✉ *Storgata
84, Lillehammer* ☎ *61–10–00–82* ⊕ *www.
heim.no* ⊘ *No lunch weekdays.*

Hvelvet
$$$ | **SCANDINAVIAN** | **FAMILY** | Considered
by locals to be one of Lillehammer's
best restaurants, Hvelvet—Norwegian
for "The Vault"—offers fine wining
and dining inside the former location
of the Norwegian Bank. The interiors
are decorated in a modern yet classic
style with handsome wood floors and
crisp white tablecloths. **Known for:** warm

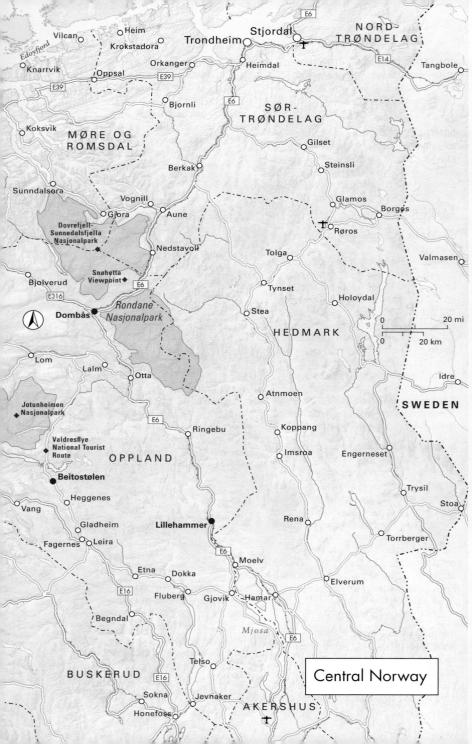

atmosphere; good children's menu; excellent value. $ *Average main: NKr 345* ✉ *Stortorget 1, Lillehammer* ☎ *907-29-100* ⊕ *www.hvelvet.no* ☉ *Closed Sun. No lunch.*

🛏 Hotels

Arctic Dome Sjusjøen

$$$$ | **RENTAL** | **FAMILY** | If the idea of glamping—glamorous camping—in the middle of the Norwegian wilderness sounds appealing, head to this spacious, luxurious tent shaped like an igloo, idyllically located in Sjusjøen (roughly 30 minutes east of Lillehammer). **Pros:** food delivered right to the tent; rent include use of two canoes; helpful and friendly staff. **Cons:** not accessible by public transportation; dogsledding not always available; outside toilet. $ *Rooms from: NKr 3750* ✉ *Sjusjøvegen, Sjusjøen* ☎ *94-84-62-70* ⊕ *no.sjusjoenhusky-tours.no* 🛏 *1 room* ⊗ *No meals.*

Mølla Hotell

$$$ | **HOTEL** | **FAMILY** | This bright yellow former mill has been transformed into a charming hotel with a reception area that feels like a private home and rooms designed in a pleasant, contemporary fashion. **Pros:** central location; cozy atmosphere; friendly staff. **Cons:** small showers; some rooms can be a bit noisy; not the largest rooms. $ *Rooms from: NKr 1425* ✉ *Elvegt. 12, Lillehammer* ☎ *61-05-70-80* ⊕ *www.mollahotell.no* 🛏 *58 rooms* ⊗ *Free breakfast.*

🛍 Shopping

Fabrikken

CERAMICS/GLASSWARE | At this creative hub you'll find different kinds of local artists in their studios making jewelry, ceramics, and other works of art. ✉ *Løkkegata 9, Lillehammer* ☎ *40-00-19-89* ⊕ *www.fabrikken.org* ☉ *Closed Sun.*

🏃 Activities

DOG SLEDDING

Sjusjøen Husky Tours

SNOW SPORTS | This outfitter offers dog-sledding in Sjusjøen, a 30-minute drive from Lillehammer. During the summer months the tours are on wheels. ✉ *Sjusjøvegen, Mesnali* ☎ *94-84-62-70* ⊕ *www.sjusjoenhuskytours.no.*

SKIING

Hafjell Alpine Resort

SKIING/SNOWBOARDING | A 15-minute drive from Lillehammer, Hafjell Alpine Resort offers both family-friendly slopes and more challenging runs for thrill-seekers. There are 18 lifts, including a gondola, leading up to 33 slopes. ✉ *Hafjell Alpine Resort, Hundervegen 122, Øyer* ☎ *40-40-15-00* ⊕ *www.hafjell.no.*

Dombås

46 km (29 miles) northwst of Otta.

In the far northern part of the Gudbrands-dalen Valley, the tiny village of Dombås is the ideal starting point for visits to Dovrefjell-Sunndalsfjella Nasjonalpark. From here you can hop aboard the scenic train to Åndalsnes.

GETTING HERE AND AROUND

At the junction of Route E6 and Route E136, Dombås is a 4 1/2-hour drive north from Oslo and a 3-hour drive south from Trondheim. The Dovre Railway runs from Oslo to Trondheim, stopping at Dombås several times a day. The ride from Oslo takes about 4 hours.

VISITOR INFORMATION

To protect the wild reindeer herds roaming Dovrefjell, the only transportation allowed to Snøheim, a starting point for hikes in Dovrefjell, is the Snøheim Shuttle Bus. Five daily departures from late June to early October.

CONTACTS Dombås Tourist Information. ✉ *Kyrkjevegen 2D, Dombås*

You can spot a majestic musk ox in Dovrefjell-Sunndalsfjella National Park.

🕾 *918–87–716* ⊕ *www.facebook.com/ dombasturistinformasjon.* **Snøheim Shuttle Bus.** ✉ *Hjerkinnhusveien 33, Hjerkinn* 🕾 *47–86–22–86* ⊕ *www.snoheim.dnt.no.*

👁 Sights

⭐ **Dovrefjell-Sunndalsfjella Nasjonalpark**

MOUNTAIN—SIGHT | Known for its dramatic contrasts, Dovrefjell-Sunndalsfjella National Park ranges from the almost alpine scenery in the northwest to the rounded mountains and drier climate in the east. Snøhetta, towering a stunning 2,286 meters (7,500 feet) from the plateau below, was for a long time thought to be the highest peak in Norway. (It's now the twenty-fourth, falling behind Jotunheimen in Rondane Nasjonalpark.) Both Kongsvold/Reinheim and Hjerkinn are good starting points for the daylong trek up this mountain. Dovrefjell is home to herds of wild reindeer, musk oxen, and Arctic foxes, among other fascinating creatures. ✉ *Dovrefjell-Sunnedalsfjella Nasjonalpark* 🕾 *61–24–14–44* ⊕ *www. nasjonalparkriket.no.*

⭐ **Snøhetta Viewpoint**

VIEWPOINT | The large Norwegian Wild Reindeer Centre Pavilion, more commonly known as Snøhetta Viewpoint, offers panoramas of Mt. Snøhetta and Dovrefjell-Sunndalsfjella National Park. The building was designed by the Norwegian architectural agency Snøhetta and functions as a warm, dry place to sit down, take a break, and enjoy the views. With a bit of luck, you might spot musk ox and wild reindeer. The building is open from June until mid-October and can be reached via the hiking trail from the Snøhetta parking lot or the train station at Hjerkinn. ✉ *Viewpoint Snøhetta, Hjerkinn* ⊕ *www.villrein.no* 🖾 *Free* ⊘ *Closed Oct.–May.*

🍽 Restaurants

Moskusgrillen

$$ | **NORWEGIAN** | **FAMILY** | In the middle of Dombås, Moskusgrillen serves traditional Norwegian dishes ranging from *potetball* (potato dumplings often served with meat) to *elgkarbonader* (elk in a cream

A Ride on the Rauma

One of the most unforgettable journeys through Norway is a spectacular train ride through the Romsdalen Valley. The 114 km-long Rauma Railway (🌐 *www.vy.no/en*), traveling between Dombås and Åndalsnes, crosses 32 bridges, including the mighty Kylling Bridge that took 10 years to build. Constructed of solid granite, it spans the Rauma River and looks postcard-perfect from the train windows. You will also get to experience the spectacular Trollveggen, the tallest vertical rock wall in Europe, and the remote and beautiful wilderness around Reinheimen National Park.

In the summer, the comfortably appointed trains slow down to give travelers the best possible photo ops. An English-language commentary informs you about what you are seeing. The sightseeing trains run from April to August. The trip from Dombås to Åndalsnes take about 90 minutes, or a little more in summer.

sauce). If you're looking for something more familiar for the kids, there are a dozen or more kinds of pizza that you can enjoy on the outside terrace. **Known for:** friendly staff; large outdoor terrace; accessible children's menu. [$] *Average main: NKr 200* ✉ *Kyrkjevegen 1, Dombås* ☎ *61–24–01–00* 🌐 *www.moskusgrillen.no.*

Hotels

Hjerkinn Mountain Lodge

$$$ | **HOTEL** | **FAMILY** | An historic mountain lodge with an active farm on the premises, Hjerkinn Mountain Lodge is currently being run by the 12th and 13th generations of the same family and is one of the country's oldest businesses. **Pros:** outdoor hot tub; serene atmosphere; friendly staff. **Cons:** meals at fixed times; few restaurants in area; not all rooms have double beds. [$] *Rooms from: NKr 1550* ✉ *Kvitdalsvegen 12, Hjerkinn* ☎ *61–21–51–00* 🌐 *www.hjerkinn.no* 🛏 *26 rooms* 🍴 *Free breakfast.*

Activities

WILDLIFE-WATCHING

Furuhaugli Musk Ox Safari

WILDLIFE-WATCHING | Dovrefjell is well known for its herd of musk ox, and watching the majestic animals in their natural habitat is a unique experience. Although you might get lucky and spot them on your own on a hiking trip, a guided trip with Furuhaugli Musk Ox Safari will increase your chances drastically. If you are lucky, you might also stumble upon a herd of reindeer. ✉ *Furuhaugli 80, Dovrefjell-Sunnedalsfjella Nasjonalpark* ☎ *61–24–00–00* 🌐 *www.furuhaugli.no.*

Beitostølen

38 km (24 miles) northwest of Fagernes, 224 km (139 miles) northwest from Oslo.

At the entrance of Jotunheimen National Park, Beitostølen is known as a great winter destination that practically guarantees snow from November to May. During the summer months, the small mountain village is a great starting point for hikes in the mountains.

From Oslo Central Station you can take the Valdresekspressen bus service to Beitostølen. You'll be traveling through the beautiful Begnadalen Valley during the journey of barely four hours. By car, it's a three-hour drive along Route E16 and Route 51.

Jotunheimen National Park covers a huge area, and is accessible from Beitostølen in the Valdrees Valley or Otta in the Gudbrandsdalen Valley. Local buses serve the most popular hiking areas during the summer months.

TOURS

Over 100 years old, the Bitihorn takes you on a trip on Lake Bygdin where you will see more than 10 of Jotunheimen's peaks topping out at over 2,000 meters (6,651 feet). If you are lucky, you might even spot reindeer. The Gjendebåten is a passenger ferry that takes you from Gjendesheim in the west to Gjendebu in the east.

CONTACTS Bitihorn . ✉ *Jernbanevegen 7, Fagernes* ☎ *61–36–16–00* ⊕ *www.jvb. no.* **Gjendebåten.** ✉ *Øygardsvegen 187, Vågå* ☎ *913–06–744* ⊕ *www.gjende. no.* **Beitostølen Tourism Office.** ✉ *Bygdinvegen 3780, Beitostølen* ☎ *61–35–94–20* ⊕ *www.valdres.no.*

👁 Sights

Beitostølen Lyskapellet (*Beitostølen Light Chapel*)
BUILDING | The late Norwegian artist Ferdinand Finne created unique painted glass in this beautiful chapel. ✉ *Sentervegen 2, Beitostølen* ⊕ *www.lyskapellet.no.*

★ Besseggen Ridge
VIEWPOINT | About 60,000 people walk the Besseggen Ridge every year, making this Norway's most popular day hike. In Jotunheimen Nasjonalpark, the mountain ridge is between Gjende and Bessvatnet, two clear alpine lakes, and the trail offers beautiful views of the landscape.

The best time to visit is when the Gjendebåten boat is running from mid-June to mid-October. Park at Reinsvangen where the shuttle bus takes you to Gjendeosen and the Gjendebåten boat. ✉ *Tessanden* ✛ *Reinsvangen* ☎ *61–24–14–44* ⊕ *www.nasjonalparkriket.no.*

★ Jotunheimen Nasjonalpark (*Jotunheimen National Park*)
NATIONAL/STATE PARK | Since the 19th century, Jotunheimen Nasjonalpark has been one of most popular areas in the country for hiking and mountain climbing. It earns its name (Jotunheimen is Norwegian for "Home of the Giants") by having the largest concentration of peaks higher than 2,000 meters (6,561 feet) in northern Europe. This includes the country's two highest mountains, Galdhøpiggen and Glittertind. Jotunheimen also features several lakes, the largest being Gjende. The national park has an extensive network of tracks and trails, and you will find hikes and treks suitable for everybody. ✉ *Jotunheimen Nasjonalpark* ☎ *61–24–14–44* ⊕ *www. nasjonalparkriket.no.*

Valdresflye National Tourist Route
SCENIC DRIVE | During this scenic drive over the mountain plateau of Valdresflye you can stop almost wherever you like, either to photograph the beautiful landscape or go for a hike in the mountains. During the summer, several local farms sell traditional foods. ⊕ *www.nasjonaleturistveger.no/en/routes/valdresflye* ⊗ *Closed Dec.–Mar.*

🍴 Restaurants

Hytta Mat and Vinhus
$$$ | **NORWEGIAN** | A hidden gem in Beitostølen, Hytta Food and Winehouse is renowned for its fine local cuisine. The restaurant is set in a traditional Norwegian cowshed, and the wooden walls and floors and reindeer skins slung across the chairs give it a rustic feel. **Known for:** amazing deer fillet; friendly hosts and

staff; authentic ambience. $ *Average main: NKr 300* ✉ *Finntøppveien 2, Beitostølen* ☎ *904–00–288* ⊕ *www.beitstolen-restaurant.com* ⊘ *Closed Mon. and Tues. No lunch.*

🛏 Hotels

★ Hindsæter Mountain Hotel

$$$ | HOTEL | FAMILY | This historic hotel has stunning views of the Sjodalen Valley and Jotunheimen National Park. **Pros:** wellness room with whirlpool and saunas; family rooms available; ski- and snowshoe rentals. **Cons:** no à la carte dinner options; rooms on the small size; books up fast. $ *Rooms from: NKr 1640* ✉ *Sjodalsveien 1549, Tessanden* ☎ *61–23–89–16* ⊕ *www.hindseter.no* ⇥ *26 rooms* ⦿ *Free breakfast.*

Bergen

Many visitors fall in love with Bergen, Norway's second-largest city, at first sight. Seven rounded lush mountains, pastel wood houses, the historic wharf, winding cobblestone streets, and Hanseatic relics all make it a place of enchantment. Its many epithets include "Trebyen" (Wooden City), "Regnbyen" (Rainy City, due to its 260 days of rain a year), and "Fjordbyen" (gateway to the fjords).

Surrounded by forested hills and glittering fjords, it's only natural that most Bergensers feel at home either on the mountains (skiing, biking, walking, or at their cabins) or at sea (fishing and boating). On any sunny day you'll often see them taking the funicular to the top of the nearby mountain for a quick hike or just to sit in the sun. As for the rainy weather, most visitors quickly learn the necessity of rain jackets and umbrellas.

Residents take legendary pride in their city and its luminaries. The composer Edvard Grieg, the violinist Ole Bull, and Ludvig Holberg, Scandinavia's answer to Molière, all made great contributions to Norwegian culture. Today their legacy lives on in nationally acclaimed theater, music, film, dance, and art. The singer Sondre Lerche, pianist Leif Ove Andsnes, choreographer Jo Strømgren, and author Gunnar Staalesen all live in Bergen. Every year a host of exciting festivals attracts national and international artists.

WHEN TO GO

The best time to visit Bergen is May through September, when the city is surprisingly temperate. It is usually warm, though only rarely do the temperature top out at close to 80 degrees. The weather does change quickly, so you'll want to carry a jacket in case you encounter a sudden downpour. Autumn is still lovely, with warm days and crisp nights. The changing colors of the leaves, especially on nearby Mount Fløyen, are the biggest draw at this time of year. Winter rarely means snow, although temperatures often fall well below freezing. The ski areas about 90 minutes from the city get all the snow, and all are very popular.

PLANNING YOUR TIME

Although it's a very compact city, you'll want several days to explore Bergen. Plan a day for exploring Bryggen and its hulking fortress, and another for Sentrum and its string of museums. The sights outside the city, such as the museum houses of Edvard Greig and Ole Bull, take at least half a day to get there and back.

If you're visiting outside of summer, remember that daylight hours are limited. Museums also have shorter hours, so get to the sights you most want to see early in the day. Even popular sights like Bergenhus Festning close earlier in winter.

GETTING HERE AND AROUND

AIR

SAS, Norwegian, and Widerøe have the
most flights into Bergen, but Air Baltic,
Air France, British Airways, Finnair, Icelandair, KLM, Lufthansa, Swiss, Vueling,
and Wizz Air also fly here. Flesland Airport is a 30-minute bus ride from Bergen.
Flybussen, the airport bus, departs every
15 minutes and drops passengers off at
the bus station in downtown Bergen.
The cost is about NKr 115. A taxi stand is
conveniently located outside the arrivals
gate. Trips downtown cost about NKr 450
to NKr 500. You can also take light rail
trains from the airport to the city center.
The trip takes about 45 minutes and
costs Nkr 38.

CONTACTS Flybussen Bergen. ⊕ www.
flybussen.no/billett/#/reise/til/
bergen-flyplass/bgo.

BOAT AND FERRY

Boats have always been Bergen's lifeline
to the world. The jewel in the crown is
the Hurtigruten coastal express, which
departs daily for the 11-day round-trip
to Kirkenes in Northern Norway. Norled
has several routes, including one to the
popular tourist destination of Flåm and
the Nordfjord area in the Western Fjords.
Fjord Line sails to Denmark.

Cruise ships dock at Skoltegrunnskaien
and Jekteviken/Dokkeskjærskaien. Both
are within a 15-minute walk of the city
center. Free shuttle buses are available
from Jekteviken/Dokkeskjærskaien. From
Skoltegrunnskaien, buses stop near the
docks.

CONTACTS Fjord Line. ☎ 51–46–40–99
⊕ www.fjordline.com. **Hurtigruten.**
☎ 77–59–72–04 ⊕ www.hurtigruten.
no. **Norled.** ☎ 51–86–87–00 press 9 for
English ⊕ www.norled.no.

BUS

Nor-Way Bussekspress operates several
daily buses between Oslo and Bergen.
The journey takes 9 to 10 hours. Buses

also connect Bergen with Stavanger and
Ålesund.

Tide is the main bus operator in Bergen,
with buses throughout the day and at
night on weekends (Friday and Saturday
until 4 am).

CONTACTS Tide. ⊕ www.tide.no/en. **Nor-
Way Bussekspress.** ⊕ www.nor-way.no.

CAR

Bergen is 462 km (287 miles) from Oslo.
There are three main routes between
Oslo and Bergen, with Route 7 across
the Hardangervidda plateau the most
scenic. The 67-km (42-miles) stretch
between Haugastøl and Eidfjord is part
of the designated National Tourist Route.
If you choose Route 52 over Hemsed-
alsfjellet or E16 over Filefjell you will pass
through the world's longest road tunnel.

From Granvin, Route 7 hugs the fjord part
of the way, making for spectacular scenery, but the road ia very narrow. A quicker
but less scenic drive is to follow Route
13 from Granvin to Voss, then take E16
from Voss to Bergen. Be aware that there
are lots of tunnels on that road. In winter,
several mountain passes are prone to
closing at short notice. The Public Roads
Administration's road information line can
give you the status of most roads.

Driving from Stavanger to Bergen
involves two ferries and a long journey
packed with stunning scenery. Downtown Bergen is enclosed by an inner
ring road. It's best to leave your car at
a parking garage (the cheapest and
most accessible is ByGarasjen, near the
train station, and Klostergarasjen, near
Nordnes) and walk.

TRAIN

There are several departures daily along
the Oslo–Bergen route, one of the most
beautiful train rides in the world. The trip
takes a little less than 7 hours and costs
about NKr 579. The main train station
in Bergen is in Sentrum, within easy

walking distance of several of the most popular hotels.

RESTAURANTS

Bergen has a world-class dining scene, with a dozen or so restaurants winning international awards. The city sits on the waterfront, so seafood features prominently on most menus. Traditional dishes are popular here, although the city's sophisticated palettes are attracted more and more to New Nordic cuisine. Most kitchens tout their use of local ingredients—often with links to specific farmers or ranchers—and change their dishes with the seasons.

HOTELS

There's a huge variety of hotels in and near the city center, ranging from smaller guesthouses to grand hotels. Boutique hotels are very popular, so this is a great city if you're into great design. If you want to be walking distance to the major sights, look for an address in Bryggen or Sentrum.

Restaurant and hotel reviews have been shortened. For full information, visit Fodors.com

NIGHTLIFE

Bergen is a university town, and the many thousand students who live and study here make the city's nightlife much more exciting than you might expect for a town of its size. Many of the most popular bars and clubs are in Sentrum, but Vågsbunnen has become more and more popular.

SHOPPING

Bergen has several cobblestoned pedestrian shopping streets, including Gamle Strandgaten, Torgallmenningen, Hollendergaten, and Marken. Stores selling Norwegian handicrafts are concentrated along the wharf in Bryggen. Near the cathedral, the tiny Skostredet has become popular with young shoppers. The small, independent specialty stores here sell everything from army surplus gear to tailored suits and designer

trinkets. Most Bergen shops are open Monday to Wednesday and Friday from 9 to 5, Thursday from 9 to 7, and Saturday from 10 to 3.

VISITOR INFORMATION

CONTACTS Visit Bergen. (*tourist information*) ☎ 55–55–20–00 ⊕ *www.visitbergen. com*.

Bryggen

◉ Sights

Bergenhus Festning (*Bergenhus Fortress*)
BUILDING | The major buildings at the medieval Bergenhus are Håkonshallen (Håkon's Hall) and Rosenkrantztårnet (Rosenkrantz Tower). Both are open to visitors. **Håkonshallen** is a royal ceremonial hall erected during the reign of Håkon Håkonsson in the mid-1200s; it sometimes closes for public holidays or special events. It was badly damaged by the explosion of a German ammunition ship in 1944 but was restored by 1961. Erected in the 1560s by the governor of Bergenhus, Erik Rosenkrantz, **Rosenkrantztårnet** served as a combined residence and fortified tower. ⊠ *Bergenhus, Bryggen* ☎ *55–30–80–30* ⊕ *www.bymuseet.no/ en/* 🖾 *NKr 100* ⊗ *Rosenkrantztårnet closed Mon.–Sat. mid-Sept.–mid-May.*

★ **Bryggen** (*Bryggen Hanseatic Wharf*)
HISTORIC SITE | A trip to this merchant city is incomplete without a trip to the historic Hanseatic harborside, Bryggen. A row of mostly reconstructed 14th-century wooden buildings that face the harbor makes this one of the most charming walkways in Europe, especially on a sunny day. Several fires, the latest in 1955, destroyed some of the original structures, but you'd never know it now. Today the old houses hold boutiques and restaurants, and wandering through the wooden alleys here will be a highlight of your trip. Bryggen has been a UNESCO World Heritage Site since 1979. ⊠ *Bryggen, Bryggen.*

Bryggens Museum

MUSEUM | This museum contains archae-ological finds from the Middle Ages. An exhibit on Bergen circa 1300 shows the town at the zenith of its importance, and has reconstructed living quarters as well as artifacts such as old tools and shoes. Back then, Bergen was the largest town in Norway, a cosmopolitan trading center and the national capital. ⊠ *Dreggsall-menningen 3, Bryggen* ☎ *55–30–80–30* ⊕ *www.bymuseet.no/en* ⊠ *NKr 100.*

Det Hanseatiske Museum og Schøtst-uene (*The Hanseatic Museum and Schøtstuene*)

MUSEUM | One of the best-preserved buildings in Bergen, the Hanseatic Museum was the 16th-century office and home of an affluent German mer-chant. The apprentices lived upstairs, in boxed-in beds with windows cut into the wall. Although claustrophobic, the snug rooms had the benefit of being relatively warm—a blessing in the unheated build-ing. In summer, there are daily guided tours in Norwegian, German, French, and English. ⊠ *Finnegården 1A, Bryggen* ☎ *53–00–61–10* ⊕ *www.museumvest.no/ english* ⊠ *NKr 160.*

Domkirke (*Bergen Cathedral*)

RELIGIOUS SITE | The cathedral's long, turbulent history has shaped the eclectic architecture of the current structure. The Gothic-style choir and the lower towers are the oldest, dating from the 13th century. Note the cannonball lodged in the tower wall—it dates from a battle between English and Dutch ships in Bergen harbor in 1665. One of the nicest ways to enjoy the cathedral is attend-ing one of the frequent organ concerts held here. ⊠ *Domkirke gt., Bryggen* ☎ *55–59–32–73.*

Fisketorget (*Bergen Fish Market*)

MARKET | In a strikingly modern building on the waterfront, the busy fish market is one of Bergen's most popular attractions. Turn-of-the-20th-century photographs of this pungent square show fishermen in Wellington boots and raincoats and wom-en in long aprons. Now the fishmongers wear bright-orange rubber overalls as they look over the day's catch. You'll want to come at lunchtime, when you can enjoy the catch of the day while watch-ing the boats in the harbor. Try a classic Bergen lunch of shrimp or salmon on a baguette with mayonnaise and cucum-ber. Fruits, vegetables, and flowers are also on offer, as are handicrafts. ⊠ *Torget 5, Bryggen* ☎ *55–55–20–00 tourist information.*

★ Fløibanen (*Mount Fløyen Funicular*)

TRANSPORTATION SITE (AIRPORT/BUS/FERRY/ TRAIN) | A magnificent view of Bergen and its suburbs can be taken in from the top of Mt. Fløyen, the most accessible of the city's seven mountains. The eight-minute ride on the funicular takes you to the top, 320 meters (1,050 feet) above the sea. A car departs at least every half hour. On the top is a restaurant and café, a shop, and a playground. Stroll along the path that goes back to downtown or explore the mountains that lead to Ulriken, the highest of the mountains surrounding Bergen. ⊠ *Vetrlidsalmenningen 21, Bryggen* ☎ *55–33–68–00* ⊕ *floyen.no/en/* ⊠ *NKr 65 each way.*

Lille Øvregaten

HISTORIC SITE | The name means "Little Upper Street," and this charming thor-oughfare is one of the oldest in the city. Along a bumpy cobblestone lane, these 19th-century clapboard houses are a glimpse of Bergen 100 years ago. ⊠ *Lille Øvregaten, Bryggen.*

Mariakirken (*St. Mary's Church*)

RELIGIOUS SITE | In continuous use since the early Middle Ages, Bergen's oldest existing building dates from around 1170. The twin-spired church's oldest treas-ures include the altarpiece from the end of 15th century, the incredibly ornate pulpit, and the remaining wall paintings depicting biblical scenes. ⊠ *Dreggen 15, Bryggen* ☎ *55–59–71–75* ⊕ *kirken. no/nb-NO/fellesrad/Bergen/menigheter/*

Did You Know?

The Fløibanen transports passengers to the top of Mt. Fløyen in just eight minutes.

bergen-domkirke-menighet/turisme/turistinformasjon 🎫 *Free mid-May–mid-Sept.; NKr 75 mid-Sept.–mid-May.* ⏲ *Closed weekends late May–mid-Sept. Closed Sat.–Mon., Wed., and Thurs. mid-Sept.–late May.*

🍴 Restaurants

Bare

$$$$ | NORWEGIAN | The elegant but spare mirrored dining room at this local favorite puts all the emphasis where it should be: on the creative dishes coming out of the kitchen. And you'll get to sample quite a few of them, depending on whether you opt for the "half menu" consisting of 7 courses or go all the way with an 11-course extravaganza. **Known for:** fine dining at its best in Bergen; wine pairings couldn't be better; attentive service. [$] *Average main: NKr 1250* ✉ *Bergen Børs Hotel, Torgallmenningen 2, Vågsbunnen* ☎ *400–02–455* 🌐 *www.barerestaurant.no* ⏲ *Closed Sun. and Mon. No lunch.*

Bryggeloftet & Stuene

$$$ | NORWEGIAN | Hearty Norwegian country fare suits the cozy dining room, which has a handsome fireplace, oil paintings depicting the city's maritime past, and wooden display cases filled with model ships and other artifacts. A reindeer fillet in a cream sauce comes highly recommended, as do the monkfish and the venison. **Known for:** great location in the center of Bryggen; the best place to try traditional fish soup; generous portions. [$] *Average main: NKr 350* ✉ *Bryggen 11, Bryggen* ☎ *55–30–20–70* 🌐 *www.bryggeloftet.no.*

Bryggeriet

$$ | NORWEGIAN | The beer couldn't be any better than at the waterfront Bryggeriet, which brews its own at its restaurant on the pier at Zachariasbryggen. The gleaming copper vats, tucked away behind a pane of glass, give the place a warm and welcoming atmosphere. **Known for:** views of the fjord are spectacular; fish comes from the nearby market; try a flight of beers. [$] *Average main: NKr 250* ✉ *Torget 2, Bryggen* ☎ *55–55–31–55* 🌐 *bryggeriet.biz* ⏲ *Closed Mon. and Tues. No lunch.*

★ **Enhjørningen**

$$$$ | NORWEGIAN | This restaurant, one of the best seafood restaurants in town, is named after the unicorn that adorns the doorway of the old wooden building in which it is housed. It may look old-fashioned, but there's nothing medieval about Enhjørningen's menu—it's contemporary Norwegian and it changes according to the day's catch. **Known for:** steamed halibut and other local seafood; traditional dishes with a modern twist; waterfront location. [$] *Average main: NKr 360* ✉ *Enhjørningsgården 29, Bryggen* ☎ *55–30–69–50* 🌐 *www.enhjorningen.no* ⏲ *Closed Sun. Sept.–mid-May. No lunch.*

Nama

$$$ | JAPANESE | The city's most popular Japanese restaurant—the name means "fresh and raw" in Japanese—has garnered enthusiastic good reviews for its *izakaya* (traditional pub) atmosphere, its *robatayaki* (barbecue) dishes, and, of course, its wide array of sushi. On one of the smaller streets just behind Bryggen, it's stylish decorated and has huge windows that let in lots of light. **Known for:** led the small plates craze in Bergen; delicious roasted meats; fine wine selection. [$] *Average main: NKr 275* ✉ *Lodin Lepps gt. 2B, Bryggen* ☎ *55–32–20–10* 🌐 *www.namasushi.no* ⏲ *No lunch Mon.–Thurs.*

Restaurant 1877

$$$$ | NORWEGIAN | Travel through time at this nostalgic venue full of traces of Bergen's proud past—from the well-used copper pots hanging on the wall down to the vintage dishes that arrive at your table with a flourish. With a great love of Norway's traditional food, the restaurant focuses on what it gets from local farmers and fishermen. **Known for:** location in the historical Kjøttbasaren; pleasant dining on the veranda; seasonal tasting menu. $ *Average main: NKr 795* ✉ *Vetrlidsallmenningen 2, Bryggen* ☎ *928–71–877* ⊕ *www.restaurant1877.no* ⊗ *Closed Sun. No lunch.*

Ridderen

$$$ | **CONTEMPORARY** | This restaurant has plenty of history: its two main dining rooms are whitewashed storage rooms that once served as potato cellars. The surroundings date back to the Middle Ages, but the food's as upscale and modern-feeling as could be, using traditional German recipes and giving them a modern twist—think mussels in a light cream sauce or pork knuckles with sauerkraut. **Known for:** perfect destination for a romantic dinner for two; located in one of the oldest parts of Bergen; near the fish market, so the seafood is fresh. $ *Average main: NKr 300* ✉ *Kong Oscars gt. 1A, Vågsbunnen* ☎ *55–32–00–70* ⊕ *ridderen.no* ⊗ *Closed Mon. No lunch Tues.–Thurs. and Sun.*

★ To Kokker

$$$$ | **NORWEGIAN** | In a 300-year-old building on the wharf, it's no surprise that the charming To Kokker has crooked floors and off-kilter molding. Ranked among Bergen's best restaurants, it serves excellent seafood and game prepared the traditional way with a contemporary twist. **Known for:** tucked away on one of Bryggen's side streets; one of the city's most tradition dining rooms; an update of old recipes. $ *Average main: NKr 595* ✉ *Enhjørningsgården 29, Bryggen* ☎ *55–30–69–55* ⊕ *www.tokokker.no* ⊗ *Closed Sun. No lunch.*

 ## Hotels

First Hotel Marin

$$$ | **HOTEL** | Along the harbor stands an elegant brick building that once housed one of Bergen's largest print shops; now it's a business hotel within walking distance of the city's top sights. **Pros:** suites are among the city's most stylish; gym room and sauna available; good deals

in off season. **Cons:** some rooms can be noisy in summer; service get mixed reviews; some rooms need renovation. $ *Rooms from: NKr 1350* ✉ *Rosenkrantzgt. 5–8, Bryggen* ☎ *53–05–15–00* ⊕ *www.firsthotels.com/Our-hotels/Hotels-in-Norway/Bergen/First-Hotel-Marin* 🛏 *151 rooms* ⊗ *Free breakfast.*

Hotel Bergen Børs

$$$ | **HOTEL** | This fashionable hotel is located on the upper floors in one of Bergen's most historic buildings, the former stock exchange. **Pros:** central location between Bryggen and Sentrum; home to one of the best restaurants in Bergen; luxurious rooms with a view. **Cons:** easy to get lost in the corridors; small seating area in the lobby; some noise from the city. $ *Rooms from: NKr 1525* ✉ *Vågsalmenningen 1, Vågsbunnen* ☎ *55–33–64–00* ⊕ *www.bergenbors.no* 🛏 *127 rooms* ⊗ *Free breakfast.*

Magic Hotel Korskirken

$$ | **HOTEL** | In one of the city's most happening neighborhoods, this centrally located lodging works its magic on the guest rooms, which compensate for their small size with smart and stylish design. **Pros:** within a stone's throw of a dozen restaurants and cafés; rooms are out of a shelter magazine; beautifully restored buildings. **Cons:** can be noisy, especially on weekends; entrance is a bit underwhelming; some rooms small for two people. $ *Rooms from: NKr 1159* ✉ *Nedre Korskirkeallmenning 1, Bryggen* ☎ *55–90–01–00* ⊕ *magichotels.no/utforsk-vare-hoteller/korskirken* 🛏 *90 rooms* ⊗ *Free breakfast.*

 ## Nightlife

Biblioteket Bar

BARS/PUBS | Enjoy a creative cocktail in this elegant lounge overlooking the busy harbor. Biblioteket has DJs and live music, but never sets the volume to a level where a conversation is no longer possible. ✉ *Vetrlidsallmenningen*

2, Bryggen ☎ 55–01–18–85 🌐 www.biblioteketbar.no.

Baklommen Bar
BARS/PUBS | With Y-shape beams holding the ceiling aloft, this intimate cocktail bar is located in one of the crooked old buildings on the wharf. ✉ *Enhjørningsgården 29, Bryggen* ☎ *55–30–69–55* 🌐 *www.tokokker.no/baklommen-bar* 🕑 *Closed Sun. and Mon.*

Shopping

Berle Bryggen
CLOTHING | Here you'l find the complete Dale of Norway collection of sweaters and cardigans, as well as trolls, pewter, down duvets, and other traditional knitwear and souvenir items. ✉ *Bryggen 5, Bryggen* ☎ *55–10–95–00* 🌐 *www.sns.no.*

Oleana
CLOTHING | The flagship store of this famous Norwegian design shop is full of gorgeous clothes and textiles with traditional and contemporary patterns, all made in Norway. ✉ *Strandkaien 2A, Bryggen* ☎ *55–31–05–20* 🌐 *www.oleana.no.*

Nordnes

Sights

Akvariet i Bergen (*Bergen Aquarium*)
ZOO | FAMILY | Focusing on fish found in the North Sea, the Bergen Aquarium is one of the largest in Europe. It has 60 tanks filled with dozen of species from massive salmon to sinewy eels (which tend to wrap around each other), and two outdoor pools that are the home of playful seals, otters, and penguins. There is also a section displaying alligators from different parts of the world on display. Kids can hold starfish and other creatures in the touch tanks, or watch as trainers feed their charges. ✉ *Nordnesbakken 4, Nordnes* ☎ *55–55–71–71* 🌐 *akvariet.no* 🎫 *NKr 285.*

Restaurants

Kafe Kippers
$$ | NORWEGIAN | In a former sardine factory, Kafe Kippers specializes in seafood dishes like arctic char with artichoke, radish, and dill or steamed mussels with herbs and garlic. This large outdoor café on the waterfront is a pleasant stop for lunch or at sunset when you can warm up with a cozy wool blanket and enjoy a spectacular view of the North Sea. **Known for:** spectacular views; trendy location; off the tourist trail. [$] *Average main: NKr220* ✉ *Georgernes Verft 12, Nordnes* ☎ *55–30–40–80* 🌐 *www.kafekippers.no.*

Hotels

Hotel Clarion Admiral
$$$ | HOTEL | If you're looking for stunning views, you won't do better than the Hotel Clarion Admiral, which looks across the water to the colorful facades of Bryggen. **Pros:** unbeatable views across to Bryggen; lavish dining room on the waterfront; walking distance to the aquarium. **Cons:** can be booked up with conferences; a bit far from the action; chain hotel feel. [$] *Rooms from: NKr 1500* ✉ *C. Sundts gt. 9, Bergen* ☎ *55–23–64–00* 🌐 *www.nordicchoicehotels.com/hotels/norway/bergen/clarion-hotel-admiral* 🛏 *210 rooms* 🍴 *Free breakfast.*

Nightlife

Altona Vinbar
BARS/PUBS | For a quiet glass of wine in an intimate and historic setting, try award-winning Altona and its 400-year-old wine cellar. The vaulted ceilings and exposed brick add a lot of atmosphere. The food is good, too. ✉ *Augustin Hotel, Strandgaten 81, Nordnes* ☎ *55–30–40–72* 🕑 *Closed Sun.*

Sentrum

👁 Sights

Grieghallen

ARTS VENUE | Home of the Bergen Philharmonic Orchestra and stage for the Bergen International Festival, this music hall is a conspicuous slab of glass and concrete that's used throughout the year for cultural events. The acoustics are marvelous. Built in 1978, the hall was named for the city's famous son, composer Edvard Grieg (1843–1907). ☒ *Edvard Griegs pl. 1, Sentrum* ☎ *55–21–61–00* ⊕ *www.grieghallen.no.*

KODE 1

MUSEUM | Looking out over the pretty Byparken, this neoclassical edifice was called the Permanenten when it first opened in doors in 1896. The centerpiece of the collection is the Sølvskatten—the Silver Treasure–a glittering display of items of gold, silver, and other precious metals created in Bergen. It also holds an eclectic collection of antiques and artworks from Europe and Asia. The Italian eatery Bien Centro is located on-site. ☒ *Nordahl Bruns gt. 9, Sentrum* ☎ *53–00–97–04* ⊕ *kodebergen.no/en/find-us/kode-1* ✉ *NKr 130 (includes 2-day admission to all KODE museums)* ⊘ *Closed Mon. mid-Sept.–mid-June.*

KODE 2

MUSEUM | Opening its doors in 1978, the newest of the museums in the KODE complex hosts temporary art exhibitions. The biggest draw here is the bookstore, which has an impressive collection of volumes on art, architecture, and design. Cafe Smakverket is a casual eatery that's perfect for a lunchtime repast or coffee in the afternoon. ☒ *Rasmus Meyers allé 3, Bryggen* ☎ *53–00–97–02* ⊕ *kodebergen. no/en/find-us/kode-2* ✉ *NKr 130 (includes 2-day admission to all KODE museums)* ⊘ *Closed Mon. mid-Sept.–mid-May.*

KODE 3

MUSEUM | If you're here to see the amazing works by Edvard Munch—the painter who gave the world *The Scream*—this is the museum for you. The museum is dedicated to Munch and other Norwegian artists like J.C. Dahl, Harriet Backer, Erik Werenskiold, and Gerhard Munthe. The building itself was designed by architect Ole Landmark in 1916 to house the huge collection amassed by businessman Rasmus Meyer. ☒ *Rasmus Meyers allé 7, Sentrum* ☎ *53–00–97–03* ⊕ *kodebergen.no/en/find-us/kode-3* ✉ *NKr 130 (includes 2-day admission to all KODE museums)* ⊘ *Closed Mon. mid-Sept.–mid-May.*

KODE 4

MUSEUM | In a building strongly resembling a huge battery—it was originally the headquarters for an electrical power company—KODE 4 lets you travel through art history with a collection ranging from the 13th to the 20th centuries, including works by international luminaries like Pablo Picasso and Norwegian favorites like Nikolai Astrup. KunstLab, an art museum geared toward children, in on the ground floor. Foodies will find themselves drawn to Lysverket, a restaurant specializing in seafood. ☒ *Rasmus Meyers allé 9, Sentrum* ☎ *53–00–97–04* ⊕ *kodebergen.no/en/find-us/kode-4* ✉ *NKr 130 (includes 2-day admission to all KODE museums)* ⊘ *Closed Mon. mid-Sept.–mid-May.*

Lepramuseet (*The Leprosy Museum*)

MUSEUM | St. George's Hospital tended to lepers for more than 500 years, and this unusual museum is now a memorial to the thousands who suffered from the disease as well as a testament to Norway's contribution to leprosy research. The building is surprisingly beautiful, especially the main ward with its tiny examining rooms and the hand-carved wood of the chapel. Many Norwegian doctors have been recognized for their efforts against leprosy, particularly Armauer Hansen,

3

Norway BERGEN

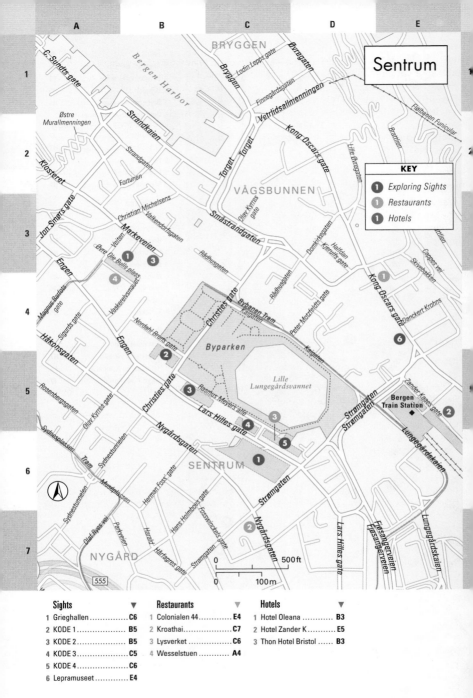

Sentrum

KEY

- ① Exploring Sights
- ① Restaurants
- ① Hotels

Sights	▼
1 Grieghallen	C6
2 KODE 1	B5
3 KODE 2	B5
4 KODE 3	C5
5 KODE 4	C6
6 Lepramuseet	E4

Restaurants	▼
1 Colonialen 44	E4
2 Kroathai	C7
3 Lysverket	C6
4 Wesselstuen	A4

Hotels	▼
1 Hotel Oleana	B3
2 Hotel Zander K	E5
3 Thon Hotel Bristol	B3

who discovered the leprosy bacteria, and after whom Hansen's disease is named. ✉ *Kong Oscars gt. 59, Sentrum* ☎ *55–30–80–37* 🌐 *www.bymuseet.no/en/museums/the-leprosy-museum-st-jorgen-hospital* 🎫 *NKr 100* ⏲ *Closed early Sept.–mid-May.*

🍴 Restaurants

Colonialen 44

$$$$ | **NORWEGIAN** | If you want to sample the best local dishes, Colonialen 44 Restaurant should be on your list. The four-course tasting menu focuses on traditional Norwegian recipes paired with international cooking techniques. **Known for:** wine pairings complement your meal; bold mixing of flavors and colors; casual seating in bar area. [$] *Average main: NKr 550* ✉ *Kong Oscars gt. 44, Sentrum* ☎ *55–90–16–00* 🌐 *colonialen.no/restaurant* ⏲ *Closed Sun. No lunch Mon.-Fri.*

Kroathai

$$ | **THAI** | With a view of the Lille Lungegårdsvann Lake, this longtime favorite offers delicious, authentic Thai dishes—some, like chicken soup with lemongrass, that you already know, and others, like steamed mussels in a pineapple sauce, that you might be meeting for the first time. There's an unusually wide range of vegetarian dishes. **Known for:** great location in the city center; surprising selection of soups; small but cozy dining room. [$] *Average main: NKr 175* ✉ *Nygårdsgaten 29, Sentrum* ☎ *55–32–58–50* 🌐 *www.kroathai.com.*

★ **Lysverket**

$$$$ | **NORWEGIAN** | With an artful location in the KODE 4 museum and next to the Grieghallen concert hall, Lysverket offers New Nordic cuisine that makes clever use of seasonal, local ingredients in dishes like roasted redfish with grilled lettuce or king crab with nasturtium purée. The spare dining room is the best of Scandinavian design, making a meal here a pleasure for both the eyes and the mouth. **Known for:** wine pairings finish your meal in style; creative dishes using fresh ingredients; cozy and stylish interior. [$] *Average main: NKr 369* ✉ *KODE 4, Rasmus Meyers allé 9, Sentrum* ☎ *55–60–31–00* 🌐 *lysverket.no* ⏲ *Closed Mon.*

Wesselstuen

$$ | **NORWEGIAN** | Housed in a 18th-century wine cellar, this atmospheric restaurant is known for its convivial atmosphere and unpretentious, authentic Norwegian fare. This is a good place to try reindeer steak or whale carpaccio. **Known for:** one of those longtime favorites that never seem to change; a great outdoor garden protected from the weather; perfect spot to try traditional dishes. [$] *Average main: NKr 250* ✉ *Øvre Ole Bulls pl. 6, Sentrum* ☎ *55–55–49–49* 🌐 *www.wesselstuen.no.*

🛏 Hotels

Hotel Oleana

$$$ | **HOTEL** | A stylish boutique lodging located in Bergen's theater district, Hotel Oleana's interior design is inspired by Ole Bull, one of the city's most famous composers and musicians. **Pros:** great location close to theater and nightlife; the sophisticated design catches the eye; excellent restaurant. **Cons:** some noise on the weekends; bar can get crowded at times; not much of a view. [$] *Rooms from: NKr 1642* ✉ *Øvre Ole Bulls pl. 5, Sentrum* ☎ *55–21–58–70* 🌐 *www.hoteloleana.com* 🛏 *97 rooms* 🍴 *Free breakfast.*

Hotel Zander K

$$$ | **HOTEL** | **FAMILY** | You notice the sophisticated Scandinavian design when you enter the inviting lobby of the stylish Hotel Zander K, located just a short walk from the main train station. **Pros:** modern and practical rooms; near public transportation; inviting and vibrant lobby. **Cons:** a long walk to the city center; no closets in standard rooms; some rooms can be noisy. [$] *Rooms from: NKr 1265*

✉ *Zander Kaaes gt. 8, Sentrum* ☎ *55–36–20–40* 🌐 *www.zanderk.no* 🛏 *249 rooms* 🍴 *Free breakfast.*

★ **Thon Hotel Bristol**
$$ | **HOTEL** | Built in the 1920s, the elegant Hotel Bristol has an enviable location that puts you within walking distance of the city's main sights. **Pros:** perfect location if you like shopping or nightlife; plenty of charm and character; great on-site eatery. **Cons:** rooms overlooking the street can be noisy; no air-conditioning, so rooms can get hot in summer; some rooms are a bit small. [$] *Rooms from: NKr 1250* ✉ *Torgallmenningen 11, Sentrum* ☎ *55–55–10–00* 🌐 *www.thonhotels.com/hotels/countrys/norway/bergen/thon-hotel-bristol-bergen/* 🛏 *123 rooms* 🍴 *Free breakfast.*

Nightlife

Jacob Aall
PIANO BARS/LOUNGES | With a clubby atmosphere, Jacob Aall lets you sink into a leather armchair and enjoy a glass of beer or wine. But the big draw is the huge rooftop terrace, open throughout the year on the top floor of a shopping center. ✉ *Xhibition Shopping Center, Småstrandgaten 3, Bergen* ☎ *55–30–71–00* 🌐 *www.jacobaall.no/bergen/kirsebaerhagen.*

Kava Roofgarden
BARS/PUBS | With two stylish bars inside and a rooftop terrace with views of the fjord, Kava attracts a young and hip crowd. The place is known for its fishbowl-sized drinks with enough straws for everyone in your group to share. ✉ *Strandgaten 15, Bergen* 🌐 *www.kava-roofgarden.no* 🕒 *Closed Sun.–Fri.*

Storm Bar
BARS/PUBS | The downstairs brasserie has plenty of aficionados, but for our money, the upstairs bar is the place to be. The heated terrace is great no matter what time of year, and the views are stellar. This is the perfect place for a drink before a show at the adjacent Ole Bull Theater. ✉ *Øvre Ole Bullsplass 3, Bergen* ☎ *55–32–11–45* 🌐 *www.olebullhuset.no/storm-bar.*

Performing Arts

★ **Bergen Jazzforum**
MUSIC | Bergensers love jazz. The Bergen Jazz Forum is *the* place to find it—there are concerts every Friday from September to May. Also, more than 40 concerts are offered in the 10-day international **Nattjazz** festival in late May and early June. ✉ *Sardinen, Georgernes Verft 12, Nordnes* ☎ *55–30–72–50* 🌐 *www.bergen-jazzforum.no.*

★ **Den Nationale Scene** (*National Theater*)
THEATER | One of the city's most majestic buildings, the art nouveau Den Nationale Scene first opened its doors in 1906 with a performance before the royal family. The National Theater is worth a visit just to see the opulent main theater, which hosts lavish Broadway-style productions. Smaller venues inside the august building include the 250-seat Småscenen and the 90-seat Lille Scene. ✉ *Engen 1, Sentrum* ☎ *55–54–97–00* 🌐 *dns.no/dns-in-english.*

Ole Bull Scene
MUSIC | On the largest theaters in Bergen, the Ole Bull Scene mounts an impressive variety of stand-up performances, rock concerts, and theatrical events. Smaller shows are presented in the Lille Ole Bull, which becomes a nightclub on weekends. ✉ *Øvre Ole Bullsplass 3, Sentrum* ☎ *55–32–11–45* 🌐 *www.olebullhuset.no.*

Shopping

Hjertholm
CERAMICS/GLASSWARE | At this gift shop, most everything is of Scandinavian design. The pottery and glassware are of

the highest quality—much of it is made by local artisans. ⊠ *Galleriet, Torgallmenningen 8, Sentrum* ☎ *55–31–70–27* ⊕ *www.hjertholm.no* ⊙ *Closed Sun.*

Norsk Flid Husfliden

CRAFTS | Established in 1895, this famous boutique sells Norwegian handicrafts, including sweaters, blankets, and leather items. You can also grab some last-minute souvenirs. ⊠ *Vågsallmenningen 3, Sentrum* ☎ *55–54–47–40* ⊕ *www.norskflid.no/bergen* ⊙ *Closed Sun.*

Sandviken

◉ Sights

★ Gamle Bergen Museum (*Old Bergen Museum*)

MUSEUM VILLAGE | FAMILY | This open-air museum transports you to the 19th century, when Bergen consisted mostly of wooden houses. Streets and narrow alleys are lined with more than 50 buildings, including a baker, dentist, photographer, and jeweler. Local artists often hold exhibitions here. The grounds and park are open free of charge year-round. ⊠ *Nyhavnsveien 4, Bergen* ☎ *55–30–80–30* ⊕ *www.bymuseet.no/en/museums/old-bergen-museum/* ⊠ *NKr 120* ⊙ *Closed Sept.–mid-May.*

Greater Bergen

◉ Sights

★ Edvard Grieg Museum

HOUSE | Built in 1885, Troldhaugen was the home of Norway's most famous composer, Edvard Grieg. He composed many of his best-known works in a garden cottage by the lakeshore. In 1867 he married his cousin Nina, a Danish soprano. They lived in the white clapboard house with green gingerbread trim for 22 years. A salon and gathering place for many Scandinavian artists then, it now houses mementos—a piano, paintings, prints—of the composer's life. The interior has been kept as it was during Grieg's time here. Concerts are held both at Troldhaugen and at the very modern Troldsalen next door. ⊠ *Troldhaugsveien 65, Paradis* ✛ *7 km (5 miles) south of Bergen* ☎ *55–92–29–92* ⊕ *griegmuseum.no/en* ⊠ *NKr 110* ⊙ *Closed mid-Dec.–mid-Jan.*

Fantoft Stavkirke (*Fantoft Stave Church*)

ARCHAEOLOGICAL SITE | During the Middle Ages, when European cathedrals were built in stone, Norway used wood to create unique stave churches. These cultural symbols stand out for their dragon heads, carved doorways, and walls of staves (vertical planks). Though as many as 750 stave churches may have once existed, only 30 remain standing. The original stave church here, built in Fortun in Sogn in 1150 and moved to Fantoft in 1883, burned down in 1992. Since then, the church has been reconstructed to resemble the original structure. Take the light rail to the town of Paradis and walk up Birkelundsbakken to the parking lot on the left hand side and follow the trail to get to the church ⊠ *Fantoftvn. 38, Paradis* ☎ *55–28–07–10* ⊕ *fantoftstavkirke.com* ⊠ *NKr 55* ⊙ *Closed mid-Sept.–mid-May.*

Ole Bull Museum (*Lysøen Island and Ole Bull's house*)

HOUSE | From 1873 onward, Lysøen ("island of light") was the home of the Norwegian violin virtuoso Ole Bull (1810–80). His over-the-top mansion has an onion dome, gingerbread gables, curved staircases, and cutwork trim, and it's surrounded by 13 km (8 miles) of pathways created by Bull; it's great for picnics, rowing, and swimming in secluded spots. During Bull's long career, he performed frequently throughout Europe and the United States, and even started a short-lived utopian colony—Oleana—in Pennsylvania. After founding the first national theater in Norway, he chose the young playwright Henrik Ibsen to write

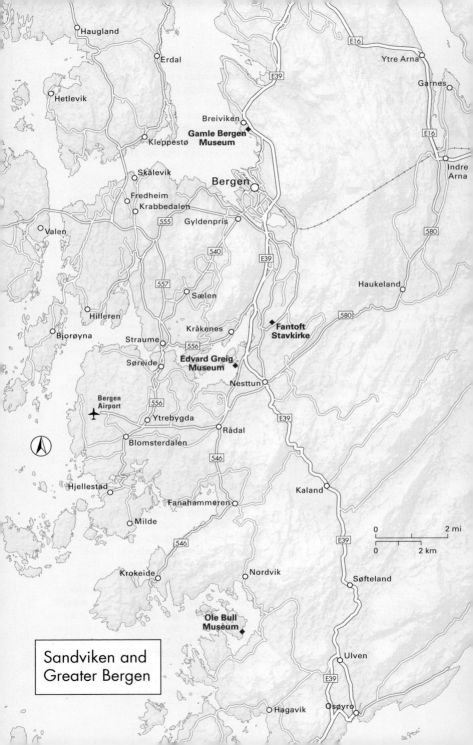

Haugland

Erdal

Ytre Arna

E16

E39

Hetlevik

Garnes

E16

Breiviken

Gamle Bergen
Museum

Indre
Arna

Kleppestø

Bergen

Skålevik

Fredheim

Krabbedalen

580

555

Gyldenpris

Valen

540

Haukeland

557

Sælen

Hilleren

580

Kråkenes

Fantoft
Stavkirke

Bjorøyna

Straume

556

Søreide

Edvard Greig
Museum

Nesttun

Bergen
Airport

556

Ytrebygda

E39

Blomsterdalen

Rådal

546

Hjellestad

Kaland

Fanahammeren

0   2 mi

E39

Milde

0   2 km

546

Krokeide

Nordvik

Søfteland

Ole Bull
Museum

Ulven

Sandviken and
Greater Bergen

E39

Osøyro

Hagavik

Composer Edvard Grieg entertained guests at Troldhaugen, an elegant country estate that is now a museum south of Bergen.

full-time for the theater, and later encouraged and promoted another neophyte—Edvard Grieg, then 15 years old. If you drive or take a bus here, the last part of the journey is on a ferry from Buena quay at Lysekloster. In the summer there are guided tours sponsored by the KODE museum in Bergen. ⊠ *Museet Lysøen, Lysekloster ✛ 25 km (13 miles) south of Bergen* ☎ *56–30–90–77* ⊕ *lysoen.no/ en* ✉ *NKr 60; ferry NKr 60 round-trip* ☉ *Closed mid-Sept.–mid-May.*

Odda

43 km (27 miles) south of Utne, 135 km (84 miles) southeast of Bergen.

A beautiful town along the Hardangerfjord, Odda is where many people choose to stay as a base for visiting Folgefonna National Park and Glacier and Trolltunga. The town is larger than any of the surrounding villages, so you'll find several restaurants and cafes where you can relax after exploring the region.

Beautiful waterfalls, blue glaciers, and deep green fjords are just some of the sights that await you in Odda.

GETTING HERE AND AROUND
The main road E134 passes through Odda, and meets Route 13 in the middle of the town. It is possible to reach Odda by public transportation, with the Haukeliekspressen bus traveling from Oslo to Odda several times a day, including one transfer at Seljestad. Line 930 takes you from Bergen to Odda.

◉ Sights

★ Folgefonna National Park
NATIONAL/STATE PARK | FAMILY | Home to Norway's third-largest glacier, Folgefonna National Park is popular for its kayaking, hiking, and, of course, hiking on the glacier. From the top of the glacier there are beautiful valleys stretching all the way down to the fjord, and visiting Folgefonna is something you will remember. The National Park has several places of entry, with Odda and Rosendal (with the visitor

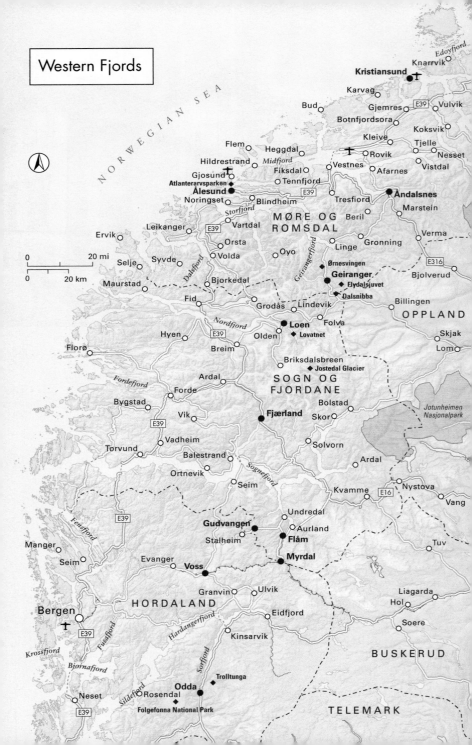

center) being two popular ones, and several hikes and glacier arms you can explore, in addition to beautiful valleys with waterfalls of melting water from the glacier. ⊠ *Skålafjæro 17, Rosendal* ☎ *53–48–42–80* ⊕ *folgefonna.info.*

Trolltunga

MOUNTAIN—SIGHT | This rock formation about 3,600 feet above sea level is one of the most breathtaking sights in Norway. From the tip of a huge sliver of stone jutting out from the mountain you can gaze down at the valley and fjord below. The hike itself takes around 10 to 12 hours, and many people find that they underestimated the level of fitness and endurance needed to make the trip. Always check weather conditions a few days ahead of time, then again the morning of the hike. The main starting point is at P2 in Skjeggedal, but it is also possible to start from P3 Mågelitopp (saving two or three hours). From Odda there are shuttle buses to P2, and between P2 and P3 there is a smaller shuttle operating in the summer season. There is parking at both P2 and P3, the latter with more limited spaces that should be booked in advance. ⊠ *Skjeggedal Carpark, Tyssedal* ⊕ *www.hardangerfjord.com/odda/ trolltunga.*

🍴 Restaurants

Glacier Restaurant

$$ | INTERNATIONAL | FAMILY | In the center of Odda, the Glacier Restaurant couldn't be more relaxed: there are picnic tables outside, a casual eatery on the main level, and a slightly more formal dining room downstairs. With Asian, European, and even Middle Eastern dishes on the menu, everyone in the family will find something to like. **Known for:** varied menu; vegetarian options; one of the few places serving cocktails. $ *Average main: NKr 239* ⊠ *Eitrheimsveien 9, Odda* ☎ *53–50–00–22* ⊕ *glacier-as.no/g/* ⊗ *No lunch Mon. or Thurs.*

🛏 Hotels

Trolltunga Hotel

$$$ | HOTEL | FAMILY | The views alone——overlooking the lake and the mountains beyond——are reason enough to chose this hotel, but it also has a relaxed atmosphere and amenities ranging from packed lunches for the trail to a gear-drying service so you don't have to pack wet clothes. **Pros:** beautiful views; renovated rooms; great breakfast. **Cons:** not all rooms offer the same view; 20-minute walk to downtown Odda; free shuttle to Trolltunga only for those hiking with a guide. $ *Rooms from: NKr 1500* ⊠ *Vasstun 1, Odda* ☎ *400–04–486* ⊕ *www.trolltungahotel.no* ⇆ *36 rooms, 2 dormitories* ⊗ *Free breakfast.*

Voss

43 km (19 miles) northwest of Ulvik, 107 km (66 miles) northeast of Bergen.

Between the Hardangerfjord and the Sognefjord, Voss is in a handy place to begin an exploration of the fjords. Once considered just a stopover, it now has a wide range of activities that invite people to linger. Its reputation is burnished by Vossajazz, an annual jazz festival, and the Sheep's Head Festival, a celebration of the region's culinary delicacies. Voss is known as the extreme sports capital of Norway. Ekstremsportveko, taking place every June, draws adrenaline enthusiasts from all over the world for paragliding, kitesurfing, base jumping, and other activities. The famous "Horgi Ned" competition includes three sports: skiing, biking, and kayaking.

GETTING HERE AND AROUND

From Bergen, Voss is a 1 1/2- to 2-hour drive along the E16. It's located on the Oslo-Bergen line, and trains are about 1 1/2 hours from Bergen, 5 1/2 hours from Oslo. Express trains run several times daily.

Sights

Voss Gondol
VIEWPOINT | This gondola is an exciting way to see Voss and the surrounding region. At the top is Hangurstoppen, which sits at 820 meters (2,690 feet) above sea level. Here you can enjoy a panoramic view from the restaurant or set off on hikes of different skill levels. ✉ *Evangervegen 5, Voss* ☎ *47–00–47–00* 🌐 *vossgondol.no* 🎟 *Nkr 750.*

Restaurants

Elvatun Restaurant
$$$ | **NORWEGIAN** | If you're looking to eat like a Viking, this long dining hall with soaring wood beams and a central fireplace should be on your list. The atmosphere is extremely cozy, especially when it's cold outside and you want to warm up by the open fire; at other times of the year, the tables out on the deck facing the lake are the most desirable (especially if you take advantage of the three outdoor hot tubs). **Known for:** an old-school vibe; plenty of local dishes; lovely location. [$] *Average main: NKr 300* ✉ *Nedkvitnesvegen 25, Voss* ☎ *56–51–05–25* 🌐 *vossactive.no.*

Hotels

★ **Fleischer's Hotel**
$$$$ | **HOTEL** | By the train station in the center of the city, this hotel dating from 1864 has plenty of details that call to mind a bygone era—bay windows, wooden balconies, and steeply pitched mansard roofs; even the newer wings have a pleasingly traditional look. **Pros:** indoor pool and sauna; central location; period charm. **Cons:** some noise from the train station; expensive rates; some amenities only open in summer. [$] *Rooms from: NKr 2100* ✉ *Evangerveien 13, Voss* ☎ *56–52–05–00* 🌐 *fleischers.no* 🛏 *110 rooms* 🍴 *Free breakfast.*

Activities

★ **Voss Active**
WHITE-WATER RAFTING | White-water rafting is just one of the activities at Voss Active, where the guides are enthusiastic about showing off what the area has to offer. They are knowledgeable about these sports and will make you feel comfortable and well taken care of, regardless of which adventure you pick. Fishing expeditions and ropes courses are among the favorite outings. ✉ *Nedkvitnesvegen 25, Skulestadmo, Voss* ☎ *56–51–05–25* 🌐 *vossactive.no.*

Gudvangen

8 km (5 miles) northeast of Stalheim.

This small village at the end of the Nærøyfjord is the final stop for cruises from both Flåm and Kaupanger. The village is a very popular destination because of the lovely views and the viking heritage.

GETTING HERE AND AROUND

Gudvangen is located along E16, the main road from Bergen and Voss. From Bergen, it takes about 2 1/2 hours by car or bus. From Flåm and Kaupanger, the most relaxing way to get here by boat.

Sights

★ **Njardarheimr Viking Village**
MUSEUM VILLAGE | You can completely immerse yourself in Viking culture at this village named for the northern god Njord. You won't be speaking with costumed performers here—the international community here is living as the Vikings did 1,000 years ago. Try your hand at axe throwing or archery, then chow down on authentic Viking grub. ✉ *Gudvangen* ☎ *46–24–54–62* 🌐 *vikingvalley.no* 🎟 *NKr 200.*

Hotels

Gudvangen Fjordtell

$$$$ | **HOTEL** | **FAMILY** | How about staying in a Viking-themed room, just a stone's throw from Norway's own Viking village of Njardarheimr? That's one of the joys of Gudvangen Fjordtell, in addition to the great location in the center of Gudvangen. **Pros:** great way to explore Viking history; lovely outdoor terrace; close to cruise ship dock. **Cons:** some rooms are drab; very remote location; restaurant has limited hours. [$] *Rooms from: NKr 1990* ✉ *Gudvangen Fjortdell, Fv 241, Gudvangen* ☎ *48–07–55–55* 🌐 *gudvangen.com* 🛏 *30 rooms* 🍴 *Free breakfast.*

Flåm

20 km (12 miles) east of Gundvagen, 64 km (40 miles) northeast of Voss.

One of the most scenic train routes in Europe zooms high into the mountains between the towns of Myrdal and Flåm. After the day-trippers have departed, it's a wonderful place to extend your tour and spend the night. Located at the end of the Sognefjord, Norway's longest fjord, this beautiful village is an ideal base for exploring the area.

GETTING HERE AND AROUND

From Voss take the E16 heading northeast—it takes about an hour to get to Flåm. The road passes the Nærøyfjord, Norway's narrowest fjord, and one of the most spectacular. Buses also link Flåm with Voss (1 hour 15 minutes) and Bergen (3 hours).

Flåm railway station is the starting point (or terminus) of the famous Flåmsbana. Trains go to Myrdal, with connections to both Voss, Geilo, Oslo and Bergen, but you take this train for the views rather than merely for transportation.

BUS CONTACTS NOR-WAY Bussekspress. ☎ *22–31–31–50* 🌐 *www.nor-way.no.*

CRUISE SHIP TRAVEL

Ships dock directly in the harbor of Flåm, within walking distance of all the sights. The train station is a five-minute walk from the pier.

VISITOR INFORMATION

CONTACTS Visit Flåm. ✉ *A-Feltvegen 11, Flåm* ☎ *57–63–14–00* 🌐 *visitflam.com.*

Sights

★ **Flåmsbana** (*Flåm Railway*)

SCENIC DRIVE | Although this trip covers only 20 km (12 miles), the one-way journey takes nearly an hour to travel through 20 tunnels and up the 2,850 feet up the steep mountain gorge. The masterpiece of Norwegian engineering took 20 years to complete, and today it's one of Norway's prime tourist attractions, drawing more than 1 million travelers each year. The train runs year-round, with 8 to 10 round-trips from mid-April through mid-October and 4 round-trips the rest of the year. Most tourists take the train round-trip, returning on the same train a few minutes after arriving in Myrdal. ✉ *Flåm Train Station, A-Feltvegen, Flåm* ☎ *57–63–14–00* 🌐 *www.visitflam.no/flamsbana* 🎫 *NKr 590.*

Flåmsbana Museet

MUSEUM | If you have a little extra time in Flåm, make sure you visit the Flåm Railway Museum. Building the railway was a remarkable feat of engineering, and this museum details the challenges the builders faced. You'll find it in the old station building, 300 feet from the one now in use. ✉ *Stasjonsvegen 8, Flåm* ☎ *57–63–14–00* 🌐 *visitflam.com/flamsbana/flamsbana-museet* 🎫 *Free.*

🍴 Restaurants

★ Ægir Bryggeri og Pub

$$$$ | **NORWEGIAN** | It started out as a straightforward microbrewery, but Ægir has been transformed into a complete culinary experience. Conveniently located near the cruise port in Flåm, its local dishes pair beautifully with the award-winning beer. **Known for:** interesting architecture; some of the region's best beer; local meats. $ *Average main: NKr 400* ✉ *A-feltvegen 23, Flåm* ☎ *57–63–20–50* ⊕ *flamsbrygga.no/aegir-bryggeripub.*

Arven

$$$ | **SCANDINAVIAN** | At the Fretheim Hotel, the Arven offeres dishes based on local ingredients—think mussels steamed in cider and herbs or monkfish with seaweed—in a sophisticated and cozy atmosphere. From the second-floor windows you can enjoy beautiful views of the Aurlandsfjord and the mountains beyond. **Known for:** views of the village; locally sourced products; top-notch service. $ *Average main: NKr 330* ✉ *Fretheim Hotel, Vikjavegen, Flåm* ☎ *57–63–63–00* ⊕ *fretheimhotel.no/nb/ mat/restaurant-arven* ⊘ *No lunch.*

★ Flåmstova

$$$ | **NORWEGIAN** | Looking for all the world like a traditional chalet, thanks to the massive beams and honey-colored wood floors, you'll feel the Scandinavian *hygge* (coziness) as soon as you walk inside. The restaurant focuses on fresh local ingredients while encouraging creativity among its chefs. **Known for:** cooks with local beer; new takes on traditional dishes; locally sourced ingredients. $ *Average main: NKr 285* ✉ *Flåmsbrygga Hotel, A-Feltvegen 25, Flåm* ☎ *57–63–20–50* ⊕ *flamsbrygga.no.*

★ Toget Cafe

$$ | **INTERNATIONAL** | With a name that means "The Train," this unique café lets you choose between tables in two converted train carriages or outside on the platform. For several summers in a row this casual eatery has served some of the best pizzas in the area. **Known for:** great pizza; unusual location; quick and efficient service. $ *Average main: NKr 180* ✉ *A-Feltvegen, Flåm* ☎ *57–63–14–00* ⊕ *visitflam.com/no/restaurants/toget-cafe* ⊘ *Closed Nov.–Mar.*

🛏 Hotels

Flåmsbrygga Hotel

$$$$ | **HOTEL** | With a wooden exterior and peaked roof that makes it look like a chalet—an extremely large chalet—this handsome lodging makes you feel right at home in no time. **Pros:** All rooms have views; delicious breakfast; central location. **Cons:** not all views are the same; very expensive rates; books up fast. $ *Rooms from: NKr 2600* ✉ *A-Feltvegen 25, Flåm* ☎ *57–63–20–50* ⊕ *flamsbrygga. no* ⇄ *41 rooms* ⊙| *No meals.*

Fretheim Hotel

$$$$ | **HOTEL** | One of western Norway's most beautiful hotels, the Fretheim has a classic, timeless look thanks to its whitewashed facade topped with a tower. **Pros:** superb location; excellent food; long history. **Cons:** not all the rooms have fjord views; expensive rates; simple decor in some rooms. $ *Rooms from: NKr 2000* ✉ *Nedre Fretheimsvegen, Flåm* ☎ *57–63–63–00* ⊕ *fretheimhotel.no/en* ⇄ *122 rooms* ⊙| *Free breakfast.*

🏃 Activities

BOATING

Fjord Cruise Nærøyfjord

BOATING | These ships have plenty of glass, ensuring that no matter the temperature you get great views of the water and the mountains on either side. Taking between 1½ and 2½ hours, depending on which vessel you choose, the journey takes you through the Nærøfjord, designated a UNESCO World Heritage Site. ✉ *Fjord Cruise Nærøyfjord, Flåm Pier, Flåm* ☎ *57–63–14–00* ⊕ *visitflam.com.*

FjordSafari

BOATING | **FAMILY** | Zoom past the slower fjord cruises on a 12-person boat, with the pilot also serving as your personal guide. This is a great way to get closer to nature, and is a truly unique experience. ✉ *Inner Harbour Flåm Center, Flåm* ✥ *Next to Pier 1* ☎ *57–63–33–23* 🌐 *fjordsafari.com.*

Myrdal

47 minutes from Flåm via the Flåm Railway, 47 minutes from Voss by train.

While there used to be a small mountain village here, few people actually lives in Myrdal today. This train station along the Oslo-Bergen Railway is where you connect to the Flåm Railway. It's also starting point for anyone wanting to hike the Flåm Valley.

GETTING HERE AND AROUND

Express trains between Oslo and Bergen stop in Myrdal several times a day, connecting to the Flåm Railway. By foot, Myrdal is accessible from Flåm via the Myrdalssvingane, a series of hairpin turns down the mountainside.

Sights

Myrdalssvingane

TRAIL | This impressive series of 21 hairpin turns takes you from Myrdal to Flåm. It's popular among hikers and cyclists, who are rewarded with spectacular views of the Kjosfossen Waterfall. Most of the trail is made up of gravel and rocks. To get to the trailhead, follow the train tracks out of Myrdal.

Restaurants

Rallarrosa Mountain Cheeses

$$ | **CAFÉ** | Rallarrosa is located at the end of the Flåm zipline, and is a great place for a bite after your adrenaline-infused trip. Those hiking or cycling the Flåm Valley will also pass Rallarrosa during their journey. **Known for:** goats roaming freely outside the fence; waffles with homemade goat cheese; traditional cheese from unpasteurized goat milk. [$] *Average main: NKr 150* ✉ *Rallarrosa Stølsysteri* ✥ *Located a 2-km (1-mile) walk from Myrdal* ☎ *48–20–95–20* 🌐 *rallarrosa.no* ⏲ *Closed in the low season.*

Hotels

Vatnahalsen Hotel

$$$ | **HOTEL** | Along the Flåm Railway, this lodging feels like a proper alpine resort (think antlers on the wall, wooden benches for seating, and lots of colorful blankets). **Pros:** mountain views; cozy and warm atmosphere; beautiful fireplaces. **Cons:** very simple furnishings; cold rooms in the winter; needs some refurbishing. [$] *Rooms from: NKr 1900* ✉ *Vatnahalsen Hotel, Aurland* ☎ *57–63–75–10* 🌐 *vatnahalsen.no* 🛏 *40 rooms* 🍴 *No meals.*

Fjærland

54 km (34 miles) northwest of Solvorn.

Fjærland is known for its proximity to the Jostedal Glacier, as well as its beautiful green fjord. The color is due to the melting glaciers nearby, and it gives the water a serene look you won't find anywhere else.

GETTING HERE AND AROUND

From Olden it's 62 km (37 miles) south to Skei, at the base of Lake Jølster, where Route 5 goes under the glacier for more than 6 km (4 miles) of the journey to Fjærland. In the summer months there are express boats running from Flåm and Balestrand to Fjærland, in addition to a "glacier bus" traveling from Fjærland to the Jostedal Glacier.

A river running through the Jostedal Glacier, the centerpiece of sprawling Jostedalsbreen Glacier National Park.

Sights

Fjærland Kyrkje (*Fjærland Church*)
RELIGIOUS SITE | This beautiful wooden church, painted a deep shade of red, dates back to 1861. It's a popular photo stop because of the snow-covered mountain peaks in the background. ✉ *Mundalsvegen 6, Mundal.*

Jostedal Glacier
SCENIC DRIVE | Covering the mountains between the Sognefjord and Nordfjord, Jostedal Glacier is the largest in Europe. Unlike many around the world, it has actually grown in recent years due to increased snowfall. There are about 100 known routes for crossing Jostedal Glacier: if you want to hike it, you must have a qualified guide. Contact the Jostedalsbreen Glacier National Park Center. Getting to Jostedalsbreen Glacier is easiest by car: from Solvorn, head north on Route 55 to Route 604. Glacier Express buses run in the summer months. ✉ *Breheimssenteret* ☎ *57–68–32–50* 🌐 *jostedal.com* 🕒 *Glacier Centre closed Oct.–Apr.*

★ **Norsk Bremuseum** (*Norwegian Glacier Museum*)
MUSEUM | One of Norway's most innovative museums, the Norsk Bremuseum lets you study glaciers up close by conducting experiments with thousand-year-old glacial ice. Take the time to watch Ivo Caprino's unforgettable film of the Jostedal Glacier. ✉ *Fjærlandsfjorden 13, Mundal* ☎ *57–63–32–88* 🌐 *bre.museum.no* 🎫 *NKr 130* 🕒 *Closed Nov.–Mar.*

Restaurants

Mikkel
$ | **CAFÉ** | **FAMILY** | In the same building as Hotel Mundal, this café serves light snacks throughout the day. It has a charming interior, including an interesting map of routes through the area. **Known for:** homemade soups; great place to stock up on snacks; simple yet charming decor. [$] *Average main: NKr 90* ✉ *Hotel*

Mundal, Fv 152, Mundal ☎ *91–90–99–90* 🌐 *hotelmundal.no/no/mat.*

Kaffistova

$ | **NORWEGIAN** | **FAMILY** | Part of the Norwegian Book Town, Kaffistova draws travelers from all over the world who want to grab a coffee and a light bite while having a read. **Known for:** a favorite of book lovers; rustic charm; great coffee. [$] *Average main: NKr 60* ✉ *Den norske bokbyen, Fv 152* ✥ *Across the street from the tourist information* ☎ *57–69–22–10* 🌐 *bokbyen.no* ⏲ *Closed Oct.–May.*

Hotels

Fjærland Fjordstove

$$$ | **HOTEL** | Sitting beside the fjord, this charming boutique hotel is a little like stepping back in time. **Pros:** historic building; the best service; unique rooms. **Cons:** no elevator; very narrow stairs; simple furnishings. [$] *Rooms from: NKr 1800* ✉ *Fjærland Fjordstove, Fv152, Mundal* ☎ *41–00–02–00* 🌐 *fjaerlandhotel.com* ⏲ *Closed Oct.–Mar.* 🛏 *14 rooms* 🍴 *Free breakfast.*

Mundal Hotel

$$$ | **HOTEL** | Artists, mountaineers, and travelers first began coming to this region in the late 1800s, many of them destined for this majestic yellow-and-white hotel. **Pros:** beautiful historic building; lovingly restored; great location on the fjord. **Cons:** some bathrooms are dated; restaurant fills up with large groups; books up fast. [$] *Rooms from: NKr 1900* ✉ *Hotel Mundal, Fv 152, Mundal* ☎ *91–90–99–90* 🌐 *hotelmundal.no* 🛏 *35 rooms* 🍴 *No meals.*

Shopping

★ **Den Norske Bokbyen**

ANTIQUES/COLLECTIBLES | Even if you can't read Norwegian, you may still be fascinated by Den Norske Bokbyen. If you look around, you may find some titles in English. In the warmer months, Norwegian Book Town has 150,000 used books, magazines, and records for sale in buildings around town, and even in little huts along the fjord. ✉ *Den Norske Bokbyen, Fv 152* ☎ *57–69–22–10* 🌐 *bokbyen.no.*

Loen

6 km (4 miles) north of Olden.

Thanks to its location near the Briksdal Glacier, Loen is a short drive from some of Norway's most spectacular hikes. It also has an unbeatable location on the eastern edge of the fjord.

GETTING HERE AND AROUND

Loen is less than a 10-minute drive from Olden along Route 60.

Sights

★ **Loen Skylift**

VIEWPOINT | This cable car whisks you to the top of Hoven Mountain, offering spectacular views of the fjord. Some people prefer to take the cable car up and walk back down the mountain. At the top there is a viewpoint and a restaurant. ✉ *Loen Skylift, Fv 60, Loen* ☎ *57–87–59–00* 🌐 *loenskylift.com* 🎫 *NKr 520* ⏲ *Closed Mon.–Thurs. Nov. and Jan.*

Lovatnet

BODY OF WATER | This beautiful lake is worth a visit for the photo ops alone. Some say it's the most beautiful lake in Norway, with its brilliant green color coming from the melting glacier water. ✉ *Lovatnet, Fv 723.*

Restaurants

Kjenndalstova

$$ | **NORWEGIAN** | This region's best-kept secret, this little red house perched at the water's edge serves up delicious traditional dishes. Close to a pristine glacier, towering mountains, cascading waterfalls, and a shimmering lake, the

scenery makes a visit to this laid-back eatery well worthwhile. **Known for:** fresh trout; homemade dishes; lovely views. [$] *Average main: NKr 220* ✉ *Kjenndalstova, Hogrenning, Loen* ☎ *91–84–87–67* 🌐 *kjenndalstova.no* ⏲ *Closed Sept.–Apr.*

★ **Hoven Restaurant**
$$$ | **SCANDINAVIAN** | At the top of Loen Skylift, this strikingly modern restaurant is perched off the edge of a cliff. One one side of the dining room is an entire wall of glass, so every table has a spectacular view. **Known for:** delicious traditional foods; a grill is open for summer lunches; rooftop café serves light fare. [$] *Average main: NKr 255* ✉ *Hoven Restaurant* ☎ *57–87–59–00* 🌐 *loenskylift.com* ⏲ *Closed Mon.–Thurs. Nov. and Jan.*

Hotels

Hotel Alexandra
$$$$ | **HOTEL** | Originally built in 1884, this longtime favorite has been transformed into a modern luxury hotel made of stone and oak. **Pros:** relaxing spa area; beautiful grounds; views are astounding. **Cons:** very expensive rates; pool can get crowded; affordable rooms book up early. [$] *Rooms from: NKr 3500* ✉ *Loen* ☎ *57–87–50–00* 🌐 *alexandra.no* 🛏 *343 rooms* 🍴 *No meals.*

Geiranger

85 km (52½ miles) southwest of Åndalsnes, 86 km (53 miles) northeast of Loen, 75 minutes by ferry east of Hellesylt.

The village of Geiranger, at the end of the fjord, is home to fewer than 300 year-round residents, but in spring and summer its population swells to 5,000 due to visitors traveling here to see the famous Geirangerfjord. In winter, snow on the mountain roads makes the village isolated.

GETTING HERE AND AROUND

The best way to take in the area's spectacular scenery is to travel by boat or ferry. The ferry between Geiranger and Hellesylt runs frequently in summer and offers stupendous views of Geirangerfjord's mighty waterfalls.

By car, the most scenic route to Geiranger from Åndalsnes is the two-hour drive along Route 63 over Trollstigen (Troll's Ladder). After that, the Ørneveien (Eagles' Road) to Geiranger, which has 11 hairpin turns, leads to the fjord.

TOURS

★ **eMobility**
TOUR—SIGHT | A fun way of exploring the area, eMobility lets you take small electric vehicles around preset routes with GPS to guide you. Each car has (just enough) space for two people. ✉ *Geirangervegen 2, Geirangerfjord* ☎ *45–50–02–22* 🌐 *emobgeiranger.no.*

Sights

Dalsnibba
VIEWPOINT | Europe's highest roadside viewpoint, Dalsnibba lets you look straight down at the village of Geiranger, as well as the famous Geirangerfjord. ✉ *Dalsnibba Utsiktspunkt, Nibbevegen* ✣ *Follow Nibbevegen from Geiranger for about 30 mins* ☎ *45–48–13–01* 🌐 *dalsnibba.no.*

Geiranger Kyrkje (*Geiranger Church*)
RELIGIOUS SITE | This church is interesting (and quite peculiar) because of its octagonal shape. Designed by architect Hans Klipe, the wooden church dating from 1842 is the third to have stood on this spot. It's especially beautiful because of the backdrop of the fjords. ✉ *Geiranger Kirke, Geirangerfjord.*

★ **Norsk Fjordsenter** (*Norwegian Fjord Centre*)
COLLEGE | An invaluable introduction to the Geirangerfjord UNESCO World Heritage Site, this excellent contemporary

museum expounds on the area's natural and cultural history, its flora and fauna, and latest technologies effecting the environment, from hydroelectric power to landslide control. Walk through the old farm buildings and learn about the old villages of the Geiranger region. Multimedia exhibits, a café, and bookshop make this a fun and interesting hour for the whole family. ✉ *Gjørvahaugen 35, Geiranger* ☎ *70–26–38–10* 🌐 *www.fjordsenter.com* 🎫 *NKr 130.*

Flydalsjuvet

VIEWPOINT | One of the best-known photo ops in Norway, this dramatic mountain plateau has two viewing platforms that put you high above Geiranger. The breathtaking views from Flydalsjuvet are well worth the trip. ✉ *Flydalsjuvet, Geirangerfjord* ✣ *Drive approximately 4 km (2½ miles) from center of Geiranger, toward Grotli* ☎ *70–26–30–09* 🌐 *www.visitnorway.com/listings/flydalsjuvet/5904.*

Ørnesvingen

VIEWPOINT | At the end of a dramatic route with 11 hairpin turns called the Ørnevegen, or Eagle Road, Ørnesvingen gives you breathtaking views of Geiranger. One of the first viewpoints in the area, it's still one of the most impressive. ✉ *Fv 63 27, Geirangerfjord* ☎ *70–26–30–99.*

🍴 Restaurants

★ Brasserie Posten

$$$ | **MODERN EUROPEAN** | Being one of the best restaurants in Geiranger may not seem such a feat (there's only a handful), but this place distinguishes itself with a stunning fjordside setting and excellent, no-nonsense cuisine that capitalizes on the area's abundant fresh, local seafood, artisanal cheeses, wild game, and produce, not to mention a huge selection of local beers. **Known for:** lovely terrace for summertime dining; great view of the fjord; central location. [$] *Average main: NKr 300* ✉ *Geirangervegen 4, Geiranger* ☎ *70–26–13–06* 🌐 *brasserieposten.no* 🕓 *Closed Nov.–Mar.*

★ Olebuda and Cafe Ole

$$$ | **MODERN EUROPEAN** | In a picturesque white clapboard house that was Geiranger's first grocery store, this restaurant is a popular choice for sophisticated, modern fare. A bright, cozy dining room on the second floor focuses on small plates with an emphasis on local veggies, seafood, and meats: wild poached salmon with parsley butter, scallops, and cauliflower purée; venison medallions with bacon and buttered beets. **Known for:** downstairs café is popular with families; homemade desserts; good coffee and pastries. [$] *Average main: NKr 325* ✉ *Gjørvahaugen, Geiranger* ☎ *70–26–32–30* 🌐 *olebuda.no* 🕓 *Restaurant closed Sept.–May. Café closed Oct.–Apr.*

Restaurant Julie

$$ | **NORWEGIAN** | If you are looking for a friendly atmosphere and a menu based on regional favorites, this is the restaurant for you. Expect original dishes with a traditional touch and great views of the Geirangerfjord. **Known for:** excellent brasserie menu; waterfront views; laidback atmosphere. [$] *Average main: NKr 230* ✉ *Hotel Union, Geirangervegen 101, Geiranger* ☎ *70–26–83–00* 🌐 *hotelunion.no.*

🛏 Hotels

Grande Fjord Hotel

$$$$ | **HOTEL** | **FAMILY** | The hotel's majestic setting on the cliffs overlooking the Geiranger fjord assures stunning views from almost every room. **Pros:** good hiking on the grounds; free coffee, tea, and hot chocolate; free parking. **Cons:** sporadic Wi-Fi; it's a trek up to the hotel; not all rooms face the fjord. [$] *Rooms from: NKr 2200* ✉ *Ørnevegen 200, Geiranger* ☎ *70–26–94–90* 🌐 *grandefjordhotel.com* 🛏 *48 rooms* 🍴 *Free breakfast.*

Hotel Union Geiranger
$$$$ | **HOTEL** | **FAMILY** | The largest hotel in the area, Hotel Union is Geiranger's closest thing to a luxury hotel. **Pros:** excellent buffet breakfast; fun classic car museum; free parking. **Cons:** pool can get crowded in summer; dining room can get uncomfortably packed; some rooms are a bit dated. [$] *Rooms from: NKr 1980* ✉ *Geirangervegen 101, Geiranger* ☎ *70–26–83–00* 🌐 *hotelunion.no* 🛏 *197 rooms* 🍴 *Free breakfast.*

Shopping

Geiranger Gallery
ART GALLERIES | Located in a historic school at the heart of Geiranger, the gallery features three floors hung floor-to-ceiling with the work of local artists, artisans, and craftspeople. There's everything from ceramics and glass to paintings and tapestries. ✉ *Maråkvegen 24, Geiranger* ⏲ *Closed Oct.–Apr.*

Activities

BOATING

Fjord Cruise Geiranger
BOATING | This classic car ferry takes you on a one-hour fjord cruise through the Geirangerfjord. Car spaces are limited, especially in the high season, so book in advance. ✉ *Geiranger ferjekai, Geiranger* ✥ *The cruise leaves from the pier in Geiranger* ☎ *57–63–14–00* 🌐 *visitflam.com/no/activities/fjord-cruise-geirangerfjord.*

★ **Geirangerfjord Safari**
BOATING | This fast-paced boat tour allows you to get closer to the famous waterfalls of the Geirangerfjord than with any other tour. The pilot is also your guide on this adventure, and it is fun and thrilling to speed along the fjord. ✉ *Geiranger Fjordservice, Fv 63, Geiranger* ✥ *Tours meet at tourist information office in Geiranger* ☎ *70–26–30–07* 🌐 *geirangerfjord.no.*

Åndalsnes

105 km (53 miles) northwest of Dombås.

Novelist Jo Nesbø's book *The Bat* says that when God created the world, he started with Åndalsnes. He spent so long crafting the scenery that he had to rush everything else in order to finish by Sunday. Åndalsnes truly is a beautiful area, nicknamed "the Mountain Peak Capital" by Norwegians. Here you'll find dramatic, snow-covered behemoths that will take your breath away.

Åndalsnes is the last stop on the railway, making it a great gateway to fjord country. Here you'll also find the Trollstigen (Troll Ladder), a serpentine roadway through the mountains, and the Trollveggen (Troll Wall), Europe's highest vertical rock face and the birthplace of rock climbing in Scandinavia.

GETTING HERE AND AROUND

Molde Airport is a 90-minute drive from Åndalsnes and has daily flights from Oslo, Bergen, and Trondheim. There are also buses running daily from Bergen and Trondheim to Åndalsnes. The Raumabanen train gets you from Oslo to Åndalsnes in approximately 5 1/2 hours.

If you're driving to Åndalsnes, follow E136 through Romsdalen Valley.

Sights

Trollstigen
SCENIC DRIVE | Norway's most popular scenic drive is in Åndalsnes. Starting in 1916, Trollstigen took 100 men 20 summers to build, and they constantly struggled against the forces of rock and water. Often described as a masterpiece of construction, the road snakes its way through 11 hairpin curves up the mountain to the peaks named Bispen (the Bishop), Kongen (the King), and Dronningen (the Queen). The road is only open in summer. ✉ *Trollstigen, Åndalsnes.*

★ **Norsk Tindemuseum** (*The Norwegian Mountaineering Museum*)
MUSEUM | One of Norway's most famous mountaineers, Arne Randers Heen (1905–91), and his wife, Bodil Roland, founded this fascinating museum dedicated to mountain climbing. Displays of Heen's equipment and descriptions of his many triumphs are among the highlights here. The mountain nearest to his heart was Romsdalshorn, rising 5,101 feet into the air. He climbed that mountain 233 times, the last time when he was 85. He was the first to reach the top of several other mountains in northern Norway. ✉ *Norsk Tindemuseum, Havnegata 2, Åndalsnes* ☎ *73–60–45–57* 🌐 *tindemuseet.no* 🎟 *NKr 160.*

🍴 Restaurants

Trollstigen Kafe
$ | **CAFÉ** | After navigating the hairpin turns of the Trollstigen, reward yourself with a stop at this café. Here you can expect an exciting menu of local dishes and spectacular views of road you just conquered. **Known for:** wide-open views; a variety of quick bites; next to a shop where you can stock up on supplies. [$] *Average main: NKr 120* ✉ *Trollstigen, Åndalsnes* 🌐 *trollstigen.no.*

🛏 Hotels

Grand Hotel Bellevue
$$$ | **HOTEL** | Travelers often begin their exploration of the region by basing themselves at this handsome hotel in the center of Åndalsnes. **Pros:** bright and beautiful rooms; close location to Trollstigen; great on-site restaurant. **Cons:** expensive rates; small lobby; so-so breakfast. [$] *Rooms from: NKr 1695* ✉ *Åndalgata 5, Åndalsnes* ☎ *71–22–75–00* 🌐 *grandhotel.no* 🛏 *86 rooms* 🍽 *Free breakfast.*

Ålesund

116 km (72 miles) west of Åndalsnes.

On three islands and between two brilliant blue fjords lies Ålesund, one of Norway's largest harbors for exporting dried and fresh fish. About two-thirds of its 1,040 wooden houses were destroyed by a fire in 1904. In the rush to shelter 10,000 people, Germany's Kaiser Wilhelm II, who often vacationed here, led a swift rebuilding that married art nouveau design with Viking flourishes. Winding streets are crammed with buildings topped with turrets, spires, gables, dragon heads, and curlicues. Today it's considered one of the few art nouveau cities in the world. Inquire at the tourism office for one of the insightful walking tours.

GETTING HERE AND AROUND

Vigra Airport is 15 km (9 miles) from the center of town. An airport bus drops you in town in 25 minutes. Buses are scheduled according to flights, leaving the airport about 10 minutes after all arrivals. SAS has nonstop flights to Ålesund from Oslo, Bergen, Trondheim, Stavanger, and several cities in Europe. Low-cost airlines Norwegian and WizzAir fly to Ålesund from Oslo, Bergen, Trondheim, London, and other European cities. KLM flies from Amsterdam.

In addition to regular ferries to nearby islands, the Hurtigruten and other boats connect Ålesund with other points along the coast. Excursions by boat can be booked through the tourist office.

From Oslo to Ålesund it's 550 km (342 miles) on Route E6 to Dombås and then E136 through Åndalsnes to Ålesund. From Bergen via the E39 it's a 390-km (242-mile) drive. It's open most of the year, and involves two ferry crossings and a few toll roads.

Spread across three islands, Ålesund is one of the region's most beautiful cities.

CONTACTS Destinasjon Ålesund og Sunnmøre. (*Destination Ålesund and Sunnmøre*) ⊠ *Skateflukaia, Ålesund* ☎ *70–16–34–30* ⊕ *visitalesund.com.* **Ålesund Taxi.** ☎ *70–10–30–00* ⊕ *alesund-taxi.no.*

👁 Sights

Ålesunds Museum

MUSEUM | This gem of a museum highlights the city's past, including the great fire of 1904 and the dangerous escape route that the Norwegian Resistance established in World War II. Handicrafts on display are done in the folk-art style of the area. You can also visit the art nouveau room and learn more about the town's unique architecture. ⊠ *Rasmus Rønnebergs gt. 16, Ålesund* ☎ *70–16–48–42* ⊕ *aalesunds.museum.no* 🎫 *NKr 60.*

Alnes Fyr (*Alnes Lighthouse*)

LOCAL INTEREST | This red-and-white lighthouse has a beautiful location on the Norwegian coastline, and from this vantage point you can see miles and miles of ocean. Alnes Fyr also has a gallery, a café that's open throughout the year, and an exhibition about the lighthouse and its history. ⊠ *Alnesgard, Godøya, Ålesund* ☎ *70–18–50–90* ⊕ *alnesfyr.no* 🎫 *Nkr 25.*

Atlanterhavsparken (*Atlantic Sea Park*)

ZOO | **FAMILY** | Teeming with aquatic life, this is one of Scandinavia's largest aquariums. Right on the ocean, 3 km (2 miles) west of town, the park emphasizes aquatic animals of the North Atlantic, including anglers, octopus, and lobster. The Humboldt penguins are popular with children. After your visit, have a picnic, hike, or take a refreshing swim at the adjoining Tueneset Park. To get here, take the Aquarium Bus (marked "Akvariebussen") from St. Olav's Plass between April and October. ⊠ *Tueneset, Ålesund* ☎ *70–10–70–60* ⊕ *atlanterhavsparken.no* 🎫 *NKr 195.*

Fiskerimuseet (*Fisheries Museum*)

MUSEUM | Learn about the people who've always been the backbone of Ålesund's fishing industry, including those who remained on shore to process the daily catch. The Fisheries Museum has several interesting exhibits, including one tracing the history of *tran* (cod liver oil), one of the many products that came from these parts. ⊠ *Molovegen 10, Ålesund* ☎ *70–16–48–42* ⊕ *sunnmore.museum. no/musea/fiskerimuseet* 🎟 *NKr 60* ☾ *Closed Sept.–Apr.*

Jugendstilsenteret (*Art Nouveau Center*)
MUSEUM | Housed in an eye-catching building topped by a graceful turret—it opened as Swan Pharmacy in 1907—the Jugendstilsenteret tells the story of how Ålesund became the art nouveau capital of the country. After the great fire of 1904 left a huge swath of the population homeless, city planners had to rebuild quickly. Europe happened to be in the middle of a love affair with art nouveau architecture, so the city ended up with a blend of this ornate style with the occasional Viking flourish. The KUBE Art Museum is part of the same complex. ⊠ *Apotekergata 16, Ålesund* ☎ *70–10–49–70* ⊕ *jugendstilsenteret.no* 🎟 *NKr 70, includes Kube Art Museum.*

★ **Kniven**
VIEWPOINT | For a splendid view of the city, one that absolutely glitters at night, take this scenic drive up the city's mountain. Most photos you've seen of Ålesund have been taken from this vantage point. ⊠ *Fjellstua Aksla, Ålesund.*

KUBE Art Museum
MUSEUM | **FAMILY** | In a branch of Norges Bank dating from 1906, this museum aims to promote the work of contemporary Norwegian artists. It is part of the complex that holds the Jugendstilsenteret. ⊠ *Apotekergata 16, Ålesund* ☎ *70–10–49–70* ⊕ *jugendstilsenteret.no* 🎟 *NKr 70, includes the Jugendstilsenteret.*

Sunnmøre Museum
MUSEUM VILLAGE | **FAMILY** | This open-air museum focuses on the traditions and history of the people who make

Off the Beaten Path ◉

Runde Perhaps Norway's most famous "bird rock"—it also happens to be one of the largest in Europe—Runde is the breeding ground for some 200 species, including puffins, gannets, and cormorants. The region's wildlife managers maintain many observation posts here. It can get quite windy during a hike, so dress accordingly. ⊠ *Ålesund* ☎ *70–16–34–30* ⊕ *www. visitalesund-geiranger.com/en/ The-bird-island-Runde.*

their home on the Norwegian coast. A five-minute drive from Ålesund, it's spread over 50 acres and consists of 55 well-kept buildings ranging from cow sheds to schoolhouses, giving insight into people's lives in this region. ⊠ *Museumsvegen 1, Ålesund* ☎ *70–16–48–70* ⊕ *sunnmore.museum.no/musea/sunnmoere-museum* 🎟 *NKr 80* ☾ *Closed Sat. Oct.–Apr.*

🍴 **Restaurants**

Egon Ålesund
$$ | **INTERNATIONAL** | **FAMILY** | The atmosphere is casual and relaxed, and perhaps a little loud at peak hours, but you won't find a better spot for a quick meal. There are wood beams, exposed brick walls, and cozy booths with rough-hewn furnishings. **Known for:** you order at the bar; great selection of starters; several vegetarian options. 💲 *Average main: NKr 210* ⊠ *Løvenvoldgt. 8, Ålesund* ☎ *70–15–78–15* ⊕ *egon.no.*

Fjellstua
$$$ | **NORWEGIAN** | **FAMILY** | This mountaintop restaurant covered with a dramatic glass canopy has tremendous views over the surrounding peaks, islands,

and fjords. It serves a mix of national and international dishes, and on the menu might be Norwegian salt cod or baked salmon. **Known for:** spectacular city views; wide variety of options; great service. [$] *Average main: NKr 300* ⊠ *Fjellstua Aksla, Ålesund* ☎ *70–10–74–00* ⊕ *fjellstua.no.*

Hotels

Thon Hotel Ålesund

$$ | **HOTEL** | **FAMILY** | This gleaming white hotel is known for its homey and casual atmosphere, with rooms that feel much more cozy than your usual chain offerings. **Pros:** lovely indoor pool; great breakfast; smart bathrooms. **Cons:** evening buffet not always available in low season; welcomes pets, so it's not for allergy sufferers; a business hotel feel. [$] *Rooms from: NKr 900* ⊠ *Kongensgate 27, Ålesund* ☎ *70–15–77–00* ⊕ *thonhotels.no/hoteller/norge/alesund/thon-hotel-alesund* ↝ *106 rooms* ⫶◯⫶ *Free breakfast.*

Kristiansund

151 km (94 miles) northeast of Ålesund, 198 km (123 miles) southwest of Tondheim.

By the 19th century, timber and *klippfisk* (fish salted and dried in the sun on slabs of rock) had made Kristiansund one of Norway's biggest ports. Today Kristiansund's lively harbor, Vågen, has a wonderful collection of historic boats. During World War II almost everything in town was destroyed except for Vågen, where some well-preserved buildings remain.

GETTING HERE AND AROUND

Kristiansund is one of the ports of call for the Hurtigruten, making this a perfect place to arrive by boat. The city's domestic airport has several daily flights from Oslo and Bergen.

This is a long drive from the country's larger cities: eight hours from Oslo, 10 from Bergen. There are buses from most places around the country (though not very frequently).

◉ Sights

★ Grip Stavkyrkje (*Grip Stave Church*)

RELIGIOUS SITE | The island of Grip is a delight, especially the little red stave church that stands at the island's highest point and dates to 1470. The fishing community itself was mostly abandoned after World War II, but locals return in summer, along with many tourists. Ferries run from Kristiansund at least once a day between June and August. If the church is closed, locals can get the key. ⊠ *Grip* ☎ *70–23–88–00.*

Kvalvik Fort

MILITARY SITE | One of Kristiansund's most beaten hiking paths is to this well-preserved World War II submarine base and fortress built by German forces. At its height, it housed 5,000 soldiers, who left several bunkers, a battery of artillery guns, and a submarine, all of which are visitable today. Tours and exhibits tell the fort's story. The pristine setting among wooded seaside hills is the second highlight and attracts many locals for fishing and barbecues. ⊠ *Kristiansund* ⊹ *13 km (8 miles) east of Kristiansund.*

★ Sundbåten

TRANSPORTATION SITE (AIRPORT/BUS/FERRY/ TRAIN) | The ferry service to connect Kristiansund's four main islands was established in 1876 and has not stopped since, making it the world's oldest public transportation in continuous use. Ferries depart two or three times per hour and provide visitors with a nice overview of the city's layout as well as views of the region's distinctive architecture, whose bright colors reflect charmingly in the water. A round-trip takes 17 minutes. ⊠ *Kirkelandet Sundbåtkai, Kristiansund* ☎ *92–85–17–44* ⊕ *sundbaten.no* ⫸ *NKr 40.*

🍴 Restaurants

Bryggekanten Restaurant/Brasserie og Bache Bar
$$$ | NORWEGIAN | Today's catch is all over the menu—crayfish, klippfisk, and grilled monkfish, to name a few—at this casual eatery. The seemingly mismatched, umbrella-shaped roof atop this rectangular blue waterfront restaurant offers a lesson in Norwegian history, culture, and cuisine: it's where locals of yesteryear dried fish by night. **Known for:** waterside patio; freshest fish available; great views of the harbor. $ *Average main: NKr 345* ⊠ *Storkaia 1, Kristiansund* ☎ *71–67–61–60* ⊕ *fireb.no* ☉ *Closed Sun. and Mon.*

Sjøstjerna
$$$ | NORWEGIAN | Another contender for the best fish restaurant crown in Kristiansund, Sjøstjerna matches its zeal for klippfisk with major skills in hospitality to create an exceedingly warm and convivial environment. In addition to intimacy of the relatively small space, the vast assortment of Norwegian folk art and fishing-related artifacts hanging from the walls adds a refreshing and well-designed layer of intrigue on an otherwise typical menu of bacalao, *blandaball* dumplings, and klippfisk. **Known for:** best bacalao in the area; live piano music in the bar; Norwegian dishes with international flair. $ *Average main: NKr 300* ⊠ *Skolegata 8, Kristiansund* ☎ *71–67–87–78* ⊕ *sjostjerna.no* ☉ *Closed Sun. No lunch.*

🛏 Hotels

Quality Hotel Grand Kristiansund
$$$ | HOTEL | This downtown hotel has modern, unfussy rooms and is well placed for local attractions, shopping, and the Caroline Cinema and Conference Center, just around the corner. **Pros:** good location; decent breakfast choices; free Wi-Fi. **Cons:** public areas full of convention attendees; cash not accepted; no in-room safes. $ *Rooms from: NKr 1700* ⊠ *Bernstorffstredet 1, Kristiansund* ☎ *71–57–13–00* ⊕ *nordic-choicehotels.no/hotell/norge/kristiansund/quality-hotel-grand-kristiansund* 🛏 *158 rooms* ❀ *Free breakfast.*

Thon Hotel Kristiansund
$$$ | HOTEL | On the north edge of Innlandet Island, this hotel is one of the region's best, with views of the harbor that receive so much praise for its natural beauty that it keeps people awake at night. **Pros:** amazing views from most rooms; popular restaurant; private beach. **Cons:** small rooms; outside city center; no gym. $ *Rooms from: NKr 1300* ⊠ *Fiskergata 12, Kristiansund* ☎ *71–57–30–00* ⊕ *thonhotels.no/hoteller/norge/kristiansund/thon-hotel-kristiansund* 🛏 *98 rooms* ❀ *Free breakfast.*

🎭 Performing Arts

Kristiansund Opera
OPERA | Kristiansund is home to Norway's oldest opera house. There are performances throughout the year, both by local troupes and visiting entertainers. ⊠ *Kong Olav V's gt. 1, Kristiansund* ☎ *71–58–99–60* ⊕ *oik.no.*

🛍 Shopping

Klippfiskbutikken
FOOD/CANDY | Pay tribute to and stock up on the mighty klippfisk at this shop, where proprietor Knut Garshol carries on the family business begun by his grandfather. A visit is also an education in the types of cod used and methods of preparation. ⊠ *Kaibakken 2, Kristiansund* ☎ *71–67–12–64* ⊕ *klippfiskbutikken.no.*

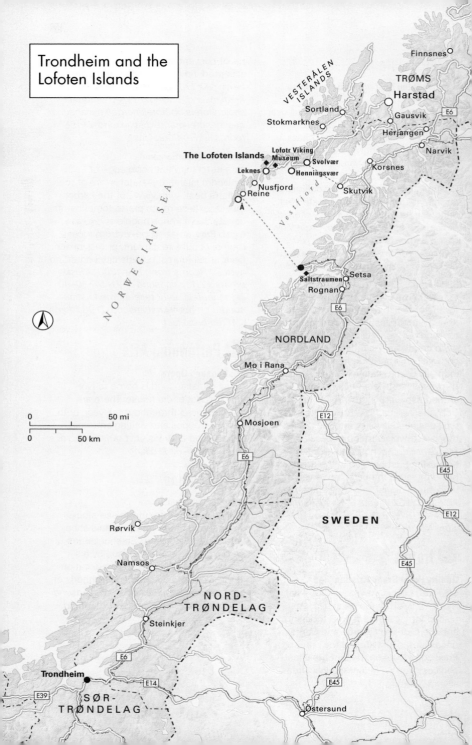

Trondheim and the Lofoten Islands

Finnsnes

TRØMS

Harstad

VESTERÅLEN ISLANDS

Sortland

Gausvik

Stokmarknes

Herjangen

The Lofoten Islands

Lofotr Viking Museum

Narvik

Leknes

Svolvær

Korsnes

Nusfjord

Henningsvær

Reine

Skutvik

Å

Vestfjord

N O R W E G I A N   S E A

Saltstraumen

Setsa

Rognan

E6

NORDLAND

Mo i Rana

0   50 mi

0   50 km

E12

Mosjoen

E6

E45

RØrvik

E12

SWEDEN

Namsos

E45

NORD-
TRØNDELAG

Steinkjer

E6

Trondheim

E14

SØR-
TRØNDELAG

E45

E39

Østersund

Trondheim

494 km (307 miles) north of Oslo, 657 km (408 miles) northeast of Bergen.

One of Scandinavia's oldest cities, Trondheim was the first capital of Norway, from 997 to 1380. Founded in 997 by Viking king Olav Tryggvason, it was first named Nidaros (still the name of the cathedral), a composite word referring to the city's location at the mouth of the Nidelva River. Today, it's Central Norway's largest (and Norway's third largest) city. The wide streets of the historic city center remain lined with brightly painted wood houses and striking warehouses. But it's no historic relic: it's also the home to NTNU (Norwegian University of Science and Technology) and is Norway's technological capital.

AIR TRAVEL

There are daily flights from Trondheim to several European cities and numerous flights to other cities in Norway. Trondheim's Værnes Airport is 32 km (21 miles) northeast of the city. SAS, Norwegian, and Widerøe offer connections throughout northern Norway. Widerøe flies to 27 destinations in the region, including Honningsvåg, the country's northernmost airport and the one closest to North Cape.

BOAT AND FERRY TRAVEL

The Hurtigruten (the coastal express boat, which goes to 35 ports from Bergen to Kirkenes) stops at Trondheim. Stops between Trondheim and North Cape include Bodø, Stamsund, and Svolvær (Lofoten Islands), Sortland (Vesterålen Islands), Harstad, Tromsø, Hammerfest, and Honningsvåg.

BUS TRAVEL

The Østerdalekspressen and Lavprisekspressen buses run from Oslo to Trondheim. Buses also connect Bergen and Ålesund with Trondheim. All local Trondheim buses stop at the Munkegata–Dronningens Gate intersection. Some routes end at the bus terminal at Trondheim Sentralstasjon.

CAR TRAVEL

Trondheim is about 494 km (308 miles) from Oslo: a seven- to eight-hour drive. The two alternatives are the E6 through Gudbrandsdalen Valley or Route 3 through Østerdalen Valley. It's 723 km (448 miles) from Trondheim to Bodø on Route E6, which goes all the way to Kirkenes. There are several toll roads in and around Trondheim. As is usual in Norway, you drive through the toll areas. If you're in a rental car, the toll will be charged directly to your credit card.

TRAIN TRAVEL

Dovrebanen has frequent departures daily on the Oslo–Trondheim route. Trains leave from Oslo Central Station (Oslo S) for the seven- to eight-hour journey. Two trains run daily in each direction on the 11-hour route between Trondheim and Bodø, to the north. The Ofotbanen has two departures daily in each direction on the Stockholm–Narvik route, a 21-hour journey.

VISITOR INFORMATION

CONTACTS Visit Trondheim. ✉ *Nordre gt. 11, Trondheim* ☎ *73–80–76–60* ⊕ *visittrondheim.no/en.*

◉ Sights

Erkebispegården (*Archbishop's Palace*)
CASTLE/PALACE | The oldest secular building in Scandinavia, Erkebispegården dates from around 1160. It was the residence of the archbishop until the Reformation in 1537. The Archbishop's Palace Museum has original sculptures from Nidaros Cathedral and archaeological pieces from throughout its history. Within Erkebispegården's inner palace is the Rustkammeret/Resistance Museum, which traces military development from Viking times to the present through displays of uniforms, swords, and daggers.

Perched on stilts, Trondheim's colorful waterfront warehouses make this one of Norway's most distinctive cities.

The dramatic events of World War II get a special emphasis. ■ TIP→ **Opening times for the various museums and wings in the Erkebispegården and for the cathedral vary greatly by season.** ⊠ *Kongsgårdsgt. 1, Trondheim* ☏ *73–89–08–00* ⊕ *www. nidarosdomen.no* ⊠ *NKr 200, includes entry to Nidaros Cathedral* ⊘ *Closed Mon. Sept.–Apr.*

Kristiansten Festning (*Kristiansten Fort*)
MILITARY SITE | Built by J. C. Cicignon after the great fire of 1681, the Kristiansten Fort saved the city from conquest by Sweden in 1718. During World War II, the German occupying forces executed members of the Norwegian Resistance here; there's a plaque in their honor. The fort has spectacular views of the city, the fjord, and the mountains. Some walls are unsecured, so take care when walking, and mind your children. ⊠ *Trondheim* ☏ *815–70–400* ⊕ *www.forsvarsbygg.no/ no/festningene/finn-din-festning/kristian- sten-festning* ⊠ *Free.*

★ **Nidarosdomen** (*Nidaros Cathedral*)
RELIGIOUS SITE | Trondheim's cathedral was built on the grave of King Olav, who formulated a Christian religious code for Norway in 1024. The town quickly became a pilgrimage site for Christians from all over northern Europe, and Olav was canonized in 1164. Construction of Nidarosdomen began in 1070, but the oldest existing parts of the cathedral date from around 1150. It has been ravaged on several occasions by fire and rebuilt each time, generally in a Gothic style. Since the Middle Ages, Norway's kings have been crowned and blessed in the cathedral, and the crown jewels are on display here. Guided tours lasting 45 minutes are offered in English from mid-June to mid-August. ⊠ *Kongsgårdsgt. 2, Trondheim* ☏ *73–89–08–00* ⊕ *www. nidarosdomen.no* ⊠ *NKr 80.*

Ringve Musikkmuseum (*Ringve Music Museum*)
MUSEUM | **FAMILY** | Taking you through the history of musical instruments in Norway and the rest of the world, the brilliant

Ringve Music Museum covers just about every type of music you can imagine. Interactive displays allow you to "play" some of the most famous instruments. After exploring the museum, take the time to explore the beautiful botanical gardens surrounding the museum. The building is over 400 years old. ✉ *Lade alle 60, Trondheim* ☎ *73–87–02–80* 🌐 *www.ringve.no* 🎫 *NKr 130* 🕒 *Closed on Mon. Sept.–May.*

★ **Stiftsgården**
BUILDING | Built in the 1770s, Stiftsgården is now the official royal residence in Trondheim. The architecture and interior are late baroque and highly representative of 18th-century high society's taste. Guided tours—the only way to see the interior—offer insight into the festivities marking the coronations and blessings of the kings in the cathedral. ✉ *Munkegt. 23, Trondheim* ☎ *73–84–28–80 guided tour information* 🌐 *www.nkim.no/stiftsgarden* 🎫 *NKr 110* 🕒 *Closed mid-Aug.–May.*

★ **Sverresborg Trøndelag Folkemuseum**
(*Sverresborg Trondelag Folk Museum*)
HISTORIC SITE | **FAMILY** | Near the ruins of King Sverre's medieval castle is this open-air historical museum that depicts everyday life in Trøndelag during the 18th and 19th centuries. The stave church here, built in the 1170s, is the northernmost preserved church of its type in Norway. In the Old Town you can visit a 1900s dentist's office and an old-fashioned grocery store that sells sweets. In the summer there are farm animals on-site, and a range of activities for children. There's a copy of the main house at Walt Disney World's Epcot in the Norway pavilion. ✉ *Sverresborg allé 13, Trondheim* ☎ *73–89–01–00* 🌐 *www.sverresborg.no* 🎫 *NKr 115* 🕒 *Closed Mon. Sept.–May.*

🍴 Restaurants

Fagn
$$$$ | **NORWEGIAN** | One of the most famous restaurants in Trondheim, Fagn has won international awards for its inventive cuisine that harkens back to the dishes that many Norwegians ate during their childhoods, then takes them in new and unexpected directions. No need to decide among the many interesting flavor combinations: you'll have a front-row seat as the chefs in the open kitchen prepare 10- or 20-course tasting menus. **Known for:** international recognition; Trøndelag's regional cuisine; relaxed atmosphere. [$] *Average main: NKr 1100* ✉ *Ørjaveita 4, Trondheim* ☎ *458–44–996* 🌐 *www.fagn.no/restaurant* 🕒 *Closed Sun. and Mon. No lunch.*

Havfruen
$$$ | **SEAFOOD** | The long-running Mermaid is Trondheim's best known and most stylish fish restaurant, located in one of the colorful historic buildings along the Nidelva River. The interior is surprisingly modern, reminiscent of the New Nordic design you will see across parts of Scandinavia. **Known for:** oysters come highly recommended; knowledgeable food and wine pairings; great views over the harbor. [$] *Average main: NKr 285* ✉ *Kjøpmannsgt. 7, Trondheim* ☎ *73–87–40–70* 🌐 *www.havfruen.no* 🕒 *Closed Sun and Mon. No lunch.*

🛏 Hotels

★ **Britannia Hotel**
$$$$ | **HOTEL** | This was Trondheim's first grand hotel when it opened in 1897, and more than a century later the Britannia remains one of the most luxurious places to stay. **Pros:** endless amenities; fine-dining restaurants; extensive fitness and spa area. **Cons:** free Wi-Fi only in common areas; decor is a little fussy for some; expensive rates. [$] *Rooms from: NKr 2300* ✉ *Dronningensgt. 5, Trondheim*

☎ *73–80–08–00* 🌐 *www.britannia.no* 🛏 *257 rooms* 🍴 *Free breakfast.*

Radisson Blu Royal Garden Hotel
$$ | **HOTEL** | This extravaganza of glass on the Nidelva River is one of Trondheim's largest hotels. **Pros:** stunning architecture; top-notch service; huge buffet breakfast. **Cons:** not for those who want something quaint; parking is extra; air-conditioning sometimes hard to operate. [$] *Rooms from: NKr 1050* ✉ *Kjøpmannsgt. 73, Trondheim* ☎ *73–80–30–00* 🌐 *www.radissonblu.com/en/hotel-trondheim* 🛏 *298 rooms* 🍴 *No meals.*

Bodø

705 km (438 miles) north of Trondheim.

The modern city of Bodø, once an important fishing village, is situated just above the Arctic Circle at the tip of a stunning coastal route where sea eagles soar and the northern lights shimmer in full splendor. In summer, the midnight sun is visible in June and early July and the polar night descends for the last two weeks of December. As the terminus of the Nordlandsbanen railroad and the Hurtigruten coastal ferry, Bodø serves as the gateway to the beautiful Lofoten Islands and the northernmost regions of Norway. The town's position on the sea makes this city the best starting point for nature walks and boat excursions to the coastal bird colonies on the Værøy Islands.

GETTING HERE AND AROUND

Scenic routes to Bodø include the Nordlandsbanen train from Trondheim and the Hurtingruten coastal ferry: both are easy and comfortable ways to traverse some of Norway's most staggeringly beautiful coastline. By car, the Rv 80 links Bodø to the E6, the main road through Norway. You can also take the Rv 17 coastal route. SAS offers several daily flights from Oslo to Bodø (80 min) to the Widerøe STOL airport.

Bodø's tourist office and your hotel are the best resources for information on getting around by bus or rental bicycle. The harbor area is best explored on foot.

VISITOR INFORMATION

CONTACTS Bodø turistinformasjon. (*Visit Bodø*) ✉ *Tollbugt. 13, Bodø* ☎ *75–54–50–80* 🌐 *www.visitbodo.com/en.*

Sights

Nordlandsmuseet (*Nordland Museum*)
MUSEUM | Housed in one of the city's oldest buildings, the Nordland Museum includes a fascinating exhibit on Sámi culture that features a 350-year-old wooden box inscribed with mysterious runes. There's also silver that dates back 1,000 years to the Rønvik era: these English and Arabic coins and jewelry were discovered in 1919. The "Byen vårres" ("Our City") exhibition reveals the history of Bodø. An open-air section has 14 historic buildings and a collection of boats, including the *Anna Karoline af Hopen*, the sole surviving Nordland cargo vessel, or *jekt.* ✉ *Prinsens gt. 116, Bodø* ☎ *75–50–35–00* 🌐 *nordlandsmuseet.no/en/nordlandsmuseet* 🎫 *NKr 70* 🕒 *Closed weekends Sept.–May.*

★ **Norsk Luftfartsmuseum** (*Norwegian Aviation Museum*)
MUSEUM | **FAMILY** | About 15 minutes from the town's center, the massive Norwegian Aviation Museum is housed in a building shaped like a propeller. The high-ceilinged rotunda illustrates "Man's Primeval Dream of Flight." On either side are smaller exhibition halls, one for civilian aviation and the other for military aviation. Here you'll find a Spitfire, a CF-104 Starfighter, a Junkers Ju 88, a U-2 spy plane, and much more. Take a turn on the flight simulators for a glimpse of the controls of an F-16. Climb the control tower for an unforgettable view of the wild landscape. ✉ *Olav V gt., Bodø* ☎ *75–50–78–50* 🌐 *luftfartsmuseum.no/en* 🎫 *NKr 175.*

★ Saltstraumen

VIEWPOINT | Truly magnificent, this 3-km-long (2-mile-long) and 500-foot-wide strait joins the inner fjord basin with the sea. During high tide the volume of water rushing through the narrow sound is so great that powerful whirlpools form. This is one of Norway's legendary maelstroms, and here you can see the strongest one in the world. The rush of water brings an abundance of fish, including cod, saithe, wolffish, and halibut, making this a popular fishing spot. ✉ *Rte. 80–17, Bodø* ✥ *33 km (20 miles) southeast of Bodø.*

Restaurants

★ Bjørk

$$$ | **ITALIAN** | **FAMILY** | This chic, modern café-restaurant is popular for its sunny terrace and straightforward food that always hits the mark—think juicy marinated jumbo shrimp, lobster soup, and a large selection of pizzas served hot from a wood-fired oven. It's an equally good stop for lunch, dinner, or an afternoon coffee with a delicious dessert. **Known for:** satisfying burgers; homemade pasta; popular with locals. [$] *Average main: NKr 300* ✉ *Storgt. 8, Bodø* ☎ *75–52–40–40* 🌐 *www.restaurantbjork.no* 🕒 *No lunch Sun.*

LystPå

$$$$ | **INTERNATIONAL** | An award-winning eatery in the heart of Bodø, LystPå that takes pride in presenting beautifully prepared dishes in an atmosphere that feels anything but pretentious. The signature dish is stockfish, but the wide-ranging menu features everything from scallops to monkfish. **Known for:** 150 wines in the cellar; friendly and relaxed atmosphere; well-prepared seafood. [$] *Average main: NKr 500* ✉ *Torghallen Postboks 417, Trondheim* ☎ *75–52–70–70* 🌐 *lystpa.no* 🕒 *Closed Sun.*

Hotels

★ Clarion Collection Hotel Grand

$$ | **HOTEL** | **FAMILY** | Overlooking the harbor, this centrally located hotel is looking spiffy after a complete renovation. **Pros:** fitness room, sauna, and steam bath; pet-friendly rooms; meals and snacks are included. **Cons:** some rooms can be noisy; some bathrooms are very small; does not accept cash. [$] *Rooms from: NKr 980* ✉ *Storgt. 3, Bodø* ☎ *75–54–61–00* 🌐 *www.nordicchoicehotels.no* 🛏 *100 rooms* 🍴 *Some meals.*

★ Thon Hotel Nordlys

$$ | **HOTEL** | Smack dab in the city center with glorious views of the sunlight reflected on the harbor, this popular Scandinavian chain hotel is a bright, modern lodging with clean, spacious rooms. **Pros:** nice outdoor terrace; friendly staff; free buffet breakfast. **Cons:** parking costs extra; some rooms are cramped; charge for some business amenities. [$] *Rooms from: NKr 900* ✉ *Moloveien 14, Bodø* ☎ *75–53–19–00* 🌐 *www.thonhotels.com/our-hotels/norway/bodo* 🛏 *147 rooms* 🍴 *Free breakfast.*

Activities

BOATING

★ Explore Salten

BOATING | This tour company that takes you on boat trips to destinations like Saltstraumen, the world's largest maelstrom. The whirlpool is at its strongest every six hours, and tours are planned accordingly. Besides safety equipment, cold-weather gear is provided if you are visiting in winter. ✉ *Dronningens gt. 18, Bodø* ☎ *941–77–962* 🌐 *exploresalten.no/Home.*

The Lofoten Islands

Extending out into the ocean north of Bodø are the Lofoten Islands, a 190-km (118-mile) chain of jagged peaks. In summer the farms, fjords, and fishing villages draw caravans of visitors, whereas in winter the coast facing the Arctic Ocean is one of Europe's stormiest. The beaches here are remarkably clear, and travelers may think they have landed in the Caribbean instead of Northern Norway. This is an adventurer's paradise with an abundance of hiking trails, boat trips, and much more. From bustling Henningsvær all the way to the photogenic village of Å, the Lofoten Islands are one of the top destinations in all of Norway.

GETTING HERE AND AROUND

Getting to the Lofoten Islands is simpler than it looks. You can take a ferry from Bodø, fly in from various other parts of Norway, or simply drive. The Islands are served by three airports: Harstad/Narvik, Leknes, and Svolvær. Once you're here, you'll want to rent a car to explore the islands at your leisure.

Henningsvær

One of the most prominent fishing villages in the Lofoten Islands, Henningsvær has a history dating back to 1556. Besides its fame as a charming fishing village, Henningsvær also offers several cafes, restaurants, workshops, and boutiques that will delight tourists. People go to Henningsvær for its quaint charm and cafes, shops, and more.

The nearest airport is Svolvær Helle Airport, reachable by bus or taxi. If you're driving, the E10 takes you most of the way from Svolvær to Henningsvær.

◉ Sights

★ Galleri Lofotens Hus

MUSEUM | One of the best-known museums in the Lofoten Islands, the family-run Galleri Lofotens Hus is home to the largest collection of northern Norwegian artwork from the last century, including renowned painters like Otto Sinding, Gunnar Berg, Even Ulving, Adelsteen Normann, Einar Berger, Ole Juul, and Thorolf Holmboe. Take a load off at the on-site café. ⊠ *Misværveien 18, Henningsvær* ☎ *915–95–083* ⊕ *www.galleri-lofoten.no/nb* 🎫 *NKr 60.*

Heimgårdsbrygga

MUSEUM | Henningsvær is quite possibly the most famous fishing village in the Lofoten Islands, and there's no better place to get a feel for its history than the harbor of Heimgårdsbrygga. It's also one of the most photogenic backdrops in the region, with many of its history structures still intact. ⊠ *Dreyers gt. 71, Henningsvær* ☎ *76–07–11–15* ⊕ *heimgardsbrygga.no/index.html.*

🍴 Restaurants

★ Henningsvær Lysstøperi and Cafe

$ | **CAFÉ** | In the heart of Henningsvær, this charming and delightful café is a favorite destination for both locals and visitors in search of a warming cup of coffee or hot chocolate. The café doubles as an arts-and-crafts store, with a range of lovely items available for sale. **Known for:** freshly baked cinnamon buns; candles and other gifts; cozy atmosphere. Ⓢ *Average main: NKr 100* ⊠ *Gammelveien 2, Henningsvær* ☎ *76-07-70-40.*

🛏 Hotels

Henningsvær Bryggehotell

$$$ | **HOTEL** | **FAMILY** | Renowned for its impeccable customer service, the Henningsvær Bryggehotell has an unbeatable location on the docks over the harbor and is a short walk from all of the main sights

in town. **Pros:** free breakfast; luggage storage; daily housekeeping service. **Cons:** older building a bit stuffy; no elevator; limited parking. $ *Rooms from: NKr 1800 ⊠ Misværveien 18, Henningsvær ☎ 76–07–47–50 ⊕ www.classicnorway. com/hotels/henningsvar-bryggehotell ⤵ 30 rooms* ⊙| *Free breakfast.*

Svolvær

An important fishing village in Northern Norway, Svolvær became a destination for travelers after 19th-century painter Gunnar Berg portrayed the lives of local fishermen. A couple of miles west is the village of Vågar, known for being Northern Norway's oldest settlement.

Svolvær Helle Airport has flights from Bodø and Oslo. Svolvær sits directly on the E10, the main highway running through the Lofoten Islands.

Sights

★ Lofotpils
WINERY/DISTILLERY | A labor of love, this brewery has been supplying the Lofoten Islands with refreshing craft beer since 2014. You can take a tour of the brewery and learn about the fermentation and brewing process. ⊠ *Fiskergata 36, Svolvær ☎ 906–37–383 ⊕ lofotpils.no.*

 Restaurants

Paleo Arctic
$$$$ | NORWEGIAN | Exploring the culinary past of the Lofoten Islands, the kitchen here has gained credibility by using as many local ingredients as possible and employing modern cooking techniques to create spectacular dishes. The menu regularly changes based on what is available that season. **Known for:** great tasting menu; good selection of wines; tasty seasonal vegetables. $ *Average main: NKr 525 ⊠ Thon Hotel Lofoten, Torget,*

Svolvær ☎ 94–86–75–67 ⊕ paleoarctic.no ⊙ Closed Sun.

🛏 Hotels

Svinøya Rorbuer
$$$$ | HOTEL | In the oldest and most atmospheric part of Svolvær Island, this cluster of *rorbuer* (fishermen's cabins) is close to the cod drying on racks and the screaming seagulls. **Pros:** cabins have a secluded feel; airport shuttle available; Wi-Fi and other amenities. **Cons:** breakfast is an extra charge; not all cabin views are the same; roads can get icy in winter. $ *Rooms from: NKr 2000 ⊠ Gunnar Bergs vei 2, Svolvær ☎ 76–06–99–30 ⊕ www. svinoya.no/en ⤵ 38 cabins* ⊙| *No meals.*

🏃 Activities

BOATING
★ Lofoten Explorer
BOATING | FAMILY | One of the most popular tours in the Lofoten Islands is the sea eagle safari offered by Lofoten Explorer. Small boats take you to the narrow and mystical Trollfjorden to see the sea eagles in their native habitat. The company provides proper winter clothing to keep you warm in sub-freezing temperatures. ⊠ *Johan E Paulsens gt. 12 N, Svolvær ☎ 971–52–248 ⊕ www.lofoten-explorer. no/en.*

Leknes

If there's any place in Norway that proves the tourist board's slogan—"Powered by Nature"—it must be Leknes. Set in the center of the Lofoten Islands on the country's northwest coast, the administrative center for the region is surrounded by dramatic landscapes of rock thrusting up from the water to form fjords at every turn.

Leknes has one of the few airports in Lofoten Islands. Getting around is easy via public transportation.

Did You Know?

The Lofoten Islands attract intrepid travelers who stay in the rustic waterfront cabins that once belonged to fishermen.

Sights

★ Lofotr Viking Museum

MUSEUM VILLAGE | FAMILY | One of the top historical sites in Europe, this museum 13 km (8 miles) north of Leknes portrays the lifestyle and culture of the Vikings through magical reconstructions of typical buildings and ships. The re-created Viking chieftain's longhouse, on the foundations of a real chieftain's home, has been built according to authentic methods, including grass-turf walls, load-bearing poles, and fireplaces. Inside, it's divided, just like the original, into a lobby, living quarters, great hall, and *byre* (barn). Nearby, several other reconstructed buildings include a smithy and boathouse, and three ships that can be boarded in summer. The exhibition halls display more Viking artifacts and show a 12-minute film about the history and people of the region. Artisans are at work on site, and there's a chance to taste Viking food. There's even an activity area for kids, which makes the museum a popular choice for families. ✉ *Vikingveien 539, Bøstad* ☎ *76–08–49–00, 76–15–40–00* 🌐 *www.lofotr.no/en* 🎟 *NKr 170* ⏲ *Closed Sun. Feb.–Apr., Sept., and Oct.*

Nasjonal turistveg Lofoten (*Lofoten National Tourist Route*)

SCENIC DRIVE | One of the most scenic road trips in the world, this route stretches 230 km (142 miles) between Raftsundet in the north and the village of Å in the south. Whether heading north or south from Leknes, the craggy rock peaks, white sand beaches, and emerald green seas make it difficult to keep your attention on the road, especially when seen as a backdrop to seaside fishing villages. At regular intervals and particularly scenic spots, rest areas, viewing platforms, observation towers, and restaurants encourage further exploration. ✉ *Leknes* 🌐 *www.nasjonaleturistveger.no/en/routes.*

Restaurants

Himmel og Havn

$$$ | NORWEGIAN | As the name translates, "Heaven and Harbor" play lead roles in the spirit of this restaurant in the village of Ballstad. Sitting on a dock moored with fishing boats, the harbor is right outside, and as picturesque as they come. **Known for:** menu that changes regularly; great views over the harbor; excellent wine selection. [$] *Average main: NKr 259* ✉ *Moloveien 45, Ballstad* ✣ *19 km (12 miles) south of Leknes* ☎ *904–70–004* 🌐 *www.himmeloghavn.no.*

Hotels

Eliassen Rorbuer

$$$ | RENTAL | The little red and yellow fishermen's huts (*rorbuer*) that populate the villages of Lofoten and appear on so many postcards also house many tourists in summer—these, dating back to the 19th century, sit along the coast of a tiny rocky island 48 km (30 miles) south of Leknes. **Pros:** pristine location; well-equipped kitchens; excellent base for outdoor activities. **Cons:** weather can be variable; price doesn't include linens; inconsistent Wi-Fi signal. [$] *Rooms from: NKr 1890* ✉ *Hamnøya* ☎ *45–81–48–45* 🌐 *www.rorbuer.no/en* 🛏 *35 cabins* 🍴 *No meals.*

Å

One of the last little fishing villages in the Lofoten Islands, photogenic Å is where you'll find some of the most epic views in the region. There is even a museum dedicated to fishing.

To get to Å, you can fly into Leknes Airport or take the ferry over from Bodø. You can also take the 18-742 bus or opt to drive.

👁 Sights

Norsk Fiskeværsmuseum

MUSEUM | This museum is dedicated to the industry that fortified this village for decades. It takes you back to a simpler time when the whole population's livelihood depended solely on what the seas brought in. It re-enacts (in a realistic manner) the old life in the Lofoten Islands, showing how people baked, worked, and did the hard labor that built the islands to what they are today. There is a café on the premises. ✉ *Å i Lofoten, Å* ☎ *76–09–14–88* ⊕ *www.museumnord.no/fiskevarsmuseum* 💰 *NKr 100* ⊘ *Closed weekends Sept.–June.*

🍴 Restaurants

★ Bakeriet på Å

$ | NORWEGIAN | FAMILY | If you drive to the end of the Lofoten Islands, you absolutely must stop at this traditional Norwegian bakery famous for its cinnamon buns. The bakers use traditional methods, so the pastries are always their freshest. **Known for:** locals say these are the region's best cinnamon buns; traditional flatbreads and other delights; freshly baked breads. 💲 *Average main: NKr 60* ✉ *Å* ☎ *76–09–14–88.*

🛏 Hotels

Å Rorbuer

$$$ | HOTEL | As with other *rorbuer,* these lodgings offer a rustic and traditional way to experience the northern Norway islands. **Pros:** terraces for warm weather; lovely gardens; one of the best local lodgings. **Cons:** rooms on the small side; walls are thin; heat can be spotty. 💲 *Rooms from: NKr 1800* ✉ *Å* ☎ *76–09–11–21* ⊕ *arorbuer.no* 🛏 *25 cabins* ⦿❘ *No meals.*

Tromsø

1,800 km (1,118 miles) north of Bergen, 250 km (155 miles) north of Narvik.

Tromsø surprised visitors in the 1800s: they thought it very sophisticated and cultured for being so close to the North Pole—hence its nickname, the Paris of the North. It looks the way a polar town should—with ice-capped mountain ridges and jagged architecture that echoes the peaks. The midnight sun shines from May 21 to July 21, and it is said that the northern lights decorate the night skies over Tromsø more than any other city in Norway. Tromsø is home to only 73,500 people, but it's very spread out—the city's total area, 2,558 square km (987 square miles), is the most expansive in Norway. The downtown area is on a small, hilly island connected to the mainland by a slender bridge. The 13,000 students at the world's northernmost university are one reason the nightlife here is uncommonly busy.

GETTING HERE AND AROUND

Tromsø, a crossroads for air traffic between northern and southern Norway, is served by SAS, Norwegian, and Widerøe. The airport is 3 km (2 miles) northwest of the town center, and easily reachable via the Flybussen airport shuttle or Tromsø Taxi.

The Hurtigruten coastal express boat calls at Tromsø. Cruise ships dock either in the city center at Prostneset or 4 km (2½ miles) north of the city center at Breivika. Step off the ship in Prostneset, and you're in the city center. A shuttle is offered between Breivika and the city center.

When coming from the south, follow the E6 (the main road north) past Narvik before taking the E8 heading west at Nordkjosbotn. Cominor is the local bus operator in the Tromsø area. There is no train station in Tromsø.

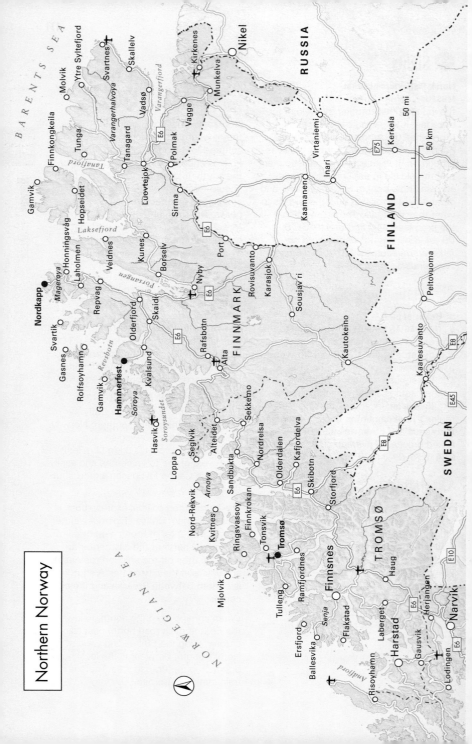

Northern Norway

◉ Sights

Fjellheisen (*Fjellheisen Cable Car*)
**TRANSPORTATION SITE (AIRPORT/BUS/
FERRY/TRAIN)** | **FAMILY** | To get a sense
of Tromsø's immensity and solitude,
take this cable car from the mainland,
just across the bridge and behind the
cathedral, up to the island's mountains.
Storsteinen (Big Rock), rising 1,386 feet
above sea level, has a great city view.
In summer a restaurant is open at the
top of the lift. ⊠ *Sollivn. 12, Tromsdalen*
☎ *77–63–87–37* ⊕ *www.fjellheisen.no/en*
🖾 *NKr 210.*

★ **Ishavskatedralen** (*Arctic Cathedral*)
RELIGIOUS SITE | Tromsø's signature struc-
ture was designed by Jan Inge Hovig to
evoke the shape of a Sami tent as well as
the iciness of a glacier. Opened in 1965,
it represents northern Norwegian nature,
culture, and faith. Also called the Arctic
Cathedral (although not a cathedral at all,
but rather a parish church), the building
is globally recognized for its interesting
structure and how different it is from the
Tromsø Cathedral, a wooden church in
the center of the city.

The immense stained-glass window
depicts the Second Coming. The Cathedral itself sits around 600 people. The
glass mosaic on the eastern side was
created by Victor Sparre, a Norwegian
painter, in 1972. In 2005, the church
received an organ from Grönlunds
Orgelbyggeri.

There are midnight sun concerts in
summer, starting at 11:30 pm. ⊠ *Hans
Nilsens v. 41, Tromsdalen, Tromsdalen*
☎ *47–68–06–68* ⊕ *www.ishavskate-
dralen.no/en* 🖾 *NKr 50.*

★ **Nordnorsk Kunstmuseum** (*Northern
Norway Art Museum*)
MUSEUM | **FAMILY** | The Northern Norway
Art Museum is a visual and interactive
art museum in the far north of Norway.
It is one of the youngest museums in

all of Norway and has exhibitions that
cater to visitors and locals of all ages and
interests. They also present a lot of local
artwork from the last 100 years. ⊠ *Sjøga-
ta 1, Tromsø* ☎ *77–64–70–20* ⊕ *www.
nnkm.no/en* 🖾 *NKr 80.*

Polarmuseet (*Polar Museum*)
MUSEUM | Inside a customs warehouse
from 1830, Polarmuseet documents the
history of the polar regions. There are
exhibitions on famous Norwegian polar
explorers like Fridtjof Nansen and Roald
Amundsen as well as the history of seal
hunting and surviving in this often hostile
climate. Part of the University of Tromsø,
the museum opened in 1978, on the
50th anniversary of Amundsen leaving
Tromsø for the last time, in search of
his missing explorer colleague Umberto
Nobile. ⊠ *Søndre Tollbodgt. 11B, Tromsø*
☎ *77–62–33–60* ⊕ *www.polarmuseum.
no* 🖾 *NKr 70.*

★ **Tromsø Botaniske Hage** (*Tromsø Botanical Garden*)
GARDEN | **FAMILY** | With plants from the
Antarctic and Arctic as well as mountainous regions all over the world, the 4-acre
Tromsø Botanical Garden has a natural
landscape that includes terraces, a
stream, and a pond. It is open all year and
has no set hours, so you can visit it by
the glow of the northern lights or while
basking in the midnight sun. Guides are
available with advance arrangement.
⊠ *Stakkevollvegen 200, Tromsø* ☎ *77–
64–50– 01* ⊕ *uit.no/tmu/botanisk.*

🍴 Restaurants

★ **Emmas Drømmekjøkken**
$$$ | **NORWEGIAN** | Emma's Dream Kitchen
specializes in the freshest seafood
imaginable, attracting both locals and
travelers who have heard about it from
fellow foodies. On the menu you'll find
everything from stockfish to whale steak
and more, all of it pleasingly presented.
Known for: tasty fish soup; small but

The breathtaking aurora borealis winds its way through the sky above the city of Tromsø.

varied menu; friendly staff. $ *Average main: NKr 300* ✉ *Kirkegata 8, Tromsø* ☎ *77–63–77–30* ⊕ *www.emmasdromme-kjokken.no* ☾ *Closed Sun.*

Rå Sushi & Bar

$$$ | **JAPANESE** | This well-known sushi bar combines the freshest Norwegian seafood with inventive Asian cooking techniques. You can find everything on the menu from fresh-caught salmon to whale sashimi. **Known for:** wide range of sushi; great decor; great views. $ *Average main: NKr 349* ✉ *Stortorget 1, Tromsø* ☎ *77–68–46–00* ⊕ *raasushi.no.*

★ Restaurant Smak

$$$$ | **NORWEGIAN** | You'll be impressed by the attention to detail shown by the chefs at this elegant dining room, with well-composed dishes that blend exciting and unexpected flavors. The menu changes with the season and takes advantage of the freshest ingredients available, with meats and cheeses from nearby farms. **Known for:** great set menu; impressive wine selection; local cheeses. $ *Average*

main: NKr 795 ✉ *Skippergata 16B, Tromsø* ☎ *941–76–110* ⊕ *www.restaurant-smak.no* ☾ *Closed Sun. and Mon.*

 ## Hotels

★ Clarion Collection Hotel With

$$$ | **HOTEL** | Often ranked as Tromsø's best place to stay, this comfortable lodging in a twin-gabled building facing the harbor puts you within walking distance of the best of the city's sights. **Pros:** breakfast and dinner included; relaxing sauna; lovely views. **Cons:** some rooms have little storage space; hard to block out light on bright summer nights; some rooms have better views than others. $ *Rooms from: NKr 1700* ✉ *Sjøgt. 35–37, Tromsø* ☎ *77–66–42–00* ⊕ *www.nordic-choicehotels.no/* ⇆ *76 rooms* ❖ *Some meals.*

Scandic Ishavshotel

$$ | **HOTEL** | Shaped like an ocean liner docked at the harbor—there's even a slender mast topped by a Norwegian flag—Tromsø's snazziest hotel stretches

over the sound toward Ishavskatedralen.
Pros: near the city and the harbor;
excellent breakfast buffet; great views
of the waterfront. **Cons:** breakfast can
get crowded with people on bus tours;
service gets mixed reviews; not all views
are created equal. $ *Rooms from: NKr
850* ⊠ *Fr. Langesgt. 2, Tromsø* ☎ *77–66–
64–00* ⊕ *www.scandichotels.no/hotell/
norge/tromso/scandic-ishavshotel/* ⤳ *214
rooms* ⦿ *Free breakfast.*

▼ Nightlife

★ Magic Ice Bar
BARS/PUBS | Everything on the premises
is made of ice, down to the barstools,
the tables, and even the glasses. Ice
sculptures of some of Norway's most
intrepid explorers make you feel like
you're getting a history lesson along with
your beer. If you're a little chilly, the staff
will loan you a parka. ⊠ *Kaigata 4, Tromsø*
☎ *413–01–050* ⊕ *www.magicice.no/
listings/tromso-norway/.*

⚡ Activities

Tromsø has more than 100 km (62 miles)
of trails for walking and hiking in the
mountains above the city. They're reachable by funicular.

BOATING
Arctic Cruise in Norway
BOATING | Arctic Cruise in Norway is a
high-quality tour provider that offers a lot
of extras on your boat trip such as prep-
ping and cooking your own self-caught
fish and much more. They offer several
different packages that will give guests a
wonderful taste of the Arctic, whether it
be under the northern lights or midnight
sun. ⊠ *Brinkvegen 41, Tromsø* ☎ *90–54–
99–97* ⊕ *www.acinorway.com/.*

WHALE-WATCHING
★ **Arctic Explorers**
WHALE-WATCHING | **FAMILY** | One of
the most reputable whale-watching

excursions in Tromsø and northern
Norway. You'll travel in speedy boats with
small groups and see humpback whales,
orcas, and other species. If you're lucky,
you may be able to see these majestic
creatures under the northern lights.
⊠ *Stortorget 1, Tromsø* ☎ *954–78–500*
⊕ *arcticholidays.org/whale-rib-tour.*

WINTER SPORTS
★ **Chasing Lights**
TOUR—SPORTS | One of the main draws to
northern Norway is the magical northern
lights, and Chasing Lights is a Tromsø-
based tour company that offers diverse
packages to help you witness this amazing natural phenomenon. As the name
suggests, the company will chase the
lights with you rather than standing still in
one spot and allowing them to come—or
not come—to you. The company also
has other activities such as snowmobile adventures and trips to the fjords.
⊠ *Storgata 64, Tromsø* ☎ *455–17–551*
⊕ *chasinglights.com.*

Hammerfest

Hammerfest is the gateway to the Barents Sea and the Arctic Ocean, making
it an ideal jumping-off point for Arctic
expeditions. More than 600 miles above
the Arctic Circle, the world's northernmost town is also one of the most widely
visited places in Northern Norway. Hammerfest means "mooring place," refering
to the town's natural harbor (remarkably
free of ice year-round thanks to the Gulf
Stream). This place has plenty of history
to explore. In 1891, residents grew tired
of the months of darkness each winter
and decided to brighten their nights. They
purchased a generator from Thomas
Edison, becoming the first city in Europe
to have electric street lamps.

GETTING HERE AND AROUND

Just minutes from the center of the city, Hammerfest Airport can be reached via the 132 bus from the downtown bus terminal. There's also a daily shuttle to and from Alta Airport. Hammerfest is small enough to navigate on foot, but there are several bus routes running throughout the town and to surrounding areas. There are also high-speed ferries operating between coastal towns.

Sights

★ Gjenreisningsmuseet
MUSEUM | Hammerfest was completely demolished by the Germans during World War II, and the Museum of Reconstruction documents how the city was painstakingly rebuilt. The museum is a place of pride for Norwegians, who flock here from all across the country. The two floors of exhibits lets you compare the historic city from 1943 with the one you see today. ✉ *Kirkegata 19, Hammerfest* ☎ *78–47–72–00* 🌐 *www.kystmuseene.no.*

Meridianstøtten
HISTORIC SITE | A UNESCO World Heritage Site, the Struve Geodetic Arc was the northernmost of 265 survey points mapped out between 1816 and 1855 by the astronomer Friedrich Georg Wilhelm Struve. This graceful column commemorates his attempt to measure the size and shape of the Earth in the 19th century. ✉ *Industrigata 5, Hammerfest.*

Restaurants

Niri Sushi and Dinner
$$$$ | **JAPANESE** | One of the most popular places in Hammerfest to grab a bite, this Japanese eatery creates amazing rolls using the freshest local seafood, from salmon to whale. During the day, the place thrives as a sushi bar, but at night DJs transform it into a happening club. **Known for:** unique varieties of sushi; vegetarian options; plenty of options available to go. [$] *Average main: NKr 400* ✉ *Storgata 22, Hammerfest* ☎ *455–00–200* 🌐 *www.nirihammerfest.no* 🕑 *Closed Sun. and Mon.*

Brygga Mathus
$$$$ | **NORWEGIAN** | Specializing in local seafood, seasonal produce, and northern Norwegian flavors, this storefront eatery in a charming brick building is a great place to sample local cuisine. Long tables encourage you to get to know your neighbors, and floor-to-ceiling windows let you gaze out at what's happening in the port. **Known for:** daily lunch specials; tasty small plates; local meats and produce. [$] *Average main: NKr 400* ✉ *Strandgata 16, Hammerfest* ☎ *401–89–600* 🌐 *bryggamathus.no* 🕑 *Closed Sun.*

Hotels

Smarthotel Hammerfest
$$ | **HOTEL** | Known for its budget-friendly accommodations, this no-nonsense lodging focuses on what you need for a great stay and jettisons the rest. **Pros:** beds are like sleeping on a cloud; architecture is bold and beautiful; free Wi-Fi and other amenities. **Cons:** no maid service on weekends; doesn't accept cash; some small rooms. [$] *Rooms from: NKr 900* ✉ *Strandgata 32, Hammerfest* ☎ *415–36–500* 🌐 *smarthotel.no/en/hammerfest* 🔑 *160 rooms* 🍴 *No meals.*

Thon Hotel Hammerfest
$$$ | **HOTEL** | One of the most popular places for for weary travelers in this part of northern Norway, the centrally located Thon Hotel Hammerfest has amenities that attract corporate clients as well as vacationers. **Pros:** eye-catching exterior design; rooms have splashes of color; best rooms have great views. **Cons:** charges for parking; no cribs for infants; some tiny rooms. [$] *Rooms from: NKr 1300* ✉ *Strandgata 2-4, Hammerfest* ☎ *78–42–96–31* 🌐 *www.thonhotels.no/hoteller/norge/hammerfest/thon-hotel-hammerfest* 🔑 *103 rooms* 🍴 *Free breakfast.*

Gazing out to the Barents Sea, Nordkapp is the northernmost point in continental Europe.

Nordkapp

34 km (21 miles) north of Honningsvåg.

Searching for a northeastern passage to India, British navigator Richard Chancellor came upon this impressive promontory in the Barents Sea in 1553. He named it North Cape, or *Nordkapp*. Europe's northernmost point is a rite of passage for nearly all Scandinavians, as well as many other adventurous type from around the world. Honningvåg's northerly location makes for long, dark winter nights and perpetually sun-filled summer days. The village serves as the gateway to Arctic exploration and the beautiful Nordkapp Plateau.

This region has an otherworldly landscape, at once rugged and delicate. You'll see an incredible treeless tundra with crumbling mountains and sparse vegetation. The subarctic environment is very vulnerable, so don't disturb the plants. Walk only on marked trails and don't

remove stones, disturb the plants, or make campfires. Because the roads are closed in winter, the only access is from the tiny fishing village of Skarsvåg via Sno-Cat, a thump-and-bump ride that's as unforgettable as the desolate view.

GETTING HERE AND AROUND

Honningsvåg Airport, 30 km (18.6 miles) south of North Cape, has direct flights from Tromsø, Kirkenes, and other towns in the far north, operated by Widerøe. Hurtigruten, the ship company, stops at Honningsvåg on its way to Kirkenes from Bergen.

The E69 goes all the way to the North Cape, with a 6.8-km (4-mile) long underwater tunnel linking the mainland with the island of Magerøya. The North Cape is 236 km (147 miles) north of Alta, and the journey takes about three hours.

Most cruise passengers visit Nordkapp from Honningsvåg, a fishing village on Magerøya Island. The journey from Honningsvåg to Nordkapp covers about

35 km (22 miles) across a landscape characterized by rocky tundra and grazing reindeer.

AIR CONTACTS Widerøe. ☎ *810–01–200* 🌐 *www.wideroe.no.*

BUS CONTACTS Visit North Cape. ✉ *Fiskerivn. 4D, Honningsvåg* ☎ *78–47–70–30* 🌐 *www.nordkapp.no/en.*

CRUISE TRAVEL

One of Northern Norway's largest ports welcomes about 100 cruise ships annually during the summer season. The port itself has no services, but within 100 yards are shops, museums, tourist information, post office, banks, restaurants, and an ice bar.

VISITOR INFORMATION

CONTACTS Nordkapp Reiseliv. ✉ *Fiskerivn. 4, Honningsvåg* ☎ *78–47–70–30* 🌐 *www.nordkapp.no/en.*

Sights

Nordkapphallen (*North Cape Hall*)
MUSEUM | Tucked away into the plateau, North Cape Hall is housed in a cave and includes exhibits tracing the history of the cape, from Richard Chancellor, an Englishman who sailed around it in 1553, to Oscar II, king of Norway and Sweden, who climbed to the top of the plateau in 1873. Celebrate your pilgrimage to 71° North at one of the cafés. The hefty admission charge covers both the exhibits and entrance to the plateau itself. If you arrive on foot or by bike, admission is free. ✉ *Nordkapp* ☎ *78–47–68–60* 🌐 *www.visitnordkapp.net/en/* 🎫 *NKr 285.*

Nordkappmuseet (*North Cape Museum*)
MUSEUM | This museum documents the history of the Arctic fishing industry and the history of tourism at North Cape. You can learn about the development of society and culture in this region. ✉ *Holmen 1, Honningsvåg* ☎ *78–47–72–00* 🌐 *www.kystmuseene.no/north-cape-museum.107296.en.html* 🎫 *NKr 60* 🕒 *Closed Sun. mid-Sept.–mid-June.*

Restaurants

★ Corner Spiseri
$$$ | NORWEGIAN | The catch of the day often dictates the menu here, but crispy cod tongue is always available. For less adventurous eaters, there's also a variety of pasta dishes. **Known for:** lovely location; incredibly tasty reindeer; great craft beers at the bar. [$] *Average main: NKr 259* ✉ *Fiskeriveien 2A, Honningsvåg* ☎ *78–47–63–40* 🌐 *www.corner.no.*

Chapter 4

SWEDEN

Updated by
Annika S. Hipple

⊙ Sights	🍴 Restaurants	🛏 Hotels	🛍 Shopping	🍸 Nightlife
★★★★★	★★★★★	★★★★★	★★★★★	★★★★☆

WELCOME TO SWEDEN

TOP REASONS TO GO

★ **Immerse yourself in nature.** A love of nature is embedded deep in the Swedish soul. The Right of Public Access gives everyone the right to enjoy it, as long as you don't damage or disturb.

★ **Delve into the past.** Walk in the footsteps of Vikings, explore castles and palaces, stroll through medieval towns, and climb imposing fortresses.

★ **Taste the flavors of the land and sea.** In recent decades, Swedish cuisine has soared to new heights, with world-class chefs creating innovative, mouthwatering dishes using only the best seasonal, locally sourced ingredients.

★ **Get out on the water.** With 1,500 miles of coastline and nearly 100,000 lakes, Sweden is made for watery fun. Take a trip on a historic steamship, dive into a sparkling lake, or paddle a kayak along a rocky shore.

★ **Take home some beautiful handicrafts.** From the world-famous Dala horse to gorgeous hand-blown glass, Sweden abounds with vibrant crafts and design.

1 Stockholm. Sweden's capital is strewn over 14 islands and offers museums, a maze-like Old Town, and urban waterways. It's a great base for exploring the remarkable beauty of the archipelago that lies to its east, as well as for nearby castles and historic towns.

2 Drottningholm. Home to the stunning royal palace and gardens.

3 Sigtuna. Known for the stone ruins of St. Olaf's and Sweden's oldest main street.

4 Mariefred. Picturesque small town with lots of history.

5 Uppsala. This lively, fascinating city is an easy day trip from Stockholm.

6 Vaxholm and the Archipelago. An hour by ferry from Stockholm, lively Vaxholm is a great base for exploring the beautiful archipelago.

7 Göteborg (Gothenburg). Sweden's standout second city.

8 Bohuslän. A stunning coastal region that buzzes with life in the summer months.

9 Lund. One of Sweden's oldest and loveliest cities.

10 Malmö. Old meets new in this multi-cultural city.

11 Ystad. Medieval market town with half-timbered houses and cobblestoned streets.

12 Kalmar. Known for the Renaissance-style Kalmar Castle and well-preserved historic buildings.

13 Öland. A hugely popular summer destination for Swedes filled with fairytale forests and wooden windmills.

14 The Kingdom of Crystal. A region in the southeast where hand-blown glass has been made since 1742.

15 Gotland. A large island off the Baltic coast, home to medieval marvel, Visby.

16 Dalarna: The Folklore District. the Country's heartland, brimming with folklore and tradition.

17 Jukkasjärvi. Famous for its extraordinary Ice Hotel.

18 Jokkmokk. The capital of Sami culture.

19 Laponia World Heritage Site. A mountainous wildlife area in Swedish Lapland.

NORWEGIAN SEA

Vestfjord

Kiruna
Jukkasjärvi 17
Laponia World
Heritage Site
19
18
Jokkmokk

Rovaniemi

Luleå

Skellefteå

NORWAY

100 mi

100 km

Trondheim

Umeå
Örnsköldsvik
Östersund
Härnösand
Sundsvall

Gulf of Bothnia

Vaasa

FINLAND

NORWAY

Lillehammer

Bergen

OSLO

Stavanger

ristiansand

Bollnäs

Gävle
16 Dalarna
Borlänge

Tampere

HELSINKI

5 Uppsala
Västerås 3 Sigtuna
Karlstad 4 Vaxholm 6
Örebro STOCKHOLM 1
Mariefred Drottningholm 2
Nyköping
Norrköping
Linköping GOTLAND

TALLINN

ESTONIA

Vannersborg

Göteborg
7

8
13 Öland
Borås Jönköping

Visby
15

RIGA

LATVIA

Mariestad

Växjö
14 Kalmar
12

DENMARK Halmstad

Helsingborg
COPENHAGEN 9 Lund
Malmö 10 Ystad 11

Karlskrona
Kristianstad

Baltic Sea

LITHUANIA

North Sea

Skagerrak

SWEDEN SNAPSHOT

AT A GLANCE

Capital: Stockholm

Population: 10,230,000

Currency: Krona (plural: kronor)

Money: ATMs common, credit cards widely accepted. Cash less widely accepted.

Language: Swedish

Country Code: 46

Emergencies: 112

Driving: On the right

Electricity: 230v/50 cycles; plugs have two round prongs

Time: Six hours ahead of New York

Documents: Up to 90 days with valid passport; Schengen rules apply

Major Mobile Companies: Telia, Tele2, Telenor, 3

WHEN TO GO

High Season: The official tourist season—when hotel rates generally go up and museum and castle doors open—runs from mid-May through mid-September. This is also Sweden's balmiest time of year; days are sunny, warm, and long. Summer is also mosquito season, especially in the north.

Low Season: Winter is November through March (sometimes longer), and brings sub-zero temperatures. Still, days can be magnificent when the snow is fresh and the sky a brilliant Nordic blue. Many of the more traditional attractions are closed for the winter, but skiing, skating, ice fishing, and sleigh riding are offered throughout the country. The northern lights are often seen in Arctic Sweden and sometimes even as far south as Stockholm.

Value Season: The weather can be bright and fresh in the spring and fall (although both can bring lots of rain), and many visitors prefer sightseeing when there are fewer people around.

BIG EVENTS

■ **April:** The last day of April is Valborgsmässoafton (Walpurgis Night), which marks the arrival of spring and is celebrated with massive bonfires throughout the country, most famously at Stockholm's Skansen.

■ **June:** Midsummer—starting on a late-June Friday evening and lasting all of Saturday—is a happy time for social gatherings, flowered hair, and maypole dancing.

■ **July–August:** One of the city's largest festivals, Stockholm Pride, celebrates the city's LGBTQ community with five days of parties, exhibits, talks, and performances. ⊕ *www.stockholmpride.org*

■ **Gothenburg Culture Festival.** For the greater part of August, streets in this university town are inundated with the finest ballet, street theater, and live music. ⊕ *gothenburg-culturefestival.com*

■ **December:** December 13 is Luciadagen (St. Lucia Day), celebrated nationwide by haunting convoys of white-robed singers, each led by a girl with a crown of lit candles.

Sweden requires the visitor to travel far, in both distance and attitude. Approximately the size of California, Sweden reaches as far north as the Arctic fringes of Europe, where glacier-topped mountains and thousands of acres of forests are broken only by wild rivers, pristine lakes, and desolate moorland. In the more populous south, roads meander through miles of softly undulating countryside, skirting lakes, and passing small villages with sharp-pointed church spires.

Once the dominant power of the region, Sweden has traditionally looked inward to find its own Nordic solutions. During the Cold War, its citizens were in effect subjected to a giant social experiment aimed at creating a perfectly just society, one that adopted the best aspects of both socialism and capitalism.

Recession in the late 1980s saw Sweden make adjustments that lessened the role of its all-embracing welfare state in the lives of its citizens. The adjustments continued through successive governments of both left- and right-wing persuasions. Today, the social safety net once so heavily relied upon by Swedes is somewhat less comprehensive, a reflection perhaps of modern economics rather than any temporary budgetary hiccup.

Sweden took off, with the rest of the globe, with the explosion of the Internet and new technology and watched with it as the bubble burst at the start of the new millennium. It continues to be one of the world's dominant players in the information-based economy, especially mobile technology, and new technology is widely used throughout Sweden.

Sweden is an arresting mixture of ancient and modern. The countryside is dotted with runic stones and timbered farmhouses, recalling its Viking past and more recent agrarian culture. Venture to the country's cities, however, and you'll find them to be modern, their shop windows filled with the latest in consumer goods and fashions.

MAJOR REGIONS

Stockholm. Built on 14 islands, Sweden's capital is an intriguing mix of global commerce and local craft, modern design and ancient architecture, bustling metropolis and peaceful green space. In the summer months, life takes to the streets—and to the water. Summer is also a great time to take in what some say is Stockholm's best attraction: its mixed, modern, self-assured, beautiful population. People-watching has never been more fun.

Sidetrips from Stockholm. Stockholm's backyard is Lake Mälaren with its many islands and deeply indented bays. The royal family makes its official home at Drottningholm Palace on an island just west of Stockholm. On the shores of Sweden's third-largest lake are many interesting sights, including the country's oldest city, Sigtuna, and one of its most impressive Renaissance castles, Gripsholm.

Also on Stockholm's doorstep, Vaxholm and the Archipelago is one of the world's most beautiful archipelagos; with more than 25,000 islands fringing the city, it's easy for everyone to find a space to call their own, even on the weekend when city dwellers flock here by the thousands.

A quick train ride north of Stockholm, Uppsala is home to both the oldest university and the tallest cathedral in the Nordic countries, both of which date from medieval times. Its rich heritage goes back more than 1,500 years to the ancient kings who lie buried in grass-covered mounds north of the city. Contrasting with all this history is the youthful spirit of its student population, which numbers more than 40,000.

Göteborg. Göteborg uses its position to its advantage. From as far back as Viking times the area has been a hub of international trade. Present-day Göteborg was established in 1621 and is a thriving, commercial, cosmopolitan place with a cultural and architectural status far beyond what you'd expect from its size. Its people remain down to earth, though,

and have a reputation for being particularly funny and vibrant.

Bohuslän. When Swedes think of the west coast, they usually picture Bohuslän, the small but extremely scenic region that stretches from just north of Göteborg to the Norwegian border. Here, picturesque fishing villages with brightly painted houses cling to smoothly rounded cliffs that slope down into narrow fjords and the brilliant blue seas that stretch to the horizon. It's no wonder many people consider this the "best coast."

The South and the Kingdom of Crystal. Dense beech forests and sun-dappled lakes are the lifeblood of Småland's isolated villages, whose names are bywords for fine crystal glassware: Kosta, Boda, and Orrefors. Farther south, the landscape opens up in Skåne where lush farmland, rolling coastal headlands, seemingly endless sandy beaches, and delightful historic cities with half-timbered houses are the main draws. Off the east coast of Småland, the long, narrow island of Öland is a favorite summer destination for many Swedes, including the royal family.

North of Öland and farther out in the Baltic is Gotland, a large island whose Viking ruins, unspoiled wilderness, and busy summer social life make for a holiday paradise. Off its northeastern tip, the island of Fårö was the beloved retreat of filmmaker Ingmar Bergman for more than 40 years.

Dalarna: The Folklore Province. Dalarna holds a special place in the hearts of Swedes, for it's here that many of the country's most beloved traditions are at their strongest. A beautiful province of forested hills surrounding Lake Siljan and rising to mountains in the west, Dalarna is the heartland of Swedish folk music and the place where everyone wants to celebrate Midsummer at some point in their life. It's also the birthplace of

Sweden's most recognizable handicraft, the red-painted Dala horse.

Swedish Lapland. Arctic Sweden is a land of big nature, from wild rivers and deep forests to vast expanses of tundra and dramatic mountains. It's the land of the midnight sun, and also of the long winter, when the darkness is brightened by a thick blanket of snow and the frequent magic of the northern lights. It's also the land of the hardy Sami people, who have inhabited this region for thousands of years and still maintain their traditional, if updated, focus on reindeer herding.

Planning

Getting Here and Around

AIR

Stockholm's main airport, 37 km north of Stockholm and nearly 40 km southeast of Uppsala, is Sweden's gateway to the world and the world's gateway to Sweden. Arlanda can be accessed by bus and train. Terminals two and five are for international flights; terminals three and four are domestic flights. Bromma Airport, just 8km from Stockholm city center, is convenient for domestic flights but it services only a handful of airlines.

Inside Sweden, Malmö Aviation, Norwegian, and SAS connect all major cities by regular flights.

AIRPORTS Stockholm Arlanda Airport. ☎ *010/1091000* ⊕ *www.swedavia.com/ arlanda.* **Göteborg Landvetter Airport.** ☎ *010/1093100* ⊕ *www.swedavia.com/ landvetter.* **Malmö Airport.** (*Sturup Airport*) ☎ *046/101094500* ⊕ *www.swedavia. se/malmo.* **Visby Airport.** ☎ *010/095200* ⊕ *www.swedavia.com/visby.*

BIKE

Cycling is a very popular sport in Sweden, and the south of the country, with its low-lying, flat landscape, is perfect for the more genteel cyclist. In fact, Sweden now has three scenic national long-distance cycling routes, all originating in the south. The 370-km (230-mile) Kattegattleden runs from Helsingborg to Göteborg, Sydostleden runs 270 km (168 miles) between Växjö and Simrishamn, and Sydkustleden connects the two with a 260-km (162-mile route) between Simrishamn and Helsingborg. All major towns and cities have bike paths and designated bike lanes. Bike-rental costs start at around SKr 100 per day. Tourist offices have information about cycling package holidays.

CONTACTS City Bikes. ☎ *077/4442424* ⊕ *www.citybikes.se.* **Cykelfrämjandet.** ✉ *Olympiahallen, Filbornavägen 11, Helsingborg* ☎ *08/54591030* ⊕ *www. cykelframjandet.nu.*

BOAT AND FERRY

Silja Line and Viking Line operate massive cruise ship–style ferries daily between Stockholm and Helsinki, either for single journeys or round-trip, two-day cruises. St. Peter Line operates a ferry service between Stockholm and St. Petersburg, Russia, with stops in Tallinn, Estonia, and Helsinki, Finland, along the way. Polferries and Unity Line operate ferries between Ystad and Świnoujście, Poland, where a minibus waits to take you to the historic city of Szczecin, Poland. Polferries also has ferry service between Nynäshamn, south of Stockholm, and Gdańsk, Poland. Stena Line has service between Göteborg and Frederikshamn, Denmark, and Kiel, Germany; between Varberg and Grenå, Denmark; between Trelleborg and Rostock and Sassnitz, both in Germany; between Karlskrona and Gdynia, Poland; and between Nynäshamn and Ventspils, Latvia. Ferries operated by ForSea and Sundbusserne shuttle back and forth between Helsingborg and nearby Helsingør, Denmark, all day long. Within Sweden, Destination Gotland has ferries between Visby on

Gotland and Nynäshamn, Oskarshamn, and Västervik on the mainland.

CONTACTS Destination Gotland.
☏ 0771/223300 ⊕ www.destinationgotland.se. **ForSea.** ☏ 042/186100 ⊕ www.forsea.se. **Polferries.** ☏ 040/121700 Ystad, 08/52068660 Nynäshamn ⊕ www.polferries.se. **Scandlines.** ☏ 042/186100 ✉ kundservice@scandlines.se ⊕ www.scandlines.se. **Stena Line.** ☏ 0770/575700 ⊕ www.stenaline.se. **St. Peter Line.** ☏ 08/4597700 ⊕ www.stpeterline.com. **Tallink/Silja Line.** ☏ 08/222140 ⊕ www.tallinksilja.se. **Unity Line.** ☏ 0411/556900 ⊕ www.unityline.se. **Viking Line.** ☏ 08/4524000 fee of SKr 50 applies to bookings made by phone ⊕ www.vikingline.se.

BUS

There is excellent bus service between all major towns and cities. When buying a single ticket for local bus journeys, it is typical to pay the driver upon boarding. Coupons or multiple tickets for longer journeys should be purchased before your journey from the relevant bus company or from a ticket machine at the relevant bus station.

CONTACTS FlixBus. ☏ 08/50513750 ⊕ www.flixbus.se. **Vy.** ☏ 0771/151515 ⊕ www.nettbuss.se.

CAR

Sweden has an excellent highway network of more than 80,000 km (50,000 miles). The fastest routes are those with numbers prefixed with an E (for "European"), some of which are the equivalent of American highways or British motorways. Öresundsbron, the 8-km (5-mile) bridge between Malmö and Copenhagen, simplifies car travel and makes train connections possible between the two countries.

Sweden's size compared to its population means that most of the country's roads are relatively traffic free, though rush hour in major cities can bring frustrating traffic jams. Drive on the right; seat belts are mandatory for everyone. You must also have at least low-beam headlights on at all times. Cars rented or bought in Sweden will have automatic headlights, which are activated every time the engine is switched on. Signs indicate five basic speed limits, ranging from 30 kph (19 mph) in school or playground areas to 110 or even 120 kph (68–75 mph) on long stretches of E roads.

CRUISE

A lovely way to experience Sweden is to go on one of the highly popular cruises on the Göta Canal, which links Göteborg, on the west coast, with Stockholm, on the east. The journey traverses rivers, lakes, and 66 locks on the coast-to-coast journey, which takes four to six days depending on whether you opt for the version where you travel by both day and night or the one where the ship moves only during the day. There are also shorter versions that cover only parts of the route. No matter which version you choose, you'll travel on one of three historic steamers, the oldest of which is the *Juno,* built in 1874. Prices start at SKr 9,190 for a double cabin.

CONTACT Rederi AB Göta Kanal .
☏ 031/806315 ⊕ www.gotacanal.se.

TRAIN

Sweden's Statens Järnvägar (SJ) is the state railway operator and has a highly efficient network of comfortable electric trains. On nearly all long-distance routes there are buffet cars and, on overnight trips, sleeping cars and couchettes in both first and second class. Seat reservations are advisable, though there are certain routes where advance seat selection is not possible. On some high-speed trains, seat reservations are compulsory. Reservations can be made right up to departure time. The high-speed X2000 train serves several routes between major cities; the Stockholm–Göteborg run takes 3 hours and Stockholm–Malmö, 3½. Travelers aged 25 and under and 65 and older travel at discounted fares.

There are also steep discounts for children traveling in the company of an adult.

CONTACTS SJ. (*State Railway Company*) ☏ *0771/757575* ⊕ *www.sj.se.*

Restaurants

Sweden's major cities offer a full range of dining choices, from traditional to international restaurants. Outside the cities, restaurants are usually more local in influence. Investments in training and successes in international competitions have spurred restaurant quality to fantastic heights in Sweden. The New Nordic cuisine movement emphasizes freshness, sustainability, and seasonality, using locally available ingredients to create innovative cuisine that combines traditional Scandinavian dishes with international influences. It is worth remembering, though, that for many years eating out was prohibitively expensive for many Swedes, giving rise to a home-socializing culture that still exists today. For this reason many smaller towns are bereft of anything approaching a varied restaurant scene.

Hotels

Two things about Swedish hotels usually surprise travelers: the relatively limited dimensions of the beds and the generous size and variety of the breakfasts, which is usually included in the room price. Otherwise, hotel guests in Sweden can expect facilities and service comparable to what's available elsewhere in Europe. Most major cities offer a full range of lodging options, from budget hostels to chic boutique accommodations and five-star business hotels. Country inns and bed-and-breakfasts can be full of character and good value for money. During the summer months and on weekends, many Swedish hotels offer reduced room rates. That said, July is the Swedish vacation month

and hotels are notoriously busy. Make reservations wherever possible. Some older hotels, particularly country inns and independently run smaller hotels in the cities, do not have private bathrooms. This is usually clearly stated in the room description on the hotel's website, but if it isn't, be sure to inquire in advance if this is important to you. Whatever their size, almost all Swedish hotels provide scrupulously clean accommodations and courteous service.

CONTACTS Countryside Hotels. ☏ *031/131870* ⊕ *www.countrysidehotels. se.*

HOTEL AND RESTAURANT PRICES *Hotel reviews have been shortened. For full information, visit Fodors.com.*

WHAT IT COSTS in Swedish Krona			
$	$$	$$$	$$$$
RESTAURANTS			
under SKr 150	SKr 150–250	SKr 250–420	over SKr 420
HOTELS			
under SKr 1,500	SKr 1,500–2,300	SKr 2,300–2,900	over SKr 2,900

Stockholm

Stockholm is a city in the flush of its second youth. Since the mid-1990s, Sweden's capital has emerged from its cold, Nordic shadow to take the stage as a truly international city. What started with entry into the European Union (EU) in 1995 gained pace with the extraordinary IT boom of the late 1990s, strengthened with the Skype-led IT second wave of 2003, and solidified with the hedge-fund invasion that is still happening today as Stockholm gains even more global confidence. And despite more recent economic turmoil, Stockholm's 1 million or so inhabitants have come to recognize

4 Sweden STOCKHOLM

that their city is one to rival Paris, London, New York, or any other great metropolis.

Positioned where the waters of Lake Mälaren rush into the Baltic, Stockholm has been an important trading site and an international city for centuries. Built on 14 islands joined by bridges crossing open bays and narrow channels, it boasts the story of its past in its glorious medieval old town, grand palaces, ancient churches, sturdy edifices, public parks, and 19th-century museums. Its history is soaked into the very fabric of its narrow lanes and its grand boulevards, built as a public display of trading glory.

Planning

PLANNING YOUR TIME

You can manage to see a satisfying amount of Stockholm in a day, though it would be tough to get too much of this place. Start near Stadshuset (City Hall) for a morning trip up to the top of its 348-foot tower. Make your way along the waterfront to Gamla Stan and the Kungliga Slottet (Royal Palace). Catch the passenger ferry from the south end of Gamla Stan to Djurgården, home to many of the city's top museums. The most unmissable is the Vasa Museum, perched on the waterfront facing the island of Skeppsholmen. From here it's a pleasant stroll back to the city center across the Djurgården Bridge and along the quays at Strandvägen. To save on dinner, try picnicking in beautiful Kungsträdgården, just across Strömsbron.

If you can linger here for a few days, take a day trip into the archipelago. Whether it be taking a sightseeing excursion by boat, venturing onto a commuter ferry for a bit of island hopping, or sea kayaking as far as your arms will let you, get thee to the water.

GETTING HERE AND AROUND

AIR

Stockholm's Arlanda International Airport, 42 km (26 miles) from the city center, is Sweden's air hub. The main regional carrier SAS flies from several North American cities. Other airlines that fly to and from Arlanda include Air France, British Airways, Finnair, Icelandair, KLM, and Norwegian. *Flygbussarna* (airport buses) leave every 10 to 15 minutes from 6:30 am to 11 pm and terminate at Cityterminalen (City Terminal), next to the central railway station. The trip takes about 49 minutes. Tickets cost SKr 119 (SKr 99 if purchased online or using the mobile app).

Alternatively, the yellow-nosed Arlanda Express train takes 20 minutes and leaves every 15 minutes (and every 10 minutes during peak hours). Single tickets cost SKr 295, though there are discounts for multiple people traveling together. There's also SL commuter rail service from Arlanda to central Stockholm. The trip takes 37 minutes and costs SKr 152 (SKr 32 plus an airport supplement of SKr 120).

■ TIP→ **With taxis, be sure to ask about a** *fast pris* **(fixed price) between Arlanda and the city. It should be around SKr 535 to a destination near the center of town.**

BICYCLE

One of the best ways to explore Stockholm is by bike. There are bike paths and special bike lanes throughout the city, making it safe and enjoyable. Bicycles can even be taken on the commuter trains (except during peak traveling times and from Stockholm City and Odenplan stations) for excursions to the suburbs.

BOAT

Silja Line and Viking Line operate massive cruise ship–style ferries daily between Stockholm and Helsinki, Finland, either for single journeys or round-trip, two-day cruises. Tallink operates cruise ferries to Tallinn, Estonia, while St. Peter Line operates a ferry service between Stockholm and St. Petersburg, Russia, with stops in Tallinn and Helsinki along the way. For boat travel closer to Stockholm, Waxholmsbolaget has a fleet of passenger ferries to destinations throughout the archipelago. Strömma Kanalbolaget also has passenger ferry service to several archipelago destinations aboard its Cinderella boats.

PUBLIC TRANSPORTATION
Stockholm has an excellent public transportation system, which is operated by SL. The *tunnelbana* (subway) system, known as T-bana (with stations marked by a blue-on-white T), is the easiest and fastest way to get around. Servicing more than 100 stations and covering more than 96 km (60 miles) of track, trains run frequently between 5 am and 3 am. Late-night bus service connects certain stations when trains stop running. The comprehensive bus network serves the entire city, including out-of-town points of interest, such as Vaxholm and Gustavsberg. Maps and timetables for all city transportation networks are available from the SL information desks at Sergels Torg and Central Station, as well as online.

Tickets work interchangeably on buses, subways, and commuter trains in the metro area. SL tickets are also valid on the Djurgården ferries and certain commuter ferries. Single tickets are valid for unlimited travel within 75 minutes.

■ TIP→ **If you plan to make extensive use of public transportation, it's worth buying an SL Access card, which costs SKr 20 and can be loaded with any amount of money you wish. Fares preloaded onto an SL Access card are significantly cheaper than purchasing individual tickets.**

Waxholmsbolaget offers 5- and 30-day travel cards for its extensive commuter network of archipelago boats; the price is SKr 445 for five days of unlimited travel.

These travel card fares can also be loaded onto an SL Access card.

CONTACTS Stockholms Lokaltrafik (SL).
☎ *08/6001000* ⊕ *www.sl.se.* **Waxholmsbolaget.** ☎ *08/6795830* ⊕ *www.waxholmsbolaget.se.*

TAXI
Taxis in Stockholm are efficient but overpriced. If you call a cab, ask the dispatcher to quote you a fast pris, which is usually lower than the metered fare. A trip of 10 km (6 miles) should cost about SKr 110 between 6 am and 7 pm, SKr 115 at night, and SKr 123 on weekends.

TRAIN
Both long-distance and commuter trains arrive at the central station in Stockholm on Vasagatan, a main boulevard in the heart of the city. There is a ticket and information office at the station where you can make reservations. Automated ticket-vending machines are also available.

TOURS
BOAT TOURS
Strömma Kanalbolaget runs excursions into the Stockholm archipelago and to destinations on Lake Mälaren, as well as boat sightseeing tours in Stockholm under the name Stockholm Sightseeing. Boats leave from the quays outside Kungliga Dramatiska Teatern (the Royal Dramatic Theater), the Grand Hôtel, and City Hall. Popular tours within the city include the Under the Bridges of Stockholm and Royal Canal tours, departing from the quay outside the Grand Hôtel, and the Historical Canal Tour, departing from the City Hall quay.

Strömma Kanalbolaget. ⊠ *Klarabergsg. 35* ☎ *08/12004000* ⊕ *www.stromma.se.*

WALKING TOURS
Free Tour Stockholm offers guided walking tours free of charge in Gamla Stan and other neighborhoods. All they ask is that you tip the guide if you are happy with the experience.

For a different perspective on central Stockholm, try the Rooftop Tour, which takes you across the rooftops of several connected buildings on Riddarholmen, the small island next to Gamla Stan. After being fitted with a climbing harness and a helmet, you'll clip into a safety cable and make your way along a catwalk on the roof. The guide stops numerous times along the way to point out landmarks and share information about Stockholm and its history. The total distance covered is less than 1,000 feet over a period of just under an hour, but the novelty of walking along the rooftops more than 140 feet up in the air makes this a memorable experience.

Free Tour Stockholm. ⊕ *www.free-tourstockholm.com.*

★ **Rooftop Tours**
⊕ *www.takvandring.com.*

Norrmalm, Vasastan, and Kungsholmen

On the mainland north of Gamla Stan, Norrmalm is at the heart of modern Stockholm. The area bounded by City Hall, Hötorget (Hay Market), and Stureplan is essentially Stockholm's downtown, where the city comes closest to feeling like a bustling metropolis. Shopping, nightlife, business, traffic, dining—all are at their most intense in this part of town. Much of this area was razed in the 1960s as part of a social experiment to move people to the new suburbs. What came in its place, a series of modernist buildings, concrete public spaces, and pedestrianized walkways, garners support and derision in equal measure. Cross one of the bridges to the west of Central Station and you reach Kungsholmen, a mostly residential island that is home to Stockholm's distinctive redbrick City Hall, as well as some delightful waterfront walking paths and cafés. At the northern edge of Norrmalm

is another residential district, Vasastan, with restaurants, the city's main library, and several attractive parks.

◉ Sights

Hötorget (*Hay Market*)
PLAZA | Once the city's hay market, this is now a popular gathering place where you're more likely to find apples, pears, and, in summer, to-die-for Swedish strawberries. Crowds come here to meet, gossip, hang out, or pick up goodies from the excellent outdoor fruit-and-vegetable market. On the east side of the square is Konserthuset (Concert Hall), fronted by a magnificent statue by Swedish American sculptor Carl Milles, portraying Orpheus playing his lyre while floating over a group of male and female figures—a representation of music's power to elevate us above the struggles and concerns of everyday life. ⊠ *Kungsg., Norrmalm* ✛ *One block west of Sveav.* ⊕ *www.stockholm.se.*

Kulturhuset Stadsteatern (*Culture House*)
ARTS VENUE | Since it opened in 1974, architect Peter Celsing's cultural center, a glass-and-stone monolith on the south side of Sergels Torg, has become a symbol of modernism in Sweden. Stockholmers are divided on the aesthetics of this building—most either love it or hate it. Here there are exhibitions for children and adults, a library, a theater, a youth center, the main Stockholm tourist office, and a restaurant. Head to Café Panorama, on the top floor, for a lunch or coffee break with a great view of Sergels Torg down below. Though still commonly referred to simply as Kulturhuset, the institution officially changed its name in 2013 to Kulturhuset Stadsteatern, reflecting the merger of the cultural center with the on-site Stockholm City Theater. ⊠ *Sergels Torg 3, Norrmalm* ☎ *08/50620200* ⊕ *www.kulturhusetstad-steatern.se.*

Stadhuset's lakeside central lawn, framed by a grid of stone paths, is a popular picnic spot after a visit to the tower.

Kungsträdgården

PLAZA | Once the royal kitchen garden, this is now Stockholm's smallest but most central park. It is often used to host festivals and events but is best seen in its everyday guise: as a pleasant sanctuary from the pulse of downtown. Several neat little glass-cube cafés sell light lunches, coffee, and snacks. ⊠ *Norrmalm* ✛ *Between Hamng. and Strömg.* ☎ *08/55510090.*

Nationalmuseum

MUSEUM | Reopened in 2018 after a five-year renovation, Sweden's leading art museum has an impressive collection of paintings, sculptures, prints, and other works of art and design. The emphasis is on Swedish and Nordic art, but other areas are well represented, particularly 17th-century Dutch and 18th-century French paintings. The collections are presented in chronological order, forming a timeline through the museum. On the ground floor, a glassed-in courtyard houses a collection of sculptures portraying Norse gods, important people from Swedish history and culture, and other figures. ⊠ *Södra Blasieholmshamnen 2, Norrmalm* ☎ *08/51954300* ⊕ *www. nationalmuseum.se* 🎟 *Free* ⊙ *Closed Mon.*

★ Stadshuset (*City Hall*)

GOVERNMENT BUILDING | The architect Ragnar Östberg, one of the founders of the National Romantic movement, completed Stockholm's City Hall in 1923. The headquarters of the city council, the building is functional but ornate: its immense **Blå Hallen** (Blue Hall) is the venue for the annual Nobel Prize dinner, Stockholm's most prestigious event. Also notable is the Golden Hall, known for its mosaics depicting people and scenes from Swedish history. Admission is by guided tour only. You can also take a trip to the top of the 348-foot tower to enjoy a breathtaking panorama of the city and Riddarfjärden. Admission to the tower is separate from the guided tour, and much but not all of the ascent can be accomplished by elevator. Tickets for the tower are timed and often go fast, so stop by

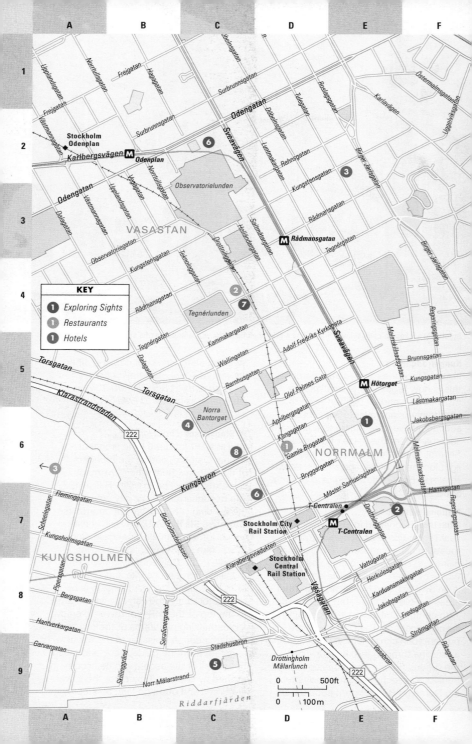

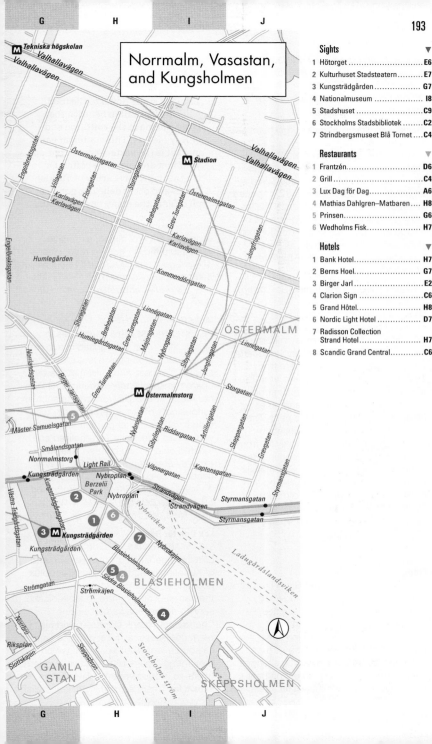

Norrmalm, Vasastan, and Kungsholmen

Sights ▼

1 Hötorget E6
2 Kulturhuset Stadsteatern E7
3 Kungsträdgården G7
4 Nationalmuseum I8
5 Stadshuset C9
6 Stockholms Stadsbibliotek C2
7 Strindbergsmuseet Blå Tornet C4

Restaurants ▼

1 Frantzén D6
2 Grill C4
3 Lux Dag för Dag A6
4 Mathias Dahlgren–Matbaren H8
5 Prinsen G6
6 Wedholms Fisk H7

Hotels ▼

1 Bank Hotel H7
2 Berns Hoel G7
3 Birger Jarl E2
4 Clarion Sign C6
5 Grand Hôtel H8
6 Nordic Light Hotel D7
7 Radisson Collection
  Strand Hotel H7
8 Scandic Grand Central C6

4

Sweden STOCKHOLM

early to guarantee a spot. ⊠ *Hantverkarg. 1, Kungsholmen* ☎ *08/50829058* ⊕ *international.stockholm.se/the-city-hall* 🖼 *SKr 90–120, tower SKr 60* 🕙 *Tower closed Oct.–Apr.*

Stockholms Stadsbibliotek (*Stockholm City Library*)

LIBRARY | The Stockholm City Library is among the most captivating buildings in town. Designed by the famous Swedish architect Gunnar Asplund and completed in 1928, the building's cylindrical, galleried main hall gives it the appearance of a large birthday cake. The collection contains some 500,000 books. ⊠ *Sveav. 73, Vasastan* ☎ *08/50830900* ⊕ *biblioteket. stockholm.se.*

Strindbergsmuseet Blå Tornet (*Strindberg Museum, Blue Tower*)

MUSEUM | Hidden away over a secondhand bookstore, this museum is dedicated to Sweden's most important author and dramatist, August Strindberg (1849–1912), who resided here from 1908 until his death four years later. The interior has been expertly reconstructed with authentic furnishings and other objects, including one of his pens. The museum also houses exhibits about various aspects of Strindberg's life, from his relationships and social engagement to his multifaceted talents, which apart from writing also included painting and music. ⊠ *Drottningg. 85, Norrmalm* ☎ *08/4419170* ⊕ *www.strindbergsmuseet.se* 🖼 *SKr 75* 🕙 *Closed Mon.*

🍴 Restaurants

Frantzén

$$$$ | **SCANDINAVIAN** | Chef Björn Frantzén creates exquisite dishes using imagination, passion, and a little science—a combination that has earned his restaurant Sweden's first (and so far only) Michelin three-star rating. The extensive tasting menu, which changes daily, is the only option, so eating here is extremely expensive. **Known for:** creative,

Refuel 🍴

Take the stairs down to the food hall **Hötorgshallen** beneath the large cinema at the southern end of Hay Market. This subterranean market is the perfect spot to put up your feet and pick up a coffee. Or try the impressive array of Turkish mezes and other delicious goodies on offer at the many bustling stalls.

sophisticated fine dining; extensive wine list; difficulty getting reservations. 💲 *Average main: SKr 3500* ⊠ *Klara Norra Kyrkogata 26, Norrmalm* ☎ *08/208580* ⊕ *www.restaurantfrantzen.com* 🕙 *Closed Sun.–Tues.*

★ Grill

$$$ | **STEAKHOUSE** | Grill specializes in high-quality meat cuts grilled in five main ways: wood-fired brick oven, rotisserie, smoke, charcoal, and grilling at the table. Share the special three-course Grill Dinner menu or choose from mains such as various cuts of steak, lamb asado, tuna teppanyaki, grilled anglerfish, or a burger with sliced pork belly, caramelized and roasted onions, and cheese. **Known for:** expertly prepared meat dishes; playful decor; three-course Grill Dinner menu. 💲 *Average main: SKr 351* ⊠ *Drottningg. 89, Vasastan* ☎ *08/314530* ⊕ *www.grill. se* 🕙 *No lunch Mon.–Thurs. or Sat.*

Lux Dag för Dag

$$$ | **SCANDINAVIAN** | On the island of Lilla Essingen, just off the western end of Kungsholmen, this former Electrolux household appliance factory (hence the name) is now a farm-to-table bistro serving delicious Swedish cuisine. Chef-owner Henrik Norström and his team use seasonal, local produce (listing its source wherever possible), which they then prepare with creative, modern twists to produce outstanding dishes. **Known for:** fresh, seasonal cuisine; stylish setting; outdoor terrace overlooking the water. [$] *Average main: SKr 271* ⊠ *Primusg. 116, Lilla Essingen* ☎ *08/6190190* ⊕ *www.luxdagfordag.se* ⊗ *Closed Sun. and Mon. No lunch Sat.*

Mathias Dahlgren–Matbaren

$$$ | SCANDINAVIAN | Located inside the Grand Hôtel, this informal bistro has large windows, colorful floor tiles, and a horseshoe-shaped bar that together create an atmosphere of casual elegance. The menu changes frequently and focuses on Swedish and international dishes such as salted cod, roast lamb, seared beef, and arctic char, beautifully prepared using fresh Scandinavian ingredients. **Known for:** casual, bistro-style fine dining; preparation that emphasizes natural flavors and textures; open kitchen. [$] *Average main: SKr 300* ⊠ *Grand Hôtel, Södra Blasieholmshamnen 6, Norrmalm* ☎ *08/6793584* ⊕ *www.mdghs. se* ⊗ *Closed Sun. No lunch Sat.*

Prinsen

$$$ | SWEDISH | Still in the same location as when it opened in 1897, "The Prince" serves both traditional and modern Swedish cuisine, but it's the traditional that brings most people here. The interior is rich with mellow, warm lighting, dark-wood paneling, and leather chairs and booths. **Known for:** classic Swedish dishes; cozy atmosphere; strong sense of history and tradition. [$] *Average main: SKr 313* ⊠ *Mäster Samuelsg. 4, Norrmalm* ☎ *08/6111331* ⊕ *www.restaurangprinsen.eu.*

Wedholms Fisk

$$$$ | SEAFOOD | Located along the Nybroviken waterfront in central Stockholm, Wedholms Fisk serves almost exclusively seafood, simply but beautifully prepared. The menu is divided by fish type, with a number of dish options for each type of fish. **Known for:** outstanding seafood; extensive wine list; elegant setting. [$] *Average main: SKr 489* ⊠ *Nybrokajen 17, Norrmalm* ☎ *08/6117874* ⊕ *www.wedholmsfisk.se* ⊗ *Closed Sun. No lunch Sat.*

🛏 Hotels

Bank Hotel

$$$$ | HOTEL | Opened in 2018, Bank Hotel—as its name suggests—occupies an elegant building from 1910 that used to be a bank. **Pros:** convenient location; luxurious design; rooftop bar. **Cons:** some rooms are quite small; street-facing rooms can be noisy; credit cards only. [$] *Rooms from: SKr 3000* ⊠ *Arsenalsg. 6, Norrmalm* ☎ *08/59858000* ⊕ *www. bankhotel.se* ⤳ *115 rooms* ⏐⊙⏐ *No meals.*

Berns Hotel

$$$ | HOTEL | This ultramodern hotel was a hotspot when it opened its doors in the late 19th century, and it retains that status today. **Pros:** stylish rooms; fantastic restaurant; great location. **Cons:** some rooms are a little small; the bar can be loud on weekends; some rooms could use updating. [$] *Rooms from: SKr 2800* ⊠ *Näckströmsg. 8, Norrmalm* ☎ *08/56632200* ⊕ *www.berns.se* ⤳ *82 rooms* ⏐⊙⏐ *No meals.*

Birger Jarl

$ | HOTEL | This stylish hotel welcomes guests to an airy lobby with a classic Scandinavian feel. **Pros:** individually designed rooms; quiet rooms; close to restaurants and supermarkets. **Cons:** some areas showing wear and tear; away from major attractions; breakfast area gets chaotic. [$] *Rooms from: SKr 1125* ⊠ *Tuleg. 8, Vasastan* ☎ *08/6741800* ⊕ *www.birgerjarl.se* ⤳ *271 rooms* ⏐⊙⏐ *Free Breakfast.*

Clarion Sign

$ | HOTEL | Neither pure business behemoth nor dictionary-definition boutique, Clarion Sign is a well-balanced and very pleasant addition to Stockholm's hotel scene. **Pros:** convenient location; great roof terrace; generous rooms. **Cons:** fee for spa and pool; crowded public areas; noisy ventilation in rooms. [$] *Rooms from: SKr 1068* ⊠ *Östra Järnvägsg. 35, Norrmalm* ☎ *08/6769800* ⊕ *www.nordicchoicehotels.se/hotell/sverige/stockholm/*

clarion-hotel-sign 🖘 558 rooms ⟊ Free Breakfast.

★ Grand Hôtel

$$$$ | HOTEL | At first glance the Grand seems like any other world-class international hotel, and in many ways it is: its location is one of the best in the city, on the quayside just across the water from the Royal Palace, and service is slick and professional. **Pros:** unadulterated luxury; location can't be beat; excellent amenities. **Cons:** gym is shared with non-guests and can be crowded; faded in parts; poor lighting in some bathrooms. Ⓢ *Rooms from: SKr 3000* ✉ *Södra Blasieholmshamnen 8, Norrmalm* ☎ *08/6793500* ⊕ *www.grandhotel.se* 🖘 *273 rooms* ⟊ *No meals.*

Nordic Light Hotel

$$ | HOTEL | Next to Central Station, this modern center for the business traveler is the perfect choice for travelers seeking cool design. **Pros:** fun lobby scene; soundproofed rooms; central location. **Cons:** average breakfast; limited menu in restaurant; some rooms are small. Ⓢ *Rooms from: SKr 1606* ✉ *Vasaplan 7, Norrmalm* ☎ *08/50563000* ⊕ *www.nordiclighthotel.se* 🖘 *169 rooms* ⟊ *Free Breakfast.*

Radisson Collection Strand Hotel

$$$ | HOTEL | This art nouveau monolith, built in 1912 for the Stockholm Olympics, has been completely and tastefully modernized. **Pros:** central location; some rooms have gorgeous views; excellent breakfast buffet. **Cons:** cheaper rooms are very small; some noise from the street and harbor; some bathrooms are cramped. Ⓢ *Rooms from: SKr 2400* ✉ *Nybrokajen 9, Norrmalm* ☎ *08/50664000* ⊕ *www.radissonhotels.com* 🖘 *170 rooms* ⟊ *No meals.*

★ Scandic Grand Central

$$ | HOTEL | The Scandic Grand Central occupies an impressive 130-year-old building just steps away from the city's main train station, right in the heart of Stockholm's downtown district. **Pros:** central to everything; quiet rooms; nice bar area. **Cons:** room cleaning must be ordered; limited bath amenities; room sizes vary. Ⓢ *Rooms from: SKr 1575* ✉ *Kungsg. 70, Norrmalm* ☎ *08/51252000* ⊕ *www.scandichotels.com* 🖘 *391 rooms* ⟊ *Free Breakfast.*

▼ Nightlife

BARS AND NIGHTCLUBS

Tranan

BARS/PUBS | The basement bar of the popular Tranan restaurant at Odenplan is a fun place to party in semidarkness to anything from ambient music to hard rock. Lots of candles, magazines, and art are inside. ✉ *Tranan, Karlbergsvägen 14, Vasastan* ☎ *08/52728100* ⊕ *www.tranan.se.*

DANCE CLUBS

Café Opera

DANCE CLUBS | This popular meeting place at the waterfront end of Kungsträdgården has fantastic 19th-century decor, including painted ceilings and elaborate chandeliers. Along with dining and drinking, the draws include roulette and major dancing after midnight. Food from the Operabaren restaurant next door is served until 1:30 am. ✉ *Karl XII:s Torg, Norrmalm* ☎ *08/6765807* ⊕ *www.cafeopera.se.*

MUSIC CLUBS

Fasching

MUSIC CLUBS | A concert venue, nightclub, and restaurant, Fasching is the best and most popular place for jazz and world music in town. International and local bands play here year-round. ✉ *Kungsg. 63, Norrmalm* ☎ *0771/477070 for tickets only* ⊕ *www.fasching.se.*

Nalen

MUSIC CLUBS | This classic club, one of Stockholm's hottest night spots from the 1930s through the 1960s, still holds major performances throughout the year, as well as themed events ranging

The Royal Swedish Opera is Sweden's national theatre for opera and ballet, founded by Gustav III in 1773.

from Rolling Stones nights to ballroom dancing. ⊠ *Regeringsg. 74, Norrmalm* ☎ *08/50529200* ⊕ *www.nalen.com.*

Pub Anchor

MUSIC CLUBS | Located on Sveavägen's main drag, the Pub Anchor is the city's downtown hard-rock and heavy metal bar. ⊠ *Sveav. 90, Norrmalm* ☎ *08/152000* ⊕ *www.pubanchor.com.*

 Performing Arts

CLASSICAL MUSIC

Konserthuset (*Concert Hall*)
CONCERTS | The home of the Royal Stockholm Philharmonic Orchestra, the city's main concert hall also hosts other Swedish and international classical music performances. ⊠ *Hötorget 8, Norrmalm* ☎ *08/50667788* ⊕ *www.konserthuset.se.*

Musikaliska

CONCERTS | This historic concert hall on the quay at Nybroviken hosts a wide variety of international classical music, jazz, and musical fusion concerts. ⊠ *Nybrokajen 11, Norrmalm* ☎ *08/54570300* ⊕ *www.musikaliska.se.*

DANCE

Dansens Hus
DANCE | When it comes to high-quality international dance in Stockholm, there's really only one place to go. Dansens Hus hosts the best Swedish and international acts, with shows ranging from traditional Japanese dance to street dance and modern ballet. You can also see ballet at Kungliga Operan (the Royal Opera House). ⊠ *Barnhusg. 12–14, Vasastan* ☎ *08/50899090* ⊕ *www.dansenshus.se.*

OPERA

It is said that Queen Lovisa Ulrika began introducing opera to her subjects in 1755. Since then Sweden has become an opera center of standing, a launchpad for such names as Jenny Lind, Jussi Björling, and Birgit Nilsson.

Kungliga Operan (*Royal Opera House*)
OPERA | The Royal Opera House is almost more famous for its restaurants and bars than for its opera and ballet productions.

But that doesn't mean an evening performance should be missed. The current baroque building dates from 1898, replacing an earlier opera house, where in 1792 King Gustav III was assassinated at a masquerade ball (the inspiration for Verdi's opera *Un Ballo in Maschera*). For about SKr 110 you can even get a listening-only seat (with no view). Guided tours of the opera house are offered on Saturday at 12:30 (more frequently in summer). ■ TIP→ **Tickets purchased by phone or at the box office carry a service charge; there's no service charge for booking online.** ⊠ *Gustav Adolfs Torg, Norrmalm* ☎ *08/7914300, 08/7914400 box office* ⊕ *www.operan.se.*

🛍 Shopping

CLOTHING

★ Filippa K

CLOTHING | One of Sweden's hottest designers, Filippa K specializes in stylish simplicity, and this store is a magnet for young Swedes seeking the latest fashions. ⊠ *Biblioteksg. 2, Norrmalm* ☎ *08/6118803* ⊕ *www.filippa-k.com.*

Gudrun Sjödén

CLOTHING | Internationally known Swedish designer Gudrun Sjödén creates brightly colored clothing and home textiles in natural fabrics for women of all ages and lifestyles. There are three locations in central Stockholm including downtown, in Gamla Stan, and on Södermalm. ⊠ *Regeringsg. 30, Norrmalm* ☎ *08/149595* ⊕ *www.gudrunsjoden.com.*

H&M

CLOTHING | H&M is one of the few Swedish-owned clothing stores to have achieved international success. Here you can find fashionable designs at reasonable prices. ⊠ *Hamng. 22, Norrmalm* ☎ *033/140000* ⊕ *www.hm.com.*

J.Lindeberg

CLOTHING | This men's store sells brightly colored and highly fashionable clothes in many styles. The golf line has been made famous by Swedish golfer Jesper Parnevik. ⊠ *Biblioteksg. 6, Norrmalm* ☎ *08/40050041* ⊕ *www.jlindeberg.se.*

DEPARTMENT STORES AND MALLS

Åhléns City

DEPARTMENT STORES | Åhléns is one of Sweden's biggest department store chains, with locations all over the country. The Stockholm flagship store, Åhléns City, is located just above the main subway station, T-Centralen, and carries everything from clothing to books to housewares and fine crystal. Prices are slightly better than at Stockholm's other major department store, NK. There's a large, well-stocked supermarket on the basement level. ⊠ *Klarabergsg. 50, Norrmalm* ☎ *08/6766000* ⊕ *www.ahlens.se.*

Gallerian

SHOPPING CENTERS/MALLS | Just down the road from Sergels Torg, this large indoor mall has designer chic to spare, selling everything from toys to fashion in beautiful surroundings. The stores are a mix of Swedish and international brands. ⊠ *Hamng. 37, Norrmalm* ☎ *073/5319496* ⊕ *www.gallerian.se.*

MOOD

SHOPPING CENTERS/MALLS | This high-end shopping destination spans an entire city block. Stylish and art filled, it has specialty boutiques and gourmet eateries that differ from the chain stores found in many Swedish shopping centers. The shops include Svenssons i Lammhult, which specializes in Nordic interior design, as well as Scandinavian fashion brands such as Samsøe & Samsøe, Jasha, and Sthlm Blvd. ⊠ *Regeringsg. 48, Norrmalm* ⊕ *www.moodstockholm.se.*

★ NK

DEPARTMENT STORES | Sweden's leading department store is the unmissable NK; the initials, pronounced enn- *koh*, stand for Nordiska Kompaniet. Almost every type of clothing can be found here, along with books, fine Swedish crystal, housewares, gourmet food, and much more. You pay for the high quality, however. ⊠ *Hamng. 18–20, Norrmalm* ⚓ *Diagonally across the street from Kungsträdgården* ☏ *08/7628000* ⊕ *www. nk.se.*

HOME

Sweden is recognized globally for its unique design sense and has contributed significantly to what is commonly referred to as Scandinavian design. All of this makes Stockholm one of the best cities in the world for shopping for furniture and home and office accessories. Swedish crystal is also renowned, with Kosta Boda and Orrefors producing the most popular and well-regarded lines of glassware.

Designtorget

HOUSEHOLD ITEMS/FURNITURE | This fun design chain sells stationery, furniture, housewares, textiles, jewelry, and assorted whimsical items, plus books on Swedish food and culture. ⊠ *Sergelgången 29, Norrmalm* ☏ *08/219150* ⊕ *www. designtorget.se.*

Fredsgatan 5

CERAMICS/GLASSWARE | Orrefors and Kosta Boda are two of the biggest names in Swedish glass, now all part of the same company. Whether you're looking for fine crystal or glass art, you'll find it at this flagship store just off the Drottninggatan pedestrian street. In addition to classic tableware, glassware, decorative bowls, vases, and candle holders, there's a gallery section filled with gorgeous, sometimes whimsical glass creations shaped like guitars, hot-air balloons, human figures, and boats. ⊠ *Fredsg. 5, Norrmalm* ☏ *08/226622* ⊕ *www.fredsgatan5.se.*

Illums Bolighus

HOUSEHOLD ITEMS/FURNITURE | The Stockholm branch of this popular Danish design chain sells furniture, clothing, housewares, and decorative items by some of Scandinavia's top design houses, including Georg Jensen silver,

Royal Copenhagen china, and Iittala glassware. ⊠ *Klarabergsg. 62, Norrmalm* ☏ *08/7185500* ⊕ *www.illumsbolighus.se.*

Målerås Flagship Store

CERAMICS/GLASSWARE | Målerås specializes in ground, engraved, and painted glass, often with nature themes such as leaves, flowers, or animals. The main level sells fine stemware, bowls, and decorative items, while the downstairs showroom houses a gallery with larger, often dramatic glass art pieces. ⊠ *Drottningg. 10, Norrmalm* ☏ *08/219686* ⊕ *www.maleras.se.*

JEWELRY

Efva Attling

JEWELRY/ACCESSORIES | A former model and pop singer, Efva Attling is now one of Scandinavia's top jewelry designers. Her award-winning creations are frequently worn by celebrities yet also remain accessible to the general public. ⊠ *Biblioteksg. 14, Norrmalm* ☏ *08/6119080* ⊕ *www.efvaattling.com.*

MARKETS

★ Hötorgshallen

OUTDOOR/FLEA/GREEN MARKETS | For a good indoor market hit Hötorgshallen, directly under the Filmstaden movie theater. The food hall is filled with butcher shops, coffee and tea shops, fresh-fish markets, and specialty food vendors. ⊠ *Hötorget, Norrmalm* ☏ *08/230001* ⊕ *www. hotorgshallen.se* ⊙ *Closed Sun.*

Gamla Stan and Skeppsholmen

Gamla Stan, Stockholm's Old Town, sits between two of the city's main islands and is the site of the original Stockholm, founded at least as far back as 1252. History, culture, and a dash of Old Europe come thick and fast here among the twisting cobbled streets lined with superbly preserved old buildings. Understandably, Gamla Stan is also a

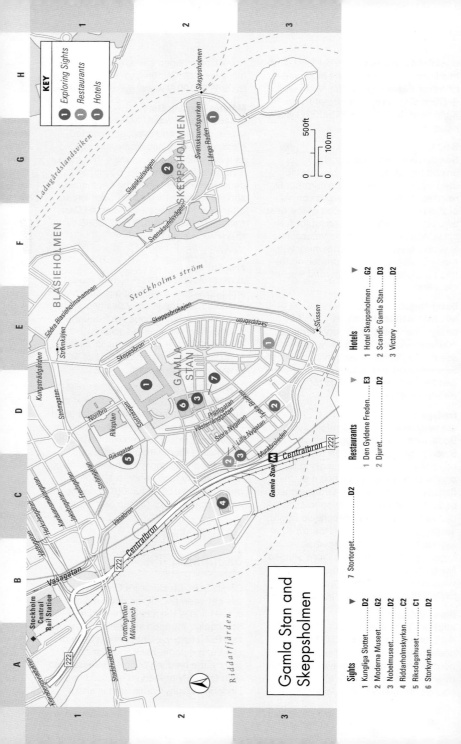

Gamla Stan and Skeppsholmen

Sights ▶

1 Kungliga Slottet..............**D2**
2 Moderna Museet..............**G2**
3 Nobelmuseet..................**D2**
4 Riddarholmskyrkan..........**C2**
5 Riksdagshuset................**C1**
6 Storkyrkan....................**D2**
7 Stortorget.....................**D2**

Restaurants ▶

1 Den Gyldene Freden.....**E3**
2 Djuret.........................**D2**

Hotels ▶

1 Hotel Skeppsholmen......**G2**
2 Scandic Gamla Stan......**D3**
3 Victory.......................**D2**

KEY

① Exploring Sights
① Restaurants
① Hotels

0 ——— 500ft
0 ——— 100m

magnet for tourists. Consequently there are plenty of substandard shops and restaurants ready to take your money for shoddy goods and bad food. Because of this, locals often make a big show of dismissing the area, but don't believe them. Secretly they love Gamla Stan. And who wouldn't? Its divine alleys, gorgeous architecture, shops, and restaurants are irresistible. Wander just a few blocks from the main tourist areas and you'll find narrow residential streets and tiny, peaceful squares. Just east of Gamla Stan is the island of Skeppsholmen, an urban oasis with tree-lined streets, colorful boats tied up alongside wooden docks, and historic maritime buildings, many now housing museums.

◉ Sights

★ Kungliga Slottet (*Royal Palace*)

CASTLE/PALACE | Designed by Nicodemus Tessin the Younger, the Royal Palace was completed in 1760 to replace the Tre Kronor palace, which burned down in 1697. Each of the four facades of the palace has a distinct style, signifying different characteristics: the west is the king's (or the male) side; the east the queen's (or female) side; the south belongs to the nation; and the north represents royalty and power in general. Watch the changing of the guard in the curved terrace entrance, and view the palace's fine furnishings and Gobelin tapestries on a tour of Representationsvåningarna (the State Apartments). Remnants of the earlier palace, as well as artifacts recovered after the fire, can be seen at the Tre Kronor Museum on the ground floor of the north side. To survey the crown jewels, which are no longer used in this self-consciously egalitarian country, head to Skattkammaren (the Treasury). Livrustkammaren (the Royal Armory)—Sweden's oldest museum, going back nearly 400 years—has an outstanding collection of weaponry, coaches, and royal regalia. Your admission ticket includes the State Apartments, the Treasury, and the Tre Kronor Museum within seven days, as well as a 50% discount off admission to the Royal Armory. ■ **TIP→ Entrances to the Treasury and Armory are on the Slottsbacken side of the palace.** ⊠ *Slottsbacken 1, Gamla Stan* ☎ *08/4026130* ⊕ *www. kungahuset.se* ☞ *Palace SKr 160, Royal Armory SKr 100.*

Moderna Museet (*Museum of Modern Art*)

MUSEUM | The museum's excellent collection includes works by Picasso, Kandinsky, Dalí, Brancusi, and other international artists. You can also view examples of significant Swedish painters and sculptors and an extensive section on photography. The building itself is striking. Designed by the well-regarded Spanish architect Rafael Moneo, it has seemingly endless hallways of blond wood and walls of glass. The building also houses the Architecture and Design Center, with exhibits including dozens of detailed architectural models of notable Swedish and international buildings. ⊠ *Exercisplan 4, Skeppsholmen* ☎ *08/520235000* ⊕ *www.modernamuseet.se* ☞ *SKr 150, combination ticket with Architecture and Design Center SKr 180* ⊗ *Closed Mon.*

Nobelmuseet

MUSEUM | The Swedish Academy meets at Börshuset (the Stock Exchange) every year to decide the winner of the Nobel Prize for literature. The building is also the home of the Nobel Museum. Along with exhibits on creativity's many forms, the museum displays scientific models, shows films, and has a full explanation of the process of choosing prizewinners. The museum does a good job covering the controversial selections made over the years. It's a must for Nobel Prize hopefuls and others. ⊠ *Börshuset, Stortorget 2, Gamla Stan* ☎ *08/53481800* ⊕ *www.nobelmuseum.se* ☞ *SKr 120* ⊗ *Closed Mon. Sept.–May.*

Riddarholmskyrkan (*Riddarholmen Church*)
HISTORIC SITE | Dating from 1270, the Greyfriars monastery is one of the oldest buildings in Stockholm; it's the burial place for two medieval kings, as well every Swedish sovereign since 1632 except Queen Kristina, who abdicated and died in Rome, and Gustav VI Adolf, the current king's predecessor, who is buried at Haga Park. The redbrick structure, distinguished by its delicate iron-fretwork spire, is rarely used for services; it's more like a museum now. The most famous figures interred within are King Gustavus Adolphus, hero of the Thirty Years' War, and the warrior King Karl XII, renowned for his daring invasion of Russia, who died in Norway in 1718. The most recent of the 17 Swedish kings to be put to rest here was Gustav V, in 1950. The different rulers' sarcophagi, usually embellished with their monograms, are visible in the small chapels dedicated to the various dynasties. Guided tours in English are offered daily. ⊠ *Riddarholmen, Kungliga slottet, Gamla Stan* ☎ *08/4026167* ⊕ *www.kungligaslotten.se/Riddarholmskyrkan* 💲 *SKr 50* ✆ *Credit cards only.*

Riksdagshuset (*Parliament Building*)
GOVERNMENT BUILDING | When in session, the Swedish Parliament meets in this neoclassical building, which was inaugurated in 1905. Above the entrance, the architect placed sculptures of a peasant, a burgher, a clergyman, and a nobleman. Take a tour of the building not only to learn about Swedish government but also to see the art within. In the former First Chamber are murals by Otte Sköld illustrating different periods in the history of Stockholm, and in the current First Chamber, a massive tapestry by Elisabet Hasselberg Olsson, *Memory of a Landscape,* hangs above the podium. An English-language guided tour is the only way to gain admission; tours are first-come, first-served and limited to 28 people, so arrive early. ⊠ *Riksg. 3A,* *Gamla Stan* ☎ *08/7864862* ⊕ *www. riksdagen.se* 💲 *Free.*

Storkyrkan (*Stockholm Cathedral*)
RELIGIOUS SITE | Dedicated to St. Nicholas, Storkyrkan (literally, the Great Church) has been at the heart of Stockholm since the 13th century. It has been modified over the years and now displays elements of a variety of architectural styles, including Gothic and baroque. Its treasures include a splendid gilded wooden sculpture of St. George and the dragon from 1489, commissioned to mark the Swedish victory over Danish forces at the Battle of Brunkeberg 18 years earlier. (A 20th-century bronze replica now stands at Köpmantorget, near Österlånggatan.) Keep an eye out for the oil painting *Vädersolstavlan,* which hangs inconspicuously near the south door. A 1636 copy of a lost original from a century earlier, it depicts an unusual atmospheric phenomenon known as a parhelion, or sun dog, and is the oldest known image of Stockholm. The Stockholm Cathedral has been the setting for many significant events such as coronations, royal weddings, and royal funerals: King Carl XVI Gustaf and Queen Silvia said their vows here in 1976, as did their eldest child, Crown Princess Victoria, and her husband Daniel Westling in 2010. ⊠ *Trångsund 1, Gamla Stan* ☎ *08/7233000* ⊕ *www.svenskakyrkan.se/stockholmsdomkyrkoforsamling* 💲 *SKr 40.*

Stortorget (*Great Square*)
PLAZA | Here in 1520 the Danish King Christian II ordered a massacre of Swedish noblemen. The slaughter paved the way for a national revolt against foreign rule and the founding of Sweden as a sovereign state under King Gustav Vasa, who ruled from 1523 to 1560. One legend holds that if it rains heavily enough on the anniversary of the massacre, the old stones still run red. Nowadays the square is lined with cafés where you can enjoy fantastic people-watching over lunch or a coffee break. During the

month before Christmas, the square fills with a market selling handicrafts, *glögg* (hot mulled wine), and other seasonal foods and gifts. ⊠ *Gamla Stan* ✛ *Near the Royal Palace.*

Restaurants

Den Gyldene Freden

$$$ | **SCANDINAVIAN** | Sweden's most famous old tavern has been open for business since 1722. The haunt of bards and barristers, artists, and advertising executives, Freden could probably serve sawdust and still be popular, but the food and staff are worthy of the restaurant's hallowed reputation. **Known for:** upscale Nordic dining; historic feel and furnishings; Swedish meatballs. $ *Average main: SKr 275* ⊠ *Österlångg. 51, Gamla Stan* ☎ *08/249760* ⊕ *www.gyldenefreden.se* ☉ *Closed Sun. No lunch weekdays.*

Djuret

$$$$ | **SWEDISH** | Vegetarians beware. At "The Animal," a cozy bistro on one of Gamla Stan's cobblestoned streets, you can dine on innovative two-week rotating meat-centric menus. **Known for:** chic decor; innovative meat dishes; impressive wine cellar. $ *Average main: SKr 595* ⊠ *Victory Hotel, Lilla Nyg. 5, Gamla Stan* ☎ *08/50640084* ⊕ *www.djuret.se* ☉ *Closed Sun. and Mon. No lunch (except sometimes on Fri.).*

Hotels

Hotel Skeppsholmen

$$ | **HOTEL** | Surrounded by trees and lawns, and just steps from the water, Hotel Skeppsholmen is an oasis of nature and tranquillity in the heart of Stockholm. **Pros:** quiet, park-like location; convenient to the Moderna and National Museum; many rooms have views of gardens and sea. **Cons:** some rooms are small; rooms lack personality and could use updates; 15–20-minute walk to more bustling parts of town. $ *Rooms from: SKr 2195*

⊠ *Gröna Gången 1, Skeppsholmen* ☎ *08/4072300* ⊕ *www.hotelskeppsholmen.se* ⤶ *74 rooms, 5 suites* ⦿ *Free Breakfast.*

Scandic Gamla Stan

$$ | **HOTEL** | The feel of historical Stockholm living is rarely stronger than in this quiet hotel tucked away on a narrow street in one of Gamla Stan's 17th-century houses. **Pros:** short walk to the Royal Palace and Nobel Museum; comfortable rooms; historic building. **Cons:** some rooms are small and unremarkable; basic facilities; 15-minute walk to Stockholm Central Station. $ *Rooms from: SKr 1595* ⊠ *Lilla Nyg. 25, Gamla Stan* ☎ *08/7237250* ⊕ *www.scandichotels.com* ⤶ *48 rooms, 4 suites* ⦿ *Free Breakfast.*

Victory

$$ | **HOTEL** | History defines this hotel, which is inside an extremely atmospheric Gamla Stan building that dates from 1640. **Pros:** great location; quirky nautical decor; superb restaurant. **Cons:** some rooms are very small; inconsistent Wi-Fi; small lobby. $ *Rooms from: SKr 1890* ⊠ *Lilla Nyg. 5, Gamla Stan* ☎ *08/50640000* ⊕ *www.thecollectorshotels.se* ⤶ *42 rooms, 3 suites* ⦿ *Free Breakfast.*

Nightlife

Le Rouge

BARS/PUBS | Le Rouge takes its cue from Le Moulin Rouge. Sit back in sumptuous surroundings of red velvet and heavy drapes and indulge in one of the most interesting cocktail menus in town. ⊠ *Brunnsgränd 2–4, Gamla Stan* ☎ *08/50524430* ⊕ *www.lerouge.se.*

Djurgården

Throughout history, Djurgården has been Stockholm's pleasure island. There was a time when only the king could enjoy this enormous green space. Today everyone comes here to breathe fresh air, visit the many museums, stroll through the forests and glades, get their pulses racing at the Gröna Lund amusement park, or just relax by the water. You can approach Djurgården from the water aboard the small ferries that leave from Slussen at the southern end of Gamla Stan. In summer, ferries also leave from Nybrokajen in front the Royal Dramatic Theater.

◉ Sights

ABBA The Museum

MUSEUM | Stockholm's newest attraction explores the phenomenon of ABBA, Sweden's most famous musical export. The crowds of visitors are a testament to the group's enduring global popularity more than three decades after its split. Exhibits trace ABBA's history from its early days and international breakthrough at the 1972 Eurovision Song Contest to the group's breakup and legacy. Outlandish stage costumes and other original memorabilia make for entertaining displays, but even more fun are the various interactive stations where you can try your hand at recording vocals, dancing like your favorite ABBA avatar, or performing on stage with holograms of the band members. Booking timed tickets in advance is strongly recommended; they can be purchased online or at the museum, tourist offices, or the SJ ticket office at Central Station. ⚠ **In-person tickets cost an additional SKr 20.** ⊠ *Djurgårdsv. 68, Djurgården* ☎ *08/12132860, 0771/757575 ticket reservations* ⊕ *www.abbathemuseum.com* ▧ *SKr 250* ⌖ *Credit cards only.*

★ Gröna Lund Tivoli

AMUSEMENT PARK/WATER PARK | Smaller than Copenhagen's Tivoli Gardens or Göteborg's Liseberg, this amusement park has managed to retain much of its historical charm, while making room for some modern, hair-raising rides among the pleasure gardens, amusement arcades, and restaurants. If you're feeling especially daring, try the Power Tower.

At 350 feet, it's one of Europe's tallest free-fall amusement-park rides and one of the best ways to see Stockholm, albeit for about three seconds, before you plummet. There isn't an adult who grew up in Stockholm who can't remember the annual excitement of Gröna Lund's April opening. Go and you will see why. Major Swedish and international artists perform on the open-air stage in the heart of the park. ⊠ *Lilla Allmänna Gränd 9, Djurgården* ☎ *08/58750100* ⊕ *www.gronalund.com* ▧ *Park entry SKr 110, concerts SKr 220, rides and attractions priced separately* ⊙ *Closed Oct.–Apr.*

Junibacken

AMUSEMENT PARK/WATER PARK | **FAMILY** | In this storybook house you travel in small carriages through the world of children's book writer Astrid Lindgren, creator of the irrepressible character Pippi Longstocking, among others. Lindgren's tales come alive as various scenes are revealed. Parents can enjoy a welcome moment of rest after the mini-train ride as the children lose themselves in the near-life-size model of Pippi Longstocking's house. It's perfect for children ages five and up. ⊠ *Galärvarsv. 8, Djurgården* ☎ *08/58723000* ⊕ *www.junibacken.se* ▧ *SKr 195.*

Nordiska Museet (*Nordic Museum*)

MUSEUM | **FAMILY** | Inside an imposing late-Victorian structure, the Nordic Museum holds exhibits on many aspects of Swedish life, including trends, traditions, clothing, costumes, folk arts, and the culture of the Sami (pronounced *sah*-mee)—the formerly seminomadic reindeer herders who inhabit the far north. Families with children should visit the delightful "village life" play area on the ground floor. ⊠ *Djurgårdsv. 6–16, Djurgården* ☎ *08/51954600* ⊕ *www.nordiskamuseet.se* ▧ *SKr 140.*

★ Rosendals Trädgård (*Rosendal's Garden*)

GARDEN | This gorgeous slice of greenery is a perfect place to spend a few hours

The Vasamuseet displays the only almost fully intact 17th-century ship that has ever been salvaged—a 64-gun warship that sank on its maiden voyage in 1628.

on a late summer afternoon. When the weather's nice, people flock to the garden café, which is in one of the greenhouses, to enjoy tasty pastries and salads made from the locally grown vegetables. Pick your own flowers from the vast flower beds (paying by weight), stroll through the creative garden displays, or take away produce from the farm shop. ⊠ *Rosendalsterrassen 12, Djurgården* ☎ *08/54581270* ⊕ *www.rosendalstradgard.se* ⊡ *Free.*

Skansen

MUSEUM VILLAGE | FAMILY | The world's first open-air museum, Skansen was founded in 1891 by philologist and ethnographer Artur Hazelius, who is buried here. Drawing from all parts of the country, he preserved examples of traditional Swedish architecture, including farmhouses, windmills, barns, a working glassblower's hut, and churches. Not only is Skansen a delightful trip out of time in the center of a modern city, but it also provides insight into the life and culture of Sweden's various regions. In addition, the park has a zoo, carnival area, aquarium, theater, and cafés. ⊠ *Djurgårdsslätten 49–51, Djurgården* ☎ *08/4428000* ⊕ *www.skansen.se* ⊡ *Park and zoo SKr 125–220, aquarium SKr 100.*

Spritmuseum (*The Museum of Spirits*) **MUSEUM |** Dedicated to alcohol and Sweden's relationship with it, this museum comes with tasting rooms, a bar, and a restaurant as well as permanent exhibits that include *Sweden: Spirits of a Nation,* which passes through the seasons of the year via scenes, scents, and sounds—all while explaining how alcohol is produced. ⊠ *Djurgårdsv. 38, Djurgården* ☎ *08/12131300* ⊕ *www.spritmuseum.se* ⊡ *SKr 100.*

★ **Vasamuseet** (*Vasa Museum*) **MUSEUM |** The warship *Vasa* sank 20 minutes into its maiden voyage in 1628, consigned to a watery grave until it was raised from the seabed in 1961. Its hull was preserved by the Baltic mud, free of the shipworms (really clams) that can eat through timbers. Now largely restored to her former glory (however short-lived it may have been), the man-of-war resides in a handsome museum. The sheer size of this cannon-laden hulk inspires awe and fear in equal measure. The political history of the world might have been different had she made it out of harbor. Daily tours are available year-round. ✉ *Galärvarvsv. 14, Djurgården* ☎ *08/51954880* 🌐 *www.vasamuseet.se* 🎫 *SKr 150.*

🍴 Restaurants

Oaxen Krog & Slip

$$$ | **SWEDISH** | This restaurant started out on the island of Oaxen in the Stockholm archipelago, where it earned a reputation as one of Sweden's best restaurants—guests were even known to arrive by helicopter on occasion. In 2013, the restaurant moved to a new, central Stockholm location on Djurgården, where its combination of seasonal, locally sourced ingredients and modern twists on classic Swedish cuisine has become more popular than ever. **Known for:** gourmet Swedish restaurant; offers casual and fine-dining options; housed in a refurbished boatyard shed. [$] *Average main: SKr 310* ✉ *Beckholmsv. 26, Djurgården* ☎ *08/55153105* 🌐 *www.oaxen.com* ⏲ *Oaxen Krog closed Sun.–Tues. and no lunch.*

Östermalm

History and money are steeped into the very bricks and mortar of Östermalm, a quietly regal residential section of central Stockholm with elegant streets lined with museums, fine shopping, and exclusive restaurants. Its crown jewel is Strandvägen, the boulevard that follows the harbor's edge from the busy downtown area to the staid diplomatic quarter. It was laid out in the late 19th century as a grand esplanade and completed just in time for the World's Fair held on Djurgården in 1897. Strolling along you can choose one of three routes. The waterside walk, with its splendid views of the city harbor, bustles with tour boats and sailboats. Parallel to the quay (away from the water) is a tree-shaded walking and bike path. Take the route farthest from the water, and you will walk past upscale shops, hotels, and expensive restaurants occupying the elegant art nouveau and Renaissance-style buildings commissioned by Stockholm's elite during the decades immediately before and after the World's Fair.

👁 Sights

Historiska Museet (*Swedish History Museum*)

MUSEUM | Viking treasures and the Gold Room are the main draw at this historical museum, but well-presented exhibitions that cover various periods of Swedish history also make the visit worthwhile. The gift shop here is excellent. ✉ *Narvav. 13–17, Östermalm* ☎ *08/51955600* 🌐 *www.historiska.se* 🎫 *Free* ⏲ *Closed Mon. Sept.–May.*

🍴 Restaurants

Sturehof

$$$ | **SCANDINAVIAN** | This massive complex of a restaurant with two huge bars is a complete social, architectural, and dining experience that surrounds you with wood paneling, leather chairs and sofas, and distinctive lighting fixtures. There's a bar directly facing Stureplan, where you can sit on a summer night and watch Stockholmers gather at the nearby Svampen (the mushroomlike concrete structure that has been the city's meeting point for years). **Known for:** excellent seafood; lively scene; good people-watching. [$] *Average main: SKr 315* ✉ *Stureplan 2, Östermalm* ☎ *08/4405730* 🌐 *www.sturehof.com.*

Hotels

Diplomat

$$ | **HOTEL** | Within easy walking distance of Djurgården, this elegant hotel is less flashy than most in its price range, but it's chic with subtle, tasteful designs and has an efficient staff. **Pros:** wonderful location; mix of old-world charm and modern comfort; fantastic views. **Cons:** antique elevator is a bit slow; some rooms are small; rooms can get hot in summer. $ *Rooms from: SKr 2100* ⊠ *Strandv. 7C, Östermalm* ☎ *08/4596800* ⊕ *www.diplomathotel.com* 130 rooms *No meals.*

★ Ett Hem

$$$$ | **HOTEL** | Feel free to grab a drink or snack from the fridge—at Ett Hem (meaning "A Home"), guests are encouraged to act like they're at home in this restored 1910 Arts and Crafts town house with only 12 rooms. **Pros:** excellent food; private-home feel; beautiful rooms and common areas. **Cons:** 20-minute walk to city center; books up fast; limited menu. $ *Rooms from: SKr 4900* ⊠ *Sköldungag. 2, Östermalm* ☎ *08/200590* ⊕ *www.etthem.se* 12 rooms *Free Breakfast.*

Hotel Esplanade

$$ | **HOTEL** | Right on the water and only a few buildings down from Stockholm's Royal Dramatic Theater, Hotel Esplanade is beautiful and offers a real touch of old Stockholm. **Pros:** great location; historic character; good breakfast. **Cons:** showing its age a little; no elevator; rooms are a little basic. $ *Rooms from: SKr 1580* ⊠ *Strandv. 7A, Östermalm* ☎ *08/6630740* ⊕ *www.hotelesplanade.se* 34 rooms *Free Breakfast.*

Nightlife

BARS AND NIGHTCLUBS

Riche

BARS/PUBS | The hangout of choice for Stockholm's wealthy elite. Sit at the bar, sip Champagne, and wonder at the glamour of it all. ⊠ *Birger Jarlsg. 4, Östermalm* ☎ *08/54503560* ⊕ *www.riche.se.*

Spy Bar

BARS/PUBS | As one of Stockholm's most exclusive clubs, Spy Bar is often filled with local celebrities and lots of glitz and glamour. ⊠ *Birger Jarlsg. 20, Östermalm* ☎ *08/54507600* ⊕ *www.spybar.se.*

Performing Arts

Berwaldhallen (*Berwald Concert Hall*)

CONCERTS | In the off-season, the Swedish Radio Symphony Orchestra plays concerts two or three times a week at this large concert hall, which is also home to the highly regarded Swedish Radio Choir. There are also occasional chamber music performances and concerts by other classical music orchestras. ⊠ *Dag Hammarskjölds Väg 3, Östermalm* ☎ *08/7841800* box office ⊕ *www.berwaldhallen.se.*

Shopping

CRAFTS

Svensk Hemslöjd

CRAFTS | From classic Dala horses to innovative textiles, jewelry, and kitchen items, this shop sells a wide range of high-quality Swedish handicrafts from some of the best artisans in the country. ⊠ *Norrlandsg. 20, Östermalm* ☎ *08/232115* ⊕ *svenskhemslojd.com.*

DEPARTMENT STORES AND MALLS

Sturegallerian

SHOPPING CENTERS/MALLS | Sturegallerian is a midsize mall on posh Stureplan that mostly carries high-end clothing and accessories by Swedish and European brands. ⊠ *Stureplan 4, Östermalm* ☎ *08/6114606* ⊕ *www.sturegallerian.se.*

HOME

Modernity

HOUSEHOLD ITEMS/FURNITURE | For-- something classic, you can't do better than Modernity, where 20th-century

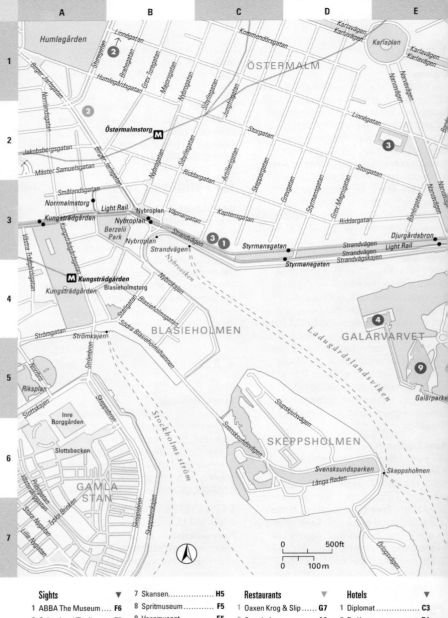

	A	B	C	D	E

Humlegården
Linnégatan
ÖSTERMALM
Karlavägen
Karlaplan
Karlavägen
Narvavägen

Storgatan
Bragehatan
Humlegårdsgatan
Grev Turegatan
Majorsgatan
Nybrogatan
Sibyllegatan
Jungfrugatan
Storgatan
Linnégatan

Birger Jarlsgatan
Nybrogatan
Sibyllegatan
Riddargatan
Artillerigatan
Skeppargatan
Grengatan
Styrmansgatan
Grev Magnigatan
Storgatan

Östermalmstorg Ⓜ

Jakobsbergsgatan
Mäster Samuelsgatan
Smålandsgatan
Norrmalmstorg Light Rail Nybroplan
Kungsträdgården Nybroplan
Berzelii Park Nybroplan
Strandvägen ❸❶ Styrmansgatan Strandvägen Light Rail
Strandvägen Strandvägskajen
Styrmansgatan Djurgårdsbron

Ⓜ Kungsträdgården
Kungsträdgården Blasieholmstorg
Stallgatan
Södra Blasieholmshamnen
BLASIEHOLMEN
Ladugårdslandsviken
GALÄRVARVET ❹

Strömgatan Strömkajen
Strömbron
Riksplan
Slottskajen
Inre Borggården
Slottsbacken
GAMLA STAN

Stockholms ström
Slupskjulsvägen
SKEPPSHOLMEN
Svensksundsvägen
Svensksundsparken Skeppsholmen
Långa Raden
Galärparken ❾

0 500ft
0 100m

Sights ▼

1 ABBA The Museum **F6**
2 Gröna Lund Tivoli **F7**
3 Historiska Museet **E2**
4 Junibacken **E4**
5 Nordiska Museet **F4**
6 Rosendals Trädgård **J5**

7 Skansen **H5**
8 Spritmuseum **F5**
9 Vasamuseet **E5**

Restaurants ▼

1 Oaxen Krog & Slip **G7**
2 Sturehof **A2**

Hotels ▼

1 Diplomat **C3**
2 Ett Hem **B1**
3 Hotel Esplanade **C3**

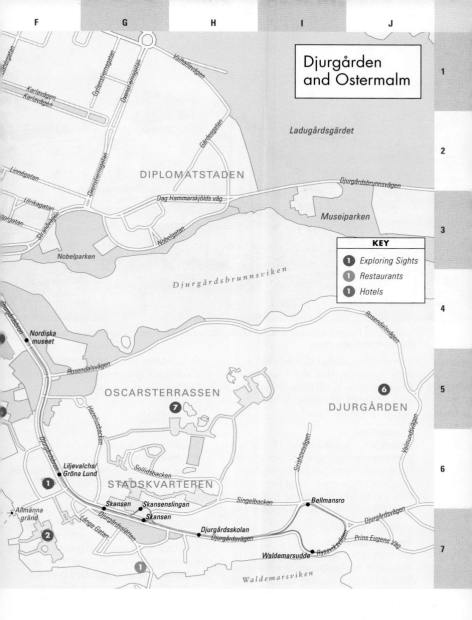

Djurgården and Ostermalm

KEY

- ① Exploring Sights
- ① Restaurants
- ① Hotels

Ladugårdsgärdet

DIPLOMATSTADEN

Museiparken

Djurgårdsbrunnsvägen

Nobelparken

Djurgårdsbrunnsviken

Nordiska museet

Rosendalsvägen

OSCARSTERRASSEN

DJURGÅRDEN ⑥

⑦

Liljevalchs/ Gröna Lund ①

STADSKVARTEREN

Sollidsbacken

Herdllnsbacken

Singelbacken

Bellmansro

Skansen

Skansenslingan

Allmänna gränd ②

Skansen

Djurgårdsslätten

Långa Gatan

Djurgårdsskolan

Djurgårdsvägen

Djurgårdsvägen

Prins Eugens Väg

①

Waldemarsudde

Ryssviksvägen

Waldemarsviken

Karlavägen
Karlavägen

Linnégatan

Ulrikagatan

...torgatan

Strandvägen

Valhallavägen

Gärdesgatan

Dag Hammarskjölds väg

Nobelgatan

Rosendalsvägen

Valmundsvägen

Strindbergsvägen

Södermalm's Fotografiska is one of the world's largest and most important photography museums and one of Stockholm's top attractions.

Scandinavian design by the likes of Arne Jacobsen, Alvar Aalto, and Poul Henningsen is in full force. ⊠ Sibylleg. 6, Östermalm ☎ 08/208025 ⊕ www.modernity.se ⊘ Closed Sun.

Svenskt Tenn

HOUSEHOLD ITEMS/FURNITURE | For elegant home furnishings, affluent Stockholmers like Svenskt Tenn, best known for its selection of designer Josef Frank's furniture and fabrics. ⊠ Strandv. 5, Östermalm ☎ 08/6701600 ⊕ www.svenskttenn.se.

MARKETS

Östermalms Saluhall

OUTDOOR/FLEA/GREEN MARKETS | If you're interested in high-quality Swedish food, try the classic European indoor market Östermalms Saluhall, where you can buy superb fish, game, bread, and vegetables—or just have a glass of wine at one of the bars and watch the world go by. The historic 1880s building has recently undergone extensive renovation to preserve and restore its original character while also ensuring its future as one of Stockholm's most popular destinations

for specialty foods. ⊠ Östermalmstorg, Östermalm ⊕ www.ostermalmshallen.se ⊘ Closed Sun.

Södermalm

South of Gamla Stan lies the island of Södermalm, usually referred to by locals simply as Söder. Long the poorest district of the city, it's now one of the most vibrant. Remnants of the old Söder can still be seen in places such as Vita Bergen and the eastern end of Åsögatan, where quaint 18th-century working-class dwellings have been preserved in isolated pockets. For the most part, however, the neighborhood is now a thoroughly modern place, filled with lively pubs, restaurants, and nightclubs, as well as an abundance of trendy shops, particularly in the district known as SoFo (South of Folkungagatan). The atmosphere is generally relaxed, with a hip, somewhat bohemian vibe. For a respite from the modern bustle, wander through Tantolunden, a large park with more than 100 community garden patches and colorful garden sheds. The steep cliffs of Söder also offer some of the city's best panoramas; head to Fjällgatan for views of Djurgården and Gamla Stan, or Monteliusvägen and Skinnarviksberget for views of City Hall, Riddarholmen, and Lake Mälaren.

Sights

★ Fotografiska

MUSEUM | Opened in 2010, this contemporary photography museum housed in a 1906 redbrick art nouveau building along the Södermalm waterfront spotlights edgy fine art photography. Past exhibitions have included celebrity photographer Annie Leibovitz and director Anton Corbijn. ⊠ *Stadsgårdshamnen 22, Södermalm* ☎ *08/50900500* ⊕ *www. fotografiska.eu* 🏷 *SKr 165.*

Stadsmuseet (*Stockholm City Museum*) **MUSEUM** | Reopened in spring 2019 after a four-year renovation, this museum traces the history of Stockholm from the 1520s to the present day. Exhibits explore the city's development during times of peace and war, how people lived during different eras, the rise of industry, and Stockholm's role in the emergence of a modern, democratic, and prosperous Sweden. ⊠ *Ryssgården, Södermalm* ☎ *08/50831620* ⊕ *stadsmuseet. stockholm.se/in-english* 🏷 *Free* ⊙ *Closed Mon.*

Restaurants

★ Hermans

$$ | VEGETARIAN | A haven for vegetarians, Hermans serves tasty, well-prepared plant-based food with influences from around the world. The glassed-in back deck and open garden both provide breathtaking vistas across the water of Stockholm Harbor, Gamla Stan, and the island of Djurgården. **Known for:** multicultural vegetarian buffets; panoramic views; cozy atmosphere. 💲 *Average*

main: SKr 189 ⊠ *Fjällg. 23B, Södermalm* ☎ *08/6439480* ⊕ *www.hermans.se.*

★ Pelikan

$$ | SCANDINAVIAN | Beer, beer, and more beer is the order of the day at this traditional drinking hall, a relic of the days when Södermalm was the dwelling place of the city's blue-collar brigade. Today's more bohemian residents find it just as enticing, with the unvarnished wood-paneled walls, faded murals, and glass globe lights fulfilling all their down-at-the-heel pretensions. **Known for:** well-prepared classic Swedish food; generous portions; salted bacon with onion sauce. 💲 *Average main: SKr 250* ⊠ *Blekingeg. 40, Södermalm* ☎ *08/55609090* ⊕ *www. pelikan.se* ☞ *No lunch Mon.-Thurs.*

Hotels

NoFo

$$ | HOTEL | Just a few blocks from busy Götgatan, this hotel is an oasis of calm in the busy urban streets of Södermalm. **Pros:** lovely setting; good-size, comfortable rooms; close to restaurants, shopping, and subway. **Cons:** some rooms are small; a bit of a walk to many attractions; soundproofing could be better. 💲 *Rooms from: SKr 1795* ⊠ *Tjärhovsg. 11, Södermalm* ☎ *08/50311200* ⊕ *www.nofo.se* 🛏 *109 rooms* ⦿| *Free Breakfast.*

★ Rival

$$ | HOTEL | Owned by ABBA frontman Benny Andersson, the Rival is cool, but never to the point of being cold. **Pros:** quiet location close to subway and Gamla Stan; lively public areas; superb breakfast. **Cons:** some rooms lack temperature controls; rooms can feel a bit dark; some very small rooms. 💲 *Rooms from: SKr 1595* ⊠ *Mariatorget 3, Södermalm* ☎ *08/54578900* ⊕ *www.rival.se* 🛏 *99 rooms* ⦿| *Free Breakfast.*

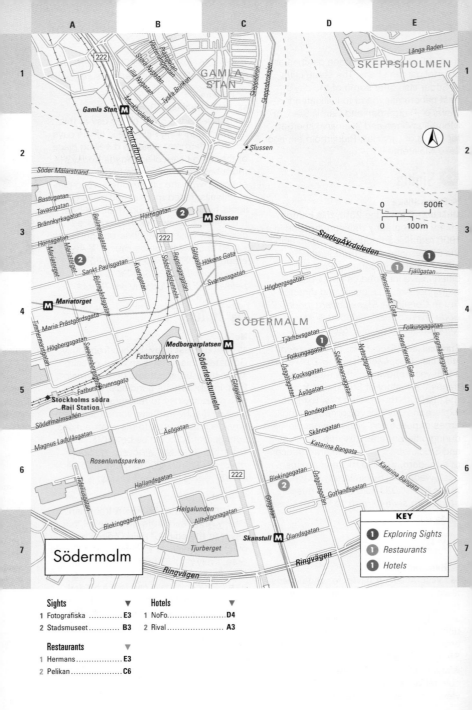

Södermalm

KEY
- **1** Exploring Sights
- **1** Restaurants
- **1** Hotels

✔ Nightlife

BARS AND NIGHTCLUBS

Akkurat

BARS/PUBS | Located just up the hill from Slussen, Akkurat is a paradise for beer and whiskey lovers. It has what's quite possibly Stockholm's best selection of draft and bottled beers, as well as a selection of nearly 400 different kinds of whiskey, particularly Scottish varieties. The menu is a cut above the usual pub grub and is especially known for its mussels prepared in various ways. There's live music on the last Sunday of every month. ⊠ *Hornsg. 18, Södermalm* ☎ *08/6440015* ⊕ *www.akkurat.se.*

Södra Teatern

BARS/PUBS | This combination indoor theater, comedy club, and outdoor café comes with a spectacular view of the city. The crowd here leans toward over-30 hipsters. ⊠ *Mosebacke Torg 1–3, Södermalm* ☎ *08/48004400* ⊕ *sodrateatern.com.*

MUSIC CLUBS

Trädgården

MUSIC CLUBS | Located under the Skanstull bridge, this hugely popular open-air club creates a festival atmosphere with multiple entertainment spaces during the summer (May to early September). In the colder months, the action moves indoors to the two-story nightclub Under Bron. ⊠ *Hammarby Slussv. 2, Södermalm* ☎ *08/6442023* ⊕ *www.tradgarden.com.*

Drottningholm

11 km (7 miles) west of downtown Stockholm.

Situated on an island in Lake Mälaren just west of Stockholm, Drottningholm is the permanent residence of Sweden's royal family, but they modestly confine themselves to only a small corner of it, leaving the rest open to the public. The interior is a riot of European design history; the beautifully manicured gardens are even more impressive.

GETTING HERE AND AROUND

The most scenic way to approach Drottningholm is by water, aboard an excursion boat from Stockholm. Strömma Kanalbolaget has daily service from the quay by City Hall between May and September, and weekend service for a month or so before and after that. Boats depart frequently—sometimes as often as every 30 minutes—and take about an hour to reach Drottningholm. Alternatively, you can take the tunnelbana to Brommaplan and the bus from there; the trip takes about half an hour. Many bus routes run from Brommaplan to Drottningholm, including routes 176, 177, and 301 to 323, so check the trip planner at ⊕ *SL.se* to find the one that best fits your schedule.

BOAT Strömma Kanalbolaget.
☎ *08/12004000* ⊕ *www.stromma.se.*

◉ Sights

Drottningholms Slott (*Drottningholm Palace*)

CASTLE/PALACE | Commissioned by Queen Hedvig Eleonora in 1662, Drottningholm Palace was designed by the court architect Nicodemus Tessin the Elder, with the finishing touches completed by his son, Nicodemus Tessin the Younger, who also designed the Royal Palace in Stockholm. During the 18th century, Queen Lovisa Ulrika put her own touches on the original baroque-style interiors, creating rooms that are a rococo riot of decoration with much gilding and trompe l'oeil. Most sections of the palace are open to the public. ⊠ *Drottningholm* ☎ *08/4016100* ⊕ *www.kungligaslotten.se* ◆ *SKr 130.*

Drottningholms Slottsteater (*Drottningholm Theater*)

ARTS VENUE | Next door to the palace is the Drottningholm Theater, the only complete theater to survive from the

Drottningholm Palace is the residence of the royal family and one of Stockholm's three World Heritage sites.

18th century anywhere in the world. Built for Queen Lovisa Ulrika in 1766, the theater experienced its glory days during the reign of her son, Gustav III, called the Theater King. It fell into disuse after his assassination at a masked ball in 1792 (dramatized in Verdi's opera *Un Ballo in Maschera*). Join a backstage tour to see the original backdrops and stage machinery and some amazing 18th-century tools used to produce such special effects as wind and thunder. To get performance tickets, book well in advance at the box office; the season runs from late May to early September. ■TIP➔ **The seats are extremely hard, so take a cushion.** ✉ *Drottningens paviljong, Drottningholm* ☎ *08/7590406* ⊕ *www.dtm.se* ✉ *SKr 110 for tours* ⊙ *Closed mid.-Dec.–Mar. and weekdays in Mar. and Nov.–mid-Dec.*

Kina Slott (*Chinese Pavilion*)
HOUSE | Located on the grounds of Drottningholm Palace Park, the Chinese Pavilion was given to Queen Lovisa Ulrika as a surprise birthday present by her husband, King Adolf Fredrik, in 1753.

At this time there was a great interest in all things Chinese due to the busy import trade conducted by the European East India companies. The rooms in the Chinese Pavilion are decorated with lacquered screens, porcelain, silk wallpaper, and other imports from China, together with Chinese-inspired, Swedish-made rococo furnishings. ✉ *Drottningholm* ☎ *08/4016100* ⊕ *www.kungligaslotten.se* ✉ *SKr 100* ⊙ *Closed Oct.–Apr.*

Sigtuna

48 km (30 miles) northwest of Stockholm.

Beautifully situated on a northern arm of Lake Mälaren, Sigtuna is Sweden's oldest town, founded around 980 by King Erik Segersäll. The main street he laid out, Stora Gatan, still follows the same course as it did a millennium ago. Though founded for political and religious reasons, the town soon became an important center for trade as well. In 1187

Sigtuna was ransacked by pirates from the eastern Baltic, and over the following centuries the town declined as cities such as Uppsala and Stockholm grew in importance and the Reformation led to the closing of the 13th-century Dominican monastery and many churches. After a long slumber, Sigtuna has come back to life over the past century and is now one of Sweden's most charming small towns, with a delightful pedestrian main street and a number of sites that reflect its long history.

GETTING HERE AND AROUND
Sigtuna can be reached by driving north from Stockholm on highway E4 to Route 263 or by taking a commuter train from Stockholm's central station to Märsta, where you change to Bus 570 or 575. The journey takes a little over an hour by public transportation. In summer you can also take a full-day boat excursion by passenger ferry to Sigtuna from Stockholm's City Hall Quay.

VISITOR INFORMATION
Sigtuna Tourist Office. ⊠ Storag. 33, Sigtuna ☎ 08/59480650 ⊕ www.destination-sigtuna.se.

◉ Sights

Mariakyrkan (*Church of St. Mary*)
RELIGIOUS SITE | The oldest building in Sigtuna, the Church of St. Mary was originally part of a monastery founded by Dominican monks in the 1230s. The church was completed around 1255 and was the first structure in Sweden to be built using the technique of firing bricks. Its style is a mix of Romanesque with early Gothic elements, and it retains much the same appearance as it did at the end of the 13th century, when the vaulted ceilings and copper roof were added. The monastery was torn down during the Reformation, but the Church of St. Mary survived and has been used as Sigtuna's parish church ever since. Its treasures include four 13th-century

crosses, two medieval triptychs, stained-glass windows from the 16th and 17th centuries, and a carved wooden pulpit from 1641. The baptismal fonts are from around 1200 and therefore predate the church itself. ⊠ Olofsg. 2, Sigtuna ☎ 08/59250454 ⊕ www.svenskakyrkan.se/sigtuna/mariakyrkan ⛉ Free.

Medieval Church Ruins
ARCHAEOLOGICAL SITE | During the early Middle Ages seven gray stone churches were constructed in Sigtuna. Most of these were allowed to fall into ruin following the Reformation. Portions of three still remain as evocative testaments to their former glory. All date from the 12th century. The best preserved are the ruins of S:t Olofs Kyrka, adjacent to the Church of St. Mary, and S:t Pers Kyrka, just beyond the western end of Prästgatan. The latter is believed to have been the seat of Sweden's archbishop until the see was moved to Uppsala in 1190. Between the two lies the ruin of S:t Lars Kyrka, of which only portions of a single tower remain. ⊠ Sigtuna ⊹ Just off Prästag. ⛉ Free.

Off the Beaten Path ◉

About 20 km (12 miles) northwest of Sigtuna is Skokloster Slott, an exquisite baroque castle with equally exquisite grounds. Commissioned in 1654 by a celebrated Swedish soldier, Field Marshal Carl Gustav Wrangel, the castle is furnished with the spoils of Wrangel's successful campaigns. The ground-floor, Wrangel, and Brahe rooms may be visited free of charge; to visit other areas you need to take a guided tour. ⊕ www.skoklosterslott.se

4

Sweden SIGTUNA

Rune Stones

ARCHAEOLOGICAL SITE | Nowhere else in the world has as dense a concentration of rune stones as Sigtuna, where there are about somewhere between 15 and 25 in the town center—more if you count fragments—and around 170 in the municipality. These stones date from the late 900s to the early 12th century, and most were raised as memorials to one or more people who died, sometimes in distant lands. One stands on Stora Gatan just outside the Sigtuna Museum, and others can be found in and around the three medieval church ruins and outside the Church of St. Mary. The tourist office and Sigtuna Museum have a brochure outlining a suggested rune stone walk, which can also be downloaded from the Destination Sigtuna website. ⊠ *Sigtuna* ⊕ *www.destinationsigtuna.se* ⊠ *Free.*

Mariefred

69 km (43 miles) southwest of Stockholm.

An idyllic small town on the south shore of Lake Mälaren, Mariefred is best known as the home of Gripsholms Slott (Gripsholm Castle), one of Sweden's most impressive Renaissance castles. The town's history dates back to the 1370s, when the powerful nobleman Bo Jonsson Grip had a castle built on the a peninsula jutting into the lake. The name Mariefred means "Peace of Mary" and comes from the name of a monastery, Pax Mariae, that was established here in the the late 15th century by Carthusian monks. A few decades later, King Gustav Vasa had the monastery torn down as part of the Reformation. He also built the present castle. Mariefred is a pretty place to walk around, with numerous well-preserved 18th- and 19th-century houses and a fine 17th-century church, whose spire is the dominating feature of the town. There are outstanding views of the castle from Mariefred's small harbor area.

GETTING HERE AND AROUND

Mariefred can be reached by taking highway E20 southwest from Stockholm to Route 223, or by taking the train to Läggesta and transferring to Bus 304 or 305. The journey takes about an hour. In summer it's also possible to take a scenic boat cruise from Stockholm to Mariefred on Läke Mälaren on the historic steamship S/S *Mariefred*. The journey takes 3½ hours each way, but you can opt to return the faster way by bus and train.

BOAT CONTACTS S/S Mariefred.
☎ *08/6698850* ⊕ *www.mariefred.info/timetable.*

VISITOR INFORMATION
Mariefreds Turistinformation. ⊠ *Kyrkog. 13* ☎ *0152/29790 Closed Sept.–May* ⊕ *www.strangnas.se/turism.*

◉ Sights

Gripsholms Slott (*Gripsholm Castle*)
CASTLE/PALACE | Built in the 16th century by King Gustav Vasa, Gripsholm Castle is an imposing redbrick structure with four round towers that occupies a small peninsula in Lake Mälaren facing the harbor of Mariefred. Its well-preserved interiors span four centuries and include Gustav Vasa's Hall of State and Duke Karl's chamber from the 1500s, as well as Gustav III's stunning 18th-century theater, located in one of the towers. Gripsholm is also home to the Swedish National Portrait Gallery, which includes more than 5,000 paintings from the 16th century to the present. A lovely park surrounds the castle, and a bit farther down the road there's a deer park with ancient oak trees and about 100 fallow deer roaming freely. ⊠ *Gripsholm, Mariefred* ☎ *0159/10194* ⊕ *www.kungligaslotten. se* ⊠ *SKr 130* ⊘ *Closed Dec.–Mar. and weekdays in Apr. and Oct.–Nov.*

Östra Södermanlands Järnväg
SCENIC DRIVE | If you're a fan of historic trains, don't miss the chance to take a ride on this narrow-gauge railway with

steam engines from the late 19th and early 20th centuries. If you just want a quick taste, you can take the 14-minute journey to Läggesta and return on the next train. For a longer option, take the train all the way to Taxinge Näsby, home of Taxinge Slott, a stately home known as the "cookie palace" for the amazing selection of baked treats in its café. The trip takes about 50 minutes. A popular alternative is the round-trip "Slott och Ånga" ("Castles and Steam") excursion, in which you travel one way between Mariefred and Taxinge by steam train and the other way aboard the historic steamship S/S *Mariefred* from 1903. Schedules vary daily, so check the website for availability. ✉ *Mariefred Station, Storg. 25, Mariefred* ☎ *0159/21000* 🌐 *www.oslj.nu* 🎫 *Mariefred–Läggesta SKr 80 one-way, SKr 100 round-trip; Mariefred–Taxinge SKr 100 one-way, SKr 140 round-trip, SKr 160 Slott och Ånga combo* 🕒 *Closed mid-Sept.–mid-May.*

🛏 Hotels

Gripsholms Värdshus

$$ | **B&B/INN** | Located along the waterfront facing Gripsholm Castle, this historic hotel sits atop the foundations of the 15th-century Carthusian monastery that gave Mariefred its name. **Pros:** perfect location; lovely front garden and terrace; comfortable beds. **Cons:** some areas in need of sprucing up; a bit expensive for what you get; service is inconsistent. [$] *Rooms from: SKr 1790* ✉ *Kyrkog. 1, Mariefred* ☎ *0159/34750* 🌐 *www.gripsholms-vardshus.se* 🛏 *46 rooms* 🍴 *Free Breakfast.*

Uppsala

67 km (41 miles) north of Stockholm.

Uppsala is home to one of Europe's oldest universities, established in 1477. It is also a historic site where pagan (and extremely gory) Viking ceremonies persisted into the 11th century. As late as the 16th century, nationwide *tings* (early parliaments) were convened here. Today it is a quiet home for about 220,000 people. Built along the banks of the Fyris River, the town has a pleasant jumble of old buildings that is dominated by its cathedral, which dates from the early 13th century.

In recent years Uppsala has shaken off the shadow of nearby Stockholm and is emerging as a destination in its own right. The town has established itself as something of a center for medical research and pharmaceuticals. Add to the mix the student population, and Uppsala has become a thriving place, with housing and office developments springing up in equal numbers to restaurants, bars, cultural venues, and shops.

GETTING HERE AND AROUND

SJ trains between Stockholm and Uppsala run twice to thrice hourly throughout the day year-round. The trip takes about 35 to 40 minutes, and ticket prices start at SKr 95 one way. SL commuter trains also run from Stockholm to Uppsala Central Station in just under an hour. A combination SL-UL (Upplands Länstrafik) ticket is required, which costs SKr 122, but if you already have a valid SL travel card, you pay only the supplementary UL fare of SKr 95.

Destination Uppsala operates staffed info points throughout the city, including at the UL Center inside Uppsala Central Station, at Gamla Uppsala Museum, and at the castle.

VISITOR INFO

Destination Uppsala. ☎ *018/7274800* 🌐 *www.destinationuppsala.se.*

👁 Sights

Gamla Uppsala (*Old Uppsala*)

ARCHAEOLOGICAL SITE | Ideally you should start your visit to the area with a trip to Old Uppsala, 5 km (3 miles) north of the

Uppsala Domkyrka is the largest and tallest cathedral in the Nordic countries, but did you know that its height is the same as its length (389 feet)?

town. Here under three huge mounds lie the graves of the first Swedish kings—Aun, Egil, and Adils—of the 6th-century Ynglinga dynasty. Close by in pagan times was a sacred grove containing a legendary oak from whose branches animal and human sacrifices were hanged. By the 10th century Christianity had eliminated such practices. A small church, which was the seat of Sweden's first archbishop, was built on the site of a former pagan temple. ⊠ *Uppsala* ✛ *North of central Uppsala, Road 290* 🖵 *Free.*

Gamla Uppsala Museum

MUSEUM | The Gamla Uppsala Museum contains exhibits and archaeological findings from the Viking burial mounds that dominate the local area. The museum distinguishes between the myth and legends about the area and what is actually known about its history. ⊠ *Disav. 15* 🕾 *018/239312, 018/239300* ⊕ *www. raa.se/gamlauppsala* 🖵 *SKr 80* ⊙ *Closed Tues., Thurs., and Fri. Oct.–Mar.*

Linnéträdgården

GARDEN | One of Uppsala's most famous sons, Carl von Linné, also known as Linnaeus, was a professor of botany at Uppsala University during the 1740s. He is best known for creating the Latin nomenclature system for plants and animals. The botanical treasures of the garden Linnaeus developed for the university have been re-created and are now on view at Linnéträdgården. Also on the grounds and included in admission is Linnémuseet, the house where Linnaeus lived with his family for 35 years. ⊠ *Svartbäcksg. 27* 🕾 *018/4712576* ⊕ *www. linnaeus.uu.se* 🖵 *SKr 100* ⊙ *Closed Oct.– Apr. and Mon. in May and Sept.*

★ Uppsala Domkyrka (*Uppsala Cathedral*)

RELIGIOUS SITE | The 390-foot twin towers of Uppsala Cathedral—whose height equals the length of the nave—dominate the city skyline. Work on the cathedral began in the early 13th century; it was consecrated in 1435 and restored between 1885 and 1893. Still the seat of Sweden's archbishop, the cathedral is also the site of the tomb of Gustav Vasa, the king who established Sweden's independence in the 16th century. Inside is a silver casket containing the relics of St. Erik, who was assassinated in 1160, as well as the burial place of other notable figures including Carl von Linné. ✉ *Domkyrkoplan* ☎ *018/4303630* 🌐 *www.uppsalacathedral.com* 🎫 *Free.*

Uppsala Universitetet (*Uppsala University*)
COLLEGE | Founded in 1477, Uppsala's university is known for the Carolina Rediviva university library, which contains a copy of every book published in Sweden, in addition to a large collection of foreign works. Two of its most interesting exhibits are the *Codex Argentus*, a Bible written in the 6th century, and Mozart's original manuscript for his 1791 opera *The Magic Flute*. ✉ *Biskopsg. 3* ☎ *018/4710000* 🌐 *www.uu.se.*

Vasaborgen Uppsala Slott (*Uppsala Castle*)
CASTLE/PALACE | Gustav Vasa began the construction of Uppsala Castle in 1549 as a symbol of royal power over the church. Occupying an imposing hilltop position, it was the site of many dramatic events, including the murder of several prominent noblemen by the mentally unstable King Erik XIV in 1567. When a devastating fire struck Uppsala in 1702 the castle was gutted. It was rebuilt some 40 years later, but the ruins of the original castle can still be seen within the southwestern section of the present structure. ✉ *Kung Jans Port* ☎ *0703/907989* 🌐 *www.vasaborgen.se* 🎫 *120 SKr* 🕒 *Closed Sept.–May except some weekends in Sept.*

🍴 Restaurants

★ Il Forno Italiano
$$$ | **ITALIAN** | From the outside, this place couldn't be more Swedish, housed as it is in a beautiful, centuries-old house opposite Uppsala's grand university building. Inside, though, a little bit of Italy takes over, with scrubbed-wood furniture, red-check tablecloths, and exposed brick and whitewashed walls. **Known for:** the best dining experience in Uppsala; personalized wine selection; authentic Italian cuisine. [$] *Average main: SKr 252* ✉ *S:t Olofsg. 8* ☎ *018/103520* 🌐 *www.ilfornoitaliano.se* 🕒 *No lunch weekdays.*

🛍 Shopping

Jaber
CLOTHING | Jaber is something of a draw for the wealthy in the area. It is a family-run clothes shop with a line of gorgeous international designs, matched only by the personal service it provides. ✉ *Fyristorg 6* ☎ *018/135050* 🌐 *www.jaber.se* 🕒 *Closed Sun.*

Öster om Ån
CRAFTS | This long-running handicraft cooperative is still hugely popular today, offering a unique and beautiful range of ceramics, knitted goods, woodwork, and jewelry. ✉ *Svartbäcksg. 18* ☎ *018/711545* 🌐 *www.osteroman.com* 🕒 *Closed Sun.*

Vaxholm and the Archipelago

32 km (20 miles) northeast of Stockholm.

Skärgården (the archipelago) is Stockholm's greatest natural asset: more than 28,000 islands and skerries (tiny, rocky islands), many uninhabited, spread across an almost tideless sea of clean, clear water. The islands closer to Stockholm are larger and more lush, with pine tree–covered rock faces and forests. There are also more year-round residents on these islands. As you move away from the mainland, the islands become smaller and more remote, turning into rugged, rocky islets. To sail among these islands aboard an old steamboat on a summer's night is a timeless delight, and throughout the warmer months Swedes flee the chaos of the city for quiet weekends on the waters.

GETTING HERE AND AROUND

For the tourist with limited time, one of the simplest ways to get a taste of the archipelago is the one-hour ferry trip to Vaxholm, an extremely pleasant, though sometimes crowded, seaside town of brightly painted wooden houses.

BOAT AND FERRY

Regular ferry service to the archipelago departs from Strömkajen, the quayside in front of Stockholm's Grand Hôtel. Boat cruises leave from the harbor in front of the Royal Palace or from Nybrokajen, across the street from the Royal Dramatic Theater, along Strandvägen. Ferries to the Fjäderholmarna run almost constantly all day long in summer (April–September) from Slussen, Strömkajen, and Nybroplan. Contact Strömma Kanalbolaget, Waxholmsbolaget, or Fjäderholmslinjen. Waxholmsbolaget's passenger ferries are part of the SL transportation network, which also includes buses, subways, and commuter trains.

TOURS

Sandhamnsguiderna. ☎ 08/6408040 ⊕ www.sandhamn.se.

VISITOR INFO

Vaxholms Turistbyrå. ✉ Rådhuset, Torget 1, Vaxholm ☎ 08/54131480 ⊕ www.vaxholm.se.

Sights

Artipelag

MUSEUM | In the archipelago, 12 miles east of Stockholm, stands this art and cultural venue, a 110,000-square-foot, primarily glass structure in which you can check out art exhibits, marvel at Swedish design, dig into local organic cuisine, or listen to world-class music. You might also just want to come to soak up the fresh breeze along the waterfront here. ✉ Artipelagstigen 1, Gustavsberg ☎ 08/57013000 ⊕ www.artipelag.se ⊴ Exhibits SKr 235.

Fjäderholmarna (*The Feather Islands*)

ISLAND | In the 19th century these four secluded islands were the last chance for archipelago residents to take a break before rowing into Stockholm to sell their produce. After more than 60 years as a military zone, the islands were opened to the public in the early 1980s. Today they are crammed with arts-and-crafts studios, shops, several restaurants and cafés, a traditional boat exhibit, an ingenious "shipwreck" playground, and a smoked-fish shop. It takes a 25-minute ferry ride to get here from Stockholm; boats depart from Slussen and Strandvägen, May to early September. ✉ Fjäderholmarna ⊕ www.fjaderholmarna.se ⊙ Closed Oct.–Apr.

Grinda

ISLAND | The island of Grinda has been popular with Stockholmers for a long time. Walking paths cut through the woods and open fields, making exploring easy. It takes just 15 minutes to walk from one end of the island to the other. If you want to stay longer, there's an inn, Grinda Wärdshus, that dates from the turn of the 20th century and also has a noted restaurant, as well as kayaks, stand-up paddleboards, and Jet Skis for rent. The trip from Stockholm to Grinda takes about two hours. ✉ Grinda ☎ 08/54249491 ⊕ www.grinda.se.

Nynäshamn

TOWN | A picturesque town at the southern edge of Stockholm's archipelago, Nynäshamn is located on the mainland but has the flavor of the islands, particularly in the lively harbor area with its seafood restaurants, fish smokery, and red huts housing tiny shops and cafés. Cruise ferries to the island of Gotland and Gdańsk in Poland depart from terminals at the north end of the harbor. At the southern end, the Nynäshamn Tourist Office has bikes for rent. A great destination for a ride is Strandvägen, a gorgeous coastal road (open to cars in one direction only) that winds along the

Constructed to defend Stockholm in the 1500s, today Vaxholm Fortress is home to the Swedish National Museum of Coastal Defense.

shore to Lövhagen, where there is a café with outdoor seating and nature trails. ✉ *Nynäshamn* ⊕ *www.visitnynashamn. se.*

Sandhamn

ISLAND | One of the most popular excursions is to Sandhamn, the main town on the island of Sandön, which is home to about 100 permanent residents. The journey takes about three hours by steamship, but there are faster boats available. The Royal Swedish Yacht Club was founded here at the turn of the 20th century, and sailing continues to be a popular sport. Sandhamn's fine-sand beaches also make it an ideal spot for swimming. Explore the village of Sandhamn and its narrow alleys and wooden houses, or stroll out to the graveyard outside the village, where tombstones bear the names of sailors from around the world. ✉ *Sandhamn* ⊕ *www.sandhamn.se.*

Trosa

TOWN | At the far southern tip of Stockholm's archipelago lies Trosa, a mainland town situated where the tiny Trosa River

empties into the Baltic Sea. The river is flanked by beautiful wooden villas painted white, red, yellow, and mint green—a reflection of Trosa's heritage as a seaside retreat for stressed but wealthy Stockholmers. Pleasures in Trosa are simple: enjoying a meal on an outdoor patio, strolling through the charming narrow streets, browsing the shops by the river, or enjoying an ice cream while watching boaters tie up along the wooden docks. ✉ *Vaxholm* ⊕ *www.trosa.com.*

Vaxholm Fortress Museum

MILITARY SITE | Built in 1544 to defend Stockholm against shipborne attacks from the east, this historic fortification on the island of Vaxholmen, just east of Vaxholm, is now a museum. Visitors see the fortress as it was in 1854, and can enter the Citadel's bombproof vaults to imagine how things were during the Crimean War. You can also visit the World War II coastal defence artillery post. ✉ *Kastellet, Vaxholm* ☎ *08/12004870* ⊕ *www.vaxholmsfastning.se/english.*

🍴 Restaurants

Dykarbaren
$$$ | **SWEDISH** | The idea for this old wooden harborside restaurant came from similar cafés in Brittany, France. Simple local dishes, mostly of fish, are served up in an informal wooden-table dining area. **Known for:** delicious comfort food; creative cocktails; lively atmosphere. [$] *Average main: SKr 272* ✉ *Strandpromenaden, Sandhamn* ☎ *08/57153554* 🌐 *www.dykarbaren.se* 🕓 *Closed Oct.–Apr.*

Fjäderholmarnas Krog & Magasin
$$$ | **SCANDINAVIAN** | A crackling fire on the hearth in the bar area welcomes the sailors who frequent this laid-back restaurant. In case you don't travel with your own sailboat, you can time your dinner to end before the last ferry returns to the mainland. **Known for:** idyllic island setting; well-presented Scandinavian dishes; cozy decor. [$] *Average main: SKr 337* ✉ *Stora Fjäderholmen, Fjäderholmarna* ☎ *08/7183355* 🌐 *www.fjaderholmarnaskrog.se* 🕓 *Closed Oct.–Apr.*

Nynäs Rökeri
$$ | **SEAFOOD** | This popular spot on Nynäshamn's waterfront is part fish shop, part casual restaurant, with seafood sourced from local fishermen. The shop sells smoked and pickled fish, shrimp, and sauces. **Known for:** smoked shrimp and fresh fish; simple yet flavorful dishes; casual pier-side dining. [$] *Average main: SKr 159* ✉ *Fiskargränd 6, Nynäshamn* ☎ *08/52010023* 🌐 *www.nynasrokeri.se.*

🛏 Hotels

The larger, more inhabited islands in the archipelago often have at least one decent hotel, if not a few, whereas some of the smaller, more remote islands have only an inn or two or camping facilities.

Bomans
$$ | **HOTEL** | Just steps from Trosa's lively harbor, this family-run hotel dates from the early 20th century. **Pros:** unique decor; intimate and charming; cozy indoor and outdoor lounge areas. **Cons:** room styles vary; rooms can be warm; some rooms and bathrooms are small. [$] *Rooms from: SKr 1850* ✉ *Östra Hamnplan 1, Trosa* ☎ *0156/52500* 🌐 *www.bomans.se* 🛏 *43 rooms* 🍴 *Free Breakfast.*

Grinda Wärdshus
$$ | **B&B/INN** | Housed in one of the archipelago's largest stone buildings, built in 1906, Grinda Wärdshus has homey rooms and bright, comfortable public areas. **Pros:** peaceful setting; gorgeous views; outdoor activities. **Cons:** rooms are a little basic; somewhat overpriced dining; uneven restaurant service. [$] *Rooms from: SKr 1990* ✉ *Södra Bryggan, Grinda* ☎ *08/54249491* 🌐 *www.grinda.se* 🛏 *30 rooms* 🍴 *Free Breakfast.*

Utö Värdshus
$ | **HOTEL** | **FAMILY** | The rooms are large and well laid out here, with traditional furniture resembling that found in a Swedish farmhouse—lots of old pine and comfy, plump cushioning. **Pros:** beautiful surroundings; lovely restaurant; variety of rooms. **Cons:** a trek from Stockholm; not right on the water; restaurant is a distance from rooms. [$] *Rooms from: SKr 1350* ✉ *Gruvbryggan, Utö* ☎ *08/50420300* 🌐 *www.utovardshus.se* 🛏 *18 rooms, 30 cabins* 🍴 *Free Breakfast.*

Göteborg (Gothenburg)

Don't tell the residents of Göteborg that they live in Sweden's "second city," but not because they will get upset (people here are known for their amiability and good humor). They just may not understand what you are talking about. People who call Göteborg (pronounced *yuh*-teh-bor; most visitors stick with the simpler Gothenburg) home seem to forget that the city is diminutive in size and status compared to Stockholm.

Spend a couple of days here and you'll forget, too. You'll find it's easier to ask what Göteborg hasn't got to offer rather than what it has. Culturally it is superb, boasting a fine opera house and theater, one of the country's best art museums, and a fantastic applied-arts museum. There's plenty of history to soak up, from the ancient port that gave the city its start in the early 1600s to the 19th-century factory buildings and workers' houses that reflect its expanding commercial power. For those looking for nature, the wild west coast and bucolic green countryside are both within striking distance. And don't forget the food—Göteborg has a dynamic culinary scene, with some of Sweden's top chefs and a strong focus on locally sourced ingredients.

GETTING HERE AND AROUND

AIR

Among the airlines operating to and from Göteborg are Air France, British Airways, Finnair, KLM, Malmö Aviation, Norwegian, and SAS. Landvetter Airport is approximately 26 km (16 miles) from the city.

Landvetter is linked to Göteborg by freeway. Buses leave Landvetter every 12–30 minutes and arrive 30 minutes later at Nils Ericsonsplatsen by the central train station, with stops at Korsvägen, Berzeliigatan, and Kungsportsplatsen. The price of the trip is SKr 119 at the airport and SKr 99 if purchased online. For more information, check Flygbussarna's website, ⊕ *www.flygbussarna.se.*

The taxi ride to the central station should cost about SKr 450, not counting possible surcharges.

TAXI

Taxi Göteborg
☎ *031/650000* ⊕ *www.taxigoteborg.se.*

PUBLIC TRANSPORTATION

Västtrafik is the regional public transportation company, which includes Göteborg's excellent transit service. Timetables and route maps are available on the Västtrafik website. Västtrafik ticket offices are located at Brunnsparken, Drottningtorget, and the Nils Ericson Terminal by Central Station. Tickets can also be purchased at convenience stores such as 7-Eleven and Pressbyrån. Single tickets cost SKr 31 for travel within the city. There are also passes available for unlimited travel within Göteborg during a 24-hour or three-day period; these cost SKr 95 and SKr 190, respectively.

TRAIN

SJ, the Swedish national rail company, has regular service from Stockholm to Göteborg, which takes a little over 4½ hours, as well as frequent high-speed (X2000) train service, which takes about three hours. The private company MTR Express also operates trains along the same route, with a journey time of just over three hours. All trains arrive at the central train station at Drottningtorget, downtown Göteborg.

TOURS

Göteborgs Turistbyrå. ⊠ *Kungsportsplatsen 2, Göteborg* ☎ *031/3684200* ⊕ *www.goteborg.com.*
Paddan Boat Tours. ⊠ *Kungsportsplatsen, Centrum* ☎ *031/609670* ⊕ *www.stromma.com.*

◉ Sights

Göteborg begs to be explored on foot. A small, neat package of a city, it can be divided up into three main areas, all of which are closely interlinked. If your feet need a rest, though, there is an excellent streetcar network that runs to all parts of town. The main artery of Göteborg is Kungsportsavenyn (more commonly referred to as Avenyn, "the Avenue"), a 60-foot-wide tree-lined boulevard that bisects the city along a northwest–southeast axis. Avenyn starts at Göteborg's cultural heart, Götaplatsen, home to the city's oldest cultural institutions, where ornate carved-stone buildings keep watch over the shady boulevards of the

Vasastan neighborhood, which are lined with exclusive restaurants and bars. Follow Avenyn north and you'll find the main commercial area, now dominated by the modern Nordstan shopping center. Beyond is the waterfront, busy with all the traffic of the port, as well as some of Göteborg's newer cultural developments, in particular its magnificent opera house.

To the west of Avenyn lies the University of Göteborg and the leafy streets of the Vasastan neighborhood, lined with restaurants and bars. Farther west still are the Haga and Linné districts. Once home to the city's dockyard, shipping, and factory workers, these areas are now chic and alive with arts-and-crafts galleries, antiques shops, boutiques selling clothes and household goods, and street cafés and restaurants.

Botaniska Trädgården (*Botanical Gardens*)
GARDEN | With 16,000 plant species, this is Sweden's largest botanical garden. It encompasses herb gardens, bamboo and rhododendron groves, a Japanese valley, forest plants, and tropical greenhouses. Once you've absorbed some inspiration, you can pick up all you need to create your own botanical garden from the on-site shop. ⊠ *Carl Skottsbergs Gata 22A, Slottsskogen* ☎ *031/4737777* ⊕ *botaniska.se* 🖻 *Park free, greenhouses SKr 20.*

Domkyrkan (*Göteborg Cathedral*)
RELIGIOUS SITE | Built in neoclassic yellow brick, Göteborg's cathedral dates from 1802—two previous cathedrals on this spot were destroyed by fire. Though plain on the outside, the interior is impressive. Two glassed-in verandas originally used for the bishop's private conversations run the length of each side of the cathedral. The altar is impressively ornate and gilt. ⊠ *Kyrkog. 28, Centrum* ☎ *031/7316130* ⊕ *www.svenskakyrkan.se/gbgdomkyrko* 🖻 *Free.*

★ **Götaplatsen** (*Göta Square*)
PLAZA | This square was built in 1923 in celebration of the city's 300th anniversary. In the center is the Swedish American sculptor Carl Milles's breathtaking fountain statue of Poseidon holding a codfish. Behind the statue stands the Göteborg Museum of Art, flanked by the city's main concert hall and municipal theater, contemporary buildings in which the city celebrates its contributions to Swedish cultural life. ⊠ *Götaplatsen* ⊕ *www.goteborg.com.*

★ **Göteborgs Konstmuseum** (*Gothenburg Museum of Art*)
MUSEUM | This impressive collection of the works of leading Scandinavian painters and sculptors captures some of the moody introspection of the artistic community in this part of the world. Holdings include works by Swedes such as Carl Milles, Johan Tobias Sergel, impressionist Anders Zorn, Victorian idealist Carl Larsson, and Prince Eugen. The collection of 19th- and 20th-century French art is the best in Sweden, and there's also a small collection of old masters. On the ground floor is the Hasselblad Center, named for the pioneering camera maker and Göteborg native Victor Hasselblad. Its changing exhibits are devoted to showcasing progress in the art of photography. ⊠ *Götaplatsen 6, Götaplatsen* ☎ *031/3683500* ⊕ *www.konstmuseum.goteborg.se* 🖻 *SKr 60* ⊙ *Closed Mon.*

Haga Nygata
HISTORIC SITE | The redbrick buildings that line this street were originally poorhouses donated by the Dickson family, the city's British industrialist forefathers; "ROBERT DICKSON" can still be seen carved into the facades of some of them. Like most buildings in Haga, the buildings' ground floors were made of stone in order to prevent the spread of fire (the upper floors are wood). Nowadays they house a diverse array of shops and cafés, including Café Husaren, which is famous for its *hagabullen,* cinnamon

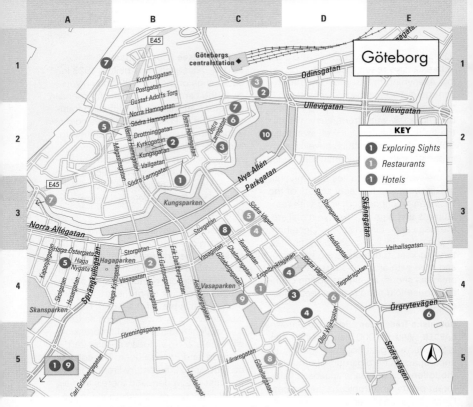

Göteborg

KEY

- ① Exploring Sights
- ① Restaurants
- ① Hotels

buns the size of salad plates. ⊠ *Haga* ☎ *070/5141328* ⊕ *www.hagashopping. se.*

Liseberg Amusement Park

AMUSEMENT PARK/WATER PARK | FAMILY | The nearly 40 attractions here—carousels, rides, roller coasters, funhouses, and the like—pull in roughly 3 million visitors each year. The park is especially mobbed around the holidays, when it throws the largest Christmas market in Sweden, with 5 million twinkling lights on display along with an ice rink, Santa's World, and stalls selling crafts, mulled wine, gingersnaps, and other seasonal goods. Big-name concerts take place regularly on the park's stages. ⊠ *Örgrytev. 5, Liseberg* ☎ *031/40222* ⊕ *www.liseberg. com* ⊡ *SKr 110 (rides priced separately)* ⊙ *Closed Jan.–Apr., closed weekdays Sept.–Oct.*

Maritiman (*Maritime Museum*)

LIGHTHOUSE | In the world's largest floating maritime museum you'll find modern naval vessels, including a destroyer, a submarine, a lightship, cargo vessels, and various tugboats, providing insight into Göteborg's historic role as a major port. Gangways lead between the ships, making it possible to explore all of them close-up. Highlights include climbing aboard the destroyer *Småland* and descending into the confined quarters of the submarine *Nordkaparen*. ⊠ *Packhusplatsen 12, Nordstan* ☎ *031/105950* ⊕ *maritiman.se* ⊡ *SKr 140* ⊙ *Closed weekdays Sept.–May.*

Röhsska Museet (*Röhsska Museum of Design and Craft*)

MUSEUM | This museum's fine collections include an eclectic mix of furniture, books and manuscripts, tapestries, silver, and East Asian arts and crafts. Artifacts date back as far as 1,000 years, but for many visitors it's the 20th-century gallery, with its collection of familiar household objects, that really strikes a chord. ⊠ *Vasag. 37–39, Vasastan*

☎ *031/3683150* ⊕ *rohsska.se* ⊡ *SKr 60* ⊙ *Closed Mon.*

Slottsskogen

CITY PARK | FAMILY | Spend some time in this stunning area of parkland containing walking trails, green lawns, natural woodlands, cafés, historical buildings, farm animals, and one of Sweden's oldest zoos, with mostly Nordic animals. A true urban oasis, Slottsskogen is one of the best parts of the city for relaxing. ⊠ *Slottsskogspromenaden, Slottsskogen* ☎ *031/3655700* ⊕ *www.goteborg.se/ slottsskogen.*

★ Trädgårdsföreningen i Göteborg (*Garden Society of Gothenburg*)

GARDEN | Beautiful open green spaces, manicured gardens, and tree-lined paths are the perfect place to escape for some peace and rest. Rose fanciers can head for the magnificent rose garden, where there are 2,500 roses of 1,200 varieties. Also worth a visit is the Palm House, whose late-19th-century design echoes that of London's Crystal Palace. ⊠ *Slussg. 1, Centrum* ☎ *031/3650000* ⊕ *tradgardsforeningen.se* ⊡ *Free.*

Gothenburg Pass ◉

Visitors who plan to explore Göteborg's attractions extensively should consider purchasing a Gothenburg Pass, which provides free admission to more than 30 top attractions, the Paddan Boat Tour, and hop-on, hop-off sightseeing by bus and boat. The pass costs SKr 395 for one day, SKr 655 for two days, SKr 855 for three days, and SKr 1135 for five days. The Gothenburg Pass can be purchased up to a year in advance online or in person at the Göteborg Tourist Offices. ⊕ *gothenburgpass.se*

🍴 Restaurants

Göteborg is filled with people who love to eat and cook. The fish and seafood here are some of the best in the world, owing to the clean, cold waters off Sweden's west coast. And Göteborg's chefs are some of the best in Sweden, as a glance at the list of recent "Swedish Chef of the Year" winners will confirm. Call ahead to be sure restaurants are open, as many are closed in July or in other summer months.

Familjen

$$$ | **SCANDINAVIAN** | Familjen's trendy warm red and green minimalist interior, along with friendly staff who manage its often-packed house with grace, both help make it one of the best restaurants in town for sampling rustic west coast–style cooking. Menus are dictated by the availability of fresh seasonal ingredients and change regularly. **Known for:** creative cocktails; covered outdoor patio; cozy room. [$] *Average main: SKr 297* ✉ *Arkivg. 7, Vasastan* ☎ *031/207979* 🌐 *www.restaurangfamiljen.se* 🕒 *Closed Sun. No lunch.*

Koka

$$$$ | **SWEDISH** | Decorated in light-colored wood with red accents, Koka provides a cozy setting for a special night out. Choose between fixed menus of three, five, or seven courses infused with flavors from the farms, forests, and waters of West Sweden. **Known for:** creative cuisine; extensive wine list; preselected wine packages. [$] *Average main: SKr 545* ✉ *Viktoriag. 12, Vasastan* ☎ *031/7017979* 🌐 *www.restaurangkoka.se* 🕒 *Closed Sun. No lunch.*

★ **Norda**

$$ | **INTERNATIONAL** | Located inside an old post office that's now the Clarion Hotel Post, Norda combines American-east-coast style with locally sourced ingredients from Sweden's west coast. The menu, overseen by superstar chef Marcus Samuelsson, includes such classics as poached cod, shrimp sandwiches, and Norda's special hamburgers, which are made with locally sourced beef topped with caramelized onions and Gruyère cheese. **Known for:** wine list; weekend brunch buffet; impressive historic interior. [$] *Average main: SKr 248* ✉ *Clarion Hotel Post, Drottningtorget 10, 2nd fl., Vasastan* ☎ *031/619060* 🌐 *restaurangnorda.se.*

Pinchos

$ | **ECLECTIC** | The thoroughly modern Pinchos takes into account the country's love for mobile technology by taking all orders through an app that diners can download onto their mobile phones. The tapas-style dishes include marinated chicken skewers, pork dumplings, Korean barbecue ribs, Caribbean fish tacos, fried prawns, quesadillas, halloumi fries, vegan spring rolls, mushroom risotto, and other international selections. **Known for:** good for groups; small plates for sharing; ordering through an app. [$] *Average main: SKr 124* ✉ *Götabergsg. 28A, Vasastan* ☎ *073/5398528* 🌐 *www.pinchos.se* 🕒 *Closed Mon. and Tues. No lunch.*

Restaurang Kometen

$$$ | **SWEDISH** | An iconic restaurant since 1934, "The Comet" is a feel-good haven for celebrities and locals alike, who come to dine on simple yet delicious seafood fare and classic Swedish dishes. Original paintings and chandeliers along with dark mahogany and red upholstery give it a 1940s saloon feel. **Known for:** old-fashioned setting; traditional cuisine; local institution. [$] *Average main: SKr 264* ✉ *Vasag. 58, Vasastan* ☎ *031/137988* 🌐 *www.restaurangkometen.se.*

Sjömagasinet

$$$$ | **SEAFOOD** | Arguably one of the best seafood restaurants in Sweden, this icon remains a leading champion of west-coast fish. In the delightful oak-beamed dining room, part of a 200-year-old renovated shipping warehouse, you can eat carefully presented, delicious fish dishes with a classical local touch. **Known**

for: summer seafood buffet; waterfront outdoor dining; extensive wine list. $ *Average main: SKr 455* ☒ *Adolf Edelsvärds Gata 5, Kiel-terminalen* ☎ *031/7755920* ⊕ *www.sjomagasinet.se* ⊘ *Closed Sun. and Mon.*

SK Mat & Människor

$$ | **SCANDINAVIAN** | The connection between people and food is at the heart of this stylish yet intimate restaurant where you can watch your meals being prepared in the completely open kitchen—in fact, chefs often bring dishes to the tables themselves. The focus is on seasonal Scandinavian cuisine expertly prepared and complemented by an extensive wine list. **Known for:** creative cuisine; relaxed fine dining; extensive wine list. $ *Average main: SKr 232* ☒ *Johannesbergsg. 24, Kiel-terminalen* ☎ *031/812580* ⊕ *www.skmat.se* ⊘ *Closed Sun. No lunch.*

★ Thörnströms Kök

$$$ | **SCANDINAVIAN** | The steep climb up the street to Thörnströms is perfect for working up a thirst: it makes sense to start with a choice from the excellent wine list. Take your table in one of the three small and elegant dining rooms and enjoy one of the four- to eight-course tasting menus featuring small dishes of modern European food made with the finest local ingredients. **Known for:** creative tasting menus; modern European cuisine; wine pairings. $ *Average main: SKr 350* ☒ *Teknologg. 3, Vasastan* ☎ *031/162066* ⊕ *www.thornstromskok.com* ⊘ *Closed Sun. No lunch.*

28+

$$$ | **SWEDISH** | Step down from the street into this former wine-and-cheese cellar to find an elegant restaurant owned by two of the best chefs in Göteborg. Finely set tables, flickering candles, and country-style artwork evoke the mood of a rustic French bistro. **Known for:** creative tasting menus; cozy atmosphere; excellent wine pairings. $ *Average main: SKr 285* ☒ *Götabergsg. 28, Vasastan*

☎ *031/202161* ⊕ *www.28plus.se* ⊘ *Closed Sun. and Mon. No lunch except for large groups by special appointment* ⛰ *Jacket required.*

Hotels

Avalon Hotel

$ | **HOTEL** | Feng shui meets Scandinavian design at this cutting-edge hotel with a rooftop swimming pool, a portion of which floats midair. **Pros:** central location; unique design; rooftop pool. **Cons:** noisy surroundings; hallways are rather dark; pool only open during afternoon. $ *Rooms from: SKr 1465* ☒ *Kungstorget 9, Centrum* ☎ *031/7510200* ⊕ *www.avalonhotel.se/en* ⇥ *101 rooms* ⦿ *Free Breakfast.*

Clarion Hotel Post

$ | **HOTEL** | Housed in a mammoth neoclassical building from the 1920s that was once a post office, the impressive Clarion Hotel Post effortlessly merges antique details and facades with a trendy Scandinavian style that includes a reception desk tricked out with sparkling crystals and a year-round rooftop pool with fantastic views of the city. **Pros:** great spa and restaurant; next to train station; lots of amenities. **Cons:** a massive building that's very busy; bar gets loud on weekends; service can be inconsistent. $ *Rooms from: SKr 1460* ☒ *Drottningtorget 10, Centrum* ⊕ *www.clarionpost.com* ⇥ *500 rooms* ⦿ *Free Breakfast.*

Dorsia

$$$ | **HOTEL** | Flamboyant, opulent, and lavish describe the Dorsia, where peacock feathers, plush indigo velvet, and French antiques are all par for the course. **Pros:** exclusive feel; unique design; central location. **Cons:** slightly over-the-top decor isn't for everyone; expensive for what you get; sooms rooms are small. $ *Rooms from: SKr 2590* ☒ *Trädgårdsg. 6, Centrum* ☎ *031/7901000* ⊕ *www.dorsia.se* ⇥ *37 rooms* ⦿ *Free Breakfast.*

Elite Park Avenue

$$ | **HOTEL** | This Göteborg institution has hosted everyone from the Beatles and Michael Jackson to George H. W. **Pros:** elegant feel; modern, comfortable rooms; historic hotel. **Cons:** street-facing rooms can be noisy; temperature control can be problematic; some rooms are small. [$] *Rooms from: SKr 1700* ✉ *Kungsportsavenyn 36–38, Centrum* ☎ *031/7271000* 🌐 *www.elite.se* 🛏 *325 rooms* 🍴 *Free Breakfast.*

Elite Plaza

$$ | **HOTEL** | An architectural attraction in its own right, the Elite Plaza occupies a palatial building that dates from 1889 and has been modernized with care to give it an air of grandeur, quality, and restfulness. **Pros:** beautiful setting; central location; mix of character and contemporary style. **Cons:** some rooms and bathrooms can be small; rooms can be stuffy in summer; soem exterior noise. [$] *Rooms from: SKr 1800* ✉ *Västra Hamng. 3, Göteborg* ☎ *031/7204000* 🌐 *www.elite.se* 🛏 *127 rooms* 🍴 *Free Breakfast.*

★ **Hotel Royal**

$$ | **HOTEL** | Göteborg's oldest hotel, built in 1852, is small, family owned, and traditional. **Pros:** charming, personal service; very comfortable beds; excellent location. **Cons:** rooms sizes vary; limited amenities; short flight of stairs to entrance. [$] *Rooms from: SKr 1975* ✉ *Drottningg. 67, Centrum* ☎ *031/7001170* 🌐 *www.hotel-royal.com* 🛏 *76 rooms* 🍴 *Free Breakfast.*

Radisson Blu Scandinavia

$ | **HOTEL** | This modern and quite spectacular international hotel stands across Drottningtorget from Central Station. **Pros:** good-sized rooms; easy access to transport links; abundant breakfast options. **Cons:** rooms overlooking atrium can be a little dark; feels corporate; bar and restaurant dark. [$] *Rooms from: SKr 1485* ✉ *Södra Hamng. 59, Centrum* ☎ *031/7585000* 🌐 *www.radissonhotels.com* 🛏 *355 rooms* 🍴 *Free Breakfast.*

Nightlife

BARS

Kino

BARS/PUBS | Quintessentially European, Kino is known for its trendy crowd and locally brewed beer as well as a spread of vegetarian sandwiches and dishes from sister café Hagabion. It's also got an outdoor terrace that faces Linnégatan. ✉ *Linnég. 21, Linnéstaden* ☎ *031/428810* 🌐 *www.hagabionscafe.se.*

★ **Locatelli**

BARS/PUBS | Göteborg's attractive young crowd heads here to sip creative cocktails that blend alcohol with flavors such as raspberry, elderberry, passion fruit, vanilla, and coriander, to name just a few. There's also a limited food menu with light dishes, burgers, and sweet treats. ✉ *Elite Park Avenue Hotel, Kungsportsavenyn 36–38, Centrum* ☎ *031/7271089* 🌐 *www.elite.se* 🕒 *Closed Mon.–Wed.*

★ **Ritz**

BARS/PUBS | With its floor-to-ceiling arched windows, the Ritz makes the most of its prime corner location in a highly coveted building that has views of the city's famous moat. The place is trendy, exclusive, and one of the hottest bars in town. ✉ *Bastionsplatsen 2, Centrum* ☎ *031/139590* 🌐 *ritz.gastrogate.com.*

JAZZ CLUBS

Jazzhuset

MUSIC CLUBS | Performers at Jazzhuset tend to play traditional, swing, and Dixieland jazz. ✉ *Eric Dahlbergsg. 3, Vasastan* ☎ *031/133544.*

Nefertiti

MUSIC CLUBS | Modern jazz enthusiasts usually head for Nefertiti, the trendy, shadowy club where the line to get in is always long. ✉ *Hvitfeldtsplatsen 6, Centrum* ☎ *031/7111533* 🌐 *www.nefertiti.se.*

🎭 Performing Arts

MUSIC, OPERA, AND THEATER

GöteborgsOperan (*Gothenburg Opera*)

OPERA | A statement in steel and glass, the opera house opened in 1994, immediately dominating this section of the waterfront with its bold lines and shape, designed to evoke the idea of a ship in the harbor. Set against a backdrop of the old docks, it makes for a striking image. The building includes an auditorium seating 1,250 and a dining area with floor-to-ceiling windows overlooking the harbor. Productions here are world class and well worth seeing if you get the chance. ✉ *Christina Nilssons Gata, Packhuskajen* ☎ *031/108000* ⊕ *en.opera.se.*

Konserthuset (*Concert Hall*)

MUSIC | The home of the highly acclaimed Göteborg Symphony Orchestra has large windows facing Götaplatsen and a main concert space noted for its fine acoustics. There's a mural by Sweden's Prince Eugen in the lobby, as well as original decor and Swedish-designed furniture from 1935. ✉ *Götaplatsen, Götaplatsen* ☎ *031/7265300* ⊕ *www.gso.se.*

🛍 Shopping

CLOTHING

Marimekko

The Finnish design chain Marimekko is known the world over for its brightly colored fabrics with bold patterns including flowers, circles, stripes, and swirls. The Göteborg store has two levels, with women's clothing and accessories downstairs and home furnishings upstairs. ✉ *Vallg. 26, Nordstan* ☎ *070/4139000* ⊕ *www.marimekko.com.*

Nudie

CLOTHING | Head here for a broad selection of Nudie Jeans, the cool streetwear label born in Göteborg. They even offer free repairs for life, though you'll have to get your jeans to a repair location, currently only in Europe. ✉ *Vallg. 15,*

Vasastan ☎ *010/1515700* ⊕ *www.nudie-jeans.com.*

Ströms

CLOTHING | In the same street-corner location for at least two generations, Ströms sells clothing of high quality and good taste. ✉ *Kungsg. 27–29, Centrum* ☎ *031/177100* ⊕ *www.stroms-gbg.se.*

CRAFTS AND DESIGN

★ Designtorget

CRAFTS | This Swedish chain sells housewares and decorative items created by both well-established and up-and-coming designers. You'll find everything from kitchen gadgets to jewelry, decorative items, and paper goods. ✉ *Vallg. 14, Nordstan* ☎ *031/7740017* ⊕ *www.designtorget.se.*

Gudrun Sjödén

TEXTILES/SEWING | At the Göteborg branch of Gudrun Sjödén you'll find the brightly colored women's clothing and home textiles that this internationally recognized Swedish designer is known for. ✉ *Södra Larmg. 18, Nordstan* ☎ *031/139930* ⊕ *www.gudrunsjoden.com.*

Kronhusbodarna

CRAFTS | If you are looking to buy Swedish arts and crafts and glassware, visit the various shops in Kronhusbodarna. They have been selling traditional, handcrafted quality goods, including silver and gold jewelry, watches, and handblown glass, since the 18th century. ✉ *Postg. 6-8, Nordstan* ⊕ *kronhuset.se.*

DEPARTMENT STORES

Åhléns

DEPARTMENT STORES | A branch of this mid-priced department-store chain is in the Nordstan mall. ✉ *Nordstan, Östra Hamng. 18, Centrum* ☎ *031/3334000* ⊕ *www.ahlens.se.*

NK

DEPARTMENT STORES | Try the local branch of NK for upscale men's and women's fashions and excellent household goods. ⊠ *Östra Hamng. 42, Centrum* 🕾 *031/7101000* ⊕ *www.nk.se.*

MARKETS

Saluhallen

FOOD/CANDY | There are several large food markets in the city area, but the most impressive is Saluhallen. Built in 1889, the barrel-roofed, wrought-iron, glass, and brick building stands like a monument to industrial architecture. Everything is available at this food hall, from fish, meat, and bakery products to deli foods, herbs and spices, coffee, chocolate, cheese, and even just people-watching. ⊠ *Kungstorget, Stora Saluhallen 46, Centrum* 🕾 *031/7117878* ⊕ *www.storasaluhallen.se* ⊗ *Closed Sun.*

SHOES

★ Haga Trätoffelfabrik

JEWELRY/ACCESSORIES | Genuine Swedish clogs in every color of the rainbow are on offer at this small shop, which has occupied the same location since 1933. The handcrafted shoes are made locally in traditional, open-toed, and Mary Jane styles. The shop also sells leather accessories including handbags, wallets, and backpacks. ⊠ *Haga Nygata 19, Nordstan* 🕾 *031/7119711.*

Bohuslän

21 km (13 miles) north of Göteborg.

This region north of Göteborg was at the crossroads of Scandinavian history for centuries, changing hands numerous times between Danes, Norwegians, and Swedes until finally becoming a fixed part of Sweden with the Peace of Roskilde in 1658. Its deeply indented coastline provides a foretaste of Norway's fjords farther north. Small towns and lovely fishing villages nestle among the distinctively rounded granite rocks and the thousands of skerries (rocky islets) and larger islands that form Sweden's western archipelago. The ideal way to explore the area is by meandering slowly north from

Göteborg, taking full advantage of the gorgeous scenery, uncluttered beaches, and colorful fishing villages.

GETTING HERE AND AROUND

The best way to explore Bohuslän is by car. The main highway is the E6, which runs the length of the coast from Göteborg north to Strömstad, close to the Norwegian border; smaller numbered routes branch off to all the major towns and tourist destinations along the coast. Rental cars are available in Göteborg, Uddevalla, and Strömstad.

BOAT AND FERRY

It's possible to make your way all the way up and down the coast of Bohuslän by boat by combining services provided by various road and passenger ferry operators. The main operators are Västtrafik, Skärgårdsbåtarna i Uddevalla, and Trafikverket, but there are also other ferries trafficking specific routes. The best way to get an overview of the services available is by downloading the Island Hopping route map available from the West Sweden Tourist Board. In the northernmost part of Bohuslän, Koster Marin operates passenger ferries between Strömstad and the Koster Islands.

VISITOR INFO

West Sweden Tourist Board. ⊕ *www.westsweden.com.*

◉ Sights

There's a bit of rivalry between Sweden's coasts, and many who favor the region north of Göteborg are quick to call it not just the west coast but the best coast. But whichever coast they favor, most Swedes are quick to agree that Bohuslän is a delight. It's a place of brilliant colors, vibrant flavors, and simple pleasures: strolling through a pretty fishing village, dining on fresh seafood at a dockside restaurant, enjoying a picnic on a sunwarmed cliff, cooling off with a dip in the ocean, and watching the sun set over the open sea—though if you're visiting in the summer, that won't happen until late in the evening, of course.

Carlstens Fästning

MILITARY SITE | Marstrand's main draw is Carlstens Fästning, the huge stone fortress that stands on the island's highest point, above the town. It was begun in the mid-17th century, after Marstrand became part of Sweden. Used as a prison as well as a defensive outpost, the fortress was captured twice by Danish Norwegian forces, in 1677 and 1719. (Both times it was returned to Sweden after negotiations.) It was finally decommissioned in 1882. During the summer there are daily guided tours (in Swedish, but guides are often willing to translate). There are also bilingual informational panels all over the fortress, so you can easily explore on your own. Don't miss the view from the tower, or the prison cells. Carlsten's most famous prisoner was Lasse-Maja, who dressed up as a woman to seduce and then rob local farmers—he spent a total of 25 years here and even managed to escape once before being recaptured and brought back to Carlsten. ✉ Marstrand ☎ 0303/61167 ⊕ www.carlsten.se ✆ SKr 95 ☉ Opening hours vary Sept.–May; call for current schedule.

Fiskebäckskil

TOWN | Located on the island of Skaftö, Fiskebäckskil is directly across the Gullmarsfjord from Lysekil, just 15 minutes away by passenger ferry. One of the oldest fishing villages in the area, Fiskebäckskil was founded in the 16th century and thrived thanks to the abundant populations of herring in the surrounding waters. Eventually it evolved into a popular seaside resort. It's now a peaceful village with a picturesque harbor and many beautiful houses that once belonged to local sea captains. You won't find many shops and services here, but if you're looking for a relaxing place to enjoy some coastal beauty and outdoor recreation, Fiskebäckskil is worth a visit. ✉ Skaftö Island, Fiskebäckskil ✛ 38 km

(24 miles) west of Uddevalla, 22 km (13½ miles) south of Lysekil by road and car ferry ⊕ www.vastsverige.com/skafto.

Kosterhavet National Park and the Koster Islands

NATIONAL/STATE PARK | Established in 2009, Sweden's only marine national park protects an area of the ocean in northern Bohuslän, where the convergence of a deep undersea channel and shallow coastal waters creates the conditions for an unusually diverse array of marine life to thrive. The main visitor center for the national park is the Naturum Kosterhavet at Ekenäs on Sydkoster Island; there are also smaller information centers in Strömstad and at nearby Rossö and Saltö. To help visitors experience its marine richness, the national park has several underwater snorkel trails with signs and blue ropes placed along the seafloor. Other water-based activities include kayaking, swimming, and diving. On land, the Koster Islands have a permanent population of around 300 people. Sydkoster has hiking trails, bike rentals, and a few options for accommodations and dining. Nordkoster is mostly a nature reserve and is a beautiful spot for hiking. There's frequent passenger ferry service to the islands from Strömstad; the journey takes about 45 minutes. ✉ Strömstad ✛ Approximately 12 km (7½ miles) from Strömstad by ferry ☎ 10/2245400 ⊕ www.nationalparksofsweden.se ✆ Free.

Lysekil

TOWN | Perched on a peninsula at the head of Gullmarsfjord—known to locals as Gullmarn—Lysekil has been one of Sweden's most popular summer resorts since the 19th century, when the country's wealthiest citizens would come to take the therapeutic waters. Back then, the small resort was made up mainly of fancy villas painted mustard and brown. Many of these can still be seen today, though the town's dominant architectural sight is its striking neo-Gothic clifftop

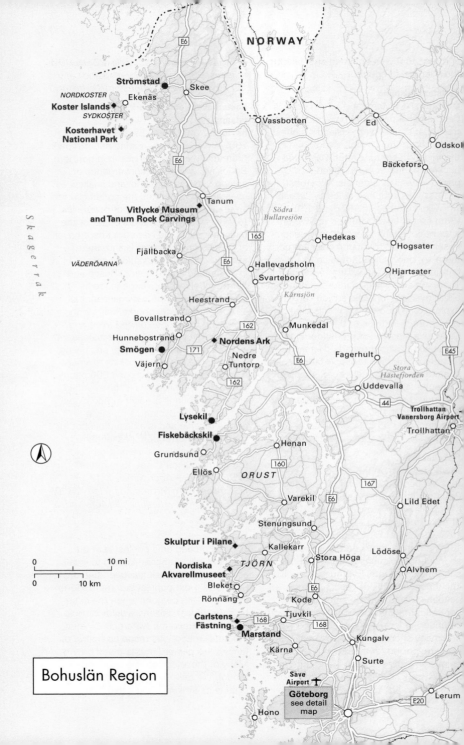

NORWAY

Strömstad
Skee
NORDKOSTER
Ekenäs
Koster Islands
SYDKOSTER
Kosterhavet
National Park

Vassbotten

Ed

Odskol

Bäckefors

E6

Tanum

Vitlycke Museum
and Tanum Rock Carvings

Södra
Bullaresjön

Hedekas

Hogsater

Hjärtsater

Fjällbacka

VÄDERÖARNA

165

Hallevadsholm
Svarteborg

E6

Kärnsjön

Heestrand

Bovallstrand

Munkedal

162

Hunnebostrand

Nordens Ark

Smögen

171

Nedre
Tuntorp

E6

Fagerhult

Stora
Hästefjorden

Väjern

162

Uddevalla

E45

44

Trollhattan
Vanersborg Airport

Lysekil

Trollhattan

Fiskebäckskil

Grundsund

Henan

Ellös

ORUST

160

Varekil

E6

167

Lild Edet

Stenungsund

Skulptur i Pilane

Kallekarr

Lödöse

Nordiska
Akvarellmuseet

TJÖRN

Stora Höga

Alvhem

Bleket

Rönnäng

Kode

E6

Carlstens
Fästning

168

Tjuvkil

168

Marstand

Kärna

Kungalv

Surte

Save
Airport ✝

Hono

Göteborg
see detail
map

Lerum

E20

Skagerrak

0   10 mi

0   10 km

▲ N

Bohuslän Region

church, which was completed in 1901. Otherwise, Lysekil's main attraction is its seaside location. The Stångehuvud Nature Reserve just west of town has great walking trails and stunning coastal views. For a different look at some local nature, take one of the regular seal safaris offered by various operators between June and August; contact the Lysekil tourist information office for details. ⊠ *Lysekil ✛ 30 km (19 miles) west of Uddevalla via E6 and Rte. 161* ⊕ *www. westsweden.com/lysekil.*

Marstrand

TOWN | Founded in the 13th century, Marstrand was an important harbor during the Middle Ages. Unusually high stocks of herring used to swim in the surrounding waters, making the town extremely rich. But with the money came greed and corruption: in the 16th century Marstrand became known as the most immoral town in Scandinavia. Eventually the fish disappeared and Marstrand experienced a period of decline. The growing popularity of seaside resorts in the 1800s led to a new golden age for Marstrand—King Oscar II (1829–1907) spent time here almost every summer during the last 20 years of his life. These days people still come to dip into the clear, blue waters and swim, sail, and fish, as well as to stroll the picturesque streets. The town is divided between a "mainland" part on the island of Koön and a car-free part on the island of Marstrand, accessible by passenger ferry. ⊠ *Marstrand ✛ 17 km (11 miles) west of Kungälv (via Rte. 168), 47 km (29 miles) northwest of Göteborg* ⊕ *www.marstrand.se.*

Nordens Ark

ZOO | A cut above the usual safari parks, Nordens Ark is a sanctuary for endangered animals, with well-respected conservation, breeding, and reintroduction programs. The tranquil park is home to approximately 80 species of amphibians, mammals, birds, reptiles, and other animals from around the world. Highlights include red pandas, lynx, snow leopards, peregrine falcons, and wolves. ⊠ *Åby Säteri, Hunnebostrand* ☎ *0523/79590* ⊕ *www.nordensark.se* 💲 *SKr 250.*

Nordiska Akvarellmuseet (Nordic Watercolor Museum)

MUSEUM | Just south of Pilane is Tjörn's other main attraction for art lovers, Nordiska Akvarellmuseet, the Nordic Watercolor Museum, which has changing exhibits by Swedish and international artists. It's located directly on the water in the pretty little town of Skärhamn. If you're inspired to try your own hand at watercolor painting, you can pick up supplies in the museum shop or join in one of the open workshops for a small materials fee. ⊠ *Södra Hamnen 6, Tjörn Island ✛ 12 km (7½ miles) south of Pilane, 67½ km (42 miles) northwest of Göteborg* ☎ *0304/600080* ⊕ *https:// www.akvarellmuseet.org/en* 💲 *SKr 50* 🕐 *Closed Mon.*

Skulptur i Pilane

PUBLIC ART | On the cliffs of the island of Tjörn, surrounding an ancient burial ground, is one of the world's most unusual sculpture parks. Its centerpiece is Anna, a 46-foot marble sculpture of a woman's head, that has found its permanent home here and is visible from miles around. Every summer the Pilane Heritage Museum stages a seasonal exhibition with other sculptures by prominent international artists. The sculptures are scattered throughout the natural landscape, surrounded by grazing sheep, scenic views, and 2,000-year-old graves. The site is open year-round, but the annual sculpture installation lasts from mid-May through September. ⊠ *Sältebo 1, Tjörn Island ✛ 53 km (32 miles) north of Marstrand via the mainland, 65 km (40 miles) northwest of Göteborg* ☎ *0304/663950* ⊕ *www.pilane.org* 💲 *Site free, exhibition SKr 140.*

★ Smögen

TOWN | A popular motif for postcards from Bohuslän, Smögen is a pretty village with red fishing huts, crystal-blue water, and boardwalks lined with restaurants and shops. To get here, take Route 171 west from Route 162 until it ends. A quick stopover is enough to get a sense of Smögen's charm, but it's worth lingering if you have time. All around Smögen there are hiking trails with beautiful views of the sea and coast, as well as good places for a dip in the ocean. From Smögen you can also take a boat trip to nearby Hållö, an island with Bohuslän's oldest lighthouse and gorgeous smooth cliffs that are perfect for sunbathing, picnicking, and swimming. Boats depart frequently from the Smögen waterfront throughout the day in summer; the crossing takes 10 minutes. ⊠ *Smögen ✛ 60 km (37 miles) west of Uddevalla, 49 km (30 miles) northwest of Lysekil ⊕ www. vastsverige.com/sotenas.*

Strömstad

TOWN | Just 20 km (12½ miles) from the Norwegian border, Strömstad has been a major shipping hub, a spa town, and the site of numerous battles between warring Danes, Norwegians, and Swedes. These days it's a popular summer resort with good shopping and easy access to the spectacular nature and recreational opportunities of the northern Bohuslän archipelago, including the Koster Islands and Kosterhavet National Park. ⊠ *Strömstad ✛ 90 km (56 miles) northwest of Uddevalla, 169 km (105 miles) north of Göteborg ⊕ www.westsweden.com/ stromstad.*

Vitlycke Museum and Tanum Rock Carvings

ARCHAEOLOGICAL SITE | Some 2,500 to 3,000 years ago, the people of what is now northern Bohuslän left their mark on the landscape in the form of rock carvings depicting scenes of love, magic, and daily life. An estimated 10,000 rock carvings are scattered over 600 sites in the area around Tanum, which is listed as a UNESCO World Heritage Site. The best place to begin your visit is at the Vitlycke Museum, which has exhibits about the carvings and life during the Bronze Age, including a replica of a Bronze Age farm. One of the most impressive concentrations of rock carvings is located just across the main road from the museum; three other signposted areas are nearby. The museum has detailed information and a downloadable map of key sites available on its website. ⊠ *Vitlycke 2, Tanumshede ✛ 60 km (37 miles) northwest of Uddevalla, 47 km (29 miles) north of Smögen ☎ 010/4414310 ⊕ www. vitlyckemuseum.se* ⊠ *Free ⊗ Museum closed Nov.–Apr.*

🛏 Hotels

Grand Hotel Marstrand

$$$ | HOTEL | History and luxury abound in this tile-roof hotel, which resembles a French château. **Pros:** historical building; beautiful setting and location; some rooms have sea views. **Cons:** the grandeur here is faded in places; rooms get warm in summer; some noise from outside. 💲 *Rooms from: SKr 2495* ⊠ *Rådhusg. 2, Marstrand ☎ 0303/60322* ⊕ *www.grandmarstrand.se* ⇥ *23 rooms* ⦿ *Free Breakfast.*

Slipens Hotel

$$ | HOTEL | This delightful small hotel overlooks the harbor in the quaint village of Fiskebäckskil on the island of Skaftö, across the fjord from Lysekil. **Pros:** cozy rooms with lots of character; beautiful waterfront location; rooms have air conditioning. **Cons:** staff nearby but not at hotel; few specific sights nearby; limited menu at restaurant. 💲 *Rooms from: SKr 2295* ⊠ *Fiskebäckskilsv. 28, Fiskebäckskil ☎ 0523/22222* ⊕ *www.slipenshotell.se* ⦿ *Free Breakfast.*

Strandflickornas Havshotell

$$ | HOTEL | This relaxed, intimate hotel occupies a restored early-20th-century rest home on a cliff overlooking the sea. **Pros:** variety of room options; wonderful location; individually designed rooms. **Cons:** limited facilities; not all rooms have sea views; not good for guests with mobility issues. $ *Rooms from: SKr 1895* ✉ *Turistg. 13, Lysekil* ☎ *0523/79750* ⊕ *www.strandflickorna.com* ⬅ *23 rooms, 22 additional rooms in annex* ⦿ *Free Breakfast.*

Lund

34 km (21 miles) southeast of Landskrona via E6/E20 and Rte. 16, 25 km (15 miles) northeast of Malmö, 183 km (113 miles) southwest of Växjö.

One of the oldest towns in Europe, Lund was founded in 990 and became the religious capital of Scandinavia in 1103. At one time the city had 27 churches and eight monasteries—until King Christian III of Denmark ordered most of them razed to use their stones for the construction of Malmöhus Castle. After that Lund was basically a backwater until 1666, when its university was established— the second-oldest university in Sweden after Uppsala. It's now a lively town with a well-preserved historic core and a youthful spirit, thanks to the 40,000 or so students who study here every year.

GETTING HERE AND AROUND

From the north, take the E4 and E6 motorways to Lund; there are lots of signs to guide you. There are daily direct trains from Stockholm (the trip takes a little over four hours) and regular connections to Malmö, just 15 minutes by train. Once in Lund, make use of the easy and extensive bus network.

VISITOR INFO

Lund Tourist Center. ✉ *Bang. 1* ☎ *046/3595040* ⊕ *www.visitlund.se.*

◉ Sights

Botaniska Trädgården (*Botanical Garden*)
GARDEN | One block east of the cathedral is Lund's botanical garden, which contains thousands of specimens of plants from all over the world, including such exotics as the paper mulberry tree, from the islands of the South Pacific. ✉ *Östra Vallg. 20* ☎ *046/2227320* ⊕ *botan.lu.se* ▧ *Free.*

Krognoshuset

MUSEUM | Krognoshuset is Lund's best-preserved medieval residence, with parts dating back to the 1300s. It houses a small but well-presented art gallery. The building itself is worth a look, but most days you will get the bonus of a contemporary art exhibition showcasing anything from industrial design to video installations. ✉ *Mårtenstorget* ☎ *046/126248* ⊕ *www.krognoshuset.se* ▧ *Free.*

★ Kulturen i Lund

MUSEUM VILLAGE | The second-oldest open-air museum in Sweden, Kulturen consists of a beautiful collection of farmhouses, town houses, a church, and other buildings that show how people have lived in southern Sweden over the centuries. Some have always stood on this spot, while others have been moved here from other locations. Step inside and see what daily life was like for people from different time periods and social classes. There are also a variety of exhibits about Lund's history, folk art and design, textiles, toys, books, and various other topics. ✉ *Stora Gråbrödersg. 11* ☎ *046/350400* ▧ *90 SKr* ⊗ *Closed Mon. mid-Sept.–Apr.*

★ Lunds Domkyrka (*Lund Cathedral*)

RELIGIOUS SITE | Lunds Cathedral, consecrated in 1145, is a monumental graystone Romanesque cathedral, the oldest in Scandinavia. Since the Reformation it has been Lutheran. Its crypt has 23 finely carved pillars, and the oldest parts of the cathedral are considered the finest Romanesque constructions in Sweden. However, the cathedral's most famous attraction is an astrological clock dating from 1380 and restored in 1923. Twice a day it comes to life with a pageant of knights jousting on horseback, trumpets blowing a medieval fanfare, and the Magi walking in procession past the Virgin and

Kulturen is both an indoor and an outdoor museum that features an extensive collection of historic buildings and beautiful gardens.

Child as the organ plays *In Dulci Jubilo*. The clock plays at noon and at 3 Monday–Saturday and at 1 and 3 on Sunday. ✉ *Kyrkog. 6* ☎ *046/718700* 🌐 *www.lundsdomkyrka.se* 🎟 *Free.*

Skissernas Museum (*Museum of Artistic Process and Public Art*)
MUSEUM | Sometimes the artistic process is as interesting and impressive as the final product. That's the idea behind this museum, which displays sketches, models, and other preliminary works by Swedish and international artists. The visual impact as you step into the high-ceilinged main exhibit hall is stunning. Be sure to pick up an exhibition guide in English as you enter, since many pieces are labeled in Swedish only. ✉ *Finng. 2* ☎ *046/2227283* 🌐 *www.skissernasmuseum.se* 🎟 *SKr 80* 🕒 *Closed Mon.*

Hotels

Grand Hotel
$$$ | **HOTEL** | This elegant red-stone hotel is in the heart of the city, on a pleasant square close to the railway station. **Pros:** wide choice of rooms; close to attractions and train station; lots of character. **Cons:** can be noisy; no parking nearby; some oddly shaped rooms. [$] *Rooms from: SKr 2345* ✉ *Bantorget 1* ☎ *046/2806100* 🌐 *www.grandilund.se* 🛏 *83 rooms* 🍴 *Free Breakfast.*

★ **Hotell Oskar**
$$ | **B&B/INN** | In this charming boutique-style inn made up of two 19th-century town houses, the rooms are spacious, modern, and bright, with white walls, colorful art, and polished oak floors. **Pros:** central location; well designed, cozy rooms; excellent breakfast. **Cons:** no restaurant; limited amenities; self-service check-in. [$] *Rooms from: SKr 1595* ✉ *Bytareg. 3* ☎ *046/188085* 🌐 *www.hotelloskar.se* 🛏 *8 rooms* 🍴 *Free Breakfast.*

Hotel Lundia
$ | **HOTEL** | Only a few hundred feet from the train station, Hotel Lundia is ideal for those who want to be near the city center. **Pros:** stylish, thoughtfully

designed rooms; rooms for visitors with allergies available; convenient location. **Cons:** limited choice in restaurant; some rooms are a little dated; can get stuffy in summer. $ *Rooms from: SKr 1100* ⊠ *Knut den Stores Torg 2* ☎ *046/2806500* ⊕ *www.lundia.se* ⟿ *97 rooms, 2 suites* ⦿ *Free Breakfast.*

🛍 Shopping

Saluhallen

FOOD/CANDY | This market hall is an adventure in itself, stocking an abundance of local products as well as delicacies from Italy, Japan, and many other places. Cheese, meats, fresh and pickled fish, chocolate, and pastries are all in great supply. It's the perfect place to grab a quick lunch at a counter or pick up some food for a picnic in one of Lund's many squares and parks. ⊠ *Mårtenstorget 1* ⊕ *lundssaluhall.se* ⊙ *Closed Sun.*

Malmö

25 km (15 miles) southwest of Lund (via E22), 198 km (123 miles) southwest of Växjö.

The capital of the province of Skåne, with a population of about 300,000, Malmö is Sweden's third-largest city, founded at the end of the 13th century. The remarkable 8-km (5-mile) bridge and tunnel from Malmö to Copenhagen has transformed travel and trade in the area, cutting both time and costs by replacing the ferries that used to shuttle between the two towns.

GETTING HERE AND AROUND

Malmö is served by the E6 motorway from Göteborg in the north and is close to the E4 motorway, which runs south from Stockholm. If you are coming from Copenhagen in Denmark, the Öresund Bridge carries car and train traffic into the heart of the city. The bridge spans nearly 8 miles and costs a hefty SKr 545 in one-way toll fees to cross by car. There's an SKr 50 discount off regular rates if you pay online in advance.

Malmö Airport (MMX), still often referred to by its old name, Sturup, is served with various daily domestic and international flights. It's approximately 30 km (19 miles) from Malmö itself and 25 km (15 miles) from Lund. Flygbussarna airport buses depart frequently for each city, with schedules based on flight arrival times. Tickets cost SKr 115 to either destination (SKr 105 if purchased online). A taxi from the airport to Malmö runs SKr 425.

Trains connect most towns in the south; contact SJ for details. There's regular service from Stockholm to Malmö; the trip takes about 4½ hours by high-speed (X2000) train and about five hours otherwise. The railway station is centrally located in Malmö. Trains between Malmö and Copenhagen take 35 minutes and run every 10–20 minutes an hour. A one-way ticket is SKr 122.

VISITOR INFO

Malmö Tourist Office. ⊠ *Börshuset, Skeppsbron 2* ☎ *040/341200* ⊕ *www.malmotown.com.*

⊙ Sights

Lilla Torg

NEIGHBORHOOD | This cobblestoned square has some of the city's oldest buildings, which date from the 17th and 18th centuries. Surrounded by cafés, restaurants, and bars, it's a great place to wander or watch the world go by. Walk into the side streets and see the traditional buildings, which were originally used mainly to store grain and produce. Check out the Saluhallen (food hall), which contains Kryddboden, one of Sweden's best coffee sellers. ⊠ *Malmö.*

Malmöhus

MUSEUM | The city's castle, Malmöhus, completed in 1542, was for many years used as a prison (James Hepburn, 4th Earl of Boswell and husband of Mary, Queen of Scots, was one of its notable inmates). Exhibits trace the dramatic history of the castle and the city of Malmö over the past 500 years. Malmöhus also houses the Malmö Art Museum and an aquarium, which together with the adjacent Technology and Maritime Museum are part of a complex called Malmö Museer. A single admission ticket gets you into all the museums. ✉ *Malmöhusv.* ☎ *040/344400* 🌐 *www.malmo.se* 🎟 *SKr 40 for all museums.*

Moderna Museet

MUSEUM | Housed in a converted power plant from 1901, this is a branch of the national modern art museum, which also includes the original Moderna Museet in Stockholm. It presents changing exhibits of 20th- and 21st-century art, including modern classics and innovative contemporary artists. ✉ *Ola Billgrens Plats 2–4* ☎ *040/6857937* 🌐 *www.modernamuseet.se/malmo/en* 🎟 *Free* 🕓 *Closed Mon.*

S:t Petri Kyrka (*St. Peter's Church*)

RELIGIOUS SITE | In Gamla Staden, the Old Town, look for Malmö's oldest church, St. Peter's Church. Dating from the 14th century, it is an impressive example of the Baltic Gothic style, with distinctive stepped gables. Inside there is a fine Renaissance altar. ✉ *Göran Olsg. 4* ☎ *040/279043* 🌐 *svenskakyrkanmalmo.se/st-petri-kyrka* 🎟 *Free.*

Restaurants

Årstiderna i Kockska Huset

$$$ | **SCANDINAVIAN** | This cozy, atmospheric restaurant occupies a series of interconnected cellar vaults in one of Malmö's best-preserved 16th-century buildings. Traditional Swedish dishes, often centered on beef, game, and seafood, are given a contemporary twist. **Known for:** traditional Swedish dishes; historic setting; excellent wine list. [$] *Average main: SKr 328* ✉ *Frans Suellsg. 3* ☎ *040/230910* 🌐 *www.arstiderna.se* 🕓 *Closed Sun. No lunch Sat.*

Johan P

$$$ | **SEAFOOD** | This extremely popular restaurant specializes in seafood and shellfish prepared in Swedish and continental styles. White walls and crisp white tablecloths give it an elegant air, which contrasts with the generally casual dress of the customers. **Known for:** well-prepared seafood; relaxed fine dining; excellent wine list. [$] *Average main: SKr 366* ✉ *Hjulhamnsg. 5* ☎ *040/971818* 🌐 *www.johanp.nu.*

Hotels

Hotel Duxiana

$$ | **HOTEL** | This intimate design hotel is so confident in the quality of its beds that it's even named after the luxurious DUX mattresses found in every room. **Pros:** very central location; some air conditioned rooms available; comfortable beds. **Cons:** limited amenities; some rooms are small; some traffic noise in street-facing rooms. [$] *Rooms from: SKr 1800* ✉ *Mäster Johansg. 1* ☎ *040/6077000* 🌐 *malmo.hotelduxiana.com* 🛏 *22 rooms* 🍴 *Free Breakfast.*

MJ's Hotel

$$ | **HOTEL** | The plain exterior of this hotel disguises a plush and meticulously crafted interior. **Pros:** central location; large, bright rooms; beautiful breakfast area. **Cons:** reception and entrance located in busy bar area; room ventilation could be better; noisy bar. [$] *Rooms from: SKr 1580* ✉ *Mäster Johansg. 13* ☎ *040/6646400* 🌐 *www.masterjohan.se* 🛏 *69 rooms* 🍴 *Free Breakfast.*

Radisson Blu Hotel

$ | **HOTEL** | Only a six-minute walk from the train station, this modern luxury hotel has spacious rooms decorated in either green and black or gray with orange accents. **Pros:** very large rooms; excellent bar; extensive breakfast buffet.

Cons: service can be inconsistent; some areas look a bit dated; rooms can be on the warm side. $ *Rooms from: SKr 1220* ✉ *Österg. 10* ☎ *040/6984000* ⊕ *www. radissonhotels.com* ⇌ *229 rooms* ⦿ *Free Breakfast.*

Nightlife
Sky Bar at Clarion
BARS/PUBS | For panoramic views of Malmö from one of the city's few high-rise buildings, head to the Sky Bar on the 25th floor of the Clarion Live Hotel. As you sip your drink you can look out over a vista that includes the castle, the harbor, the Öresund Bridge, and Turning Torso, Scandinavia's tallest building. If you'd prefer a full meal, make a reservation at the adjoining Kitchen & Table restaurant, whose menu is overseen by celebrity chef Marcus Samuelsson. ✉ *Clarion Live Hotel, Dag Hammarskjölds Torg 2, 25th fl.* ☎ *040/207500* ⊕ *www.kitchenandtable.se/malmo.*

 Performing Arts

Malmö Live Konserthus
CONCERTS | Opened in 2015, the Malmö Live concert house boasts world-class acoustics and several performance spaces, making it the city's top venue for live music. It's home to Malmö SymfoniOrkester, a symphony orchestra that has a reputation across Europe as a class act. Other performances include a chamber music series and a wide range of jazz, world, pop, and other shows. ✉ *Dag Hammarskjölds Torg 4* ☎ *040/343500* ⊕ *www.malmolive.se.*

Shopping

Formargruppen
CRAFTS | As an arts-and-crafts cooperative, Formargruppen is owned and operated by its 20 members. It sells high-quality woodwork (including cabinets), ceramics, textiles, metalwork, and jewelry. ✉ *Engelbrektsg. 8*

☎ *073/9841699* ⊕ *www.formargruppen. se* ⊙ *Closed Sun.*

★ Form/Design Center
BOOKS/STATIONERY | Form/Design Center is a hub for knowledge, exploration, and exchange in the areas of design and architecture. Look here for the very latest in Scandinavian interior design and crafts. The center also sells products related to its changing exhibitions on related topics. ✉ *Lilla Torg 9* ☎ *040/6645150* ⊕ *www. formdesigncenter.com* ⊙ *Closed Mon.*

Malmö Saluhall
SHOPPING CENTERS/MALLS | Opened in 2016, Malmö's market hall is bursting with everything from gorgeous fruits and vegetables to cheese, tea, chocolate, ice cream, and fresh-baked bread. Its many cafés make it a wonderful spot to grab lunch. You'll find seafood, sandwiches, salads, falafel, burgers, noodles, pizza, and more. ✉ *Gibraltarg.* ☎ *040/6267730* ⊕ *www.malmosaluhall.se.*

Möllevångstorget
OUTDOOR/FLEA/GREEN MARKETS | This square's lively year-round market usually has a wonderful array of flowers, fruit, and vegetables. It is an old working-class area that is now one of Malmö's most international districts. Nearby are many restaurants serving food from all corners of the globe. ✉ *Möllevångstorget* ⊙ *Market closed Sun.*

Ystad

64 km (40 miles) southeast of Malmö (via E65), 205 km (127 miles) southwest of Växjö.

A small city with a long history dating back to the 12th century, Ystad has preserved its medieval character with winding narrow streets and hundreds of half-timbered houses built over a span of five centuries. During the Napoleonic Wars, Ystad became a smuggling center, and in recent years it has become

Scandinavia's hub for another kind of crime—the fictional kind. Dozens of internationally successful crime films and television series have been filmed in and around Ystad, including many based on the late Swedish author Henning Mankell's beloved novels about the moody Ystad police detective Kurt Wallander. A good place to begin exploring is the main square, Stortorget.

GETTING HERE AND AROUND

Ystad is easily reachable by train from Malmö in about 50 minutes, but if you intend to explore the surrounding countryside you'll want a car. The drive from Malmö also takes just under an hour. Once in Ystad, the town center is small enough to get around by foot (and pretty enough to want to do so).

VISITOR INFORMATION

Ystad Visitor Center. ⊠ *S:t Knuts Torg* ☎ *0411/577681* ⊕ *www.ystad.se/turism.*

Sights

Ales Stenar

ARCHAEOLOGICAL SITE | Less than half an hour's drive east of Ystad lies Ales Stenar, Sweden's largest and best-preserved stone ship setting. Erected sometime between AD 500 and 1000, it consists of 59 stones of various sizes, arranged in the shape of a ship and perfectly positioned along a northwest-to-southeast axis to align with sunrise and sunset during the annual equinoxes and solstices. Roughly 220 feet long and 62 feet wide, the ship setting is positioned on a windswept clifftop overlooking the Baltic Sea, on the edge of the village of Kåseberga. From the free parking lot on the edge of town it's a 15-minute walk to the stones. ⊠ *Ales Väg* ⊕ *www.ystad.se/turism* 🎫 *Free.*

Klostret i Ystad

RELIGIOUS SITE | The Franciscan monastery Gråbrödraklostret, which adjoins St. Peter's Church, is one of the best-preserved cloisters in Sweden. The oldest parts date from 1267. Together, the church and monastery are considered the most important historical site in Ystad. Exhibits inside the cloisters trace the history of the Greyfriars order and the abbey, as well as other notable events in Ystad's past. ⊠ *S:t Petri Kyrkoplan* ☎ *0411/577286* ⊕ *www.ystad.se/klostret* 🎫 *SKr 50.*

S:ta Maria Kyrka (*St. Mary's Church*)

RELIGIOUS SITE | Ystad's oldest church, also known as Mariakyrkan, was built shortly after 1220 as a basilica in the Romanesque style, though there have been later alterations. Among its treasures are a 15th-century wooden altarpiece from Germany, an iron chandelier from the 1300s, and a Baroque stone pulpit from 1626. Since 1748 a watchman has sounded a copper horn from the church tower every 15 minutes from 9:15 pm to 1 am. It's to proclaim that "all is well." ⊠ *Stortorget 1* ⊕ *www.svenskakyrkan.se/ystad/ sta-maria-kyrka* 🎫 *Free.*

Ystad Studios Visitor Center

FILM STUDIO | Since 2004, Ystad has been home to Scandinavia's largest film studio and has been riding a wave of global enthusiasm for the Nordic noir genre of crime fiction, including Henning Mankell's Wallander series, set in Ystad. So far there have been 44 Wallander movies in Swedish, as well as 12 English-language BBC films starring Kenneth Branagh—all of them filmed almost entirely in and around Ystad. At the Ystad Studios Visitor Center, you can step into Wallander's living room and office, explore the filmmaking process, and see costumes worn by actors in the Swedish Danish television series *The Bridge*, another international hit filmed largely in the area. ⊠ *Elis Nilssons Väg 14* ☎ *0709/477057* ⊕ *www.ystad.se/ysvc* 🎫 *120 SKr* 🕐 *Closed Fri., Sun.*

🍴 Restaurants

Möllers Bryggeri
$$ | **SCANDINAVIAN** | Inside a lovely cross-timbered inn, this restaurant brews its own beer—there are two large copper boilers near the bar. It has a pleasant garden, and the brick vaulting of the dimly lighted interior gives it the appearance of an underground cavern. Juicy steaks are a specialty. **Known for:** juicy steaks; regional cuisine; traditional setting. [$] *Average main: SKr 173* ✉ *Långg. 20* ☎ *0411/69999* 🌐 *mollersbryggeri.se* 🕒 *Closed Sun.–Wed. No lunch Thurs.–Fri.*

🛏 Hotels

Anno 1793 Sekelgården Hotel
$ | **HOTEL** | A short walk from the main square in the heart of Ystad, this small and comfortable family-owned hotel occupies several interconnected half-timbered buildings from the late 18th century, centered around a leafy green courtyard where breakfast is served in summer. **Pros:** on-site microbrewery; central location; historic character. **Cons:** some rooms very small; limited amenities; bells and horn blowing at nearby church may bother light sleepers. [$] *Rooms from: SKr 1495* ✉ *Långg. 18* ☎ *0411/73900* 🌐 *www.sekelgarden.se* 🛏 *26 rooms* 🍽 *Free Breakfast.*

★ **Hotell Continental du Sud**
$$ | **HOTEL** | The Continental opened in 1829, and is a truly stunning building, both inside and out. **Pros:** lots of character; great location; elegant, historic building. **Cons:** some small rooms; reception closes at 10 pm; traffic noise. [$] *Rooms from: SKr 2250* ✉ *Hamng. 13* ☎ *0411/13700* 🌐 *www.hotellcontinental.se* 🛏 *52 rooms* 🍽 *Free Breakfast.*

Ystad Saltsjöbad
$$$ | **RESORT** | A seaside retreat since 1897, Ystad Saltsjöbad has expanded into a complex of interconnected buildings with facilities that include indoor and outdoor pools, spa treatment rooms, a gym, and four restaurants. **Pros:** wide range of room options; abundant amenities; Baltic Sea setting. **Cons:** can feel like a maze; spa treatments must be reserved far in advance; not convenient for walking to Ystad attractions. [$] *Rooms from: SKr 2550* ✉ *Saltsjöbadsv. 15* ☎ *0411/13630* 🌐 *www.ysb.se* 🛏 *139 rooms* 🍽 *Free Breakfast.*

🛍 Shopping

★ **Konsthantverkarna i Ystad**
CRAFTS | Occupying three floors in a 17th-century half-timbered house, this shop is run by a collective of local artisans and designers. Here you'll find everything from handknit sweaters and printed fabrics to handmade leather goods, jewelry, pottery, woodcrafts, and more. ✉ *Tvättorget 2* ☎ *0411/12699* 🌐 *www.kiy.se* 🕒 *Closed Sun. Sept.–Nov. and Jan.–June.*

Kalmar

269 km (40 miles) northwest of Ystad (via E22).

Southern Sweden is considered, even by many Swedes, to be a world of its own. Once a part of Denmark, the region is clearly distinguished from the rest of the country by its geography, culture, and history. Småland, the northernmost of Sweden's southern provinces, is also the largest, but its harsh countryside and poorer, bleaker way of life led thousands to emigrate to the United States in the 19th and 20th centuries. Those who stayed behind developed a reputation for inventiveness. The area has many small glassblowing firms, and it is these glassworks, such as the world-renowned Kosta Boda and Orrefors, that have given the area the nickname the Kingdom of Crystal. Kalmar was a rather important outpost from the 13th to the 17th centuries because it was one of the southernmost cities in Sweden. However, in the Treaty of Roskilde, the King of Denmark–Norway was forced to cede what is now southern Sweden, and the town's importance diminished gradually over the years as its fortress no longer defended the country's southern border. Now the Öland Bridge makes it the gateway to that island.

👁 Sights

Kalmar Domkyrka (*Kalmar Cathedral*)
RELIGIOUS SITE | This highly impressive building was designed by Nicodemus Tessin the Elder in 1660 in the Italian baroque style. Inside, the massive open spaces create stunning light effects. There are noon concerts on Wednesday and sometimes on other weekdays. ✉ *Stortorget, Västra Sjög. 19* ☎ *0480/12300* ⊕ *www.kalmardomkyrka. se* ✉ *Free.*

★ Kalmar Läns Museum

MUSEUM | The highlight of this museum is the exhibit of the remains of the royal warship *Kronan,* which sank in battle off Öland in 1676. Of the 850 people on board, only 42 survived. Since the wreck was discovered in 1980, more than 35,000 objects including cannons, wood sculptures, old coins, and a variety of items belonging to the ship's ill-fated crew have been raised from the seabed—many of them astonishingly well preserved thanks to the low salt content and oxygen-poor environment of the Baltic Sea. On the top floor of the museum is an exhibit focusing on the Kalmar-born artist Jenny Nyström, famous for her paintings of gnomes. ✉ *Skeppsbrog. 51* ☎ *0480/451300* ⊕ *www.kalmarlansmuseum.se* ✉ *SKr 100.*

★ Kalmar Slott (*Kalmar Castle*)

CASTLE/PALACE | Kalmar's top attraction is the imposing Kalmar Castle, which sits on a small island facing the downtown and the harbor. Begun as a defense tower in the 1100s and expanded over

the following century, it held an important strategic position along what was then the border between Sweden and Denmark. In 1397 the castle was the site of one of the most significant events in medieval Scandinavia history, the establishment of the Kalmar Union, which joined Sweden, Norway, and Denmark under one crown. The castle was rebuilt by the Vasa kings during the 16th century and remains the best-preserved Renaissance castle in northern Europe today. It contains a number of well-preserved chambers, as well as interesting displays on the castle's development and Kalmar's importance in Swedish history. ✉ *Kungsg. 1* ☎ *0480/451490* ⊕ *www. kalmarslott.se* ✉ *SKr 110–155* 🕑 *Closed weekdays Nov.–Feb.*

Öland

99 km (62 miles) northeast of Karlskrona via E22, 300 km (161 miles) northeast of Malmö, 117 km (73 miles) southeast of Växjö.

The island of Öland is a magical and ancient place—and the smallest province in Sweden. The area was first settled some 4,000 years ago and is fringed with fine sandy beaches and dotted with old windmills, churches, and archaeological remains.

The island also has spectacular birdlife—swallows, cranes, geese, and birds of prey. Many birds migrate to Öland from as far away as Africa and Siberia. The southern part of the island, known as Stora Alvaret, is a UNESCO World Heritage Site in large part due to its stark beauty and unique flora and fauna. After you cross the bridge from Kalmar on the mainland, be sure to pick up a tourist information map (follow the signs as soon as you get on the island); most of the scattered sights have no address.

GETTING HERE AND AROUND

It's easiest to get to Öland by car. Other methods are likely to be either too slow (bus) or too expensive (taxi). We also suggest hiring a car for traveling around the island itself. The closest major car rental companies are in Kalmar. To get onto the island take Route E22 through the town of Kalmar and across the 6-km (4-mile) bridge.

VISITOR INFO

Ölands Turistbyrå
✉ *Träffpunkt Öland 102, Färjestaden* ☎ *0485/88800* 🌐 *www.oland.se.*

Hotels

Guntorps Herrgård
$ | **B&B/INN** | Spacious parkland surrounds this manor house, which is half a mile from the center of Borgholm. **Pros:** electric bikes available for rent; nice spa area; peaceful location. **Cons:** limited facilities; no food during the day; bathrooms are on the small side. [$] *Rooms from: SKr 1495* ✉ *Guntorpsg. 2, Borgholm* ☎ *0485/13000* 🌐 *www.guntorpsherrgard.se* 🛏 *32 rooms* 🍴 *Free Breakfast.*

The Kingdom of Crystal

Stretching roughly 109 km (68 miles) between Kalmar and Växjö.

The rocky, heavily forested province of Småland is home to the world-famous Swedish glass industry, a spectacular creative art that was at its height in the late 19th century. The conditions were perfect: large quantities of wood to fuel the furnaces and plenty of water from streams and rivers. At the time, demand for glass was such that the furnaces burned 24 hours a day.

Scattered throughout the countryside of the southeastern Småland province are isolated villages whose names are synonymous with high-quality crystal glassware. The region is still home to around a dozen major glassworks, many of them created through the merging of the smaller firms. You can still see glass being blown and crystal being etched by skilled craftspeople. Most glassworks also have shops selling quality firsts and not-so-perfect seconds at a discount.

GETTING HERE AND AROUND

To explore this area properly you need a car. Head to Kalmar or Växjö to rent one or to pick up things like cash or pharmacy supplies. There are also services in the small town of Nybro, which is accessible from all the glassworks and has regular train links from Kalmar, Växjö, Göteborg, and Malmö/Copenhagen.

VISITOR INFORMATION

Glasriket Tourist Information. ☎ *0481/45215* 🌐 *www.glasriket.se.*

Sights

Boda Glasbruk (*The Glass Factory*)
FACTORY | The Glass Factory, part of the Kosta Boda Company, is the second-oldest glassworks here, founded in 1864. At the Glass Factory, young and innovative glass artists and designers have the chance to experiment through residency programs and collaboration. Visitors can try their hand at painting or engraving on glass. There's also an on-site museum with permanent and changing exhibitions related to glass. ✉ *Storg. 5, Boda Glasbruk* ✥ *Just off Rte. 25, 42 km (26 miles) west of Kalmar* ☎ *0471/249360* 🌐 *www.theglassfactory.se* 🎟 *SKr 50* 🕐 *Closed Mon. and Tues. mid-Sept.–late Apr.*

Kosta Boda Glasbruk
FACTORY | The Kingdom of Crystal's oldest works, dating from 1742, was named for the two former generals who founded it, Anders Koskull and Georg Bogislaus Stael von Holstein. Faced with a dearth of local talent, they initially imported glassblowers from Bohemia. The Kosta works pioneered the production of crystal (to qualify for that label, glass must contain at least 24% lead oxide).

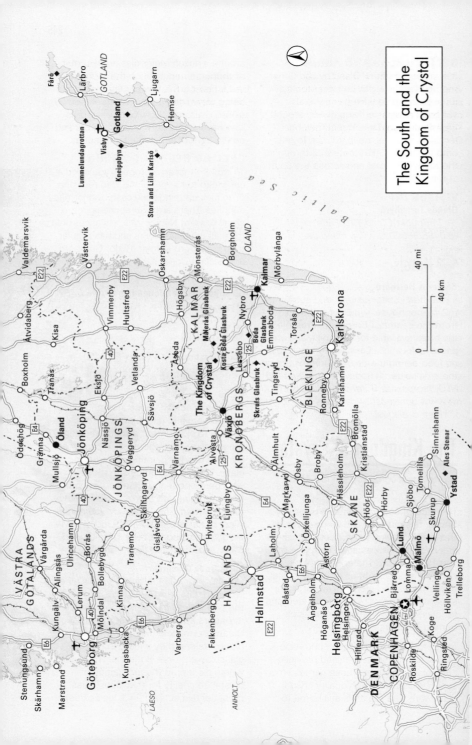

The South and the
Kingdom of Crystal

The Kosta complex includes a glass hut where you can watch glassblowers at work, a glass art gallery, outlet stores, and a glass studio where you can try your own hand at glassblowing. Since 1990 Kosta Boda also owns the renowned Orrefors glass brand, which has its own outlet shop here. To get to the village of Kosta from Kalmar, drive 49 km (30 miles) west on Route 25, then 14 km (9 miles) north on Route 28. ✉ *Stora Vägen 96, Kosta* ☎ *0478/34500* 🌐 *www.kostaboda.se* 🎟 *SKr 100 for guided tours (reservations required).*

Målerås Glasbruk

FACTORY | Målerås specializes in ground, engraved, and painted glass art and decorative glass items. The glassworks's lead designer and primary owner, Mats Jonasson, is known internationally for his stylized crystal animal heads and engraved figures, which can be seen in the exhibition gallery and shop. You can see glassblowing here every day of the year, and guided hot shop shows take place three times a day during the summer. ✉ *Mackamålav. 7, Målerås* ✣ *Just off Rte. 31, 31 km (19 miles) northwest of Nybro* ☎ *0481/31400* 🌐 *www.maleras.se* 🎟 *Free.*

Skrufs Glasbruk

FACTORY | The royal family, the ministry of foreign affairs, and parliament have all commissioned work from Skruf, which started in 1896. Local farmers encouraged the development of the glassworks because they wanted a market for their wood. The factory specializes in lead-free crystal, which has a unique iridescence and form. ✉ *Kajv. 4, Skruv* ✣ *10 km (6 miles) south of Lessebo. Turn left at Åkerby* ☎ *0478/20133* 🌐 *www.skrufsglasbruk.se* 🎟 *Free.*

🛏 Hotels

★ **Kosta Boda Art Hotel**

$$ | **HOTEL** | This hotel pays homage to all things glass, particularly Kosta Boda glass—from an impressive blue-glass bar to the artworks and centerpieces in the Linnéa Art Restaurant. **Pros:** stylish rooms; located next to glassworks and outlet stores; nice spa. **Cons:** be careful—glass everywhere; limited menu in restaurants; not much to do in the area beyond glass. [$] *Rooms from: SKr 1850* ✉ *Stora Vägen 75, Kosta* ☎ *0478/34830* 🌐 *www.kostabodaarthotel.com* 🛏 *102 rooms* 🍴 *Free Breakfast.*

Gotland

85 km (53 miles) south of Stockholm.

Gotland is Sweden's main holiday island, a place of ancient history, a relaxed summer-party vibe, wide sandy beaches, and wild cliff formations called *raukar,* the remnants of reefs formed more than 400 million years ago. Measuring 125 km (78 miles) long and 52 km (32 miles) at its widest point, Gotland is where Swedish sheep farming has its home. In its charming glades, 35 varieties of wild orchids thrive, attracting botanists from all over the world.

GETTING HERE AND AROUND

Regular and high-speed car ferries sail from the small port of Nynäshamn, an hour south of Stockholm by car, bus, or commuter rail. Ferry timetables change frequently, so it is best to consult the operating company, Destination Gotland, before departure. The ferry takes 3½ hours. Boats also leave from Oskarshamn, farther down the coast and closer to Gotland by about an hour. BRA flies from Stockholm's Bromma and Arlanda airports to Visby on Gotland. Flights are daily in the summer.

Exploring beyond Visby is most easily done by car. Avis, Hertz, and Europcar have offices in Visby.

BOAT AND FERRY Destination Gotland. ✉ *Korsg. 2, Visby* ☎ *0771/223300* 🌐 *www.destinationgotland.se.*

VISITOR INFO
Destination Gotland. ☎ *0498/201800*
⊕ *www.destinationgotland.se.*

⊙ Sights

★ Fårö

ISLAND | It takes a five-minute ferry cross-
ing to reach tiny, secluded Fårö from
Gotland, to the south. A popular summer
retreat for Scandinavians, the island has
just 600 year-round residents. Legendary
Swedish filmmaker Ingmar Bergman
once called this island home; every June,
film fanatics head over to celebrate Bergman Week. And in September, the island
celebrates Fårönatta—a night when its
shops, restaurants, and attractions stay
open all night and the church holds a
midnight mass. Head to the Digerhuvud
area to find some impressive natural
"sea stacks," weather rock formations
known as raukar. They often take on
human profiles, fueling local myths and
legends. Note that basic services, including police, medical services, and banks,
are virtually nonexistent on Fårö itself. If
you really want to retreat from the world,
Fårö is it. ⊕ *www.gotland.com.*

★ Fornsalen, Gotlands Museum

MUSEUM | The Gotland county museum's
historical section, Fornsalen, contains
examples of medieval artwork and armor,
prehistoric gravestones and skeletons,
and silver hoards from Viking times. Be
sure to also check out the ornate "picture
stones" from AD 400–600, which depict
ships, people, houses, and animals. Other exhibits highlight significant aspects of
the Middle Ages, when Gotland was an
important mercantile center, controlling
much of the trade between western
Europe and Russia. ⊠ *Strandg. 14, Visby*
☎ *0498/292700* ⊕ *www.gotlandsmuse-
um.se* ⌷ *SKr 100–150.*

Kneippbyn

AMUSEMENT PARK/WATER PARK | **FAMILY** |
This resort with a water park and amusement park brings droves of families

in summer. Locations from the Pippi
Longstocking TV show, including her
house, Villa Villekulla, are here, along with
more than 50 rides, waterslides, and
other attractions. There's a wide range
of accommodation available, including hotel rooms, cabins, apartments,
furnished glamping tents, and campsites.
⊠ *Visby ✈ 3 km (2 miles) south of Visby*
☎ *0498/296150* ⊕ *www.kneippbyn.se*
⌷ *SKr 195–345* ⊗ *Closed Sept.–Apr.*

★ Lummelundagrottan

CAVE | The 4 km (2½ miles) of stalactite
caves at Lummelunda, about 18 km (11
miles) north of Visby on the coastal road,
are unique in this part of the world and
well worth a visit. ⊠ *Lummelundsbruk
520, Visby* ☎ *0498/273050* ⊕ *www.lum-
melundagrottan.se* ⌷ *SKr 150* ⊗ *Closed
Oct.–Apr.*

★ Stora and Lilla Karlsö

ISLAND | These two islands off the south-
west coast of Gotland are bird sanc-
tuaries, known primarily for their large
populations of guillemots and razorbills,
which nest on the islands' steep cliffs
and narrow ledges. Stora Karlsö is also
known for its spring flowers, including
thousands of orchids in late May or early
June. The islands are open to visitors
from early May through August. Boat
tours operate from Klintehamn south of
Visby to Stora Karlsö; from mid-May to
mid-August they also stop at Lilla Karlsö.
The trip includes a guided walking tour
on the island. Overnight accommodations on Stora Karlsö include a hostel and
rooms in the old lighthouse and lighthouse keeper's cottage. ☎ *0498/240500*
⊕ *www.storakarlso.se* ⌷ *SKr 370*
⊗ *Closed Sept.–Apr.*

Visby

TOWN | Gotland's capital, Visby, is a
delightful hilly town of about 24,000
people. Medieval houses, ruined fortifications, churches, and cottage-lined
cobbled lanes make Visby look like something out of a fairy tale. Thanks to a very
gentle climate, the roses that grow along

In several places along Gotland's coastline, you will find the wild vertical rock formations known as sea stacks or "raukar."

many of the town's facades bloom even in November. In its heyday Visby was protected by a wall, of which 3 km (2 mi) survive today, along with 44 towers and numerous gateways. It is considered one of the best-preserved medieval city walls in Europe. Take a stroll to the north gate for an unsurpassed view of the wall. ⊠ *Visby* ⊕ *www.gotland.info.*

★ **Visby Domkyrka** (*Visby Cathedral*)
RELIGIOUS SITE | Visby's cathedral, also known as S:t Maria Kyrka (the Church of St. Mary), is the only one of the town's 13 medieval churches that is still intact and in use. Built between 1190 and 1225 as a place of worship for the town's German parishioners, the church has few of its original fittings because of the extensive and sometimes clumsy restoration work done over the years. That said, the sandstone font and the unusually ugly angels decorating the pulpit are both original features worth a look. ⊠ *Norra Kyrkog. 2, Visby* ☎ *0498/206800* ⊕ *www. svenskakyrkan.se/visby* ⌕ *Free.*

🍴 Restaurants

★ **Bakfickan**
$$ | **SWEDISH** | It may have one of the best locations in town—right in Stora Torget next to medieval ruins of St. Karin—but this restaurant is decorated in what could be called Fisherman's Shack Rustic, with wood benches, shellfish and seafood displays, details from fishing boats, small metal buckets resting on shelves, and menus scribbled on chalkboards. Expect a tight squeeze—there isn't much space to maneuver inside. **Known for:** maritime decor; simple but flavorful seasonal seafood; Baltic herring with mashed potatoes. $ *Average main: SKr 214* ⊠ *Stora Torget 1, Visby* ☎ *0498/271807* ⊕ *www. bakfickan-visby.nu.*

🛏 Hotels

Best Western Strand Hotel
$$ | **HOTEL** | **FAMILY** | What was once the old Visby brewery is now a hotel with lap pool, sauna, steam room, and bright, comfortable rooms. **Pros:** convenient

Visby is Scandinavia's best-preserved medieval town and one of Sweden's most photogenic destinations.

to sightseeing; energy-efficient heating and cooling systems; warm service. **Cons:** several interconnected buildings make hotel something of a maze; limited parking; breakfast gets very crowded. $ *Rooms from: SKr 2195* ✉ *Strandg. 34, Visby* ☎ *0498/258800* ⊕ *www.strandhotel.se* ⇨ *124 rooms* ⏀ *Free Breakfast.*

★ Clarion Hotel Wisby

$$ | **HOTEL** | **FAMILY** | A hotel since 1855, the tall, thin building that's now the Clarion Hotel Wisby dates from the 1200s and sits at the junction of two narrow medieval streets. **Pros:** convenient location; charming mix of old and new; lively bar and lounge. **Cons:** some areas showing wear and tear; spa and pool access are additional fee; crowded breakfast area. $ *Rooms from: SKr 1870* ✉ *Strandg. 6, Visby* ☎ *0498/257500* ⊕ *www.nordicchoicehotels.com* ⇨ *212 rooms* ⏀ *Free Breakfast.*

Hotel Helgeand Wisby

$$ | **HOTEL** | Head to Hotel Helgeand if you want a room that evokes the Middle Ages, when Visby's importance was at

its height. **Pros:** historic atmosphere; quiet location; can choose specific room when booking. **Cons:** some rooms are small; reception open limited hours; extra charge for sauna and hot tub. $ *Rooms from: SKr 2195* ✉ *N:a Kyrkog. 3–7, Visby* ☎ *0498/291230* ⊕ *www.hotelhelgeand. se* ⇨ *17 rooms* ⏀ *Free Breakfast.*

▾ Nightlife

There are many bars and drinking establishments on Gotland, but the best are in Visby. The town comes alive on summer nights; the best way to experience it is simply to wander the streets, follow the loudest noise, and go with the flow. Most clubs in Visby are only open from June to August.

● Performing Arts

Medeltidsveckan

FESTIVALS | Medieval Week, celebrated in early August, is a citywide festival celebrating Visby's rich medieval heritage and marking the invasion of Gotland by the Danish king Valdemar Atterdag in 1361. Celebrations begin with a parade and continue with battle reenactments, jousts, an open-air market, live music, and street-theater performances re-creating the period. On the final day, King Valdemar makes his grand entrance procession following his defeat of Visby's defenders outside the city walls. If you plan to visit Gotland during this time, book early, since hotels fill up well in advance. ⊕ *www.medeltidsveckan.se.*

🏃 Activities

★ Gotland Active Store
BICYCLING | Adventure tours and packages that cover Gotland and nearby islands are available from this company. ✉ *Hamng. 4, Visby* ☎ *0498/230300* ⊕ *www.gotlandactive.se.*

Gotlands Cykeluthyrning
BICYCLING | Bicycles, tents, and camping equipment can be rented from Gotlands Cykeluthyrning. ✉ *Skeppsbron 2, Visby* ☎ *0498/214133* ⊕ *www.gotlandscykeluthyrning.com.*

Dalarna: The Folklore District

A place of forests, mountains, and red-painted wooden farmhouses and cottages by pristine, sun-dappled lakes, Dalarna is considered the most traditional of all the country's 25 provinces. It is the favorite center for Midsummer celebrations, when Swedes don folk costumes and dance to fiddle and accordion music around maypoles covered with wildflower garlands. Midsummer also kicks off Siljansrodden, in which teams of rowers compete in "church boats," traditional longboats that were once used to transport people across Lake Siljan to Sunday church services. Races are held in various communities around the lake over a two-week period. Also in late

June, the towns of Rättvik and Leksand host Musik vid Siljan, a week-long festival with dozens of folk music and classical music concerts, folk dancing, and other musical events.

GETTING HERE AND AROUND
The best way to explore Dalarna is by car. From Stockholm take E18 to Enköping and follow Route 70 northwest. From Göteborg take E20 to Örebro and Route 60 north from there. Villages are well signposted.

There are currently no flights available to the region, but there are frequent train and bus connections to the region from Stockholm. SJ, the state railway company, has regular daily train service from Stockholm to all the major communities in Dalarna, including Borlänge, Falun, Leksand, Rättvik, and Mora, as well as points in between. The journey takes from 2½ to 3 hours to Borlänge and Falun, and between 3 and 4 hours to Leksand, Rättvik, and Mora.

VISITOR INFORMATION
Visit Dalarna. ☎ *0771/626262* ⊕ *www. visitdalarna.se.*

👁 Sights

Dalhalla
ARTS VENUE | Once a lucrative open chalk mine, the huge multi-tier quarry left at Dalhalla has become one of the world's most beautiful outdoor stages. Opera, rock concerts, and amazing light shows are all presented here, where the sound is enhanced by the quarry's incredible acoustics. Regularly scheduled guided tours are available during the summer. ✉ *Rättvik ✛ 7 km (4½ miles) north of Rättvik off Sätra Dalhallavägen* ☎ *0248/797950* ⊕ *www.dalhalla. se* 🎟 *SKr 140 for guided tour* 🕐 *Closed Sept.–May.*

Falu Gruva (*Falun Mine*)
MINE | The town of Falun is famous for its copper mine. It began in the Middle

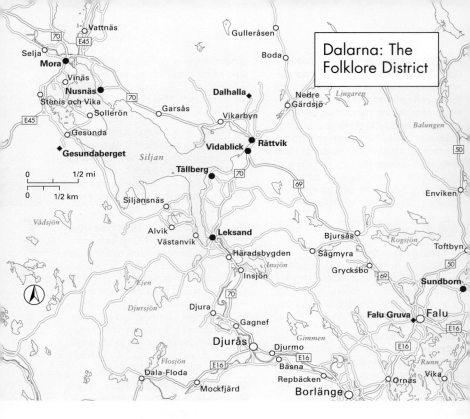

Ages, fueled Sweden's Age of Great Power in the 17th century, and generally held its own until a collapse in 1687; it eventually closed in 1992. Today the mine site is Falun's principal tourist attraction. The guided tour begins with a descent through a network of old shafts and tunnels, 220 feet underground. Wear old shoes and warm clothing, since the copper-tinged mud can stain footwear and it's cold down there. The museum at surface level has interactive exhibits where you can explore the mine's history and experience what life was like for the miners who worked here. Fun fact: the dark red paint color that is so ubiquitous on houses throughout the Swedish countryside is called Falu *röd* (Falun red) and is made from a by-product of the copper mine. ☒ *Gruvplatsen 1, Falun* ✛ *230 km (143 miles) northwest of Stockholm via E18 and Rte. 70* ☎ *023/782030* ⊕ *www.*

falugruva.se ✉ *Mine and museum SKr 210–230.*

Gesundaberget

MOUNTAIN—SIGHT | A chairlift from Gesunda, a pleasant little village, will take you to the top of a mountain for unbeatable views over Lake Siljan. The peak of Gesundaberget is 1,686 feet above sea level (1,158 feet above the lake). In winter, the mountain is a popular local ski area. In summer, there's a bike park, a ropes course, and above all, that glorious view. You can hike up the mountain from the parking lot at about 1,000 feet in elevation, or take the chairlift up. At the top there's a restaurant, Toppstugan, as well as a café that sells sandwiches and snacks and also has bikes for rent. Both are open daily mid-June to mid-August and weekends in early June and from mid-August to early October, as well as during ski season, which lasts from just before the holidays to early April. ✉ Gesunda Ski Resort, Gesundabergsv. 106, Gesunda ✛ 42 km (26 miles) northwest of Leksand, 19 km (12 miles) south of Mora ☎ 0250/21400 ⊕ www.gesundaberget.se ⌨ SKr 89 round-trip lift ticket (summer).

Leksand

TOWN | At the southern end of Lake Siljan, Leksand is famous for the largest Midsummer celebrations in all of Sweden. In the early evening on Midsummer Eve, folk musicians in traditional costumes arrive by church boat and fiddle their way to Gropen, an amphitheater-like depression created by glaciers during the last Ice Age. Here Sweden's tallest maypole is decorated and raised, with thousands of people joining in the traditional dancing and festivities. Leksand also has a lovely church with an unusual onion-domed spire. The church has had its present appearance since 1715, though its oldest sections date from the 1200s. Its lovely cemetery contains the grave of Hugo Alfvén (1872–1960), one of Sweden's best-known composers, who lived just in the Leksand area for the last two decades of his life. Classical and folk music concerts are held in the summer at his home, Alfvéngården, which is now a museum dedicated to the composer. ✛ 12 km (7½ miles) south of Tällberg via Hjortnäs Siljansvägen, 21 km (13 miles) southwest of Rättvik via Rte. 70.

Mora

TOWN | Mora is best known as the finishing point for the world's longest cross-country ski race, Vasaloppet. Held in March, it begins 90 km (56 miles) away at Sälen, a ski resort close to the Norwegian border. The race commemorates a fundamental piece of Swedish history: the successful attempt by Gustav Vasa in 1521 to rally local peasants to the cause of ridding Sweden of Danish occupation. It attracts thousands of competitors from all over the world, including

members of the Swedish royal family. There is a spectacular mass start at Sälen before the field thins out. The finish is eagerly awaited in Mora, where a statue of Gustav Vasa by Anders Zorn stands by the portal marking the finish line; there's also a small free museum about Vasaloppet that's worth a quick look, though most information is only in Swedish. By the Mora waterfront there's a 12-foot Dala horse that's reputedly the biggest wooden Dala horse in the world. (The huge one at Avesta is made of concrete.) ✉ Mora ✛ 37 km (23 miles) northwest of Rättvik via Rte. 70.

★ Nusnäs

TOWN | The lakeside village of Nusnäs is where the famous painted wooden Dala horses are made. These were originally carved by the peasants of Dalarna as toys for their children, but their popularity rapidly spread in the 20th century. In 1939 they achieved international popularity after being shown at the New York World's Fair, and since then they have become a Swedish symbol. Founded in the 1920s by brothers from a poor family, the companies Grannas A. Olsson Hemslöjd ⊕ www.grannas.com and Nils

Olsson Dalahästar ⊕ *www.nilsolsson.
se* still make Dala horses today. At their
factories you can see the horses being
made and purchase finished horses in
many different sizes and colors, including
the classic bright red. You can even have
them personalized with your name or other text while you wait. ⊠ *Nusnäs.*

Rättvik

TOWN | On the eastern tip of Lake Siljan,
Rättvik is a pleasant town of timbered
houses surrounded by wooded slopes.
A center for local folklore, the town has
several shops that sell handmade articles
and local produce. Rättvik is a great place
to experience Dalarna's Midsummer celebrations, which include the festive arrival
of church boats on Midsummer Day,
bringing people in traditional costumes
to attend services in the town's white-
washed 13th-century church, just as they
would have arrived by boat each Sunday
in bygone days when church attendance
was mandatory. The church occupies a
pretty spot on the shore of the lake, and
its interior contains some fine examples of local religious art. In downtown
Rättvik, a mile down the shore, the main
square has a fountain with charming
sculptures of folk dancers. ⊠ *Rättvik
✛ 50 km (31 miles) northwest of Falun
via Rte. 69.*

Sundborn

HOUSE | In this small village you can visit
Carl Larsson-gården, the lakeside home
of the internationally famous Swedish
artist (1853–1915), especially known for
his watercolor paintings of his family's
busy domestic life. The house itself was
creatively painted and decorated by
Larsson's wife, Karin, also trained as an
artist. Admission is by guided tour only,
and tickets are timed; advance booking
is recommended, especially in summer.
If you do need to wait you can stroll
around the garden or lake, visit the café,
or browse the shop, which sells items
based on designs in the house and other
work by the Larssons. In summer tour

tickets also include entry to the Kvarnen
Gallery, which has special exhibits related
to Carl Larsson and his work. ⊠ *Carl
Larsson-gården, Carl Larssons Väg 12,
Sundborn ✛ 14 km (8½ miles) northeast
of Falun* ☎ *023/60053* ⊕ *www.carllars-
son.se* ☜ *SKr 195–220* ⊘ *Guided tours
only; only one English tour per day Oct.–
Apr. Check website for times.*

★ Tällberg

TOWN | Tällberg is considered by many to
be the real Dalarna. It was a sleepy town
that few knew about, but an 1850 visit
from Hans Christian Andersen put an end
to all that. He extolled its virtues—tiny
flower-strewn cottages, sweet-smelling
grass meadows, stunning lake views—
to such an extent that Tällberg quickly
became a major tourist stop. This little
village, which has fewer than 900 permanent residents, has eight hotels—nearly
one for every 100 locals. ⊠ *Tällberg ✛ 13
km (8½ miles) south of Rättvik via Rte.
70.*

Vidablick

VIEWPOINT | In the forest just south of
Rättvik is Vidablick, a tall wooden tower
situated on a high ridge. More than 100
years old, the tower offers some of the
most stunning views across Lake Siljan
to be found anywhere. At the base of
the tower there's a shop selling handicrafts made by local artisans. ⊠ *Rättvik
✛ 5 km (3 miles) south of Rättvik on
Vidablicksvägen* ☎ *073/8406358* ⊕ *www.
vidablickhantverk.se* ☜ *Free* ⊘ *Closed
late Aug.–early June.*

🛍 Shopping

★ Mora Hemslöjd

CRAFTS | Hand-knitted mittens and hats,
brass candle holders, traditional painted
wooden animals, woven blankets,
embroidered pillows, and local Mora
folk costumes are just some of the
things you'll find at this handicrafts
store. ⊠ *Kyrkog. 4, Mora* ☎ *0250/10225*
⊕ *www.morahemslojd.se* ⊘ *Closed Sun.*

Jukkasjärvi's Icehotel is rebuilt every year from December to April.

★ **Nittsjö Keramik**

CRAFTS | One of the oldest crafts companies in Sweden, Nittsjö has been producing fine ceramics for well over a century. At the factory you can watch master artisans at work, while in the shop you'll find a wide range of ceramic products including tableware, vases, Christmas decorations, and other items both useful and purely decorative. ✉ *Nittsjö Keramikvägen 31, Rättvik* ☎ *0248/17130* 🌐 *www.nittsjokeramik.se* 🕒 *Factory closed weekends. Shop closed Sun. Sept.–May.*

Jukkasjärvi

Located in the frigid, wind-swept north of Sweden's Lapland province, tiny Jukkasjärvi is home to just 675 souls (at last count). While the town's main claim to fame is its spectacular Icehotel, the very first of its kind, Jukkasjärvi also has two- to three-day snowmobile and dogsled excursions through the tundra—a thrilling way to experience this wild, desolate region of the world. There are also a variety of northern lights tours available—though whether or not you'll get lucky is up to nature, of course. If you want to give yourself a good chance of seeing the aurora, it's best to plan a stay of several days.

🛏 Hotels

★ **Icehotel**

$$ | **HOTEL** | It's no wonder that Jukkasjärvi's famed Icehotel was first conceived and constructed as an art installation in 1990—this fantastical structure is a sensory extravaganza. **Pros:** cool accommodations, both literally and figuratively; beautiful riverside setting; gorgeous ice art everywhere. **Cons:** ice rooms are expensive; some guests find it hard to sleep in the cold, despite warm sleeping bags; bathroom use at night requires some unwrapping. [$] *Rooms from: SKr 2242* ✉ *Marknadsv. 63, Jukkasjärvi* ☎ *0980/66800* 🌐 *www.icehotel.com* 🛏 *64 ice rooms, 43 warm accommodations, 12 chalets* 🍴 *Free Breakfast.*

Jokkmokk

170 km (106 miles) northwest of Luleå,
207 km (129 miles) south of Jukkasjärvi.

Located just a few kilometers north of the Arctic Circle, Jokkmokk is an important cultural center for the indigenous Sami people, whose territory spreads over the far north of four countries: Norway, Sweden, Finland, and Russia. Every year since 1605, this town of about 3,000 people has been the site of the Jokkmokk Market, a winter gathering that takes place over several days in early February, drawing more than 35,000 visitors including Sami from throughout northern Scandinavia, as well as other travelers who come to join in the festivities. In addition to market stalls selling traditional foods, handicrafts, and more, there is a full program of cultural events, concerts, lectures, and winter activities such as skiing, northern lights viewing, dogsled riding, and reindeer racing. Plan well ahead if you're interested in attending, as accommodation fills up fast.

◉ Sights

★ Ájtte, Swedish Mountain and Sami Museum

MUSEUM | At first glance, this museum looks quite simple, but once you enter the heart of the museum you'll find exhibit areas opening off a central core like petals on a flower, exploring the culture and history of the Sami people. There are impressive displays of Sami crafts and traditional clothing, as well as exhibits about culture, reindeer herding, religion, education, the Arctic landscape and wildlife, and the impact of outside settlers on the Sami way of life. Many exhibits are labeled in English, but there are also printed museum guides and

After Ice, Stay in the Trees 🛏

About three hours south of Jukkasjärvi's famous Icehotel, you'll find what looks like an outdoor museum with a series of seven glass cubes and other unusual structures suspended among the pine trees of a Swedish forest. However, this is not an art installation—it's a hotel. Family-owned and operated, the eco-friendly, low-impact property offers rooms set at various heights above the ground (ranging from 13 to 33 feet), and each one is different in shape and furnishings. Choose from a mirror cube, a bird's nest, a UFO, or other uniquely designed accommodation and enjoy the feeling of unwinding in a natural setting. ☎ *928/10300* ⊕ *www.treehotel.se*

audio guides available. ⊠ *Kyrkog. 3, Jukkasjärvi* ☎ *0971/17070* ⊕ *www.ajtte.com/english* 🎫 *SKr 90* ⊗ *Closed Mon. mid-Aug.–mid-June and Sun. mid-Sept.–Apr.*

🛏 Hotels

Hotel Akerlund

$$ | HOTEL | Located just off the main street in Jokkmokk, this small hotel has 24 simple but comfortable rooms on two floors. **Pros:** convenient location; nice lounge area; excellent breakfast buffet. **Cons:** no elevator; reception is not 24/7; limited amenities. 🅂 *Rooms from: SKr 1695* ⊠ *Herrev. 1* ☎ *0971/10012* ⊕ *www.hotelakerlund.se* 🛏 *24 rooms* ⦿ *Free Breakfast.*

Laponia World Heritage Site

141 km (88 miles) northwest of Jokkmokk. Take the E45 highway to just north of Porjus, then turn left on Road 827, following signs for Stora Sjöfallet and Björkudden.

A wild and stunningly beautiful area of mountains, lakes, rushing rivers, and bogs, Laponia encompasses four national parks: Padjelanta, Sarek, Muddus, and Stora Sjöfallet. The region received its World Heritage designation from UNESCO not just for its natural value but also for its importance to the local Sami people, who have herded reindeer in the region for thousands of years. If you're looking to experience the nature of the north, this is a relatively accessible place to do so.

Sights

Naturum Laponia

INFO CENTER | Perched on the north shore of Lake Langas, this visitor center is built in a style that resembles the rounded shape of traditional Sami dwellings. It tells the story of the people and nature of the area, through exhibits that explore life during the eight distinct seasons recognized by the Sami. There are also listening stations where you can hear the personal stories of different people who live or spend time in the area. A café serves sandwiches, waffles, and other light meals and snacks. ✉ *Stora Sjöfallet National Park , Rd. 827, Jukkasjärvi* ☎ *0973/22020* 🌐 *www.laponia.nu* 🎟 *Free* 🕑 *Hours vary, check website.*

Hotels

Saltoluokta Fjällstation (*Saltoluokta Mountain Station*)

$ | **B&B/INN** | Given the area's remoteness, you'll have to sacrifice some comfort if you want to stay overnight in the Laponia area, but if you don't mind basic rooms and shared bathroom facilities, the Saltoluokta Mountain Station makes a good base for hiking and enjoying some spectacular scenery. **Pros:** gorgeous setting; outdoor equipment rental; lovely sauna. **Cons:** hostel-style rooms—you make up your own bed and do your own cleaning; creaky floors; toilets and showers can be some distance from rooms. [$] *Rooms from: SKr 850* ✉ *Saltoluokta* ✥ *Across the lake from Kebnats* ☎ *0973/41010* 🌐 *www.swedishtouristassociation.com/saltoluokta* 🕑 *Closed mid-Sept.–late Feb. and late Apr.–mid-June* 🛏 *33 rooms* 🍴 *Free Breakfast.*

Chapter 5

DENMARK

Updated by
Michelle Arrouas

👁 Sights	🍽 Restaurants	🛏 Hotels	💼 Shopping	🍸 Nightlife
★★★★☆	★★★★★	★★★★★	★★★★★	★★★★★

WELCOME TO DENMARK

TOP REASONS TO GO

★ **Fairytale castles.** From Egeskov to Rosenborg and Frederiksborg to Hamlet's Kronborg (Castle Elsinore, per Shakespeare), there are hundreds of historic castles across this small country.

★ **Bornholm.** Once a sleepy fisherman's island, today it's the Danish Cape Cod with ambitious restaurants and beautiful beaches.

★ **Hans Christian Andersen.** The 19th-century writer of such stories as *The Ugly Duckling* and *The Emperor's New Clothes* is a national hero in Denmark. Look for statues, festivals, and museums.

★ **Vintage amusement parks.** Dyrehavsbakken, north of Copenhagen, is the world's oldest amusement park, and Tivoli, in the heart of the city, is the world's second oldest.

★ **All the food.** From traditional Danish fare to the New Nordic foodie revolution, you'll want to pack your stretchy pants.

1 Copenhagen.

2 Klampenborg, Bakken, and Dyrehaven.

3 Humlebæk.

4 Lyngby.

5 Hellerup.

6 Charlottenlund.

7 Dragør and Store Magleby.

8 Ishøj.

9 Gisselfeld Kloster and Tårn.

10 Helsingør.

11 Hornbæk and the Danish Riviera.

12 Hillerød.

13 Roskilde.

14 Møn.

15 Bornholm.

16 Odense.

17 Svendborg.

18 Ærø.

19 Ribe.

20 Billund.

21 Aarhus.

22 Samsø.

23 Aalborg.

24 Skagen.

25 Klitmøller and Thy.

26 Tórshavn and the Faroe Islands.

Skagen
Hirtshals
Göteborg
Borås
Jönköping
Frederikshavn
VENDSYSSEL-THY
LÆSØ
Aalborg
SWEDEN
Baltic Sea
ANHOLT
Växjö
Halmstad
Karlskrona
Aarhus
DENMARK
Hornbæk
Helsingborg
Hillerød
Helsingør
Kristianstad
SAMSØ
Humlebaek
Lyngby
Charlottenlund
Roskilde
COPENHAGEN
Ishøj
Dragør
Malmö
Odense
Sorø
ZEALAND
Ystad
FUNEN
Gisselfeld Kloster
Tårn
Svendborg
Ronne
BORNHOLM
ÆRØ
MØN
Baltic Sea
FALSTER
LOLLAND
Kiel
0   25 mi
GERMANY
Stralsund
0   25 km

DENMARK SNAPSHOT

DENMARK AT A GLANCE

- **Capital:** Copenhagen
- **Population:** 5,814,400
- **Currency:** Krone
- **Money:** ATMs are common, almost every establishment accepts credit cards, and euros are widely accepted
- **Language:** Danish
- **Country Code:** 45
- **Emergencies:** 112
- **Driving:** On the right
- **Electricity:** 200v/50 cycles; electrical plugs have two round prongs
- **Time:** Six hours ahead of New York
- **Documents:** Up to 90 days with valid passport; Schengen rules apply
- **Mobile Phones:** GSM (900 and 1800 bands)
- **Major Mobile Companies:** TDC, Telia, Telenor, and 3

WHEN TO GO

High Season: The lingering sun of summertime—June, July, and August—brings out the best in the climate and the Danes and is the best time to visit. Prices are accordingly at their highest of the year, and hotels are often at capacity.

Low Season: Winter—November through March—is dark and misty, and rather cold, but it's the best time to find cheaper flights and hotel rates. Some attractions and tour offices are closed. The weeks preceding Christmas are particularly charming.

Value Season: May and September are ideal months to visit Denmark. Prices tend to be a bit cheaper for both flights and hotels, and temperatures are generally pleasant. April and October are a safer bet than the winter months.

BIG EVENTS

- **May:** The colorful, week-long Aalborg Carnival is northern Europe's largest, drawing more than 100,000 revelers. ⊕ *www.aalborg-karneval.dk*
- Heartland Festival is an eclectic, three-day music, visual, and culinary arts festival set in the stunning Egeskov Castle and Gardens. ⊕ *www.heartland-festival.dk*
- **June and July:** The Roskilde Festival is one of Europe's oldest and biggest annual rock music events. ⊕ *www.roskilde-festival.dk*
- **August:** Odense is known for being a festival city but one of its most popular is a tribute to its most famous son, Hans Christian Andersen with a week of cabaret, concerts, parades, and artistic experiences. ⊕ *www.hcafestivals.com*
- **August and September:** The ten-day Aarhus Festival showcases arts and culture with a different theme each year. ⊕ *www.aarhusfestuge.dk*
- **November and December:** More than a million visitors flock to the pretty Christmas market at Copenhagen's famed Tivoli Gardens. ⊕ *www.tivoli.dk*

Denmark is a liberal, modern state with a strong focus on equality, the environment, and European integration, where historical traditions are mixed with new ideas, where age-old buildings stand next to cutting-edge restaurants serving New Nordic cuisine, and where many residents still ride their bicycles to work and to play.

The history of this little country stretches back 250,000 years, when Jutland was inhabited by nomadic hunters, but it wasn't until AD 500 that a tribe from Sweden, called the Danes, migrated south and christened the land Denmark. The Viking expansion that followed was based on the country's strategic position in the north. Intrepid navies navigated to Europe and Canada, invading and often pillaging, until, under King Knud (Canute) the Great (995–1035), they captured England by 1018.

After the British conquest, Viking supremacy declined as feudal Europe learned to defend itself. Under the leadership of Valdemar IV (1340–75), Sweden, Norway, Iceland, Greenland, and the Faroe Islands became a part of Denmark. Sweden broke away by the mid-15th century and battled Denmark for much of the next several hundred years, whereas Norway remained under Danish rule until 1814 and Iceland until 1943. Greenland and the Faroe Islands are still self-governing Danish provinces.

By the 18th century, absolute monarchy had given way to representative democracy, and culture flourished. Then—in what turned out to be a fatal mistake— Denmark refused to surrender its navy to the English during the Napoleonic Wars. Lord Nelson famously turned a blind eye to the destruction and bombed Copenhagen to bits. The defeated King Frederik VI handed Norway to Sweden. Denmark's days of glory were over.

Though Denmark was unaligned during World War II, the Nazis invaded in 1940. The small but strong resistance movement that was active throughout the war years is greatly celebrated. After the war, Denmark focused inward, concentrating on its main industries of agriculture, shipping, and financial and technical services. It's become an outspoken member of the European Union (EU), championing environmental responsibility and supporting development in emerging economies, and it has a highly developed social-welfare system. Hefty taxes are the subject of grumbles and jokes, but Danes are proud of their state-funded medical and educational systems and high standard of living. And the Danes' lifestyle is certainly enviable. In fact, almost everything about the country—from the nature to the climate and temperament—is temperate. The landscape is mellow and mild; in the cities the pace is set by pedestrians, not traffic; and the social climate is such that everyone can be friends, despite their differences.

MAJOR REGIONS

Copenhagen. The starting point for most travelers to Denmark, Copenhagen provides a wonderful introduction to the country. Visitors to Denmark's capital can jump into harbor baths, dine at world-famous restaurants, bike winding lanes, and explore rapidly transforming neighborhoods such as Refshaleøen, a former shipyard turned urban playground. From Copenhagen it's easy to travel to the rest of Denmark—whether you're getting there by car, train, plane, bus, or bike—as well as onward to Sweden and Norway.

Side Trips from Copenhagen. Copenhagen is surrounded by forests, coastal areas, affluent suburbs, and cultural institutions, and no trip to the city is complete without a getaway from it. A raft of museums and theme parks—including the oldest amusement park in the world—can be found in the towns around Copenhagen. Most are reachable by bus or S-train and make for easy excursions from the capital.

Zealand. Slightly larger than the state of Delaware, Zealand is the largest of the Danish islands. It is home to Copenhagen as well as the countryside surrounding Copenhagen, which is beautiful and easily explored on day-trips from the capital—almost any point on Zealand can be reached in an hour and a half, making it the most-traveled portion of the country. Hike the white chalk cliffs of Møns Klint; wander around the castle in Hillerød; visit a 12th-century, UNESCO-listed cathedral that once served as northern Europe's spiritual center in Roskilde, medieval Denmark's most important town; relax on the beaches surrounding Hornbæk, with their summer cottages, white dunes, and calm waters; and travel through the many small vacation towns that have become known as the Danish Riviera. To the north, explore Frederiksborg, considered one of the most magnificent Renaissance castles in Europe, and walk through the Kronborg Castle of *Hamlet* fame, which crowns Helsingør; along the pretty beach highway between Copenhagen and Helsingør are the suburbs that play home to Denmark's wealthiest citizens. This area is still referred to as the "whiskey belt"—so named because whiskey was a preferred drink of the wealthy residents in this area. To the south are rural towns and fine white beaches, often surrounded by forests. Even more unspoiled are the tiny islands around southern Zealand, virtually unchanged over the past century.

Bornholm. Off the coast of southern Sweden, the Danish island of Bornholm beckons with its wild scenery, relaxed atmosphere, and white-sand beaches. Those who make the trek tend to find it is worth the effort.

Jutland. The only part of the country naturally connected to mainland Europe, Denmark's western peninsula of Jutland is the geographical link between Denmark and continental Europe; its southern boundary is the frontier with Germany. The landscape of Jutland is the most severe, with Ice Age–chiseled fjords and hills, sheepishly called mountains by the Danes. In the cities of Aarhus and Aalborg, you can find museums and harbor baths that rival Copenhagen's, although the cities' nightlife is more subdued. The holiday island Samsø is known for its organic farms and beautiful beaches, while Skagen has been attracting artists—and wealthier vacationers—for centuries with its special light and storied hotels. The northwest Jutland town of Klitmøller, also known as Cold Hawaii, is a recent addition to most travelers' itinerary, while southwest Jutland's historic Ribe, Denmark's oldest town, has been drawing crowds for long, and in its medieval town center you'll find the country's earliest church. Ribe is also the departure point for trips to Rømø and Fanø, islands of windswept beaches and traditional villages. The center of Jutland is dotted with gentle, rolling hills, castles, parklands, and the famed Legoland. Nearly three times the size of the rest of Denmark, with long distances between towns, the peninsula of Jutland can easily take several days, even weeks, to explore. If you are pressed for time, concentrate on a single tour or a couple of cities.

Funen and the Central Islands. Christened the Garden of Denmark by its most famous son, Hans Christian Andersen, Funen (Fyn) is the smaller of the country's two major islands and is the geographical heart of Denmark (thus easy to explore on your way between the major cities). The city of Odense, Hans Christian Andersen's birthplace, is cobbled with crooked old streets and Lilliputian cottages, while Svendborg's maritime history is still alive and well. A patchwork of vegetable fields and flower gardens, the flat countryside is also sprinkled with beech glades and swan ponds. Manor houses and castles pop up from the countryside like magnificent mirages. Some of northern Europe's best-preserved castles are here: the 12th-century Nyborg Slot, the classic beauty Egeskov Slot, and the lavish Valdemars Slot. The fairy-tale cliché often attributed to Denmark is due to Funen, where the only place with modern vigor or stress seems to be Odense, its capital. Trimmed with thatch-roof houses and green parks, the city makes the most of the Andersen legacy but surprises with a rich arts community at the Brandts, a former textile factory turned museum. Towns in Funen are best explored by car. It's even quick and easy to reach the smaller islands of Langeland and Tåsinge—both are connected to Funen by bridges. Slightly more isolated is the small Baltic island of Ærø, where the town of Ærøskøbing, with its colorfully painted half-timbered houses and winding streets, seems caught in a time warp or fairy tale.

The Faroe Islands. The 18 volcanic, rocky, and rugged islands that make up the Faroe Islands, a self-governing archipelago located between Iceland, Scotland, and Norway, are home to dramatic mountains, steep coastal cliffs, and green heathlands where wild-roaming sheep grass. The islands have been attracting nature lovers for decades, but in recent years Tórshavn's restaurants, hotels, and shops have begun attracting urban travelers, too.

Planning

Getting Here and Around

AIR

Kastrup International Airport (CPH), 10 km (6 miles) from the center of Copenhagen, is the hub of Scandinavian and international air travel in Denmark. Jutland has regional hubs in Aalborg (AAL), Aarhus (AAR), and Billund (BLL), which handle mainly domestic and some European traffic. SAS, the main carrier, flies to the capital from several North American cities, as does Norwegian, a low-cost carrier. United Airlines and Delta offer direct flights to Copenhagen from New York in the summer. KLM, Air France, Lufthansa, Icelandair, and Finnair have numerous connecting flights to Copenhagen via Amsterdam, Paris, Frankfurt, Reykjavík, and Helsinki, respectively.

From New York, flights to Copenhagen take 7 hours, 40 minutes. From Chicago, they take 9 hours, 30 minutes. From Seattle and Los Angeles the flight time is about 10 hours, 55 minutes. Flight times within the country are all less than one hour.

AIRPORTS Copenhagen Airport (CPH). ✉ Lufthavnsboulevarden 6, Kastrup ☎ 32/31–32–31 ⊕ www.cph.dk. **Aarhus Airport (AAR).** ✉ Ny Lufthavnsvej 24, Århus ☎ 87/75–70–00 ⊕ www.aar.dk.

Billund Airport. ✉ *Passagerterminalen 10, Billund* ☎ *76/50–50–50* ⊕ *www.billund-airport.dk.*

BOAT AND FERRY

Although more people drive or take buses and trains over new bridges spanning the waters, ferries are still a good way to explore Denmark and Scandinavia, especially if you have a rail pass. The Eurail Scandinavia Pass, for travel anywhere within Scandinavia (Denmark, Sweden, Norway, and Finland), is valid on some ferry crossings.

DFDS sails to Oslo from Copenhagen. Fjord Line is another company with service between Denmark and Norway, though only from northern Denmark. Scandlines connects Denmark with Sweden and Germany.

Vehicle-bearing hydrofoils operate between Jutland's Ebeltoft or Aarhus to Odden on Zealand; the trip takes about one hour. You can also take the slower (2 hours, 40 minutes), but less expensive, car ferry from Aarhus to Kalundborg on Zealand. From there, Route 23 leads to Copenhagen. Make reservations for the ferry in advance through Molslinjen. (Note: During the busy summer months, passengers without reservations for their vehicles may have to wait hours.) The Helsingør/Helsingborg vehicle and passenger ferry (Scandlines) takes only 20 minutes.

CONTACTS DFDS Seaways. ✉ *Sundkrogsgade 11, Copenhagen* ⊕ *www.dfdsseaways.dk.* **Molslinjen.** ⊕ *www.molslinjen.dk.* **Scandlines.** ⊕ *www.scandlines.com.*

BUS

Private bus operators and Danish State Railways (DSB) have collaborated to create an online travel planner called Rejseplanen, which consolidates schedule and route information for the country's trains and buses.

While train travel is more common, a number of coach lines operate an extensive network of efficient and reasonably priced routes that include more remote areas. FlixBus links the principal Danish cities to major European cities, with several dozen departures every day. Säfflebussen offers routes to Sweden. Domestic companies include Thinggaard Express and Gråhundbus. Abildskou (which is a partner of FlixBus) offers service from Copenhagen to several major cities. Bus tickets are usually sold online or on board the buses immediately before departure.

CONTACTS Abildskou. ☎ *70/21–08–88* ⊕ *www.abildskou.com.* **FlixBus.** ☎ *32/72–93–86* ⊕ *www.flixbus.dk.* **Gråhundbus.** ☎ *44/68–44–00* ⊕ *www.graahundbus.dk.* **Rejseplanen.** ⊕ *www.rejseplanen.dk.*

CAR

Car rental can be expensive, but overall, traveling by car in Denmark is a great way to get off the beaten path. Roads and signage are excellent, and traffic is generally light. Ferries to the islands have reasonable car rates but should be booked in advance.

The only part of Denmark that's connected to the European continent is Jutland, via the E45 highway from Germany. The E20 highway then leads to Funen and Zealand. Storebæltsbroen (the Storebælt Bridge) connects Funen and Zealand via the E20 highway; the E20 then continues east, over the Lillebælt Bridge, to Copenhagen. You can reach many of the smaller islands via toll bridges.

Øresundsbroen, the monumental bridge that connects Denmark with Sweden, was inaugurated in 2000. The drive that takes you across it from Copenhagen to Malmö takes approximately 45 minutes.

Rental rates in Copenhagen begin at DKr 550 a day and DKr 2,220 a week. This doesn't include potential additional per-kilometer fees and any insurance you purchase; there's also a 25% tax on car rentals. The good news? Most companies have special weekend offers.

⚠ **It's illegal to talk on the phone while driving.**

TRAIN

Denmark's train system is thorough, efficient, and reasonably priced, and trains within Europe are well connected to Denmark, with Copenhagen serving as the main hub. Traveling by train, however, is often not much cheaper than flying, especially if you make your arrangements from the United States. The DSB and a few private companies cover the country with a dense network of service, supplemented by buses in remote areas. Hourly InterCity trains connect the main towns in Jutland and Funen with Copenhagen and Zealand; faster InterCityLyn trains run on the most important stretches.

You can reserve seats (for an extra DKr 30) on most longer-distance routes. When traveling on InterCity and InterCityLyn, reservations are a good idea as some trains often sell out. Buy tickets online in advance or at stations. Call Arriva for train travel in central and western Jutland or the DSB Travel Office for the rest of the country. The Eurail Denmark Pass allows for unlimited train travel within Denmark for either three or seven days within a month.

Journeys by train (as well as bus and city transit) can be easily mapped out at ⊕ *http://www.rejseplanen.dk.*

CONTACTS Arriva. ☎ *70/27–74–82* ⊕ *www.arriva.dk.* **DSB.** ☎ *70/13–14–15* ⊕ *www.dsb.dk.*

Hotels

All hotels listed have private bathrooms unless otherwise noted. Many Danes prefer a shower to a bath, so if you particularly want a bath, ask for it—and be prepared to pay more. Older hotels may have rooms described as "double," which in fact have one double bed plus one fold-out sofa big enough for two people.

Two things about hotels usually surprise North Americans: the small size of Scandinavian beds and the generous size of Scandinavian breakfasts. Scandinavian double beds are often about 60 inches wide or slightly less, close in size to the U.S. queen size. King-size beds (72 inches wide) are difficult to find, though they're becoming more normal at newer hotels. It's a good idea to make a special request when you place your reservation to find out if the hotel offers king-size beds. Breakfast, on the other hand, which is normally included in hotel rates, consists of a huge buffet of meats, cheeses, fish, marmalade, etc., and is enough to satisfy the heartiest of appetites.

Restaurants

In the big cities you can find traditional Danish restaurants, but with Denmark's recent culinary revolution, you are probably more likely to find many New Nordic gourmet restaurants, shops selling vegan smoothies, salad bars, and international cuisine options, including French bistros, Italian trattorias, European wine bars, Middle Eastern kebab joints, and street-food stalls with food from all over the world.

Traditional Danish fare, which is found in most rural areas, relies on provisions native to the region: grains, potatoes, pork, beef, and fish. At the most traditional restaurants many meals begin with *sild,* or pickled herring of various flavors, served on *rugbrød,* a very dark and dense rye-based bread. This bread also provides the basis for what used to be the most common Danish lunch: *smørrebrød*— open-face sandwiches piled high with various meats, vegetables, and condiments. These days that lunch is often reserved for special visits to the traditional lunch restaurants, often around Christmas or special occasions, but it generally makes for both a nutritious and low-cost meal in Copenhagen, especially in the less central Nørrebro and Østerbro neighborhoods. For dinner, try *flæskesteg*, pork roast with a crispy rind, which is commonly served with *rødkål* (stewed red cabbage) and potatoes; this is also a traditional Danish Christmas meal.

Denmark's major cities have a good selection of restaurants serving both traditional Danish and international cuisines. Danes start the workday early, which means they generally eat lunch at noon and consume their evening meal on the early side. Make your dinner reservations for no later than 9 pm. Bars and cafés stay open later, and most offer at least light fare.

HOTEL AND RESTAURANT PRICES

Hotel prices in the reviews are the lowest cost of a standard double room in high season. Restaurant prices in the reviews are the average cost of a main course at dinner, or if dinner is not served, at lunch.

WHAT IT COSTS in Danish kroner

	$	$$	$$$	$$$$
RESTAURANTS				
	Under DKr 100	DKr 100–DKr 300	DKr 301–DKr 600	Over DKr 600
HOTELS				
	Under DKr 750	DKr 751–DKr 1,200	DKr 1,201–1,800	Over DKr 1,800

Copenhagen

Copenhagen—København in Danish—is the gateway to Sweden and the other Scandinavian countries, as well as the perfect place to start or base oneself on a visit to Denmark. The city regards itself as the cultural and culinary capital of the region, and with its many museums and

Danish Fare 🍽

Smørrebrød: buttered dark rye bread topped with meat, fish, and cheese.

Æbleflæsk: bacon fried with apples, onions, and sugar.

Frikadeller: pan-fried minced-meat dumplings.

Gule ærter: Danish split-pea soup with salted pork and carrots.

Rødgrød med fløde: red berry pudding served with cream.

Wienerbrød: ironically, the Danish name for Danish pastry translates to "Viennese bread."

cultural institutions and its position as a vanguard of the New Nordic cuisine, it's easy to understand why. Though the city is packed with gourmet restaurants, specialized bars, and ambitious cafés and attracts an ever-growing number of foreign visitors, Copenhagen still has a relaxed and homey atmosphere. The capital city has no glittering skylines and little of the high-stress bustle of most big cities. Instead the morning air in the pedestrian streets of the city's core is redolent of baked bread and soap-scrubbed storefronts, and it's here that mothers safely park baby carriages outside bakeries, outdoor cafés fill with cappuccino sippers, and lanky Danes pedal to work in lanes thick with bicycle traffic. On the weekends, locals flock to the many harbor baths, vast parks, and romantic gardens of the royal castles.

The town was a fishing colony until 1157, when Valdemar the Great gave it to Bishop Absalon, who built a palace on the site of what is now the parliament, Christiansborg. It grew as a center on the Baltic trade route and became known as *købmændenes havn* (merchants' harbor) and eventually København.

In the 15th century it became the royal residence and the capital of Norway and Sweden. From 1596 to 1648 Christian IV, a Renaissance king obsessed with fine architecture, began a building boom that crowned the city with towers and castles, many of which still stand. They're almost all that remain of the city's 800-year history; much of Copenhagen was destroyed by two major fires in the 18th century and by British bombing during the Napoleonic Wars.

When you walk through the historic heart of the city, with its castles and palaces, gardens, and quiet, crooked streets filled with colorful houses, the past doesn't seem far away. If you bike through the more urban and residential neighborhoods, though, or cross the bridge to Refshaleøen, a formerly industrial island that's being transformed into an urban playground with bars, harbor baths, and galleries, you'll witness the city's casual, contemporary feel. The city is small and inherently walk- and bikeable, making it easy to switch between the two sides of Copenhagen. If there's such a thing as a cozy city, this is it.

PLANNING YOUR TIME

If you have just one day in Copenhagen, start at Kongens Nytorv and Nyhavn in Indre By (the city center) and walk along the canals in the direction of Rådhuspladsen (City Hall Square). You can see Christiansborg and/or Rosenborg Slot (Rosenborg Castle) along the way, depending on your chosen route. If you're not up for a walk, one of the guided canal tours will give you a good sense of the city. In summer or around Christmastime, round off your day with a relaxed stroll and nightcap in Tivoli.

With additional days, make sure to head to the more urban residential neighborhoods outside of Indre By, but also reserve time to peruse some of the city's cultural institutions; among the most exciting of these are the Statens Museum for Kunst, Nationalmuseet (National Museum), Ny Carlsberg Glyptotek, and Copenhagen Contemporary. Copenhagen is a culinary hub that attracts foodies from all over the world, so a visit to one of the many restaurants that subscribe to the New Nordic Food Manifesto is in order; Noma is, of course, the most famous one, but Amass, Relæ, AOC, and Geranium are other celebrated options. The harbor is an integral part of the city, and all year round you'll see locals swimming in the many harbor baths. Most of them are located close to the café-lined canals of Christianshavn, which is also the gateway to the freetown Christiania and Refshaleøen, a former industrial shipyard that's now home to galleries, harbor baths, restaurants, and breweries.

GETTING HERE AND AROUND

Copenhagen is small, with most sights within 2½ square km (1 square mile) of its center. Sightseeing, especially downtown, is best done on foot at an unhurried pace. Or follow the example of the Danes and rent a bike. That said, excellent bus and train systems can come to the rescue of weary legs. Also, be it sea or canal, water surrounds Copenhagen. A network of bridges and drawbridges connects the two main islands—Zealand and Amager—on which Copenhagen is built. The neighborhood with the most attractions is Indre By, the city center; a small eastern section of it, Frederiksstaden, is where the royal palace and the Little Mermaid are.

AIR

Copenhagen Airport is located 10 km (6 miles) southeast of downtown in Kastrup. The 20-minute taxi ride downtown costs DKr 200–DKr 300, depending on route and time of day. The city's sleek and affordable subterranean train system takes about 14 minutes to zip passengers into Copenhagen's main train station. Buy a ticket (DKr 36) upstairs in the airport

The Nyhavn Waterfront in Copenhagen is famous for its bars and restaurants, but it was also once home to the famous children's author, Hans Christian Andersen.

train station at Terminal 3. Trains depart every 4 minutes during the day and every 15 minutes during night hours. Trains also travel from the airport directly to Malmö, Sweden (DKr 60), leaving every 20 minutes and taking 20 minutes in transit. Trains run from 5 am to midnight. On Thursday, Friday, and Saturday, trains run all night. A new metro line, which runs 24 hours, seven days a week, travels between the airport and Kongens Nytorv (downtown) in 15 minutes. Tickets can be bought from machines in Terminal 3 (or even by SMS on your mobile phone). Note that a free airport bus connects the international terminal with the domestic terminal.

BICYCLE

More Danes bike to work than drive. Bikes are well suited to Copenhagen's flat terrain, rentals are readily available, and most roads have bike lanes. Rentals cost DKr 75–DKr 300 a day, with a deposit of DKr 100–DKr 1,000, depending on the price of the bike. You may also chance upon a free City Bike chained up at racks in various spots around town, including Nørreport and Nyhavn.

BOAT

DFDS Seaways sails to Oslo from Copenhagen. Scandlines connects Denmark with Sweden and Germany. The Eurail Scandinavia Pass, for travel anywhere within Scandinavia (Denmark, Sweden, Norway, and Finland), is valid on some ferry crossings.

CAR

If you're only planning to sightsee in central Copenhagen, however, a car won't be convenient. Parking spaces are at a premium and, when available, are expensive. A maze of one-way streets and bicycle lanes make it even more complicated. If you're going to drive, choose a small car that's easy to parallel park.

CRUISE

The city's main cruise port at Langelinie Pier is one of the best in Europe. Although it's a five-minute drive or 20-minute walk from the downtown core, the port is within walking distance of the

Little Mermaid and the attractions of the seafront. Taxis wait outside the cruise terminal. The on-site Copenhagen Cruise Information Center is run by the city tourist office, and there is a selection of shops housed in the renovated old wharf warehouses selling typical souvenirs.

Some ships dock at the Freeport Terminal, which is a further 30 minutes on foot from the downtown core (i.e., a full hour's walk from the center). Taxis wait outside the terminal, and the cost is around DKr 125 for the trip into town. A small number of ships (primarily smaller vessels) dock at the quayside at Nordre Toldbod, which sits beside the Little Mermaid and is a 10-minute walk from the city center; however, there are no passenger facilities here.

A water-taxi service to the city center leaves from the end of Langelinie Pier hourly. The boat stops at various parts of the city, and you can hop on and off as you wish. A one-day ticket costs DKr 40. A taxi directly to downtown (10 to 15 minutes) costs around DKr 70–DKr 90 from Langelinie.

PUBLIC TRANSPORT

Within Copenhagen, Metro trains and buses operate around the clock on the same ticket system and divide Copenhagen and surrounding areas into three zones. Unlimited travel within two zones (inner-city area) for one hour costs DKr 24 for an adult. A city pass good for unlimited travel in four zones for 24 hours costs DKr 80. A Copenhagen Card includes admission to attractions as well as public transit for 24 to 120 hours beginning at DKr 399. By far the cheapest way to get around with public transport is to purchase a rejsekort; it halves the price of most trips and can be purchased at the airport, most stations, and in some 7-Elevens.

The harbor buses are small ferries that travel along the canal, with stops along the way. The boats are a great way to sightsee and get around the city. They run from 7 am to 11 pm (10 am to 11 pm on weekends). Standard bus fares and tickets apply.

The Metro system runs nonstop. There are currently three Metro lines in operation, and two more are on their way (one to be completed in 2020, the other in 2024). The major Metro hubs in central Copenhagen are Nørreport Station and Kongens Nytorv. Stations are marked with a dark-red Metro logo.

TAXI

The computer-metered Mercedes and Volvo cabs aren't cheap. The base charge is around DKr 39–DKr 79, plus DKr 8.50–DKr 17 per kilometer, depending on the hour. A cab is available when it displays the sign *Fri* (free); you can hail cabs, pick them up at stands, or call for one (more expensive). The latter option is your best bet outside the city center.

TRAIN

Copenhagen's Hovedbanegården (Central Station) is the hub of the DSB rail network and is connected to most major cities in Europe. InterCity trains run regularly (usually every hour) from 5 am to midnight for principal towns in Funen and Jutland.

TOURS

BICYCLE TOURS
Bike Tours Copenhagen
BICYCLE TOURS | This operator offers guided biking tours of Copenhagen as well as bike rentals and recommendations on the best routes. ✉ *Nikolaj Pl. 34, Indre By* ☎ *22/28–24–00* ⊕ *tourscopenhagen.com.*

BOAT TOURS
Canal Tours' Grand Tour
BOAT TOURS | The company organizes lunch and dinner cruises and a one-hour tour of the harbor and canals that leaves from Gammel Strand and Nyhavn every half hour in summer. Additionally, heated and roofed boats are in service throughout most of the winter. ✉ *Copenhagen* ☎ *32/96–30–00* ⊕ *www.stromma.dk.*

Netto-Bådene (*Netto Boats*)

BOAT TOURS | For about half the price of its competitors, this outfitter offers hour-long boat tours that depart from Kvæst-husbroen, Holmens Kirke, Nuhavn, and Den Lille Havfrue twice hourly from 9 am to 7 pm. ✉ *Copenhagen* ☎ *32/54–41–02* ⊕ *www.havnerundfart.dk.*

BUS TOURS
Copenhagen City Sightseeing

BUS TOURS | This company offers three different routes, all on a hop-on hop-off basis. One route travels past the classic sights of Copenhagen, a second through the more urban part of the city, and the third past Christiania, Christianshavn, and Refshaleøen. ✉ *Copenhagen* ☎ *32/96–30–00* ⊕ *www.stromma.com.*

DINING IN COPENHAGEN

Copenhagen has undergone a culinary revolution since is the New Nordic Food Manifesto was coined by chefs Claus Meyer and René Redzepi in the early 2000s. They were the masterminds behind the restaurant Noma, which opened in 2003 and was ranked by www.theworlds50best.com as the best restaurant in the world in 2011, 2012, and 2014 (in 2019, when the restaurant reopened, it was ranked the world's second best). Noma has been at the forefront of the revolution, but many other restaurants—some of them run by Noma alumni—have joined and developed the movement. The repercussions have resonated through Copenhagen's culinary scene, leading to a dramatic rise in food quality whether you're biting into a flaky, buttery croissant from one of the city's many celebrated bakeries, stopping for tacos at a street truck run by a former dessert chef at Noma, having a cocktail made of aquavit from one of the city's new distilleries, or treating yourself to a 20-course dinner at one of the city's 17 Michelin-starred restaurants.

It's not all about the New Nordic cuisine, though; the many traditional Danish restaurants, often focusing on open-face sandwiches, are still going strong, and the number of high-quality international restaurants keeps growing. Copenhagen's culinary scene is as playful as it is ambitious and as traditional as it is groundbreaking; be sure to make eating and drinking an integral part of your trip.

LODGING IN COPENHAGEN

There's been a boom on Copenhagen's hotel scene in recent years, and many of them are stylish designer hotels. Many hotels are home to restaurants and bars that have become staples in Copenhagen's dining and nightlife scene.

NIGHTLIFE IN COPENHAGEN

Beer remains a defining element of Danish culture. In fact, Denmark has the most breweries per capita of any country in the world. Although the traditional Carlsberg and Tuborg pilsner varieties are still the main options at most bars and restaurants, there are more brews on offer than ever before. The number of brewpubs with handcrafted brews has increased, especially outside of the city center, and so has the number of beer-pairing menus. Copenhagen is also peppered with wine bars and traditional pubs where you can sample foreign and domestic beer. The city has seen a rise in places that specialize in cocktails—both traditional and experimental.

Copenhagen's jazz scene is thriving, and on most nights of the week you can groove to local talent and international headliners, especially in July, when the Copenhagen Jazz Festival spills over into the clubs.

Copenhagen's rock clubs almost all are filled with young, fashionable crowds. There are a few long-lived legends—Vega, Loppen, Rust, Stengade, Pumpe-huset, and Loppen are among them—and many smaller clubs that tend to open and go out of business frequently. You can get free entertainment newspapers and flyers advertising gigs at almost any café.

SHOPPING IN COPENHAGEN

A showcase for world-famous Danish design and craftsmanship, Copenhagen seems to have been set up with shoppers in mind. In fact, the city's name means "merchants' harbor." Crystal, porcelain, and silver are among the best finds on a Danish shopping experience. Danish classics such as Holmegaard Glassworks and Royal Copenhagen porcelain are timeless (albeit fragile) treasures to take back home. Many department stores hold the latest collections and settings; however you can often find secondhand pieces at antiques stores and markets for reduced prices. Signed art glass is always more expensive, but be on the lookout for seconds as well as secondhand and unsigned pieces. Throughout summer and into autumn, there are six major markets every weekend, many of which sell antiques and secondhand porcelain, silver, and glassware. Bargaining is expected. Also, keep an eye out for offers and sales (*tilbud* or *udsalg* in Danish).

Check the silver standard of a piece by its stamp. Three towers and "925S" (which means 925 parts out of 1,000) mark sterling. Two towers are used for silver plate. The "826S" stamp (also denoting sterling, but less pure) was used until the 1920s. Even with shipping charges, you can expect to save 50% compared to American prices when buying Danish silver (especially used) at the source.

If you're on the prowl for the newest Danish threads, you'll find a burgeoning number of cooperatives and designer-owned stores around town, particularly along Kronprinsensgade, near the Strøget.

VISITOR INFORMATION

You can buy a Copenhagen Card to save on attractions throughout the city. This money-saving card (available at ⊕ *www. copenhagencard.com*) comes in one-, two-, three-, and five-day versions, grants entrance to more than 70 local attractions, and provides you with free public transport.

CONTACTS Copenhagen Visitor Service. ⊠ *Vesterbrogade 4, Vesterbro* ☎ *70/22–24–42* ⊕ *visitcopenhagen.com.* **VisitDenmark.** (*Danish Tourist Board*) ☎ ⊕ *www. visitdenmark.com.*

Indre By

Indre By, Copenhagen's city center and historic heart, surrounds Christiansborg, the hub of Danish government. The neighborhood is packed with shops, restaurants, and businesses, as well as the crowning architectural achievements of King Christian IV. Its boundaries roughly match the fortified borders under his reign (1588–1648), when the city was surrounded by fortified walls and moats. The city center is home to most of Copenhagen's cultural and historical attractions and its parliament, businesses, and hotels, and many of the city's most ambitious restaurants and bars are located in the winding lanes between them. The area is residential, and it's lively all hours of the day and night, especially on weekends.

Indre By is cut by the city's pedestrian and commercial spine, a 1.8-km (roughly 1-mile) series of streets called Strøget (pronounced *stroy*-et), Europe's longest pedestrian shopping strip; the five streets are Frederiksberggade, Nygade, Vimmelskaftet, Amagertorv, and Østergade. Some locals love Strøget, but many love to hate it; the smaller streets surrounding it hold much more charm. By midmorning, particularly on Saturday, it's congested with people, baby strollers, and motionless-until-paid mimes. To the south and north of Strøget, you will find smaller, more peaceful shopping streets with smaller brands and more personal service.

To the north of Strøget, you will find the smaller, calmer shopping streets of

The walls of Christiansborg Slot's Great Hall are decorated with Bjørn Nørgaard's colorful tapestries and yellow marbling, while Venetian glass chandeliers hang from the ceiling.

Købmagergade, Fiolstræde, and Nørregade. Kronprinsensgade, off Købmagergade, is another street known for trendy boutiques and cafés. The area spreads from Strøget to the lakes that divide central Copenhagen from the boroughs of Vesterbro, Frederiksberg, Nørrebro, and Østerbro and consists of many mini neighborhoods: the city's Latin Quarter, called Pisserenden; an area around Nansensgade; and the quieter, posher areas around Kongens Have (King's Garden). Wherever you go there will be people, bars, and bustling big-city life.

Plan to explore Strøget and its side streets and grand squares on foot. A hurried walk (20 minutes or so) will take you from Kongens Nytorv in the east to City Hall Square and Tivoli, which border Vesterbro in the west. But to fully experience the area, consider spending a few hours or even a full day on shopping, visiting cafés, and taking in notable sights.

Shops along Strøget tend to keep longer hours than those elsewhere. Strøget is good for major stores, posh boutiques,

porcelain shops, and street performances. If you prefer unique, nonchain shops, head to the colloquially named Strædet (composed of Kompagnistræde and Læderstræde), one block south, which runs parallel to the main drag from the area just south of City Hall Square to Højbro Plads and Amagertorv. This quieter strip has cafés, design stores, and antiques dealers.

◉ Sights

Arbejdermuseet (*Workers Museum*)
MUSEUM | This museum chronicles the working class from 1870 to the present, with evocative life-size "day in the life of" exhibits, among them reconstructions of a city street and re-creations of apartments, including the home of a brewery worker, his wife, and eight children. Changing exhibits focusing on Danish and international social issues are often excellent. The exhibitions have explanatory texts in English. The museum also has a 19th-century-style café and beer hall serving old-fashioned

Danish specialties and a 1950s-style coffee shop. ✉ Rømersgade 22, Indre By ☎ 33/93–25–75 ⊕ www.arbejdermuseet. dk 🎫 DKr 90.

Børsen (Stock Exchange)

BANK | This masterpiece of fantasy and architecture is Europe's oldest stock exchange. Børsen was built between 1619 and 1640, with the majority of the construction in the 1620s. Christian IV commissioned the building in large part because he wanted to make Denmark the economic superpower and cross-roads of Europe. Rumor has it that when it was being built he was the one who twisted the dragons' tails on the spire that tops the building. When it was first opened, it was used as a medieval mar-ket, filled with shopping stalls. Though parts of Børsen still operate as a stock exchange, the bulk of the building hous-es the chamber of commerce, and the interior isn't open to the public, except on special occasions such as Culture Night, held in mid-October. Across the canal, look for a square, modern building: the Nationalbanken (Denmark's central bank), designed by the famed Danish designer and architect Arne Jacobsen. ✉ Børsgade 1, Indre By ☎ 33/74–65–73 ⊕ www. borsbygningen.dk.

Botanisk Have (Botanical Garden)

GARDEN | Trees, flowers, ponds, sculp-tures, and a spectacular 19th-century Palmehuset (Palm House) of tropical and subtropical plants blanket the garden's 25-plus acres. There's also an observato-ry and a geological museum. Take time to explore the gardens and watch the pensioners feed the birds. Some have been coming here so long that the birds actually land on their fingers. ✉ Øster Farimagsgade 2B, Indre By ☎ 35/32–22–22 ⊕ botanik.snm.ku.dk/english 🎫 Free.

★ Christiansborg Slot (Christiansborg Palace)

GOVERNMENT BUILDING | Surrounded by canals on three sides, the massive granite Christiansborg Palace is where the queen officially receives guests and from where the parliament—and the prime minister—rules the country. From 1441 until the fire of 1795, it was used as the royal residence. Even though the first two castles on the site were burned, Christiansborg remains an impressive neobaroque and neoclassical compound. Several parts of the palace can be visited, including the **Royal Reception Chambers**, **Ruins of Bishop Abasalon's Castle**, the **Royal Kitchen**, and the **Royal Stables**, all of which have separate admission fees unless you buy a combination ticket. The tower, which is free to access, offers wonderful views over Copenhagen.

While Christiansborg was being rebuilt around 1900, the National Museum exca-vated the ruins of Bishop Absalon's castle beneath it. The resulting dark, subterrane-an maze contains fascinating models and architectural relics.

At the Kongelige Repræsentationslokaler, you're asked to don slippers to pro-tect the floors in this impossibly grand space. ✉ Prins Jørgens Gård 1, Indre By ✛ Bordered by Børsgade, Vindebrogade, and Frederiksholms Kanal ☎ 33/92–64–92 ⊕ kongeligeslotte.dk 🎫 Tower free, Royal Reception Chamber Dkr 95, combination ticket DKr 160 ⊗ Closed Mon.

Dansk Jødisk Museum (Danish Jewish Museum)

MUSEUM | In a wing of Det Kongelige Bibliotek (Royal Library), this national center of Jewish culture, art, and history holds objects of both secular and reli-gious interest, including paintings, prints, jewelry, scrapbooks, and films. The site was designed by the famed architect Daniel Libeskind. The museum also gives extensive coverage to the Danish resistance movement, whose work during World War II helped bring nearly all of Denmark's 7,000 Jews to safety in Sweden. The museum has information in English. ✉ Proviantpassegen 6, Indre By ☎ 33/11–22–18 ⊕ www.jewmus.dk 🎫 DKr 50 ⊗ Closed Mon.

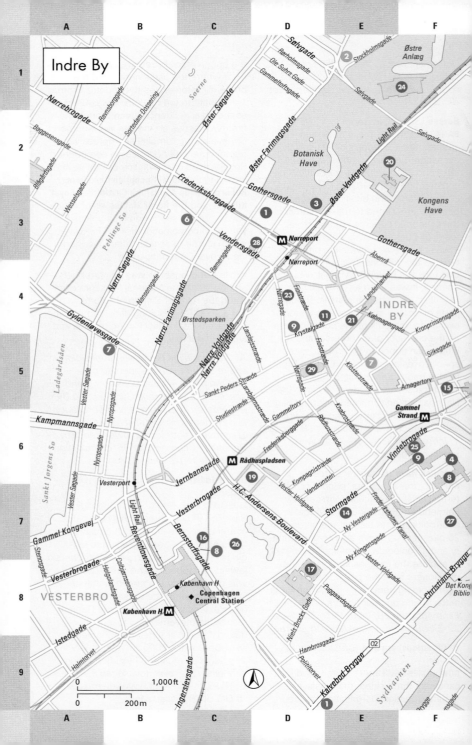

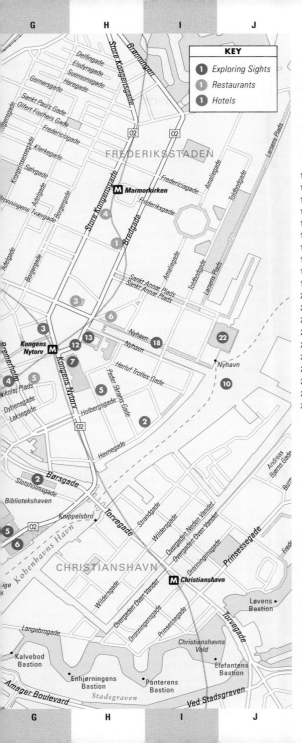

Sights ▼

1 Arbejdermuseet................... D3
2 Børsen G6
3 Botanisk Have..................... D3
4 Christiansborg Slot F6
5 Dansk Jødisk Museum............. G7
6 Det Kongelige Bibliotek........... G7
7 Det Kongelige Teater.............. H5
8 Folketinget........................ F6
9 Højesteret F6
10 Inderhavnsbroen J5
11 Københavns Synagoge E4
12 Kongens Nytorv.................... H5
13 Kunsthal Charlottenborg.......... H5
14 Nationalmuseet.................... E7
15 Nikolaj Kunsthal F5
16 Nimb.............................. C7
17 Ny Carlsberg Glyptotek D8
18 Nyhavn............................ I5
19 Rådhuspladsen D6
20 Rosenborg Slot.................... E2
21 Rundetårn E4
22 Skuespilhuset..................... J5
23 Sømods Bolcher................... D4
24 Statens Museum for Kunst........ F1
25 Thorvaldsens Museum F6
26 Tivoli.............................. C7
27 Tøjhusmuseet F7
28 TorvehallerneKBH D3
29 Vor Frue Kirke D5

Restaurants ▼

1 AOC.............................. H3
2 Clou.............................. E1
3 Geist.............................. H4
4 Ida Davidsen H3
5 Kong Hans Kælder................. G5
6 Nyhavns Færgekro H4
7 Peder Oxe E5

Hotels ▼

1 Copenhagen Marriott Hotel E9
2 Copenhagen Strand................ I6
3 Hotel d'Angleterre................. G4
4 Hotel Herman K G5
5 Hotel Sanders..................... H5
6 Ibsens hotel C3
7 Manon Les Suites B5
8 Nimb Hotel........................ C7
9 Skt. Petri D4

Det Kongelige Bibliotek (*Royal Library*)
LIBRARY | If you like grand architecture and great views, you really should visit the majestic Royal Library. Among its more than 2 million volumes are accounts of Viking journeys to America and Greenland and original manuscripts by Hans Christian Andersen and Karen Blixen (Isak Dinesen). Peer through the glass opening in the door to the old, ornate reading room, which is open only to readers.

The library's massive new glass-and-granite addition, called the Black Diamond, looms between the main building and the waterfront. The Black Diamond hosts temporary historical exhibits that often feature books, manuscripts, and artifacts culled from the library's extensive holdings. The National Museum of Photography, also housed in the Black Diamond, contains temporary exhibitions with handouts and wall texts in English.

Escalators that lift you from sea level to the main study areas provide spectacular views of both the harbor and an impressive ceiling mural by the Danish artist Per Kirkeby. The small park that lies hidden between the library and the parliament is a lovely place for a stroll or a pensive rest. ⊠ *Søren Kierkegaards Pl. 1, Indre By* ☎ *33/47–47–47* ⊕ *www.kb.dk* ✉ *Library free, temporary exhibits DKr 40* ☾ *Closed Sun.*

Det Kongelige Teater (*Royal Theater*)
ARTS VENUE | The old, pillared Royal Theater, dubbed Gamle Scene (the old stage) after the openings of the Opera and the Skuespilhuset (Royal Danish Playhouse), is almost as beautiful on the outside as on the inside; the main stage is located in what might just be the most stunning place in all of Denmark. The theater was established in 1748, although the facade dates from 1874. Since the division of the Royal Theater into separate venues, the original building is primarily devoted to ballets performed by the world-renowned Royal Danish Ballet. Statues of

Danish poet Adam Oehlenschläger and author Ludvig Holberg—whose works remain the core of Danish theater—flank the facade. ⊠ *Kongens Nytorv 9, Indre By* ☎ *33/69–69–69 for tickets* ⊕ *www. kglteater.dk.*

Folketinget (*Parliament House*)
GOVERNMENT BUILDING | Free tours of the Folketinget are given on weekends, holidays, and certain other days. A full list of the days the parliament building accepts visitors is on its website. You can sign up for a tour in advance or pick up a ticket when they are distributed at 10 am on tour days. You can also visit the tower and see the view for free most days. ⊠ *Christiansborg Palace, Prins Jørgens Gård 1, Indre By* ☎ *33/37–55–00* ⊕ *www. folketinget.dk* ✉ *Free* ☾ *Tower closed Sun. and Mon.*

Højesteret (*Supreme Court*)
GOVERNMENT BUILDING | The Højesteret was built on the site of the city's first fortress. The guards at the entrance are knowledgeable and friendly; ask them about the court's complicated opening hours. ⊠ *Prins Jørgens Gård 13, Indre By* ⊕ *hoejesteret.dk* ✉ *Free.*

★ **Inderhavnsbroen**
BRIDGE/TUNNEL | It transformed the city when Inderhavsbroen, a bridge linking the most historical part of Copenhagen with one of the most enticing, new areas, opened in 2016. The bridge has brought Refshaleøen and Holmen closer to the rest of the city, and as a result both areas have blossomed. The bridge itself offers beautiful views over Copenhagen's harbor. There's a street-food market where the bridge meets Christianshavn. ⊠ *Indre By.*

Københavns Synagoge (*Copenhagen Synagogue*)
RELIGIOUS SITE | The contemporary architect Gustav Friedrich Hetsch borrowed from the Doric and Egyptian styles to create the ark-like Copenhagen Synagogue. Women sit in the upper galleries,

while the men are seated below. Access to the synagogue is limited, so call ahead, or visit on a Tuesday afternoon or Thursday morning. ✉ *Krystalgade 12, Indre By* ☎ *33/12–88–68.*

Kongens Nytorv

MARKET | A mounted statue of Christian V dominates Kongens Nytorv, King's New Square. The square is the beautiful center of the royal, historic, and affluent part of the city. The statue was crafted in 1688 by the French sculptor Abraham-César Lamoureux, and the subject is conspicuously depicted as a Roman emperor. Every year, at the end of June, graduating high school students arrive in truckloads and dance beneath the furrowed brow of the sober statue. ✉ *Indre By.*

Kunsthal Charlottenborg

ARTS VENUE | This Dutch baroque–style castle on Kongens Nytorv was built by Frederik III's half brother in 1670. Since 1754 the garden-flanked property has housed the faculty and students of the Royal Danish Academy of Fine Art. A section of the building is devoted to exhibitions of contemporary art and is open to the public. The canteen, Apollo Bar and Kantine, is a popular place to stop by for breakfast, lunch, dinner, or just a coffee. ✉ *Nyhavn 2, Indre By* ☎ *33/36–90–50* ⊕ *www.kunsthalcharlottenborg.dk* 🎟 *DKr 90* ⊗ *Closed Mon.*

★ Nationalmuseet (*National Museum*)

MUSEUM | FAMILY | One of the best museums of its kind in Europe, the National Museum sits inside an 18th-century royal residence that's peaked by massive overhead windows. Extensive permanent exhibits chronicle Danish cultural history from prehistoric to modern times. The museum has one of the largest collections of Stone Age tools in the world, as well as Egyptian, Greek, and Roman antiquities. The exhibit on Danish prehistory features a great section on Viking times. The children's museum, with replicas of period clothing and a scalable copy of a real Viking ship, makes history fun

for those under 12. Displays have English labels, and the do-it-yourself walking tour "History of Denmark in 60 Minutes" offers a good introduction to Denmark; the guide is free at the information desk. ✉ *Prinsens Palæ, Ny Vestergade 10, Indre By* ☎ *33/13–44–11* ⊕ *www.natmus.dk* 🎟 *DKr 95* ⊗ *Closed Mon.*

Nikolaj Kunsthal (*Nicholas Art Gallery*)

MUSEUM | Though the green spire of the imposing Nicholas Church—named for the patron saint of seafarers—appears as old as the surrounding medieval streets, it's actually relatively young. The current building was finished in 1914; the previous structure, which dated from the 13th century, was destroyed in the 1795 fire. Today the church is a contemporary art gallery that often has good exhibitions. ■**TIP**➔ **Entry is free on Wednesday.** ✉ *Nikolaj Pl. 10, Indre By* ☎ *33/18–17–80* ⊕ *www.nikolajkunsthal.dk* 🎟 *Exhibit DKr 70, tower DKr 70, combination ticket DKr 100* ⊗ *Closed Mon.*

Nimb

BUILDING | Nimb, accessed from inside the Tivoli gardens as well as from outside year-round, is a complex dating from 1909. It has Moorish-inspired architecture and was once a bazaar. It was also one of the first buildings here to house a restaurant—a place for the jet-set crowd in the '20s and '30s. Today it's a modernized, multipurpose, high-class playground with a luxury all-suite hotel, bar, gourmet restaurant, bistro, dairy, chocolate factory, and well-stocked wine cellar. ✉ *Bernstorffsgade 5, Indre By* ☎ *88/70–00–00* ⊕ *www.nimb.dk.*

★ Ny Carlsberg Glyptotek

MUSEUM | The exquisite antiquities and a world-class collection of impressionist masterpieces make this one of Copenhagen's most important museums. The neoclassical building was donated in 1888 by Carl Jacobsen, son of the founder of the Carlsberg Brewery. Surrounding its lush indoor garden, a series of rooms house works by Pissarro, Degas, Monet,

Sisley, Rodin, and Gauguin. The museum is also renowned for its extensive assemblage of Egyptian and Greek pieces, not to mention Europe's finest collection of Roman portraits and the best collection of Etruscan art outside Italy. A modern wing, designed by the acclaimed Danish architect Henning Larsen, provides a luminous entry to the French painting section. From June to September, guided English-language tours start at 2. The café Picnic, overlooking the winter garden, is well known among Copenhageners for its delicious small dishes. ■TIP→ **The museum is free on Tuesday.** ✉ *Dantes Pl. 7, Indre By* ☎ *33/41–81–41* ⊕ *www.glyptoteket.dk* ✆ *DKr 115* ☯ *Closed Mon.*

Nyhavn

NEIGHBORHOOD | This pretty harborfront neighborhood, whose name means "new harbor," perhaps the most photographed location in Copenhagen, was built 300 years ago to attract traffic and commerce to the city center. Until 1970 the area was a favorite haunt of sailors. Though restaurants, boutiques, and antiques stores now outnumber tattoo parlors, many old buildings have been well preserved and retain the harbor's authentic 18th-century maritime character; you can even see a fleet of old-time sailing ships from the quay. Hans Christian Andersen lived at various times in the Nyhavn houses at numbers 18, 20, and 67. ✉ *Indre By.*

Rådhuspladsen (*City Hall Square*)

PLAZA | City Hall Square is dominated by the 1905 mock-Renaissance Rådhus (City Hall). Architect Martin Nyrop's creation was popular from the start, perhaps because he envisioned that it should give "gaiety to everyday life and spontaneous pleasure to all." A statue of Copenhagen's 12th-century founder, Bishop Absalon, sits atop the main entrance.

Besides being an important ceremonial meeting place for Danish VIPs and a popular wedding hall for locals, the intricately decorated City Hall contains the first world clock. The multi-dial, highly accurate astronomical timepiece has a 570,000-year calendar and took inventor Jens Olsen 27 years to complete before it was put into action in 1955.

Topped by two Vikings blowing an ancient trumpet called a *lur,* the Lurblæserne (Lur Blower Column) displays a good deal of artistic license—the lur dates from the Bronze Age, 1500 BC, whereas the Vikings lived a mere 1,000 years ago. City tours often start at this landmark, which was erected in 1914. Look up to see one of the city's most charming bronze sculptures, created by the Danish artist E. Utzon Frank in 1936. Across H. C. Andersens Boulevard, atop a corner office building, are an old neon thermometer and a gilded barometer. On sunny days there's a golden sculpture of a girl on a bicycle; come rain, a girl with an umbrella appears. ✉ *Indre By* ⊹ *Bounded by H. C. Andersens Blvd., Vester Voldgade, and Bag Rådhuset* ☎ *33/66–25–82* ✆ *Free, guided tours DKr 60.*

★ **Rosenborg Slot** (*Rosenborg Castle*)

CASTLE/PALACE | The Dutch Renaissance Rosenborg Castle contains ballrooms, halls, and reception chambers, but for all of its grandeur there's an intimacy that makes you think the king might return any minute. Thousands of objects are displayed, including beer glasses, gilded clocks, golden swords, family portraits, a pearl-studded saddle, and gem-encrusted tables; the underground treasury contains the crown jewels. The castle's setting is equally welcoming. It's in the middle of King's Garden, amid lawns, park benches, and shady walking paths.

King Christian IV built Rosenborg Castle as a summer residence but loved it so much that he ended up living here until his death. In 1849, when the absolute monarchy was abolished, all the royal castles became state property except for Rosenborg, which is still passed down

Rosenborg Castle was built by one of the most famous Scandinavian kings, Christian IV, in the early 17th century.

from monarch to monarch. ✉ Øster Voldgade 4A, Indre By ☎ 33/15–32–86 ⊕ www.kongernessamling.dk/rosenborg 💰 DKr 115 ⊘ Closed some Mon.

Rundetårn (Round Tower)

VIEWPOINT | Instead of climbing the stout Round Tower's stairs, visitors scale a smooth, 600-foot spiral ramp. Supposedly, Peter the Great of Russia once ascended this ramp on a horse alongside his wife, Catherine, who took a carriage. From its top, you enjoy a panoramic view of the twisted streets and crooked roofs of Copenhagen. The unusual building was constructed as an observatory in 1642 by Christian IV and is still maintained as Europe's oldest such structure.

The art gallery has changing exhibits, and occasional concerts are held within its massive stone walls. An observatory and telescope are open to the public evenings mid-October through mid-March, and an astronomer is on hand to answer questions. ✉ Købmagergade 52A, Indre By ☎ 33/73–03–73 ⊕ www.rundetaarn.dk 💰 DKr 25.

Skuespilhuset (Royal Danish Playhouse)

ARTS VENUE | Completed in 2008, the newest addition to the Royal Theater focuses mainly on drama. While theater stagings are primarily in Danish, more accessible dance and music performances are also featured. A beautiful wooden ramp extends in front of the striking glass building. In summer, the café and restaurant move onto this deck and offer one of the best views of the Copenhagen harbor. Behind the theater a new square and public beach, Ofelia Plads, has been created; there are frequent events and it's a popular place to while away a summer evening. ✉ Skt. Annæ Pl. 36, Indre By ☎ 33–69–69–69 for tickets ⊕ kglteater.dk.

Sømods Bolcher

STORE/MALL | Near Copenhagen University stands this Danish confectioner, which has been on the scene since the late 19th century. You are able to stop by the factory to see the production of the preservative-free candy (check website for production-viewing times). Children and candy lovers relish seeing the hard candy pulled and cut by hand. ⊠ *Nørregade 36B, Indre By* ☎ *33/12–60–46* ⊕ *www. soemods-bolcher.dk.*

Statens Museum for Kunst

MUSEUM | FAMILY | Old-master paintings— including works by Rubens, Rembrandt, Titian, El Greco, and Fragonard—as well as a comprehensive array of antique and 20th-century Danish art make up the National Art Gallery collection. Also notable is the modern art, which includes pieces by Henri Matisse, Edvard Munch, Henri Laurens, Emil Nolde, and Georges Braque. The space also contains a children's museum, which puts on shows for different age groups at kids' eye level. Wall texts are in English. The bookstore and café, which was recently taken over by Frederik Bille Brahe, one of Copenhagen's most hyped chefs, are also worth a visit. ⊠ *Sølvgade 48–50, Indre By* ☎ *33/74–84–94* ⊕ *www.smk.dk* ⊠ *DKr 120* ⊙ *Closed Mon.*

Thorvaldsens Museum

MUSEUM | The 19th-century artist Bertel Thorvaldsen (1770–1844) is buried at the center of this museum in a simple, ivy-covered tomb. Strongly influenced by the statues and reliefs of classical antiquity, Thorvaldsen is one of the world's greatest neoclassical artists, having completed commissions all over Europe. The museum, once a coach house for Christiansborg, now houses Thorvaldsen's interpretations of classical and mythological figures, and an extensive collection of paintings and drawings by other artists that Thorvaldsen assembled in Rome, where he lived for most of his life. The outside frieze by Jørgen Sonne depicts the sculptor's triumphant return to Copenhagen after years abroad. A free English audio guide is available.
■TIP➜ **The museum is free on Wednesday.** ⊠ *Bertel Thorvaldsens Pl. 2, Indre By* ☎ *33/32–15–32* ⊕ *www.thorvaldsensmuseum.dk* ⊠ *DKr 70* ⊙ *Closed Mon.*

★ Tivoli

AMUSEMENT PARK/WATER PARK | FAMILY | Tivoli is not only Copenhagen's best-known attraction, but it's also the most charming one. The amusement park, the second-oldest in the world, is located conveniently next to the city's main train station and attracts an astounding 4.4 million people from mid-April to mid-September. Tivoli is a pleasure garden as well as an amusement park; among its attractions are a pantomime theater, an open-air stage, several dozen restaurants (some of them very elegant and with Michelin stars), and frequent concerts, which cover the spectrum from classical to rock to jazz. Fantastic flower exhibits color the lush gardens and float on the swan-filled ponds. The park was established in the 1840s, when Danish architect George Carstensen persuaded a worried King Christian VIII to let him build an amusement park on the edge of the city's fortifications, rationalizing that "when people amuse themselves, they forget politics." Try to see Tivoli at least once by night, when 100,000 colored lanterns illuminate the Chinese pagoda and the main fountain. Tivoli is also open select hours around Halloween and in the winter season. ⊠ *Vesterbrogade 3, Indre By* ☎ *33/15–10–01* ⊕ *www.tivoli.dk* ⊠ *DKr 130–140, entrance and unlimited ride pass DKr 350* ⊙ *Closed late Sept.– mid-Oct., early to mid-Nov., most of Jan., and late Feb.–May.*

Tøjhusmuseet (*Danish War Museum*)

MUSEUM | FAMILY | This Renaissance structure—built by King Christian IV and one of central Copenhagen's oldest—contains impressive displays of uniforms, weapons, and armor in a 600-foot-long arched hall. Children usually like this museum, but it's very much a look-but-don't-touch place. Each artifact has a label in English. ⊠ *Tøjhusgade 3, Indre By* ☎ *33/11–60–37* ⊕ *www.thm.dk* ⊠ *DKr 80* ⊙ *Closed Mon.*

TorvehallerneKBH
MARKET | FAMILY | Ever since opening in 2011, this covered marketplace with vendors selling culinary specialties has been busy and popular. Vendors range from natural wine bars to stalls selling Vietnamese sandwiches, Danish licorice, raw food, and specialty coffee. There are many stalls selling delicacies to go and fresh vegetables, fish, meat, and poultry as well. ✉ *Frederiksborggade 21, Indre By* ☎ *70/10–60–70* 🌐 *torvehallernekbh.dk.*

★ **Vor Frue Kirke** (*Church of Our Lady*)
RELIGIOUS SITE | The site of Denmark's main cathedral, the Church of Our Lady, has drawn worshippers since the 13th century, when Bishop Absalon built a chapel here. The previous church, consecrated in 1738, was burned to the ground in 1807 during the Napoleonic Wars. Despite the country's poverty after the defeat, the city built a new place of worship, in the then-modern neoclassical style. Inside you can see sculptor Bertel Thorvaldsen's marble sculptures depicting Christ and the 12 apostles, and Moses and David cast in bronze. The funerals of both Søren Kierkegaard and Hans Christian Andersen were held here. ✉ *Nørregade 8, Indre By* ☎ *33/15–10–78* 🌐 *www.domkirken.dk* 🎟 *Free.*

🍴 Restaurants

AOC
$$$$ | SCANDINAVIAN | When international foodies visit Copenhagen, AOC is high on the list of restaurants to visit. The restaurant, which has two Michelin stars, offers tasting menus—with five, seven, or ten dishes—with a strong focus on sensory pleasure, Nordic produce, and imaginative cooking. **Known for:** ultra-fresh ingredients from Scandinavia; seasonal menu; beautifully presented dishes. [$] *Average main: DKr 2000* ✉ *Dronningens Tværgade 2, Indre By* ☎ *33/11–11–45* 🌐 *restaurantaoc.dk* 🕒 *Closed Sun. and Mon. No lunch.*

Clou
$$$$ | SCANDINAVIAN | Four nights a week Clou serves a 20-course dinner for 12–20 lucky guests. Rather than creating a menu and finding wines to go with it, Clou starts with the wines—cult wines are chosen, and then the chefs get to work creating dishes that will complement them. **Known for:** amazing wines; food served by the chef himself; bright, homey atmosphere. [$] *Average main: DKr 1600* ✉ *Øster Farimagsgade 8, Indre By* ☎ *91/92–72–30* 🌐 *restaurant-clou.dk* 🕒 *Closed Sun.–Tues. No lunch.*

★ **Geist**
$$$ | SCANDINAVIAN | This restaurant is stylish and lively with its concrete floors, dark wood, and open kitchen. Many of the 30 dishes on Geist's a la carte menu have become legendary, and so has the concept: there's no distinction between starters and mains. **Known for:** fashionable crowd; perhaps the best tiramisu in Copenhagen; simple, clever, unfussy cooking. [$] *Average main: DKr 500* ✉ *Kongens Nytorv 8, Indre By* ☎ *33/13–37–13* 🌐 *restaurantgeist.dk.*

Ida Davidsen
$$ | SCANDINAVIAN | This five-generations-old, world-renowned lunch spot is synonymous with *smørrebrød*, the Danish open-face sandwich. The often-packed dining area is dimly lighted, with worn wooden tables and news clippings of famous visitors on the walls. **Known for:** a large selection of creative sandwiches; atmospheric setting; smoked duck. [$] *Average main: DKr 200* ✉ *Store Kongensgade 70, Indre By* ☎ *33/91–36–55* 🌐 *www.idadavidsen.dk* 🕒 *Closed weekends. No dinner.*

Kong Hans Kælder
$$$$ | SCANDINAVIAN | Five centuries ago this was a vineyard; now it's the site of one of Scandinavia's finest restaurants. Chef Mark Lundgaard's French- and Danish-inspired dishes employ local ingredients and are served in a medieval subterranean space with whitewashed

walls and vaulted ceilings. **Known for:** first Michelin-starred restaurant in Copenhagen; extensive, expensive wine list; classic French cuisine. [$] *Average main: DKr 1700* ✉ *Vingaardsstræde 6, Indre By* ☎ *33/11–68–68* 🌐 *www.konghans.dk* 🕑 *Closed Sun.–Tues. No lunch.*

Nyhavns Færgekro

$$ | **SCANDINAVIAN** | Among the dozens of restaurants and cafés lining Nyhavn, Nyhavns Færgekro is one of the most atmospheric, with moderately priced Danish treats served in a cozy dining room. Its windows date back to the building's early incarnation as a home to the shipping company White Star Line, which ominously sold tickets for the *Titanic*. **Known for:** homemade flavored schnapps; all-you-can-eat lunch buffet of pickled herring; Danish specialties. [$] *Average main: DKr 275* ✉ *Nyhavn 5, Indre By* ☎ *33/15–15–88* 🌐 *www.nyhavnsfaergekro.dk.*

Peder Oxe

$$ | **BISTRO** | On a 17th-century square, this lively, countrified bistro has rustic tables (set with simple white linens, heavy cutlery, and opened bottles of hearty French wine) and 15th-century Portuguese tiles. All entrées—among them grilled steaks, fish, and the best burgers in town—come with salad from the excellent self-service bar. **Known for:** location on atmospheric Gråbrødretorv; open-face sandwiches; good-value prix-fixe menus. [$] *Average main: DKr 195* ✉ *Gråbrødretorv 11, Indre By* ☎ *33/11–00–77* 🌐 *www.restaurantpederoxe.com.*

Hotels

Copenhagen Marriott Hotel

$$$$ | **HOTEL** | Featuring a great view of the canal and Christianshavn through floor-to-ceiling windows, this large Marriott on the waterfront is a well-oiled machine. **Pros:** all rooms have both tub and shower combo; all rooms have a view (either city or canal); good facilities for business travelers. **Cons:** no restaurants nearby; small windows in the rooms; slightly generic and lacks local flavor. [$] *Rooms from: DKr 2000* ✉ *Kalvebod Brygge 5, Indre By* ☎ *88/33–99–00* 🌐 *www.marriott.com/cphdk* 🛏 *411 rooms* 🍴 *No meals.*

Copenhagen Strand

$$$ | **HOTEL** | You can't stay closer to the harbor than at this pleasant hotel housed in an 1869 waterfront warehouse just a five-minute walk from Nyhavn. **Pros:** close to city attractions; most bathrooms have both a tub and shower; minimalist decor. **Cons:** restaurant only serves breakfast; tight quarters; morning street noise. [$] *Rooms from: DKr 1385* ✉ *Havnegade 37, Indre By* ☎ *33/48–99–00* 🌐 *www.copenhagenstrand.dk* 🛏 *176 rooms* 🍴 *Free Breakfast.*

★ Hotel d'Angleterre

$$$$ | **HOTEL** | Widely considered the best luxury hotel in Copenhagen, this elegant establishment dates back to 1755 and has been brought back up to its peak with a complete renovation. **Pros:** newly renovated rooms; central location; great service. **Cons:** pricey; restaurant and spa can be busy; breakfast service can be spotty. [$] *Rooms from: DKr 4350* ✉ *Kongens Nytorv 34, Indre By* ☎ *33/12–00–95* 🌐 *www.dangleterre.dk* 🛏 *92 rooms* 🍴 *No meals.*

Hotel Herman K

$$$$ | **HOTEL** | One of the most hyped recent hotel openings in the center of Copenhagen, Herman K wows with its stylish interior, great restaurant, and high-class lobby bar. **Pros:** many rooms have balconies; inspiring, bustling common areas; organic breakfast. **Cons:** small rooms; located on busy, noisy street; no reception desk, and the café can be busy. [$] *Rooms from: DKr 2750* ✉ *Bremerholm 6, Indre By* ☎ *33/12–42–00* 🌐 *www.brochner-hotels.dk/hotel-herman-k* 🛏 *33 rooms* 🍴 *Free Breakfast.*

★ Hotel Sanders

$$$$ | **HOTEL** | A challenger for the title of Copenhagen's best hotel, Hotel Sanders

is all about quiet, casual, understated luxury. **Pros:** exquisite design throughout the hotel; stylish, casual crowd; excellent service. **Cons:** rooms are pricey; the bar and café can be busy with non-guests; some rooms are small. $ *Rooms from: DKr 2900* ✉ *Tordenskjoldsgade 15, Indre By* ☎ *46/40–00–40* ⊕ *hotelsanders.com* ◄ *52 rooms* ¶◉¶ *Free Breakfast.*

Ibsens Hotel

$$$ | **HOTEL** | Located in the bohemian neighborhood surrounding Nansensgade, this hotel is a solid choice for travelers wishing to be close to the city's main attractions. **Pros:** great location; minimalist rooms with good beds; great views from the rooms. **Cons:** area can be noisy; breakfast (not included in price) could be better; some rooms are small. $ *Rooms from: DKr 1611* ✉ *Vendersgade 23, Indre By* ☎ *33/45–77–44* ⊕ *www.arthurhotels. dk/ibsens-hotel* ◄ *118 rooms* ¶◉¶ *No meals.*

Manon Les Suites

$$$ | **HOTEL** | It's easy to forget you're in Copenhagen when you walk into this hotel and see the indoor pool, surrounded by jungle-like plants and plush daybeds—you may think you're in Bali. **Pros:** stylish interior and common areas; popular with Copenhagen creatives; great location. **Cons:** pool area can be noisy; popular with non-guests; windows don't open in some rooms. $ *Rooms from: DKr 1395* ✉ *Gyldenløvesgade 19, Indre By* ☎ *45/70–00–15* ⊕ *guldsmeden-hotels.com/manon-les-suites* ◄ *87 suites* ¶◉¶ *Free Breakfast.*

★ Nimb Hotel

$$$$ | **B&B/INN** | It's the first hotel in Tivoli Gardens and one of the most exclusive hotels in the city, with prices to match. **Pros:** very comfortable; superb location; great views. **Cons:** sky-high rates; awkward spaces throughout due to building limitations; not all rooms have views of the Tivoli garden. $ *Rooms from: DKr 4900* ✉ *Bernstorffsgade 5, Indre By* ☎ *88/70–00–00* ⊕ *www.nimb.dk* ◄ *38 rooms* ¶◉¶ *Free Breakfast.*

Skt. Petri

$$$$ | **HOTEL** | For the better part of a century, a beloved budget department store nicknamed Dalle Valle occupied this site, which is now a relaxed luxury hotel that's a hit with interior designers, fashionistas, and celebrities. **Pros:** great design everywhere; beautiful terrace; sleek cocktail bar. **Cons:** on the pretentious side; small rooms; street noise. $ *Rooms from: DKr 2250* ✉ *Krystalgade 22, Indre By* ☎ *33/45–91–00* ⊕ *sktpetri.com* ◄ *268 rooms* ¶◉¶ *Free Breakfast.*

▼ Nightlife

BARS AND LOUNGES

Brewpub

BREWPUBS/BEER GARDENS | The Brewpub microbrewery and restaurant has a beer garden with 11 beers on tap as well as a beer-sampler menu and dishes made using beer. ✉ *Vestergade 29, Indre By* ☎ *33/32–00–60* ⊕ *www.brewpub.dk.*

Centralhjørnet

BARS/PUBS | The small Centralhjørnet is in a house that dates from 1802. Now a bar catering to gays and lesbians, it has a busy events calendar with drag shows, live music, and holiday-themed events. ✉ *Kattesundet 18, Indre By* ☎ *33/11–85–49* ⊕ *www.centralhjornet.dk.*

★ Hviids Vinstue

BARS/PUBS | Around since the 1720s, Hviids Vinstue attracts all kinds, young and old, singles and couples, for a glass of wine or cognac in its atmospheric basement with dark, wooden furniture, stained-glass windows, and leather couches. ✉ *Kongens Nytorv 19, Indre By* ☎ *33/15–10–64* ⊕ *www.hviidsvinstue.dk.*

Masken Bar and Café

BARS/PUBS | This relaxed gay bar welcomes both men and women, young and old. ✉ *Studiestræde 33, Indre By* ☎ *33/91–09–37.*

Nimb Bar and Vinotek

BARS/PUBS | In what used to be a ballroom, this second-floor hotel bar has an enormous fireplace and crystal chandeliers. You can come for the afternoon tea and coffee service or for a drink. The impressive basement wine cellar has candlelit wooden picnic tables and glass-lined walls displaying bottles from every corner of the globe. The list has an unprecedented 1,300 varieties, many available by the glass. There are also Danish-inspired tapas (oysters, smoked salmon, quail eggs, Skagen ham, and cheese) to accompany tastings. ✉ *Nimb Hotel, Bernstorffsgade 5, Indre By* ☎ *88/70–00–00* ⊕ *nimb.dk.*

Oscar Bar and Café

BARS/PUBS | Popular with gay women and men, Oscar is a relaxed spot for a drink or a cup of coffee and a chat with locals. ✉ *Rådhuspladsen 77, Indre By* ☎ *33/12–09–99* ⊕ *www.oscarbarcafe.dk.*

★ Palæ Bar

BARS/PUBS | One of Denmark's most legendary bars, this beloved institution has served beer, wine, and stronger spirits for decades. It's long been popular among journalists and in the publishing world. ✉ *Ny Adelgade 5, Indre By* ☎ *33/12–54–71* ⊕ *palaebar.dk.*

★ Ruby

BARS/PUBS | Ruby was one of the first serious cocktail bars to open up in Copenhagen, and it's still one of the best. Inside an unmarked building, Ruby feels more like a private party in a luxury apartment than a cocktail lounge. It buzzes with a mixed clientele. The cocktail bars Lidkøb and Brønnum are run by the same team. ✉ *Nybrogade 10, Indre By* ☎ *33/93–12–03* ⊕ *rby.dk.*

JAZZ CLUBS

Jazzhus Montmartre

MUSIC CLUBS | From 1959 to 1976 Montmartre was one of the most legendary jazz venues in the world, and jazz giants like Dexter Gordon, Ben Webster, Stan Getz, and Kenny Drew played here on a regular basis. In 2010 Jazzhus Montmartre reopened, in a new location and with slightly fewer world stars on the stage, but still with a good lineup. There's also a popular restaurant and bar. ✉ *Store Regnegade 19A, Indre By* ☎ *91/19–19–19* ⊕ *jazzhusmontmartre.dk.*

★ La Fontaine

MUSIC CLUBS | A must for jazz lovers. This is Copenhagen's quintessential jazz dive, with sagging curtains, impenetrable smoke (although there is a room for smokers), nights that turn into mornings without you noticing it, and hepcats. ✉ *Kompagnistræde 11, Indre By* ☎ *33/11–60–98* ⊕ *www.lafontaine.dk.*

WINE BARS

Beau Marché

WINE BARS—NIGHTLIFE | Whether you're looking to buy vintage furniture or just have a glass of wine, you've come to the right place. This Francophile combined coffee shop, wine bar, and furniture store is a delight for the eyes and taste buds. ✉ *Ny Østergade 32, Indre By* ☎ *55/77–14–30* ⊕ *beaumarche.dk.*

Ved Stranden 10

WINE BARS—NIGHTLIFE | With a view of Christiansborg and an ever-popular terrace on the canal, this wine bar and shop is as famed for its location as its wine list. There's a focus on wine from Eastern Europe, tastings on Wednesday, and staff-like dinners on Monday. ✉ *Ved Stranden 10, Indre By* ☎ *35/42–40–40* ⊕ *vedstranden10.dk.*

⛁ Shopping

CLOTHING AND ACCESSORIES

Ganni

CLOTHING | Printed dresses, graphic tees, and playful patterns have made this Danish brand rise to megastardom—in Denmark as well as internationally—in no time. ✉ *Store Regnegade 12, Indre By* ☎ *20/88–53–11* ⊕ *www.ganni.com* ☉ *Closed Sun.*

Copenhagen Cafés

Café life appeared in Copenhagen in the 1970s and quickly became a compulsory part of city living. As the cheapest sit-down eateries (a cappuccino and sandwich often cost less than DKr 150), cafés often transform from daytime eateries into lively and relaxed nightspots. The crowd is usually an interesting mix. On weekends many cafés offer brunch, a Copenhagen classic. Most streets in central Copenhagen have cafés, but a few are known for their high concentration of them: Istedgade and Sønder Boulevard in Vesterbro; Ravnsborggade, Griffenfeldsgade, and Jægersborggade in Nørrebro; Værnedamsvej in Frederiksberg; and most of Indre By.

Cafés in Indre By

Café Atelier September The food is as photogenic as the decor at this café, and the avocado toast is legendary. The window seats are perfect for watching the world pass by. ⊠ Gothersgade 30, Indre By ⊕ cafeatelierseptember.com.

Café Norden Substantial portions make up for minimal table space at this classic art nouveau–style café, which is at Købmagergade and Strøget. ⊠ Østergade 61, Indre By ☎ 33/11–77–91 ⊕ www.cafenorden.dk.

The Log Lady Café The velvet curtains, comfy couches, and cherry pie at this café and bar, which is heavily inspired by *Twin Peaks*, provides the perfect living room setting. Sink into a couch, order a coffee (or something stronger), and stay for a while. ⊠ Studiestræde 27, Indre By ☎ 26/27–93–62 ⊙ Closed Sun. and Mon.

Paludan Bog and Café Given its location on lovely Fiolstræde, the middle of the Latin Quarter, surrounded by century-old university buildings, it makes sense that this combined café and bookstore is always packed with students and professors as well as other book lovers. The café serves good coffee and affordable, honest food. ⊠ Fiolstræde 10, Indre By ☎ 33/15–06–75 ⊕ paludan-cafe.dk.

Cafés in Nørrebro

Mahalle True to Nørrebro's multi-cultural setting, this Lebanese café, which has three locations in Copenhagen, serves everything from breakfast *menemen* (Turkish style-scrambled eggs) to *halloumi* (hard, unripened brie cheese) salads, *fattoush* (Levantine salad with mixed greens, toasted bread, radishes and tomatoes), and a few meaty dishes. ⊠ Birkegade 6, Nørrebro ☎ 23/91–83–33 ⊕ mahalle.dk.

House of Amber

CLOTHING | Carrying a wide selection of amber jewelry and other objects, this shop and museum has another location on Strøget. ⊠ Kongens Nytorv 2, Indre By ☎ 33/11–67–00 ⊕ www.houseofamber.com.

Mads Nørgaard

CLOTHING | An institution on Copenhagen's fashion scene, Mads Nørgaard sells classic and contemporary pieces that fit into any wardrobe. ⊠ Amagertorv 13–15, Indre By ☎ 33/12–24–28 ⊕ www.madsnorgaard.dk ⊙ Closed Sun.

MUNTHE

CLOTHING | Visit this brand's store for innovative and playful—and pricey—Danish designs. ⊠ Store Regnegade 2, Indre By ☎ 33/32–03–12 ⊕ www.munthe.com.

★ Stine Goya

CLOTHING | The most celebrated, hyped, and beloved fashion brand in Copenhagen might just be Stine Goya, run by and named for a model turned designer. She sells colorful silk dresses, playful suits, and embellished shorts that are relatively affordable, given the hype and the high quality of the clothing. Goya made international headlines when she designed a pink, embellished suit for Michelle Obama in 2019. ⊠ *Gothersgade 58, Indre By* ☎ *32/17–10–00* ⊕ *stinegoya. com* ⊘ *Closed Sun.*

Wood Wood

CLOTHING | This contemporary fashion brand from Copenhagen mixes high-end fashion with street- and sportswear. It collaborates with brands such as Nike, Lego, and Adidas. ⊠ *Grønnegade 1, Indre By* ☎ *35/35–62–64* ⊕ *www.woodwood. com* ⊘ *Closed Sun.*

CRYSTAL AND PORCELAIN

Royal Copenhagen

CERAMICS/GLASSWARE | The flagship store for Royal Copenhagen beautifully displays its famous porcelain ware and settings fit for a king. The shop also has a museum on the second floor, where you can see the painters in action. ⊠ *Amagertorv 6, Indre By* ☎ *33/13–71–81* ⊕ *www.royalcopenhagen.dk.*

DEPARTMENT STORES

Illum

DEPARTMENT STORES | Not to be confused with Illums Bolighus, this well-stocked department store has a lovely rooftop café and excellent basement grocery shops. ⊠ *Østergade 52, Indre By* ☎ *33/14–40–02* ⊕ *illum.dk.*

Magasin

DEPARTMENT STORES | At Scandinavia's largest department store, there's also a top-quality basement marketplace. ⊠ *Kongens Nytorv 13, Indre By* ☎ *33/11–44–33* ⊕ *www.magasin.dk.*

HOME

Bang & Olufsen

CAMERAS/ELECTRONICS | The high-tech design and acoustics of Bang & Olufsen products are so renowned that many are in the permanent design collection of New York's Museum of Modern Art. ⊠ *Østergade 18, Indre By* ☎ *33/11–14–15* ⊕ *www.bang-olufsen.dk.*

Hay House

ART GALLERIES | This is one of the most popular design houses for contemporary Danish furniture and interior design pieces. ⊠ *Østergade 61, 2nd fl., Indre By* ☎ *99/42–44–40* ⊕ *www.hay.dk.*

Illums Bolighus

ART GALLERIES | Part gallery and part department store, Illums Bolighus will surround you with cutting-edge Danish and international design—art glass, porcelain, silverware, carpets, and loads of grown-up toys. Staff will help you file your V.A.T. refund on-site—don't forget to get some documents stamped at customs upon leaving Denmark and mail them back. ⊠ *Amagertorv 10, Indre By* ☎ *33/14–19–41* ⊕ *www.illumsbolighus. dk.*

SILVER

Georg Jensen

JEWELRY/ACCESSORIES | This elegant, austere shop is aglitter with sterling, which is what you'd expect from one of the most recognized names in international silver. Jensen has its own museum next door. ⊠ *Amagertorv 4, Indre By* ☎ *33/11–40–80* ⊕ *www.georgjensen.com.*

Frederiksstaden and East Indre By

Northeast of Kongens Nytorv is the posh thoroughfare of Bredgade, which intersects Frederiksstaden, a royal quarter commissioned by Frederik V in the mid-1700s. It's home to the palace of Amalienborg. Time your visit with

Amalienborg, the home of the Danish royal family, consists of four identical classical palace façades with Rococo interiors around an octagonal courtyard.

the noon changing of the guard. The old sailors' neighborhood of Nyboder is west of the fortification of Kastellet.

For a pleasant 1½-hour stroll, depart from Kongens Nytorv, and loop around Nyhavn before continuing northeast along Bredgade. Turn off to see Marmorkirken (the Marble Church) and admire the rococo palace of Amalienborg. Carry on to the water or head down Amaliegade to the Frihedsmuseet (Museum of Danish Resistance), Gefion Springvandet (Gefion Fountain), and Kastellet fortress, ending up at the Little Mermaid in Langelinie.

◉ Sights

★ Amalienborg

CASTLE/PALACE | The four identical rococo buildings occupying this square have housed royals since 1784. It's still the queen's winter residence. The Christian VIII Palace across from the royal's wing houses the Amalienborg Museum, which displays the second part of the Royal Collection (the first is at Rosenborg Castle)

and chronicles royal lifestyles between 1863 and 1947. Here you can view the study of King Christian IX (1818–1906) and the drawing room of his wife, Queen Louise. Rooms are packed with royal heirlooms and treasures.

On Amalienborg's harborside is the garden of Amaliehaven, at the foot of which the queen's ship often docks. In the square's center is a magnificent equestrian statue of King Frederik V by the French sculptor Jacques François Joseph Saly. It reputedly cost as much as all the buildings combined. Every day at noon, the Royal Guard and band march from Rosenborg Castle through the city for the changing of the guard. At noon on April 16, Queen Margrethe's birthday, crowds of Danes gather for a special treat: their monarch stands and waves from her balcony at Amalienborg and the Danes cheer her on with many a "Hurra!" Queen Margrethe has been on the throne since 1972. ⊠ *Amalienborg Slotsplads, Frederiksstaden* ☎ *33/12– 21–86* ⊕ *www.kongernessamling.dk/*

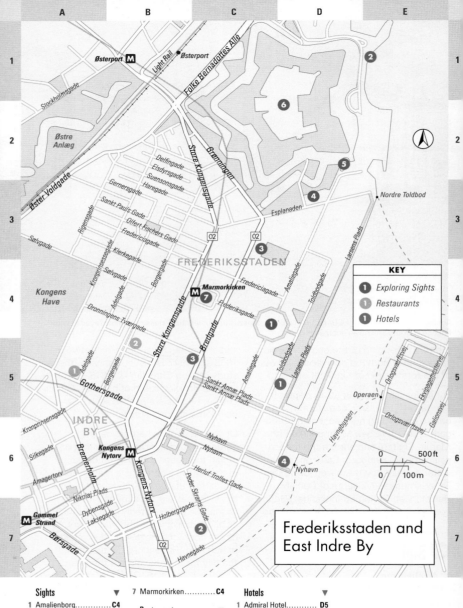

Frederiksstaden and East Indre By

KEY

1 Exploring Sights
1 Restaurants
1 Hotels

en/amalienborg ✉ *Museum DKr 95* ⊙ *Closed some Mon.*

Den Lille Havfrue (*The Little Mermaid*)
PUBLIC ART | Somewhat overhyped, this 1913 statue commemorates Hans Christian Andersen's lovelorn Little Mermaid. (You may want to read the original Hans Christian Andersen tale in advance; it's a heartrending story that's a far cry from the Disney animated movie.) Donated to the city by Carl Jacobsen, the son of the founder of the Carlsberg Brewery, the innocent waif has also been the subject of some cruel practical jokes, including decapitation and the loss of an arm, but she's currently in one piece. The Langelinie promenade is thronged with Danes and visitors making their pilgrimage to the statue, especially on sunny Sundays. Although the statue itself is modest, the views of the surrounding harbor are not. ✉ *Langelinie Promenade, East Indre By.*

Designmuseum Danmark
MUSEUM | Originally built in the 18th century as a royal hospital, the fine rococo Danish Museum of Art and Design houses a large selection of European and Asian crafts. The focus is on design from the 19th century. Also on display are ceramics, silverware, tapestries, and special exhibitions that often focus on contemporary design. There are labels in English. A small café also operates here. ✉ *Bredgade 68, Frederiksstaden* ☎ *33/18–56–56* ⊕ *www.designmuseum. dk* ✉ *DKr 115* ⊙ *Closed Mon.*

Frihedsmuseet (*Museum of Danish Resistance*)
MUSEUM | Evocative, often moving displays commemorate the heroic Danish resistance movement, which saved 7,000 Jews from the Nazis by hiding and then smuggling them to Sweden. The homemade tank outside was used to spread the news of the Nazi surrender after World War II. The displays have information in English. The museum was recently renovated and is set to reopen in mid-2020. ✉ *Churchillparken 6,*

Frederiksstaden ☎ *33/47–39–21* ⊕ *www. frihedsmuseet.dk* ✉ *Free.*

Gefion Springvandet (*Gefion Fountain*)
FOUNTAIN | Not far from the Little Mermaid, this fountain illustrates another dramatic myth. The goddess Gefion was promised as much of Sweden as she could plow in a night. The story goes that she changed her sons into oxen and used them to portion off what is now the island of Zealand. ✉ *Churchillparken, Frederiksstaden* ✛ *East of Frihedsmuseet.*

Kastellet
CASTLE/PALACE | At the end of Amaliegade, the beautiful Churchill Park surrounds the spired Anglican church St. Alban's. From here, walk north on the main path to reach the fortification of Kastellet. The peaceful walking paths, grazing sheep, and greenery welcome joggers and lovebirds to this still-operative military structure. Built in the aftermath of the Swedish siege of the city on February 10, 1659, the double moats were among the improvements made to the city's defense. The citadel served as the city's main fortress into the 18th century; in a grim reversal during World War II, the Germans used it as headquarters during their occupation. ✉ *Kastellet 1, East Indre By* ☎ *72/81–11–41* ✉ *Free.*

★ **Marmorkirken** (*Marble Church*)
RELIGIOUS SITE | Officially the Frederiks Kirke, this ponderous baroque sanctuary of precious Norwegian marble was begun in 1749 and remained unworked on from 1770 to 1874 due to budget constraints. It was finally completed and consecrated in 1894. Around the exterior are 16 statues of various religious leaders from Moses to Luther, and below them stand sculptures of outstanding Danish ministers and bishops. The hardy can scale 273 steps to the outdoor balcony on the top of the church for great views of the queen's palace and the Opera, across the canal. Afterward, you can continue along Bredgade to the exotic gilded

onion domes of the Russisk Ortodoks Kirke (Russian Orthodox Church). ✉ *Frederiksgade 4, off Bredgade, Frederiksstaden, Frederiksstaden* ☎ *33/15–01–44* 🌐 *www.marmorkirken.dk* 🎫 *Church free, dome DKr 25.*

🍴 Restaurants

Pastis

$$ | **FRENCH** | This lively eatery, which looks exactly like your favorite brasserie in Paris, is the place to go for French dishes. Its accomplished chef and owner, Mikkel Egelund, satisfies with classics like entrecote with béarnaise and crispy fries, *moules marinière* (mussels steamed in white wine and herbs), or salade niçoise. **Known for:** classic French bistro atmosphere; great wine list; festive mood and a stylish clientele. [$] *Average main: DKr 225* ✉ *Gothersgade 52, Frederiksstaden, Indre By* ☎ *33/93–44–11* 🌐 *bistro-pastis.dk.*

Pluto

$$ | **MODERN EUROPEAN** | The food at this centrally located restaurant is delicious and unpretentious, and the service is impeccable. Decked out in dark wood and concrete, the dining room here is stylish in an understated way. **Known for:** meals served family style; well-priced set menus; cocktail bar after restaurant hours. [$] *Average main: DKr 225* ✉ *Borgergade 16, Frederiksstaden, Indre By* ☎ *33/16–00–16* 🌐 *restaurantpluto.dk* ⏲ *No lunch* 💳 *No credit cards.*

🛏 Hotels

Admiral Hotel

$$$$ | **HOTEL** | A five-minute stroll from Nyhavn, overlooking old Copenhagen and Amalienborg, the massive Admiral was once a grain warehouse (circa 1787) but today is one of the least expensive top hotels, cutting frills and prices but retaining charm. **Pros:** great restaurant; convenient waterfront location; atmospheric building. **Cons:** standard rooms aren't that big; all rooms can get stuffy, particularly in summer; busy part of town. [$] *Rooms from: DKr 2180* ✉ *Toldbodgade 24–28, Frederiksstaden, Indre By* ☎ *33/74–14–14* 🌐 *www.admiralhotel.dk* 🛏 *366 rooms* 🍽 *Free Breakfast.*

Best Western Hotel City

$$ | **HOTEL** | This no-frills Best Western is on a side street a short walk from Kongens Nytorv, Nyhavn, the Royal Theater, the Opera, and the royal palace. **Pros:** great location; good number of amenities; reasonable price. **Cons:** some room furnishings are outdated; restaurant serves only breakfast; slightly generic design. [$] *Rooms from: DKr 1080* ✉ *Peder Skrams Gade 24, Frederiksstaden* ☎ *33/13–06–66* 🌐 *www.hotelcity.dk* 🛏 *81 rooms* 🍽 *Free Breakfast.*

Phoenix

$$$ | **HOTEL** | The hotel was originally built in the 1680s but was torn down and rebuilt—rising from its rubble, just like the mythical phoenix rose from its ashes—in 1847 as a plush, Victorian-style hotel. **Pros:** central location; most baths have tubs; elegant rooms. **Cons:** small rooms; slightly run down; less-than-efficient service. [$] *Rooms from: DKr 1700* ✉ *Bredgade 37, Frederiksstaden* ☎ *33/95–95–00* 🌐 *www.phoenixcopenhagen.com* 🛏 *213 rooms* 🍽 *No meals.*

71 Nyhavn Hotel

$$$ | **HOTEL** | In this well-preserved former spice warehouse, the rooms are tiny but cozy, with warm woolen spreads, dark woods, soft leather furniture, and crisscrossing timbers. **Pros:** superb location; elegant furnishings; excellent service. **Cons:** small rooms and bathrooms; located in touristy part of town; some rooms are pricey for their size. [$] *Rooms from: DKr 1800* ✉ *Nyhavn 71, Frederiksstaden* ☎ *33/43–62–00* 🌐 *www.71nyhavnhotel.com* 🛏 *158 rooms* 🍽 *Free Breakfast.*

The Danish Royals

The equitable Danes may believe that excessive pride is best kept hidden, but ask about their queen and this philosophy promptly flies out the window. The passion for Queen Margrethe II is infectious, and before long you may find yourself waving the Dannebrog along with the rest of them when the queen passes by. Graceful and gregarious, Queen Margrethe II is the embodiment of the new Danish crown, a monarchy that is steeped in history yet decidedly modern in its outlook.

Denmark's royal lineage has its roots in the 10th-century Kingdom of Gorm the Old. His son, Harald Bluetooth, established the royal headquarters in Zealand, where it remains to this day. Copenhagen's stately Amalienborg has been the official royal residence since 1784. From here Queen Margrethe reigns in a true Danish style marked by sociability, not stuffiness. Renowned for her informal charm, the queen has fostered an open, familial relationship between the royal house and the Danish public. Queen Margrethe's nurturing role has evolved naturally in a country of Denmark's petite size and population. Though she lives in Copenhagen, the queen is far from Zealand-bound.

Margrethe wasn't always destined to be queen. When she was born in 1940, the law of succession was limited to sons, and it wasn't until 1953 that the law was ratified to include female accession of the throne. She was groomed to become queen, and on her 18th birthday stepped into her position as heir apparent to the crown. She studied archaeology and political science both at home and abroad, at the universities of Copenhagen,

Aarhus, Cambridge, and the Sorbonne. In 1967 Margrethe married the French-born Prince Henrik, born a count near Cahors, France. He passed away in 2018.

Today's modern monarchy is perhaps best exemplified by what the queen does when she takes off her crown. An accomplished artist and illustrator, she designed the costumes for the acclaimed 1987 television production of Hans Christian Andersen's *The Shepherdess and the Chimney Sweep*. She also illustrated an edition of J. R. R. Tolkien's *The Lord of the Rings*. Her paintings have been exhibited in galleries, where they command top prices; she donates all of the proceeds to charity.

If there's anyone else in the royal circle who has captured the public's hearts like Queen Margrethe, it's the elegant, stylish, Tasmanian-born Crown Princess Mary, who married Margrethe's son Crown Prince Frederik in 2004 at Copenhagen's Church of Our Lady. Some 180 million people worldwide watched the event. The couple now has four children; the first-born, Christian, who will one day become king, was born in 2005.

Frederik's younger brother also went abroad for love. Prince Joachim married Hong Kong–born Alexandra in 1995, but the couple divorced in 2004. Both have since remarried—Joachim to the French Marie Cavallier, who is fast catching up to Mary in terms of style and popularity. When in Denmark, you will become familiar with the faces of all of these royals, since they often occupy the front pages of the Danish tabloids sold at the front of every convenience store.

Kastellet is one of the best-preserved fortresses in northern Europe.

🍸 Nightlife

Charlie's Bar

BREWPUBS/BEER GARDENS | Charlie's Bar is a small, no-frills establishment that has 19 drafts, six of which are cask-conditioned ale—unfiltered, unpasteurized beer served from casks. There's a wide range of international and Danish beer, including the house lagers Hancock and Thisted. ✉ *Pilestræde 33, Frederiksstaden* ☎ *33/32–22–89.*

Christianshavn, Refshaleøen, Islands Brygge, and Amager

Across the capital's main harbor stands the smaller, 17th-century Christianshavn, where the seafaring atmosphere is indelible. South of Christianshavn is a residential area, Islands Brygge, and north of it lies Refshaleøen, a former industrial site on a once-separate island that's been annexed to the rest of Amager. The entire area is divided up by canals, lakes, and the harbor, and in the summertime the quays are swarming with swimmers, sailors, and sunbathers.

In the early 1600s this area was mostly a series of shallows between land, which were eventually dammed. Today Christianshavn's colorful boats and postcard maritime character make it one of the toniest parts of town. To get there, walk from the Christiansborg area in Indre By across the Knippelsbro Bridge or across Inderhavsbroen, which links Kongens Nytorv with Christianshavn and Holmen. Cobbled avenues, antique street lamps, and bohemian charm are all part of one of the city's oldest neighborhoods, while the rough charm of Refshaleøen has made it one of the city's hippest areas to explore. In the 17th century, Christian IV offered people patches of partially flooded land for free and with additional tax benefits; in return, takers would have to fill them in and construct sturdy buildings for trade, commerce, housing for ship builders, and defense against sea attacks. Gentrified today, the area harbors restaurants, cafés, and shops, and its ramparts are edged with green areas and walking paths, making it the perfect neighborhood for an afternoon or evening amble. The central square, Christianshavn Torv, is where all activity emanates from, and Torvegade, a bustling shopping street, is the main thoroughfare.

Prinsessegade leads you past Christiania, the hippie commune, through Holmen and out to Refshaleøen, where new bars, restaurants, and harbor baths seem to open up on a monthly basis.

⊙ Sights

★ Christiania

TOWN | FAMILY | En route from Christianshavn to Refshaleøen is Copenhagen's legendary freetown Christiania, which was founded in 1971, when students occupied army barracks. It's now a peaceful community of nonconformists, consisting of 630 adults and 130 kids, where wall cartoons preach drugs and peace. There are a number of businesses here, including a bike shop, a smithy, a rock-music club, and several good organic eateries. When exploring Christiania, make sure to leave the central, busy part of the community to walk around on the idyllic, pedestrian paths that run through the forest, past the riding school, along the lake, and between the imaginative self-built houses.

A group of residents recount their experiences as well as the history of Christiania on daily English-language tours, which are a great way to discover the nooks and crannies of this quirky community. ⚠ **Many inhabitants are not fond of cameras, and picture taking is forbidden on Pusher Street.** ⊠ *Prinsessegade and Bådsmansstr, Christianshavn* ✛ *Walking from Christianshavn, take Torvegade and make a left on Prinsessegade, which takes you*

to the main gate. ☎ *32/57–96–70 guided tours* 🎟 *Tours Dkr 40.*

Copenhagen Opera House

ARTS VENUE | Once isolated from central Copenhagen, the former navy base north of Christianshavn dating from the 17th century is now an attractive area for arts, culture, and chic living. The Royal Academy's schools of theater, film, music, and architecture are all housed in old barracks here on the island of Holmen. The most famous resident of the island, however, is the new opera house, designed by the famous Danish architect Henning Larsen and placed symmetrically opposite the Marble Church and Amalienborg. Operas are in their original language with Danish subtitles. The building opens three hours prior to performances and includes a café and restaurant, the latter only for ticket holders. ⊠ *Ekvipagemestervej 10, Holmen* ✛ *The arts area is most easily accessed by the bridge that connects Nyhavn with Holmen, Refshaleøen, and Christianshavn.* ☎ *33/69–69–69 tickets* ⊕ *kglteater.dk.*

Havnebadet Islands Brygge

BEACH—SIGHT | FAMILY | Islands Brygge's main claim to fame is its harbor bath, which draws visitors from all over the city on summer days. The bath consists of five pools that are filled with water from the harbor and several jumping boards. In the winter there's a club for ice swimmers, complete with a sauna. ⊠ *Islands Brygge 14, Christianshavn* ☎ *30/89–04–69* 🎟 *Free.*

★ Refshaleøen

NEIGHBORHOOD | This cultural and culinary hub used to be an artificial island home to a historical shipyard, but the island has been annexed with the rest of Amager, and the shipping industry is long gone. Instead, Refshaleøen's former factories are being turned into art galleries, not-so-micro-breweries, busy beach bars, music venues, and gourmet restaurants (including several of Copenhagen's most influential restaurants, most notably

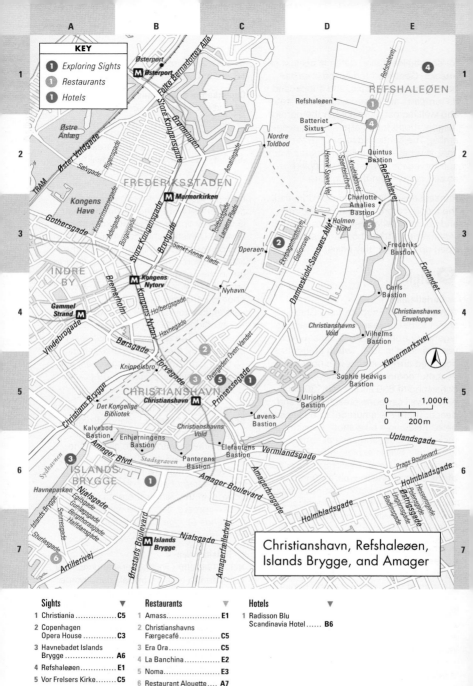

Christianshavn, Refshaleøen,
Islands Brygge, and Amager

Sights ▼	Restaurants ▼	Hotels ▼
1 Christiania **C5**	1 Amass.................... **E1**	1 Radisson Blu Scandinavia Hotel **B6**
2 Copenhagen Opera House **C3**	2 Christianshavns Færgecafé................ **C5**	
3 Havnebadet Islands Brygge **A6**	3 Era Ora.................. **C5**	
4 Refshaleøen.............. **E1**	4 La Banchina............. **E2**	
5 Vor Frelsers Kirke........ **C5**	5 Noma..................... **E3**	
	6 Restaurant Alouette.... **A7**	

Noma and Amass). Additionally, Copenhagen Contemporary (🌐 *copenhagen-contemporary.org/en*) has become one of the city's most important venues for contemporary art. ✉ *Refshaleøen.*

Vor Frelsers Kirke (*Our Savior Church*)
RELIGIOUS SITE | FAMILY | With one of the most beautiful spires puncturing the sky over Copenhagen, Our Savior Church is one of the city's most beloved landmarks. It's possible to scale the 398 steps leading up to the top of the spire, which has stunning views over Copenhagen's harbor and Christiania. ✉ *Skt. Annæ Gade 29, Christianshavn* ☎ *32/54–68–83* 🌐 *www.vorfrelserskirke.dk/English* 🎫 *Church free, spire Dkr 50 in peak season, Dkr 35 in shoulder season* ⏲ *Tower closed mid-Dec.–Feb.*

🍴 Restaurants

★ Amass

$$$$ | SCANDINAVIAN | The Californian Matt Orlando worked at some of the world's best restaurants—Noma, Per Se, and The Fat Duck—before opening his own fine dining establishment on the formerly industrial island Refshaleøen. Overlooking the former docks, the restaurant has graffitied concrete walls and an artsy, industrial-chic sort of interior—the backdrop for a lovely experience of trying flavorful dishes that are beautifully presented. **Known for:** delicious tasting menus; use of almost 100% organic produce; one of the world's most ambitious sustainability practices. [$] *Average main: DKr 1095* ✉ *Refshalevej 153, Christianshavn* ☎ *43/58–43–30* 🌐 *amassrestaurant.com* ⏲ *Closed Sun. and Mon. No lunch Tues.–Thurs.*

Christianshavns Færgecafé

$$ | SCANDINAVIAN | FAMILY | Located on one of Christianshavn's quiet backstreets, this café serves traditional Danish food, with plenty of aquavit to go with it. It's been doing so for more than 150 years, and the beautiful setting perfectly matches the food. **Known for:** traditional fare, with a focus on beloved classics; lovely location on the canal; atmospheric, old-school decor. [$] *Average main: DKr 150* ✉ *Strandgade 50, Christianshavn* ☎ *32/54–46–24* 🌐 *faergecafeen.dk.*

Era Ora

$$$$ | ITALIAN | Since 1983 this premier Italian restaurant has been known for its changing tasting menus and its huge cellar, with 80,000 bottles of Italian wine. Burnt-umber walls and black, chocolate-brown, and white accents predominate in the dining room. **Known for:** only Italian Michelin-starred restaurant in Scandinavia; romantic, canalside setting; innovative dishes based on ingredients imported from Italy. [$] *Average main: DKr 980* ✉ *Overgaden Neden Vandet 33B, Christianshavn* ☎ *32/54–06–93* 🌐 *www.era-ora.dk* ⏲ *Closed Sun.*

★ La Banchina

$$ | EUROPEAN | This wine bar and restaurant is known for its tasty dinners and natural wines as well as for its sauna and bathing jetties, which are impossibly popular with Copenhageners on summer days. The restaurant looks a bit like a boat shed, and dinner is cooked in a small kitchen outdoors. **Known for:** natural wines; casual, urban atmosphere; taking harbor-front hygge to new heights. [$] *Average main: DKr 100* ✉ *Refshalevej 141, Christianshavn* ☎ *31/26–65–61* 🌐 *www.labanchina.dk.*

★ Noma

$$$$ | SCANDINAVIAN | It made international headlines in 2017 when René Redzepi, one of the world's most influential chefs, shut down Noma, widely considered to be one of the world's best restaurants and the place that started the New Nordic food revolution. But one year later Noma reopened in a new location and was awarded two Michelin stars; it draws such large crowds that it's almost impossible to get a table. **Known for:** beautifully presented dishes in the New Nordic cuisine; impeccable service;

Freetown Christiania was once known for its open cannabis trade and "Green Light District" along Pusher Street, but today it is clear of all drug activity.

location on a lake facing Christiania. [$] *Average main: DKr 2500* ✉ *Refshalevej 96, Christianshavn* ☎ *32/96–32–97* 🌐 *noma.dk* ⏲ *Closed Sun. and Mon. No lunch.*

Restaurant Alouette
$$$$ | **MODERN EUROPEAN** | The Danish-American couple behind this restaurant met when Camilla Hansen walked into Nick Curtin's restaurant in New York to go on a blind date with another man, and the rest is history. The restaurant, which serves French-inspired menus in a former band room in Islands Brygge, recently got its first Michelin star. **Known for:** transforming high-quality ingredients into playful dishes; elegant setting; seasonal approach. [$] *Average main: DKr 695* ✉ *Sturlasgade 14, Christianshavn* ☎ *31/67–66–06* 🌐 *www.restaurant-alouette.dk* ⏲ *Closed Sun.–Wed. No lunch.*

Hotels

Radisson Blu Scandinavia Hotel
$$$ | **HOTEL** | Across the Stadsgraven from Christianshavn to the south stands one of Denmark's largest hotels, which houses Copenhagen's only casino. **Pros:** good-size rooms with great city views; several on-site restaurants; good area for walks. **Cons:** it's about a mile to the city center; feels like the business hotel it is, which isn't to everyone's taste; rather pricey. [$] *Rooms from: DKr 1605* ✉ *Amager Blvd. 70, Amager* ☎ *33/96–50–00* 🌐 *www.radissonblu.dk/scandinaviahotel-koebenhavn* 🛏 *584 rooms* 🍴 *No meals.*

Nightlife

Broaden and Build
BREWPUBS/BEER GARDENS | This combined brewery and bar, opened by Amass, has taken over a huge hall in Refshaleøen. It's ambitious with the food—ranging from bar snacks to a full meal—as well as the beer, and the chicken wings are probably the best in Copenhagen. ✉ *Refshalevej 175A, Christianshavn* ☎ *73/70–81–70* 🌐 *broadenbuildcph.com.*

Casino Copenhagen

CASINOS | The Casino Copenhagen has American roulette, blackjack, poker, and slot machines. You must be 18 years old to enter, and there's a strictly enforced dress code: jackets are required, and no athletic clothing is allowed. Outerwear must be left at the coat check for a fee. Dealers and croupiers aren't shy about reminding winners that a tip of a certain percentage is customary. The casino is open daily 2 pm to 4 am, and admission is DKr 95. ⊠ *Radisson Blu Scandinavia Hotel, Amager Blvd. 70, Amager* ☎ *33/96–59–65* ⊕ *casinocopenhagen.dk/en.*

★ Christianshavn Bådudlejning

CAFES—NIGHTLIFE | One of Copenhagen's most charming cafés isn't just located by the water but is directly on it. This combined café, restaurant, and bar is floating on Christianshavn Kanal, giving it one of the best locations in the city. Stop by for coffee, light lunch, or dinner, or just a glass of wine. It's closed in the fall and spring but usually open in December when the enterprising owner adds a roof, walls, and a wood-burning stove to the platform. ⊠ *Overgaden Neden Vandet 29, Christianshavn* ☎ *32/96–53–53* ⊕ *baadudlejningen.dk.*

★ The Corner 108

WINE BARS—NIGHTLIFE | This bar serves coffee during the day and wine at night, and everything is as tasty as you'd expect, given the owners (it's run by Restaurant 108, Noma's unofficial little brother). The Danish pastries and sourdough bread are amazing, and so are the light lunch dishes, the selection of natural wines, and the coffee. ⊠ *Strandgade 108, Christianshavn* ☎ *32/96–32–92* ⊕ *108.dk/the-corner-2/kaffebar.*

★ Loppen *(MusikLoppen)*

MUSIC CLUBS | Some of the bigger names in Danish music (pop, rock, and urban) and budding artists from abroad play at this medium-size venue in Christiania, which is run by volunteers and known for spotting the next big thing on the international alternative rock and indie scene. Covers range from DKr 50 to DKr 350. ⊠ *Sydområdet 4B, 1st fl., Christianshavn* ☎ *32/57–84–22* ⊕ *www.loppen.dk.*

Mikkeller Baghaven

BREWPUBS/BEER GARDENS | The microbrewing empire Mikkeller seems aimed at world domination, and with breweries in the United States, and bars in locations such as Bangkok, Seoul, Bucharest, New York, and Madrid, the microbrewery is well on its way. In Copenhagen, Mikkeller runs restaurants—Mexican La Neta and Japanese Ramen to Biiru are especially popular—as well as coffee shops and biergartens. The massive beer garden next to the water in hip Refshaleøen is one of the best places to taste the beers. ⊠ *Refshalevej 169B, Christianshavn* ☎ *22/89–85–32* ⊕ *mikkeller.dk.*

🏃 Activities

BOATING

The best way to experience Copenhagen is from the sea, and the most fun way to go boating is to rent your own. Several companies rent out boats for a few hours or a day.

FriendShips

Take up to seven companions with you and explore Copenhagen at your own pace via electric boat. FriendShips is located at the canal in Christianshavn. Rentals are DKr 420 for one hour, DKr 750 for two hours, and DKr 999 for three hours. ⊠ *Trangravsvej 1, Christianshavn* ☎ *53/83–78–78* ⊕ *www.friendships.dk* ⊗ *Closed in winter.*

★ GoBoat

BOATING | Located next to the harbor bath in Islands Brygge, GoBoat offers one-, two-, and three-hour rentals at a cost of DKr 449, DKr 799, and DKr 1049, respectively. *Typically closed mid-October to mid-March but exact dates depend on the weather; call ahead to confirm.* ⊠ *Islands Brygge 10, Christianshavn* ☎ *40/26–10–25* ⊕ *goboat.dk.*

🛍 Shopping

The Apartment

HOUSEHOLD ITEMS/FURNITURE | Visiting this furniture shop feels more like stopping by the home of your most stylish friend, as it's decorated as an apartment where everything is for sale. The design gallery is located in a beautiful apartment on Christianshavn, and there's a focus on vintage design from the 1920s to the 1970s as well as on contemporary designers. *Contact tsb@theapartment. dk for opening hours; they tend to change.* ⊠ *Overgaden Neden Vandet 33, 1st fl., Christianshavn* ☎ *31/62–04–02* ⊕ *theapartment.dk.*

Vesterbro

To the west of Indre By lies the vibrant neighborhood of Vesterbro. Formerly home to mostly working-class inhabitants and a red-light district, immigrants and trendy young folk have since moved in and seem to live quite harmoniously with the original populations. The buildings date from the late 1800s and were constructed during the industrial revolution. A number of popular cafés now surround the spruced-up Halmtorvet Square, which was previously notorious for its late-night prostitution, as well as Kødbyen, the former meatpacking district. No longer an area reserved for porn shops and massage parlors, the colorful, diversified neighborhood is now full of low-key cafés and trendy boutiques that serve the neighborhood's rapidly growing population of creatives, artists, and the students that can still afford to live here.

Vesterbrogade, Istedgade, and Sønder Boulevard are the main arteries in the neighborhood, the latter two leading from the Central Station to Enghave Plads. These streets are some of the most hip and happening places in Copenhagen to enjoy a snack, a coffee, or a beer in the sun. The street of Vesterbrogade runs west from City Hall Square to the neighborhood of Valby, where Carlsberg has its headquarters, although the company now only brews specialty beers here.

👁 Sights

Carlsberg Bryggeri (*Carlsberg Brewery*)

WINERY/DISTILLERY | A large, ornate chimney makes this mid-19th-century brewery visible from a distance. J. C. Jacobsen, one of Denmark's most important historical figures, named the brewery after his son Carl; berg, or mountain, signifies the brewery's location on Valby Hill. The four giant granite elephants that guard the main entrance were inspired by Bernini's famous obelisk in Rome. In the visitor center, interactive displays, also in English, take you step by step through the brewing process. At the end of your visit, you can sample some of the company's beers for an extra DKr 45. The Carlsberg Museum, also on the grounds, tells the story of the Jacobsen family, their beer empire, and Carlsberg's extensive philanthropy, which still greatly benefits Danish culture. Large-scale beer production has now moved outside of the city and the old brewery complex is being transformed into a combined neighborhood for arts, culture, and living. ⊠ *Gamle Carlsberg Vej 11, Vesterbro* ☎ *33/27–12–82* ⊕ *www.visitcarlsberg.com.*

★ **Kødbyen**

NEIGHBORHOOD | Copenhagen's former meat-packing district has transformed into a hipster neighborhood with galleries, coworking spaces, fashion boutiques, restaurants, bars, coffee shops, and nightclubs. The area is small and easy to explore on foot. Galleri Bo Bjerggaard, V1 Gallery, and Fotografisk Center are some of the best galleries, and the pizzeria Mother, the gourmet restaurant Gorilla, the brewpub Warpigs, and the bustling, bistro-like wine bar Paté Paté are some of the best places to eat. After dark, Mesteren & Lærlingen draws a casual crowd with its strong drinks and happy DJs. ✉ *Vesterbro.*

Tycho Brahe Planetarium

OBSERVATORY | **FAMILY** | Situated at the western end of the lakes that divide Copenhagen, this modern, cylindrical planetarium appears to be sliced at an angle. It's Denmark's most advanced center for popularizing astronomy and space research and promoting knowledge of natural science. The on-site IMAX theater is devoted to visual odysseys of the natural environment—below the sea, through the jungle, or into outer space. These films aren't recommended for children under age seven. Admission includes access to an IMAX movie and a 3-D movie. ✉ *Gl. Kongevej 10, Vesterbro* ☎ *33/12–12–24* 🌐 *planetariet.dk* 🎟 *DKr 160.*

🍴 Restaurants

★ H15

$ | **SCANDINAVIAN** | This combined cafeteria, bar, and venue in an old carrier hall is one of the best places to go for a cheap but delicious breakfast, a glass of wine with a friend, an organic cup of coffee, or a light lunch or bigger dinner. The service is casual and friendly, and the dishes are creative and inexpensive despite their outstanding quality. **Known for:** local clientele; organic vegetable-focused dishes; casual atmosphere with communal tables and self-service at the bar. [$] *Average main: DKr 90* ✉ *Halmtorvet 15, Vesterbro* ☎ *26/13–68–46* 🌐 *h15.dk.*

★ Jah Izakaya and Sake Bar

$$$ | **JAPANESE** | This small *izakaya* (informal Japanese pub with grub) and sake bar is the best place in Denmark to get an authentic taste of Japan. The dining room is simple and beautiful, with its light, wooden furniture. **Known for:** creative classic and seasonal dishes; omakase menu; excellent sashimi and sushi. [$] *Average main: DKr 375* ✉ *Gasværksvej 21, Vesterbro* ☎ *38/41–27–21* 🌐 *jahizakaya.dk* 🕒 *No lunch.*

Pony

$$$ | **SCANDINAVIAN** | The team behind Michelin-starred Kadeau in Bornholm (and also in Copenhagen) has opened a sister restaurant where the dishes are simpler, the prices are lower, and the atmosphere is more casual. The vision is the same, though, and you'll dine on Danish products such as fried scallops with corn crème and sage, veal sweetbreads with baked tomatoes, and salted cod with cauliflower. **Known for:** organic wine list with a focus on small producers; playful but ambitious chefs; four-course menu that's a steal. [$] *Average main: DKr 445* ✉ *Vesterbrogade 135, Vesterbro* ☎ *33/22–10–00* 🌐 *ponykbh.dk* 🕒 *Closed Mon. No lunch.*

Sanchez

$$ | **MODERN MEXICAN** | Noma's former dessert chef has been drawing a crowd since she opened a street-food stall at Torvehallerne (still going strong), where she serves the best tacos in Copenhagen. Now she's opened a full-service restaurant, too, on hip Istedgade, where the tacos are just as good. **Known for:** best tacos in town; festive atmosphere; weekend brunch. [$] *Average main: DKr 160* ✉ *Istedgade 60, Vesterbro* ☎ *31/11–66–40* 🌐 *lovesanchez.com* 🕒 *No lunch weekdays.*

🛏 Hotels

DGI-byen Hotel

$$ | **HOTEL** | This place seemingly has everything: rooms with an exquisite blend of simple Danish design; a buffet breakfast included in the rates; and a state-of-the-art recreation center with a bowling alley, climbing wall, shooting range, swimming pool, and spa. **Pros:** lots of recreational activities; good amenities and discounts; very central location. **Cons:** slightly off the beaten track from main attractions; occasional noise from trains; slightly generic design and architecture. [$] *Rooms from: DKr 798* ✉ *Tietgensgade 65, Vesterbro* ☎ *33/29–80–50* 🌐 *www.*

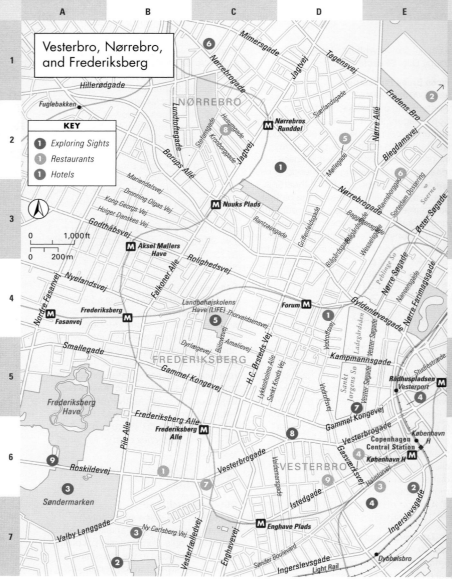

Vesterbro, Nørrebro, and Frederiksberg

KEY

1 Exploring Sights

1 Restaurants

1 Hotels

dgi-byen.dk ⟿ 104 rooms ⎮◎⎮ Free Breakfast.

★ Hotel Ottilia

$$$ | HOTEL | Formerly the old Carlsberg brewery, this hotel with an industrial look opened in 2019 to much fanfare. **Pros:** beautiful furniture and plush beds; affordable, considering the quality; big breakfast buffet (included with all suites). **Cons:** close to Enghave Plads but a few stops from the city center; neighborhood gets quiet at night; noise from nearby construction. $ *Rooms from: DKr 1335* ✉ *Bryggernes Pl. 7, Vesterbro* ☎ *33/38–70–30* ⊕ *www.brochner-hotels.dk* ⟿ *156 rooms* ⎮◎⎮ *Free Breakfast.*

★ Radisson Blu Royal Hotel

$$$ | HOTEL | This 1960 Arne Jacobsen high-rise has been fully restored as a paean to the legendary designer and will appeal to those who want classic midcentury design along with more modern comforts. **Pros:** great views; beautiful Danish design throughout; large fitness area. **Cons:** some furnishings are worn; service can be spotty; very busy and central location. $ *Rooms from: DKr 1435* ✉ *Hammerichsgade 1, Vesterbro* ☎ *33/42–60–00* ⊕ *www.radissonblu.com/royalhotel-copenhagen* ⟿ *284 rooms* ⎮◎⎮ *No meals.*

ⓨ Nightlife

Bang & Jensen

CAFES—NIGHTLIFE | This cozy café and bar was one of the first hip places to open on Istedgade, and it's still a favorite among locals. ✉ *Istedgade 130, Vesterbro* ☎ *33/25–53–18* ⊕ *www.bangogjensen.dk.*

★ Library Bar

BARS/PUBS | Located in the heart of a historic hotel, this bar is an elegant and romantic spot for a quiet but pricey drink. It has golden wood, leather chairs, and walls carpeted by books. In December, a Christmas tree hangs from the atrium—upside down. ✉ *Copenhagen Plaza Hotel,* *Bernstorffsgade 4, Vesterbro* ☎ *33/14–92–62* ⊕ *www.librarybar.dk.*

Nørrebro

Nørrebro, a neighborhood that grew enormously to accommodate working people during the industrial revolution, is now known for being home to a large immigrant population as well as many of Copenhagen's young hipsters. These days, ethnic stores and kebab joints live side by side with intellectual bookshops, casual cafés, vintage stores, and hip restaurants. Intersecting the whole neighborhood is the long street Nørrebrogade, which is packed with shops and kebab joints. The area is crisscrossed by small, charming streets filled with wine bars, designer shops, cafés, and international restaurants; Ravnsborggade, Elmegade, Sankt Hans Torv, Blågårdsgade, Rantzausgade, Griffenfeldsgade, Jægersborggade, and Stefansgade are the busiest. The leafy cemetery Assistens Kirkegård (where Hans Christian Andersen is buried) is the only major park in the neighborhood, but there are countless playgrounds aimed at the growing number of young families, and a walk along the lakes provide locals with some fresh air and nature.

◉ Sights

★ Assistens Kirkegård (*Assistens Cemetery*)

CEMETERY | This peaceful, leafy cemetery in the heart of Nørrebro is the final resting place of numerous great Danes, including Søren Kierkegaard (whose last name actually means "cemetery"), Hans Christian Andersen, and physicist Niels Bohr. In summer the cemetery takes on a cheerful, city-park air as picnicking families, young couples, and sunbathers relax on the sloping lawns amid the dearly departed. ✉ *Kapelvej 4, Nørrebro* ☎ *35/37–19–17* ⊕ *www.assistens.dk* ⊠ *Free.*

Superkilen

PLAZA | This photogenic public park is the stuff that city planning dreams are made of. Designed by Superflex and Bjarke Ingels Group, the urban park has skate ramps, barbecue grills, a green park, and much more, making it popular among skaters, young parents with kids, dog walkers, and retired people going for a stroll. ✉ *Nørrebrogade 210, Nørrebro.*

🍴 Restaurants

★ Geranium

$$$$ | SCANDINAVIAN | This modern northern European kitchen might be located in Parken, Denmark's national football (soccer) stadium, but the three-Michelin-starred restaurant is giving acclaimed Noma a run for its money. Chefs Rasmus Kofoed and Søren Ledet put a modern touch on classic Scandinavian cooking by using molecular gastronomy and sourcing products from biodynamic farmers (that is, those who follow a system of organic and holistic cultivation). **Known for:** wine pairings; reputation among the world's top 50 restaurants; vegetable-centric masterpieces. [$] *Average main: DKr 698* ✉ *Parken, Per Henrik Lings Allé 4, 8th fl., Østerbro* ☎ *69/96–00–20* 🌐 *www.geranium.dk* 🕓 *Closed Sun.–Tues., no lunch Wed.–Thurs.*

★ Kiin Kiin

$$$$ | THAI | At this trendy and inventive Asian Michelin-starred restaurant, whose name means "eat, eat" (implying dinner's ready), the fragrance of cinnamon may well whet your appetite for such typical Thai street snacks as lotus-flower chips, satay, and fish cakes. Gilded Buddhas grace the walls, hand-woven wicker chairs made from water hyacinth beckon, and cream-color bamboo lamps illuminate the space. **Known for:** dishes flavored with green curry, fresh coriander, and ginger; wine pairings with every course; four-course theater menu available from 5:30 to 7:30 pm for DKr 495. [$] *Average main: DKr 975* ✉ *Guldbergsgade 21, Nørrebro* ☎ *35/35–75–55* 🌐 *www.kiin.dk* 🕓 *Closed Sun. and July. No lunch.*

Nørrebro Bryghus

$$$ | EUROPEAN | Seating 160, this award-winning microbrewery and two-story restaurant (plus beer garden in summer) was an instant hit when it opened in 2003. Lunches include salads, sandwiches, and burgers; in the evening you can order prix-fixe dinners of between three and four courses. **Known for:** more than 50 beers with a dozen on tap; beer pairings; dishes featuring beer as an ingredient. [$] *Average main: DKr 350* ✉ *Ryesgade 3, Nørrebro* ☎ *35/30–05–30* 🌐 *www.noerrebrobryghus.dk.*

Relæ

$$$ | SCANDINAVIAN | The Danish-Sicilian chef Christian Puglisi is one of the brightest stars on Denmark's culinary scene, and this Michelin-starred restaurant is his brainchild. The casual, no-nonsense approach and atmosphere is combined with lofty culinary ambitions, and the result is incredibly tasty food served in unpretentious settings. **Known for:** unfussy atmosphere; great service; creative food. [$] *Average main: DKr 495* ✉ *Jægersborggade 41, Nørrebro* ☎ *36/96–66–09* 🌐 *restaurant-relae.dk* 🕓 *Closed Sun. and Mon. No lunch Tues.–Thurs.*

🍸 Nightlife

BARS AND LOUNGES

★ Lygtens Kro

BREWPUBS/BEER GARDENS | Heavy rock meets German beers and good food—the kitchen serves everything from moules frites to bratwurst—at Lygtens Kro. This bar might just be the coziest in Copenhagen, and it's a good place to meet locals. ✉ *Lygten 29, Nørrebro* ☎ *26/36–90–86* 🌐 *lygtens-kro.dk.*

Oak Room

BARS/PUBS | Serving specialty cocktails, this bar is in the popular nightlife corridor near Elmegade. ⊠ *Birkegade 10, Nørrebro* ☎ *38/60–38–60* ⊕ *oakroom.dk.*

Ølbaren

BREWPUBS/BEER GARDENS | This local favorite carries about 115 Danish and international beers by the bottle and nine on tap. It also offers beer tastings "on demand." ⊠ *Elmegade 2, Nørrebro* ☎ *35/35–45–34* ⊕ *oelbaren.dk.*

Pompette

WINE BARS—NIGHTLIFE | Democratic wine bars, aka bars where commoners can actually afford a glass of wine, are all the rage in Copenhagen these days. This friendly bar and shop sells natural wines by the glass and bottle, served with a good selection of cheese and charcuterie. ⊠ *Møllegade 3, Nørrebro* ⊕ *pompette.dk.*

Sidecar

CAFES—NIGHTLIFE | Though it's mostly known as a cocktail bar, this Nørrebro favorite doubles as a café by day. The breakfast and brunch are as good as the whiskey drinks. ⊠ *Skyttegade 5, Nørrebro* ☎ *20/99–97–27* ⊕ *sidecarnoerrebro. dk.*

Snack and Blues

BARS/PUBS | It's greasy, it's sticky, and it's good. Stop by this bar and restaurant for tasty chicken wings, strong cocktails, and the soundtrack—all blues. ⊠ *Guldbergsgade 7A, Nørrebro* ☎ *42/45–81–22* ⊕ *snackandblues.com.*

JAZZ CLUBS

⭐ **Alice**

MUSIC CLUBS | When Jazzhouse, one of Copenhagen's best jazz and night clubs, joined forces with the music venue Global, this venue was created. It's home to the city's scene for jazz, experimental electronic, global, and folk, and it's located in a lovely brick building in an idyllic courtyard in inner Nørrebro. ⊠ *Nørre Allé 7, Nørrebro* ☎ *50/58–08–41* ⊕ *alicecph. com.*

🛍 Shopping

Galleri Dansk Møbelkunst

ART GALLERIES | You may find pieces by Arne Jacobsen, Kaare Klint, and Finn Juhl at this spacious and elegant store, which has one of the city's largest collections of vintage furniture. ⊠ *Bredgade 5, Frederiksberg* ☎ *33/32–38–37* ⊕ *www. dmk.dk.*

Frederiksberg

Originally a farming area that supplied the royal households with fresh produce, Frederiksberg is now known for its residences of the well-heeled and the city zoo. Though technically its own town, Frederiksberg is encircled by the rest of Copenhagen. The affluent area is known for its leafy boulevards, quiet residential streets, good shopping, and many dining options. Side streets tend to be calm, but the main thoroughfares— Gammel Kongevej, Frederiksberg Allé, H.C. Ørstedsvej, and Allegade/Falkoner Allé— are bustling with life. Some of Copehagen's most romantic gardens are located here: Frederiksberg Have and Landbohøjskolens Have are among them.

👁 Sights

⭐ **Cisternerne**

MUSEUM | A former water reservoir has been transformed into one of Copenhagen's most popular venues for contemporary art. The exhibitions change and it can be difficult to find the entrance to the underground reservoir; check the website for information before you head out. ⊠ *Bag Søndermarken, Frederiksberg* ☎ *30/73–80–32* ⊕ *cisternerne.dk* 💷 *70 DKr* ⊗ *Closed Mon.*

Landbohøjskolens Have

GARDEN | This lovely garden was created in 1858, and since then it's been one of the most charming green areas in Copenhagen. There's a pond, a creek, a seemingly endless number of different plants and flowers, and a cute café. ⊠ *Bülowsvej 17, Frederiksberg* ☎ *35/32–26–26* 🎫 *Free.*

Værnedamsvej

NEIGHBORHOOD | It might be one of Copenhagen's shortest streets, but Værnedamsvej is also one of the most charming. The mix of cafés (Granola is a beloved institution), cheese and flower shops, bookshops, wine bars, bistros, and designer boutiques gives the street a Parisian feel, and it's lovely from early morning to late night. ⊠ *Frederiksberg.*

Zoologisk Have

ZOO | FAMILY | Established in 1859, the Copenhagen Zoo blends the old with the new. The elephant house, by acclaimed architect Norman Foster, is an elegant structure topped by two glass domes, providing its inhabitants with plenty of light and stomping ground. Modern glass enclosures for hippos and polar bears also make for spectacular viewing. But children are just as likely to gravitate to the small petting zoo and playground, which includes friendly cows, horses, rabbits, goats, and hens. The indoor rain forest has butterflies, sloths, alligators, and other tropical creatures. On sunny weekends, the line to enter can be long, so come early. *There are often extended weekend and summer opening hours.* ⊠ *Roskildevej 32, Frederiksberg* ☎ *70/20–02–00* ⊕ *www.zoo.dk* 🎫 *DKr 195.*

 Restaurants

Formel B

$$$$ | EUROPEAN | The name stands for "basic formula," but this French-Danish restaurant is anything but basic. Young chefs Rune Jochumsen and Kristian Moeller serve classic French cuisine based on seasonal Danish ingredients in an interior of leather, glass, marble, and steel. **Known for:** seafood dishes; creative desserts; nice wine list. $ *Average main: DKr 995* ⊠ *Vesterbrogade 182,* *Frederiksberg* ☎ *33/25–10–66* ⊕ *www. formel-b.dk* ⊙ *Closed Sun. No lunch.*

 Hotels

CABINN Scandinavia Hotel

$ | HOTEL | This impeccably maintained, bright budget hotel is just west of the lakes and Vesterport Station. **Pros:** functional and practical; affordable given the location; centrally located. **Cons:** tiny rooms; occasional mix-ups make it a good idea to reconfirm your reservation; generic decor. $ *Rooms from: DKr 625* ⊠ *Vodroffsvej 55, Frederiksberg* ☎ *35/36–11–11* ⊕ *www.cabinn.com* 🛏 *201 rooms* 🍴 *No meals.*

ⓨ Nightlife

★ Café Intime

BARS/PUBS | This bohemian institution, which first opened in 1922, is popular among intellectuals, artists, and the LGBT community for its cocktails. Every day a pianist plays on the grand piano, and every Sunday there's live jazz. ⊠ *Allegade 25, Frederiksberg* ☎ *38/34–19–58* ⊕ *www.cafeintime.dk.*

Rouge Oyster

WINE BARS—NIGHTLIFE | Located on one of Copenhagen's busiest streets, this combined wine and oyster bar is the perfect place to head for some fresh or canned seafood, affordable wine, enjoyable people-watching, and interesting art (the walls are adorned with contemporary art). ⊠ *Gl. Kongevej 43, Frederiksberg.*

🛍 Shopping

Royal Copenhagen Factory Outlet

CERAMICS/GLASSWARE | The Royal Copenhagen Factory Outlet has a good deal of stock, often at reduced prices. You can also buy Holmegaard glass at the Royal Copenhagen store in Indre By and this factory outlet. ⊠ *Søndre Fasanvej 9, Frederiksberg* ☎ *38/34–10–04* ⊕ *www. royalcopenhagen.com.*

Klampenborg, Bakken, and Dyrehaven

15 km (9 miles) north of Copenhagen.

If you only have time for one day trip, then head north of Copenhagen to explore Dyrehaven (and, if you have the time, the museum Louisiana in Humlebæk). As you follow the beautiful coast north of Copenhagen, you'll come upon the wealthy enclave of Klampenborg. Flocks of deer munch away on the well-kept soccer pitches in Dyrehaven—the "animal garden" that was planned as the official royal hunting terrain in the 1670s—while roller coaster–fatigued revelers in the amusement park of Bakken happily consume sausages, beer, and lollipops.

GETTING HERE AND AROUND

To reach Klampenborg take a regional train (in the direction of Nivå) or S-train C to Klampenborg Station; both leave from the major train stations in Copenhagen. The trip takes about 15 minutes and traverses four zones (DKr 40 for a one-way ticket). Both Bakken and Dyrehaven are walking distance from Klampenborg Station. For Bellevue Beach, take Bus 14 from Klampenborg Station. Horse-drawn carriages are available for hire in Dyrehaven.

Sights

Bakken

AMUSEMENT PARK/WATER PARK | FAMILY | Located in the peaceful Dyrehaven, Bakken is the world's oldest amusement park—it opened in 1583!—and one of Denmark's most popular attractions. Here a mostly working-class crowd lunches on hot dogs and cotton candy and, perhaps most importantly, plenty of beer. Tivoli, with its trimmed hedges, dazzling firework displays, and evening concerts, is still Copenhagen's reigning queen, but unpretentious Bakken is unabashedly about having a good time. Bakken has more than 30 rides, from quaint, rickety roller coasters (free of Disney gloss) to newer, faster rides and little-kid favorites such as Kaffekoppen, the Danish version of spinning teacups, where you sit in traditional Royal Copenhagen–style blue-and-white coffee cups. ✉ *Dyrehavevej 62, Klampenborg* ⌖ *Take a train to Klampenborg Station* ☎ *39/63–35–44* ⊕ *www.bakken.dk* 🎟 *Entrance free, ride pass DKr 269 (full day in peak season).*

★ Dyrehaven (*Deer Garden*)

NATIONAL/STATE PARK | Herds of deer roam freely in the verdant, 2,500-acre Dyrehaven. Once the favored hunting grounds of Danish royals, today the park has become a cherished weekend oasis for Copenhageners. Hiking and biking trails traverse the park, and lush fields beckon nature-seekers and families with picnic baskets. The deer are everywhere; in the less-trafficked regions of the park you may find yourself surrounded by an entire herd of deer delicately stepping through the fields. The park's centerpiece is the copper-top, 17th-century Eremitagen, formerly a royal hunting lodge. It is closed to the public but is sometimes rented for private events. Dyrehaven is a retreat for hikers and bikers, but you can also go in for the royal treatment and enjoy it from the high seat of a horse-drawn carriage. The carriages gather at the park entrance near the station. ✉ *Klampenborg* ⌖ *Park entrance near Klampenborg S-train station* 🎟 *Free.*

🏖 Beaches

Bellevue Strand

BEACH—SIGHT | The residents of Klampenborg are lucky enough to have this pleasant beach nearby. In summer this luck may seem double-edged, when scores of city-weary sunseekers pile out at the Klampenborg S-train station and head for the sand. The Danes have a perfect word for this: they call Bellevue

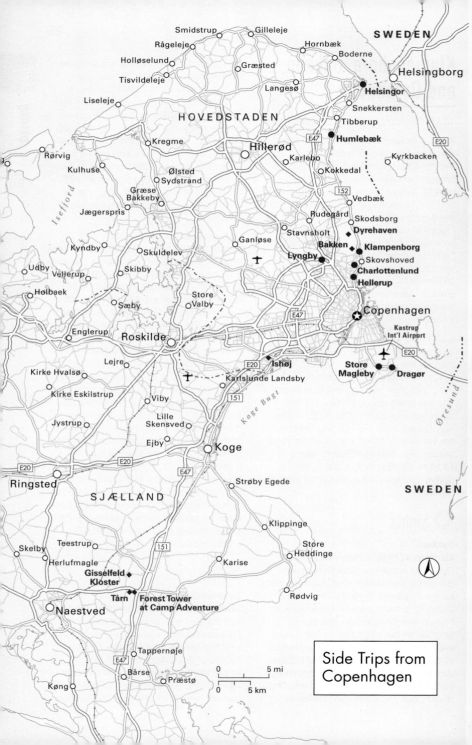

Side Trips from Copenhagen

a *fluepapir* (flypaper) beach. Bellevue is still an appealing seaside spot to soak up some rays. **Amenities:** lifeguards, showers, toilets. **Best for:** partiers, swimming. ⊠ *Strandvejen 340, Klampenborg* ✛ *A 15-minute train ride from Copenhagen.*

Humlebæk

31 km (19 miles) north of Copenhagen.

Historically a fishing village, this elegant seaside town with a population of about 6,000 is now a suburb of Copenhagen. It's also home to Louisiana, a fantastic modern art museum. In summer the town's many cottages fill with vacationers, and the gardens come alive with vibrant colors. The town takes its name from the plant *humle* (hops), which is abundant in the area.

GETTING HERE AND AROUND
Trains run to Humlebæk from Copenhagen every 20 minutes. These trains originate in the Swedish city of Malmö and run in the other direction from Helsingør. The 30-minute trip costs DKr 92, and you can buy tickets from machines in any station.

TRAIN INFO DSB. ☎ *70/13–14–15* ⊕ *www.dsb.dk.*

◉ Sights

Karen Blixen Museum
MUSEUM | This museum is in the elegant, airy manor of Baroness Karen Blixen, who wrote *Out of Africa* under the pen name Isak Dinesen. The manor house, to which she returned in 1931 to write her most famous works, now displays Blixen's manuscripts, sketches, photographs, and memorabilia documenting her years in Africa. Leave time to wander around the gorgeous gardens, which also function as a bird sanctuary. ⊠ *Rungsted Strandvej 111, Rungsted* ✛ *Take Bus 388 from Louisiana to the Blixen museum* ☎ *45/57–10–57* ⊕ *www.karen-blixen.dk*

⊞ *DKr 100* ⊘ *Closed Mon. Sept.–June and Tues. Oct.–Apr.*

★ Louisiana
MUSEUM | FAMILY | The must-see Louisiana is a modern-art museum with fresh, often-witty temporary exhibitions and an impressive permanent collection that includes Picasso, Giacometti, and Warhol. Even if you're not an art lover, it's well worth the 30-minute trip from Copenhagen to see this beautiful combination of a 19th-century villa and modern Danish architecture, with its large sculpture garden and dramatic view of the Øresund waters. There's a children's section as well, where kids can draw and paint under the supervision of museum staff. In late August the museum is home to a literature festival with visits from some of the literary world's biggest names. ⊠ *Gl. Strandvej 13* ✛ *About 10 minutes' walk north from the station* ☎ *49/19–07–19* ⊕ *www.louisiana.dk* ⊞ *DKr 125* ⊘ *Closed Mon.*

Lyngby

16 km (10 miles) northwest of Copenhagen.

◉ Sights

Frilandsmuseet
MUSEUM | FAMILY | North of Copenhagen is Lyngby, whose main draw is this open-air museum. About 50 Danish farmhouses and cottages from the period 1650–1950 have been painstakingly dismantled, moved here, reconstructed, and filled with period furniture and tools. Trees, farm animals, and gardens surround the museum; bring lunch and plan to spend the day. For children, the farm animals and history-theme pantomime performances are the biggest draw. ⊠ *Kongevejen 100, Lyngby* ✛ *Take the B Line S-train from all major Copenhagen stations to Sorgenfri Station, then walk right and follow the signs. The trip from*

Copenhagen encompasses five travel zones. ☎ *33/47–34-81* ⊕ *www.frilands-museet.dk* ✉ *Free* ⊘ *Closed mid-Dec.–mid-Apr., weekdays in early Dec., and Mon.*

Hellerup

8 km (5 miles) north of Copenhagen.

Sights

Experimentarium
MUSEUM | FAMILY | At a former bottling plant, in the beachside town of Hellerup, more than 300 exhibitions are clustered in various "Discovery Islands," each exploring a different facet of science, technology, and natural phenomena. A dozen hands-on exhibits allow you to do things like blow giant soap bubbles, feel an earthquake, stir up magnetic goop, play ball on a jet stream, and gyrate to gyroscopes. The center also organizes interactive temporary exhibitions. Exhibit texts are in English. ⊠ *Tuborg Havnevej 7, Hellerup* ⊕ *From downtown Copenhagen, take Bus 14 (from Rådhuspladsen) or 1A (from Kongens Nytorv or the Central Station). Alternatively, take the S-train to Svanemøllen Station, then walk north for 10 minutes.* ☎ *39/27–33–33* ⊕ *www.experimentarium.dk* ✉ *DKr 195.*

Charlottenlund

10 km (6 miles) north of Copenhagen.

Just north of Copenhagen is the leafy, affluent coastal suburb of Charlottenlund, with a small, appealing beach that gets predictably crowded on sunny weekends. A little farther north is Charlottenlund Slot (Charlottenlund Palace), a graceful mansion that has housed various Danish royals since the 17th century. The palace isn't open to the public, but the surrounding peaceful palace gardens are, and

Copenhageners enjoy coming up here for weekend ambles and picnics.

GETTING HERE AND AROUND
Charlottenlund is a 15-minute S-train ride from Central Station on the C line. Trains leave every 10 minutes. Alternatively, take Bus 14, which leaves from several points in Copenhagen. For the Ordrupgaard museum, take the S-train from major Copenhagen stations to Klampenborg or Lyngby Station where you can catch Bus 388. Bus 169 leaves from Charlottenlund Station. Get off at Hovmarksvej, a 15-minute walk from the museum. Alternatively, take the train from Charlottenlund Station to Klampenborg Station and follow the above directions. Bus and train rides from Copenhagen to Charlottenlund cross three zones, so a one-way ticket costs DKr 36.

◉ Sights

★ Ordrupgaard
MUSEUM | Temporarily closed for renovation until late 2020, Ordrupgaard is one of the largest museum collections of French impressionism in Europe outside France itself. Most of the great 19th-century French artists are represented, including Manet, Monet, Matisse, Cézanne, Renoir, Degas, Gauguin, Sisley, Delacroix, and Pissarro. Ordrupgaard also has a superb collection of Danish Golden Age painters and spectacular works by Vilhelm Hammershøi, whose deft use of light and space creates haunting settings for his mostly solitary figures. The paintings hang on the walls of what was once the home of museum founder and art collector Wilhelm Hansen. The interior of this manor, dating from 1918, has been left just as it was when Hansen and his wife Henny lived here. In 2005 a black, curvaceous addition, designed by the acclaimed Iraqi-British architect Zaha Hadid, joined the main building. In addition to extra exhibition space, the new structure made room for a spacious café that overlooks the park. There

are labels in English. ✉ *Vilvordevej 110* ☎ *39/64–11–83* ⊕ *www.ordrupgaard.dk* 🎫 *DKr 85* ⏱ *Closed Mon.*

🍽 Restaurants

Café Jorden Rundt

$ | | **FAMILY** | Strandvejen, the coastal road that showcases private mansions like beads on a string, is the location of this café, whose name means "around the world." It features striking views of Øresund, the sound between Denmark and Sweden. **Known for:** sizable sandwiches; salads and soups; cakes. 🍴 *Average main: DKr8* ✉ *Strandvejen 152* ☎ *39/63–73–81* ⊕ *www.cafejordenrundt.dk* 💳 *No credit cards.*

🛏 Hotels

Skovshoved Hotel

$$$ | **B&B/INN** | This delightful, art-filled inn is near a few old fishing cottages, beside the yacht harbor. **Pros:** quiet; close to the beach; highly regarded restaurant. **Cons:** far from shopping or other conveniences; maybe a little pretentious; rather pricey. 🍴 *Rooms from: DKr 1595* ✉ *Strandvejen 267* ✥ *Take the S-train to Charlottenlund and walk 15 minutes from the station* ☎ *39/64–00–28* ⊕ *www.skovshovedhotel.com* 🛏 *24 rooms* 🍽 *No meals.*

Dragør and Store Magleby

22 km (14 miles) southeast of Copenhagen.

On the island of Amager the quaint fishing towns of Dragør (pronounced *drah*-wer) and Store Magleby, both less than a half hour from Copenhagen, feel far away in distance and time. The two adjacent villages are part of Dragør municipality. If it weren't for the planes whizzing to and from the nearby Copenhagen Airport, then the bobbing wooden

Street Mirrors 👁

As you're wandering around Dragør, and other old Danish villages, notice that many of the older houses have an angled mirror contraption attached to their street-level windows. This *gade spejl* (street mirror), unique to Scandinavia, was—and perhaps still is—used by the occupants of the house to "spy" on the street activity. Usually positioned at seat level, the curious (often the older ladies of town) could pull up a chair and observe all the comings and goings of the neighborhood from the warmth and privacy of their homes.

boats, cobbled streets, small squares, and well-preserved thatched-roof houses might make you think you'd gone back in time. The town is set apart from the rest of the area around Copenhagen because it was settled by Dutch farmers in the 16th century. King Christian II ordered the community to provide fresh produce and flowers for the royal court. Today neat rows of houses, covered with terra-cotta roofs, wandering ivy, and roses, characterize the still meticulously maintained community. If there's one color that characterizes Dragør, it's the lovely pale yellow (called Dragør *gul,* or Dragør yellow) of its houses.

GETTING HERE AND AROUND

Several buses leave every 20 minutes from City Hall Square. Bus 350S leaves every 5 to 10 minutes from Nørreport; the trip takes about 45 minutes. The ride from Copenhagen traverses three zones (DKr 36 for a one-way ticket); the ride from the airport covers only two zones (DKr 24).

ESSENTIALS

VISITOR INFORMATION Dragør Harbor Office. ✉ *Lodsgaarden A 111, Dragør* 🌐 *www.visitdragoer.dk.*

🍴 Restaurants

Restaurant Beghuset

$$ | **SCANDINAVIAN** | This handsome restaurant in the center of the town has rustic stone floors and green-and-gold painted doors. It's named Beghuset (Pitch House) because this is where Dragør's fishermen used to boil the pitch that waterproofed their wooden ships. **Known for:** traditional decor; Danish–French fusion cuisine; set on a cobblestone street in Dragør. [$] *Average main: DKr 225* ✉ *Strandgade 14, Dragør* ☎ *32/53–01–36* 🌐 *www.beghuset.dk* 🕒 *Closed Sun.–Tues. No lunch.*

Ishøj

20 km (12 miles) southwest of Copenhagen.

👁 Sights

ARKEN Museum for Moderne Kunst

MUSEUM | Architect Søren Robert Lund was just 25 and still a student when he was awarded the commission for the ARKEN Museum for Moderne Kunst, which is set against the flat coast southwest of Copenhagen. ARKEN, or "the ark," which opened in 1996, is a building with a ship's features: sail-like protrusions and narrow red corridors that evoke a submarine. The museum's massive sculpture room exhibits both modern Danish and international art. The hall is narrow in one end and wider in the other to provoke illusions of space and proximity, depending on where you stand. The café, which looks like a ship's bridge, offers nice views of Køge Bugt. ✉ *Skovvej 100, Ishøj* ✥ *S-trains C and E leave from all major Copenhagen train stations. From Copenhagen, you cross five zones. From there, take Bus 128, which lets you off in front of the museum.* ☎ *43/54–02–22* 🌐 *www.arken.dk* 🎟 *DKr 150* 🕒 *Closed Mon.*

Gisselfeld Kloster and Tårn

69 km (42 miles) southwest of Copenhagen.

👁 Sights

★ **The Forest Tower at Camp Adventure**

VIEWPOINT | Since opening in 2019, this forest tower has been one of the most popular day-trips from Copenhagen. The 45-meter (148-foot) tall spiraling wooden structure towers over the trees below, and it's as much an architectural masterpiece as it is a way to experience nature from a new angle. It's part of Camp Adventure, a nature camp with a climbing park and a café. The tower is open year-round. **■ TIP→ Price discounts for the climbing park are available online; children younger than 15 also pay a lower rate for the climbing park.** ✉ *Denderupvej 9A, Rønnede* ✥ *A one-hour drive from Copenhagen. Alternatively, take the train to Næstved and from there Bus 630R to Faxe Ladeplads; it takes close to two hours.* ☎ *38/15–00–30* 🌐 *www.campadventure.dk* 🎟 *Tower DKr 150, climbing park DKr 325* 🕒 *Climbing park closed Dec.–Mar.; Mon.–Wed. Apr.–June, Sept., and Oct.; and Sun.–Fri. Nov.*

Helsingør

14 km (9 miles) north of Humlebæk, 45 km (28 miles) north of Copenhagen.

Helsingør's name is derived from *hals,* or "neck," after the narrow neck of water separating it from Sweden's Helsingborg. That slim waterway made the town wealthy in the 1420s, when Erik of Pomerania established a tariff for all ships passing through it. Shakespeare anglicized the town's name to Elsinore and made its massive castle the home of his fictional character Hamlet. Today about 34,000 people live in Helsingør, which still has a maritime flavor.

GETTING HERE AND AROUND

Trains run every 20 minutes from Copenhagen, and the 45-minute journey to Helsingør costs DKr 66. These trains originate in the Swedish city of Malmö.

Ferries, including some that take cars, also run every half hour between Helsingør and its Swedish twin city, Helsingborg, with a round trip costing from DKr 166. Helsingør is also the starting point for a regional railway that provides excellent connections to Fredensborg and Hornbæk. *Veterantog* (antique trains) periodically run on this line in the summer.

CONTACTS ForSea. ✉ *Færgevej 12* ☎ *49/26–01–55* ⊕ *www.forsea.dk.*

VISITOR INFORMATION

CONTACTS Helsingør Turistbureau. ✉ *Allegade 2* ☎ *49/21–13–33* ⊕ *www. visitnordsjaelland.com.*

◉ Sights

Carmelite Kloster (*Carmelite Convent*)
RELIGIOUS SITE | Close to Sankt Olai Kirke stands Sankt Marie Kirke; the 15th-century Carmelite Convent is one of the best-preserved examples of medieval architecture in Scandinavia. ✉ *Skt. Annægade 38* ☎ *49/21–17–74* 🎫 *Free, tour DKr 20.*

⭐ **Kronborg Slot** (*Kronborg Castle*)
CASTLE/PALACE | Kronborg Castle dominates the city of Helsingør. Built in the late 1500s, it's the inspiration for Elsinore castle in Shakespeare's *Hamlet* (1601). Shakespeare probably never saw the castle in person, but he managed to capture its spirit—it's a gloomy, chilly

To Be or Not to Be?

Shakespeare Festival Each August, Kronborg Castle is the site of the Shakespeare Festival, featuring outdoor performances of Shakespeare plays . The schedule varies from year to year. In 2019, productions were *Richard III* by HamletScenen, the house theater company, and *Songs of Lear* by a visiting theater troupe. ✉ *Hamletscenen, Kronborg 13* ☎ *49/21–69–79* ⊕ *www. hamletscenen.dk.*

place, where it's clear that an ordinary person today lives much better than kings once did. The castle was built as a Renaissance tollbooth: from its cannon-studded bastions, forces collected a tariff from all ships crossing the sliver of water between Denmark and Sweden. Well worth seeing are the 200-foot-long dining hall and the dungeons, where there is a brooding statue of Holger Danske (Ogier the Dane). According to legend, the sleeping Viking chief will awaken to defend Denmark when it's in danger. (The largest Danish resistance group during World War II called itself Holger Danske.) ✉ *Kronborg 2C* ⊹ *At the point, on the harbor front* ☎ *49/21–30–78* ⊕ *kongeligeslotte.dk* 🎫 *DKr 95–145* ⊙ *Closed Mon. Oct.–Mar.*

Sankt Olai Kirke (*St. Olaf's Church*)
RELIGIOUS SITE | On the corner of Stengade and Sankt Annægade near the harbor is Sankt Olai Kirke, worth a peek for its elaborately carved wooden altar. Also in downtown are whole streets of medieval-era merchants' and ferrymen's houses—they're now modern shops. ✉ *Skt. Annægade 12* ☎ *49/21–04–43* ⊕ *www.helsingoerdomkirke.dk* 🎫 *Free.*

🍴 Restaurants

Most simple cafés and inexpensive eateries are in the city center, along the main shopping street on Stengade and around Axeltorv, the city's main square. If you are in Helsingør mainly to visit Kronborg, consider having a picnic on the castle grounds at the picnic area just left of the main entrance.

Rådmand Davids Hus
$$ | **SCANDINAVIAN** | This classic Danish lunch restaurant is in a creaky, half-timbered building dating from 1694 with off-kilter floors, low ceilings, and lots of charm. It's a good place to stop for a "shopping lunch," a hearty platter with homemade Danish specialties. **Known for:** atmospheric, charming building; traditional Danish specialties; homemade rye bread and famous Grand Marnier pancakes. [$] *Average main: DKr 195* ✉ *Strandgade 70* ☎ *49/26–10–43* 🕓 *No dinner. Closed Sun.*

🛏 Hotels

Marienlyst
$$$ | **HOTEL** | The historic hotel dates from 1860, when it was the country's first waterfront property. **Pros:** beach location while still being close to Copenhagen; super views; family friendly. **Cons:** a major conference and party hotel; some room furnishings show signs of wear; can be noisy, particularly on weekends. [$] *Rooms from: DKr 1695* ✉ *Nordre Strandvej 2* ☎ *49/21–40–00* 🌐 *www.marienlyst.dk* 🛏 *227 rooms* 🍽 *Free Breakfast.*

👜 Shopping

Beneath its well-restored medieval charm, Helsingør is a working-class town with a substantial population of immigrants. Although you won't find the fancy boutiques that dot the rest of northern Zealand, on Helsingør's pedestrian shopping streets—Stengade, Sternegade, and Bjergegade—there's a great selection of traditional food providers that will offer memorable snacks. From April to November an outdoor market with fresh fruit, cheese, and fish takes place on Wednesday, Friday, and Saturday at Axeltorv, in the center of town.

★ **Brostræde Is**
FOOD/CANDY | Follow the delectable smell of home-baked waffle cones—or just follow the crowds—to Brostræde Is. It has been making summer days more tasty since 1922. ✉ *Brostræde 2* ☎ *49/21–35–91.*

Hornbæk and the Danish Riviera

60 km (37 miles) from Copenhagen.

North Zealand has historically been the favorite holiday spot for Denmark's most affluent families, and the area from Hornbæk to Hundested—known as the Danish Riviera—is home to a lovely selection of traditional beach hotels, picturesque former fishing villages, beautiful vacation homes, and a host of restaurants, bars, and delicatessen shops. The seemingly endless stretch of sandy beaches is broken only by green forests, small marinas, and holiday homes. Base yourself in a traditional beach hotel and spend a few days walking in the woods, lounging on the beaches, and visiting some of North Zealand's many museums. The main villages worth visiting are pretty Hornbæk, Gilleleje, Tisvildeleje, and Liseleje. All towns are home to several ice cream parlors, fishmongers, cafés, and restaurants.

GETTING HERE AND AROUND

It's quick and easy to get to North Zealand's idyllic beach towns. In a car it takes around one hour; take Route 16 or 19 north of town. The trip is also doable by train. Take the train to Hillerød. From here you can change to the regional trains linking the small beach towns with the bigger towns in the area. The trip takes around 1½ hours and costs around DKr 115.

 Sights

Rudolph Tegners Museum og Statue Park

MUSEUM | This museum is set in the middle of a wild, uncultivated part of North Zealand called Russia. On the heath-covered grounds there are 14 outdoor statues, and inside the stunning museum—designed by the sculptor and architect Rudolph Tegner himself—there are many, many more. Tegner was a controversial figure because of the monumental scale and content of his sculptures, but in recent years his art has gained more recognition. ⊠ *Muse-umsvej 19, Dronninmølle* ☎ *49/71–91–77* ⊕ *www.rudolphtegner.dk* 🎟 *Dkr 60* ☉ *Closed Mon.*

★ Tisvildeleje

TOWN | North Zealand's most happening historic seaside town is charming Tisvildeleje. Copenhagen's creative elite has been vacationing in the town for decades, leading to an influx in classy hotels, fine dining options, designer boutiques, and stylish, casual cafés. Most of the town consists of private vacation homes, but the main street—which ends at the beach—is where most of the action takes place. There are two lovely, sandy beaches, and a forest just west of the town, Tisvilde Hegn, is an ideal spot for a stroll. ⊠ *Tisvildeleje.*

🍴 Restaurants

Adamsens Fisk

$ | SCANDINAVIAN | Zealand's largest fishmonger has been in the same family for three generations. You can stop by to buy fish and delicacies, and sit down on the benches outside of the store with your sushi, grilled fish fillets, or seafood platter. **Known for:** wide variety of fresh and prepared fish; generous portions; great location on the harbor. $ *Average*

main: DKr 98 ⊠ *Havnen 2, Gilleleje* ☎ *48/30–09–27* ⊕ *adamsensfisk.dk.*

🛏 Hotels

Gilleleje Badehotel

$$$ | HOTEL | This nostalgic gem of a beach hotel has been receiving wealthy vacationers since 1895, and it's as popular as ever. **Pros:** beautiful location; historic charm has been preserved; popular restaurant. **Cons:** some rooms are on the small side; no direct access to the beach; a bit pricey. $ *Rooms from: DKr 1790* ⊠ *Hulsøvej 15, Gilleleje* ☎ *48/30–13–47* ⊕ *gillelejebadehotel.dk* 🛏 *24 rooms* ❏ *Free Breakfast.*

★ Helenekilde Badehotel

$$$$ | HOTEL | Perched atop the steep cliffs leading down to a pretty beach and offering grand views of the sea, this beachside beauty, in business since 1904, is one of the best hotels in Denmark. **Pros:** many rooms have sea views and some have terraces; beautiful decor; excellent restaurant and bar. **Cons:** books out months in advance in peak season; sometimes booked by weddings or conferences; luxury comes with a price. $ *Rooms from: DKr 1995* ⊠ *Strand-vejen 25, Tisvildeleje* ☎ *48/70–70–01* ⊕ *helenekilde.com* 🛏 *27 rooms* ❏ *Free Breakfast.*

Hillerød

10 km (6 miles) southwest of Fredens-borg, 40 km (25 miles) northwest of Copenhagen.

Surrounded by forests, Hillerød is an ordinary small city with some extraordinary features: it's home to the lovely Frederiksborg Slot (Frederiksborg Castle) and within a short drive of the ruins of two medieval monasteries, at Æbelholt and Esrum. Nowadays the town, founded in the 15th century, is an important industrial area.

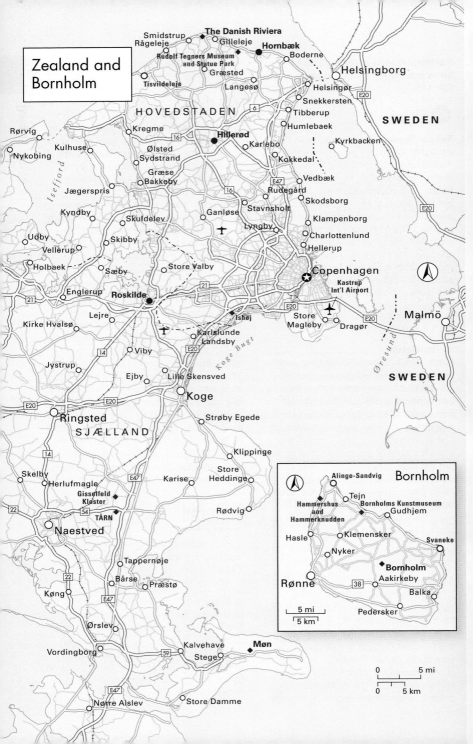

GETTING HERE AND AROUND

S-trains run every 10–20 minutes between Copenhagen and Hillerød. The 55-minute trip costs DKr 55.

CONTACTS DSB. ☎ *70/13–14–15* 🌐 *www.dsb.dk.*

Sights

★ **Frederiksborg Slot** (*Frederiksborg Castle*)

CASTLE/PALACE | The Danish royal family's castles are a motley lot, and Hillerød's Frederiksborg Castle is one of the few that can be called a true beauty. Danish builder King Christian IV tore down a previous castle on the site and built this Dutch Renaissance version in the early 1600s. The building is enclosed by a moat, covers three islets, and is topped with dozens of gables, spires, and turrets. Devastated by a fire in 1859, the castle was reconstructed with the support of the Carlsberg Foundation and now includes Denmark's Nationalhistoriske Museum (National History Museum), which contains the country's best collection of portraits and historical paintings. It also has an activity area where kids can dress up as historical figures.

Don't miss the gorgeous castle chapel Slotskirke, with its lacy ornamentation: Danish monarchs were crowned here for more than 200 years, and the house organ dates from 1610. The Baroque Gardens, rebuilt according to J. C. Krieger's layout from 1725, include a series of wide waterfalls that make the neatly trimmed park a lovely place for a stroll. Don't miss the floral sculptures of the current royals' official monograms. ✉ *Hillerød* ☎ *48/26–04–39* 🌐 *www.dnm.dk* 🎟 *DKr 75, gardens free.*

Restaurants

Spisestedet Leonora

$ | **SCANDINAVIAN** | **FAMILY** | In the shadow of Frederiksborg Castle, this family restaurant thrives in what used to be the castle stables. Inside, walls feature hanging prints and paintings of royalty and the castle; outside you'll find a large patio with great views of the castle. **Known for:** patios with castle views; open-face sandwiches; traditional Danish brunch. [$] *Average main: DKr 72* ✉ *Frederiksborgslot 5* ☎ *48/26–75–16* 🌐 *www.leonora.dk* 🕓 *No dinner.*

Hotels

Hotel Hillerød

$$ | **HOTEL** | About a 25-minute walk from Frederiksborg Castle, this hotel has a decor that consists of sensible Danish design and luxurious lighting. **Pros:** central location near shopping and sights; friendly, helpful staff; good value. **Cons:** often used as a conference hotel; not a lot of local charm; relatively pricey. [$] *Rooms from: DKr 915* ✉ *Milnersvej 41* ☎ *48/24–08–00* 🌐 *www.hotelhillerod.dk* 🛏 *113 rooms* 🍴 *Free Breakfast.*

Roskilde

36 km (22 miles) west of Copenhagen (on Rte. 156).

Roskilde is Zealand's second-largest town and one of its oldest, having been founded in 998. The town is named for a Viking king called Ro, who, according to legend, built the city around a lovely spring—*kilde* in Danish. In the Middle Ages, Roskilde was one of northern Europe's largest and most important cities, with a population of 5,000–10,000. Its eccentric, enormous cathedral, built in 1170, is a UNESCO World Heritage Site. These days Roskilde is a university town

Roskilde's Vikingeskibsmuseet is Denmark's national museum for ships, seafaring, and boat-building in the prehistoric and medieval period.

known for hosting an enormous rock festival every summer. It makes a great base for exploring nearby historic areas like Lejre and Skibby.

GETTING HERE AND AROUND

Trains run from Copenhagen to Roskilde every half hour. The 20-minute journey costs DKr 49. Within Roskilde, there's an excellent bus network. If you'd like to take a scenic boat ride, the M/S *Sagafjord* makes regular trips on Roskilde Fjord and has a restaurant onboard. Tickets cost DKr 135.

⊙ Sights

★ Lejre Forsøgscenter (*Lejre Archaeological Research Center*)

MUSEUM | FAMILY | Back in the Iron Age, Lejre was the capital of the Lejre Kingdom; some scholars believe it's mentioned in *Beowulf*. These days it's best known as the home of the 50-acre Lejre Forsøgscenter, a pioneer in the field of "experimental archeology." In summer a

handful of hardy Danish families live here under the observation of researchers; they go about their daily routine grinding grain, herding goats, and wearing furs and skins, providing a clearer picture of ancient ways of life. You can experience a Stone Age camp, a Viking market, and 19th-century farmhouses, and there's a large children's area. ✉ *Slangealleen 2* ☎ *46/48–08–78* ⊕ *www.sagnlandet.dk* 🎫 *DKr 165* ⊙ *Closed late Oct.–mid-Apr. and Mon. in May, June, Aug., and Sept.*

★ Roskilde Domkirke (*Roskilde Cathedral*)

RELIGIOUS SITE | Construction began on Roskilde Cathedral around 1170 on the site of a church erected 200 years earlier by the Viking hero Harald Bluetooth. It was made possible by the introduction of brickmaking to Denmark—it is made up of more than 3 million bricks—and a commission by the powerful Bishop Absalon, who's also considered one of the founders of Copenhagen. The cathedral made the city one of the spiritual capitals of northern Europe. These days, its best known as the mausoleum of the royals: 38 Danish monarchs are entombed here, including the first Queen Margrethe (1353–1412), and there's reason to believe that Queen Margrethe II will ultimately find her resting place in or near the cathedral, like her father, Frederik IX. Don't miss the 16th-century clock depicting St. George charging a dragon, whose hisses and howls throughout the church cause Peter Døver, "the Deafener," to sound the hour. A squeamish Kirsten Kiemer, "the Chimer," shakes her head in fright but manages to strike the quarter hours. ⊠ *Domkirkestræde 10* ☎ *46/35–16–24* ⊕ *roskildedomkirke.dk* 🎫 *DKr 60.*

Vikingeskibsmuseet (*Viking Ship Museum*)

MUSEUM | Less than 1 km (½ mile) north of the cathedral, on the fjord, is the modern Viking Ship Museum, containing five Viking ships sunk in the fjord 1,000 years ago. Submerged to block the passage of enemy ships, they were discovered in 1957. The painstaking recovery involved building a watertight dam and then draining the water from that section of the fjord. The splinters of wreckage were then preserved and reassembled. A deep-sea trader, warship, ferry, merchant ship, and fierce 92½-foot man-of-war attest to the Vikings' sophisticated and artful boat-making skills. ⊠ *Vindeboder 12* ☎ *46/30–02–00* ⊕ *www.vikingeskibsmuseet.dk* 🎫 *DKr 110–150.*

 **Restaurants**

Raadhuskælderen

$$ | **SCANDINAVIAN** | The basement of city hall, near the cathedral, houses this charming and popular café-restaurant with exposed brick walls, curved white ceilings, and low lights. The dinner menu features French Danish dishes and various cuts of beef and lamb grilled on a lava-rock barbecue. **Known for:** open-face sandwiches; cake and coffee; a courtyard

Rock On 🎫

Roskilde Festival At the end of June, Roskilde hosts one of Europe's biggest rock and pop music gatherings, the Roskilde Festival. Some 100,000 people show up every year to see the world's biggest names play outdoors. ⊕ *www.roskilde-festival.dk.*

with town views. **$** *Average main: DKr 188* ⊠ *Fondens Bro 1* ☎ *46/36–01–00* ⊕ *www.raadhuskaelderen.dk* ☾ *Closed Sun.*

Store Børs

$$ | **SEAFOOD** | Located on the Roskilde Harbor, this seafood restaurant has views of the Roskilde Cathedral. Menus here change monthly; its seven-course Torve Taste menu, with matching wines, represents the best of each season. **Known for:** house-smoked salmon and housemade cheese; fresh herbs from the restaurant's own garden; locally brewed Gourmetbryggeriet beer pairings. **$** *Average main: DKr 195* ⊠ *Havnevej 43* ☎ *46/32–50–45* ⊕ *www.store-bors.dk* ☾ *Closed Mon. No dinner Sun.*

🛏 **Hotels**

⭐ Zleep Hotel Roskilde

$$ | **HOTEL** | Licensed since 1695, this hotel in the heart of Roskilde is one of Denmark's oldest, though technically it closed down temporarily in 2015 until it was reopened by a new owner. **Pros:** superb location in the middle of the pedestrian shopping street; good service; historic building. **Cons:** rooms and bathrooms are small; some street noise; busy on weekends. **$** *Rooms from: DKr 1029* ⊠ *Algade 13* ☎ *70/23–56–35* ⊕ *www.zleep.com/da/hotel/roskilde* 🛏 *73 rooms* ⦿ *Free Breakfast.*

Møn

122 km (75 miles) south of Copenhagen.

The island of Møn makes for a wonderful side trip from Copenhagen, especially in summer. Its main attraction is the white chalk cliffs along the coast, some of the most dramatic nature Denmark has to offer. The local beaches are unspoiled and uncrowded. Hikers will enjoy its network of trails, bird watchers can observe local and migrating specimens, and lovers of wild orchids will find the greatest selection in all of Denmark. Although it has fewer than 12,000 year-round inhabitants, Møn comes alive in summer, with vacationers from around Europe attracted to its holiday cottages.

GETTING HERE AND AROUND

You can reach Møn by car across bridges linking it to Zealand and the nearby island of Falster. It's about a 90-minute drive from Copenhagen. There's no direct train link to Møn: you must take a train to Falster and then switch to a bus.

VISITOR INFORMATION

CONTACTS House of Møn. ⊠ *Storegade 2, Stege* ☎ *52/24–63–88* ⊕ *www.sydkystdanmark.dk.*

👁 Sights

GeoCenter Møns Klint

MUSEUM | FAMILY | While in town, you may want to join the Danish families hunting for fossils at the base of Møns Klint. Then have your fossils identified at the GeoCenter Møns Klint, a spectacular natural history museum with aquariums, interactive exhibits, and a *Mosasaurus* skeleton. ⊠ *Stengårdvej 8, Borre* ☎ *55/86–36–00* ⊕ *www.moensklint.dk* 🚗 *DKr 145* 🕙 *Closed Nov.–Sat. before Easter.*

★ Møns Klint

NATURE SITE | The island of Møn is most famous for its dramatic chalk cliffs, known in Danish as Møns Klint. Circled by a beech forest, the milky-white bluffs

plunge 400 feet to a small, craggy beach with jade-green waters—accessible by more than 500 steps. Fossils on the beach suggest that the cliffs are 70 million years old. The cliffs attract tens of thousands of visitors each year, who come for the views and to be close to nature. ■ TIP→ **Visit on a sunny day if you can, and park at the top of the cliff and walk down.** ⊠ *Borre* 🚗 *Free.*

🍴 Restaurants

Bryghuset Møn

$$ | CAFÉ | This café-restaurant serves its own beer produced on the premises, with up to six varieties on tap and many more bottled. The café serves sandwiches and a popular fresh-vegetable-laden "brewery burger." A quality carvery buffet, with freshly sliced roasted meats and salads, and an a la carte menu are available in the restaurant. **Known for:** beautiful view of the fjord from the dining room; big selection of home-brewed beers; gourmet burgers, cakes, and gastropub dishes. $ *Average main: DKr 199* ⊠ *Priorsvej 1, Stege* ☎ *55/81–20–00* ⊕ *www.bryghusetmoen.dk* 🕙 *Closed Sun.–Tues.*

David's

$$ | SCANDINAVIAN | FAMILY | At this charming café with a garden patio, the kitchen satisfies its many patrons with delicious Danish French dishes. Brunch is served daily, as are a good variety of sandwiches, tapas, vegetarian options, warm dishes like quiche Lorraine and soups, and children's plates. **Known for:** great lunches; loyal local following; French-inspired plates of cheese and charcuterie. $ *Average main: DKr 100* ⊠ *Storegade 11, Stege* ☎ *33/13–80–57* ⊕ *www.davids.nu.*

🛏 Hotels

Bakkegård Gæstgiveri

$ | B&B/INN | FAMILY | Between the views of the Baltic Sea and the Klinteskov

Forest, this small hotel farm dating from 1910 offers the best of the island. **Pros:** lots of comfortable common areas; nice views; accessible by bus. **Cons:** rooms have sinks, but toilets and baths are shared; more accessible if you have your own transport; sells out in peak season. [$] *Rooms from: DKr 600* ✉ *Busenevej 64, Borre* ☎ *55/81–93–01* 🌐 *www.bakkegaarden64.dk* 💳 *No credit cards* 🛏 *16 rooms* 🍴 *Free Breakfast.*

Hotel Præstekilde

$ | HOTEL | On a small island, this hotel has a splendid view of Stege Bay from the middle of the golf course. **Pros:** a bus comes to the hotel's door every day; golf, hiking, and biking opportunities; great location for walks. **Cons:** rooms are small and simple; about 5 km (3 miles) from shopping; busy during summer season. [$] *Rooms from: DKr 690* ✉ *Klintevej 116, Keldby* ☎ *55/86–87–88* 🌐 *www.praestekilde.dk* 🕒 *Closed Oct.–Mar.* 🛏 *46 rooms* 🍴 *Free Breakfast.*

Bornholm

156 km (97 miles) from Copenhagen, by way of Sweden.

Bornholm is a far cry from the rest of Denmark, geographically as well as culturally. With its eastern location (the island lies closer to to Sweden and Germany than the rest of Denmark), rugged beauty, and local traditions, flag, and dialect, it feels a bit like visiting a separate country. The island used to be a sleepy former fisherman's island with dropping population rates, but the last decade has seen it transform into one of Denmark's most beloved and hyped vacation spots. Copenhagen's creative elite flock to vacation houses in the pretty villages that dot the coast. Traditional smokehouses and Michelin restaurants vie for the attention and appetite of locals as well as visitors. The island's nature is more mountainous and wild than the rest of the country's, and the beaches—and cliffs—are perfect for swimming.

Though the island is home to beautiful forests and lakes, most visitors base themselves in one of the coastal villages; Allinge and Svaneke are the most lively of the lot. Ferries and flights arrive in Rønne, the island's capital. Off the coast you'll find Christiansø, a tiny island home to historical buildings that is a popular day-trip from Bornholm.

GETTING HERE AND AROUND

Though Bornholm is closer to Sweden and Germany than the Danish mainland, it's relatively cheap and easy to visit the island. If you're driving, take the Øresundsbro to Sweden and drive to Ystad; from there, you can take the ferry to Bornholm. The trip takes around three hours. The Øresundsbro costs DKr 450, and the ferry from Ystad costs as little as DKr 149 for a small car with one passenger, if you book in advance. The cheapest and fastest way to get to Bornholm if you don't have a car is to take a bus to Ystad and then the ferry to Bornholm; several bus companies sell a ticket that combines the two, starting at DKr 100. It's also possible to fly, which takes around half an hour.

CONTACTS Bornholmslinjen. ☎ *70/90–01–00* 🌐 *www.bornholmslinjen.dk.* **Danish Air Traffic (DAT).** 🌐 *dat.dk.*

VISITOR INFO

Feriøen Bornholm. ✉ *Nordre Kystvej 3, Rønne* ☎ *56/95–95–00* 🌐 *bornholm.info.*

Sights

Allinge-Sandvig

TOWN | United by a stretch of cliffs that are popular to swim from, Allinge and Sandvig used to be two separate coastal towns, but both have grown and they've now joined forces. The towns are home to sandy beaches, small guesthouses, a bustling music venue, and several yacht harbors and smokehouses. There are beautiful walks to take along the cliffy coast north of Sandvig and south of Allinge. ⊠ *Allinge.*

Bornholms Kunstmuseum

MUSEUM | **FAMILY** | Perched atop the dramatic stretch of cliffs called Helligdomsklipperne is this light-filled, white museum with a permanent collection mostly focused on Danish artists with a connection to Bornholm. Though the art is beautiful, the architecture and surroundings are as much of a reason to visit. Make sure to walk down to the coast after visiting the museum; the walk from the museum to Gudhjem is one of Bornholm's most spectacular, and you can get aboard the lovely M/S *Thor,* which cruises between Gudhjem and Helligdomsklipperne in the summer months, and sail back. ⊠ *Otto Bruuns Pl. 1, Gudhjem* ☎ *56/48–43–86* ⊕ *bornholms-kunstmuseum.dk* ⊠ *DKr 90* ⊗ *Closed Mon.–Wed. Nov.–Mar. and Mon. in Sept., Oct., Apr., and May.*

★ Hammershus and Hammerknudden

ARCHAEOLOGICAL SITE | **FAMILY** | Hammerknuden, the northernmost tip of Bornholm is home to the island's most dramatic cliffs and some stunning coastal walks and also to northern Europe's biggest fortress ruin, Hammershus. The medieval fortress is perched atop a windy cliff with views of the Baltic Sea, and it's the perfect crowning of a walk around the coast. Close to the ruin you'll find Opalsøen, a jade-green lake in a former granite quarry. It's popular for swimming, and the brave try the 8-meter (26-foot) cliffside jump. Scale the steep hill behind the lake to access a heath-clad area where sheep graze between lighthouses. The top of the island offers stunning view of Hammershus and a beautiful walk around the tip of Bornholm and back into charming Sandvig. ⊠ *Langebjergvej 26* ☎ *56/48–11–40* ⊠ *Free.*

Svaneke

TOWN | **FAMILY** | This town is known for its pretty houses, which are dressed in hollyhocks and painted the same shade of yellow. The area between the bustling harbor and the small main square is packed with ice cream parlors, cute cafés, small restaurants, design shops, and a number of artisan candy shops producing everything from caramel to licorice. There's also a brewery with a restaurant and a very ambitious and creative bakery with a flower shop attached to it. Walk south through the idyllic streets and pass the lighthouse to reach a small beach, a peaceful camping spot, and one of Denmark's best beach bars. ⊠ *Svaneke.*

⊕ Beaches

Dueodde

BEACH—SIGHT | **FAMILY** | Bornholm's most famous beach is known for its blinding, fine-grained sand, which you reach after walking through a beautiful pine forest. The sand is easily moved by the wind, and the beach is made up of an ever-changing landscape of shifting dunes as well as a wide, windswept area leading down to the coast. The beach stretches for 30 km (19 miles) without interruption, and it's popular year-round with beachgoers, picnickers, and dog walkers. **Amenities:** lifeguards, parking (no fee). **Best for:** solitude, swimming, walking, sunrise, sunset. ⊠ *Skrokkegårdsvejen 17, Snogebæk.*

⊕ Restaurants

Bornholm's culinary game is strong, whether it comes to traditional smokehouses or groundbreaking, contemporary restaurants. There's a small smokehouse in almost every coastal city, and plenty of ice cream parlors, cafés, and restaurants too.

★ Kadeau

$$$$ | SCANDINAVIAN | Located in the sand dunes on the idyllic southern stretch of the island, this New Nordic disciple serves Michelin-starred dishes with a strong focus on local produce. It looks like a traditional Danish summer house, but the food is anything but traditional; the lofty ambitions and equally high culinary capabilities of the young chefs have made it one of Denmark's most daring, darling restaurants. **Known for:** beautiful location on sandy beach; ambitious, creative dishes; good wine list. $ Average main: DKr 1550 ⊠ Baunevej 18, Aakirkeby ☎ 56/97–82–50 ⊕ www.kadeau.dk ⊗ Closed late Oct.–mid-Apr.

★ Kalas Bornholm

$ | SCANDINAVIAN | Bornholm's ice cream game is strong, with several artisanal producers, but this family-run ice cream parlor and café takes the prize. That's because of both the ice cream—organic milk from Bornholm is paired with local fruit, berries, and herbs—and the location in a former smokehouse located directly on the coast with a beautiful view of the sea and cliffs. **Known for:** creative ice creams; good coffee and some cocktails; reputation as a friendly, family-run place. $ Average main: DKr 37 ⊠ Strandpromenaden 14, Allinge ☎ 60/19–13–84 ⊕ kalasbornholm.dk ⊗ Closed late Oct.–early Apr.; shop closed Sun.–Tues. yearround.

Nordbornholms Røgeri

$$ | SCANDINAVIAN | FAMILY | Locals get into heated arguments about which smokehouse on Bornholm is the best, but most can agree that Nordbornholms Røgeri, with its great views of the sea and an idyllic beach, is one of the best. The buffet—featuring smoked, baked, fried, and fresh fish—is popular, but you also can also order a la carte dishes. **Known for:** big fish and seafood buffet; great location; fairly cheap prices. $ Average main: DKr 100 ⊠ Kæmpestranden 2, Allinge ☎ 56/48–07–30 ⊕ nbr.dk/en.

🛏 Hotels

★ Hullehavn Campingplads

$ | RENTAL | FAMILY | Bornholm has been blessed with a number of prime camping spots, many of them located directly on the beach. **Pros:** located on the beach; most tents will have sea view; good facilities. **Cons:** short walk from Svaneke; gets busy in peak season; some tents will not have direct views of the sea. $ Rooms from: DKr 89 ⊠ Sydskovvej 9, Svaneke ☎ 56 /49–63–63 ⊕ hullehavn.dk ⇌ camping site ¶O¶ No meals.

Melsted Badehotel

$$$ | HOTEL | Located in a quiet cove just south of the pretty but touristy coastal town Gudhjem, this white-washed beach hotel is a haven of peace and style. **Pros:** beautiful location on the beach; great restaurant; quiet and close to nature. **Cons:** 15-minute walk to Gudhjem; far from other restaurants; closes down in the winter. $ Rooms from: DKr 1575 ⊠ Melstedvej 27, Gudhjem ☎ 56/48–51–00 ⊕ melsted-badehotel.dk ⊗ Closed in the winter (except around Christmas) ⇌ 21 rooms ¶O¶ Free Breakfast.

★ Nordlandet

$$$ | HOTEL | Perched atop the cliff that separates Allinge from Sandvig, this contemporary hotel boasts grand views of the Baltic Sea, one of Bornholm's best restaurants (Pony X Nordlandet), and bright, airy rooms and apartments dressed in a mix of classic and contemporary designer furniture. **Pros:** great sea views; excellent restaurant and hotel bar; location at the meeting point between Allinge and Sandvig. **Cons:** not all rooms are in the main building; café and bar can be busy with non-guests; pricey. $ Rooms from: DKr 1290 ⊠ Strandvejen 68, Allinge ☎ 56/48–03–44 ⊕ hotelnordlandet.com ⊗ Closed Jan.–Mar., Mon.–Wed. in Apr., and Mon. and Tues. Oct.–Dec. ⇌ 27 rooms ¶O¶ Free Breakfast.

▼ Nightlife

★ Gæstgiveren

MUSIC CLUBS | Though only open for six weeks every summer, Gæstgiveren–called "Gæsten" by everyone, including the owners–has become a fixture on Bornholm's nightlife scene. The venue has become known for hosting Denmark's biggest names—including superstars like Mø and Lukas Graham—in the idyllic courtyard garden. Before the concerts there's a buffet with tasty organic meat, poultry, fish, and salads, and after the shows, the bar is a popular place for a drink. On concert nights the party continues at Pilen, a pub across the road from Gæsten. ⊠ *Theaterstræde 2* ☎ *56/44–62–30* ⊕ *gaestgiveren.dk.*

★ Provianten

BARS/PUBS | This cozy harbor-front café is a gathering point for locals throughout the year and is popular with tourists in the summer. There are also a few daily dishes, a good selection of organic wine, beer, and alcohol-free drinks, and a long list of delicious bar snacks. You can buy wines to go, but it'd be a shame to miss the action of Gudhjem's busy harbor. ⊠ *Ejnar Mikkelsensvej 28, Gudhjem* ☎ *21/68–00–19.*

Odense

20 km (12 miles) southwest of Ladby on Rte. 165, 144 km (90 miles) west of Copenhagen.

Odense, the capital of Funen and Denmark's third-largest city, is reminiscent of a storybook village—perhaps because much of its charm is built on the legend of its most famous son, author Hans Christian Andersen. The historical half-timbered houses and the fairy-tale charm are only part of the city, though, and locals pride themselves on its more contemporary aspects, such as the art museum and the gastronomic scene.

The town is named after another famous Scandinavian, Odin, the king of the Nordic gods.

GETTING HERE AND AROUND

Direct trains from Copenhagen's main station depart for the 75-minute trip to Odense every half hour and cost DKr 282. You also can take the train to Odense directly from Copenhagen airport. The Odense station is central, close to hotels and sights. If you're traveling from Copenhagen to Odense by car, you'll want to take E20 heading west. If you're traveling from the north or south of Denmark, take E45.

FlixBus runs the only bus service connecting Copenhagen and Odense. The ride takes approximately two hours and costs DKr 79. It travels more than a dozen times a day, heading in both directions. FynBus runs the bus system within Odense. You can rent bikes through City Cykler in Odense or at several hotels.

TOURS

CONTACTS Odense Aafart. ☎ *66/10–70–80* ⊕ *www.aafart.dk.*

VISITOR INFO

The Odense tourist office has a helpful map of cycle routes in and around Odense.

CONTACTS VisitOdense. ☎ *63/75–75–20* ⊕ *www.visitodense.com.*

◉ Sights

★ Brandts

MUSEUM | Occupying a former textile factory, this four-story building is home to one of Denmark's best—and first—museums of art and visual culture, an educational center specializing in the same subjects, and an art bookstore with a wide range of books. National and international exhibits shown here vary widely, but there's a focus on photography and visual art. ⊠ *Amfipladsen 7 ✛ North of the river and parallel to Kongensgade* ☎ *65/20–70–00* ⊕ *www.*

brandts.dk 🎟 *DKr 95, free Thurs. evening* 🕒 *Closed Mon.*

★ H. C. Andersen Museum

MUSEUM | This museum tells the story of Hans Christian Andersen's life through 32,000 items related to the Danish author, from his vintage travel suitcases to his top hat, handwritten manuscripts, and poetic paper cuttings. The museum is a temporary holdover until a new museum and garden, designed by the Japanese architect Kengo Kuma, will open in 2020. Ticket price includes one-day admission to five Hans Christian Andersen attractions. ✉ *Claus Bergs Gade 11* ☎ *65/51–46–01* 🌐 *hcandersensodense.dk* 🎟 *DKr 125–135* 🕒 *Closed Mon.*

H. C. Andersens Barndomshjem (*Hans Christian Andersen's Childhood Home*)

MUSEUM | In Hans Christian Andersen's childhood home, where he lived in the early 1800s, the young boy and his parents lived in three tiny rooms. The rooms are outfitted with rustic, period furnishings (chairs, lamps, a table) and little else. Ticket price includes one-day admission to five Hans Christian Andersen attractions. ✉ *Møntestræde 1* ☎ *65/51–46–01* 🌐 *hcandersensodense.dk* 🎟 *DKr 125–135* 🕒 *Closed Mon.*

★ H. C. Andersens Hus (*Hans Christian Andersen's Birthplace*)

MUSEUM | If you walk east on Østre Stationsvej to Thomas B. Thriges Gade and Hans Jensens Stræde, you'll come to the Hans Christian Andersen's Birthplace. The house clearly depicts the poverty the author-to-be was born into, though it now sits in an idyllic location amid half-timbered houses and cobbled streets. Ticket price includes one-day admission to five Hans Christian Andersen attractions. ✉ *Hans Jensens Stræde 45* ☎ *65/51–46–01* 🌐 *hcandersensodense.dk* 🎟 *DKr 125–135* 🕒 *Closed Mon.*

Sankt Knuds Kirke (*Odense Cathedral*)

RELIGIOUS SITE | Constructed between the 13th and 15th century, this is Denmark's only purely Gothic cathedral. The intricate wooden altar covered with gold leaf was carved by German sculptor Claus Berg. Beneath the sepulcher are the bones of St. (King) Knud, killed during a farmers' uprising in 1086, and his brother. ✉ *Klosterbakken 2* ✥ *Toward pedestrian zone of Skt. Knuds Kirkestræde, in front of Andersen Park* ☎ *66/12–03–92* 🌐 *www.odensedomkirke.dk* 🎟 *Free.*

Vikingemuseet Ladby (*Viking Museum Ladby*)

MUSEUM | The village of Ladby, 16 km (10 miles) east of Odense, is best known as the home of the 1,100-year-old remains of this ship, which belonged to a Viking chieftain and is now the centerpiece of the Viking Museum. The chieftain was buried here, along with the hunting dogs and horses he would need for Valhalla—the afterlife. ✉ *Vikingevej 123, Ladby* ☎ *65/32–16–67* 🌐 *www.vikingemuseetladby.dk* 🎟 *DKr 80* 🕒 *Closed Mon. Sept.–May.*

🍴 Restaurants

Den Gamle Kro

$$ | **FRENCH** | Built within the courtyards of several 17th-century homes, this popular restaurant has walls of ancient stone topped by a sliding glass roof. Though the menu is mostly French, you can still order inexpensive smørrebrød for lunch. **Known for:** open-face sandwiches and other traditional Danish dishes; use of almost exclusively local produce; changing set menus (such as Provence and Fall). [$] *Average main: DKr 225* ✉ *Overgade 23* ☎ *66/12–14–33* 🌐 *www.dengamlekro.eu.*

★ GOMA

$$$ | **JAPANESE** | One of Denmark's best Japanese restaurants is located in Odense, and the omakase menus alone are worth the trip from Copenhagen. Regulars stop by for a single serving of

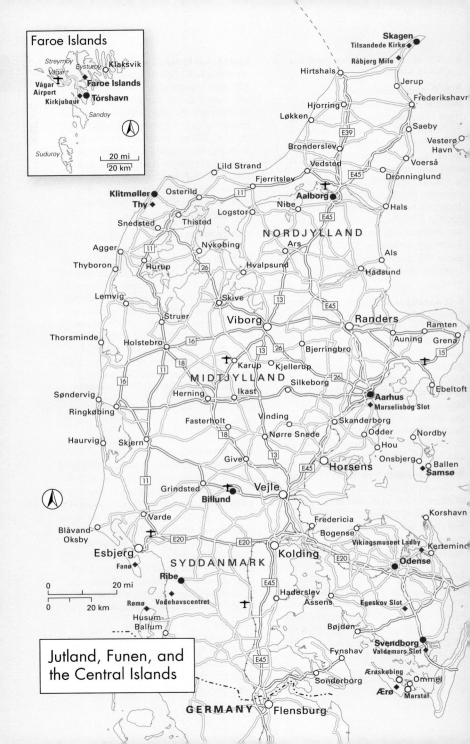

Faroe Islands

Streymoy
Vágar *Eysturoy* Klaksvik
Vágar **Faroe Islands**
Airport
Kirkjubøur ● **Tórshavn**

Sandoy

Suduroy

20 mi
20 km

Skagen
Tilsandede Kirke
Råbjerg Mile
Hirtshals
Jerup
Frederikshavn
Hjørring
Saeby
Løkken
Vesterø
Havn
Bronderslev
Voerså
Vedsted
Dronninglund
Lild Strand
Fjerritslev
Klitmøller
Osterild
Aalborg
Thy
Nibe
Hals
Snedsted
Logstor
Thisted
NORDJYLLAND
Agger
Nykøbing
Ars
Thyboron
Hurup
Hvalpsund
Als
Hadsund
Lemvig
Skive
Struer
Viborg
13
Randers
Ramten
Thorsminde
Holstebro
Bjerringbro
Auning
Grenå
16
Karup
15
11
18
Kjellerup
Ebeltoft
Søndervig
MIDTJYLLAND
Silkeborg
16
Herning
Ikast
Aarhus
Ringkøbing
Marselisbog Slot
Fasterholt
Skanderborg
Haurvig
18
Vinding
Odder
Nordby
Skjern
Nørre Snede
Hou
Onsbjerg
Ballen
Give
13
Horsens
Samsø
11
Grindsted
Vejle
Billund
Korshavn
Varde
Fredericia
Blåvand-
Bogense
Vikingsmuseet Ladby
Oksby
E20
E20
Kertemind
Esbjerg
SYDDANMARK
Kolding
Odense
Fanø
E20
Ribe
E45
Haderslev
Egeskov Slot
Rømø
Assens
Vadehavscentret
Bøjden
Svendborg
Husum-
Valdemars Slot
Ballum
Fynshav
Ærøskøbing
Ommel
Sonderborg
Ærø
Marstal
GERMANY Flensburg

Jutland, Funen, and the Central Islands

0   20 mi
0   20 km

E39
E45
E45
26
26
E45
11
16
13
26
18
13
11
E20
E45

sushi or for the all-evening chef's menu—or just for a late-night drink and dessert.
Known for: omakase menus; creative gin cocktails; relaxed atmosphere. $ *Average main: DKr 335* ✉ *Kongensgade 66–68* ☎ *66/14–45–00* ⊕ *goma.nu* ☾ *Closed Sun. No lunch.*

Restaurant Under Lindetræet
$$$ | EUROPEAN | The snug corner restaurant, situated in the same cozy, cobblestone neighborhood as the Hans Christian Andersen's Birthplace, serves seasonal Italian- and French-inspired dishes using Danish ingredients, such as grilled redfish with boiled potatoes.
Known for: three- and five-course dinner menus; ambitious and creative dishes; the Fairy Tale Menu (the signature of the restaurant). $ *Average main: DKr 545* ✉ *Ramsherred 2* ☎ *66/12–92–86* ⊕ *www. underlindetraet.dk* ☾ *Closed Mon. No lunch Tues.–Fri.*

Vår
$$$ | MODERN EUROPEAN | The six tables at Vår are a popular place to get a taste of Funen, as the small restaurant uses only organic produce from local farms. You can opt for either five or ten small dishes, such as scallops with buckwheat, zucchini, and peas, and pair them with organic and natural wines from Europe. **Known for:** organic produce from Funen; natural wines; casual atmosphere and informal service. $ *Average main: DKr 550* ✉ *Vintapperstræde 10* ☎ *26/49–26–44* ⊕ *vaar. dk* ☾ *Closed Sun.–Tues. No lunch.*

🛏 Hotels

First Hotel Grand Odense
$$ | HOTEL | More than a century old, with renovated fin-de-siècle charm, this imposing four-story, brick-front hotel greets guests with old-fashioned luxury.
Pros: close to Odense attractions and the train; atmospheric hotel bar; good breakfast buffet. **Cons:** not recommended for people with disabilities; pricey drinks; small fitness area. $ *Rooms from: DKr*

1050 ✉ *Jernabanegade 18* ☎ *66/11–71–71* ⊕ *www.firsthotels.com* ⊃ *135 rooms* ⦿ *Free Breakfast.*

★ Hotel Odeon
$$$ | HOTEL | This sleek, new design hotel with big rooms, plush beds, an atmospheric bar, and a lounge area with an open fireplace has quickly become popular with business travelers and vacationers alike. **Pros:** close to the train station in the city center; well-designed rooms with big beds; good restaurant. **Cons:** relatively pricey; construction in the surrounding area; lacks historical charm. $ *Rooms from: DKr 1325* ✉ *Odeons Kvarter 11* ☎ *65/42–05–00* ⊕ *hotelodeon. dk* ⊃ *234 rooms* ⦿ *Free Breakfast.*

Milling Hotel Plaza
$$ | HOTEL | A five-minute walk from the train station, this stately hotel dates from 1915 and overlooks Odense's leafy central park, Kongens Have. **Pros:** seven suites; charming park view; good restaurant at the hotel. **Cons:** some rooms are noisy; some rooms are dusty; in need of renovation. $ *Rooms from: DKr 979* ✉ *Østre Stationsvej 24* ☎ *66/11–77–45* ⊕ *millinghotels.dk* ⊃ *75 rooms* ⦿ *Free Breakfast.*

Radisson Blu–H. C. Andersen Hotel
$$ | HOTEL | Around the corner from Hans Christian Andersen's Birthplace, this blocky brick conference hotel has a plant-filled lobby and rooms done in shades of red and yellow. **Pros:** close to top attractions; casino; adjacent to concert hall. **Cons:** lacks charm; no single rooms; construction noise in the area. $ *Rooms from: DKr 875* ✉ *Claus Bergs Gade 7* ☎ *66/14–78–00* ⊕ *www.radissonhotels. com* ⊃ *145 rooms* ⦿ *Free Breakfast.*

🍸 Nightlife

Odense's central arcade is an entertainment mall, with bars, restaurants, and a variety of live music. Lately, smaller, more intimate bars have opened up, many of them with a focus on wine or cocktails.

BARS
⭐ Lalou
WINE BARS—NIGHTLIFE | Everything about this gem of a wine bar is ambitious, from the wines to the bar snacks. Order the sardines with pickled lemon or the foie gras terrine with truffle mustard, and settle in. ■**TIP→ Ask the waiter, usually one of the two owners, for recommendations.** ⊠ *Pogestræde 31* ☎ *52/19–35–65* ⊕ *lalouvinbar.dk.*

⭐ S'vineriet Vinapotek
WINE BARS—NIGHTLIFE | There are few places in Denmark better suited for a dark night than this cellar-like wine bar. Let the owners guide you through the eclectic, international, and very fairly priced wine list. For dining, don't miss out on the smoked duck breast, wild swine rillette, or Danish cheese. ■**TIP→ Don't make any plans for immediately after; you'll want to stay for a while.** ⊠ *Klaregade 34–36* ☎ *93/93–17–19* ⊕ *svinerietvinapotek.dk.*

CAFÉS
Café Biografen
CAFES—NIGHTLIFE | For a quiet evening, stop by Café Biografen for an espresso, beer, or light snack, or settle in to see one of the films screened here. ⊠ *Amfipladsen 13* ☎ *66/13–16–16* ⊕ *cafebio.dk.*

Cafe Fleuri
CAFES—NIGHTLIFE | This cutesy café is a mixture of Provençal charm and Danish retro design. You can have a light, organic lunch, a sumptuous piece of cake, or a cup of coffee amid the plants, pottery, and cozy tables, or buy local delicacies to go. ⊠ *Nørregade 28* ☎ *23/63–93–30* ⊕ *fleuri.dk.*

JAZZ CLUBS
Dexter
MUSIC CLUBS | Dexter has all kinds of jazz—from Dixieland to fusion—as well as blues, rock, world, and folk music. ⊠ *Vindergade 65* ☎ *63/11–27–28* ⊕ *www.dexter.dk.*

Grøntorvet Café and Bar
MUSIC CLUBS | There's live jazz here the first Saturday of every month. ⊠ *Sortebrødre Torv 9* ☎ *63/12–33–00.*

🛍 Shopping

Odense's compact city center has clothing, furniture, and shoe stores and a Magasin department store. The main shopping strips are Vestergade and Kongensgade. Rosengårdcentret, one of northern Europe's largest malls, is 5 km (3 miles) west of Odense. It has more than 150 shops and food outlets but lacks local charm. At the Brandts museum you can buy art books, prints, and other arty accessories.

Denmark is well known for its paper cutouts, inspired, in part, by Hans Christian Andersen. Using a small pair of scissors and white paper, he would create cutouts to illustrate his fairy tales. Today replicas of Andersen's cutouts are sold at several Odense gift stores. Also popular are mobiles, often depicting Andersen-inspired themes like swans and mermaids. Uniquely Danish—and light on the suitcase—they make great gifts to take home.

Klods Hans
GIFTS/SOUVENIRS | This store opened just after World War II to cater to all the American soldiers on leave who wanted to bring back Danish gifts. It's still jam-packed with mobiles, cutouts, and Danish flags and dolls. ⊠ *Hans Jensens Stræde 34* ☎ *66/11–09–40.*

Svendborg

45 km (30 miles) from Odense.

With a rich maritime history, a charming, cobblestoned historic center, and a location making it the starting point for island hopping in the South Funen Archipelago, Svendborg is one of Denmark's most atmospheric towns. Spend a day or two exploring the town, the strait, and the nearby castles before heading south to Ærø, Tåsinge, or the even smaller islands.

GETTING HERE AND AROUND

There are several direct trains every hour from Odense to Svendborg, taking 40 minutes and costing 79 DKr. Exploring the area around the town is best done by bike or car; it's possible to rent both at multiple locations throughout the town. From Svendborg you can take ferries to nearby islands such as Ærø.

VISITOR INFORMATION

There's a helpful tourist information office in an old warehouse at the harbor.

CONTACTS Svendborg Tourist Information. ✉ *Havnepladsen 2, Svendborg* ☎ *62/23–69–51* 🌐 *www.visitsvendborg.dk.*

Sights

★ **Egeskov Slot** (*Egeskov Castle*)
CASTLE/PALACE | **FAMILY** | There are castles, and then there are castles. With its Renaissance main building, impressive moat, delicate spires, gigantic garden, and even grander knight's hall, Egeskov is one of Europe's most extraordinary buildings. After losing yourself in the grand halls, leave time for tree-top walking and exploring the forest, as well as for perusing the exhibitions about classic cars, historic dresses, and airplanes. The castle is home to the yearly Heartland Festival, which brings together Denmark's creative elite for three days of contemporary art and music, intellectual debates, and fine dining. ✉ *Egeskovgade 18, Kværndrup* ✣ *Roughly halfway between Odense and Svendborg* ☎ *62/27–10–16* 🌐 *www.egeskov.dk* 🎫 *Park, exhibitions, and castle DKr 229.*

★ **M/S Helge**
MARINA | The real star of Svendborg is the strait the town is located on, and the best way to explore it is by getting aboard the classic ship M/S *Helge*. Onboard, you'll cruise past landing stages, former fisherman's towns, thatched-roof houses, yachtsmen taking their boats out, impossibly green lawns, and idyllic beaches. The tour ends at Valdemars Slot (Valdemar's Castle) before heading back to Svendborg, but you can get on or off board at several landing stages in the strait. The schedule changes seasonally, so check at the tourist office. ✉ *Jessens Mole 5, Svendborg* ☎ *62/23–30–80* 🌐 *www.svendborg-havn.dk* 🎫 *DKr 70–140, depending on length of trip.*

★ **Valdemars Slot** (*Valdemar's Castle*)
CASTLE/PALACE | One of Denmark's best-preserved castles is located on the island of Tåsinge, immediately south of Svendborg. There's a restaurant, a tea pavilion, an orchard to get lost in, and several stately buildings to explore. The castle was built in the 17th century for a Danish prince, but it now belongs to a wealthy family. ✉ *Slotsalléen 100, Troense* ☎ *62/22–61–06* 🌐 *valdemarsslot.dk* 🎫 *DKr 120* 🕒 *Closed Mon.*

Restaurants

Svendborg is home to a combination of contemporary and traditional restaurants, most of them located along the harbor and in the cobblestoned streets of the historic center.

Bendixens Fiskehandel
$ | **SEAFOOD** | **FAMILY** | This fishmonger doubles as a lunch spot. Whether you're in the mood for smoked salmon and oysters to go or fried fish fillet with fries on the harbor, you'll find it at this beloved local institution. **Known for:** big selection of fish and shellfish; harborside setting; knowledgeable sales assistants. [$] *Average main: DKr 50* ✉ *Jessens Mole 2, Svendborg* ☎ *62/21–18–75* 🌐 *www.bendixens-fiskehandel.dk* 🕒 *Closed Sun.*

★ **Resumé**
$$$ | **MODERN EUROPEAN** | This small restaurant draws a full house almost every night with its New Nordic–inspired

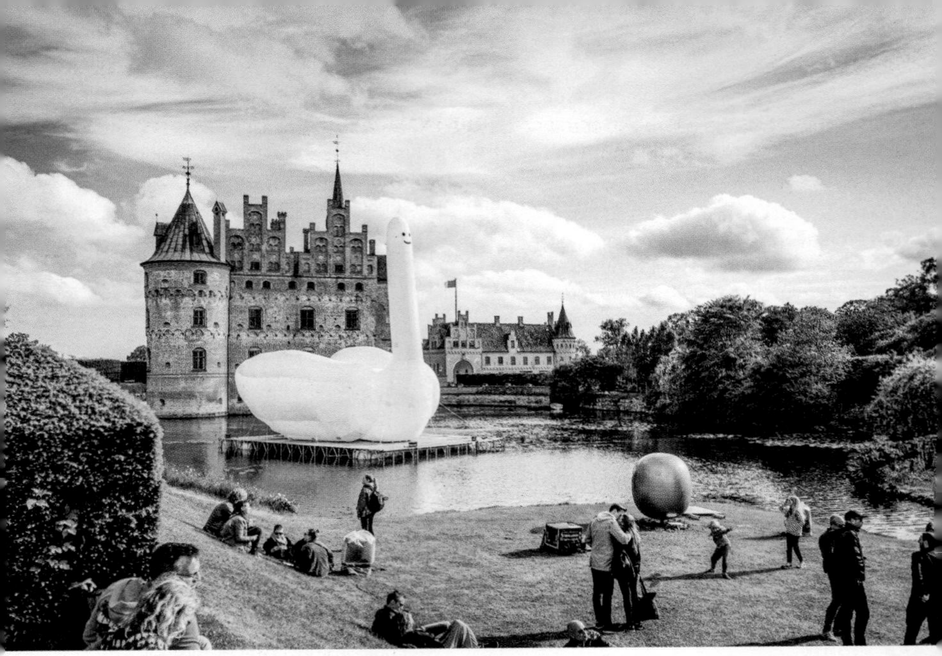

Egeskov is famous for being the best preserved moat castle in Europe and for its three-day Heartland festival in May.

prix-fixe menu. You will start out with a selection of creative snacks; continue with starters like burned salmon with a sauce of fermented cucumber, avocado, and salt-pickled lemon; have duck prepared in several ways with new carrots as a main; and finish off with a dessert of pears with rosemary cream. **Known for:** assortment of creative starters; using local ingredients; prix-fixe menu that includes wine. [$] *Average main: DKr 500* ✉ *Møllergade 35A, Svendborg* ☎ *60/38–86–42* 🌐 *www.restaurantresume.dk* 🕒 *Closed Sun. and Mon. No lunch.*

Hotels

Hotel Ærø
$$ | **HOTEL** | Svendborg's most atmospheric hotel is located on the harbor, and the maritime setting is mirrored in the beautiful but dated decor. **Pros:** harborside setting; oozes old-school charm; popular restaurant and bar. **Cons:** some rooms can be noisy; breakfast can be underwhelming; some rooms are dark. [$] *Rooms from: DKr 850* ✉ *Brogade 1–3, Svendborg* ☎ *62/21–07–60* 🌐 *hotelaeroe.dk* 🛏 *58 rooms* 🍴 *Free Breakfast.*

Hotel Christiansminde
$$ | **HOTEL** | **FAMILY** | This hotel is located on a beach a bit away from the heart of town, but the walk there, along the pretty coast, is worth the visit in itself. **Pros:** located on a beautiful beach; big breakfast buffet; free bike rental. **Cons:** decor is slightly dated; 20-minute walk from town; lacks historic charm. [$] *Rooms from: DKr 900* ✉ *Christiansmindevej 16, Svendborg* ☎ *62/21–90–00* 🌐 *christiansminde.dk* 🛏 *98 rooms* 🍴 *Free Breakfast.*

Nightlife

★ **Hansted**
BARS/PUBS | With live music, friendly bartenders, and a big assortment of beer, Hansted has long been a favorite of locals, which means it's a good hangout for visitors, too. Stop by for the concerts, quiz nights, or talks, and stay around for the chance to strike up friendly chatter

with locals. ⊠ *Vestergade 2A, Svendborg* ☎ *62/21–21–70* ⊕ *www.hansted.nu.*

Strandbar and Kammerateriet

BARS/PUBS | Frederiksø is a tiny island with an industrial past, and it's floating in Svendborg's harbor. There are several music venues, bars, and museums, but the most popular place to go for a drink is Strandbar, a beach bar with Berlin-like, laid-back vibes. It's run by the music venue Kammerateriet and only open during summer months; the music venue, however, is home to concerts year-round. ⊠ *Frederiksø 2, Svendborg* ☎ *70/50–57–00* ⊕ *kammerateriet.com.*

Ærø

77 km (47 miles) from Odense.

This jewel of an island is located in the heart of the South Funen Archipelago. It's the ideal starting point for an island-hopping exhibition, but chances are you'll never leave; the bustling harbors, friendly locals, cobblestoned streets, and half-timbered, thatched-roof houses—not to mention the beautiful beaches with their colorful beach houses— make it easy to stay. Small towns dot the coast, but most people base themselves in either Ærøskøbing or Marstal. There's a web of bike routes and hiking paths around the island's gently rolling hills, as well as free buses criscrossing the island.

GETTING HERE AND AROUND

You need to board a boat to get to Ærø, whether you're bringing a car or not. The most frequent route is between Svendborg and Ærøskøbing (which takes 75 minutes), but there are also ferry connections to Søby and Fynshavn. It costs DKr 224 for a round-trip ticket per person, or DKr 488 if you're traveling with a car. There are cheaper tickets outside of the peak, summer season.

CONTACTS Ærøfærgerne. ☎ *62/52–40–00* ⊕ *aeroe-ferry.dk.*

VISITOR INFORMATION

Ærø Tourism Office. (*Ærø Turist and Erhvervskontor*) ⊠ *Ærøskøbing Havn 4, Ærøskøbing* ☎ *62/52–13–00* ⊕ *www.visitaeroe.com.*

◉ Sights

★ Ærøskøbing

TOWN | Time seems to stand still in Ærø's main town, where the half-timbered houses and cobblestoned, winding streets look exactly like they did a century ago. The heart of town is full of small restaurants, cafés, inns, and galleries, but the harbor and the beach—where a seemingly endless column of charming, colorful beach houses stands guard—beg to be explored too. A quirky museum sheds light on the island's rich maritime history. ⊠ *Ærøskøbing.*

Marstal

TOWN | **FAMILY** | The yacht harbor is the biggest attraction in Marstal, a small town with a long, maritime history. The town itself is not as pretty as Ærøskøbing, but the museum dedicated to documenting the island's seafaring history (Marstal Søfartsmuseum) makes it worth a visit. South of town you'll find Eriks Hale, a narrow tongue of land with beach on either side. The isthmus is home to a long row of incredibly photogenic beach houses, and there's a bathing bridge popular with young families. ⊠ *Marstal.*

Voderup Klint

BEACH—SIGHT | **FAMILY** | These cliffs, leading down to Ærø's southern coast, are some of the most spectacular nature to be found on the island. The grassy, terrace-like giant steps link the rolling hills of Ærø's heartland with one of Denmark's southernmost coastal areas, and it's an excellent place to go for a hike. ⊠ *Mølledamsvej 1, Ærøskøbing* ▣ *Free.*

🍴 Restaurants

Den Gamle Købmandsgaard

$$ | **SCANDINAVIAN** | This combined farmers' market, café, and bar is the main meeting point on the town's central square. Stop by for local products—such as locally produced clothes, pottery, whiskey, soap, mustard, vinegar, or beer—or for a meal in the atmospheric café. **Known for:** local delicacies; traditional dishes; historical atmosphere. [$] *Average main: DKr 100* ✉ *Torvet 5, Ærøskøbing* ☎ *64/81–14–57* 🌐 *dgkshop.com* 🕒 *No dinner.*

The Monica

$$$$ | **EUROPEAN** | This tiny luxury guesthouse, café, and boutique has a certain international flair, perhaps because of the owner's impeccable taste and former life in the fashion world. The small restaurant is styled as a kitchen, the service is warm, and the boutique sells some of Ærø's most stylish garments, shoes, and accessories. **Known for:** tasty homemade cakes; beautiful courtyard and garden; excellent shop. [$] *Average main: DKr 240* ✉ *Brogade 16, Ærøskøbing* ☎ *25/63–09–01* 🌐 *themonica.dk.*

🛏 Hotels

Andelen Guesthouse

$$ | **B&B/INN** | A charming Brit has converted a historic building, which is also home to Denmark's smallest cinema, into a charming guesthouse. **Pros:** charming host and setting; located in the middle of Ærøskøbing; historic details have been preserved. **Cons:** not many rooms to choose from; sells out in advance; more historical charm than modern amenities. [$] *Rooms from: DKr 900* ✉ *Søndergade 28A, Ærøskøbing* ☎ *61/26–75–11* 🌐 *www.andelenguesthouse.com* 🛏 *6 rooms* 🍴 *Free Breakfast.*

★ **Arnfeldt Hotel and Restaurant**

$$$ | **HOTEL** | This small family-run hotel charms with bright rooms set in a beautiful, old half-timbered house in the heart of Ærøskøbing. **Pros:** excellent on-site restaurant; beautiful rooms with preserved historic details; friendly, family-run atmosphere. **Cons:** bathrooms are small (but lovely); must book well in advance; rooms and dinners are pricey. [$] *Rooms from: DKr 1250* ✉ *Smedegade 33, Ærøskøbing* ☎ *62/52–23–00* 🌐 *arnfeldthotel.dk* 🛏 *5 rooms* 🍴 *Free Breakfast.*

Ribe

60 km (36 miles) southwest of Kolding, 150 km (103 miles) southwest of Aarhus.

In the southwestern corner of Jutland, the country's oldest town is well worth the detour for its medieval center preserved by the Danish National Trust. As you stroll around, note the detailed doors and facades of the buildings and the antique streetlights. From May to October (as well as during Easter) a night watchman circles the town, recalling its history and singing traditional songs. If you want to accompany him, gather at the main square at 8 and, in June, July, and August, at 10 pm.

GETTING HERE AND AROUND

From Sønderborg, take Route 41 to Åbenrå, then take E45, followed by Route 429 or Route 24 to Ribe. The drive takes approximately 1½ hours.

From other parts of Denmark, the easiest way to get to Ribe is by train. Take DSB service to Tønder or Esbjerg; if you're coming from Copenhagen or other cities in east Denmark, you'll transfer at Bramming to the Arriva service to Ribe (the trip costs DKr 382 from Copenhagen and takes 3 to 3½ hours).

Once in Ribe, take Sydtrafik Bus 717 to the Viking Center and the 712 to Vadehavscentret in Vester Vedsted. In Vester Vedsted, you can buy the DKr 60 ticket for the so-called tractor buses—run by

Manboebussem and Vadehadffafari—to Mandø, a small, verdant island accessible only at low tide.

VISITOR INFORMATION
CONTACTS Ribe Tourist Office. ✉ *Torvet 3* ☎ *75/42–15–00* ⊕ *www.visitribe.dk.*

Sights

Fanø
ISLAND | FAMILY | In the 19th century, the tiny island of Fanø (30 km [19 miles] northwest of Ribe—plus a 12-minute ferry from Esbjerg) had an enormous shipbuilding industry and a fleet second only to Copenhagen's. The shipping industry deteriorated, but the maritime heritage remains. Today Fanø is a summer oasis for legions of Danes and other northern Europeans. Silky sand beaches unfold along the west coast, buffered by windswept dunes and green reeds. Cars are allowed on the beach, and it's well worth taking a ride along the flat sandy coast between the ferry port in Nordby, Fanø's capital, and the traditional town of Sønderho, 13 km (8 miles) to the south. Spinning along the white sandy expanse is like crossing a desert; only the dark blue sea off in the distance reminds you of your island whereabouts. The beach is so level and wide that the military used to train here. In the off-season, when summer visitors have returned home, the Fanø shore becomes a tranquil retreat, hauntingly silent save for the rustle of reeds and the far-off squawk of a bird.

Museet Ribes Vikinger (*Ribe Viking Museum*)
MUSEUM | FAMILY | The Ribe Viking Museum chronicles Viking history with conventional exhibits of household goods, tools, and clothing. There's a multimedia room with an interactive computer screen where you can search for more Viking information in the form of text, pictures, and videos. ✉ *Odins Pl. 1* ☎ *76/16–39–60* ⊕ *www.ribesvikinger.dk* ✑ *DKr 85* ⊙ *Closed Mon. Sept.–May.*

Ribe Domkirke (*Ribe Cathedral*)
BUILDING | Ribe Cathedral stands on the site of one of Denmark's earliest churches, built around AD 860. The present structure, which dates from the 12th century, is built of a volcanic tufa stone, transported by boats from quarries in Cologne, France. Note the Cat Head Door, said to be for the exclusive use of the devil. The 14th-century brick bell tower once clanged out flood and fire warnings to Ribe's citizens and today affords sweeping views of the town's red-slate rooftops and surrounding marshes. A museum dedicated to the story of the church, as well as to religious life in the area before and after the Reformation, is part of the church. ✉ *Torvet 19* ☎ *75/42–06–19* ⊕ *www.ribe-domkirke.dk* ✑ *DKr 20.*

Ribe VikingeCenter
MUSEUM | FAMILY | This outdoor exhibit, 2 km (1 mile) south of the Ribe railway station, details how the Vikings lived day to day, with demonstrations about homes, food, and crafts. ✉ *Lustrupholm, Lustrupvej 4* ☎ *75/41–16–11* ⊕ *www.ribevikingecenter.dk* ✑ *DKr 130* ⊙ *Closed Nov.–March, Sat.–Tues. in Apr., and Sat. and Sun. in May, June, Sept., and Oct.*

★ Rømø
ISLAND | FAMILY | The lush island of Rømø, 35 km (22 miles) southwest of Ribe, has one of Denmark's widest beaches, which unfurls along a sunny western coast and has protected areas for windsurfers, horseback riders, nudists, and dune-buggy riders—space for everyone, it seems. Rømø has fewer than 600 permanent residents, but masses of vacationing German and Danish families increase this number tenfold in summer. It's a haven for campers, cyclists, and budget vacationers. A causeway crosses green fields and marshy wetlands to connect Rømø to the mainland. Many birds live here, feeding off the seaweed and shellfish washed up by the tides. Summer houses dot the island; most of Rømø's services

and accommodations are in and around the village of Havneby, 8 km (5 miles) south of the causeway, and in the camping and shopping complex of Lakkolk, in the west.

★ **Vadehavscentret** (*Wadden Sea Centre*)
NATURE PRESERVE | FAMILY | The UNESCO World Heritage Site national park is a flat, wet, and large marshland stretching from southern Denmark to the Netherlands. The dynamic landscape is home to many migratory birds and, since 2017, a visitor center designed by the Danish starchitect Bjarke Ingels. The building blends into the flat marshland and has become as much of an attraction as the mudflat area itself. It is home to changing exhibitions, guided tours, acitivities, and teaching programs for schools. ✉ *Okholmvej 5* ☎ *75/44–61–61* 🌐 *www.vadehavscentret.dk* 🎫 *DKr 100* 🕐 *Closed Jan.*

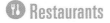

🍴 Restaurants

Sælhunden
$$ | SCANDINAVIAN | FAMILY | The 400-year-old canal-side tavern named after the seals often spotted on the nearby coast can seat up to 60 people, but it feels smaller, and its coziness draws both wayfarers and locals. The only seal mementos left are a few skins and pictures, but you can still order a "seal's special" of cold shrimp, sautéed potatoes, and scrambled eggs. **Known for:** beautiful setting in traditional half-timber house; big selection of open-face sandwiches; cozy, casual atmosphere. [$] *Average main: DKr 179* ✉ *Skibbroen 13* ☎ *75/42–09–46* 🌐 *www.saelhunden.dk.*

🛏 Hotels

Den Gamle Arrest
$$ | HOTEL | Spend the night in the clink at "The Old Jail," a simple, cozy hotel housed in what was Ribe's main jail from 1893 to 1989. **Pros:** historical building; modern, with fun prison twist; location in the center of Ribe. **Cons:** few in-room amenities; restaurant gets mediocre reviews; some rooms are dated. [$] *Rooms from: DKr 790* ✉ *Torvet 11* ☎ *75/42–37–00* 🌐 *www.dengamlearrest.dk* 🛏 *11 rooms* 🍴 *Free Breakfast.*

★ **Hotel Dagmar**
$$ | HOTEL | Originally built in 1581 by a city alderman, the Dagmar became an inn by 1800. **Pros:** well-regarded restaurant; historical hotel; located next to tourist office and cathedral. **Cons:** parking fee DKr 90/day; some rooms are small; pricey for the town. [$] *Rooms from: DKr 1045* ✉ *Torvet 1* ☎ *75/42–00–33* 🌐 *www.hoteldagmar.dk* 🛏 *48 rooms* 🍴 *Free Breakfast.*

Billund

40 km (25 miles) northwest of Kolding, 59 km (37 miles) northeast of Ribe, 101 km (63 miles) southwest of Aarhus.

Billund is the site of Denmark's second-biggest tourist attraction outside Copenhagen: Legoland. The son of the founder of the Lego Company, Godtfred Christiansen, invented the Lego toy brick in Billund in 1949; today the Lego Company employs approximately 19,000 people worldwide. Over the years, the company has manufactured more than 400 billion Lego bricks, all of which trace back to the modest facilities of the family home, which still stands on Main Street here.

Billund has grown exponentially with the Lego success, and today has its own international airport (constructed by the Lego Company and then given to the community) and a large community center (also donated by Lego). However, outside of Legoland there's not much to keep you here—the bank in town is larger than the town hall, and you're in and out of the little metropolis before you know it.

GETTING HERE AND AROUND

Billund Airport is 3 km (2 miles) northeast of downtown. Car rentals are available here, but several buses (43, 119, 143, 166, and 944X) can take you into the city center in approximately 15 minutes. (Bus 406 also runs directly to Kolding.) A free shuttle bus goes to Hotel Legoland. Other buses will take you to Aarhus, Esbjerg, Kolding, Vejle, or Odense.

If you're coming by car from Ribe, follow Route 32 approximately 10 km (6 miles) out of town, then take Route 425 toward Billund Airport. The drive takes approximately 45 minutes.

Sights

★ Legoland

AMUSEMENT PARK/WATER PARK | FAMILY | At Legoland just about everything is constructed from Lego bricks—more than 58 million of them. Among its incredible structures are scaled-down versions of cities and villages from around the world (Miniland), with working harbors and airports; the Statue of Liberty; a statue of Sitting Bull; Mt. Rushmore; a safari park; and Pirate Land.

Some of the park's other attractions are more interactive than the impressive constructions. The Falck Fire Brigade, for example, allows a family or group to race eight mini fire engines. The Power Builder Robots allow children and adults to sit inside robots as they program their own ride. ✉ *Nordmarksvej 9* ☎ *75/33–13–33* 🌐 *www.legoland.dk* 🎫 *DKr 395* 🕒 *Closed early-Nov.–late Mar.*

Hotels

Hotel Legoland

$$$ | HOTEL | FAMILY | It may be a bit pricier than other area hotels, but it is inside Legoland Village, and your room rate includes two days' admission to the park, as well as direct access to the park through the hotel so that you avoid the long lines at the usual entrance. **Pros:** family friendly; activities for kids in summer; access to Legoland included in rates. **Cons:** no in-room safes; rooms near the bar get noisy; pricier than other hotels in the area. [$] *Rooms from: DKr 1375* ✉ *Aastvej 10* ☎ *75/33–12–44* 🌐 *www.legoland.dk* 🛏 *200 rooms* 🍴 *Free Breakfast.*

Hotel Propellen

$$ | HOTEL | Very close to the airport (and to Legoland), this hotel is owned by the Danish Air Pilots Union. **Pros:** sauna; all-you-can-eat ice-cream bar in summer; good for families. **Cons:** few overall amenities for the price; lacks style; far from the city center. [$] *Rooms from: DKr 1000* ✉ *Nordmarksvej 3* ☎ *75/33–81–33* 🌐 *www.propellen.dk* 🛏 *91 rooms* 🍴 *Free Breakfast.*

Aarhus

101 km (63 miles) northeast of Billund.

Aarhus is Denmark's second-largest city. With its world-class art museum, vibrant college community, and vicinity to forests and beaches, it's one of the country's most pleasant cities. Cutting through the center of town is a canal called the Creek, and an amalgam of bars, cafés, and restaurants has sprouted along its banks. The city's pretty Latin Quarter is home to ambitious restaurants, wine bars, coffee shops, designer boutiques, and small galleries, while the neighborhood of Vesterbro is home to a younger, more urban side of the city. At all hours of the day and night the city is abuzz with crowds that hang out on the outdoor terraces of the city's many cafés, bars, and restaurants.

The VisitAarhus tourist office has information about the Aarhus Passport, which includes passage on buses, free or discounted admission to the 12 most popular museums and sites in the city, and tours.

GETTING HERE AND AROUND

AIR

The easiest way to get to Aarhus is by train; the trip to Copenhagen takes less than three hours and costs DKr 383, but if you book well in advance you can get tickets for as little as DKr 109. There are several departures hourly with DSB, and from Aarhus you can take the train onward to towns all across Jutland. There are also frequent buses connecting Aarhus and Copenhagen; FlixBus runs more-than-hourly connections between the two cities for DKr 99, the trip taking around three hours.

Aarhus airport, 45 km (28 miles) northeast of the city, has regular flights to Copenhagen, Göteborg, Stockholm, Oslo, and London, as well as charters to southern Europe. Hourly buses run between Aarhus Airport and the train station in town. The trip takes around 50 minutes and costs DKr 90. There's also bus service (Bus 217) between Aarhus Airport and Randers and Ebeltoft, as well as frequent connections to bigger towns all across Jutland. A taxi ride from the airport to central Aarhus takes 45 minutes and costs well over DKr 500.

BOAT AND FERRY

For direct Zealand-to-Jutland passage, you can take a car-ferry hydrofoil from Zealand's Odden to Aarhus (one hour). You can also take the slower, but less expensive, car ferry from Kalundborg (on Zealand) to Aarhus (2 hours, 40 minutes). Both ferries travel five times daily on weekdays and slightly less often on weekends. For ferry schedules and information, call Molslinjen.

BUS

FlixBus offers the cheapest bus service from Copenhagen to Aarhus, at DKr 99.

CAR TRAVEL

From Copenhagen, follow E20 toward Esbjerg via the Storebælt Bridge (toll DKr 245). At the highway, bear right after Exit 60 Fredericia V and continue on E45 north toward Aarhus/Vejle. Stay on E45 until you reach Aarhus.

CRUISE

Cruise ships dock at Pier 2, a 10-minute walk from the city center. If your ship calls in summer, you may arrive in time for one of Aarhus's many festivals.

TRAIN

The DSB train takes just under three hours and costs DKr 387; if you book well in advance you can get unrefundable, discounted tickets for as little as DKr 109.

VISITOR INFORMATION

CONTACTS VisitAarhus. ⊠ *Store Torv* ☎ *87/31–50–10* ⊕ *www.visitaarhus.com.*

◉ Sights

Aarhus Domkirke (*Aarhus Cathedral*)
RELIGIOUS SITE | Rising gracefully over the center of town, the Aarhus Cathedral was originally built in 1201 in a Romanesque style but was expanded and redesigned into a Gothic cathedral in the 15th century. Its soaring, whitewashed nave is one of the country's longest. The cathedral's highlights include its chalk frescoes in shades of lavender, yellow, red, and black, which grace the high arches and towering walls. Dating from the Middle Ages, they depict biblical scenes and the valiant St. George slaying a dragon and saving a maiden princess in distress. Also illustrated is the martyrdom of St. Clement, who was drowned with an anchor tied around his neck. He became a patron saint of sailors. Climb the tower for bird's-eye views of the rooftops and streets of Aarhus. ⊠ *Store Torv 1* ☎ *86/20–54–00* ⊕ *aarhusdomkirke. dk/english* ⊠ *DKr 20.*

★ **ARoS Aarhus Kunstmuseum**
MUSEUM | A hit from the day it opened in 2004, this museum displays the more than 9,000 artworks dating from 1770 to the present that make up its own, impressive collection, as well as internationally known visiting exhibits.

There are several cafés, a museum shop, and a much-Instagrammed rooftop terrace in the form of a rainbow, an artwork by Olafur Eliasson. ✉ *Aros Allé 2* ☎ *87/30–66–00* 🌐 *www.aros.dk* 🎫 *DKr 20* 🕒 *Closed Mon.*

Den Gamle By (*Old Town*)
MUSEUM VILLAGE | Don't miss the town's open-air museum, known as Den Gamle By. Its 75 historic buildings—including 70 half-timbered houses and a mill—and its millstream were carefully moved from locations throughout Denmark and meticulously re-created, inside and out. ✉ *Viborgvej 2* ☎ *86/12–31–88* 🌐 *www.dengamleby.dk* 🎫 *DKr 135.*

★ **Latin Quarter**
NEIGHBORHOOD | **FAMILY** | Aarhus's historic heart is a jumble of quaint, cobblestoned streets, cute cafés, and colorful houses. Spend at least one day strolling through Graven, Volden, Klostergade, Badstuegade, Borggade, and Rosensgade, whiling away hours at the many coffee shops, designer boutiques, and restaurants in the area. ✉ *Århus.*

★ **Marselisborg Slot** (*Marselisborg Palace*)
GARDEN | Just south of the city is Marselisborg Palace, the summer residence of the royal family. The changing of the guard takes place daily at noon when the queen is here. When the royal family is away (generally in winter and spring), the grounds, including a sumptuous rose garden, are open to the public. It's worth checking out Marselisborg Beach and especially the Infinite Bridge, a circular bridge floating over the water, while in the area. You can get here on Bus 17, 18, or 100. ✉ *Kongevejen 100* 🌐 *www.kongehuset.dk* 🎫 *Free.*

★ **Moesgaard Museum**
MUSEUM | **FAMILY** | Prehistory might not sound exiting to all, but at Moesgaard Museum it's presented in a way that's anything but dusty and dated. The exhibitions are created with care and creativity, but the architectural and natural settings are so stunning that you have to force yourself to focus on the exhibits rather than the forest and sea surrounding the remarkable museum. ✉ *Moesgård Allé 15* ☎ *87/39–40–00* 🌐 *www.moesgaardmuseum.dk* 🎫 *DKr 140* 🕒 *Closed most Mon. Sept.–May.*

🍴 Restaurants

In addition to traditional sit-down restaurants, Aarhus has a selection of international street-food vendors (🌐 *www.aarhusstreetfood.com*). Buses that used to occupy the former bus station (✉ *Ny Banegårdsgade 46*) in Aarhus have been replaced with colorful containers from which vendors sell street food from all over the world. The sprawling outdoor terrace here is also home to wine and beer bars and coffee shops.

★ **Domestic**
$$$ | **SCANDINAVIAN** | The brick walls, wooden floors, and high-beamed ceilings wow visitors at this gourmet restaurant, but only until the snacks arrive; then it's all about the food. The menu—four or eight courses—changes depending on the season, but it's always based on high-quality local ingredients and imaginative culinary thinking. **Known for:** meals starting with eight creative snacks; excellent wine and juice pairings; a contemporary take on the roulade, a traditional Danish dessert. [$] *Average main: DKr 595* ✉ *Mejlgade 35B* ☎ *61/43–70–10* 🌐 *restaurantdomestic.dk* 🕒 *Closed Sun. and Mon. No lunch.*

Frederikshøj
$$$$ | **SCANDINAVIAN** | One of Denmark's most celebrated and uncompromising chefs, Wassim Hallal, concocts brilliant dishes at this Michelin-starred restaurant with floor-to-ceiling windows offering views of a beautiful garden and the sea. The menus, consisting of 7 or 10 courses, are a tour de force of local ingredients and sky-high gastronomic ambitions.

Known for: elaborate, elegant dishes; first-class local produce; contemporary design and service. [$] *Average main: DKr 1200* ✉ *Oddervej 19* ☎ *86/14–22–80* 🌐 *frederikshoj.com* 🕓 *Closed Sun.–Tues. No lunch.*

La Cabra

$ | **SCANDINAVIAN** | Open since 2012, this bustling coffee shop is as popular for its coffee as it is for its baked goods. The almond croissant is legendary, and so is the bread. **Known for:** excellent coffee—and beans to go; ambitious bakery; cozy atmosphere. [$] *Average main: DKr 28* ✉ *Graven 20* 🌐 *www.lacabra.dk.*

Langhoff & Juel

$$ | **SCANDINAVIAN** | This restaurant is as popular for brunch as for dinner, which has as much to do with the excellent food as the beautiful, rustic, light-filled dining room it's served in. Certain classics—such as the signature brunch; lunch dishes like steamed plaice with burnt carrot; or mains such as chicken breast with pickled rhubarb—stay on the menu, but much of the menu rotates with the seasons. **Known for:** creative brunch servings; communal, rustic tables and wooden chairs; photogenic dining room. [$] *Average main: DKr 128* ✉ *Guldsmedgade 30* ☎ *30/30–00–18* 🌐 *langhoffogjuul.dk.*

★ **Restaurant ET**

$$ | **FRENCH** | The culinary ambitions are lofty, the portions are huge, the produce is excellent, and the wine list is extensive, which are just some of the reasons why locals keep coming back to this lovely French restaurant. The service and the setting equal that of a much fancier place, but the prices remain low, especially considering the quality of the food. **Known for:** perfecting French brasserie fare; very extensive wine list; knowledgeable sommeliers. [$] *Average main: DKr 169* ✉ *Åboulevarden 7* ☎ *86/13–88–00* 🌐 *restaurant-et.dk* 🕓 *Closed Sun.*

Restaurant Seafood

$$$ | **SEAFOOD** | Just south of town lies Marselis Harbor, a bustling little sailboat cove surrounded by waterfront restaurants and cafés that draw big crowds on sunny summer weekends. Restaurant Seafood has an interior of light-blue walls, and its signature dish is a seafood bouillabaisse heaped with tiger prawns, squid, Norwegian lobster, and mussels and served with aioli on the side. **Known for:** maritime-inspired decor; fresh local seafood; festive place on a summer evening. [$] *Average main: DKr 350* ✉ *Marselisborg Havnevej 44* ☎ *86/18–56–55* 🌐 *restaurantseafood.dk.*

🛏 Hotels

Helnan Marselis Hotel

$$$ | **HOTEL** | This beachside hotel easily boasts the best views in town, with all rooms facing east, toward the sea. **Pros:** quiet surroundings; within walking distance of a gorgeous hilltop park inhabitated by dozens of deer; floor-to-ceiling windows on east wall of room. **Cons:** not within walking distance of center of town; room furniture a bit dated; slightly pricey. [$] *Rooms from: DKr 1435* ✉ *Strandvejen 25* ☎ *86/14–44–11* 🌐 *www.helnan.info* 🛏 *163 rooms* 🍴 *Free Breakfast.*

Hotel Ferdinand

$$$ | **HOTEL** | Occupying a prime spot along the canal, this hotel has lodgings that are divided between eight suites and 11 luxurious studio apartments. **Pros:** large rooms; beautiful views; on-site brasserie. **Cons:** gets noisy outside; no no-smoking rooms; only two parking spaces. [$] *Rooms from: DKr 1550* ✉ *Åboulevarden 28* ☎ *87/32–14–44* 🌐 *www.hotelferdinand.dk* 🛏 *19 rooms* 🍴 *No meals.*

Hotel Guldsmeden

$$$ | **HOTEL** | This intimate hotel with many personal touches is in a renovated 19th-century town house. **Pros:** organic

breakfast; courtyard and terrace; French colonial rooms. **Cons:** only five parking spaces that are only available at certain times of day; not all rooms have private baths; some rooms are small. [$] *Rooms from: DKr 1215* ✉ *Guldsmedgade 40* ☎ *86/13–45–50* 🌐 *guldsmedenhotels.com* 🛏 *27 rooms* 🍴 *Free Breakfast.*

Hotel Oasia Aarhus

$$ | **HOTEL** | Located close to the train station and the happening Jægergårdsgade, this pleasant hotel is a good base for exploring the city. **Pros:** good location; most rooms have view of the train tracks and the greenery surrounding them; good breakfast buffet. **Cons:** a few minutes' walk from the center; rooms can be a little generic; some rooms are small. [$] *Rooms from: DKr 899* ✉ *Kriegersvej 27* ☎ *87/32–37–15* 🌐 *www.hoteloasia.dk* 🛏 *100 rooms* 🍴 *Free Breakfast.*

Hotel Royal

$$$$ | **HOTEL** | In operation since 1838, Aarhus's grand hotel has welcomed such greats as the pianist Arthur Rubinstein and the singer Marian Anderson. **Pros:** discounts at nearby golf course; luxurious decor; great location. **Cons:** parking costs an additional DKr 100; rooms are pricey; some rooms are a little dated. [$] *Rooms from: DKr 1995* ✉ *Store Torv 4* ☎ *86/12–00–11* 🌐 *www.hotelroyal.dk* 🛏 *69 rooms* 🍴 *Free Breakfast.*

★ **Villa Provence**

$$ | **HOTEL** | **FAMILY** | As promised by the name, this boutique hotel is a little slice of Provence in the heart of Aarhus. **Pros:** atmospheric courtyard and lounge areas; excellent breakfast with handpicked cheeses, fresh fruit, and homemade bread; friendly owners. **Cons:** some rooms are newer than others; breakfast room is cute but small; some rooms are decorated with more love than others. [$] *Rooms from: DKr 1195* ✉ *Fredens Torv 12* ☎ *86/18–24–00* 🌐 *villaprovence.dk* 🛏 *39 rooms* 🍴 *Free Breakfast.*

Nightlife

The nightlife scene in Aarhus, which has been known for its festive vibes since the first popular cafés opened in the 1980s, is growing constantly. The Latin Quarter is one popular nightlife area, and so is the area running along Åen, or the Creek, which is bordered by bars and cafés on either side. In recent years Jægergårdsgade, located on the other side of the train tracks, has seen a surge of cocktail bars, French cafés, hip restaurants, and microbreweries open their doors.

BARS

St. Pauls Apothek

BARS/PUBS | Jægergårdsgade is home to an ever-growing number of cafés, bars, and shops, but this remains one of the best. It doubles as a restaurant, with a focus on local, organic produce. Stop by for a cocktail before an evening out on Jægergårdsgade. ✉ *Jægergårdsgade 76* ☎ *86/12–08–33* 🌐 *stpaulsapothek.dk.*

CAFÉS

Café Drudenfuss

CAFES—NIGHTLIFE | It's difficult to find a better place to people-watch than this ivy-clad café that occupies a corner in the middle of Aarhus's Latin Quarter. ✉ *Graven 30* ☎ *86/12–82–72* 🌐 *drudenfuss.dk.*

★ **Café Englen**

CAFES—NIGHTLIFE | Models, movie stars, and musicians have been hanging out at this Parisian-inspired café since 1984, along with the rest of Aarhus. The beloved institution serves café classics such as croque monsieur sandwiches, but many patrons don't come for the food but just to linger over a cup of coffee or glass of wine by the marbled bar, in the cozy courtyard, or by the heated outdoor terrace tables. ✉ *Studsgade 3* ☎ *86/13–06–44.*

Café Jorden

CAFES—NIGHTLIFE | The friendly but slightly dated Café Jorden has a brass-and-wood bar and a heated outdoor terrace with a red awning. Students and young professionals mix with the chatty bar staff. ⊠ *Badstuegade 3* ☎ *86/19–72–22.*

★ **Café Paradis**

CAFES—NIGHTLIFE | This café, known locally as "the last stop," is a popular place to head for a nightcap (or three). It's located on top of the beloved landmark Øst for Paradis, one of Aarhus's best cinemas. The dance floor is as popular as the bar. ⊠ *Paradisgade 7* ☎ *61/26–22–67.*

Café Under Masken (*Under the Mask Café*)

CAFES—NIGHTLIFE | The Café Under Masken, next door to the Royal Hotel, is the creation of Aarhus artist Hans Krull, who also designed the iron sculptures at the entrance to the hotel. The surreal bar is crammed with every type of mask imaginable, including grinning Balinese wooden masks and black-and-yellow African visages. Pygmy statues and stuffed tropical birds and fish line the shelves, and the back wall is lined with aquariums filled with exotic fish. Everything was collected by Krull and bar patrons. As the manager puts it, "Everyone's welcome. This bar is a no-man's-land, a place for all the 'funny fish' of the world." If that's not enough of a draw, consider that the drink prices are some of the lowest in town, and more than 30 kinds of beer are on offer. It's open Monday through Saturday until 2 am and Sunday until midnight. ⊠ *Bispegade 3* ☎ *86/18–22–66.*

Carlton

CAFES—NIGHTLIFE | At this classy bar and restaurant, which is presided over by a carousel horse, you can sip cocktails in the front bar-café or dine on French fare in the dining room. ⊠ *Rosensgade 23* ☎ *86/20–21–22* ⊕ *www.carlton.dk.*

Cockney Pub

CAFES—NIGHTLIFE | The Cockney Pub is just that, and a bit more, with an exclusive line of beers and a wide selection

of whiskeys. ⊠ *Maren Smeds Gyde 8* ☎ *86/19–45–77* ⊕ *www.cockneypub.dk.*

🛍 Shopping

With several hundred small shops, several department stores, and many pedestrian streets (Strøget, Fredericksgade, Sankt Clemens Stræde, Store Torv, and Lille Torv), this is a great place to play havoc with your credit cards. As befits a student town, Aarhus also has its Latin Quarter, a jumble of cobbled streets around the cathedral, with designer boutiques, antiques shops, and glass and ceramic galleries. On Vestergade, you can turn on Grønnegade and stroll along Møllestien to see its charming old homes.

Bülow Duus Glass

CERAMICS/GLASSWARE | At Bülow Duus Glass you can browse among delicate and colorful items, including fishbowls and candle holders. While you're here, visit Mette Bülow Duus's workshop and see how all this beautiful glassware gets made. ⊠ *Studsgade 12* ☎ *86/12–72–86* ⊕ *www.bulow-duus.dk* ⊗ *Closed Sun.*

Georg Jensen

JEWELRY/ACCESSORIES | For the best selection of Georg Jensen designs, head to the official Georg Jensen store. It stocks Jensen-designed and-inspired watches, jewelry, table settings, and art nouveau vases. The textile designs of Georg Jensen Damask, in a separate department, are truly beautiful. ⊠ *Søndergade 1* ☎ *86/12–01–00* ⊕ *www.georgjensen.com* ⊗ *Closed Sun.*

Salling Aarhus

DEPARTMENT STORES | What separates Salling from other department stores is its rooftop complex, complete with cafés, bars, leveled terraces, and viewpoints. ⊠ *Søndergade 27* ☎ *87/78–60–00* ⊕ *salling.dk.*

Samsø

40 km (25 miles) from Aarhus.

Organic farms with roadside vegetable stands, half-timbered houses with thatched roofs, sandy beaches overgrown with wild roses, and cute town centers with cafés, beach hotels, and hollyhocks galore—Samsø is the essence of summer in Denmark. In recent years a younger generation of chefs, bed-and-breakfast owners, and holiday makers have given the vacation island a more contemporary feel.

GETTING HERE AND AROUND

You can take a ferry to Samsø from either Hou, south of Aarhus, or Kalundborg on Zealand. There are many daily departures, especially in the summer, and the prices are reasonable: a single ticket for passengers without a car costs DKr 64–104, while it costs DKr 130–467 with a car. Cheaper tickets are available outside of the summer season. The ferry ride takes around one hour.

VISITOR INFORMATION

CONTACTS Samsølinjen. ☎ *70/25–10–25* 🌐 *samsoelinjen.dk.* **Samsø Rederi.** ☎ *70/22–59–00* 🌐 *tilsamsoe.dk.* **VisitSamsø.** ✉ *Anton Rosens Pl. 3* ☎ *86/59–00–05* 🌐 *visitsamsoe.dk.*

Sights

Ballen
TOWN | FAMILY | This charming coastal town, one of Samsø's largest, is bustling in summer, when the yacht harbor is busy, the restaurants are packed, and most hotels and B&Bs book up weeks in advance. The sandy beach just south of the town is child friendly with its mild, shallow waters, while the beach stretching up north of town is more stony. There's an idyllic camping spot, Ballen Strandcamping, just north of the city; it's located directly on a beautiful, sandy beach, with tents perched between the pines.

★ **Issehoved and Ballebjerg**
BEACH—SIGHT | FAMILY | Samsø's northern peninsula is home to two stunning natural areas, Ballebjerg (on the west coast of the island) and Issehoved, the island's northernmost point. The round, sloping hills are a joy to walk in, and from the top of them you can see Jutland, Zealand, and several small islands. There's a beautiful beach at Issehoved, while Ballebjerg—which is the island's highest point—is one of the most beautiful sunset spots in Denmark. ✉ *Issehoved, Nordby.*

Nordby
TOWN | FAMILY | Samsø's cutest town—and that says a lot—might be Nordby, an idyllic town on the so-called northern island, a peninsula jutting out from the rest of Samsø. The town consists entirely of winding lanes with fairy-tale-like half-timbered houses in bright colors, all clad in hollyhocks. There are several good cafés, B&Bs, and restaurants and a huge labyrinth just north of the town.

Restaurants

★ **Nordby 13**
$$$ | BRASSERIE | Samsø is known across Denmark for its vegetable produce—the potatoes and strawberries, especially, are popular—and many restaurants on Samsø benefit from that. This one, located in Nordby, is one of the best; at lunch the chefs prepare traditional, Danish classics, but at night the restaurant transforms into one of the best bistro cuisines in Denmark, giving the local produce some French flair. **Known for:** use of local, organic produce; elegant dining room and atmospheric terrace; brasserie-style cooking. [$] *Average main: DKr 350* ✉ *Nordby Hovedgade 13, Nordby* ☎ *86/59–65–13* 🌐 *www.nordby13.dk* 🕒 *Closed Mon. and Tues.*

Skipperly
$ | **SCANDINAVIAN** | **FAMILY** | The harbor-facing garden at this boisterous restaurant is always packed, which has as much to do with the excellent open-face sandwiches as the prime location on the harbor. **Known for:** open-face sandwiches with a focus on fish and seafood; schnapps-fueled lunches; atmospheric setting. [$] *Average main: DKr 90* ✉ *Havnevej 9, Ballen* ☎ *86/59–10–18* 🌐 *skipperly.dk.*

Hotels

Ballen Badehotel
$$ | **HOTEL** | Located in the heart of Ballen is Samsø's classiest hotel, a traditional beach hotel full of charm. **Pros:** beautifully decorated; modern amenities; excellent restaurant and breakfast buffet. **Cons:** books out months in advance during peak season; not directly located on the beach; some rooms are on the small side. [$] *Rooms from: DKr 1000* ✉ *Aavej 21, Ballen* ☎ *86/59–17–99* 🌐 *www.ballen-badehotel.dk* 🛏 *39* 🍴 *Free Breakfast.*

Stay by Stage
$$ | **HOTEL** | **FAMILY** | This small B&B in the heart of pretty Nordby is a good choice for a simple stay in a place run by a friendly couple. **Pros:** garden adds charm; beautiful garden; good breakfast buffet with food from local producers. **Cons:** some rooms are small; books out weeks in advance in peak season; not much historical charm. [$] *Rooms from: DKr 795* ✉ *Nordby Hovedgade 8, Nordby* ☎ *28/92–27–83* 🌐 *samsoebystage.dk* 🛏 *14 rooms* 🍴 *Free Breakfast.*

Shopping

★ **Sams Island Distillery**
WINE/SPIRITS | The gin at this small distillery is made partially out of ants from Samsø, the vodka is made of the island's famed potatoes, and the rum is aged on oak from, you guessed it, Samsø. The shop and tasting room is located in a courtyard in Tranebjerg, and the distillery's charming and enterprising masterminds are happy to show guests around. ✉ *Langgade 19, Tranebjerg* ☎ *28/96–83–05* 🌐 *samsisland.dk* 🕒 *Closed Mon. and Tues.*

Smagen af Øen
FOOD/CANDY | The decor of this grocery is straight out of the 1950s, but the wares on the shelves are all from present-day producers revolutionizing Samsø's farming. You'll find beers from the island's microbreweries, dairy products from its farmers, and other delicacies and specialties from all over the island. There's a charming café serving coffee, cakes, and light lunches too. ✉ *Nordby Hovedgade 15, Nordby* ☎ *86/59–66–65* 🌐 *www.smagenafoen.dk.*

Aalborg

119 km (73 miles) miles from Aarhus.

There's a rough charm to Aalborg, Denmark's fourth-biggest city. Its industrial past is still evident, especially on the waterfront, though the city has transformed itself from an industrial powerhouse into a cultural and educational hub. The buildings that used to be home to the fishing industry, textile plants, and aquavit distilleries have been torn down, and in their place architectural masterpieces home to museums, music venues, and restaurants have shot up. There's a strong focus on community, user-driven projects, and cultural entrepreneurship, perhaps because of the city's working-class past.

GETTING HERE AND AROUND

It takes one hour and 20 minutes to drive from Aarhus to Aalborg. The train, which leaves twice every hour, takes the same amount of time and costs DKr 188.

VISITOR INFORMATION

InfoCenter Aalborg. ✉ *Kjellerups Torv 5, Aalborg* ☎ *99/31–75–00* 🌐 *visitaalborg.dk/aalborg/turistinformation.*

◉ Sights

★ Aalborg Waterfront

NEIGHBORHOOD | Aalborg lies on the Limfjord, and the waterfront used to be busy with fishermen and factory workers. These days you're more likely to run into sunbathers, joggers, or museum goers on the waterfront, which has been rebuilt and is now home to several cultural institutions, restaurants, and restorative areas. The Utzon Center is one highlight; it's the last building that Jørgen Utzon, who designed the Sydney Opera House, built before his death, and it's home to a museum about his work, a lovely café, and a first floor with beautiful views of the Limfjord. ✉ *Aalborg* ✛ *The waterfront stretches from the Limfjord Bridge to the Limfjord Tunnel. Most activity is between the bridge and the eastern harbor.*

★ Fjordbyen

NEIGHBORHOOD | **FAMILY** | Locals call it "mini Christiania" for good reason: There are several similarities between Copenhagen's freetown and this harbor-front community centered around more than 100 self-constructed houses. Most of them are based on former firshermen's sheds, but nowadays the community is home to freethinkers of all income levels. There's a street-food market and a harbor bath close to the community's imaginative houses, so set aside at least half a day for exploring the area. ✉ *Aalborg.*

★ Kunsten Museum of Modern Art Aalborg

MUSEUM | **FAMILY** | It might be tempting to spend the day in the sculpture garden, which is surrounded by forest and home to sculptures by Olafur Eliasson, Jeppe Hein, and Bjørn Nørgaard, but Aalborg's museum of modern art has much more to offer. Wander through the airy, light-filled galleries and divide your time between the permanent and changing exhibitions and the building itself, an architectural masterpiece by Alvar Aalto. The café has an ambitious lunch menu and is a wonderful spot to stop for a light meal or a coffee. There's free admission to the sculpture garden, which is open 24/7, outside of the museum's opening hours. ✉ *Kong Christians Alle 50, Aalborg* ☏ *99/82–41–00* ⊕ *kunsten.dk* 💰 *DKr 110* ⊗ *Closed Mon.*

★ Musikkens Hus

ARTS VENUE | Classical ensembles, pop and rock stars, jazz virtuosos, and intellectual superstars from near and far grace the stages at this venue. The main stage is known for its incredible acoustics, but the building itself, designed by Coop Himmelb(l)au and garnished with artworks by artists such as Jeppe Hein, is worth a visit in itself. ✉ *Musikkens Pl. 1, Aalborg* ☏ *60/20–30–00* ⊕ *musikkenshus.dk* 💰 *Free, event prices vary.*

Nordkraft

ARTS VENUE | **FAMILY** | Aalborg's former power station has been turned into a cultural instution. These days, the brutalist concrete halls are home to a music venue; an art hall for experimental, contemporary art; a cinema; public areas; and several clubs organizing everything from martial arts to poetry readings. ✉ *Kjellerups Torv 1, Aalborg* ☏ *99/82–41–30* ⊕ *nordkraft.dk* 💰 *Free.*

Street art murals

PUBLIC ART | **FAMILY** | Aalborg has made it its mission to attract street artists from all over the world, and at the time of this writing there were 70 murals giving the city a pop of color. Some of them are found along busy intersections on the highway, others are hidden in residential courtyards, while a few are found along the pedestrian streets in the city. Stop by the tourist information office for an updated list and map of the murals. ✉ *Aalborg.*

◉ Restaurants

Aalborg's citizens have borne witness to a culinary revolution. From gourmet restaurants and classic bistros to street food, the gastronomic options available in the city now weren't there just a few years ago.

Dejavú

$$$ | **BISTRO** | Located in an atmospheric basement, complete with brick walls, velvet dining chairs, and low ceilings, this restaurant might look like a speakeasy jazz club in New York, but it's one of the best brasseries in Aalborg. The chef, who also runs the popular restaurant Applaus, mixes Danish produce with French bistro cooking, bringing both to perfection. **Known for:** funky wine list with many natural wines; classic, ambitious bistro cuisine; creative desserts. [$] *Average main: DKr 395* ✉ *Ved Stranden 7D, Aalborg* ☎ *40/30–49–28* 🌐 *bistrodejavu.dk* 🕓 *Closed Sun. and Mon.*

Fusion

$$$ | **ASIAN FUSION** | This was the first restaurant to open on Aalborg's waterfront nine years ago, and it's still the best place in the city for French Japanese fusion cuisine. It makes perfect sense to surrender to an evening of endless fish and seafood dishes while looking out at the Limfjord, and the service and wine list is as impeccable as the many small dishes. **Known for:** excellent fish and seafood dishes; well-executed merging of French and Japanese cuisines; extensive wine list and good cocktails. [$] *Average main: DKr 565* ✉ *Strandvejen 4, Aalborg* ☎ *35/12–33–31* 🌐 *restaurantfusion.dk* 🕓 *Closed Sun. No lunch weekdays.*

★ **La Bottega**

$ | **ITALIAN** | **FAMILY** | This is the Italian restaurant all cities derserve to have at least one of. You have many choices—settle in for interesting Italian wines and pasta in the atmospheric courtyard, get a juicy panini on your lunch break, order a pizza (delicious, if a little pricey) to go, or stop by for Italian delicacies for a picnic—and all of them are good options. **Known for:** wide range of excellent pasta dishes; some of the best pizzas outside of Copenhagen; great selection of antipasti and desserts. [$] *Average main: DKr 99* ✉ *Cortesgyde 6, Aalborg* ☎ *23/95–07–01* 🌐 *la-bottega.dk* 🕓 *Closed Sun.*

★ **Tabu**

$$$$ | **SCANDINAVIAN** | At Tabu the seafood, fish, meat, and produce of northern Denmark's windswept fjords, coasts, heaths, and fields are translated into ambitious tasting menus. Each of the six dishes are beautifully presented, inviting you to savor the tastes slowly as you sip some wine and relax in a warm setting, accentuated with exposed brick walls and linen-clad tables. *The menus are less expensive and more casual on Wednesday and Thursday, where you'll get five dishes (plus snacks) instead of six.* The restaurateurs behind Tabu also run the popular Ubat Veggie and Glashuset, two nearby establishments that are a step down in price. **Known for:** perfect seafood dishes; taking the New Nordic philosophy to Denmark's north; fixed-price tasting menus. [$] *Average main: DKr 850* ✉ *Vesterå 5, Aalborg* ☎ *88/19–60–58* 🌐 *ta-bu.dk* 🕓 *Closed Sun.*

🛏 Hotels

First Hotel Aalborg

$ | **HOTEL** | With a prime location on the waterfront, between the Utzon Center and Musikkens Hus, this hotel is an excellent starting point for exploring the city. **Pros:** great views of the Limfjord; prime location; friendly service. **Cons:** breakfast room can be crowded; some rooms only have city views; generic lobby. [$] *Rooms from: DKr 727* ✉ *Rendsburggade 5, Aalborg* ☎ *98/10–14–00* 🌐 *www.firsthotels.dk* 🛏 *156 rooms* 🍴 *Free Breakfast.*

Radisson Blu Limfjord Hotel

$$ | **HOTEL** | **FAMILY** | This Radisson has a location close to many of the city's best restaurants and attractions, making it a comfortable and convenient stop for travelers. **Pros:** good breakfast buffet; great views of the fjord; atmospheric cocktail bar. **Cons:** rooms can be a little

generic; not all rooms have fjord views; small fitness center. $ *Rooms from: DKr 1076* ⊠ *Ved Stranden 14–16, Aalborg* ☎ *98/16–43–33* ⊕ *radissonhotels.com* ⥲ *188 rooms* ⊙l *Free Breakfast.*

Nightlife

In recent years Aalborg has seen an explosion in the number of good bars and nightlife options. The scene used to take place along Jomfru Ane Gade, an infamous party street that mostly attracts youngsters, but these days the city is home to a growing number of beer, wine, and cocktail bars; most of them are located within walking distance of one another—and most hotels—in the heart of the city.

★ Café Ulla Terkelsen London

CAFES—NIGHTLIFE | FAMILY | This café is a beloved institution, especially among street artists and hipsters. It's as well known for its tasty, classic café food as for the colorful, vintage furniture it's been decorated with. ■**TIP→ The brunch is especially popular.** ⊠ *Kastetvej 36, Aalborg* ☎ *98/15–80–00* ⊕ *cafeullaterkelsenlondon.dk.*

1000Fryd

BARS/PUBS | A long-standing semi-anarchist darling run by volunteers, 1000Fryd is home to a music venue, an art room, and a café selling organic beer and sustainable coffee. You can raffle to decide the price of a beer. ⊠ *Kattesundet 10, Aalborg* ☎ *98/13–22–21* ⊕ *1000fryd.dk.*

⬤ Shopping

Lange Kunsthåndværk

CERAMICS/GLASSWARE | FAMILY | This arts and crafts center is home to a glass and ceramics workshop, a gallery, a sculpture garden, and a shop. It's run by the third generation of the family and located in a beautiful building in the heart of Hjelmerstad, Aalborg's historical center with crooked, cobblestoned streets, and lopsided houses. ⊠ *Hjelmerstald 15, Aalborg* ☎ *98/13–82–68* ⊕ *www.langekeramik.dk* ⊙ *Closed Sun.*

Skagen

88 km (55 miles) northeast of Aalborg.

For more than a century, Skagen (pronounced *skane*), a picturesque area where the North Sea meets the Baltic Sea, has been a favorite destination of well-off travelers, artists, and architects. This 600-year-old market town on Jutland's windswept northern tip has long pebbly beaches and huge open skies, which shower the beach town in an almost mythical lights. Sunsets are tremendous events, drawing crowds to the beaches, while nights are spent dining, drinking, and dancing at romantic beach hotels, scenic bistros, and small bars. Skagen's main industry has traditionally been fishing, but tourism has long replaced it as the town's main source of income. Denmark's northernmost point has been known for its natural light and beauty for centuries, not least because of the group of painters who tried to recreate the light in their paintings. Head to the village of Skagen to experience the light and beaches for yourself.

GETTING HERE AND AROUND
From Aalborg, drive north on E45 to Frederikshavn, then continue north on Route 40 to Skagen. The drive should take approximately 90 minutes. Those traveling by train must transfer at Frederikshavn to Nordjyske Jernbaner, a local service that operates hourly on most days. The ride from Aalborg to Skagen costs DKr 143 and takes just over two hours.

CONTACTS Nordjyske Jernbaner. ☎ *98/45–45–10* ⊕ *njba.dk.*

VISITOR INFORMATION
CONTACTS Skagen Turistbureau – Turisthus Nord. ✉ *Vestre Strandvej 10* ☎ *98/44–13–77* ⊕ *www.skagen-tourist.dk.*

Sights

Anchers Hus
HOUSE | Michael and Anna Ancher are Skagen's—if not Denmark's—most famous artist couple, and their meticulously restored 1820 home and studio, Anchers Hus, is now a museum. Old oil lamps and lace curtains decorate the parlor; the doors throughout the house were painted by Michael. Anna's studio, complete with easel, is awash in the famed Skagen light. More than 240 paintings by Michael, Anna, and their daughter, Helga, grace the walls. ✉ *Markvej 2–4* ☎ *98/44–30–09* ⊕ *skagenskunstmuseer.dk* 🎫 *DKr 80, combined ticket for three museums DKr 180* 🕐 *Closed Nov.–Mar. and Mon. in Apr., May, Sept., and Oct.*

Grenen
BEACH—SIGHT | At Denmark's nothern tip, the North Sea meets the Baltic Sea, and you can literally stand with each foot in a different sea. The water can be calm on one side and quite choppy on the other. Many a ship found its end here where the two seas clash, so don't go swimming in these dangerous waters. ✉ *Skagen* ✚ *To get to the tip, walk for about a mile along the beach or take a tractor trailer called the "Sandworm" from the nearby parking lot.*

Råbjerg Mile
NATURE SITE | Even more famed than the area's sand-buried church is the west coast's dramatic Råbjerg Mile, a protected desert-like migrating dune that moves about 50 feet a year. You can reach it on foot from the Kandestederne. ✉ *Raabjerg Mile Vej* 🎫 *Free.*

★ Skagens Museum
MUSEUM | The 19th-century Danish artist and poet Holger Drachmann (1846–1908) and his friends, including the well-known P. S. Krøyer and Michael and Anna Ancher, founded the Skagen School of painting, which sought to capture the special quality of light and idyllic seascapes here. They and their contemporaries depicted everyday life in Skagen primarily from the turn of the 20th century until the 1920s, and you can see their efforts on display in the Skagens Museum. It's a wonderful homage to this talented group of Danes, and you'll become mesmerized by some of the portraits, which seem more like a photographic collection of days gone by. The light and the landscape, however, remain the same, and it's a magical experience to recognize scenes from the paintings when you walk on the beach or in the dunes. The museum store sells posters, postcards, and other souvenirs depicting the Skagen paintings. ✉ *Brøndumsvej 4* ☎ *98/44–64–44* ⊕ *www.skagensmuseum.dk* 🎫 *DKr 110, combined ticket to three museums DKr 180* 🕐 *Closed Mon. Sept.–May.*

★ Tilsandede Kirke *(Sand-Buried Church)*
ARCHAEOLOGICAL SITE | Denmark's northernmost point is so thrashed by storms and roiling waters that the 18th-century Sand-Buried Church, 2 km (1 mile) south of town, is almost completely covered by dunes; only its tower rises above the sand. It's a beautiful if windswept area to go for a walk. ✉ *Gamle Landevej 63* ☎ *72/54–30–00* 🎫 *Free* 🕐 *Closed Sat. and Sun.*

🍴 Restaurants

★ Brøndums Hotel Restaurant
$$ | SCANDINAVIAN | Skagen's grand dame of a hotel is home to one of the town's most storied and popular bistros. The kitchen focuses on Danish French bistro fare, some of it more contemporary and some of it classic, such as the open-face sandwiches, the fish soup, and the whole plaice. **Known for:** being a hangout for famous artists, dead and alive; dishes prepared in front of the guests; beautiful setting. 💲 *Average main: DKr 235*

✉ *Anchersvej 3* ☎ *98/44–15–55* 🌐 *www.broendums-hotel.dk.*

★ **De2Have**
$$ | **SCANDINAVIAN** | At the very top of Denmark and at the tip of Skagen lies De2Have, possibly the most spectacularly located restaurant in Denmark. The open-face sandwiches are popular for lunch, and it's a must to book well in advance for the popular Sunday brunch, but the a la carte menu is excellent too. **Known for:** location at the top of Grenen with a different sea on each side; extensive wine list; excellent fish and seafood dishes. [$] *Average main: DKr 296* ✉ *Fyrvej 42* ☎ *98/44–24–35* 🌐 *www.restaurantde2have.dk* 🕓 *Closed Sun. No dinner Mon. Sept.–Apr.*

Iscafeen
$ | **SCANDINAVIAN** | **FAMILY** | The ice creams and the pancakes are the real people pleasers at this small café, but the open-face sandwiches and light lunch meals are popular too. There is outdoor seating available. **Known for:** pretty courtyard; high-quality pancakes; good ice cream. [$] *Average main: DKr 68* ✉ *Oddevaj 2A* ☎ *98/44–21–08* 🕓 *No dinner.*

Pakhuset Restaurant
$$ | **SEAFOOD** | In this quaint harbor setting, you'll be able to savor fresh fish done right. The restaurant displays numerous replicas of figureheads that had washed ashore—the flotsam from the many shipwrecks that have happened around Skagen over the years. **Known for:** maritime-inspired decor; setting on the harbor of Skagen; live music on summer evenings. [$] *Average main: DKr 139* ✉ *Rødspættevej 6* ☎ *98/44–20–00* 🌐 *www.pakhuset-skagen.dk* 🕓 *Closed Mon.*

Skagen Fiskerestaurant
$$ | **SEAFOOD** | **FAMILY** | At first this place seems very unassuming, but it faces one of the two marinas that dock private yachts, and in the summer the restaurant's terrace is the place to see and be seen by the denizens of these vessels. Whether you dine on the ground floor in the pub or upstairs in the blue-and-white restaurant that resembles a warehouse attic, you must try the *fiskefrikadeller* (fish cakes). **Known for:** traditional Danish seafood dishes; fashionable clientele in the summer; atmospheric decor and setting. [$] *Average main: DKr 125* ✉ *Fiskehuskaj 13* ☎ *98/44–35–44* 🌐 *www.skagen-fiskerestaurant.dk.*

Hotels

★ **Brøndums Hotel**
$ | **HOTEL** | Located between the most interesting attractions in Skagen and steeped in local history, this beach hotel is one of the most charming places to stay not only in Skagen but in all of Denmark. **Pros:** atmospheric rooms and beautiful main building; first-class Danish French bistro restaurant; excellent location. **Cons:** books up in the summer; not located directly on the beach; not all rooms are in the main building. [$] *Rooms from: DKr 595* ✉ *Anchersvej 3* ☎ *98/44–15–55* 🌐 *www.broendums-hotel.dk* 🛏 *47 rooms* 🍴 *Free Breakfast.*

Plesner Hotel and Restaurant
$$$ | **HOTEL** | Designed by Ulrik Plesner, a famous local architect responsible for many buildings in Skagen, this appealing hotel is a three-minute walk from the train station. **Pros:** fresh and clean; beautiful garden; rooms 21 and 22 have French windows. **Cons:** no spa or similar frills; restaurant closes in the winter; rather pricey. [$] *Rooms from: DKr 1380* ✉ *Holstvej 8* ☎ *98/44–68–44* 🌐 *www.hotelplesner.dk* 🛏 *17 rooms* 🍴 *Free Breakfast.*

★ **Ruths Hotel**
$$$$ | **HOTEL** | One of the most glitzy and historical places to stay in Skagen was built by Emma and Hans Christian Ruth before World War I. Since then it's been completely rebuilt with modern facilities, and its main restaurant, Ruths Gourmet,

is one of the most popular restaurants in town. **Pros:** luxury amenities; close to beach; impecable service. **Cons:** room service not available 24 hours; early reservations essential for restaurant and hotel in peak season; pricier than other hotels in town. $ *Rooms from: DKr 1900* ✉ *Hans Ruths Vej 1* ☎ *98/44–11–24* ⊕ *www.ruths-hotel.dk* 🛏 *52 rooms* ⦿ *Free Breakfast.*

💼 Shopping

Skagen's artistic heritage and light-drenched landscapes continue to draw painters and craftspeople, meaning you'll find better-than-average souvenirs in town. The pedestrian street has a fascinating and intimate shopping atmosphere with stores as fine as those you'd see in Copenhagen.

Glaspusterblæser

CERAMICS/GLASSWARE | For colorful, innovative handblown glass, head to this large glassblowing workshop. ✉ *Skt. Laurentii Vej 29* ☎ *98/44–58–75.*

Klitmøller and Thy

105 km (65 miles) from Aalborg.

Denmark's northwestern coast has long been known for its windswept, sandy dune beaches and remote, unspoiled nature. The wind used to be something to avoid, but these days it's why most people go. Klitmøller, a small, coastal town, attracts surfers from all over the world and has earned the nickname Cold Hawaii because of its waves and growing surf community. The interest in Klitmøller has led to a number of hip new hotel and restaurant openings.

The coast becomes quieter the farther north you travel, and Jammerbugten is home to sophisticated beach hotels set between pine tree forests and quiet dunes. The area is also home to Denmark's national park Thy.

GETTING HERE AND AROUND

It's difficult to travel around this remote part of Denmark without your own wheels. Though there are some buses and trains in the region, none of them take you directly to the region's main hub, Aalborg. You can transfer in Thisted, in which case the trip would take close to three hours and cost DKr 85 (take Bus 70/970X to Thisted and transfer to Bus 322 to Klitmøller).

👁 Sights

★ Nationalpark Thy

NATIONAL/STATE PARK | Nationalpark Thy is known as the first national park and last wilderness in Denmark, and it's worth taking a day to explore the windy coast, beautiful heaths, quiet meadows, and sandy dunes that make up the area. There are plenty of walking routes you can embark on yourself, but it's also possible to hire a nature guide, book a horse-back-riding trip, or go fishing, biking, or hiking. You even can stay overnight in the wooden shelters (check their availability with the tourist office). ✉ *Nationalpark Thy, Hurup* ⊹ *Route 181 from the south; Route 26/571 from island Mors* ☎ *72/54–15–00* ⊕ *nationalparkthy.dk* 🎟 *Free.*

🍴 Restaurants

The influx of surfers has led to a new wave of restaurants in Klitmøller, which is home to a *poké* bar (Hawaiian restaurant serving a dish traditionally made with fresh raw fish and toppings like onions and seaweed), an organic ice cream parlor, a rotisserie, a pizzeria, and a street-food truck on top of the traditional smokehouse. Most of the restaurants and cafés are located on Ørhagevej.

Haandpluk

$ | **EUROPEAN** | **FAMILY** | Locals stop by this small café for well-made flat whites and homemade bread with local cheese. They also come for the drinks, including excellent glasses of wine and beer that's been brewed in the brewery in the back room. **Known for:** great coffee; homemade snacks and cheese/charcuterie boards; hangout for locals. $ *Average main: DKr 50 ⊠ Vestermøllevej 18, Aalborg 🕾 31/22–80–88 ⊕ haandpluk.dk ⊗ Closed Sun. and Mon. No dinner Fri.–Wed.*

★ Hanstholm Madbar

$$ | SCANDINAVIAN | FAMILY | Located on the top of a hill, next to a lighthouse and looking directly down on the wild North Sea and an industrial harbor, this restaurant has a view that is stunning. The food includes well-executed comfort classics (think fish-and-chips, moules frites, and fish burgers) and more exotic starters such as a salad with halloumi, *burrata* (fresh cow milk cheese made from cream and mozzarella) with cherry tomatoes, and *vitello tonnato* (sliced veal covered with a tuna-mayonnaise sauce.) **Known for:** cozy atmosphere; good drinks and live music; classic comfort food. $ *Average main: DKr 129 ⊠ Helshagevej 98, Handstholm 🕾 81/71–19–12 ⊕ www. hanstholmmadbar.dk ⊗ Closed Mon.– Wed. Aug.– May.*

🛏 Hotels

★ Svinkløv Badehotel

$$ | HOTEL | It made national headlines when one of Denmark's most beloved beach hotels burned to the ground in 2016, but also when it reopened after having been rebuilt in 2019. **Pros:** stunning location on beautiful beach; lovingly rebuilt after fire; one of the best restaurants outside of Copenhagen. **Cons:** both restaurant and hotel fill quickly; difficult to reach with public transportion; very busy in the summer. $ *Rooms from: DKr 1050 ⊠ Svinkløvvej 593, Fjerritslev 🕾 98/21–70–02 ⊕ www.svinkloev-bade-hotel.dk ➦ 36 rooms ⋈ Free Breakfast.*

🏃 Activities

It's all about the wind in Klitmøller— aka Cold Hawaii—and whether you're into kite-, wind- or old-school surfing, the waves will take care of you. There are several places in town renting out boards, offering lessons, and providing surfers with advice; most of them are located at the end of Ørhagevej.

Cold Hawaii Surf Camp

SURFING | FAMILY | The fact that owners Mor and Vahine—from Israel and Tahiti, respectively—have left their sunny homelands behind to open up a surf shop in Klitmøller tells you a lot about just how seductive the waves are here. The couple organizes surf camps for beginners as well as for pros, has stand-up paddle-board (SUP) lessons, sells surf gear, and offers free advice in their board shop. ⊠ *Ørhagevej 151, Klitmøller 🕾 29/10–88–73 ⊕ www.coldhawaiisurfcamp.com.*

Tórshavn and the Faroe Islands

Once the gathering site of Viking chieftains, "Thor's Harbor" retains its command and respect as the capital of the Faroe Islands. It's windswept and rainy, but Tórshavn's inhabitants find many ways to keep warm outside and in, whether it's boat racing across the harbor or bouncing between cozy cafés and pubs along the twisted medieval streets.

👁 Sights

Kirkjubøur

BUILDING | The first settlers in the Tórshavn area, believed to be Irish monks, settled on the southernmost tip of the island at Streymoy, just 10 km (6 miles) outside of the capital. Although the cathedral, built around 1300, remains unfinished, it's still the largest medieval structure on the islands. Next door is one

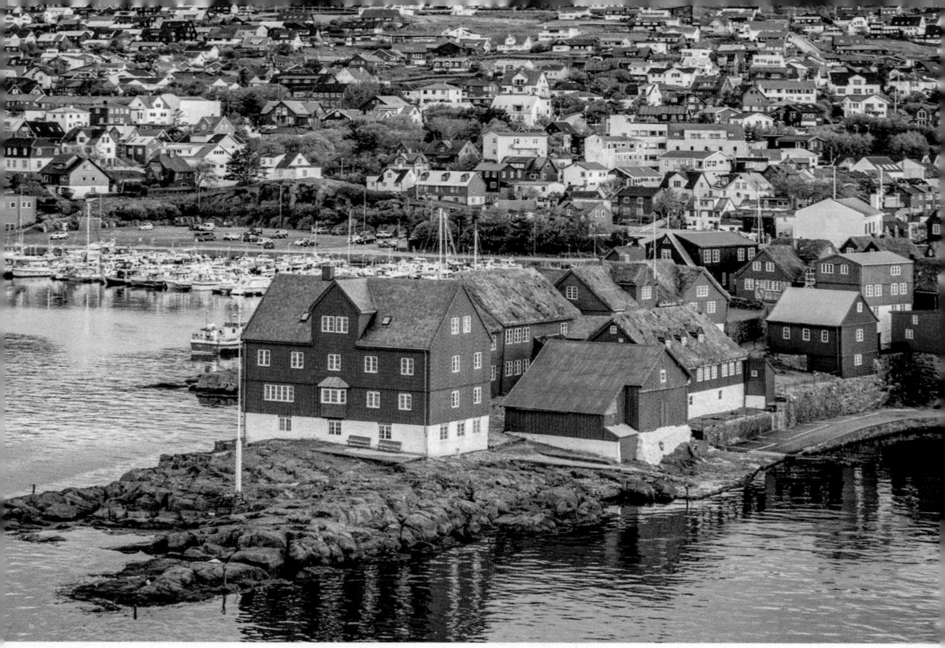

Tórshavn, the capital city of the Faroe Islands, is known for its wooden turf-roofed houses on a small peninsula.

of the world's oldest inhabited wooden houses, the Roykstovan farmhouse, which dates to the 11th century and has been occupied by the same family since 1550. ✉ *Kirkjubøur.*

Steinprent

ARTS VENUE | The workspace in this 1887 factory building overlooking the harbor is still being put to good use by regional lithographers and designers, who create and display their artwork in the spacious studio. Exhibitions in visual art by artists like Peter Carlsen occur regularly, as do book and poetry readings and live music. ✉ *Skálatrøð 16* ☎ *298/316–386* 🌐 *www.steinprent.com* 🎟 *Free.*

Tinganes

GOVERNMENT BUILDING | A postcard favorite, this rocky promontory dividing the harbor has been the home of the Faroese parliament for more than 1,000 years. It also hosts a bundle of red sod-roofed cottages built in the 16th and 17th centuries that are cute enough to pinch. The prime minister's office is in the last building, but the marks of Viking chieftains long gone are still visible in the rocks to practiced eyes. A guide is recommended. ✉ *Tórshavn.*

🍴 Restaurants

Hafnia

$ | **SCANDINAVIAN** | Hotel Hafnia has several restaurants and one café. The main restaurant is open for breakfast and lunch, and offers a generous buffet with a selection of local dishes—with a heavy focus on lamb and seafood—and international classics. **Known for:** homemade bread; mixture of local and international dishes; many seafood dishes. [$] *Average main: DKr 149* ✉ *Aarvegur 4–10* ☎ *298/313–233* 🌐 *www.hafnia.fo.*

★ Koks

$$$$ | **SCANDINAVIAN** | One of the most celebrated New Nordic restaurants in Scandinavia, KOKS is the only Michelin-restaurant on the archipelago. The restaurant is known for its playful tasting menu, the modern takes on local classics and experimenting with ræst, a local kind of fermentation. **Known for:** internationally celebrated chef; 17-course tasting menu; rural setting. $ *Average main: DKr 1900* ⊠ *Frammi við Gjónna, Leynavatn* ☎ *298/333–999* ⊕ *www.koks.fo* ⊘ *Closed Sun.–Mon.*

Áarstova

$$$ | SCANDINAVIAN | Drawing from the tenets of the New Nordic philosophy, the chef at this "house by the brook" sources his ingredients locally and fills the tasting menu with simple, earthy meals like langoustine bisque, smoked salmon, poached cod, and his famous braised lamb. However, the most special occasion to visit is late March, when, for three days only, Áarstova serves a rare white Faroe Bank cod. **Known for:** authentic location in Tórshavn's old heart; tasting menu only; cozy rooms in historic building. $ *Average main: DKr 500* ⊠ *Gongin 1* ☎ *298/333–000* ⊕ *www.aarstova.fo* ⊘ *No lunch.*

 ## Hotels

Hotel Føroyar

$$ | HOTEL | High in the hills above Tórshavn, and high in guests' estimation, this is considered to be one of the best accommodations in town, combining boutique design sensibilities with the natural life of the island. **Pros:** fabulous views; interesting architecture; nature setting. **Cons:** a 20- to 30-minute walk to town, uphill on the way back; some rooms are a little dated; no elevator. $ *Rooms from: DKr 1095* ⊠ *Oyggjarvegur 45* ☎ *298/317–500* ⊕ *www.hotelforoyar.com* ⇆ *106 rooms* ◎l *Free Breakfast.*

Hotel Hafnia

$$ | HOTEL | Within walking distance of city sights, services, and transportation links, Hotel Hafnia has been hosting guests since 1950, when Christian Restorff demolished his estate to build the best accommodations in town. **Pros:** panoramic views; convenient location; nice lunch buffet. **Cons:** rooms a bit small; very small

bathrooms; thin pillows. $ *Rooms from: DKr 850* ⊠ *Áarvegur 4–10* ☎ *298/313–233* ⊕ *www.hafnia.fo* ⇆ *74 rooms* ◎l *Free Breakfast.*

Hotel Tórshavn

$$ | HOTEL | For location, it's hard to beat this three-star boutique hotel just steps from the harbor. **Pros:** couldn't be more central; great views; helpful staff. **Cons:** nighttime noise from surrounding streets; some rooms showing wear and tear; small rooms. $ *Rooms from: DKr 1090* ⊠ *Tórsgøta 2* ☎ *298/350–000* ⊕ *www.hoteltorshavn.fo* ⇆ *43 rooms* ◎l *Free Breakfast.*

🛍 Shopping

Andreas í Vágsbotni

CERAMICS/GLASSWARE | Stock up on costumed dolls, cuddly stuffed puffins, and other island gifts at this harborside shop. The knitwear by designers like Snaeldan and Toting is especially prized for its local lanolin-rich wool. ⊠ *Vágsbotnur 4* ☎ *298/312–040* ⊘ *Closed Sun.*

Glarsmiðjan

ART GALLERIES | Discover the Faroese art scene at this downtown gallery showcasing oil paintings, watercolors, lithographs, and prints by island artists like Anita K. Petersen, Bjørg Mohr Anderssen, and Torhild Tolfsen—both on display and for sale. ⊠ *Dr. Jakobsensgøta 7* ☎ *298/310–623* ⊕ *www.glarsmidjan.fo* ⊘ *Closed Sat.–Mon.*

Guðrun & Guðrun

CLOTHING | With so many sheep on the Faroe Islands, it's no wonder wool products are featured in most gift shops. At the luxury level is this shop run by two local women, who use the Faroes' isolation and natural beauty as inspiration for their designs of sweaters, hats, cardigans, vests, and dresses. ⊠ *Niels Finsensgøta 13* ☎ *298/315–166* ⊕ *www.gudrungudrun.com.*

Chapter 6

FINLAND

Updated by
Timothy Bird

⊙ Sights	🍴 Restaurants	🛏 Hotels	🛍 Shopping	🍸 Nightlife
★★★★★	★★★★☆	★★★★☆	★★★★☆	★★★☆☆

WELCOME TO FINLAND

TOP REASONS TO GO

★ **Enjoy comfort close to nature.** Explore vast expanses of unspoiled forests, lakes, rivers, and sweeping fells, then relax in a luxe hotel or cabin.

★ **Sample the "real" sauna.** Finland is the cultural and spiritual home of the sauna, ideally experienced between dips in a nearby lake or the sea. Locals will often be keen for you to give it a go.

★ **Discover Finland's cultural riches.** Marvel at elegant architecture, the music of Sibelius, exquisite design, and classical and modern art. Small towns come alive for summer festivals of opera, rock, and jazz.

★ **Wow at the northern lights.** Away from the city lights, Finland offers great viewing of the aurora borealis and expertise on how to witness this most memorable of natural phenomena.

★ **Explore the wonders of winter.** Finland is a winter activity paradise, with options ranging from skiing, snowshoeing, and skating to ice-hole fishing, ice swimming, and reindeer safaris.

Finland extends well over 1,000 km (600 miles) from its capital, Helsinki, in the south to its northern tip above the Arctic Circle. The capital region on the Baltic coast of the Gulf of Finland also comprises the neighboring cities of Espoo and Vantaa. The coast fragments into the excitingly rugged Southwest Finland archipelago and the Åland Islands grouping. Most of Lapland, containing Europe's wildest wilderness, is above the Arctic Circle; its provincial capital, Rovaniemi, is directly on the circle. Breezy towns including Joensuu, Kuopio, and Savonlinna are located on the shores of the expansive lake systems of the east, close to the long border with Russia.

1 **Helsinki.**

2 **Gallen-Kallela Estate.**

3 **Hvitträsk.**

4 **Ainola.**

5 **Porvoo.**

6 **Fiskars Village.**

7 **Savonlinna.**

8 **Kuopio.**

9 **Tampere.**

10 **Turku.**

11 **Hanko.**

12 **Naantali.**

13 **Pargas (Parainen).**

14 **Mariehamn and the Åland Islands.**

15 **Rovaniemi.**

16 **Saariselkä.**

17 **Ivalo and Inari.**

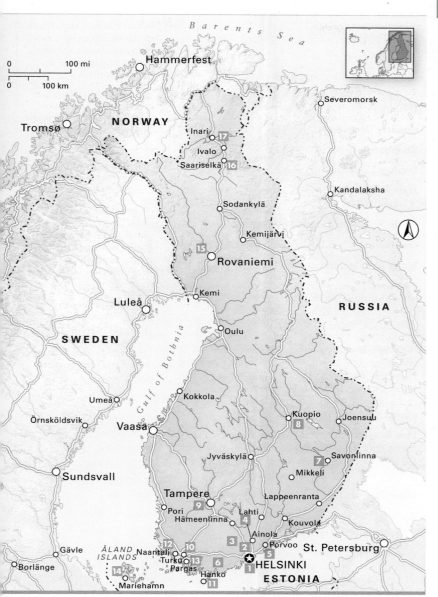

B a r e n t s   S e a

0 ___ 100 mi
0 ___ 100 km

Hammerfest

Severomorsk

NORWAY

Tromsø

Inari

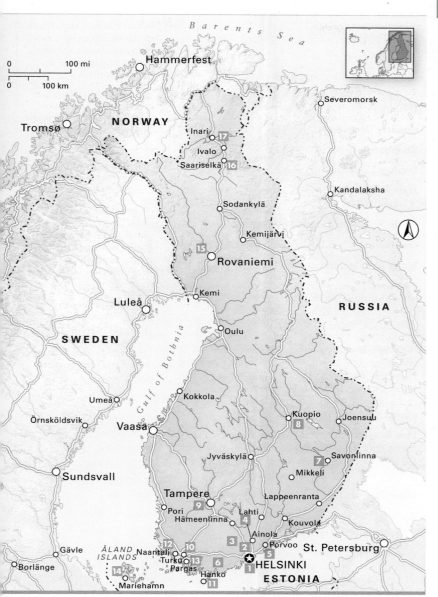17

Ivalo

Sariselkä 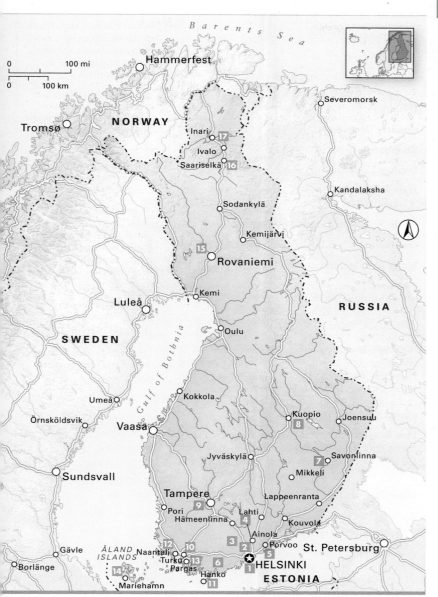16

Kandalaksha

Sodankylä

Kemijärvi

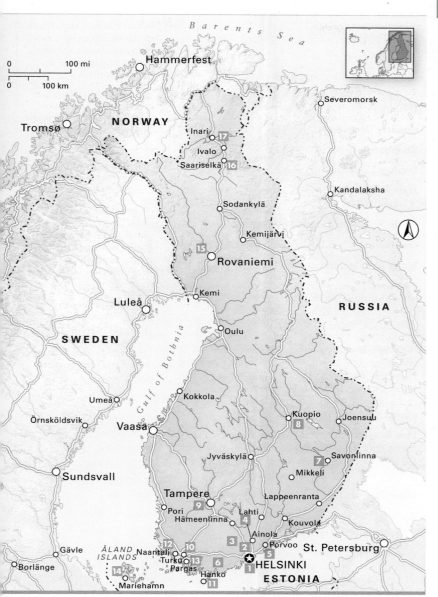15 ○Rovaniemi

Kemi

Luleå

RUSSIA

SWEDEN

Gulf of Bothnia

Oulu

Umeå○

Kokkola

Örnsköldsvik○

Vaasa

Kuopio

Joensuu

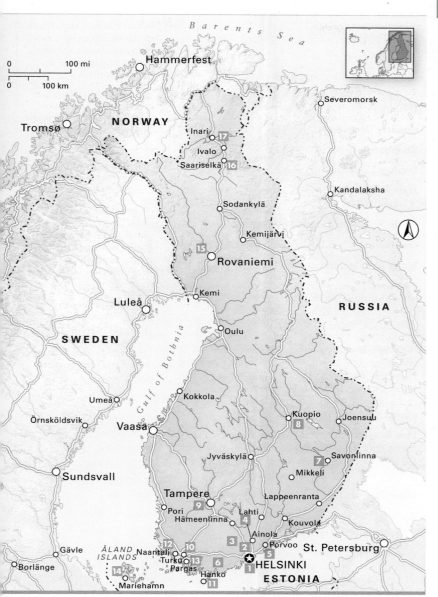8

Jyväskylä

Savonlinna

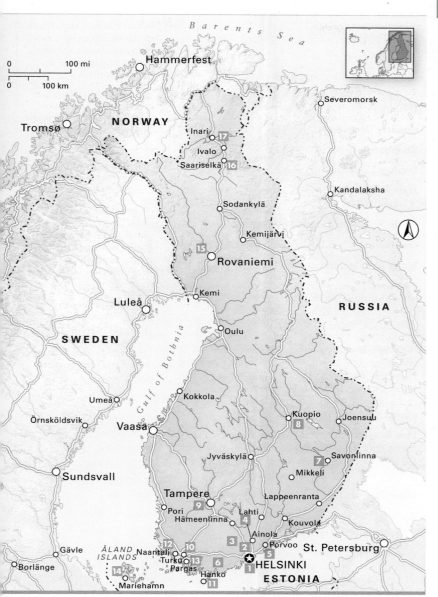7

Sundsvall

Mikkeli

Tampere

Lappeenranta

Pori 9

Lahti

Hämeenlinna 4

Kouvola

Ainola

Gävle

ÅLAND
ISLANDS Naantali 12 10

3

Porvoo

St. Petersburg

Turku 13

2

Borlänge

Pargas

6

5

Hanko

★ HELSINKI

14

1

Mariehamn

11

ESTONIA

FINLAND SNAPSHOT

AT A GLANCE

Capital: Helsinki

Population: 5,530,000

Currency: Euro

Money: ATMs common, credit cards widely accepted

Language: Finnish, Swedish

Country Code: 358

Emergencies: 112

Driving: On the right

Electricity: 230v/50 cycles; plugs have two round prongs

Time: Seven hours ahead of New York

Documents: Up to 90 days with valid passport

Major Mobile Companies: Telia, Elisa, DNA

Websites: ⊕ www.visitfinland.com, ⊕ www.visithelsinki.fi, ⊕ www.discoveringfinland.com

WHEN TO GO

High Season: June, July, and August are the warmest months, with very long days when the sun never fully sets in the far north. July, however, is when most Finns have their summer holidays, and some businesses, including restaurants, will be closed.

Low Season: Except for a December price spike during the Christmas lead-up, November to March is the cheapest time to visit. It's also the coldest and darkest, with very short days near year's end.

Value Season: April can still be a bit risky temperature-wise, but May is usually quite lovely, and hotel and flight prices are a bit lower than at their summer peak. This is also true of September and October, but fall is generally wetter than spring.

BIG EVENTS

■ **July:** One of Europe's oldest and best-known jazz festivals is the nine-day Pori Jazz, held in the western coastal town of Pori. ⊕ www.porijazz.fi

■ **August:** What began as a joke in the 1990s is now the annual Air Guitar World Championships in Oulu—one of many odd "sports" and annual activities pursued across the country. ⊕ www.airguitarworld-championships.com

■ **August–September:** Helsinki Festival is a two-week multi-arts event incorporating local and international music, theater, dance, and film. ⊕ www.helsingin-juhlaviikot.fi

■ **December:** Numerous cities and towns around Finland (including Helsinki, Turku, and Porvoo) host bright and colorful Christmas markets throughout December.

Mother Nature dictates life in this Nordic land, where winter brings perpetual darkness, and summer, perpetual light. Crystal-clear streams run through vast forests lighted by the midnight sun, and reindeer roam free. The architecture of Alvar Aalto and the Saarinens—Eliel and son Eero—visible in many U.S. cities, demonstrates the Finnish affinity for nature, with soaring spaces evocative of Finland's moss-floored forests. And the music of Jean Sibelius, Finland's most famous son, swings from a somber nocturne of midwinter darkness to the tremolo of sunlight slanting through pine and birch.

Until 1917, Finland was under the domination of its nearest neighbors, Sweden and Russia, who fought over it for centuries. After more than 600 years under the Swedish crown and 100 under Russian czars, the country inevitably bears many traces of the two cultures, including a small (just under 6%) but influential Swedish-speaking population and a scattering of Orthodox churches.

There is a tough, resilient quality to the Finns, descended from wandering tribes who probably migrated from the south and southwest before the Christian era. Finland is one of the few countries that shared a border with the Soviet Union in 1939 and retained its independence. Indeed, no country fought the Soviets to a standstill as the Finns did in the grueling 105-day Winter War of 1939–40. This resilience stems from the turbulence of the country's past and from the people's determination to work the land and survive the long, dark winters.

The average Finn has become harder to define, as a new, more urbanized, well-traveled, and often multilingual generation comes to the fore, gradually eroding the surly, reticent stereotype. Make the first approach—although you may not need to—and you may have a friend for life. Finns still like their silent spaces, though, and won't appreciate backslapping familiarity—least of all in the sauna, still regarded by many as a spiritual as well as cleansing experience. You might also notice an annual cycle of character more pronounced than elsewhere, whereby the gloom of midwinter is reflected in introspection, and the continuous light of the northern summer is expressed in more extroverted behavior.

MAJOR REGIONS

Helsinki. A city on the sea, Helsinki was built along a series of odd-shape peninsulas and islands jutting into Baltic Coast along the Gulf of Finland. Today, the lively capital is the meeting point of Eastern and Western Europe, which is reflected in its cosmopolitan image.

Side Trips from Helsinki. The capital is within easy reach of some rewarding day-trips that give a taste of the milieus and cultural heritage in the rest of the country as a whole. These include museum homes such as Ainola, onetime home of Sibelius; Hvitträsk, a fabulous architectural fantasy; and artist Akseli Gallen-Kallela's studio in Espoo. A short voyage through the rugged Baltic archipelago to idyllic Porvoo and a manageable drive to the old iron foundry village of Fiskars, home of the famous scissors, are other options. Charming wooden towns and waterside former homes of iconic musicians and architects, now engaging museums, are within easy reach of the capital by boat or bus. Two national parks are within an hour's drive from the city center, offering a taste of the greater wilderness beyond.

The Lakelands. Finland is perhaps best known for its lakes, numbering about 188,000, and you don't need to travel far in this region to appreciate their beauty, whether in winter or summer. Almost every lake, big or small, is fringed with tiny cabins. The lake cabin is a Finnish institution, and until the advent of cheap package tours abroad, nearly every Finnish family vacationed in the same way: in its cabin on a lake. Savonlinna is the best-placed town in the Lakeland and can make a convenient base from which to begin exploring the region. Lake Saimaa is home to the rare freshwater ringed seal, and if you're lucky you might see a seal head or two pop up in the lake. To the west, the smaller Hämeenlinna has its own lakeside castle. North of Hämeenlinna, Tampere has vibrant cultural variety and is nestled between two large lakes. There are small medieval churches scattered throughout the Lakeland, the most famous of which is the stone church in Hattula just outside Hämeenlinna, its interior a gallery of medieval painted scenes. Tampere and Hämeenlinna are short train rides from Helsinki and make good daylong excursions from the capital city. Savonlinna takes over four hours to reach but could still be visited in a day with an early start.

Southwest Finland Archipelago, including the Åland Islands. A magical world of islands stretches along Finland's coastline. In the Gulf of Finland and the Baltic Sea, more than 30,000 islands form a magnificent archipelago. The rugged and fascinating Åland Islands group lies west of Turku, forming an autonomous province of its own. Turku, the former capital of Finland, was the main gateway through which cultural influences reached the nation over the centuries, while nearby Naantali is a charming old harbor town and home of the Moominworld theme park. A trip to Turku via Hanko and Ekenäs will give you a taste of Finland at its most historic and scenic. Many of Finland's oldest towns lie in this southwest region of the country, having been chartered by Swedish kings—hence the predominance of the Swedish language here. Mariehamn, with its rich maritime heritage, is the provincial capital of the autonomous Åland archipelago.

Lapland. The far north boasts winter sports resorts, the reindeer-herding Sami people, exhilarating trekking trails—and Santa Claus's "true home" right on the Arctic Circle. A magical blue light persists during winter's *kaamos* period when the sun barely dares to rise, while summer days are dazzling.

Planning

Getting Here and Around

AIR

Finnair offers domestic and international flights, with direct service from New York (JFK), Chicago, Miami, San Francisco, and Los Angeles and code share flights from other U.S. destinations. Other airlines offer links through the other Nordic hubs of Copenhagen and Stockholm. Flying time from New York to Helsinki is about eight hours, and nine hours for the return trip.

All international flights arrive at Helsinki–Vantaa International Airport (HEL), also known as Helsinki Airport, 20 km (12 miles) north of city center.

AIRPORT Helsinki Airport. (*HEL*) ☏ *0200/14636* ⊕ *www.finavia.fi.* **Rovaniemi Airport (RVN) .** ☏ *020/7086506* ⊕ *www.finavia.fi/en/airports/rovaniemi.* **Tampere-Pirkkala Airport (TMP).** ⊠ *Tornikaari 50, Tampere* ☏ *020/7085521* ⊕ *www.finavia.fi/en/airports/tampere-pirkkala.*

BOAT

From Stockholm, Silja and Viking Line ships cross to the Finnish Åland Islands (7 hours), Turku (11 hours), and Helsinki (15 hours), generally with one departure daily in each direction. The same shipping lines, in addition to Eckerö Line, ply the route between Helsinki and Tallinn (two hours).

The car ferries that cruise the Baltic to the Åland Islands and Sweden have saunas, children's playrooms, casinos, a host of bars and cafés, and superb restaurants. There are storage boxes for luggage in the Helsinki and Stockholm terminals if you are planning a day of sightseeing in either city.

In Helsinki the Tallink Silja Line terminal for ships arriving from Stockholm is at Olympialaituri (Olympia Terminal), on the west side of the Eteläsatama (South Harbour). The Viking Line terminal for ships arriving from Stockholm is at Katajanokanlaituri (Katajanokka Terminal), on the east side of the South Harbour. Both Silja and Viking have downtown agencies where information and tickets are available. Ask about half-price fares for bus and train travel in conjunction with ferry trips.

CONTACTS Eckerö Line. ☏ *0600/04300* ⊕ *www.eckeroline.fi.* **Suomenlinna Ferry.** ⊹ *The public ferry terminal is in the eastern corner of the Market Square in the South Harbour* ☏ *09/3102–1000* ⊕ *www.slloy.fi.* **Tallink Silja Line.** ☏ *040/547541222 international customer service, 0600/15700 in Finland* ✉ *international.sales@tallinksilja.com* ⊕ *www.tallinksilja.com.* **Viking Line.** ⊠ *Katajanokka Terminal, South Harbour* ☏ *09/123–574 in Helsinki* ⊕ *www.vikingline.fi.*

BUS

The Finnish bus network, Matkahuolto, is extensive, and fares are reasonable.

CONTACTS Matkahuolto. ☏ *0200/4000 €1.99/min + local network charge* ⊕ *www.matkahuolto.com.* **OnniBus.** ☏ *0600/02010 €0.99/minute* ⊕ *www.onnibus.com.*

CAR

Driving is pleasant on Finland's relatively uncongested roads. Car rental daily rates start at around €25.

Late autumn and spring are the most hazardous times to drive. Roads are often icy in autumn, and the spring thaw can make for potholes in the more rural areas. Driving is on the right-hand side of the road. You must use headlights at all times, and seat belts are compulsory for everyone. Yield to cars coming from the right at most intersections. The use of cell phones while driving is not permitted. There are strict drinking-and-driving laws in Finland, with occasional police breathalyzer checkpoints. Remember to watch out for elk and reindeer signs, placed where the animals are known to cross the road. Elk (moose) don't budge when cars approach and can cause collisions, while reindeer wander freely in the far north, often onto the roads.

Outside urban areas, speed limits vary between 60 kph and 100 kph (37 mph and 62 mph), with a general speed limit of about 80 kph (50 mph). In towns the limit is 40 kph to 60 kph (25 mph to 37 mph), and on motorways it's 100 kph to 120 kph (62 mph to 75 mph).

Gasoline costs about €1.55 per liter. Nearly all gas stations are self-service. Those in Helsinki and on major roadways are open 24 hours.

CONTACTS Automobile and Touring Club of Finland. ☎ *09/7258–4400 in Helsinki, 0200/8080 24-hr road service* ⊕ *www. autoliitto.fi.*

CRUISE

Helsinki is a busy cruise destination and sees many ships throughout the season. Ships dock at one of three distinct areas.

The quay at Katajanokka Terminal has a souvenir shop, toilets, and a taxi station. From Katajanokka Terminal, local Bus 13 or Tram 4 or 4T will take you to Helsinki city center, but this is also reachable on foot.

South Harbour has quays at the Olympia Terminal—with shopping, information, a taxi rank, currency exchange, and Internet access—and the Makasiini Terminal. It's a 15-minute walk into downtown from the South Harbour port entrance.

Trams 1A, 3B, and 3T run from the port into town.

Hernesaari Harbor has two quays with access to the dedicated cruise terminal, with shops, information desk, taxi rank, and Internet access. It's a longer walk into Helsinki from here, but the terminal is served by bus routes 14B and 16.

Taxis wait at all terminals to take visitors downtown, and this may be the most convenient way to travel if you don't want to take the cruise shuttle service. Journey times are short from all the terminals, the longest being around 15 minutes. Taxis are plentiful (albeit expensive) and make a convenient way to link attractions. A 5-km (3-mile) trip is about €10, while a 10-km (6-mile) trip is about €16.

TAXI

Taxis go everywhere in Finland. The meter starts at about €9. The price per kilometer increases with the number of passengers. In cities people generally go to one of the numerous taxi stands and take the first one available. Generally, taxis cannot be hailed, and a yellow "vacant" light means that the car is on its way to a stand. Most taxi drivers take credit cards. Tipping is unnecessary; if you want to leave something, round up to the nearest euro. The Finnish for a receipt is *kuitti.*

CONTACTS Taksi Helsinki. ☎ *0100/0700 €2.76 plus 35 cents per 10 minutes; queuing is free up to 85 seconds, 0100/06000 same charges apply; for advance bookings* ⊕ *www.taksihelsinki.fi.*

TRAIN

Passenger trains leave Helsinki twice daily for St. Petersburg, a roughly three-hour trip, and once daily on an overnighter to Moscow (13 hours). Remember that you need a visa to travel to Russia. To get to northern Sweden or Norway, you must combine train-bus or train-boat travel.

The Finnish State Railways, or VR, serve southern Finland well, but connections in the central and northern sections are scarcer and are supplemented by buses. Helsinki is the main junction, with Riihimäki to the north a major hub. You can get as far north as Rovaniemi and Kemijärvi by rail, but to penetrate farther into Lapland, you'll need to rely on buses, domestic flights, or local taxis.

Note that all train travelers (apart from those on commuter services in the Helsinki region) in Finland must have a reserved seat, but it is possible to buy a seat ticket on the train. Special fast trains (InterCity and Pendolino) are more expensive but also more comfortable. First- and second-class seats are available on all express trains.

CONTACTS Finnish State Railways. (*VR*) ☎ *0600/41900 €1.99 plus local network charge* ⊕ *www.vr.fi.* **Rail Europe.** ☎ *888/382–7245, 800/622–8600 in the United States* ⊕ *www.raileurope.com.*

Hotels

Expect private baths and/or showers in rooms unless otherwise noted. Prices almost always include a generous breakfast and sauna privileges.

Look for room-rate discounts on weekends and in summer months, especially between *juhannus* (Midsummer, the summer solstice holiday in late June) and July 31, when prices are usually 30% to 50% lower.

HOTEL AND RESTAURANT PRICES
Hotel prices in the reviews are the lowest cost of a standard double room in high season. Restaurant prices in the reviews are the average cost of a main course at dinner, or if dinner is not served, at lunch.

WHAT IT COSTS In Euros

	$	$$	$$$	$$$$
RESTAURANTS				
	under €20	€20-25	€25-35	over €35
HOTELS				
	under €150	€150-200	€200-250	over €250

Restaurants

Most restaurants open at 11 for lunch, switch to a dinner menu at 4, and close their kitchens around 11; many non-hotel restaurants are closed on Sunday. Finns generally prefer to eat at 7 or 7:30 when dining out, so it's rarely necessary to make a reservation to eat before 7 or after 9 but always wise to check, especially for upmarket gourmet dining. No dress codes are stated and jackets are rarely required; however, at top restaurants smart casual is the order of the day. Take note that restaurants in the bigger cities are often closed in July.

Finnish food emphasizes freshness rather than variety, although in keeping with European trends, restaurants are becoming more innovative and expanding on classic Finnish ingredients from forest, lake, and sea.

The better Finnish restaurants offer some of the country's most stunning game—reindeer, elk (moose), grouse, and very rarely, bear—accompanied by wild-berry compotes and exotic mushroom sauces. The chanterelle grows wild in Finland, as do dozens of other edible mushrooms, including the tasty morel. Fish is served in many ways, and is especially savored smoked. Crayfish season kicks off from late July.

Alcohol is expensive here, but beer lovers should not miss the well-made Finnish brews. More coffee is consumed per capita in Finland than in any other country, and you'll see a staggering number of cafés and coffee bars throughout the country. Particularly in Helsinki, patrons of cafés downtown and around the waterfront spill outside onto the streets in fine weather.

Visitor Information

CONTACTS Visit Finland. ⊕ *www.visitfinland.com.* **Museum Card.** ☎ *044/784–5745* ⊕ *museot.fi.*

Helsinki

A city of the sea, Helsinki was built along a series of oddly shaped peninsulas and islands jutting into the Baltic coast along the Gulf of Finland. Streets and avenues curve around bays, bridges reach to nearby islands, and ferries ply among offshore islands. Many of the Finnish capital's main attractions are in a compact central area—an attraction in itself—although an affordable and varied mass transit system is also available for visitors.

Although the center is compact, the city as a whole has grown dramatically since World War II. Helsinki now absorbs more than one-tenth of the Finnish population. The metro area covers 764 square km (474 square miles) and 315 islands. Most sights, hotels, and restaurants cluster on one peninsula, forming a compact central hub. The greater Helsinki metropolitan area has a total population of more than 1 million people and includes Espoo and Vantaa, officially cities in their own right but effectively extended suburban outskirts. It's a continuously developing and expanding city, with new suburbs, such as Kalasatama to the east and Jätkäsaari to the west, still rising and expanding and existing ones, such as Pasila, being redeveloped.

For three centuries, Helsinki (Helsingfors in Swedish) had its ups and downs as a trading town. Turku, to the west, remained Finland's capital and intellectual center. However, Helsinki's fortunes improved when Finland fell under Russian rule as an autonomous grand duchy. Czar Alexander I wanted Finland's political center closer to Russia and, in 1812, selected Helsinki as the new capital. Shortly afterward, Turku suffered a disastrous fire, forcing the university to move to Helsinki. The town's future was secure.

Just before the czar's proclamation, a fire destroyed many of Helsinki's traditional wooden structures, precipitating the construction of new buildings suitable for a nation's capital. The German-born architect Carl Ludvig Engel was commissioned to rebuild the city, and as a result, Helsinki has some of the purest neoclassical architecture in the world. Add to this foundation the influence of Stockholm and St. Petersburg with the local inspiration of 20th-century Finnish design, and the result is a European capital city that is as architecturally eye-catching as it is distinct from other Scandinavian capitals. You are bound to discover endless engaging details: a grimacing gargoyle; a foursome of males supporting a balcony's weight on their shoulders; a building painted in striking colors with contrasting flowers in the windows. The city's 400 or so parks and the proximity to the sea, with many shorelines skirted by pleasant woodland, make it particularly inviting in summer.

Today, Helsinki is still a meeting point of eastern and western Europe, which is reflected in its cosmopolitan image, the influx of Russians and Estonians, and a generally multilingual population. Outdoor summer bars (*terassit* as the locals call them) and cafés in the city center are perfect for people-watching on a summer afternoon.

The temperature in the sea water pool in Helsinki's Allas Sea Pool is equivalent to that of the Baltic Sea, so you'll want to wear a woolly hat.

GETTING HERE AND AROUND

AIR

All domestic and international flights are to Helsinki Airport, 20 km (12 miles) north of the city center.

Local Bus 615 runs between the airport and the main railway station downtown from 4:50 am to 1:20 am, taking 40 minutes. Finnair buses carry travelers to and from the railway station (Finnair's City Terminal) every 25 minutes, with a stop at Hesperia Park and by request at a number of other stops on the route. Travel time from Hesperia Park to the airport is about 35 minutes.

A rail loop runs from the main railway station. Travelers can take a train in either direction from the airport to get to the city center. The trip takes about half an hour. Tickets can be bought from machines near the entrance to the underground station or on the platform but should be bought before boarding the train.

Confusingly for bleary-eyed arriving travelers, there are several competing taxi companies operating from Helsinki Airport. Fares vary slightly from company to company and depending on the number of passengers, and they are displayed at the head of each company's separate stand. Expect to pay in the region of €40 to get to central Helsinki.

BUS AND TRAM

Many of Helsinki's main attractions are reachable on foot within the central downtown area, but public city transport is an efficient alternative. Public transit networks are extensive, and service is frequent, with fewer buses at nights and on Sunday. Pick up a route map at the tourist office—many stops do not have them. A zonal system is in place, for which the best option for short-term visitors is to purchase day tickets, costing from €8 for one day to €32 for seven days for unlimited travel on all transport in central zones A and B. Extensive information on routes, fares, and timetables is available from the Helsinki City Transport website.

Mass transit in the Helsinki region includes buses, streetcars, local commuter trains, a metro, and ferries to the Suomenlinna fortress. All local trains start from Helsinki Central Railway Station and stop at the Pasila district station. For trips in the downtown area, trams are often the quickest and most convenient option. Visit the website or call the service number for details. A metro line runs from eastern Helsinki to the stations in the neighboring city of Espoo to the west, and there are a number of stations in the downtown area, including the Central Railway Station. Hotel reception staff are generally very well informed about local transport options.

The Helsinki Card allows unlimited travel on city public transportation, in addition to free entry to many museums, a free sightseeing tour, and other discounts. Visit the Helsinki Card website for pricing details. You can buy it online as well as at more than 70 places, including airport information desks, ferry terminals, some hotels and travel agencies, the Stockmann department store, the Hotel Booking Centre, and the Helsinki City Tourist Office. Visit the Helsinki City Transport (HSL) website at ⊕ *www.hsl.fi* for details and fares, or call Customer Service on ☎ *09 4766 4000.*

TAXI

There are numerous taxi stands; central stands are at Rautatientori (Railway Station Square); the main bus station, or *linja-autoasema*; and in the Esplanade. In general, taxis will not stop if hailed; the yellow "vacant" light means that they are on their way to a stand. Taxis fares are quite high, but drivers are usually safe and reliable, as are the vehicles. An average taxi ride in downtown Helsinki can cost around €20; a taxi from the airport can cost €40 or more. All taxis in Helsinki go through the Taxi Center. Call 0100–0700 or visit www.taksihelsinki.fi.

TOURS

Tours run most frequently in the summer, but some do not operate in early June or September.

BY BOAT

Most major boat tours depart from the Market Square (Kauppatori). The easiest way to choose one is to go to the square in the morning and read the information boards describing the tours. Most tours run in summer only. You can go as far afield as Porvoo or take a short jaunt to the Helsinki Zoo on the island of Korkeasaari.

BY BUS

Stromma Helsinki

Bus tours are a good way to get oriented in Helsinki. Stromma's Hop On Hop Off guided bus sightseeing tour of central Helsinki sites runs from April to October and is free with the Helsinki Card; otherwise it's €27. Recorded commentary is available on a headset. Tours stop at the Senaatintori (Senate Square), Cafe Ursula near Kaivopuisto Park, the Hietalahti Market Square, the Temppeliaukio Church, and many other popular sights. Stromma offers a variety of other tours, including sightseeing by boat on a number of scenic routes. It also issues a variety of discount cards, most notably the Helsinki Card. ⊠ *Helsinki ✛ Ticket sales in the Esplanade, Market Square, Senate Square, and Katajanokka and Olympia ferry terminals* ☎ *09/2288–1600* ⊕ *www. stromma.com.*

ON FOOT

The Helsinki Tourist Information office employs "Helsinki Helpers," dressed in green and white to walk the streets in the city center and harbor area in summer to answer questions and give directions. Helsinki Expert is a multipurpose travel agent and guide-booking center that will arrange personal tour guides. The City Tourist Office also has an excellent brochure, *Helsinki on Foot,* with six walks covering most points of interest.

VISITOR INFORMATION
CONTACTS Helsinki Tourist Information.
✉ *Central Railway Station, Kaivokatu 1, Keskusta/Rautatieasema* ☎ *09/3101–3300* ⊕ *www.visithelsinki.fi.*

👁 Sights

The city center is compact and easily explored on foot, with the main tourist sites grouped in several clusters; nearby islands are easily accessible by ferry. Pleasant residential suburbs spread across leafy islands such as Lauttasaari to the west and Kulosaari to the east, and several of the city's attractions are located on islands. Just west of the residential Katajanokka promontory, the Senate Square and its Lutheran cathedral mark the beginning of the city center, which extends westward along Aleksanterinkatu. The wide street Mannerheimintie moves diagonally past the major attractions of the city center before terminating at the western end of the Esplanade. The orange tents of the Market Square brighten even the coldest snowy winter months with fresh flowers, fish, crafts, and produce. In warm weather, the bazaar fills with shoppers who stop for the ubiquitous coffee and munkki or doughnuts, with the seaborne traffic in the South Harbour as a backdrop. From here you can take the local ferry service to the Suomenlinna fortress or to Korkeasaari, home of the zoo, or take a walk through the neighborhoods of Helsinki encompassing the harbor; city center shopping district; tree-lined Bulevardi; and indoor Hietalahdentori, another marketplace.

Several of the main sights are grouped to the west of the Central Railway Station. These include the Amos Rex art museum, Museum of Contemporary Art Kiasma, Oodi Central Library, Music Center, and Parliament House. The largely residential districts, adjacent to the center, of Eira, with its fabulous art nouveau buildings, Punavuori, Töölö, and Kruunuhaka

are a tangle of smaller streets, some of them curving and some of which run for just a few blocks before changing their names; carry a good map while exploring this area. The revitalized area of Kallio, with its hipster bars and restaurants, lies to the north of the center.

Outlying suburbs include the new and still expanding districts of Ruoholahti to the west and Kalasatama to the east. Pasila, 2 kilometres to the north, is a cluster of modern residential, corporate and administrative buildings and the focus of a major ongoing architectural face lift. All trains out of Helsinki, local and regional, also stop at Pasila.

★ Allas Sea Pool
SWIMMING | Finland's love affair with the sauna—one of the very few originally Finnish words that are internationally recognizable—has never diminished, but this very traditional national pursuit has been enjoying a resurgence in popularity, not least with a younger crowd. You are not obliged to sample this most Finnish of activities at the hugely popular Allas Sea Pool in the South Harbour, but a dip in one of the year-round pools built into the sea—one of which is heated—wouldn't really be complete without a visit to the mixed sauna (swimsuits and towels are available for rent). The Allas concept also embraces events and concerts and has food and drinks available from the separately managed Allas Cafe and Terrace (a prime harborside sun-trap), which serves breakfast to prework bathers and wholesome lunches. ✉ *Katajanokanlaituri 2A, Katajanokka* ☎ *040/565-6582* ⊕ *www.allasseapool.fi.*

★ Amos Rex
MUSEUM | Opened in 2018 beneath the newly renovated 1930s Lasipalatsi (Glass Palace), this impressive new contemporary art museum with 24,000 square feet of subterranean exhibition space is the expanded new home of the Amos Anderson Art Museum, the 590-seat handsome Bio Rex cinema (restored to

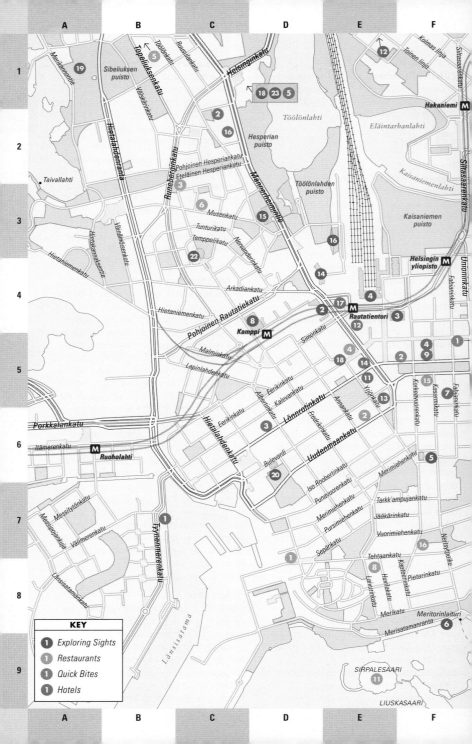

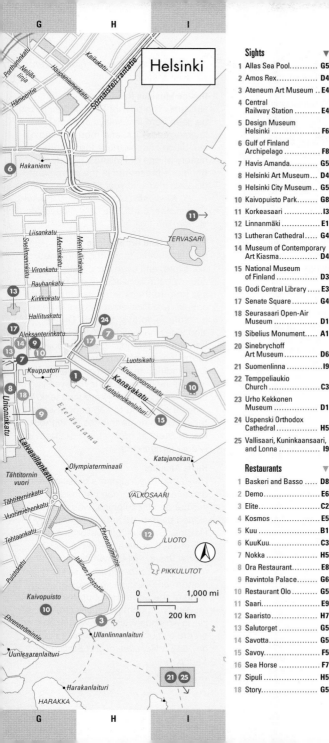

Helsinki

Sights ▼

1. Allas Sea Pool **G5**
2. Amos Rex **D4**
3. Ateneum Art Museum .. **E4**
4. Central Railway Station **E4**
5. Design Museum Helsinki **F6**
6. Gulf of Finland Archipelago **F8**
7. Havis Amanda **G5**
8. Helsinki Art Museum ... **D4**
9. Helsinki City Museum .. **G5**
10. Kaivopuisto Park **G8**
11. Korkeasaari **I3**
12. Linnanmäki **E1**
13. Lutheran Cathedral **G4**
14. Museum of Contemporary Art Kiasma **D4**
15. National Museum of Finland **D3**
16. Oodi Central Library **E3**
17. Senate Square **G4**
18. Seurasaari Open-Air Museum **D1**
19. Sibelius Monument **A1**
20. Sinebrychoff Art Museum **D6**
21. Suomenlinna **I9**
22. Temppeliaukio Church **C3**
23. Urho Kekkonen Museum **D1**
24. Uspenski Orthodox Cathedral **H5**
25. Vallisaari, Kuninkaansaari, and Lonna **I9**

Restaurants ▼

1. Baskeri and Basso **D8**
2. Demo **E6**
3. Elite **C2**
4. Kosmos **E5**
5. Kuu **B1**
6. KuuKuu **C3**
7. Nokka **H5**
8. Ora Restaurant **E8**
9. Ravintola Palace **G6**
10. Restaurant Olo **G5**
11. Saari **E9**
12. Saaristo **H7**
13. Salutorget **G5**
14. Savotta **G5**
15. Savoy **F5**
16. Sea Horse **F7**
17. Sipuli **H5**
18. Story **G5**

Quick Bites ▼

1. Café Engel **G5**
2. Café Esplanad **F5**
3. Cafe Ursula **H8**

Hotels ▼

1. Clarion Hotel Helsinki .. **B7**
2. Crowne Plaza Helsinki .. **C2**
3. GLO Hotel Art **D6**
4. GLO Hotel Kluuvi **F5**
5. Hilton Helsinki Kalastajatorppa **D1**
6. Hilton Helsinki Strand .. **G2**
7. Hotel F6 .... **F5**
8. Hotel Haven **G5**
9. Hotel Kämp **F5**
10. Hotel Katajanokka **I5**
11. Hotel St. George **E5**
12. Hotel Seurahuone **E4**
13. Klaus K **E5**
14. Marski by Scandic **E5**
15. Scandic Grand Marina Helsinki **H5**
16. Scandic Park Helsinki ... **C2**
17. Sokos Hotel Vaakuna ... **E4**
18. Solo Sokos Hotel Torni **E5**

its 1930s glory), a café, and a restaurant. The roof of the sizeable exhibition hall is a series of giant domes with angled roof lights that frame surrounding views and light the galleries. From outside, the roof's gently rolling forms are part of a popular public square that beckons to children and skateboarders and serves as a a very modern counterpoint to the 1930s functionalist surroundings. Originally dedicated to Finnish and Swedish art of the 19th and 20th centuries, the museum is now also focused on international contemporary art. ⊠ *Mannerheimintie 22–24, Keskusta* ☎ *09/6844–4633* ⊕ *amosrex.fi* 🖃 *€15* ☽ *Closed Tues.* Ⓜ *Central Railway Station.*

Ateneum Art Museum

MUSEUM | The best traditional Finnish art is housed in this splendid neoclassical complex occupying one side of the Railway Station Square, one of three museums organized under the Finnish National Gallery umbrella. The gallery holds major European works, but the outstanding attraction is the Finnish art, particularly the dramatic and moody works of Akseli Gallen-Kallela, inspired by the national epic, *The Kalevala.* The rustic portraits by Albert Edelfelt are enchanting, and many contemporary Finnish artists are well represented. The two other museums that make up the National Gallery are **Kiasma** and **Sinebrychoff.** ⊠ *Kaivokatu 2, Keskusta* ☎ *0294/500–401 information* ⊕ *www. ateneum.fi* 🖃 *€17* ☽ *Closed Mon.*

Central Railway Station

TRANSPORTATION SITE (AIRPORT/BUS/FERRY/ TRAIN) | The train station, the terminus for routes all across the country and to St. Petersburg and Moscow in Russia, and its adjoining Railway Station Square are the city's bustling commuter hub. The station's huge quirky granite figures are by Emil Wikström; the solid granite building they adorn was designed by Eliel Saarinen, one of the founders of the early-20th-century National Romantic style. ⊠ *Kaivokatu 1, Keskusta/Rautatieasema*

☎ *0600/41900* ⊕ *www.vr.fi/en* Ⓜ *Central Railway Station.*

Design Museum Helsinki

MUSEUM | The best of Finnish design can be seen here in displays of furnishings, jewelry, ceramics, and more. Changing exhibitions supplement the absorbing history of one of Finland's proudest traditions presented in the permanent displays and archives. ⊠ *Korkeavuorenkatu 23, Keskusta* ☎ *09/622–0540* ⊕ *www. designmuseum.fi* 🖃 *€12* ☽ *Closed Mon.* Ⓜ *Tram 10.*

Gulf of Finland Archipelago

NEIGHBORHOOD | In winter, Finns walk, ski, skate, and even cycle with dogs and even strollers across the frozen sea here to the nearby islands. Visitors should take local advice about where it is safe to do this, though. On the land side, the facades of the Eira and Kaivopuisto districts' grandest buildings form a parade of architectural splendor. One tradition that remains, even in this upscale neighborhood, is rug washing in the sea—an incredibly arduous task. You may be surprised to see people leave their rugs to dry in the sea air without fear of theft. ⊠ *Merisatama* ✛ *South of Merisatamanranta.*

Havis Amanda

FOUNTAIN | This fountain's brass centerpiece, a young woman perched on rocks surrounded by dolphins, was commissioned by the city fathers to embody Helsinki. Sculptor Ville Vallgren completed her in 1908 using a Parisian girl as his model. It's a well-known landmark and meeting place for locals, marking the eastern end of the Esplanade and the edge of the South Harbour. Partying university students annually crown the Havis Amanda with their white caps on the eve of Vappu, the May 1 holiday. ⊠ *Eteläesplanadi and Eteläranta, Kauppatori.*

The Amos Rex museum's domed subterranean galleries bubble up through the ground to create a playful outdoor landscape.

⭐ Helsinki Art Museum (HAM)

MUSEUM | Housed in the converted 1930s Tennispalatsi (Tennis Palace), the Helsinki Art Museum (HAM) is one of Helsinki's brightest, most engaging art museums, with a collection of almost 10,000 works of contemporary art. The first-floor halls are dedicated to the museum's collection of Finnish modern art and works of the beloved Finnish artist Tove Jansson, creator of the much-loved but peculiar Finnish Moomin characters. ⊠ *Eteläinen Rautatiekatu 8, Keskusta* ☎ *09/3108–7001* ⊕ *hamhelsinki.fi* 🎫 *€12* ☉ *Closed Mon.* Ⓜ *Kamppi.*

Kaivopuisto Park

CITY PARK | This large, shady, path-filled park close to the Baltic shoreline was once the site of a popular spa that drew people from St. Petersburg, Tallinn, and all of Scandinavia until its popularity faded during the Crimean War. All the spa structures were eventually destroyed (the main spa building was destroyed during World War II) except one, the Kaivo-huone, now a popular bar-restaurant.

From the Ursa Observatory at the top of the hill (a favorite local spot for winter sledding), sea views extend across the harbor entrance and islands including the Suomenlinna sea fortress. Across from the entrance to the Kaivohuone, take Kaivohuoneenrinne through the park past a grand Empire-style villa built by Albert Edelfelt, father of the famous Finnish painter who bore the same name. Built in 1839, it is the oldest preserved villa in the park. Many embassies, including those of the United States, the United Kingdom, and France, and diplomats' residences are located on the eastern side of the park, one of Helsinki's most beautiful residential areas. ⊠ *Kaivopuis-to* ⊹ *Waterfront park, close to the Eira district* ☎ *09/169–2278* Ⓜ *Tram 3.*

Korkeasaari (Helsinki Zoo)

ZOO | FAMILY | Snow leopards and reindeer like the cold climate here, one of the world's northernmost zoos. Korkeasaari has a good reputation for breeding and conserving endangered species and is home to a wildlife hospital. Entirely within the limits of this small island, the winding paths make the zoo seem larger than it actually is. Between May and September, ferries depart from the Market Square and from a quay in the Hakaniemi district. Tickets, bought on the ferry, cost €7 round trip and are free for children under 18. Zoo tickets are sold at the zoo entrance. The trip takes 15 minutes; arrival and departure times are posted at the harbor. Alternatively, you can take the metro to the Kulosaari stop, cross under the tracks, and follow the signs for a 20-minute walk to the zoo. Bus 16 runs to the zoo from the Central Railway Station. ⊠ *Mustikkamaanpolku 12, Korkeasaari* ☎ *050/352–5989* ⊕ *www. korkeasaari.fi* ⊠ *Day ticket €18, evening ticket €12* Ⓜ *Kulosaari.*

Helsinki City Museum

MUSEUM | Housed in five of Helsinki's oldest buildings opposite the Lutheran Cathedral on the southeast corner of the Senate Square, the main premises of the Helsinki City Museum holds exhibitions on the history and culture of the capital. The Museum is also an umbrella for various other 'satellite' museums across the city. ⊠ *Aleksanterinkatu 16, Senaatintori* ☎ *09/310–36630* ⊕ *www.helsinginkau-punginmuseo.fi* Ⓜ *Helsinki University.*

★ Lutheran Cathedral

RELIGIOUS SITE | The steep steps and green domes of the church dominate the Senate Square, and its silhouette is a classic emblem of the city. Completed in 1852, it is the work of German architect Carl Ludvig Engel, who was commissioned to design a focus for the newly appointed capital during Russian rule and who also designed parts of Tallinn and St. Petersburg. Wander through the tasteful blue-gray interior, with its white moldings and the statues of German reformers Martin Luther and Philipp Melanchthon, as well as the Finnish bishop Mikael Agricola. Concerts are frequently held inside the church, and the expansive square in front of it is a venue for

Tack on a Day Trip 👁

The country's role as a crossroads between East and West is vibrantly reflected in Helsinki, from which it has become increasingly convenient to arrange brief tours to Tallinn, Estonia, and St. Petersburg, Russia. The architectural echoes of St. Petersburg in Helsinki are particularly striking in the "white night" light of June. Tallinn, with its medieval Old Town and bargain shopping, is a popular trip that can be done in a day. Traveling there takes 1½ hours by hydrofoil, 3½ by ferry. ⊕ *www.eckeroline.fi*

national celebrations and gatherings. The crypt at the rear is the site of frequent historic and architectural exhibitions and bazaars. ⊠ *Unioninkatu 29, Senaatintori* ☎ *09/2340–6100* ⊕ *www.helsinginseura-kunnat.fi* ⊠ *Free* Ⓜ *Helsinki University.*

Museum of Contemporary Art Kiasma

MUSEUM | Praised for the boldness of its curved steel shell conceived by American architect Steven Holl, but initially scorned for its encroachment on the territory of the iconic Mannerheim statue, this striking museum displays a wealth of Finnish and foreign art from the 1960s to the present and stages provocative and throught-provoking changing exhibitions. Look for the "butterfly" windows, and don't miss the view of Töölö Bay from the north side of the fifth-floor gallery. ⊠ *Mannerheiminaukio 2, Keskusta* ☎ *0294/500–501* ⊕ *www.kiasma.fi* ⊠ *€15* ⊗ *Closed Mon.* Ⓜ *Central Railway Station.*

National Museum of Finland

MUSEUM | Architect Eliel Saarinen and his partners combined the language of Finnish medieval church architecture with elements of art nouveau to create this vintage example of the National Romantic style. The result resembles something from Tolkien fantasy, with granite embellishments and a sturdy stone bear guarding the steps to the main entrance. The museum's collection of archaeological, cultural, and ethnological artifacts gives you an insight into Finland's past, while changing exhibitions delve into other cultures. Be sure to admire the fabulous fresco in the entrance hall, depicting scenes from the national epic, *The Kalevala*, painted by Akseli Gallen-Kallela. ⊠ *Mannerheimintie 34, Keskusta* ☏ *029/533–6000, 09/4050–9552 guided tours* ⊕ *www.kansallismuseo.fi* ✉ *€12* Ⓜ *Trams 4, 10 to National Museum/Kansallismuseo.*

★ Oodi Central Library

LIBRARY | Opened at the beginning of 2019 and conceived as a gift to its citizens marking the centenary of Finland's independence in 1917, sleek, ultramodern Oodi, made of steel, glass, and wood, is much more than a conventional book-lending library, although it serves that function too. A huge, convivial living room for the people, it houses two cafés, a kids' area, 3-D printers, sewing machines, computer workstations, and a movie theater. The view from the balcony on the top floor (closed in the slippery winter months) extends across a broad plaza to the Music Center and Finlandia Hall. It is a manifestation of Nordic service planning at its finest and most elegant. ⊠ *Töölönlahdenkatu 4, Keskusta/Rautatieasema* ☏ *09/3108–5000* ⊕ *www.oodihelsinki.fi* Ⓜ *Central Railway Station.*

Senate Square (*Senaatintori*)

HISTORIC SITE | The harmony of the three buildings flanking this spacious square exemplifies one of the purest styles of European architecture, as envisioned and designed by German architect Carl Ludvig Engel. This is the heart of neoclassical Helsinki. On the square's west side is one of the main buildings of

Helsinki University, and up the hill is the university library. On the east side is the pale yellow Council of State, completed in 1822 and once the seat during Russian rule of the autonomous grand duchy of Finland's Imperial Senate. At the lower end of the square, stores and restaurants now occupy former merchants' homes. ⊠ *Senaatintori* ⊹ *Bounded by Aleksanterinkatu to the south and Yliopistonkatu to the north* Ⓜ *Helsinki University.*

Sibelius Monument

MEMORIAL | The Sibelius Monument is the main feature of the Sibelius Park on the shoreline of a Baltic inlet in the Töölö district northwest of the center. This tribute to Finland's great composer, designed by Eila Hiltunen and unveiled in 1967, resembles a cluster of soaring silver organ pipes—600 of them—and is a popular stop on coach tours of the city. ⊠ *Sibelius Park, Töölö* ⊹ *West of Mechelininkatu.*

Sinebrychoff Art Museum (*Sinebrychoff Museum of Foreign Art*)

MUSEUM | The wealthy Russian Sinebrychoffs owned a brewing company (the Koff beer for sale throughout Helsinki is their legacy) and lived in this splendid yellow-and-white 1840 neo-Renaissance mansion filled with wildly opulent furniture. The family's home and foreign art collection are now a public museum containing old European collections forming part of the Finnish National Gallery. Dutch, Swedish, Italian, and French works are on show, with a mixture of 17th- and 18th-century portraits, landscapes, miniatures, and porcelain and the mansion's original decorative furniture. ⊠ *Bulevardi 40, Hietalahti* ☏ *0294/500–460 ticket sales and information* ⊕ *www.sinebrychoffintaidemuseo.fi* ✉ *€15, free first Wed. every month 5–8 pm* ☉ *Closed Mon.* Ⓜ *Tram 6.*

★ Suomenlinna (*Fortress of Finland*)

HISTORIC SITE | A former island fortress and a must for any visitor, Suomenlinna is a perennially popular collection of fortifications, museums, parks, and

The Helsinki Central Library Oodi is topped with a large open-plan reading room under an undulating roof with circular skylights.

gardens and has been designated a UNESCO World Heritage Site. In 1748 the Swedish rulers started to build the impregnable fortress, long referred to as the Gibraltar of the North, across a series of interlinked islands. Although Suomenlinna has never been taken by assault, it came under Russian governance with the rest of Finland in 1808 and came under fire from British and French ships in 1855 during the Crimean War. Today Suomenlinna makes a lovely excursion from Helsinki at any time of the year but particularly in early summer when the island is carpeted by wildflowers and engulfed in a mauve-and-purple mist of lilacs, introduced from Versailles by the Finnish marshal and founder of the fortress Augustin Ehrensvärd.

Suomenlinna is easily reached by city ferry (€5, return valid for 12 hours) or JT-Line water-bus (€3.50 one way, €5.50 round trip), both of which leave from Helsinki's Market Square. One-hour guided English-language tours (€11 for adults, €4 for children) leave daily from the Suomenlinna Museum; call for information about times. The Suomenlinna Museum is on the shore of Tykistö Bay, about 400 yards south of the main ferry terminal and close to the private ferry quay.

⚠ Opening days and hours of sites are limited off-season. ✉ *Suomenlinna Museum, Suomenlinna C74, Suomenlinna* ✛ *At the bridge between Iso Mustasaari and Susisaari islands* ☎ *0295/338–410* ⊕ *www.suomenlinna.fi/en* 🎫 *Fortress free, museum €7, other fees vary.*

Temppeliaukio Church (*"The Church in the Rock"*)
BUILDING | Topped with a copper dome, the church looks like a half-buried spaceship from the outside. It's really a modern Lutheran church carved into the rock outcrops below. The sun shines in from above, illuminating a stunning interior with birch pews, modern pipe organ, and cavernous walls. Ecumenical and Lutheran services in various languages are held throughout the week; during services the church is closed to tourists.

✉ *Lutherinkatu 3, Töölö* ☎ *09/2340–5940*
⊕ *www.temppeliaukionkirkko.fi* 🚋 *Free*
Ⓜ *Trams 1, 2, 4, 10.*

Uspenski Orthodox Cathedral
RELIGIOUS SITE | Perched atop a small rocky cliff in Katajanokka is the main cathedral of the Orthodox Church in Finland. Its brilliant gold onion domes are its hallmark, but its imposing redbrick edifice, decorated by 19th-century Russian artists, is no less distinctive. The cathedral was built and dedicated in 1868 in the Byzantine-Slavonic style and remains the biggest Orthodox church in Scandinavia. ✉ *Kanavakatu 1, Katajanokka* ☎ *09/8564–6100* ⊕ *www.hos.fi* 🚋 *Free* ☽ *Closed Mon.* Ⓜ *Tram 4.*

OFF THE BEATEN PATH
Linnanmäki
AMUSEMENT PARK/WATER PARK | **FAMILY** | Helsinki's amusement park, to the north of the city, is a great option for families and one of the most popular attractions in terms of visitor numbers in the whole country. It includes the Sea Life aquarium and stages its annual Carnival of Light to brighten up the onset of fall in October. ✉ *Tivolikuja 1, Linnanmäki* ☎ *0105/722–200* ⊕ *www.linnanmaki.fi* 🚋 *Entry free, wristbands and tickets for attractions vary* Ⓜ *Tram 3.*

★ Seurasaari Open-Air Museum
ISLAND | The Seurasaari Open-Air Museum was founded in 1909 to preserve rural Finnish architecture. The old farmhouses and barns that were brought to this island, which is about 3 km (2 miles) northwest of the city center, came from all over the country. Many are rough-hewn log buildings dating from the 17th century, a style that was a major inspiration to the late-19th-century architects of the national revivalist movement. All exhibits are marked by signposts along the trails; don't miss the church boat and the gabled church—and watch out for the very sociable red squirrels! Seurasaari is connected to land by a pedestrian bridge and is a restful place for walking throughout the year, with its forest trails and ocean views. You can walk there in about 40 minutes from the Opera House; follow Mannerheimintie northeast, then turn left onto Linnankoskenkatu and follow signs along the coast. Alternatively, take Bus 24 from the city center, in front of the Swedish Theater at the west end of Pohjoisesplanadi; its last stop is by the bridge to the island. It's free to enter and wander around the traffic-free island at any time of the year, but there is a €10 fee if you want to go into the museum buildings, open from May 15 to September 15, and the ticket includes daily guided tours at 3 pm in summer. There is a naturist beach on the north side of the island, well shielded from public view. Plan on spending at least three hours exploring and getting to the museum. ✉ *Seurasaari* ☎ *0295/336–912* ⊕ *www.kansallismuseo.fi/en/seurasaarenulkomuseo* 🚋 *€10* ☽ *Closed mid-Sept.–mid-May.*

Urho Kekkonen Museum (*Tamminiemi*)
BUILDING | The grand house overlooking Seurasaari from the mainland is where the late Finnish president Urho Kekkonen lived from 1956 to 1986. Originally known as Villa Nissen, this grand house known as Tamminiemi was built in 1904. Inside are the scores of gifts presented to Finland's longest-serving president by leaders from around the world. His study is the most fascinating room, with its gift from the United States: a cupboard full of *National Geographic* maps of the world. To ensure an English-speaking guide, call ahead. ✉ *Seurasaarentie 15, Seurasaari* ☎ *029/533–6921* ⊕ *www.kansallismuseo.fi/en/tamminiemi* 🚋 *€10* ☽ *Closed weekdays Oct.–Mar.*

★ Vallisaari, Kuninkaansaari, and Lonna
ISLAND | From May to September, JT-Line water-buses run the 20–25-minute voyage from a quay at the Market Square to the two connected islands of Vallisaari and Kuninkaansaari. On some departures the water-bus also stops off at the smaller island of Lonna, site of a popular

summer restaurant, and it also calls in at the Suomenlinna sea fortress on its return voyage. All three islands were closed to public access until recently due to their military functions. On Vallisaari, visitors must stick to the trails running through designated areas to protect the unique and beautifully wooded natural environment. The trail leads to a viewing platform above fortifications built as part of the 18th-century Suomenlinna sea fortress project. The views are glorious, stretching back to the city across Suomenlinna and out to the open sea, and there is the occasional spectacle of cruise ships and ferries slipping through the narrow straits between islands. The island has a quayside café and bar, picnic benches, and a marina for visiting boats. Guided nature, history, and photography tours are available through Finland National Parks, which maintains and manages the island. One can reach the smaller Kuninkaansaari across a causeway and explore the old gun emplacements. **■ TIP→ First departures are at 9:30 am and the last return at 7:30 pm.** ✉ *Helsinki* ✥ *Market Square "Kolera allas" quayside for JT-Line ferries* ☎ *045/329–0501 Market Square ticket office* 🌐 *www.nationalparks.fi/en/vallisaari.*

🍴 Restaurants

Helsinki is dotted with cozy yet decidedly modern-looking venues offering reindeer, herring, and pike accompanied by delicious Finnish mushrooms or wild-berry sauces. Don't be turned off by spare menu descriptions such as "reindeer with lingonberry sauce and chanterelles"—it's a classic example of the Finnish tendency toward understatement, and the skill will be evident in the taste. You'll find everything from Mexican to Nepalese (quite popular with locals) in the city, though not at every price point. Expect European-size entrées, excellent location, and service at a steep price. A strong café culture makes it easy to find a tasty, reasonably priced lunch.

Baskeri and Basso

$$$ | SCANDINAVIAN | The entrance is hidden away in a courtyard close to the Hietalahti shipyard, but this bustling bistro is worth the effort to hunt down. An open kitchen serves tapas-style meals at candlelit tables, and the adjacent Basbas wine bar also serves snacks to accompany its fine selection of wines. **Known for:** lively spot; great wine list; shared plates. [$] *Average main: €34* ✉ *Tehtaankatu 27–29, Punavuori* ✥ *Entrance through the courtyard at the back* ☎ *050/467–3400* 🌐 *basbas.fi* ⏲ *Closed Sat.–Mon. and July. No lunch.* [M] *Tram 6.*

Demo

$$$$ | FRENCH | Opened in 2003 by chefs Tommi Tuominen and Teemu Aura and the holder of a Michelin star since 2007, Demo serves food of the very best quality without the stuffiness of some high-end restaurants; this is a place where you can comfortably laugh out loud. The core menu is classical French, and the restaurant offers four-, five-, six-, and seven-course chef's menus, which change daily. **Known for:** daily chef's menus; Michelin star; extensive wine list. [$] *Average main: €62* ✉ *Uudenmaankatu 9–11, Keskusta* ☎ *09/2289–0840* 🌐 *www.restaurantdemo.fi* ⏲ *Closed Sun. and Mon. No lunch* [M] *Tram 10.*

Elite

$$ | EUROPEAN | A short distance from the town center, Elite makes a welcome place to recharge after visiting Temppeliaukio Church, which is a five-minute walk away, and the Sibelius Monument—especially in summer, when there's outdoor seating. Its simple art deco interior and spacious layout are popular with artists and writers. **Known for:** art deco interior; fried Baltic herring; artsy crowd. [$] *Average main: €24* ✉ *Etelä Hesperiankatu 22, Töölö* ☎ *09/6128–5200* 🌐 *www.elite.fi* [M] *Trams 1, 2.*

Just a 15-minute ferry ride from Helsinki, Suomenlinna offers ocean views, fortress buildings and tunnels, and great walking paths and swimming areas.

★ Kosmos

$$ | **SCANDINAVIAN** | Just a short walk from the Stockmann department store, this cozy restaurant has become a lunchtime favorite. Come evening, it's given over to artists and journalists. **Known for:** Scandinavian-Russian fusion dishes; cozy alcoves; historic hangout. [$] *Average main: €24* ✉ *Kalevankatu 3, Keskusta* ☎ *09/647–255* 🌐 *www.kosmos.fi* 🕒 *Closed Sun. and July. No lunch Sat.*

Kuu

$$$ | **SCANDINAVIAN** | If you like finding the true character of a city and enjoy local color, try looking in simple, friendly restaurants like this one, whose name means "moon." The menu combines Finnish specialties such as perch, salmon, and reindeer with imaginative international fare. It's especially convenient for nights at the opera, and the delightful covered terrace is open year-round. **Known for:** pre-opera dining; authentic Helsinki character; covered dining terrace. [$] *Average main: €30* ✉ *Töölönkatu 27, Töölö* ☎ *09/2709–0973* 🌐 *www.ravintolakuu.fi* [M] *Tram 10.*

KuuKuu

$$ | **SCANDINAVIAN** | **FAMILY** | A five-minute walk from the somewhat austere neoclassical Parliament House and on the same street as the National Museum, this local gem is the kind of restaurant travelers delight to discover. The main courses have a pan-European flavor, but the "classics"—the sort of hearty food that grandma used to make—are what this place is about. **Known for:** seasonal menu; reservations necessary; classic Finnish cooking. [$] *Average main: €24* ✉ *Museokatu 17, Töölö* ☎ *09/2709-0974* 🌐 *www.kuukuu.fi* [M] *Tram 10.*

Nokka

$$$$ | **SCANDINAVIAN** | Look for a giant propeller and anchor to find the main door of Nokka in the redbrick buildings near the Uspenski Orthodox Cathedral in Katanajanokka, overlooking the marina. This innovative restaurant specializes in seasonal fare with fresh Finnish ingredients provided by smallholdings across the country

and the forests of Lapland. **Known for:** waterside dining; locally sourced, organic ingredients; excellent vegetarian options. [$] *Average main: €60* ✉ *Kanavaranta 7F, Katajanokka* ☎ *09/6128–5600* 🌐 *www.ravintolanokka.fi* ⏲ *Closed Sun. No lunch Sat. and July and Aug.* [M] *Trams 4, 5.*

★ **Ora Restaurant**
$$$$ | MODERN EUROPEAN | Hidden away in the Eira district on Helsinki's most elegant art nouveau residential street, tiny Ora is the antithesis of pretentious gourmet dining, although its creativity and sense of fun has earned it a Michelin star. Intimacy is not sacrificed in what feels like an expanded home dining room, with tables turned toward the open kitchen. **Known for:** open kitchen; exciting and innovative menu; Michelin star. [$] *Average main: €89* ✉ *Huvilakatu 28A, Eira* ☎ *0400/959–440* 🌐 *orarestaurant.fi* ⏲ *Closed Sun.–Tues.* [M] *Tram 3.*

★ **Ravintola Palace**
$$$$ | SCANDINAVIAN | This hotel restaurant has a magnificent view of the South Harbour. Chef Eero Vottonen has steered it to Michelin-star status with a sumptuous seven-part menu that covers almost every conceivable fresh Nordic ingredient, from crispy rye sourdough bread and smoked trout roe to Norwegian king crab and scallops with asparagus. **Known for:** midcentury modern design; harbor views; Michelin star–quality dining. [$] *Average main: €164* ✉ *Eteläranta 10, 10th fl., Kauppatori* ☎ *050/505-0718* 🌐 *www.palacerestaurant.fi* ⏲ *Closed weekends and July* [M] *Trams 2, 3.*

Restaurant Olo
$$$$ | FUSION | Restaurant Olo is perfectly located close to the historic Senate Square and the harborside Market Square. Its Michelin-star-winning menu, inspired by chef Jari Vesivalo's childhood memories, varies from season to season. **Known for:** seasonal, Michelin-starred menu; bistro brunches; great location near South Harbour. [$] *Average main: €127* ✉ *Pohjoisesplanadi 5, Esplanadi* ☎ *010/320–6250* 🌐 *www.olo-ravintola.fi* ⏲ *Closed Mon.* [M] *Trams 2, 3; Metro Helsinki University.*

Saari
$$$$ | SCANDINAVIAN | There's the flavor of Hyannis Port and the Kennedys in this lovely restaurant—stunning views of yachts and mansions and other islands in the Baltic Sea abound. The boat trip to this island (€6 added to the bill for the ferry trip there and back) from the Ursininlaituri jetty only takes a few minutes, and it's well worth it. **Known for:** island location; summer crayfish party; vegetarian options. [$] *Average main: €59* ✉ *Sirpalesaari, Eira* ✣ *Ferries depart from quayside near the Cafe Carusel* ☎ *09/7425–5566* 🌐 *www.ravintolasaari.fi* ⏲ *Closed Oct.–Apr. and Sun. in Sept.*

Saaristo
$$$ | SCANDINAVIAN | Sitting at the mouth of Helsinki's South Harbour, Saaristo sits on Klippan island in a magnificent wooden pavilion. There's hardly a seat in the whole restaurant that doesn't offer a stunning view: from the Empire-era buildings to the north to the massive sea fortress of Suomenlinna to the south, with yachts and cruise ships floating by. **Known for:** beautiful views; fresh seafood; spectacular pavilion building. [$] *Average main: €30* ✉ *Luoto (Klippan), Keskusta/Kauppatori* ☎ *09/7425–5590* 🌐 *www.ravintolasaaristo.fi* ⏲ *Closed Oct.–Apr. and weekends. No lunch.* ☞ *€6.50 is added to your bill for the return ferry ticket* [M] *Tram 3.*

Salutorget
$$ | SCANDINAVIAN | Right beside city hall and a handy place to take a break from shopping in Market Square, this building retains marble columns and deep wood panels that harken back to the days when it was a bank rather than an elegant restaurant, fitted as it is today with very plush and luxurious furniture. Toast Skagen, a Nordic classic, is a good bet—it's shrimp, mayo, and chives on toasted bread, topped with a generous dollop of

whitefish roe. **Known for:** afternoon tea; close to Market Square; elegant setting in a renovated bank. $ *Average main: €24* ✉ *Pohjoisesplanadi 15, Esplanadi* ☎ *09/6128–5950* ⊕ *www.salutorget.fi/en* ⊙ *Closed Sun.* Ⓜ *Tram 3.*

Savotta
$$ | SCANDINAVIAN | *Savotta* means "lumber camp," and the hearty food those lumberjacks would want is reflected on the menu here. Located on Senate Square, directly across from the Lutheran cathedral, the 250-year-old building is adorned with knickknacks from a bygone era. **Known for:** authentic Finnish food; meat-heavy menu; locally brewed beer. $ *Average main: €23* ✉ *Aleksanterinkatu 22, Senaatintori* ☎ *09/7425–5588* ⊕ *www.ravintolasavotta.fi* ⊙ *No lunch Sun.* Ⓜ *Trams 2, 3, 4, 5, 7.*

Savoy
$$$$ | MODERN EUROPEAN | Given that its airy dining room was designed by Alvar Aalto and overlooks the Esplanade, it's no surprise that the Savoy is a popular spot for business lunches or occasion dining. This was Finnish statesman Marshal Carl Gustaf Mannerheim's favorite restaurant (in the late 1800s); he is rumored to have introduced the *vorschmack* (minced lamb and anchovies) recipe here. **Known for:** rooftop views; historic reputation; vorschmack (minced lamb and anchovies). $ *Average main: €45* ✉ *Eteläesplanadi 14, Esplanadi* ☎ *09/6128–5300* ⊕ *www.ravintolasavoy.fi/en* ⊙ *Closed Sun. No lunch Sat.* Ⓜ *Helsinki University.*

Sea Horse
$$ | EUROPEAN | At the foot of village-like Korkeavuorenkatu—"high hill street"— within easy reach of a cluster of boutiques and cozy cafés, Sea Horse was founded in 1934. Originally famed for its fried Baltic herring and authentically local feel, it gained a higher profile in the 1990s when lauded in national and European publications for its excellent steaks. **Known for:** seahorse mural; traditional restaurant; generous portions. $ *Average*

main: €25 ✉ *Kapteeninkatu 11, Punavuori* ☎ *09/628–169* ⊕ *www.seahorse.fi* Ⓜ *Trams 3, 10.*

Sipuli
$$$ | FRENCH | Standing at the foot of the Uspenski Orthodox Cathedral, Sipuli gets its name, "onion," from the church's bulbous golden cupolas. The restaurant is in a 19th-century warehouse building, with redbrick walls, dark-wood panels, and a skylight with a spectacular view of the cathedral. **Known for:** cathedral views; former warehouse setting; French-Finnish dishes. $ *Average main: €29* ✉ *Kanavaranta 7, Katajanokka* ☎ *09/6128–5500* ⊕ *www.ravintolasipuli.fi* ⊙ *Closed weekends (except for group dinners) and July* Ⓜ *Trams 4, 5.*

Story
$ | MODERN EUROPEAN | Story has three "chapters": Story Kauppahalli in the Old Market Hall, Story Kortteli on the restaurant floor above the Kamppi Center shopping mall, and Story Tripla in the new Tripla mall in the Pasila district. Describing themselves as "café restaurants" specializing in quick bites, they offer tasty and affordable snacks, breakfasts, brunches, lunches, and dinners. **Known for:** quick bites; great burgers; popular with shoppers. $ *Average main: €15* ✉ *Old Market Hall, Eteläranta, Kauppatori* ☎ *010/666–8458* ⊕ *story-restaurants.fi* Ⓜ *Tram 3.*

☕ Coffee and Quick Bites

Café Engel
$$ | SCANDINAVIAN | Named for the architect Carl Ludvig Engel, this café on Senate Square serves traditional lunch fare, and it's also open for breakfast. Portions are hearty—you can fill up on a huge bowl of the tomato basil soup or the cold smoked salmon sandwich; for a lighter snack, try a savory karjalanpiirakka or one of the smaller open-faced cold-cut sandwiches. **Known for:** Senate Square location; soups and sandwiches;

lingonberry cheesecake. $ *Average main:* ✉ *Aleksanterinkatu 26, Senaatintori* ☎ *09/652–776* ⊕ *www.cafeengel.fi/en* Ⓜ *Helsinki University; Tram 3.*

★ Café Esplanad

$$ | SCANDINAVIAN | Situated on the north side of the Esplanade amid stylish design boutiques, this café is a great place to sample a giant version of the *korvapuusti*, roughly translated as a "slap around the ear"—a sweet bun fresh from the oven and made all the more delicious by virtue of the cinnamon spinkled between its folded layers. Salads, filled bread rolls, and other enormous confectioneries are on offer, eased down with some of Helsinki's best coffee or something stronger if required. **Known for:** generous portions; fresh cinnamon buns; popular meeting spot. $ *Average main:* ✉ *Pohjoisesplanadi 37, Esplanadi* ☎ *09/665–496* ⊕ *www.esplanad.fi* Ⓜ *Metro Helsinki University.*

Café Ursula

$$ | SCANDINAVIAN | Located by the sea, with views across to Suomenlinna, this café has been a favorite with locals since the 1950s. They come for the coffee, ice cream, pastries, and light lunches that include soups and salads made with traditional Finnish ingredients and to sit on the terrace on sunny days after seaside strolls in and around nearby Kaivopuisto Park. **Known for:** seaside terrace; warm-up spot for winter walkers; convenient to U.S. and U.K. Embassies. $ *Average main:* ✉ *Ehrenströmintie 3, Kaivopuisto* ⊹ *Walk through Kaivopuisto park from tram stop* ☎ *09/652–817* ⊕ *www.ursula.fi* ▭ *No credit cards* Ⓜ *Tram 3.*

🛏 Hotels

In recent years, Helsinki has been noted for its high-end design hotels, which emphasize room decor, layout, and in-house restaurants and bars. Top hotels are on the pricey side, generally have small rooms, and cater to business travelers as well as more discerning tourists. Standards are high, and the level of service usually corresponds to the price. Rates can plummet by as much as 50% on weekends, and most include a generous breakfast buffet, wifi and sauna privileges.

Clarion Hotel Helsinki

$$ | HOTEL | This quayside hotel has been described as the trendiest hotel in Helsinki. **Pros:** wonderful city and harbor views; interesting quayside location; modern amenities. **Cons:** distance from city center; pricey bar tariff; check-in sometimes understaffed. $ *Rooms from: €180* ✉ *Tyynenmerenkatu 2, Hietalahti* ☎ *010/850–3820* ⊕ *nordicchoicehotels.com* ⇗ *425 rooms* ❍ *Free Breakfast.*

Crowne Plaza Helsinki

$$$ | HOTEL | On Helsinki's main avenue, facing Hesperia Park and across the street from the Opera House, this upscale property has relatively spacious rooms with a modern Finnish flair; business-class rooms, including dedicated quiet zone rooms, and suites are also available. **Pros:** good-size rooms; parkside location; good transport links to downtown. **Cons:** slightly corporate feel; location near a busy main road; removed from downtown proper. $ *Rooms from: €240* ✉ *Mannerheimintie 50, Töölö* ☎ *09/2521–0000* ⊕ *www.ihg.com* ⇗ *344 rooms* ❍ *Free Breakfast* Ⓜ *Trams 4, 7, 10.*

★ GLO Hotel Art

$ | HOTEL | This small luxury hotel, in the center of Helsinki's Design District, distinguishes itself through a rare combination of character, consistency, and service. **Pros:** quiet location; pleasant rooms; generous closet space. **Cons:** dark furnishings; mix of room styles makes for inconsistent experience; slightly confusing layout. $ *Rooms from: €109* ✉ *Lönnrotinkatu 29, Hietalahti* ☎ *09/5840–9445* ⊕ *www.glohotels.fi/en/hotels/glo-art* ⇗ *47 rooms* ❍ *Free Breakfast.*

Finland Culture Primer

Listen to This

Värttinä. Soulful female vocalists performing traditional Finnish folk with a melodic rock-pop sensibility.

Imsomnium. Finnish heavy rock at its loudest and darkest.

Alma. Pop singer-songwriter with an international following.

Jaakko Kuusisto. One of many classical Finnish composers following in the Sibelius tradition.

Read This

The Summer Book, Tove Jansson. An artist and her young granddaughter get acquainted on a small island in the Gulf of Finland.

Little Siberia, Antti Tuomainen. 'Helsinki noir' black-comic tale about the consequences of a meteorite landing in a small Finnish town.

The Kalevala, Elias Lönnrot. Finland's national folk epic, as collected from ancient tales and compiled in the 19th century.

Watch This

The Man without a Past. Dark comedy from famed director Aki Kaurismäki about a man with amnesia restarting his life in Helsinki's underbelly.

Ambush. Epic World War II romance on the Finnish-Russian border.

Lapland Odyssey. Three young northern men go on a comic quest for a digital TV box.

Eat This

Lihapullat: small round meatballs of ground beef (and sometimes pork), fried or baked.

Kaalikääryleet: cabbage leaves stuffed with ground meat, rice, cream, eggs, and spices, glazed with molasses and butter and then baked.

Karjalanpiirakkat (Karelian pasties): small rye-crusted pies filled with rice, spread on top with butter and sometimes a boiled egg.

Hernekeitto: green pea soup cooked with smoked pork shank, carrots, onions, and spices, often served with pancakes for dessert.

Korvapuusti: an irresistible wrap of sweet dough baked with cinnamon.

Runebergintorttu (Runeberg torte): a cake served in winter flavored with almonds and rum, topped with raspberry jam within a glazed sugar ring.

⭐ GLO Hotel Kluuvi

$ | HOTEL | Well-dressed locals meet in the lobby lounge while a largely international business clientele heads upstairs to unwind in what are Helsinki's slickest hotel rooms. **Pros:** gorgeous rooms and amenities; excellent weekend deals; great location. **Cons:** breakfast, gym, and sauna cost extra if in standard room; self-conscious design theme; busy location. ⓢ *Rooms from: €119* ✉ *Kluuvikatu 4,*

Keskusta ☎ *010/344–4400* ⊕ *www.glohotels.fi/en/hotels/glo-kluuvi* ✈ *131 rooms* ⓘ◎ⓘ *No meals* Ⓜ *Helsinki University.*

⭐ Hilton Helsinki Kalastajatorppa

$ | HOTEL | Located in the plush and leafy western Munkkiniemi neighborhood, a 15-minute taxi ride or 20-minute tram hop from the city center, this hotel routinely hosts statesmen, celebrities, and honeymooning couples and bills itself as

Saunas

👁

An authentic Finnish sauna (it's the only Finnish word to have properly entered world vocabulary) is an obligatory experience and not hard to find: there are 1.6 million saunas in this country of just more than 5 million people—even the parliament has its own sauna. The traditional Finnish sauna—which involves relaxing on wooden benches, pouring water onto hot stones, and swatting your neighbor's back with birch branches—is an integral part of cabin life and now city life, too, as many apartments are outfitted with small saunas in their bathrooms. Almost every hotel has at least one sauna available free of charge, usually at standard times in the morning or evening for men and women to use separately. Larger hotels offer a private sauna in the higher-class rooms and suites. Public saunas (with swimsuits required) are becoming increasingly popular, even in winter, when sauna goers momentarily leave the sauna to jump into the sea through a large hole in the ice (a practice called *avantouinti*). Public swimming pools are also equipped with saunas that can be used at no extra charge.

"A Resort in the City." The best rooms are in the seaside annex, but all are large and airy, with clear pine and birchwood paneling. **Pros:** luxuriously appointed rooms; beachfront; peace and quiet. **Cons:** not in the center of town; dispersed layout; walk to tram stop. $ *Rooms from: €138* ✉ *Kalastajatorpantie 1, Munkkiniemi* ☎ *09/45811* ⊕ *www.hilton.com* ⬅ *238 rooms* ⦿*I Free Breakfast* Ⓜ *Tram 4.*

Hilton Helsinki Strand

$$ | **HOTEL** | With tastefully furnished rooftop saunas; large, crisply decorated rooms; bathrooms with heated floors; and even a car-wash service in the basement garage, this hotel pampers you. **Pros:** lavish rooms; regal lobby; great views. **Cons:** slightly removed from city center; extra fee for underground parking; erratic AC in rooms. $ *Rooms from: €185* ✉ *John Stenbergin Ranta 4, Hakaniemi* ☎ *09/39351* ⊕ *www.hilton.com* ⬅ *184 rooms* ⦿*I Free Breakfast* Ⓜ *Hakaniemi.*

Hotel F6

$$$ | **HOTEL** | Getting its name from the Fabianinkatu 6 address, family-owned F6 is a welcome addition to the gradually expanding portfolio of Helsinki boutique hotels. **Pros:** central location; authentic sustainability; cheerful staff. **Cons:** erratic AC; no dinner restaurant; rather somber dark floors in some rooms. $ *Rooms from: €230* ✉ *Fabianinkatu 6, Esplanadi* ☎ *09/6899–9666* ⊕ *www.hotelf6.fi* ⬅ *66 rooms* ⦿*I Free Breakfast* Ⓜ *Helsinki University.*

Hotel Haven

$$ | **HOTEL** | Haven's prime harborside location and luxury amenities place it among Helsinki's finest hotels and grant it membership into the Small Luxury Hotels of the World. **Pros:** lavish room amenities; harbor views; Elemis bath and spa products. **Cons:** some rooms face plain side streets; no sauna; erratic heating control. $ *Rooms from: €185* ✉ *Unioninkatu 17, Esplanadi* ☎ *09/681–930* ⊕ *www.hotelhaven.fi* ⬅ *76 rooms, 1 suite* ⦿*I Free Breakfast* Ⓜ *Helsinki University.*

★ Hotel Kämp

$$$$ | **HOTEL** | Situated opposite the Esplanade, this luxurious, late-19th-century cultural landmark has long been the meeting point for Finland's most prominent politicians, artists, and celebrities,

including Carl Gustaf Mannerheim, Eliel Saarinen, Akseli Gallen-Kallela, and Sibelius who dedicated a song to it. **Pros:** lavish rooms; five-star service; fantastic spa. **Cons:** breakfast costs extra; gym and sauna costs €10 extra if in standard room; high rates. $ *Rooms from: €300* ✉ *Pohjoisesplanadi 29, Keskusta* ☎ *09/576–111* ⊕ *www.hotelkamp.com* ⍟ *179 rooms* ❍| *No meals* Ⓜ *Helsinki University.*

Hotel Katajanokka

$ | HOTEL | Located in a quiet part of town full of fascinating art nouveau detail and close to the South Harbour, the Katajanokka is not a bad place to do time, which makes perfect sense when you realize that the building originally served as a county jail in 1888. **Pros:** comfortable rooms with heated bathroom floors; good breakfast; quirky former-jail theme. **Cons:** slightly removed from city center; not a prime area for attractions or restaurants; too-busy carpet design in some rooms. $ *Rooms from: €133* ✉ *Merikasarminkatu 1A, Katajanokka* ☎ *09/686–450* ⊕ *www.bwkatajanokka. fi/en* ⍟ *103 rooms* ❍| *Free Breakfast* Ⓜ *Trams 4, 5.*

Hotel Seurahuone

$ | HOTEL | Built in 1913, this Viennese-style town-house hotel across from the train station has a loyal clientele won over by its ageless charm and cosmopolitan interiors. **Pros:** elegant decor; city-center location; good breakfast. **Cons:** fading charm; rooms can be too warm; very busy and noisy location. $ *Rooms from: €120* ✉ *Kaivokatu 12, Rautatieasema* ☎ *09/6899–9035* ⊕ *www.hotelliseurahuone.fi* ⍟ *118 rooms* ❍| *Free Breakfast* Ⓜ *Central Railway Station.*

★ Hotel St. George

$$$$ | HOTEL | The pinnacle of luxury in Helsinki and a member of the Design Hotels group, the St. George opened in 2018 in converted apartment buildings on one corner of the Vanha Kirkkopuisto (Old Church Park). **Pros:** stylish and luxurious;

park and city rooftop views on the upper floors; excellent restaurant. **Cons:** pricey; confusing reception entrance; art not to everyone's taste. $ *Rooms from: €350* ✉ *Yrjönkatu 13, Bulevardi* ☎ *09/4246–0011* ⊕ *www.stgeorgehelsinki.com* ⍟ *153 rooms* ❍| *No meals* Ⓜ *Trams 4, 6, 10.*

Klaus K

$$$ | HOTEL | Klaus K is on the pleasant, centrally located Bulevardi street, and its inconspicuous entrance might not prepare guests for the ultra-cool design themes concealed within. **Pros:** Helsinki's best breakfast; fantastic location just off the Esplanade; imaginatively designed rooms. **Cons:** some standard rooms are small; some guests might find the design features distracting; high rates. $ *Rooms from: €200* ✉ *Bulevardi 2–4* ☎ *020/770–4700* ⊕ *www.klauskhotel.com* ⍟ *171 rooms* ❍| *Free Breakfast.*

Marski by Scandic

$$$ | HOTEL | The Marski has always been favored for its absolutely central location, on the main Mannerheimintie artery and opposite the Stockmann department store. **Pros:** relaxing street-level café; ideal location; everything new after recent renovations. **Cons:** low light fittings in restaurant; crowded breakfast; bathrooms a little somber. $ *Rooms from: €160* ✉ *Mannerheimintie 10, Keskusta* ☎ *09/68061* ⊕ *www.scandichotels.com/ hotels/finland/helsinki/marski-by-scandic* ⍟ *289 rooms* ❍| *Free Breakfast* Ⓜ *Trams 4, 7, 10.*

Scandic Grand Marina Helsinki

$ | HOTEL | Housed inside an early-19th-century customs warehouse in the well-heeled Katajanokka promontory neighborhood, the Grand Marina has one of the best convention centers in Finland. **Pros:** family friendly; location near the harbor and Market Square; ample breakfast buffet. **Cons:** some rooms have poor views and small windows; breakfast can be hectic; reception sometimes crowded with arriving groups. $ *Rooms from:*

€149 ✉ Katajanokanlaituri 7, Katajanokka ☎ 09/16661 ⊕ www.scandichotels.com ⤳ 442 rooms ‖○‖ Free Breakfast Ⓜ Trams 4, 5.

Scandic Park Helsinki

$$ | HOTEL | FAMILY | One of the most popular hotels in Helsinki, this local institution is modern, central, and particularly popular with business travelers from the United States. **Pros:** excellent location; sauna and swimming pool on the top floor; recently refurbished. **Cons:** corporate feel; AC issues reported; noise of elevators in some rooms. Ⓢ *Rooms from: €166* ✉ *Mannerheimintie 46, Töölö* ☎ *09/47371* ⊕ *www.scandichotels.com* ⤳ *523 rooms* ‖○‖ *Free Breakfast* Ⓜ *Trams 4, 10.*

Sokos Hotel Vaakuna

$$ | HOTEL | The quirky 1950s architecture and interior design of the Vaakuna dates back to the 1952 Helsinki Olympics. **Pros:** soundproof windows; brilliant rooftop views; central location. **Cons:** busy location; dull furnishings; crowded breakfast. Ⓢ *Rooms from: €160* ✉ *Asemaaukio 2, Rautatieasema* ☎ *020/123–4610* ⊕ *www. sokoshotels.fi* ⤳ *258 rooms* ‖○‖ *Free Breakfast* Ⓜ *Metro Central Railway Station.*

Solo Sokos Hotel Torni

$ | HOTEL | The original part of this hotel was built in 1903, and its towers (*torni* means "tower") and internal details still reflect some of the more fanciful touches of Helsinki's Jugendstil period. **Pros:** unique character; fabulous views from the upper floors; convenient location. **Cons:** elevator noise with some rooms; small rooms; some lower-floor rooms catch street noise. Ⓢ *Rooms from: €130* ✉ *Yrjönkatu 26, Keskusta* ☎ *020/123–4604* ⊕ *www.sokoshotels.fi* ⤳ *138 rooms* ‖○‖ *Free Breakfast* Ⓜ *Metro Kamppi.*

ⓨ Nightlife

Originally known for its rock and heavy metal clubs, Helsinki has recently developed a suave bar-lounge scene, now flourishing in a number of carpeted, couch-lined venues combining loungy tunes with great cocktails. The compact size of the city center makes it easy to barhop.

BARS AND LOUNGES

Angleterre

BARS/PUBS | An affluent crowd frequents this English pub, one of the first of its kind when it opened back in the 1970s. It's popular with the more sedate English-speaking expat set but also frequented by fine real-ale aficionados. ✉ *Fredrikinkatu 47, Keskusta* ☎ *010/766–3580* ⊕ *www.raflaamo.fi/fi/helsinki/angleterre* Ⓜ *Kamppi.*

★ Ateljee Bar

BARS/PUBS | Perched atop the historical Solo Sokos Hotel Torni, the Ateljee Bar is a modest space, accessed by means of elevator and narrow spiral staircase, that's big enough to serve its purpose: serving cocktails and other drinks. Though the drinks are expensive, the views of the city from its balconies—and famously, from its bathrooms—are second to none. Art exhibitions are an added attraction. ✉ *Solo Sokos Hotel Torni, Yrjönkatu 26, Keskusta* ☎ *010/784–2080* ⊕ *www.raflaamo.fi/fi/helsinki/ateljee-bar* Ⓜ *Trams 4, 9, 10.*

Gate A21

BARS/PUBS | Finland's finest cocktails are mixed at A21, a bar and music club playing on the airport gate theme, even to the extent that it has a replica propeller plane hanging from the ceiling. ✉ *Annankatu 21, Keskusta* ☎ *044/765–5783* ⊕ *www.a21.fi* Ⓜ *Trams 3, 4, 6.*

Juttutupa

BARS/PUBS | Steeped in history, this bar was first opened in 1906 by the Helsinki Workers' Association. It hosts great jazz,

With its golden cupolas and redbrick facade, Uspenski Cathedral is one of the clearest symbols of the Russian impact on Finnish history.

blues, and other music nights (admission is free Wednesday and Saturday) and has a convivial, authentically Helsinki atmosphere, making it one of the city's best live music venues. At the bar's "revolutionary table," Vladimir Lenin met with fellow conspirators and plotted Russia's revolution, just one element of a fascinating and eventful history. The bar is inside the Graniittilinna restaurant, behind the Scandic Paasi hotel, a magnificent National Romantic–style stone fortress overlooking an inlet from the sea. The menu includes good pizzas and salads, and there is an outdoor terrace that catches the evening sun. ⊠ *Graniittilinna, Säästöpankinranta 6, Hakaniemi* 🕾 *020/742–4240* ⊕ *www.juttutupa.fi* Ⓜ *Hakaniemi.*

Kaisla

BARS/PUBS | Larger than it appears from the outside, this bar—actually two conjoined bars with two separate entrances—offers a huge range of beers, ales, ciders, and whiskies from across the globe as well as bar snacks, including doorstop toast sandwiches. Popular with students (Helsinki University buildings are nearby), after-work drinkers, and board game enthusiasts, it's a lively haunt especially for discerning beer drinkers. ⊠ *Vilhonkatu 4, Keskusta* 🕾 *010/766–3850* ⊕ *www.raflaamo.fi/fi/helsinki/kaisla* Ⓜ *Metro Helsinki University.*

Kappeli

BARS/PUBS | The windows of this ornate, classic 19th-century Esplanade venue—containing a café, bar, and restaurant as well as offering one of Helsinki's most popular summer terraces—provide an excellent view of the Havis Amanda statue and the western edge of the Market Square. The terrace is a great place to sip a drink while enjoying afternoon performances on the bandstand on the other side of the Esplanade. ⊠ *Eteläesplanadi 1, Esplanadi* 🕾 *010/766–3880 8 cents/ call + 12 cents/min* ⊕ *www.kappeli.fi* Ⓜ *Tram 3.*

Molly Malone's

BARS/PUBS | There's nightly live music upstairs at this popular Irish pub. ✉ *Kaisaniemenkatu 1C, Keskusta* ☎ *020/719–1970* ⊕ *www.mollymalones.fi.*

O'Malley's

BARS/PUBS | This was the first Irish pub in Helsinki, and it hosts occasional Irish jam sessions and attracts a loyal regular crowd as well as guests at the Solo Sokos Hotel Torni. The courtyard serves as a pleasant outdoor terrace in summer. ✉ *Solo Sokos Hotel Torni, Yrjönkatu 26, Keskusta* ☎ *010/784–2050* ⊕ *www. raflaamo.fi/fi/helsinki/pub-omalleys-torni* Ⓜ *Trams 3, 10, Metro Kamppi.*

Ravintola Teatteri

BARS/PUBS | Located on the Esplanade side of the Swedish Theater, Teatteri takes full advantage of its sexy Esplanade location with a perennially cool (and expensive) nightclub and two bar-lounges. ✉ *Pohjoisesplanadi 2, Esplanadi* ☎ *09/6128–5000* ⊕ *www.teatteri.fi* Ⓜ *Tram 6, 10.*

Teerenpeli Helsinki

BARS/PUBS | Located on the edge of the Kamppi Center mall, Teerenpeli Kamppi serves excellent on-tap and bottled beers from its on-site microbrewery, its own whiskey, and substantial snacks and tapas plates. ✉ *Olavinkatu 2, Keskusta* ☎ *042/492–5260* ⊕ *www.teerenpeli.com/en* Ⓜ *Kamppi.*

Vltava

BARS/PUBS | This four-story, Jugendstil building next to the main railway station is now a bar and restaurant with the best selection of Czech beers in the city. ✉ *Elielinaukio 2, Keskusta* ☎ *010/766–3650* ⊕ *www.vltava.fi* Ⓜ *Central Railway Station.*

William K. Tennispalatsi

BARS/PUBS | Situated on one side of the Tennispalatsi cinema and art museum complex, cleverly converted from a previous sports hall, this is the most central of a group of William K. bars, originally modeled on the Dutch ale house concept, specializing in a large selection of good Finnish and European craft beers. ✉ *Fredrikinkatu 65, Keskusta* ☎ *010/766–4420* Ⓜ *Kamppi.*

Woolshed

BARS/PUBS | Probably the best sports bar in Helsinki, the Woolshed is an Australian gastropub serving a great selection of beers and good-value pub meals such as fish-and-chips and burgers. There are special discounts on certain evenings. A plethora of well-placed TVs with access to major sports channels show the most popular sporting events, including ice hockey, soccer, rugby, and cricket, making it popular with expats as well as locals. It has a spacious outdoor terrace, too, and a back door that opens onto the railway station platforms. ✉ *Töölönlahdenkatu 3B 1, Keskusta/Rautatieasema* ✛ *Close to Oodi library, behind the main railway station* ☎ *044/760–4086* ⊕ *woolshed.eu* Ⓜ *Central Railway Station.*

LGBTQ BARS

DTM

BARS/PUBS | Short for "Don't Tell Mama," DTM is the largest and best-known gay club in Finland, combining a nightclub, bar, and event venue with VIP bookings and welcoming "every letter of LGBTIQ." There's an age minimum of 20 on Saturday and 18 on other days. Open Wednesday to Sunday, 10 to 5. Check website for entry fees. ✉ *Mannerheimintie 6B, Keskusta* ☎ *010/841–6996* ⊕ *www. dtm.fi* Ⓜ *Trams 3, 4, 6, 10.*

MUSIC CLUBS

Circus

MUSIC CLUBS | This newly popular venue satisfies young Finns' appetite for heavy rock. Other kinds of Finnish and international music acts, from pop to electronica, also get an airing. ✉ *Salomonkatu 1–3* ✛ *Close to Kamppi Center mall* ☎ *010/423–3231* ⊕ *thecircus.fi.*

Singalong Nation

Considering the Finns' reputation for reserve and reticence, which in any case is sometimes doubtful, it might come as a surprise to discover their passion for a decidedly extroverted pursuit: karaoke. A gutsy, tear-jerking bellow of a Finnish pop classic after a few *tuopit*, or large beers, seems to proffer emotional therapy on a weekend evening for many a Finn, whether in the capital or in a remote Lapland bar, and it's a popular way to finish up a Tallinn day-trip on the return ferry. If you are seeking an archetypal, down-to-earth Helsinki nightlife experience, drop into one of the several karaoke bars around town, where vocal enthusiasm is never in short supply and performances continue long into the early hours. Top of the list is Pataässä (Ace of Spades), a Helsinki institution where sessions continue every morning until 5 am (and on weekends get going again four hours later). It's at Snellmaninkatu 13, behind the Lutheran cathedral. ⊕ *www.karaokebar.net/pataassa*

Storyville

MUSIC CLUBS | Helsinki's most popular jazz club has live jazz, blues, rock and roll, and dancing Monday–Saturday. ✉ *Museokatu 8, Keskusta* ☎ *050/363–2664* ⊕ *www. storyville.fi* Ⓜ *Trams 4, 10.*

NIGHTCLUBS

Kaivohuone

DANCE CLUBS | This old spa structure in beautiful Kaivopuisto Park is open from May to August on Wednesday, Friday, and Saturday and often packed with a trendy young set. Weekend parties are sometimes open to the public at other times; check the website for details. ✉ *Iso Puistotie 1, Kaivopuisto* ☎ *020/775–9825* ⊕ *www.kaivohuone.fi* Ⓜ *Tram 3.*

Manala

MUSIC CLUBS | The first-floor restaurant in this lively three-floor complex is open until 2 am Sunday–Thursday and 4 am on weekends—the longest opening hours of any kitchen in Helsinki. Entertainment to accompany your late-night or early-morning pizza include stand-up comedy, Sunday lounge music, and after-work jazz. ✉ *Dagmarinkatu 2, Töölö* ☎ *09/5807–7707* ⊕ *manala.fi* Ⓜ *Tram 4, 10.*

Tavastia Club

DANCE CLUBS | The university-owned Tavastia Club is one of the best and most atmospheric rock clubs for top Finnish talent and some solid imports. Be prepared for some good-natured rowdiness and late starts for bands. ✉ *Urho Kekkosenkatu 4–6, Keskusta* ☎ *09/7746–7420* ⊕ *www.tavastiaklubi.fi* Ⓜ *Kamppi.*

Performing Arts

VENUES

Helsinki Music Center (*Musiikkitalo*)
CONCERTS | Since it opened in 2011, the Helsinki Music Center has been praised for its acoustics and daring design, dominating one side of the Kansalaistori square and facing the Kiasma art museum and the Oodi Central Library. It's home to the Sibelius Academy and two symphony orchestras. Guided tours are available, but most are in Finnish—check the website for details. The one-hour guided walking tour introduces participants to what happens here as well as to the architecture, main audience, and the concert hall. In the summer there are free afternoon concerts in the main foyer. There's also a café and

the Terrace Restaurant, and the Fuga classical CD and record store is housed here too. ✉ *Mannerheimintie 13A, Töölö* ☎ *020/707–0400 service desk and contact info* ⊕ *www.musiikkitalo.fi* Ⓜ *Trams 4, 10.*

Finlandia Hall (*Finlandia-talo*)
CONCERTS | This white, winged concert and congress hall was one of Alvar Aalto's last and most conspicuous creations, a venue for concerts, exhibitions, and conferences. Perhaps most famously, it hosted the Cold War–era summit between U.S. president Gerald Ford and Soviet president Leonid Brezhnev in 1975. It's especially impressive on foggy days or at night when its illuminated facade is reflected in the Töölö Bay. If you can't make it to a concert here, try to take a guided tour or enjoy a coffee at the Cafe Veranda. ✉ *Mannerheimintie 13E, Keskusta* ☎ *09/40241* ⊕ *www.finlandiatalo.fi* ⏰ *Guided tours €11.50 Wed. at 2 pm* Ⓜ *Trams 4, 7, 10.*

Finnish National Opera
CONCERTS | Grand gilded operas, classical ballets, and booming concerts all take place in Helsinki's splendid Opera House, a striking example of modern Scandinavian architecture. All events at the Opera House draw crowds, so buy your tickets early. ✉ *Helsinginkatu 58, Keskusta* ☎ *09/4030–2210 tours, 09/4030–2211 box office* ⊕ *www.opera.fi/en* Ⓜ *Trams 3, 4, 10.*

Finnish National Theater
THEATER | Productions in the three theaters here are in Finnish, with the very occasional English-language show. The elegant granite facade overlooking Railway Station Square is decorated with quirky relief typical of the Finnish National Romantic style. In front is a statue of writer Aleksis Kivi. ✉ *Läntinen Teatterikuja 1, Keskusta/Rautatieasema* ✛ *North side of Railway Station Square* ☎ *010/73311* ⊕ *www.nationaltheatre.fi* Ⓜ *Central Railway Station.*

🛍 Shopping

The area south and west of Mannerheimintie, including the tree-lined Esplanade with its design brand stores, has been branded Design District Helsinki. It includes roughly 170 venues, most of them smaller boutiques and designer-run shops selling handmade everything from jewelry and clothing to housewares. The majority are located on Fredrikinkatu and Annankatu; look for a black Design District Helsinki sticker in the window. You can pick up a map detailing the shops in the district at most participating stores. Kiosks are open late and on weekends; they sell basics such as milk, juice, camera film, and tissues. Stores in Asematunneli are open weekdays 10–10 and weekends noon–10.

Alcohol sales in Finland are controlled by the Finnish state monopoly, Alko. This might sound severe, but in fact Helsinki liquor and wine stores are extremely well stocked and staffed by very knowledgeable salespeople. Prices are relatively high, however. These stores are your only option for full-strength wines and spirits. Rules in groceries have relaxed to the extent that they can now sell stronger beers and ciders (up to 5.5%).

CERAMICS AND ACCESSORIES
Aarikka
JEWELRY/ACCESSORIES | Aarikka specializes in quality wooden jewelry and decorative items. Earrings and Christmas decorations are especially popular and make perfect, very Finnish gifts. The classic Pässi sheep, made from small wooden spheres, are less compact but no less charming. ✉ *Pohjoisesplanadi 27, Esplanadi* ☎ *044/422–0204* ⊕ *www.aarikka. com* Ⓜ *Helsinki University.*

Iittala and Arabia Design Centre Store
CERAMICS/GLASSWARE | Arabia, Hackman, and Iittala tableware, glassware, cutlery, and cookware are sold here at outlet prices, along with Finlayson textiles and Fiskars garden tools and scissors.

Marimekko

When the world's fashion-conscious think "Finland," they think Marimekko. Founded by a Finnish couple in 1951, the company got its big international break when Jacqueline Kennedy appeared in front of JFK on the cover of *Sports Illustrated* magazine wearing a Marimekko dress during the 1960 presidential campaign. More recently, Manolo Blahnik took the company's prints as one of the inspirations for his Spring/Summer 2008 collection. One of Marimekko's best-known designs is artist Maija Isola's "Unikko," comprising large poppies in bright, bold colors, created in 1964 and still in production on items from dresses to bedding. Another of the company's timeless designs is "Piccolo," a vivid striped pattern that first took the form of the "Jokapoika" shirt (1956) and is today printed on clothing and accessories found in Marimekko stores. The company introduces dozens of new fabric designs every year, with an emphasis on bold, uncluttered patterns.

The shop is on the site of the old Arabia factory in the Arabiankeskus (Arabia center) and is some way out of central Helsinki in the Arabianranta district, but it's worth the diversion if you are looking for a one-stop shop for practical Finnish design items for your home or as gifts. It's a great spot to find Moomin character mugs! ⊠ *Hämeentie 135, Arabianranta* ☎ *020/439–3507* ⊕ *www.designcentre-helsinki.com* Ⓜ *Tram 6.*

Pentik

CERAMICS/GLASSWARE | This company, with several stores in and around Helsinki, is known for its classy but country-home style of ceramic dishes and other housewares, including bed linens, cushion covers, and duvet covers (the Peony design is a classic). Inventive gift items and cards are also for sale. The main store is in the Forum mall, right in the center of town. ⊠ *Forum, Mannerheimintie 20, 3rd fl., Keskusta* ☎ *040/839–4423* ⊕ *www.pentik.com* Ⓜ *Kamppi.*

CLOTHING

Ivana Helsinki House and Gallery Shop

CLOTHING | Ivana Helsinki has earned international recognition for its women's whimsical sweaters and dresses, done in either solid colors or bold and bright patterns and designed by its founder, the talented Paola Suhonen. You need to venture out to the Marjaniemi suburb to visit her charming and elegant gallery shop. ⊠ *Palopirtintie 15, Punavuori* ⊹ *Metro to Itäkeskus, then a 15-minute walk* ☎ *05/0505–1626* ⊕ *www.ivanahelsinki. com* ⊙ *Closed Sun.–Tues. and mornings* Ⓜ *Itäkeskus.*

Marimekko

CLOTHING | Since the 1950s Marimekko has been selling bright, unusual clothes for men, women, and children in quality fabrics, and it is perhaps the most durable, recognizable, and iconic of all Finnish design brands, popular globally. Though the products are expensive, they're worth a look even if you don't plan to buy. There are several locations in central Helsinki and others throughout Finland, in addition to this flagship concept store. ⊠ *Galleria Esplanad, Mikonkatu 1, Esplanadi* ☎ *09/75871* ⊕ *www.marimekko. com* Ⓜ *Helsinki University.*

DEPARTMENT STORES

Stockmann

DEPARTMENT STORES | This is Helsinki's premier department store. A one-stop shop for Finnish interior design and top-label clothing and established in the 19th century, Stockmann occupies a single block at the southern end of the Keskuskatu pedestrian street and is a favorite with well-heeled clientele. The entrance on Aleksanterinkatu, under the clock and opposite the Three Smiths statue, is a traditional rendezvous for locals meeting up in town. The food market in the basement is a good (although not the cheapest) place to stock up on edible souvenirs and picnic ingredients, including an excellent choice of fresh breads, cheeses, fruit, and (when in season) berries. There are also branches in the Itäkeskus suburb, in Tapiola in Espoo, in the Jumbo mall in Vantaa, and in the cities of Turku and Tampere. ⊠ *Aleksanterinkatu 52B, Keskusta* ☎ *09/1211* ⊕ *www.stockmann. fi* Ⓜ *Central Railway Station.*

HOME DESIGN

Artek

HOUSEHOLD ITEMS/FURNITURE | Artek Helsinki, opposite the Stockmann department store on the Keskuskatu pedestrian street, offers two floors of classic Finnish design items in addition to international brands. Artek's original product range comprised items by Alvar Aalto, probably the country's best-known designer and architect, including the classic three-legged stool and other bent-birch furniture. These have stood the test of time and are still on show and for purchase at Artek. Many other smaller accessories, tableware, books, magazines, and wellness products are also for sale. ⊠ *Keskuskatu 1B, Keskusta* ☎ *010/617–3480* ☾ *Closed Sun.* Ⓜ *Helsinki University.*

Iittala

SPECIALTY STORES | Iittala glass and kitchenware represents the best and most stylish of Finnish design and makes classy souvenirs and gifts. There are two Iittala stores in central Helsinki, one in the corner of the Amos Rex art museum and a flagship store on the north side of

the Esplanade. ⊠ *Pohjoisesplanadi 23, Keskusta* ☎ *020/439–3501* ⊕ *iittala.com* Ⓜ *Helsinki University.*

JEWELRY

Kalevala Koru

JEWELRY/ACCESSORIES | This company bases its designs on traditional motifs dating back as far as the Iron Age and inspired in part by the imagery of the Finnish national epic, *The Kalevala*. Its designs are also available at most jewelry shops around Finland and in the Stockmann department store. ⊠ *Pohjoisesplanadi 25–27, Keskusta* ☎ *020/761–1380* ⊕ *www.kalevalakoru.fi* Ⓜ *Metro Helsinki University.*

STREET MARKETS

Hietalahti Market Hall and Flea Market (*Hietalahden Kauppahalli*)

MARKET | The 115-year-old redbrick market hall, close to the shipyard, houses a variety of small restaurants serving everythng from sushi and soups to meze and ramen. It's an excellent venue for lunch or to shop for local breads, cheeses, and smoked meats and fish. An outdoor flea market offers the rejects of countless Helsinki attics and cellars in the adjacent market square through the summer, a colorful and lively mecca for vintage bargain hunters. ⊠ *Bulevardi and Hietalahdenkatu, Hietalahti* ☎ *09/3102–3555* ⊕ *www.hietalahdenkauppahalli.fi/en* ☾ *Market Hall closed Sun.* Ⓜ *Tram 6.*

★ Market Square (*Kauppatori*)

MARKET | At this Helsinki institution, open year-round on the South Harbour quayside, wooden stands with orange and gold awnings bustle in the mornings when everyone—tourists and locals alike—comes to shop, browse, or sit and enjoy coffee and conversation. You can buy a freshly caught perch for the evening's dinner along with an array of forest mushrooms, a bouquet of bright flowers for a friend, or a fur pelt. In summer the fruit, berry, and vegetable stalls are supplemented by an arts-and-crafts and souvenir market. The crepes, made to order by one of the tented vendors, are excellent, while locals swear by the meat pies and fresh jam-filled doughnuts. In summer there are several vendors selling lunch plates. ⊠ *Eteläranta and Pohjoisesplanadi, Kauppatori* Ⓜ *Tram 3.*

Old Market Hall (*Vanha Kauppahalli*) LOCAL INTEREST | Fish, meat, fruit, berries, fresh vegetables, bread and pastries, local cheeses, spices, coffee, and tea—the brick Old Market Hall on the waterfront, close to the outdoor Market Square, is a treasury of delicacies. A soup station, café, and seafood bar make it ideal for a quick lunch, and there is even a small branch of the Alko wine and liquor outlet. Permanent stalls are adorned with decorative carved woodwork, giving the hall a historic feel. ⊠ *Eteläranta along the South Harbour, Kauppatori* ☎ *09/3102–3550* ⊕ *vanhakauppahalli.fi* Ⓜ *Tram 3.*

Gallen-Kallela Estate

10 km (6 miles) northwest of Helsinki.

GETTING HERE AND AROUND
To get to the estate from Helsinki, take Tram 4 from in front of the Sokos department store on Mannerheimintie and get out at the Munkkiniemi stop. From there, walk 2 km (1 mile) following the scenic path along the seashore and across a couple of footbridges, or rent a City Bike from the stand near the tram stop.

◉ Sights

★ Gallen-Kallela Estate
HOUSE | Set at the edge of the sea and surrounded by towering, wind-bent pines, the turreted brick-and-stucco Gallen-Kallela Estate on the Tarvaspää promontory was the self-designed studio and home of the Finnish Romantic painter Akseli Gallen-Kallela. Gallen-Kallela

(1865–1931) lived in the mansion on and off from its completion in 1913 until his death. Inside, the open rooms of the painter's former work spaces make the perfect exhibition hall for his paintings. Also displayed are some of his posters and sketches of the ceiling murals he made for the Paris Art Exhibition at the turn of the 20th century. There is a very good and popular café selling pastries, ice cream, and lunches in the villa opposite the museum. ⊠ *Gallen-Kallelantie 27, Espoo* ☎ *010/406–8840* ⊕ *www.gallen-kallela.fi* ⊠ *€9.*

Hvitträsk

40 km (25 miles) west of Helsinki.

GETTING HERE AND AROUND
Hvitträsk can be reached independently from Helsinki by taking the E, L, S, or U train to Kauklahti and then calling a taxi. It is not the most accessible out-of-town attraction but is definitely one of the most rewarding.

◉ Sights

★ Hvitträsk
BUILDING | In an idyllic position at the top of a wooded slope is Hvitträsk, the studio home of architects Herman Gesellius, Armas Lindgren, and Eliel Saarinen, a wonderful day or half-day excursion destination from Helsinki. The property dates back to the turn of the 20th century and is now a charming museum. The whimsical main house reveals the national art nouveau style, with its rustic detail and paintings by Akseli Gallen-Kallela; Saarinen lived here, and his grave is nearby in the woods that slope down to the lakeside. A café and restaurant are set up in one of the architects' houses. ⊠ *Hvitträskintie 166, Luoma* ☎ *295/336–951* ⊕ *www.hvittrask.fi* ⊠ *€10* ⊗ *Closed Oct.–Apr.*

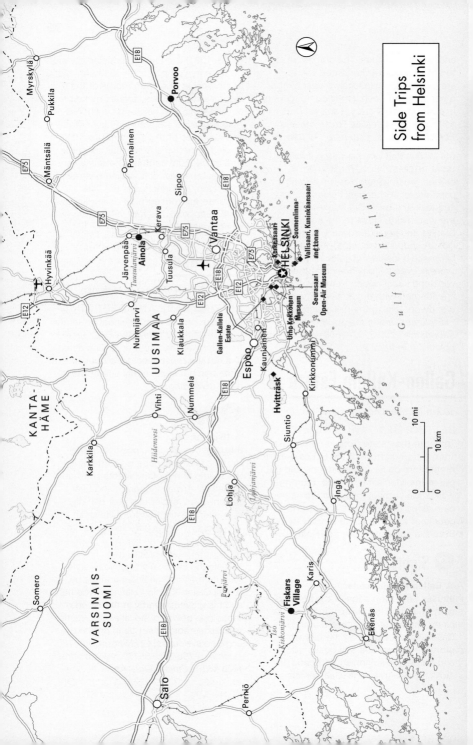

Side Trips
from Helsinki

The architect trio Gesellius, Lindgren, and Saarinen built their studio home, Hvitträsk, at Lake Vittträsk; today, it's a museum and must for architecture and design fans.

Ainola

50 km (31 miles) north of Helsinki.

GETTING HERE AND AROUND
Take a bus from the Helsinki bus station or a local train first to the town of Järvenpää; Ainola is 2 km (1 mile) farther by bus or taxi.

Sights

Ainola
MUSEUM | The former home of Finland's most famous son, composer Jean Sibelius, was designed by Lars Sonck in 1904 and takes its name from his wife, Aino. From late spring through summer, the intimate wooden house set in secluded woodland is open to the public as a museum. Cafe Aulis, in an adjacent modern building, serves refreshments, pastries, and cakes. A guided tour is included in the ticket price if booked in advance. ⊠ *Ainolankatu, Järvenpää*
☎ *09/287–322* ⊕ *www.ainola.fi* ✉ *€10* ☉ *Closed Nov.–May.*

Porvoo

50 km (31 miles) east of Helsinki.

Porvoo is a living record of the past, with its old stone streets and painted wooden houses lining the riverbank. Artisan boutiques around the old Town Hall Square invite exploration. Take a stroll into the Old Town to see the multicolor wooden houses. Porvoo is also known locally as Borgå, the Swedish name for the city. There are many Swedish speakers in this area.

GETTING HERE AND AROUND
Part of the fun of visiting Porvoo is the journey you take to get there. On five summer Saturdays (July through the end of August, except Midsummer Day) there's a train connection along the historical museum rail between Helsinki and Porvoo, on board the old trains from the 1950s and 1960s. Prices are €20

one-way, €30 round-trip. Contact the Porvoo Museum Railway Society for details.

Far more regular than the historic train journey is the **boat service.** May through September, cruises depart from Helsinki's South Harbor regularly (check the website for exact dates and times): the *J.L. Runeberg* takes 3½ hours, and the round-trip costs €39. The *King* takes three hours each way and costs €39 for a round-trip. You will be taken westward through dozens of islands before landing at Porvoo. For more information, contact the boat companies or the Porvoo City Tourist Office. By bus, take the Porvoo bus from Kanppi Station in Helsinki one-hour to Porvoo Station near the marketplace, which is a five-minute walk from the harbor. By car, take the E18 freeway to the old road 170 into Porvoo.

TRAIN CONTACTS Porvoo Museum Railway Society. ☎ 0400/700–717 ⊕ www.porvoonmuseorautatie.fi.

VISITOR INFORMATION CONTACTS Porvoo City Tourist Office. ✉ Läntinen Aleksanterinkatu 1 ☎ 40/489–9801 tourist office ⊕ www.porvoo.fi/tourism.

👁 Sights

Albert Edelfelt's Studio
MUSEUM | Near Porvoo in Haikko stands the studio of the painter Albert Edelfelt in a quaint wooden cottage tucked away in the woods. Edelfelt was born into a well-to-do Swedish-speaking family in 1854 and was one of the first Finnish painters to find international fame. He introduced the realist movement to his native country and was active in encouraging young aspiring artists to find success in Paris. In this studio he completed some 220 of his works, and it's here where he died in 1905, surrounded by the beautiful landscape that inspired so many of his works. ✉ Edelfeltinpolku 3 ☎ 019/577–414 ⊕ www.albertedelfeltinateljee.fi 🖾 €5.

Home of J. L. Runeberg
LOCAL INTEREST | The home of Finland's national poet is a fantastically authentic museum displaying the poet and his wife's original furnishings and paintings exactly as they were when he died in 1877. The Runeberg story is told by museum staff, and there's an exhibit related to Finnish history. ✉ Aleksanterinkatu 3 ☎ 019/574–7500 ⊕ https://www.visitporvoo.fi/jl-runebergs-home 🖾 €8.

Porvoo Cathedral
BUILDING | At this 15th-century stone-and-wood cathedral, the diet of the first duchy of Finland was opened in 1809, making Finland semiautonomous as part of the Russian Empire. This is one of the oldest churches of its kind in Finland—it's survived being burned to the ground by both Danish and Russian armies on several occasions and more recently in 2006 by home-grown arsonists, after which it was impressively and lovingly restored. Inside, you can make out some of the original Catholic artwork, before the Protestant Reformation led to the whitewashing of its walls. Just outside the front gate are some of the best views of the surrounding town. ✉ Kirkkotori 1 ☎ 019/661–1250 ⊕ www.porvoonseurakunnat.fi 🖾 Free.

Porvoo Museum
HISTORIC SITE | The Porvoo Museum, inside the historic town hall built in 1764, captures the region's social and cultural history through exhibits on daily life and household objects. ✉ Jokikatu 45 ☎ 040/197–5557 ⊕ www.porvoonmuseo.fi 🖾 €8.

🛍 Shopping

Atelier Ann Helene Nordlund
CLOTHING | Atelier AN sells smart-looking handmade sweaters, hats, coats, and jackets produced from wool and from local reindeer, lamb, and elk skins. ✉ Jokikatu 12A 4 ☎ 040/565–5625.

Brunberg Chocolate

FOOD/CANDY | At the Brunberg shop on the edge of the Old Town you can sample and buy chocolate-mint chips, chocolate-orange chips, and other combinations, as well as individually wrapped melt-in-your-mouth chocolate truffles and marshmallow kisses adored throughout the country, at the best prices in Finland. You can also visit the factory shop outside the center at Teollisuustie 19. ⊠ *Välikatu 4* ☏ *019/548–4235* ⊕ *www. brunberg.fi.*

Fiskars Village

90 km (56 miles) west of Helsinki.

This ironworks village is best known as the place where the Fiskars company began producing its orange scissors in 1967. The company has since relocated production but the picturesque lake-dotted, tree-lined village, where artists, designers, and their families have settled, remains. At any given time, the village features exhibitions, most notably the Fiskars Village Art and Design Biennale, a modest museum, a couple of rather good restaurants, and a small hotel. There are many little shops and boutiques, including a candlemaker, a goldsmith, a brewery and beer shop, a cider shop, a photography gallery, a paper maker, a ceramics studio, other handicraft artisans, and a Fiskars shop selling the eponymous goods and those of Arabia, Hackman, and Iittala.

GETTING HERE AND AROUND

From Helsinki, it's best to rent a car for the easy 75-minute drive. Alternatively, you can take a 50- to 55-minute train ride to Karjaa, from which point it's a 15-minute taxi ride; buses from Karjaa are infrequent and connections from the train are few.

VISITOR INFORMATION

CONTACTS Fiskars Village. ⊠ *Peltorivi 1, Fiskars* ☏ *20/439 2099* ⊕ *www.fiskars-village.fi.*

 Sights

Bianco Blu

MUSEUM VILLAGE | **FAMILY** | At Bianco Blu visitors can try their hand at blowing their own glass item during a 1½-hour-long guided session or shop the many professionally made pieces. ⊠ *Kuparivasarantie 7A, Fiskars* ☏ *045/139–0020* ⊕ *www. biancoblu.fi* 🎟 *Glassblowing session €30 and up.*

Fiskars Museum

MUSEUM | **FAMILY** | The Fiskars Museum gives a modest overview of the things produced in the village, its culture, and the living conditions of 19th-century families. ⊠ *Peltorivi 13, Fiskars* ☏ *019/237–013* ⊕ *www.fiskarsmuseum.fi* 🎟 *€3, free on Tues.*

🛍 Shopping

Onoma

CRAFTS | Onoma features work by a cooperative of Fiskars artisans, designers, and artists, one of whom is nearly always manning the shop. The selection includes exquisitely crafted wood items, candles, visual art, cards, ceramics, and hanging mobiles. ⊠ *Clocktower, Fiskarsintie 352, Fiskars* ☏ *0400/850–250* ⊕ *www.onoma. fi/en.*

Sassi

JEWELRY/ACCESSORIES | Silver jewelry in flowing designs is available at this family-owned store and workshop. ⊠ *Fiskarsintie 366B, Fiskars* ☏ *044/757–2480* ⊕ *www.sassidesign.fi.*

Sirius

CERAMICS/GLASSWARE | This shops sells gorgeous glassware designed by Camilla Moberg, who lives above the shop. ⊠ *Fiskarsintie 38, Fiskars* ☏ *050/590–9961* ⊕ *www.camillamoberg.fi.*

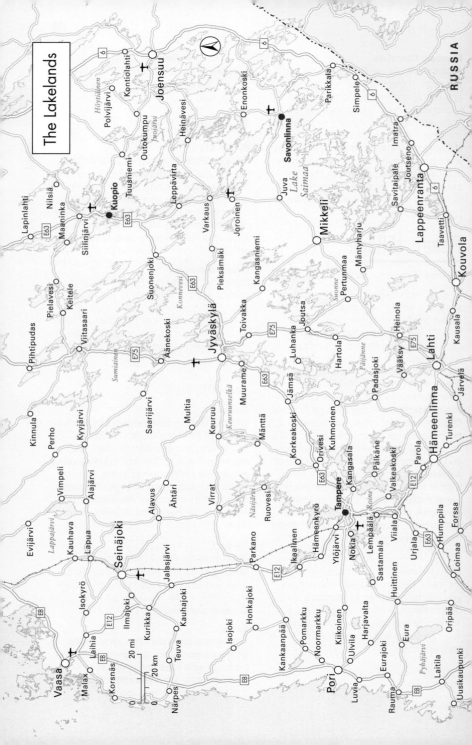

Takopaja

GIFTS/SOUVENIRS | This shop and workshop offers the unique opportunity to observe and chat with a blacksmith at work as you peruse his wares, which include keychains, jewelry, knives, lanterns, and candle holders, which are popular at Christmas. ✉ *Kuparivasarantie, Fiskars ⊹ Across from Bianco Blu* ☎ *050/590–2797* ⊕ *www.takopaja.fi* ⊗ *Closed weekends.*

Savonlinna

335 km (208 miles) northeast of Helsinki.

Although it is home to just 35,000 people, Savonlinna is one of the larger Lakeland towns, best known for having the finest castle in all of Finland. The town takes advantage of this stunning attraction by holding the annual opera festival in the castle courtyard.

GETTING HERE AND AROUND

Buses are the best form of public transport into the region, with frequent connections to lake destinations from most major towns. An express bus from Helsinki can take more than four hours. It's a six-hour ride/drive from Helsinki to Savonlinna traveling Route 5 to Route 14 in Juva, then another 60 km (37 miles) from Juva. The train trip from Helsinki to Savonlinna takes 4½ hours. The islands that make up Savonlinna center are linked by bridges. First, visit the open-air market that flourishes along the main passenger quay, and indulge in a coffee from one of the several stands with a *lörtsy,* a local specialty in the form of a flat semicircular pastry envelope filled with fruit jam or savory meat. From here you can catch the boat to Kuopio and Lappeenranta. You can take scenic and lunch cruises aboard one of several old steamboats June through August.

BOAT Saimaan Laivamatkat. ☎ *015/250–250* ⊕ *www.mspuijo.fi/info.* **Vip Cruise.** ☎ *050/368–2287* ⊕ *www.vipcruise.info.*

VISITOR INFORMATION

Savonlinna Tourist Information. ✉ *Tottinkatu 6A, Savonlinna* ☎ *044/417–4466* ⊕ *www.visitsavonlinna.fi.*

⊙ Sights

Kerimäki Church

Believed to be the biggest wooden church in the world at 45 meters in length and 42 meters wide, the church at Kerimäki has the capacity to seat 3,000 worshippers, with another 2,000 standing. There is a nice story about how the size of the church was due to the architect's confusion about centimeters and inches, but in fact it was meant to be this big, in order to accommodate half of the people living in the area. The church is a 30-minute drive east of Savonlinna on Lake Puruvesi, or take a train from Savonlinna to Kerimäki station (about 15 minutes) and call a taxi (the number is on a sign at the station) to cover the remaining 12 km (8 miles). ✉ *Hälväntie 1* ☎ *015/ 576–800, 044/776–8009 for guides* ⊠ *Free.*

★ Olavinlinna

HISTORIC SITE | A 10-minute stroll from the quay to the southeast brings you to Savonlinna's most famous site, the castle Olavinlinna. First built in 1475 to protect Finland's eastern border, the castle retains its medieval character and is one of Scandinavia's best-preserved historic monuments. Still surrounded by water that once bolstered its defensive strength, the fortress rises majestically out of the lake. Every July the Savonlinna Opera Festival is held in the castle's courtyard, which creates a spell-binding combination of music and surroundings. The festival is a showcase for Finnish opera, but it also hosts foreign companies. You will need to make reservations well in advance for both tickets and hotel rooms (note higher hotel rates during the festival), as Savonlinna draws many music lovers. The festival also includes arts and crafts exhibits around town.

✉ *Savonlinna* ☎ *029/533–6942* 🌐 *www.kansallismuseo.fi/en/olavinlinna* 🎫 *€10, combined one-day ticket with Riihisaari museum €12.*

Riihisaari–Lake Saimaa Nature and Museum Centre

MUSEUM | Also housing Savonlinna Tourist Information, the museum on the island of Riihisaari, adjacent to Olavinlinna, offers a glimpse into the history of lake traffic, including the fascinating floating timber trains still a common sight on Lake Saimaa today. Steamships moored on the island are open in summer. ✉ *Tottinkatu 6A, Savonlinna* ☎ *044/417–4466* 🌐 *www.savonlinna.fi/riihisaari* 🎫 *€8, Olavinlinna Castle and Riihisaari combined €12.*

Saimaa Ringed Seal Lake Trip

SCENIC DRIVE | The rare Saimaa ringed seal owes it freshwater existence to the retreat of the ice sheets some 8,000 years ago, when it began to be effectively cut off from other Baltic seals. Springtime boat safaris in the company of experts have a high spot success rate. There are almost 400 of the animals in the lake, representing a conservation success story for a species that had dropped to a dangerously low population. Savonlinna Tourist Information has details about responsible tour operators. ✉ *Savonlinna Tourist Information, Tottinkatu 6A, Savonlinna* ☎ *044/ 417–4466* 🌐 *www.savonlinna.fi.*

🍴 Restaurants

Huvila Brewery Restaurant

$$ | **SCANDINAVIAN** | Boasting nine homemade brews as home to the Waahto microbrewery, a waterfront locale with an outdoor patio and live music, and a gastronomic cuisine, Huvila is a fantastic surprise so far from a big city. It seems a shame that restaurants like this are only open in summer. **Known for:** beer brewed on the spot; live music in summer; poker evenings. [$] *Average main: €25* ✉ *Puistokatu 4, Savonlinna* ☎ *015/555–0555* 🕒 *Closed Sept.–May.*

Paviljonki

$$ | **SCANDINAVIAN** | The restaurant of the Savonlinna restaurant school opens for lunch (from 11 till 3) on weekdays, and at other times only by arrangement. The menu is short but sweet; the fried vendace, a classic local dish, is good when available, as is the pepper steak. **Known for:** affordable lunches; lakeside location; airy conservatory dining room. [$] *Average main: €23* ✉ *Rajalahdenkatu 4, Savonlinna* ☎ *044/550–6303* 🌐 *www.ravintolapaviljonki.fi* 🕒 *Closed weekends.*

Pizzeria Capero

$ | **PIZZA** | This Savonlinna institution has been satisfying locals with its excellent, affordable pizzas and pasta dishes in its split-level, tavern-like space for more than 25 years. An equally big draw, however, are its "pots"—combinations of rice and ingredients including chicken, shrimp, mussels, and mushrooms, baked together with a crispy cheese overlay. **Known for:** central location; good value; generous portions. [$] *Average main: €10* ✉ *Olavinkatu 48, Savonlinna* ☎ *015/533–955* 🌐 *www.pizzeriacapero.net.*

🛏 Hotels

Hotel Hospitz

$$ | **HOTEL** | In the heart of Savonlinna overlooking the lake, this 1930s building on historic Linnankatu has small, unpretentious rooms, all individually decorated in period styles. **Pros:** central location; lake views from some rooms; lakeside terrace. **Cons:** simple bathrooms; dated decor; no elevator. [$] *Rooms from: €125* ✉ *Linnankatu 20, Savonlinna* ☎ *015/515–661* 🌐 *www.hospitz.com* 🛏 *21 rooms* 🍽 *Free Breakfast.*

★ **Hotel Punkaharju**

$$$ | **HOTEL** | Situated on the idyllic Punkaharju esker ridge a 30-minute drive southeast of Savonlinna, surrounded by quintessential Finnish lake and forest

scenery, this is one of the most beautifully located hotels in Finland, if not *the* most beautifully located. **Pros:** scenic location; modern with historic character; excellent restaurant. **Cons:** some rooms are a little small; weak Wi-Fi; distance from other dining options and amenities. $ *Rooms from: €190* ⊠ *Punkaharjun Harjutie 596, Punkaharju* ☎ *015/ 511–311* ⊕ *www.hotellipunkaharju.fi* ⤳ *11 rooms, 12 forest cabins* ⑩ *Free Breakfast.*

Kuopio

185 km (115 miles) northwest of Savonlinna.

See firsthand Finland's cultural connections with Russia in Kuopio, with its Russian Orthodox Church Museum. The area is characterized by forest-covered hills and countless lakes and is a great place for boating, hiking, and fishing. The Tahko tourism center is an hour's drive away and is a popular winter sports destination and general outdoor activity hub.

GETTING HERE AND AROUND
Kuopio's airport, 20 km (12 miles) from the town center, is a one-hour flight from Helsinki on Finnair, which operates flights up to seven times daily. It's a 10–15-minute drive into town, and Bus 40 operates between the airport and the city center. Expect to pay €20–25 for the taxi into town. A drive to Kuopio from Helsinki takes four hours along Route E63, passing through Mikkeli; bus services from Helsinki run up to seven times a day and take at least six hours to complete the trip. VR trains run from Helsinki seven times a day, with the fastest Pendolino train making the journey in five hours.

VISITOR INFORMATION
Kuopio Tourism. ⊠ *Tulliportinkatu 31, Kuopio* ☎ *0800/182–050* ⊕ *www.kuopi-otahko.fi.*

◉ Sights

Market Square
PLAZA | Called *maailman napa*—the belly button of the world—by locals, Kuopio's Market Square should be one of your first stops, as it is one of the most colorful outdoor markets in Finland. Try the famous *kalakukko* (fish and bacon baked in a rye crust). Kuopio's tourist office is nearby. ⊠ *Kauppakatu 45, Kuopio.*

Puijo Observation Tower
BUILDING | The slender Puijo Tower, 3 km (2 miles) northwest of Kuopio, is best visited at sunset, when the lakes shimmer with reflected light. It has two observation decks and is crowned by a café and revolving restaurant with marvelous views. ⊠ *Puijontie 135, Kuopio* ☎ *044/975–0225* ⊕ *www.visitpuijo.com* 🎟 *€6.*

Rauhalahti Spa
SPA—SIGHT | Traditional lumberjack evenings take place at the Jätkänkämppä log lodge in the expansive lakeside grounds of the Rauhalahti Spa Hotel on Tuesday throughout the year, with live accordion music, dancing, and a delicious buffet as well as log-rolling demonstrations on the lake. Nearby is the world's biggest smoke sauna, with capacity for 70 bathers at one time. ⊠ *Katiskaniementie 8, Kuopio* ☎ *030/608–3100* ⊕ *www. rauhalahti.fi* 🎟 *€13.*

RIISA – Orthodox Church Museum of Finland
MUSEUM | The Orthodox Church Museum possesses one of the most interesting and unusual collections of its kind. When parts of Karelia (the eastern province of Finland) were ceded to the Soviet Union after World War II, religious art was taken out of the monasteries and brought to Kuopio. The collection is eclectic and includes one of the most beautiful icon collections in the world, as well as embroidered church textiles. ⊠ *Karjalankatu 1, Kuopio* ☎ *020/610–0266* ⊕ *riisa.fi* 🎟 *€10* ⊙ *Closed Sun. and Mon.*

Valamo Monastery

RELIGIOUS SITE | If you were fascinated by the treasures in the Orthodox Church Museum, you'll want to visit the Orthodox Valamo Monastery in Heinävesi, between Varkaus and Joensuu. As a major center for Russian Orthodox religious and cultural life in Finland, the monastery hosts daily services. Precious 18th-century icons and sacred objects are housed in the main church and in the icon conservation center. The Orthodox library is the most extensive in Finland and is open to visitors. A café-restaurant is on the grounds, and very modest hotel and hostel accommodations are available at the monastery. ✉ *Valamontie 42, Kuopio* ☎ *017/570–111* 🌐 *www.valamo.fi* 🎟 *Free.*

🍴 Restaurants

Isä Camillo

$$ | **SCANDINAVIAN** | This popular restaurant is in a former Bank of Finland building and serves Finnish and international cuisine—steaks and pastas are particularly popular—at reasonable prices. Ask to eat in the bank vault. **Known for:** unique setting; outdoor seating; great cocktails. [$] *Average main: €25* ✉ *Kauppakatu 25–27, Kuopio* ☎ *017/581–0450* 🌐 *isacamillo.ravintolamestarit.net.*

Muikkuravintola Sampo

$ | **SCANDINAVIAN** | The first word of the name means "vendace restaurant," and the eponymous little lake fish is the dominant item on the menu. In the town center, Sampo was founded in 1931, and its Scandinavian furniture dates from the 1950s. **Known for:** muikku whitefish; history as a local institution; traditional shorefish soup. [$] *Average main: €17* ✉ *Kauppakatu 13, Kuopio* ☎ *020/762–4818* 🌐 *www.restel.fi/ravintolat/muikkuravintola-sampo.*

Musta Lammas

$$$ | **SCANDINAVIAN** | Situated near the passenger harbor, Musta Lammas is in the basement of a brewery founded in 1862. It has been attractively adapted from its beer-cellar days, retaining the original redbrick walls and beer barrels. **Known for:** innovative dishes; rooftop garden; Finnish fish. [$] *Average main: €25* ✉ *Satamakatu 4, Kuopio* ☎ *017/581–0458* 🌐 *mustalammas.ravintolamestarit.net.*

Sisu

For centuries the Lakeland region was a much-contested buffer zone between the warring empires of Sweden and Russia. After visiting the people of the Lakeland, you should have a basic understanding of the Finnish word *sisu*, a quality of perseverance or guts that defines the Finnish identity.

🛏 Hotels

Scandic Kuopio

$$$ | **HOTEL** | One of the most modern local hotels, rooms here are spacious by European standards, with large beds and generous towels. **Pros:** on the lakefront and close to town; recently renovated rooms; good restaurant. **Cons:** chain-hotel feel; inconsistent service; Wi-Fi can be temperamental. [$] *Rooms from: €150* ✉ *Satamakatu 1, Kuopio* ☎ *017/195–111* 🌐 *www.scandichotels.com* 🛏 *138 rooms* 🍴 *Free Breakfast.*

Spa Hotel Rauhalahti

$$ | **RESORT** | **FAMILY** | About 5 km (3 miles) from the town's center, Rauhalahti is near Lake Kallavesi and has no-frills rooms and apartments and a full-service spa. **Pros:** six restaurants on-site; variety of room types; full-service spa. **Cons:** removed from city center; fading decor; nightclub and family-friendly amenities can make it busy. [$] *Rooms from: €150* ✉ *Katiskaniementie 8, Kuopio* ☎ *030/60830* 🌐 *www.rauhalahti.fi* 🛏 *106 rooms* 🍴 *Free Breakfast.*

Tampere

174 km (108 miles) northwest of Helsinki.

Although cotton and textile manufacturers put Tampere on the map as a traditional center of industry, the city has more recently garnered attention for its high-tech companies and large universities. Tampere's more than 200,000 inhabitants also nurture an unusually sophisticated cultural environment, with international festivals of short film (March) and theater (August) among the most popular offerings. An isthmus little more than a half mile wide at its narrowest point separates Lakes Näsi and Pyhä, and at one spot the Tammerkoski Rapids provide an outlet for the waters of one to cascade through to the other. These rapids once provided the electrical power on which the town's livelihood depended. Their natural beauty has been preserved in spite of the factories on either bank.

Just outside the center is the scenic Pyynikki ridge, affording great views across both lakes and whose steep slopes are occupied by clusters of attractive, wooden former workers' houses, a reminder of the city's industrial culture. For local flavor, try the famous Tampere version of blood sausage—*mustamakkara*—at the Tapola kiosk in the Tammelantori square, and head up to the stone observation tower café on the Pyynikki ridge for one of its famous fresh doughnuts.

GETTING HERE AND AROUND

Finnair flies to Tampere from Helsinki, and the city is also on the networks of SAS, Ryanair, and Air Baltic. Tampere's airport is 17 km (11 miles) from the city center. Public Bus 1A will take you from the city center for €6. The 30-minute taxi ride from the airport to the city center will cost around €35. Finnish State Railways offers excellent and frequent train connections from Helsinki, ranging from 1½ to two hours, depending on the train.

Driving from Helsinki, take Highway 3. The drive will take around an hour and 45 minutes. The Tampere tourist office offers helpful services such as walking and bus tours and free bicycle rentals.

VISITOR INFORMATION

CONTACT Visit Tampere. ✉ *Rautatienkatu 25, Tampere* ☎ *03/5656–6800* ⊕ *www. visittampere.fi.*

◉ Sights

Amuri Museum of Workers' Housing

MUSEUM VILLAGE | One of the city's best museums, the Amuri Museum of Workers' Housing consists of more than 30 apartments in a collection of wooden houses, plus a sauna, a bakery, a haberdashery, and more from the 1880s to the 1970s. Its cozy Café Amurin Helmi has garden seating in summer and serves fresh bread baked on the premises with breakfast and a soup lunch. ✉ *Satakunnankatu 49, Tampere* ☎ *040/804–8765* ⊕ *www.museokortteli.fi* ⌐ *€8* ⊗ *Closed mid-Sept.–mid-May and Mon.*

Cathedral

BUILDING | Most buildings in Tampere, including this cathedral, are comparatively modern. It was built in 1906, designed by National Romantic architect Lars Sonck in that style, and houses some stunning masterpieces of Finnish art, including Hugo Simberg's *Wounded Angel* and *Garden of Death* and Magnus Enckell's *The Resurrection.* ✉ *Juhannuskylänkatu 3, Tampere* ☎ *040/804–8765* ⊕ *tampereenseurakunnat.fi* ⌐ *Free.*

Moomin Museum

MUSEUM | FAMILY | Finland's best-loved fictional characters, the Moomins, created by Tove Jansson, are celebrated at the world's only Moomin Museum. It's in the Tampere Hall, the city's main concert and conference hall, and is a dream come true for Moomin fans, where you can relive some of the Moomintroll stories and see a collection of Moomin art. There is a Moomin Museum Reading Room and a gift shop selling all things Moomin. Free guided tours are at 1 pm, Saturday and Sunday. ✉ *Yliopistonkatu 55, Tampere* ☎ *03/243–4111* 🌐 *www.muumimuseo.fi* 🎟 *€12* ⏲ *Closed Mon.*

★ Poet's Way

SCENIC DRIVE | One of the most popular excursions from Tampere is the Poet's Way steamboat tour along Lake Näsi and through the Murole Canal. The *Tarjanne,* built in 1908, passes through the agricultural parish of Ruovesi, where J. L. Runeberg, Finland's national poet, once lived. Shortly before the boat docks at Virrat, you'll pass through the straits of Visuvesi, where many artists and writers spend their summers. The Hopealinjat line also offers cruises as far south as Hämeenlinna, a nearly nine-hour voyage through wonderful Lakeland scenery, as well as a variety of other cruises and routes. ✉ *Ticket office at Laukontori harbor, Laukontori 10 LH 2, Tampere* ☎ *010/422–5600* 🌐 *www.hopealinjat.fi* 🎟 *One way €30, lunch €20.*

🍴 Restaurants

Periscope

$$$ | **MODERN EUROPEAN** | With great views over Lake Pyhä at the city stadium, this trendy new endeavor combines a restaurant, lounge bar, and rooftop terrace, serving superb local dishes and international cuisine. Try *tom yam* salmon from the starter list, followed by Asian ribs, a Korean burger, or "the most wanted Finnish Caesar salad," with goat cheese and crispy rye. **Known for:** famous Finnish salad; rooftop terrace; imaginative menus for the table. [$] *Average main: €39* ✉ *Vuolteenkatu 1, Tampere* ☎ *050 /599–9188* 🌐 *www.ravintolaperiscope.fi* ⏲ *Closed 2–3 on weekdays.*

Tiiliholvi

$$$ | **SCANDINAVIAN** | A romantic cellar in an art nouveau building with a colorful 50-year history, Tiiliholvi serves Finnish haute cuisine on a fixed menu and the finest wine selection in Tampere. Fresh, seasonal ingredients like mushrooms, reindeer, pike perch, and salmon are often paired with unexpected wine or liquor sauces or fresh herb vinaigrettes. **Known for:** pike perch from Lake Näsi; historic setting; great wine selection. [$] *Average main: €40* ✉ *Kauppakatu 10, Tampere* ☎ *0207/669–061* 🌐 *tiiliholvi.fi/en* ⏲ *Closed Sun. No lunch in July.*

Tillikka

$$ | **SCANDINAVIAN** | Long known as a hangout for leftist intellectuals, Tillikka now prepares hearty meals overlooking the rapids for patrons of every political persuasion. House specialties include vendace, fried pike perch, steaks, warm sandwiches, and *pyttipannu,* a no-nonsense fry-up of pork sausage, potato, and onion topped with gherkins and fried egg—much more appetizing than it might sound. **Known for:** pyttipannu; local brews; waterside location. [$] *Average main: €20* ✉ *Teatteritalo, Hämeenkatu 14, Tampere* ☎ *050/309–0161* 🌐 *www.tampereelle.fi.*

🛏 Hotels

Scandic Tampere City

$$ | **HOTEL** | This Scandic property in the heart of the city center, directly opposite the train station, offers newly renovated rooms that exude a restrained and tidy Nordic elegance. **Pros:** convenient location; contemporary design; reliable brand. **Cons:** central location is also a busy location; disappointing breakfast selection; chain feel. [$] *Rooms from: €155* ✉ *Hämeenkatu 1, Tampere* ☎ *03/244–6111* 🌐 *www.scandichotels.com* 🛏 *263 rooms* 🍴 *Free Breakfast.*

Solo Sokos Hotel Torni Tampere

$$$ | **HOTEL** | Torni means "tower," which gives you an idea of what to expect with this 88-meter-tall building on the edge of converted rail yards, with decor and rooms referencing various elements of Tampere culture and history. **Pros:**

fabulous views; fresh and modern design; convenient to railway station. **Cons:** lobby gets busy with visitors heading to the Sky Bar; decor can be overworked in places; dark tiled bathrooms. $ *Rooms from: €170* ✉ *Ratapihankatu 43, Tampere* ☎ *020/123–4634* ⊕ *www.sokoshotels.fi* ⤵ *305 rooms* ❐ *Free Breakfast.*

🛍 Shopping

The major malls in central Tampere are Koskikeskus, near the rapids running through the center of the city, and Ratina near the city stadium, both with many of the stores familiar to shoppers in other malls across the country. Also interesting are the smaller design and fashion shops scattered individually around the downtown district and in the redbrick, formerly industrial areas.

Finlayson

HOUSEHOLD ITEMS/FURNITURE | Practical souvenirs to brighten up your home—that's what's on offer at Tampere's Finlayson stores. Find room in your suitcase for cushion and pillow covers, duvet covers, and sheets from the longest-established quality brand in Finland's second city. ✉ *Kuninkaankatu 3, Tampere* ☎ *0400/193–1133* ⊕ *www.finlayson.fi.*

Verkaranta Arts and Crafts Center

CRAFTS | You'll find a colorful selection of locally made gifts and handicrafts by a collective of artisans and designers at this former textile-dyeing workshop close to the rapids and near the Koskikeskus mall. ✉ *Vuolteentori 2, Tampere* ☎ *03/225–1409* ⊕ *www.taitopirkanmaa.fi.*

🍸 Nightlife

Tampere has a lively pub and beer-bar scene. Look for quiz nights in local pubs, a popular Tampere pastime, particularly in the winter.

Moro Sky Bar

BARS/PUBS | Situated on the 25th floor of the Sokos Hotel Torni, and with an outdoor terrace in summer and terrific city views, Moro Sky Bar is the coolest spot in town. ✉ *Solo Sokos Hotel Torni Tampere, Ratapihankatu 43, 25th fl., Tampere* ☎ *020/123–4634.*

Plevna

BREWPUBS/BEER GARDENS | Try the in-house brews at this highly regarded and lively microbrewery bar set in one of the redbrick, former Finlayson mill buildings near the rapids. A lively German-style brass band plays during Oktoberfest and at Christmas. ✉ *Itäinenkatu 8, Tampere* ☎ *03/260–1200.*

★ Salhojankadun Pub

BARS/PUBS | This authentic wood-panel bar founded in 1969 is one of the oldest English-style pubs not just in Tampere but anywhere in Finland, and an institution as such. ✉ *Salhojankatu 29, Tampere* ☎ *03/255–3376.*

Turku

166 km (103 miles) west of Helsinki.

Founded at the beginning of the 13th century, Turku is the nation's oldest and fourth-largest city and was the original capital of Finland. Turku has a long history as a commercial, cultural, and intellectual center. Once the site of the first Finnish university, it has two major universities, the Finnish University of Turku and the Swedish-speaking Åbo Akademi. Turku has a population of about 200,000 and a busy, year-round harbor. In summer the banks of the river come alive with boat and ship cafés. A lively artistic community thrives in Turku, and like most Finnish towns, it comes into its own in the summer.

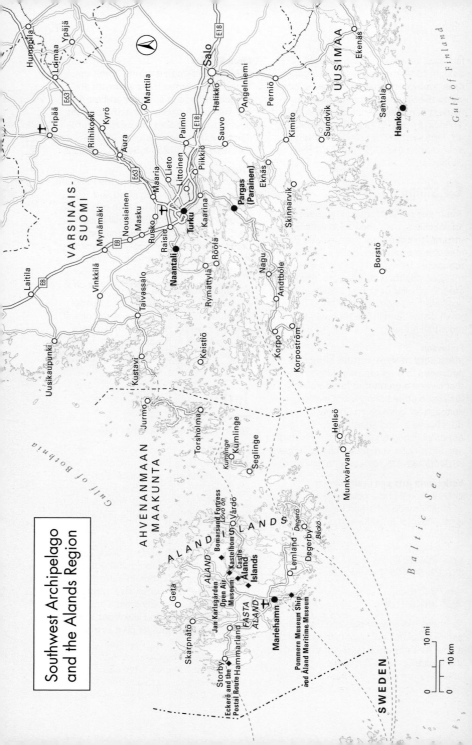

GETTING HERE AND AROUND

Turku's airport is a 15-minute taxi ride from the town's center, which will cost €25–€30. Alternatively, you can take Bus 1, which leaves from in front of the Hamburger Bors Hotel every 20 minutes and goes straight to the airport for €3. Finnair provides service to and from Helsinki. The Helsinki–Turku drive is 166 km (103 miles) on E18. There are regular train services between Helsinki and Turku and between Tampere and Turku. Turku has three stations: one in the suburb of Kupittaa; in the main Turku station; and at Turku's harbor (*satama*), served by connections with Stockholm ferry departures.

VISITOR INFORMATION

Visit Turku. ✉ *Aurakatu 4, Turku* ☎ *02/262–7444* ⊕ *www.visitturku.fi.*

👁 Sights

Aboa Vetus/Ars Nova

MUSEUM | This museum of history and contemporary art in Turku displays a unique combination of the two elements. Begun as a straightforward extension of the Villa von Rettig collection, the museum's concept changed when workers discovered archaeological remains, which were excavated and incorporated into the museum. Modern art in the old villa, part of the Matti Koivuranta Foundation Collection, includes works by Auguste Herbin (1882–1960) and Max Ernst (1891–1976), as well as works by Picasso, Warhol, and Hockney, although not all works are always on display. The preserved excavations, revealing the sunken former street level of the city, in the Aboa Vetus section date to as early as the 13th century. ✉ *Itäinen Rantakatu 4–6, Turku* ☎ *0207/181–640* ⊕ *www. aboavetusarsnova.fi* 🎫 *€10.*

Forum Marinum

MUSEUM | Close to the castle, toward the seaward end of the Aura River, and signaled by the magnificent *Suomen*

Joutsen (Swan of Finland) three-mast, full-rigger sailing ship berthed nearby, Forum Marinum contains a nautical museum and the museum of the Finnish navy and stages exhibitions and conferences connected to seafaring. In summer, you can also visit the *Suomen Joutsen,* the *Bore* ferry (also used as a hostel), and two naval vessels, namely a corvette and a minelayer. ✉ *Linnankatu 72, Turku* ☎ *02/267–951* ⊕ *forum-marinum.fi/en* 🎫 *€10, extra fees for ship visits.*

⭐ Luostarinmäki Handicrafts Museum

MUSEUM | Outdoor museums like Luostarinmäki are a Nordic tradition. This authentic collection of wooden structures escaped the city's major 1827 fire and now contains shops and workshops where traditional crafts are demonstrated and sold. Ask staff about the history of a particular workshop or call ahead for a schedule of guided tours, offered several times daily in summer. ✉ *Vartiovuorenkatu 2, Turku* ☎ *02/262–0350* ⊕ *www. turku.fi/en/handicraftsmuseum* 🎫 *€5, with guide €7* 🕐 *Closed Mon., closed Feb.–Mar.*

⭐ Turku Art Museum

MUSEUM | Finland's most famous paintings, including works by Akseli Gallen-Kallela, and a broad selection of turn-of-the-20th-century Finnish art and contemporary works are housed in this impressive granite building. Situated along Puolala Park, the building was completed in 1904 and in itself is worth the visit. Call ahead for information on guided tours. ✉ *Aurakatu 26, Turku* ☎ *02/262–7100* ⊕ *www.turuntaidemuseo.fi* 🎫 *€10* 🕐 *Closed Mon.*

⭐ Turku Castle

CASTLE/PALACE | Where the Aura flows into the sea stands Turku Castle, one of the city's most important historical monuments. The oldest part of the fortress was built at the end of the 13th century, and the newer part dates from the 16th century. The castle was damaged by bombing in 1941, and its restoration was completed in 1961. The vaulted chambers themselves give you a sense of the domestic lives of the Swedish royals. Linger for a while in the decent gift shop and pleasant café on the castle grounds. ✉ *Linnankatu 80, Turku* ☎ *02/262–0300* 🌐 *www.turku.fi/museo* 🎟 *€12* ⏲ *Closed Mon. in winter.*

🍴 Restaurants

★ Mami

$$$ | **SCANDINAVIAN** | The name means "mom," and the regulars at this small-yet-airy riverside bistro feel right at home. The bright green-and-white dining room is outfitted with chairs from the 1960s and floor-to-ceiling windows overlooking the river. **Known for:** fresh fish dishes; central location; river views. [$] *Average main: € 25* ✉ *Linnankatu 3, Turku* ☎ *02/231–1111* 🌐 *www.mami.fi* ⏲ *Closed Sun. and Mon. No lunch Sat.*

Pinella

$$$ | **SCANDINAVIAN** | A riverfront restaurant with a long terrace under classical pillars close to the cathedral, Pinella is popular for lunch and dinner and with both locals and visitors. Scandinavian elements dominate the menu, with the a la carte menu including the classic toast Skagen—prawns on a grilled brioche and laced with dill—and spicy ribs. **Known for:** classic toast Skagen; riverside terrace; close to sights. [$] *Average main: €25* ✉ *Vanha Suurtori 2, Turku* ☎ *02/445–6500* 🌐 *www.pinella.fi* ⏲ *Closed Sun. and Mon.*

★ Smör

$$$ | **SCANDINAVIAN** | An elegant riverside restaurant, Smör (Swedish for "butter") prides itself on being an "ambassador of local food and a master of Nordic cuisine," and is beloved for its discerning wine cellar filled with small vineyard labels. Finger-food snacks are available as well as fully fledged, all-Nordic-ingredient set menus. **Known for:** new menu every eight weeks; all-Nordic ingredients; carefully curated wine cellar. [$] *Average main: €29* ✉ *Läntinen Rantakatu 3, Turku* ☎ *02/536–9444* 🌐 *smor.fi* ⏲ *Closed July and Sun. No lunch.*

★ Suomalainen Pohja

$$$ | **SCANDINAVIAN** | This classic Finnish restaurant is decorated in dark wood and has large windows offering a splendid view of an adjacent park. The a la carte menu makes up for its brevity with quality. **Known for:** park views; seafood; good wine list. [$] *Average main: €27* ✉ *Aurakatu 24A, Turku* ☎ *02/251–2000* 🌐 *ravintolasuomalainenpohja.fi* ⏲ *Closed weekends.*

🛏 Hotels

Original Sokos Hotel Wiklund

$$$ | **HOTEL** | The Wiklund is at the heart of Turku's city life, located on one corner of the Market Square on the site of the historic Wiklund hardware store and within a two- to three-minute walk of the scenic riverfront. **Pros:** heart-of-it-all location; good restaurant and rooftop bar; modern. **Cons:** chain feel; central location also means noisy surrounding area; shower and toilet concealed behind transparent glass wall by curtain. [$] *Rooms from: €150* ✉ *Eerikinkatu 11, Turku* ☎ *010/786–5000* 🌐 *www.sokoshotels.fi* 🛏 *112 rooms* 🍽 *Free Breakfast.*

Park Hotel

$$$ | **HOTEL** | Built in 1902 in the art nouveau style, the Park Hotel offers individual rooms with high ceilings and antique furniture and all the amenities of a modern hotel. **Pros:** unique and quirky atmosphere; in-house parrot; central location. **Cons:** room sizes vary considerably; bathrooms could use an update; style is a little jaded. [$] *Rooms from: € 150* ✉ *Rauhankatu 1, Turku* ☎ *02/273–2555* 🌐 *www.parkhotelturku.fi* 🛏 *22 rooms* 🍽 *Free Breakfast.*

In its 700 years, Turku Castle has seen its share of battles and sieges. Today, it is a must-see museum.

ⓨ Nightlife

Turku is home to a large number of students, and this is reflected in a lively bar scene, including a number of boat bars on the river that come to life in the summer. The city also has several distinctive and quirky bars in converted historic buildings.

Koulu (*School*)

BREWPUBS/BEER GARDENS | This brewery-restaurant serves excellent beers and good pub food in what used to be a school for girls, built in the 1880s. School desks are given a second life, and there are school maps on the walls. ⊠ *Eerikinkatu 18, Turku* ☎ *02/274–5757.*

★ Old Bank

BARS/PUBS | Located near the Market Square, Old Bank is one of the most popular bars in Turku, housed in a former bank and offering 150 brands of beer from all over the world. ⊠ *Aurakatu 3, Turku* ☎ *02/274–5700.*

Puutorin Vessa (*Toilet*)

BARS/PUBS | Decidedly Turku's most unique pub setting, Puutorin Vessa is located in a functionalist building and once served as a public restroom. Rest assured it is a pleasant-smelling bar these days. ⊠ *Puu Square, Puutori, Turku* ☎ *02/233–8123.*

Uusi Apteekki (*New Pharmacy*)

BARS/PUBS | If you have a prescription for a wide selection of beers on tap, then this bar in an old apothecary is your spot. ⊠ *Kaskenkatu 1, Turku* ☎ *02/250–2595.*

🛍 Shopping

Market Square

MUSIC STORES | Market Square is a village of red tents selling flowers, fruits, and vegetables as well as baked goods, clothing, and trinkets. It's also the site of a charming Christmas market. *The market is undergoing extensive renovations to add an underground parking lot, which is due for completion in late 2021.* ⊠ *Keskusta, Turku.*

Hanko

141 km (88 miles) southeast of Turku.

GETTING HERE AND AROUND

Hanko can be reached by car along Route 25, by train from Helsinki or Turku with a connection at Karjaa, and by bus from either city.

VISITOR INFORMATION

Visit Hanko. ✉ *Raatihuoneentori 5, Hanko* ☎ *019/220–3411* ⊕ *tourism.hanko.fi/en.*

◉ Sights

★ Hanko

TOWN | In the coastal town of Hanko (Hangö), you'll find long stretches of beach—about 30 km (19 miles) of it—some sandy and some with sea-smoothed boulders. Sailing abounds here, thanks to Finland's largest guest harbor. A sampling of the grandest and most fanciful private homes in Finland dot the coast, their porches edged with gingerbread iron detail and woodwork and crazy towers sprouting from their roofs. Favorite pastimes here are beach-side strolls; bike rides along well-kept paths; and, best of all, long walks along the main avenue past the great wooden houses with their wraparound porches. Hanko is Finland's southernmost town and its ultimate destination for beach-combers. Clean sands and shallow waters make it a popular tourist hotspot, especially during the Hanko Regatta yacht race held every July.

This customs port has a rich history. Fortified in the 18th century, Hanko defenses were destroyed by the Russians in 1854 during the Crimean War. Later it became a popular spa town for Russians, then the port from which more than 300,000 Finns emigrated to North America between 1880 and 1930. ✉ *Hanko.*

Water Tower

BUILDING | **FAMILY** | Through the telescope of the water tower, you can follow the

comings and goings of the town's marine traffic and get a grand view of some of the very small islands sprinkled around the peninsula's edges. ✉ *Vartiovuori, Hanko* ☎ *019/220–3411* 🎫 *€2.*

Woolly Traffic Jams

Naantali's extremely narrow cobblestone lanes gave rise to a very odd law. During periods when economic conditions were poor, Naantali's people earned their keep by knitting socks and exporting them by the tens of thousands. Men, women, and children all knitted so feverishly that the town council forbade groups of more than six from meeting in narrow lanes with their knitting—and causing road obstructions.

Naantali

20 km (12 miles) west of Turku.

Built around a convent of the Order of Saint Birgitta in the 15th century, the picturesque coastal town of Naantali is an aging medieval settlement, former pilgrimage destination, artists' colony, and modern resort all rolled into one. Many of its buildings date from the 17th century, following a massive rebuilding after the Great Fire of 1628. You'll also see a number of 18th- and 19th-century buildings, which form the basis of the Old Town—a settlement by the water's edge. These shingled wooden buildings were originally built as private residences, and many remain so, although a few now house small galleries. Naantali is home to Moominworld, a fantasy theme park on a lovely island devoted to Finland's most famous fictional characters, the Moomins.

GETTING HERE AND AROUND

From Turku, a number of buses run frequently from the Market Square. By car, take Route 185, 8, or E8 through the city of Raisio to either Route 40 or the Raisiontie to the Aurinkotie into Naantali. In summer, you can take a 3½- to four-hour steamship cruise through the labyrinthine archipelago between Turku and Naantali, which includes a smorgasbord lunch or dinner while drifting around the islands (€24–€29, not including meals); cruises run from mid-June to mid-August. Contact the Naantali tourist office or the steamship SS *Ukkopekka*.

CONTACTS Steamship SS Ukkopekka. ✉ *Linnankatu 38–40, Naantali* ☎ *02/515–3300* 🌐 *www.ukkopekka.fi.*

VISITOR INFORMATION

Visit Naantali. ✉ *Nunnakatu 2, Naantali* ☎ *02/435–9800* 🌐 *www.visitnaantali.com.*

Sights

Kultaranta Park

GARDEN | Surrounding the house of the same name which is the summer residence for Finland's presidents, this huge park has numerous gardens, greenhouses, and more than 3,500 rosebushes and is one of the area's top attractions. The rose gardens peak in summer. ✉ *Kordelininkatu 1, Naantali* ☎ *02/435–9800* 🎫 *Free.*

★ Moominworld

AMUSEMENT PARK/WATER PARK | **FAMILY** | The Moominworld theme park brings to life all the famous characters of the beloved children's stories written by Finnish author Tove Jansson. The stories emphasize family, respect for the environment, and new adventures. Obviously, it's a very popular family destination, but it's also a draw for tourists of all ages. Sadly, it's only open in summer. ✉ *Kaivokatu 5, Naantali* ☎ *02/511–1111* 🌐 *www.moominworld.fi* 🎫 *€29, 2-day ticket €37* 🕒 *Closed mid-Aug.–mid-June.*

Naantali Church

RELIGIOUS SITE | Founded in 1443 and completed in 1462, this church housed both monks and nuns and operated under the aegis of the Catholic Church until it was dissolved by the Reformation in the 16th century. Buildings fell into disrepair, then were restored from 1963 to 1965 and again in 2011–12. The church is all that remains of the convent. It's now a wonderful venue for concerts during the Naantali Music Festival. ✉ *Nunnakatu 1, Naantali* ☎ *040/130–8300* 🎫 *Free.*

Restaurants

★ Merisali

$$ | **SCANDINAVIAN** | Housed in a delightful harborside pavilion, this is the best-loved, most romantic eatery in town, where you can find live music in summer. **Known for:** seafood specialties; live music in summer; pretty location. [$] *Average main: €16* ✉ *Nunnakatu 14, Naantali* ☎ *02/435–2451* 🌐 *www.visitnaantali.com.*

Naantalin Kaivohuone

$$ | **FAST FOOD** | **FAMILY** | A summer restaurant in a historic wooden building on the waterfront, Kaivohuone boasts barbecue ribs, burgers, pizzas, and salads on its terrace menu. Live music by top Finnish bands in the main hall adds some extra bounce to summer evenings. **Known for:** pub grub; waterfront setting; live music. [$] *Average main: €16* ✉ *Nunnakatu 4, Naantali* ☎ *02/445–5999* 🌐 *www.naantalinkaivohuone.fi.*

Uusi Kilta

$$ | **EUROPEAN** | A superb waterfront location and a menu comprising fresh local products such as fish, game, mushrooms, and berries, in addition to a pleasant outdoor terrace in summer, are the main attractions of Uusi Kilta. **Known for:** seafood; waterfront location; terrace seating. [$] *Average main: €16* ✉ *Mannerheimintie 1, Naantali* ☎ *02/435–1066* 🌐 *www.uusikilta.fi.*

Often referred to as a "mini-Versailles," Kultaranta has been the summer residence of Finnish presidents since 1922.

🛏 Hotels

⭐ Naantali Spa Hotel and Spa Residence

$$$ | RESORT | This modern spa complex offers spiritual and physical replenishment in a tranquil seaside setting and is often voted Finland's best hotel in travel awards. **Pros:** 100 listed spa treatments; variety of restaurants and bars; seaside location. **Cons:** lacks the intimacy of smaller retreats; menu of treatments can be confusing; slightly at odds with small-town local atmosphere. $ *Rooms from: €210* ⊠ *Matkailijantie 2, Naantali* ☎ *02/445–5100* ⊕ *www.naantalispa. fi* ⇌ *129 rooms, 40 apartments* ⧖ *Free Breakfast.*

Pargas (Parainen)

40 km (25 miles) southeast of Turku.

The town of Pargas (Parainen; population 15,500), the only Finnish town to be surrounded by water on all sides, is the gateway to the islands spreading out to the southeast of Turku and the smaller archipelago villages of Nagu (Nauvo) and Korpo (Korpoo). The islands are linked by bridges and by a car and passenger ferry system that operates as an extension of the road network—even in the winter when ice can clog up the waterways. The roads and trails through the islands here are very popular with cyclists, too, and it's possible to complete an archipelago circuit across the islands back to Turku. Swedish is widely spoken as the first language in this region. The town itself has a small marina and a pleasant Old Town and is a stocking-up stop for Finns on their way to island holiday homes or boating trips.

GETTING HERE AND AROUND

Pargas can be reached by the regular 40-minute Bus 801. It's a 20- to 25-minute drive from the center of Turku.

Sights

Nagu Church

RELIGIOUS SITE | Perhaps the best example of the well-preserved churches in the islands and a landmark on the St. Olav pilgrimage route, the 13th-century church at Nagu (Nauvo), close to red boathouses and a bustling marina, is surrounded by a well-tended and restful cemetery. ⊠ *Kyrkvallen 1, Turku* ☎ *040/312–4430.*

★ **Old Town** (*Gamla Malmen*)

TOWN | The cluster of old wooden buildings is picturesque, if compact, and includes narrow alleyways, a district museum, and an industrial museum (an enormous limestone mine is just outside the town). Its crowning glory is the stone church, typical of the sturdy places of Lutheran worship in the region, the earliest parts of which date back to the 13th century. ⊠ *Kyrkoesplanaden 4* ☎ *040/312–4400.*

Mariehamn and the Åland Islands

155 km (93 miles) west of Turku.

The Åland Islands, one of Europe's best-kept secrets in terms of rugged maritime and pastoral beauty, are composed of more than 6,500 small rocky islands and skerries, inhabited in large part by families that fish or run small farms. Virtually all of the more than 25,000 locals speak Swedish and are very proud of their largely autonomous status, which includes having their own flag and stamps. Their connection with the sea is indelible and their seafaring traditions revered. Åland is demilitarized and has special privileges within the European Union (EU) that allow duty-free sales on ferries between Finland and Sweden. The gently undulating islands are perfect for cycling tours.

Pargas Pilgrims

Pargas is on the St. Olav pilgrimage route extending from the cathedral of Turku to that of Trondheim in Norway, passing through the southwest archipelago and the Åland Islands before crossing Sweden. You can experience the Finnish section of this scenic trekking trail (cycling sections are also an option) by following the pilgrimage signs through forest and along seashores and quaint fishing villages. You can get a special "pilgrimage passport" and have it stamped at significant locations along the way. ⊕ *www.stolavwaterway.com.*

Mariehamn (Maariahamina), on the main island, is the capital (population 11,600) and hub of Åland life. At its important port, some of the greatest grain ships sailing the seas were built by the Gustaf Erikson family.

GETTING HERE AND AROUND

Mariehamn's airport is 5 km (3 miles) from the town center and a €15–€20, 10-minute taxi ride. Finnair provides service to and from Helsinki.

Åland is most affordably reached by boat from Helsinki or Turku. Call the Tallink Silja or Viking Line in Turku, Mariehamn, Tampere, or Helsinki. You can also reach the islands from the mainland by Alandstrafiken ferry, which runs on four routes—northern, southern, a cross line, and the Föglö line—and can be booked online, advisable especially if traveling with a vehicle during peak season. Book online or at the harbor.

BOAT Alandstrafiken. ☎ *018/25600* ⊕ *www.alandstrafiken.ax.* **Tallink Silja.** ☎ *060/015-700* ⊕ *www.tallinksilja.com.*

Hammarland's Church of St. Catherine was constructed with local Åland red granite, rapakivi.

Viking Line. ☎ 09/123–574 for international customer service and sales ⊕ www.vikingline.fi.

VISITOR INFORMATION

Visit Åland. ✉ Storagatan 8, Mariehamn ☎ 018/24000 ⊕ www.visitaland.com.

◉ Sights

Bomarsund Fortress

BUILDING | About 8 km (5 miles) from the village of Kastelholm in Sund are the scattered ruins of a huge naval fortress, which was built by the Russians in the early 19th century. It was only half-finished when it was destroyed by Anglo-French forces during the Crimean War. The fortress is open for touring at all times and has explanatory signs. For more information, you'll want to pick up a pamphlet from the small visitor center if it's open. ☎ 018/25730 ⊕ bomarsund.ax/en ⊠ Free.

Eckerö and the Postal Route

BUILDING | Eckerö is a small community some 40 km (24 miles) northwest of Mariehamn and the site of one of its most interesting and unusual attractions: the Post and Customs House. The building, designed by Carl Ludvig Engel, who also planned Helsinki's Senate Square, was constructed in 1828, and houses a postal museum. Here you can see the postal route that took mail by small boats and overland from Stockholm, crossing Åland to Turku and onward to the Russian capital at the time, St. Petersburg. A similar system persisted until 1910, when Åland was still part of the Russian Empire. The route extends for 65 km (39 miles) through the islands and is marked with information signs at places of interest. There is also a separate mail route museum in the Berghamn area, close to the Eckerö Line ferry terminal. ⊠ Sandmovägen 111–113 ☎ 0457/530–1435 ⊠ Free ⊘ Closed Oct.–Apr.

Hammarland Church
BUILDING | Åland is known for its many beautiful stone churches adorned with votive ships. One of the best examples is at Hammarland, a village about 30 km (18 miles) northwest of Mariehamn, with 12th-century origins. ✉ *Prästgårdsgatan 41* ✥ *On the road from Mariehamn to Eckerö* ☎ *018/36029* 🎫 *Free.*

Jan Karlsgården Open Air Museum
LOCAL INTEREST | At this popular museum near Kastelholm, the buildings and outhouses from the 18th century show what farming life was like on the island 200 years ago. A traditional maypole, which is a typical feature of the Åland landscape, is erected here on Midsummer Eve. ✉ *Kungsgårdsallén 5, Kastelholm* ☎ *018/432–150* 🎫 *Free* 🕒 *Closed mid-Sept.–Apr.*

Kastelholm Castle
BUILDING | **FAMILY** | Kastelholm is a wonderfully preserved medieval castle, with 14th-century origins, built by the Swedes to strengthen their presence on Åland. The nearby 18th-century Vita Björn prison is also worth a visit, and there is a treasure hunt and period costumes for the children, making this a great family destination. By turns, the castle has been a seat of Swedish royal bailiffs and a hunting lodge as well as the victim of damaging fires and sieges. Visits out of season can be made by arrangement. ✉ *Kastelholm* ☎ *018/25000* 🌐 *kastelholm.ax/en* 🎫 *€7* 🕒 *Closed Oct.–Apr.*

Pommern Museum Ship and Åland Maritime Museum
LOCAL INTEREST | **FAMILY** | The *Pommern* is one of the last existing grain ships in the world and the only four-masted steel barque remaining anywhere. Once owned by the sailing fleet of the Mariehamn shipping magnate Gustaf Erikson, the ship carried wheat between Australia and England from 1923 to 1939. The ship has reopened after extensive restoration work at a new, more accessible dock just below the Åland Maritime Museum, where you'll find a fascinating collection of seafaring items and a great children's section. The *Pommern* includes interactive aspects that describe the hardships of life onboard the ship as well as an audio tale for children by Karin Erlandsson called *Ruby's Voyage.* ✉ *Hamngatan 2, Mariehamn* ☎ *018/19930* 🌐 *www.sjofartsmuseum.ax/eng* 🎫 *€14* 🕒 *Pommern closed Oct.–Apr.*

🍴 Restaurants

The islands' dining options are concentrated in Mariehamn, but there are some fine options also in small seaside and rural villages. Seafood is obviously worth looking out for, but Åland is also known for its lamb, cheese, potatoes, local beer, and fruit wines.

ÅSS Paviljongen
$$ | **SCANDINAVIAN** | Very popular in summer due to its sheltered seaside outdoor terrace, Paviljongen (Pavilion) spills out from a fabulous wooden Mariehamn yacht club building and offers a reasonably priced menu of fish, beef, and lamb. There is a good pizza menu in the adjacent Pub Albin. **Known for:** waterside setting; traditional wooden style; good value. [$] *Average main: €29* ✉ *Sjöpromenaden, Mariehamn* ✥ *Follow the coastline from the Pommern Museum Ship and Åland Maritime Museum* ☎ *018/19141* 🌐 *paviljongen.ax* 🕒 *Closed Oct.–May.*

Indigo Bar and Restaurant
$$ | **SCANDINAVIAN** | Indigo is in a brick building in the heart of Mariehamn, with a main restaurant on the first floor, a bistro, and a bar. Finnish beef and arctic char feature on the a la carte menu, with "tapas of the sea" and Åland beef tartare as starters. **Known for:** seafood tapas; central location; family friendly. [$] *Average main: €35* ✉ *Nygatan 1, Mariehamn* ☎ *018 /16550* 🌐 *indigo.ax* 🕒 *Closed Sun.*

If Kastelholm Castle's walls could talk they'd tell stories that date back to 12 AD.

Park Restaurant and Bar

$$ | SCANDINAVIAN | The Park Alandia Hotel in Mariehamn's lovely leafy Esplanade has a popular restaurant, reopened after renovations in 2019, in addition to a great bistro menu in its bar. The restaurant's classic dish is Russian spiced beef a la Park, a delicious fillet with honey gherkins, red cabbage, beans, and pan-fried garlic potatoes. **Known for:** Russian spiced beef a la Park; local beers; open Sunday. $ *Average main: €32* ⊠ *Park Alandia Hotel, Norra Esplanadgatan 3, Mariehamn* ☎ *018/14130* ⊕ *www.parkalandia. com.*

🛏 Hotels

★ Björnhofvda Gård

$$ | HOTEL | Run by a charming couple and at the end of a remote rustic lane, just a 30-minute drive from Mariehamn and close to Eckerö, Björnhofvda Gård is one of the best country-lodge hotels in the archipelago. **Pros:** nature escape; old-style wood-burning sauna; homely service. **Cons:** distance from other amenities; limited dinner menu; higher-than-average rates. $ *Rooms from: €140* ⊠ *Fjärdvägen 14* ☎ *045/7344–7727* ⊕ *www.bjornhofvda.com* ❑ *Free Breakfast.*

Hotel Arkipelag

$$$ | HOTEL | In the heart of Mariehamn, the bayside Hotel Arkipelag is known for its fine marina and lively Arken nightclub. **Pros:** indoor and outdoor pool; great views from seaside rooms; several restaurants. **Cons:** party goes late; unattractive architecture; rooms vary. $ *Rooms from: €150* ⊠ *Strandgatan 35, Mariehamn* ☎ *018/24020* ⊕ *www. hotellarkipelag.com* 🛏 *86 rooms* ❑ *Free Breakfast.*

🏃 Activities

BIKING

Bikes of various kinds are available from RO-NO Rent in Mariehamn, situated opposite the main ferry terminal. Mopeds, boats, and canoes are also avilable for rent here, as well as cycling accessories such as helmets, carts, and baskets. A standard bike costs €12 per day (€60 per week), while an eight-gear bike costs €22 a day (€110 a week). The fine scenery and the terrain, alternately dead flat and gently rolling, make for ideal cycling. The roads are not busy once you leave the highway, and often there are cycle paths running parallel to the main roads.

Ålandsresor

BICYCLING | Ålandsresor arranges individual and group outdoor travel, including cycling and boating packages, throughout the islands, usually starting from Mariehamn. Contact through the company's website. ⊠ *Alandia Trade Center, Torgattan 2, Suite 249, Mariehamn* ⊕ *www. alandsresor.fi.*

Viking Line

BICYCLING | This bike-friendly outfit offers 200 cottage rentals, ranging from remote cabins to camping resorts, in Åland through its website. ⊠ *Storagatan 2, Mariehamn* ☎ *018/262–198 weekdays* ⊕ *sales.viking.com.*

BOATING

These are great sailing waters for experienced mariners. Boats can be rented through the Åland tourist office.

Ålandsresor

BOATING | The Åland Islands are a paradise for fishermen all year around. Ålandsresor offers fishing packages in the Ålands, which include equipment, a cottage, and a license for three or four days from €161.50. ⊠ *Alandia Trade Center, Torgattan 2, Suite 249, Mariehamn* ☎ *018/280–40* ⊕ *www.alandsresor.fi/en.*

Rovaniemi

832 km (516 miles) north of Helsinki.

The best place to start your tour of Lapland is Rovaniemi, where the Ounas and Kemi Rivers meet almost on the Arctic Circle. A gateway to Lapland in terms of transport and culture, Rovaniemi is also

the administrative hub and communications center of the province.

If you're expecting an Arctic shantytown, you're in for a surprise. After Rovaniemi was all but razed by the retreating German army in 1944, Alvar Aalto directed its rebuilding and devised an unusual street layout: from the air, the layout was designed to mimic the shape of reindeer antlers! During rebuilding, the population rose from 8,000 to its present-day size of around 62,000—so be prepared for a contemporary city, university town, and cultural center on the edge of the wilderness.

GETTING HERE AND AROUND

Rovaniemi is connected with Helsinki and the south by road, rail, and air links; there is even a car train from Helsinki. There are flights, stepped up in the busy Holiday season, from the United Kingdom, Ireland, and central Europe. There is a Finnair service every day but Sunday between Rovaniemi and Ivalo. Norwegian Air also operates frequent flights to Lapland from Helsinki. The Rovaniemi airport is 10 km (6 miles) from the town center. A €7 Airport Express shuttle goes to the major hotels, then heads to the airport one hour before scheduled flights. A taxi to or from the airport will cost around €20 and take 10–15 minutes. Trains leave twice daily from Helsinki, with one in the morning and one overnight. Sodankyla, 130 km (81 miles) north of the Rovaniemi airport, can be reached by a 1½-hour bus ride.

◉ Sights

Arktikum

MUSEUM | One of the best ways to tune in to the Finnish far north culture is to visit Arktikum, housed in a long, glass-roofed, north-facing building above the banks of the Ounas River. Arktikum combines a science center and museum, introducing and explaining the nature, culture, and history of the region, in permanent and

changing exhibitions. The Arktikum Beach Park has a pleasant garden, and in winter it's one of the best spots in town to view the northern lights. ⊠ *Pohjoisranta 4, Rovaniemi* ☎ *016/322–3260* ⊕ *www. arktikum.fi* ☞ *€13.*

Korundi

ARTS VENUE | Underlining Rovaniemi's proud status as the cultural capital of northern Finland, Korundi is a cultural center combining the Rovaniemi Art Museum and the home venue of the Lapland Chamber Orchestra, a world-class ensemble that performs regular concerts in the beautifully designed auditorium, renowned for its great acoustics. Korundi is an absorbing alternative to the Santa attractions and safaris on extra-brisk winter days. ⊠ *Lapinkävijäntie 4, Rovaniemi* ☎ *016/322–2822* ⊕ *www. korundi.fi* ☞ *€9* ⊙ *Closed Mon.*

Luosto

TOWN | Lapland is dominated by great moor-like expanses. The modern tourist center of Luosto, 105 km (65 miles) north of Rovaniemi, is in the heart of the moor district of southern Lapland—an area of superb hiking, mountain cycling, orienteering, and skiing. If you don't have a car, a daily bus makes the 60-km (37-mile) trip from Kemijärvi. Kemijärvi is 87 km (54 miles) north of Rovaniemi and can be reached via local train. ⊠ *Luosto* ⊕ *www.laplandluosto.fi.*

★ Santa Claus Village on the Arctic Circle

TOWN | Santa Claus is big business in northern Finland, and Rovaniemi likes to declare itself as the one true home of the one and only true Santa. The main attraction, located directly on the Arctic Circle some 8 km (5 miles) out of town, is Santa Claus Village, where you can visit Santa's Main Post Office and the old fellow himself in his grotto. There are restaurants and souvenir shops, and especially in winter, with the thick snow and frost on the trees, it's an enchanting place to visit, obviously especially for younger family members. You can even pick up

an Arctic Circle Crossing Certificate at the information office. Take local Bus 8 or Santa's Express Bus from Rovaniemi; see website for timetables. ⊠ *Tähtikuja 1, Rovaniemi* ☎ *016/356–2096* ⊕ *www. santaclausvillage.info.*

★ SantaPark

CITY PARK | **FAMILY** | An imaginative, subterranean, Christmas theme park built into the side of a hill just a few miles outside Rovaniemi, SantaPark sports a magic train, an ice gallery, a lively elf show, a Christmas post office, and naturally another chance to meet the man of the moment, Santa Claus. ⊠ *Tarvantie 1, Rovaniemi* ☎ *0600/301–203* ⊕ *www. santaparkarcticworld.com* ☞ *Hours and fees vary so check website before you visit* ⊙ *Closed Feb.–Oct.*

Science Center Pilke

MUSEUM | **FAMILY** | This science center, directly adjacent to Arktikum, offers an interactive introduction to everything connected with the forests of northern Finland, from their trees, plants, and animals to the machinery used to harvest their timber. ⊠ *Ounasjoentie 6, Rovaniemi* ☎ *0206/397820* ⊕ *www. tiedekeskus-pilke.fi* ☞ *€7* ⊙ *Closed Mon. Sept.–Nov., Jan.–May.*

🍴 Restaurants

Arctic Restaurant

$$$ | **SCANDINAVIAN** | The restaurant of one of Rovaniemi's best hotels, the Arctic Light Hotel, offers a great dinner menu selection in a calm and stylish setting. Main courses range from pasta with chanterelle king crab sauce, reindeer burgers, sautéed reindeer, smoked salmon, and a mushroom-based vegetarian option. **Known for:** seafood and wild game; sophisticated but cozy; no frills, hearty food. $ *Average main: €30* ⊠ *Valtakatu 18, Rovaniemi* ☎ *20/171–0100* ⊕ *www.arcticboulevard.fi* ⊙ *Closed Sun.*

Nili

$$$ | SCANDINAVIAN | Probably the coziest and best place in town to sample authentic, top quality Lapp dishes, Nili offers a Rovaniemi Menu for 62 euros, kicking off with bear meat stock, moving through caramelized pork side, Arctic pike perch, and finishing up with homemade oven cheese. The a la carte includes sautéed reindeer – *poronkäristys* – with mashed potatoes and lingonberry, a local classic. **Known for:** sautéed reindeer; authentic Lapp dishes; rustic wood-and-hide decor. $ *Average main: €30* ⊠ *Valtakatu 20, Rovaniemi* ☎ *400/369–669* ⊕ *www.nili.fi* ⊘ *Closed Sun., no lunch.*

★ Lumimaa Snowland

$$$$ | SCANDINAVIAN | It's hard to argue with a restaurant that declares itself "the coolest restaurant in the world" when it is set in an igloo. That is indeed cool so dress accordingly (the restaurant has added blankets to keep you warm at your ice table). **Known for:** unique igloo experience; ice sculptures and ice cups; magical setting. $ *Average main: €99* ⊠ *Kajaanintie 1, Rovaniemi* ☎ *40/762–5744* ⊕ *www.snowland.fi.*

Yuca

$$ | | If you're not already surprised to find Mexican food in Lapland, you'll be even more surprised to find authentic and good Mexican food here. A sister property to the cool and popular Café and Bar 21 next door, this Mexican theme eatery brought in a chef and bartender from Mexico to train the staff in creating authentic flavors and dishes. **Known for:** great taco combinations; good cocktails; welcome alternative to Lapp cuisine. $ *Average main: €17* ⊠ *Rovakatu 21, Rovaniemi* ☎ *400/998–754* ⊕ *www.yuka.fi* ⊘ *Closed Sun.*

Saariselkä

265 km (165 miles) north of Rovaniemi.

You could hike and ski for days in the area around Saariselkä. What used to be a village has developed into a resort very popular with Finns from the south on winter skiing holidays. It has several hotels and is a good central base from which to set off on a trip into the wilderness. Marked trails traverse forests and moors, where little has changed since the last Ice Age. The town of Tankavaara, 40 km (25 miles) south of Saariselkä, is the most accessible and the best developed of several gold-panning areas.

GETTING HERE AND AROUND

A one-hour Airport Express shuttle connects Saariselkä and Ivalo Airport.

CONTACTS Saariselkä Booking. ⊠ *Restaurant Pirkonpirtti, Honkapolku 2, Saariselkä* ☎ *016/554–0500* ⊕ *www.saariselka.com.*

🛏 Hotels

Holiday Club Saariselkä

$$ | RESORT | FAMILY | This luxurious spa center in rural Lapland offers rooms with casual Scandinavian style and more rustic cabins with fireplaces, as well as a glass-dome swimming area crammed with foliage, fountains, waterslides, wave machines, and a hot tub. **Pros:** spa facilities are included; solarium, saunas, and Turkish baths; variety of accommodations. **Cons:** on-site family theme park means it can be overrun with families; cheaper rooms are in need of renovation; experience can vary wildly depending on room. $ *Rooms from: €90* ⊠ *Saariseläntie 7, Saariselkä* ☎ *0300/870–966* ⊕ *www.holidayclubresorts.com* ⌁ *139 rooms, 89 holiday homes, 33 villa apartments* ❑ *Free Breakfast.*

Follow in the snowy footsteps of the Sami people as you travel in the age-old way: on a reindeer-pulled sleigh through Lappish forests.

★ Kakslauttanen Arctic Resort
$$$ | **RESORT** | What started as a roadside restaurant grew into a cozy scattering of wood cabins and eventually a sprawling resort with a variety of lodgings from traditional log cabins to glass igloos, snow igloos, and apartment-sized chalets with hemispherical glass extensions for aurora viewing. **Pros:** variety of unique lodging styles; beautiful location surrounded by forest; amenities include reindeer farm and smoke saunas. **Cons:** resort feel, especially in the west village; continuous expansion; pricey. [$] *Rooms from: €300* ✉ *Kiilopääntie 9, Saariselkä* ☎ *016/667–100* 🌐 *www.kakslauttanen.fi* 🍴 *Free Breakfast.*

★ Muotka Wilderness Hotel
$$ | **HOTEL** | One of the best examples of elevated luxury in one of Europe's most remote and wild landscapes, lodging options here include riverside log cabins and en suite glass-roofed pods, some with their own saunas, designed for watching the northern lights in luxurious comfort. **Pros:** very comfortable; stunning remote location; tour and activity options on-site. **Cons:** Aurora Cabins are expensive; restaurant on the pricey side; remote location not for everyone. [$] *Rooms from: €169* ✉ *Muotkantie 204, Saariselkä* ☎ *050/430–7600* 🌐 *nellim.fi* 🍴 *Free Breakfast.*

Santa's Hotel Tunturi
$$$ | **HOTEL** | This recent addition at the edge of the enormous Urho Kekkonen National Park, with its endless ski tracks and hiking trails, offers comfortable, well-heated rooms with balconies. **Pros:** variety of room sizes is good for groups and families; location in the heart of Saariselkä; traditional tepee barbecue. **Cons:** rooms vary wildly; style a little faded; bathrooms could use an update. [$] *Rooms from: €180* ✉ *Lutontie 3, Saariselkä* ☎ *016/68111* 🌐 *www.santashotels.fi/en* 🛏 *200 rooms, 5 studios with saunas, 48 apartments* 🍴 *Free Breakfast.*

What a Gem

If you're looking for a distraction from your hunt for Santa Claus or the aurora borealis, you might be interested to hear that you can prospect for gold in Lapland. In fact, commercial gold mining has enjoyed a quiet resurgence in Finland. Finns have been panning for this precious substance for a century and a half, and the practice is kept alive at a more fun level at the Tankavaara Village, where visitors put on their rubber boots, wade into the stream with their pans under expert guidance, and mutter quiet prayers that their dreams of sudden fortune are about to come true. The quantities on offer are unlikely for that to happen, but modest finds are possible, and in any case, where else can you have this kind of fun in Europe or even in the rest of the world?

Gold Prospector Museum The Gold Prospector Museum charts the history of gold mining in Finland since 1868, when one Johan Konrad Lihr discovered traces in the Ivalo River, sparking a mini gold rush to the far north. Sapphires and rubies have also been found in the region, and in February 2019 the first ever diamond was unearthed at Tankavaara. ✉ *Tankavaarantie 11C, Tankavaara* ☎ *016/626–171* ⊕ *www.kultamuseo.fi* 🎫 *€12* ⊙ *Closed weekends Oct.–May.*

Lampivaara Amethyst Mine On the edge of the magnificent Ukko-Luosto National Park, near Luosto, this mine presents another opportunity for a Lapland treasure hunt. Visitors are able to dig for their own gem souvenir at the covered mine, and there is no extra charge for the precious stone that you might discover. Hours change seasonally so check ahead. ✉ *Luostontie 4, Luosto* ☎ *016/624–334* ⊕ *www.amethystmine.fi* 🎫 *€19.*

🏃 Activities

Saariselkä is a great base for all the outdoor activities Lapland offers at different times of the year. These include skiing, snowshoeing, snowmobiling, taking husky and reindeer safaris, tubing, river fishing, rafting, fell walking, berry and mushroom picking, mountain biking, and northern lights viewing. All of these are options in or around the adjacent and enormous 2,550-square-km (995-square-mile) Urho Kekkonen National Park.

★ Lapland Safaris

SNOW SPORTS | Lapland Safaris is the most experienced and versatile tour operator in the region, with appropriate guides and experts at its disposal all over Lapland, including Saariselkä. ✉ *Saariseläntie 13, Saariselkä* ☎ *016/331–1280* ⊕ *www.laplandsafaris.com.*

Ivalo and Inari

287 and 326 km (178 and 202 miles) north of Rovaniemi.

The village of Ivalo is the main center for northern Lapland and the largest village in the Inari region, with 4,300 inhabitants. Inari is the municipality containing Ivalo, as well as the name of a small village about 40 km (24 miles) further north. Inari connects major snowmobile routes in winter and attracts anglers to its lakes, which have a reputation for bountiful fishing in summer. This is also the heart of the Sami (indigenous Lapp) community.

GETTING HERE AND AROUND
Finnair runs 1½-hour flights a day to Ivalo, some of them stopping at Rovaniemi on the way. In winter, groups sometimes charter flights from London and Paris to

Finland's Aurora Borealis

The aurora borealis is a natural phenomenon that occurs in a roughly oval belt around the Arctic zone as a reaction in the earth's magnetic fields to solar activity. Known more commonly as the northern lights, the aurora is matched in the south polar region by the aurora australis, and together they are the most mesmerizing, magical, and spectacular natural apparitions that the world has to offer.

Finnish Lapland is one of the most accessible places with the highest probability for aurora viewing in the world. Statistically, the aurora is visible here every second clear night between September and March. Nothing is ever guaranteed when it comes to natural phenomena, and good sightings depend also on the weather, but this is the region for potentially optimal viewing. Happily, it's not a big challenge to escape the light pollution from the relatively sparse settlements, as this can spoil chances in built-up areas. Although snow-laden trees and icebound lakes are favorite backdrops for aurora photos, the most vivid and exciting sightings often occur in autumn, casting eerie reflections on the still-unfrozen lakes and rivers.

Photography

Aurora photography is an art in itself, and Lapland is now well populated with photographers and other experts leading tours and workshops, advising on techniques and equipment, and providing a feel for the best locations and conditions. Many hotels ring a bell or similar alert when a "show" begins. An aurora hunt is one of the most exhilarating Lapland activities—and potentially the most memorable. Find more tips and info at ⊕ *www.visitfinland.com*. Stay informed and sign up for the Finnish Meteorological Institute's Auroras Now email alerts at ⊕ *www.aurorasnow.fmi.fi*.

Ivalo en route to visiting the Santa Claus Village. From the airport, your only option is a 10-minute, €15 taxi ride into town; there are usually taxis waiting. Buses leave six times daily from Rovaniemi to Ivalo (four hours). Tourist information can be found in Saariselkä.

Buses leave from the Ivalo town center to Inari and cost €7. A taxi from Ivalo will take about 40 minutes. Buses leave four times daily from Rovaniemi to Inari (five to six hours). Lake Lines Inari offers Sami tours that include a visit to Siida, the Sami Museum in Inari, and a cruise on Lake Inari.

◉ Sights

★ Reindeer Farm Petri Mattus

FARM/RANCH | Visits to this (actual working) reindeer farm, located near Lake Menes toward the Lemmenjoki National Park, are hosted by the owner, Petri Mattus. He'll show you the reindeer and let you hand-feed them, and if you're there at the right time, you can watch a spectacular roundup or witness calves being born and earmarked in spring. Coffee, tea, and light lunch can be included in the program price. ✉ *Kittiläntie 3070B, Inari* ☎ *0400/193–950* ✉ *petri.mattus@gmail.com* ⊕ *www.reindeerfarmpetrimattus.com* ✉ *Price depends on the group size.*

Siida

MUSEUM | The museum of the culture of the Sami people, Siida, is close to the westernmost corner of Lake Inari in the village of Inari and houses an absorbing exhibition describing every aspect of Sami history and life. It also gives fascinating explanations of the natural environment and harsh Arctic climate in which these people, predominantly reindeer herders, have traditionally forged a seminomadic livelihood. There's an open-air museum behind the main building, comprising traditional Lapp dwellings and farm buildings. There is a souvenir shop selling Sami handicrafts, and the café-restaurant Sarrit serves good lunches. *Expansion and renovation starting in April 2021 will be complete in May 2022.* ✉ *Inarintie 46, Inari* ☎ *0400/898–212* 🌐 *www.siida.fi* 🎟 *€10* 🕒 *Closed Mon. Oct.–May.*

Hotels

Hotel Ivalo

$$ | **HOTEL** | Modern and well equipped for couples and families, this hotel is 1 km (half a mile) from Ivalo, right on the Ivalo River. **Pros:** river views; spacious and modern rooms; restaurant serves Lappish dishes. **Cons:** slight motel feel; the town is quiet; service is inconsistent. [$] *Rooms from: €90* ✉ *Ivalontie 34, Ivalo* ☎ *016/688–111* 🌐 *www.hotelivalo.fi* 🛏 *94 rooms.*

Hotel Kultahovi

$$ | **HOTEL** | This cozy inn is on the wooded banks of the swiftly flowing Juutua River rapids. **Pros:** rooms in the new building have their own saunas; riverside setting; good aurora and salmon-spawning viewing. **Cons:** river rapids too strong for swimming; average breakfast spread; thin room walls. [$] *Rooms from: €110* ✉ *Saarikoskentie 2, Inari* ☎ *016/511–7100* 🌐 *www.hotelkultahovi.fi* 🛏 *45 rooms* 🍴 *Free Breakfast.*

Chapter 7

ICELAND

Updated by Erika Owen
and Birna Stefánsdóttir

7

◉ Sights   🍴 Restaurants   🛏 Hotels   🛍 Shopping   🍸 Nightlife

WELCOME TO ICELAND

TOP REASONS TO GO

★ **Art:** See live music in the capital and visit museums all over the country.

★ **Divine Cuisine:** The best lamb and langoustines you'll ever try.

★ **Protected Natural Wonders:** National parks here are UNESCO World Heritage sites.

★ **Year-Round Adventure:** Swim between tectonic plates; hike atop glaciers; horseback ride to waterfalls.

★ **Swimming:** From city pools to the world-famous Blue Lagoon and hidden hot springs.

★ **Night Sky:** Stargaze, seek out the northern lights, or bask in the midnight sun.

1 Reykjavík. The nation's capital, home to half the island's population.

2 Ísafjörður. A town in the northern region of the Westfjords with 18th- and 19th-century wooden homes.

3 Flateyri. There's an interesting and devastating history of avalanches in this area.

4 Þingeyri. A good spot to fill up on gas, groceries, and views.

5 Patreksfjörður. The largest town in the Southern Westfjords.

6 Hólmavík. Discover tales of the region's history of witchcraft.

7 Drangsnes. Catch boat ferries to Grimsey Island here.

8 Akranes. A great place for groceries, coffee, and baked goods.

9 Borganes. A cozy fishing town on the Borgarfjörður with ocean views in every direction.

10 Reykholt. Home to one of Iceland's oldest structures, waterfalls, and hot springs.

11 Húsafell. Amazing hiking trails.

12 Snæfellsjökull National Park. The park has every natural formation you could think of in one place.

13 Hellissandur. This area dates back to the 16th century—don't miss the maritime museum.

14 Ólafsvík. This scenic town that used to be a major port for trade with Denmark.

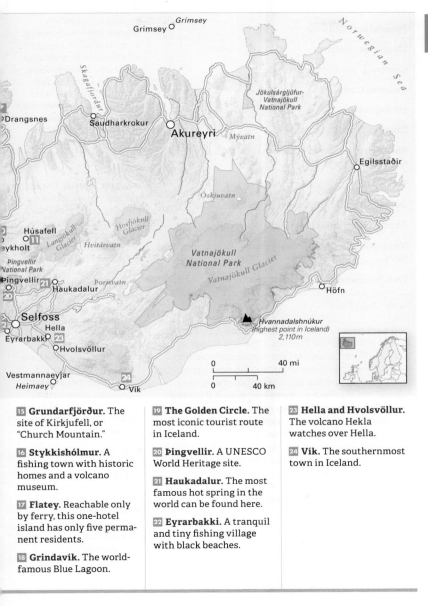

15 Grundarfjörður. The site of Kirkjufell, or "Church Mountain."

16 Stykkishólmur. A fishing town with historic homes and a volcano museum.

17 Flatey. Reachable only by ferry, this one-hotel island has only five permanent residents.

18 Grindavík. The world-famous Blue Lagoon.

19 The Golden Circle. The most iconic tourist route in Iceland.

20 Þingvellir. A UNESCO World Heritage site.

21 Haukadalur. The most famous hot spring in the world can be found here.

22 Eyrarbakki. A tranquil and tiny fishing village with black beaches.

23 Hella and Hvolsvöllur. The volcano Hekla watches over Hella.

24 Vík. The southernmost town in Iceland.

ICELAND SNAPSHOT

AT A GLANCE

Capital: Reykjavík

Population: 340,000

Language: Icelandic

Currency: Icelandic króna

Country Code: 354

Emergencies: 112

Driving: On the right side

Electricity: 220 volts/50 cycles; electrical plugs have two round prongs

Time: Four hours ahead of New York

Documents: Up to 90 days with valid passport.

Airport: Keflavík Airport (KEF)

Major Mobile Companies: Síminn, Vodafone, and Nova.

Web Resources: ⊕ *www.inspiredbyiceland.com*

WHEN TO GO

The best time to visit Iceland is entirely based on personal preference. For those seeking a peek at the northern lights, traveling between September and March is the best time to go, but the weather can be more intense and the lack of sunlight during the winter months can be oppressive, even if it is ideal for aurora-spotting. Summer is the best time to visit for (slightly) more stable weather, which is great for road-tripping; it's also the most popular time of year for tourists, and the lack of darkness can be similarly strange. There isn't really a bad time to visit Iceland, so just decide what appeals to you about the country and then pick a season to match. Note that in winter some activities may be unavailable, as will certain roads.

BIG EVENTS

■ **Þorrablót** Iceland's pagan past is joyfully celebrated each midwinter in the festival of Þorrablót, which includes recitations of poetry, speeches, and a feast now known as Þorramatur. This feast is the origin of the most notorious Icelandic dishes, and many of them are eaten exclusively during this time of year. ⊕ *www.inspiredbyiceland.com.*

■ **Secret Solstice** The summer solstice marks the longest day in the year, which in Iceland means the sun won't set at any point. This is the best time to witness the marvelous midnight sun and take advantage of all the fun summer activities, particularly the Secret Solstice music and culture festival. They've been steadily adding unique locations to the festival playlist, including the Lava Tunnel, a 5,200-year-old magma chamber, and Into the Glacier, home to the world's only rave inside of a glacial cave. ⊕ *www.secretsolstice.is.*

■ **Reykjavik Pride** Pride is one of the most attended annual events in the country, and a fun one at that. The parade takes place on a Saturday in August—the final day of an 11-day citywide celebration. ⊕ *www.hinsegindagar.is.*

Iceland is like no place on earth. Its landscapes are so otherworldly that they represent fictional worlds in many fantasy epics. Glacial-topped volcanoes, black sand beaches, towering sea stacks, and azure geothermal waters tell stories of Vikings and whisper local folklore. The capital city of Reykjavík breeds immense artistic and musical talent and pride. Visitors come to party in the capital, or to ride horseback through the interior Highlands to the edges of the sea, whether in ash-streaked snow or midnight sun.

MAJOR REGIONS

Reykjavík. A quaint and colorful harbor city, Reykjavík is also the warmest part of the country and home to half of Iceland's population. The main streets of Skólavörðustígur and Laugavegur are tourist-filled shopping strips. To the east of Lækjargata, **City Center East**, is the extremely recognizable Hallgrímskirkja church, a helpful point from which to orient yourself. The western part of the city center, **City Center West**, encapsulates the Old West Side, Reykjavík's historic quarter. Reykjavík **Old Harbor** is a hub of industrial activity, and home to Harpa, the behemoth concert hall. **Vesturbær** (the West Town) is home to museums and the revitalized harbor. In **Greater Reykjavík**, beyond the city center, you will find noteworthy museums like Perlan and Viðey, the site of Yoko Ono's Imagine Peace Tower. To the far west of Reykjavík is Seltjarnes peninsula, with large golf courses. At the tip of the peninsula is Grótta island.

The Westfjords. Despite its natural beauty, it happens to be one of the least-traveled regions of the country. But perhaps that should come as no surprise: The Westfjords occupy one-third of the Icelandic coastline, so getting from place to place takes a lot of driving, plus it's so far from other must-see Icelandic destinations that a trip here demands its own itinerary. Head here for mountains, waterfalls, pink-sand beaches, hot springs, and bird-watching cliffs.

The Westfjords are really accessible only during the summer months (late May—if you're lucky—through August). The area receives a massive amount of snowfall every year, and roads are often closed in winter for safety reasons. The only way to get around the region is by car, so it can be nearly impossible to drive as early as September and through April. When you're traveling to the Westfjords, it's important to keep a close eye on the weather to anticipate any road closures or obstacles. Even in summer, expect quick changes in weather—rain, sleet, hail, sunshine, sometimes even snow. Pack extra layers and always make sure you check in on the weather radar frequently, especially if you're venturing out on a multiday hike or camping trip—trails and fields can get windy, and you don't want to be unprepared.

West Iceland and Snæfellsnes Peninsula. If you're traveling to Iceland and have only a few days in the country, West Iceland is the perfect region to explore. Many of the photos and stories from people who have been to the island come from outside city limits, and it's one of a dwindling number of places in the world where you can put yourself in the middle of nature without any distractions.

Reykjanes Peninsula and the South Coast. Iceland's southern "left leg" (if looking at the map as a crooked duck) contains both the Golden Circle and the Blue Lagoon—arguably two of the country's most popular and breathtaking attractions—as well as the Reykjanes Peninsula. The Southwest is also home to some of Iceland's most iconic landscapes—from steep black cliffs, lonely lighthouses, and bubbling mud pots to spouting geysers, dormant volcanoes, and some of the largest white-water cascades in all of Europe. Streams of hot water shoot from geysers up to the skies, while the shopping mall–size Gullfoss waterfall plummets at incredible speed and volume down from the lava-bed highlands towards the unforgiving North Atlantic ocean. And here's the best

bit: all of these attractions and more can be accessed comfortably in day trips from Reykjavík. Hundreds of thousands of tourists visit the three famous sights of the Golden Circle each year, which has allowed the neighboring towns to flourish. Numerous restaurants and shops have popped up—each more inventive than the next—all around the area. It is highly recommended to stop in smaller, out-of-the-way places in search of hidden gems.

Planning

Getting Here and Around

Getting around Iceland is an adventure in and of itself, but with proper planning it can be easily mastered. Most of Iceland is accessible by well-maintained asphalt roads. When in Reykjavík, note that there is no metro system, nor are there rideshare services like Uber and Lyft. Buses are readily available, affordable, and clean—many locals choose to travel this way because of the convenience and the helpfulness of the bus system's website and app (⊕ straeto.is). Most of Reykjavík's restaurants and activities are in the downtown area, a very walkable district that takes no more than 30 minutes to cross on foot. Taxis are also available but quite pricey: a trip from the airport to Reykjavík, for example, can cost more than ISK 16,000, or about $130.

Outside of Reykjavík, other villages and attractions are extremely spread out, making cars the transportation method of choice when seeing more than just the capital. The Ring Road (Route 1) conveniently circles the country, and it's a very popular choice for people traveling by car, bike, or even foot. If self-guiding—especially when going off-road—it helps to have a GPS system to avoid becoming the latest beneficiary of Iceland's superb volunteer rescue squad. Domestic flights are also a very popular way for locals to move between cities, and an affordable one at that: Flying from Reykjavík to Akureyri should cost less than $100. (However, weather makes flying unpredictable.) Main and local bus lines can be used for cross-country travel, but planning is necessary. For more information on public transit, a wealth of information (in English) can be found at ⊕ *publictransport.is*, which was created by cyclists, so it's particularly useful in that area.

AIR

All international flights from each of the 28 airlines serving this destination land and depart from Keflavík Airport (KEF), which is about 45 minutes and 50 km (31 miles) away from the city of Reykjavík. When searching for tickets, this airport will be coded or written as Reykjavík, which can give the false impression of proximity. This is not to be confused with the Reykjavík Airport (RVK), the country's main *domestic* airport, which is actually just outside the city proper. Airport pickup services tend to know that when visitors say "Reykjavík Airport," they mean Keflavík, and will typically ask for clarification to be sure.

The Reykjavík FlyBus runs round-trip between Keflavík Airport (from directly outside the terminal building) and the BSÍ Bus Terminal in Reykjavík. From there, you can take one of the connections to larger hotels and guesthouses, or you can take a taxi to your final destination. FlyBuses are scheduled according to flight arrivals and departures. The ride takes around 45 minutes, and the fare is ISK 3,299 per person one-way or ISK 6,299 round-trip.

If you need a quicker transfer from the airport, a taxi may be the most efficient option (as well as the most expensive). The ride from Keflavík Airport to Reykjavík is a little faster than the FlyBus and costs around ISK 10,500 during daytime and around ISK 13,500 in the evenings for a smaller car. A large car, which seats

five to eight passengers, costs around ISK 13,500 during the day and around ISK 17,800 at night, depending on the taxi company or service. There are direct phones to taxi companies in the arrivals hall. From the Reykjavík Airport a taxi to your hotel costs around ISK 1,500. Municipal Bus 15 also stops in front of the main domestic terminal.

AIRPORTS Reiykjavík Keflavík Airport (KEF). ✉ *Keflavíkurflugvöllur, 235 Keflavík, Reykjavík* ☎ *354/424–4000 general info on Icelandic airports* ⊕ *www.isavia.is/en/keflavik-airport.* **Reykjavík Airport (RVK).** ✉ *Reykjavík Airport, 101 Reykjavík, Reykjavík* ☎ *354/424-4000* ⊕ *www.isavia.is/en/reykjavik-airport.* **Akureyri Airport (AEY).** ✉ *Urðargil 15, Akureyri* ☎ *354/424–4000* ⊕ *www.isavia.is/en/akureyri-airport.*

AIRPORT TRANSFERS Airport Taxi. ✉ *260 Reykjanesbæ* ☎ *354/420–1212* ⊕ *www.airporttaxi.is.* **Hreyfill.** ✉ *Fellsmúla 26 , 108 Reykjavík* ☎ *354/588–5522* ⊕ *www.hreyfill.is.* **Reykjavík FlyBus.** ✉ *BSÍ Bus Terminal , 101 Reykjavík* ☎ *354/580–5400* ⊕ *www.flybus.is.*

BUS

The municipal bus service, affectionately nicknamed "Strætó" (pronounced *stry*-toe), provides extensive, cheap, and reliable service throughout Reykjavík and its surrounding municipalities. Buses are yellow, with an "S" logo on a red circular background. They begin service around 6:30 am, and the last buses of the day tend to depart around 11 pm. Express buses run every 15 minutes during peak times and every half hour during evenings and weekends. Route booklets are available at the main terminals of Hlemmur, Mjódd, and Ártún, as well as at most tourist information centers. A new "Strætó bs" app is available for iOS, offering mobile planners, payments, and real-time travel information. The flat fare within the sprawling capital area is ISK 400, payable to the driver in exact change on boarding. You can also buy strips of tickets at a lower price from the driver or at main bus terminals. A single fare allows you to travel any distance in the metro area. Depending on your destination, you may have to change buses; if so, ask for *skiptimiða* (*skiff*-teh-mee-tha), a transfer ticket that you give the second bus driver.

If you plan an extended stay in the Reykjavík area, it may be worthwhile to spend ISK 10,900 on the Green Card, a monthly pass valid on all routes. For shorter stays, a practical investment is the Reykjavík City Card, available at most of the city's museums and tourist information centers, which permits unlimited bus usage and admission to any of the capital city's eight pools, the Fjölskyldugarðurinn Family Park, the ferry to Viðey Island, and city-run museums.

CONTACTS Strætó. ⊠ Þönglabakka 4, *Pósthólf 9140, 109 Reykjavík, Reykjavík* ☎ *354/540–2700* ⊕ *www.bus.is.*

TAXI
Most taxicabs are new, fully equipped passenger sedans. They have small "taxi" signs on top and can be hailed anywhere on the street; the "laus" sign indicates that the cab is available. There are taxi stands in a few locations around the city, but it is common to order a taxi by phone—normally you have to wait only a few minutes. Most taxis accept major credit and debit cards. Fares are regulated by meter; rides around Reykjavík run between ISK 1,500 and ISK 4,500. There is no tipping.

CONTACTS BSR Taxi. ⊠ Skógarhlíð 18, *Reykjavík* ☎ *354/561–0000* ⊕ *www.bsr. is.* **Hreyfill Taxi.** ⊠ *Fellsmúli 26, Reykjavík* ☎ *354/588–5522* ⊕ *www.hreyfill.is.*

Restaurants

The dining scene in Reykjavík has diversified a great deal in the past few years: traditional Icelandic restaurants now face competition from restaurants serving Asian, Italian, Mexican, Indian, and vegetarian fare. A recent trend has seen the emergence of several upscale establishments emphasizing locally grown ingredients and New Nordic cuisine.

Hotels

Lodging ranges from modern, first-class Scandinavian-style hotels to inexpensive guesthouses and B&Bs offering basic amenities at relatively low prices. Iceland's climate makes air-conditioning unnecessary. Most hotel rooms have televisions, though not always cable TV. Lower-price hotels sometimes have a television lounge in lieu of a TV in each room. Ask if your hotel offers complimentary admission to the closest swimming pool.

HOTEL AND RESTAURANT PRICES
Hotel prices in the reviews are the lowest cost of a standard double room in high season. Restaurant prices in the reviews are the average cost of a main course at dinner, or if dinner is not served, at lunch.

WHAT IT COSTS in ISK			
$	$$	$$$	$$$$
RESTAURANTS			
under ISK 2,500	ISK 2,500–4,000	ISK 4,100–5,500	over ISK 5,500
HOTELS			
under ISK 21,000	ISK 21,000–28,000	ISK 29,000–35,000	over ISK 35,000

Nightlife

Through most of the year, Reykjavík has an active cultural life, which is especially strong in music and the visual arts. The classical performing arts scene tends to quiet down somewhat in summer, though a growing number of rock and jazz concerts—as well as a new chamber music festival held in Harpa, called Reykjavík Midsummer Music—have been helping to fill in the gap. The Reykjavík Arts Festival is held annually in May; past festivals have drawn Luciano Pavarotti and David Bowie, among other stars. Check out the *Reykjavík Grapevine* (⊕ *grapevine.is*) for up-to-date listings; it's biweekly in summer, monthly in winter.

Nightlife in Reykjavík essentially means two types of establishments: nightclubs with dancing and live music, and pubs. Icelanders tend to dress up for going out, but visitors can get away with being a bit more casual. On weekends, unless you start before 11 pm, be prepared to wait in line, especially if the weather is good. After midnight during the first weekends of summer, excessive drinking can result in some raucous and aggressive behavior. Suffice it to say, Icelanders party en masse.

Shopping

The main shopping downtown is on and around Austurstræti, Aðalstræti, Hafnarstræti, Hverfisgata, Bankastræti, Laugavegur, and Skólavörðustígur.

Tours

Ferðafélag Íslands, or the Iceland Touring Association (ITA), owns and operates numerous mountain huts where hikers and other travelers can get a sleeping bag accommodation (prebooking necessary). The ITA also offers a variety of programs year-round: day tours (hiking, cross-country skiing, or bus tours), weekend tours (Friday evening through Sunday), and longer tours.

Arcanum offers snowmobiling tours, and Dog Sledding Iceland offers dog-sled tours; both companies can take you to see a glacier. Icelandic Mountain Guides is the go-to tour company for a wide range of quality adventures and activities, covering everything from superjeep tours, day trips to popular natural wonders, and glacial excursions to memorable multiday or monthlong expeditions. Arctic Rafting specializes in rafting tours, but also offers quad biking, climbing, trekking, biking, and a number of other activities.

Several bus companies, including Reykjavík Excursions and Gray Line, also run bus tours that include museums and art galleries, shopping centers, and the like, in around three hours. Reykjavík Excursions also operates a hop-on, hop-off bus service in the city during the summer.

Arcanum
ADVENTURE TOURS | One of Iceland's main tour operators, Arcanum specializes in glacier walks, ATV tours, snowmobiling, and jeep tours. Activities take place on or around Sólheimajökull, one of the magnificent glacial tongues of the Mýrdalsjökull ice cap. Most tours include an option for a pick-up in Reykjavík, if you're staying in the capital city. ⊠ *Sólheimaskála, Ytri Sólheimum 1, Vík* ☎ *354/487–1500* ⊕ *www.arcanum.is.*

Arctic Rafting
ADVENTURE TOURS | Arctic Rafting specializes in river rafting tours, but also offers quad biking, climbing, trekking, biking, and a number of other exciting activities that will get you out of the city. ⊠ *Laugavegur 11, Reykjavík* ☎ *354/564–7000* ⊕ *www.arcticrafting.com.*

DIVE.IS
SPECIAL-INTEREST | The folks at Dive.is specialize in snorkeling and diving tours of the stunning Silfra Fissure—an area where the American and Eurasian tectonic plates meet, at Þingvellir National Park—as well as a number of other locations in Iceland. ⊠ *Hólmaslóð 2, 101 Reykjavík* ☎ *354/578–6200* ⊕ *www.dive.is.*

Dog Sledding Iceland

ADVENTURE TOURS | One-hour mush tours, with real Greenland dogs, on top of Langjökull glacier are available from this family-run business between May and August, with some slightly cheaper, dry-land tours offered from either Skálafell or their Hólmasel base in Selfoss, at other times of the year. Glacier tours, with transfer from Reykjavík, cost ISK 44,500. They include a bit of sightseeing and can take up to nine hours. If you have your own 4X4 transport, you can drive to the glacier basecamp yourself (around two hours from Reykjavík) and take the tour for ISK 29,900 instead. ✉ *Hólmasel–Gaulverjabæjarhreppi, Selfoss* ☎ *354/863–6733* ⊕ *www.dogsledding.is.*

Ferðafélag Íslands (*Iceland Touring Association*)

WALKING TOURS | The Iceland Touring Association is the best place to sign up for hiking tours, especially for the famous Laugavegur hiking trail. ✉ *Mörkinni 6, Reykjavík* ☎ *354/568–2533* ⊕ *www.fi.is.*

Gray Line Iceland (*Iceland Excursions*)

ADVENTURE TOURS | From a *Game of Thrones*–themed bus tour to hunting down the northern lights on an ATV, Iceland Excursions offers experiences as simple as riding a Highland road from Reykjavík to Akureyri to the more complicated task of hiking Landmannalaugar. Gray Line also offers transfers between Reykjavík and Keflavík International Airport (from $25). Day tours—like a hop-on, hop-off city sightseeing experience—start at $33. ✉ *Hafnarstræti 20, Reykjavík* ☎ *354/540–1313* ⊕ *www.grayline.is.*

★ Iceland Adventure Tours

ADVENTURE TOURS | This company offers an impressive array of ways to see the natural environment that Iceland's so famous for. From snorkeling or diving into Silfra Fissure to hiking down into a volcanic crater, the friendly tour guides will be there to make sure you're comfortable every step of the way. Bonus: They take photos for you, so all you have to think about is enjoying yourself. ✉ *Bildshofði 14, Reykjavík* ☎ *354/519–3777* ⊕ *icelandadventuretours.is.*

Icelandic Mountain Guides

ADVENTURE TOURS | The go-to tour company for a wide range of quality adventures and activities covers everything from glacier walks and super-jeep day tours of popular natural wonders to memorable month-long expeditions. ✉ *Stórhöfði 33, Reykjavík* ☎ *354/587–9999* ⊕ *www.mountainguides.is.*

★ Íshestar (*Icelandic Riding Tours*)

HORSEBACK RIDING | One- to seven-hour rides and a variety of half- to multiday tours include guides and transportation from Reykjavík hotels (it's only a 15-minute drive out of town). The most unique way to spend time in the stunning Icelandic countryside is on horseback; you can experience Icelandic horses' special fifth gait, the *tölt*. ✉ *Sörlaskeiði 26, Hafnarfjörður* ☎ *354/555–7000* ⊕ *www.ishestar.is.*

Reykjavík Excursions

ADVENTURE TOURS | You can join one of many single- or multiday hiking journeys straight from the capital city. Reykjavík Excursions also offers shorter adventures like whale watching from Reykjavík, northern lights tours, and city sightseeing on a double-decker bus, as well as more involved experiences like hiking Þórsmörk. ✉ *BSÍ Bus Terminal, Vatnsmýrarvegi 10,, Reykjavík* ☎ *354/580–5400* ⊕ *www.re.is.*

Reykjavík Sailors

BOAT TOURS | Whale-watching, puffin-spotting, northern lights hunting, sea angling—Reykjavík Sailors does it all. You can also request a private tour for any of the company's offerings, if you're traveling with a group. ✉ *Hlésgata Vesturbugt F101, Reykjavík* ☎ *354/571–2222* ⊕ *www.reykjaviksailors.is.*

★ Special Tours

BOAT TOURS | While Special Tours offers all of the regular tours—whale-watching, puffin-watching, and sea angling—the one you should not miss, if you're visiting during the wintertime, is the three-hour northern lights cruise. There's no better way to see the aurora than afloat in the bay. ✉ Ægisgarður 13, Reykjavík ☏ 354/560–8800 ⊕ www.specialtours.is.

TukTuk Tours

GUIDED TOURS | Inspired by the auto rickshaws of South Asia, these battery-operated three-wheelers, with trademark yellow-and-black rain covers, can be spotted all over town, taking visitors on a variety of eco-friendly sightseeing tours. It's best to book in advance via the website, but there's always the possibility that you could hop on one at the TukTuk stand in front of Harpa Concert Hall. It's certainly a cheap and cheerful way to discover the city and stock up on a few pearls of local wisdom. Note that seats are low but nicely heated. ✉ Harpa Music Hall , Austurbakki 2, Reykjavík ☏ 354/788–5500 ⊕ www.tuktuktours.is.

Útivist Travel Association

WALKING TOURS | This expert guide service is famous for summer solstice hikes across the Fimmvörðuháls mountain trail, which passes between the ice caps of both Eyjafjallajökull and Mýrdalsjökull. ✉ Ferðafélagið Útivist, Laugavegur 178, Reykjavík ☏ 354/562–1000 ⊕ www.utivist.is.

Visitor Information

The Reykjavík Tourist Information Center, in the classic Geysishús at Aðalstræti 2, is open daily 8:30–7, June through September 15. For the rest of the year it's open weekdays 9–6, Saturday 10–4, and Sunday 10–2.

Reykjavík Tourist Information Center

The official tourist information center of Reykjavík is staffed by a team of multilingual personnel offering up-to-date information on all the city's services, lodgings, and tours, as well as the best spots for your preferred dining experience. You can also book tours, exchange currency, and purchase maps, stamps, and the Reykjavík City Card. ✉ Tjarnargata 11, Reykjavík ☏ 354/411–6040 ⊕ www.visitreykjavik.is.

Reykjavík

On a bay overlooked by proud Mt. Esja (pronounced eh-shyuh), with its everchanging hues, the city is a pleasant sight, its concrete houses painted in light colors and topped by vibrant red, blue, and green roofs. In contrast to the almost treeless countryside, Reykjavík has many tall native birches, rowans, and willows, as well as imported aspen, pines, and spruces.

City Center East

⊙ Sights

★ **Hallgrímskirkja** (Hallgrímur's Church)
RELIGIOUS SITE | FAMILY | Completed in 1986 after more than 40 years of construction, the church is named for the 17th-century hymn writer Hallgrímur Pétursson. It has a stylized concrete facade recalling both organ pipes and the distinctive columnar basalt formations you can see around Iceland. For ISK 900, you can climb to the top of the church for incredible views of greater Reykjavík. You may luck into hearing a performance or practice on the church's huge pipe organ. In front of Hallgrímskirkja is a statue of Leif Erikson, the Icelander who discovered America 500 years before Columbus. (Leif's father was Eric the Red, who discovered Greenland.) The statue, by American sculptor Alexander Calder, was presented to Iceland by the United States in 1930 to mark the millennium of the Alþing parliament. ✉ Hallgrímstorg 1, Miðbær ☏ 354/510–1000 ⊕ www.hallgrimskirkja.is ⛫ Tower ISK 900.

Northern lights over Hallgrímskirkja church and the Leif Eriksson Memorial in Reykjavík.

Höfði

HISTORIC SITE | The Höfði house stands out for both its architectural and historical importance. It was here, in 1986, that President Ronald Reagan and President Mikhail Gorbachev met and officially marked the end of the Cold War. The house is not open to visitors, but it's worth spending some time exploring the exterior. ✉ *Borgartún 105, Hlíðar* ☎ *354/552–5375* ⊕ *www.visitreykjavik.is.*

★ Iceland Phallological Museum

LOCAL INTEREST | This iconic museum could easily be described as the city's most … interesting attraction. The Phallological Museum is exactly what it sounds like—an ode to the male genitalia of mammals from around the world. But don't be alarmed: this is truly an educational experience. The museum houses 280 specimens from 93 different species. The gift shop is not to be missed. ✉ *Laugavegur 116, Miðbær* ☎ *354/561–6663* ⊕ *www.phallus.is* 🎫 *ISK 1700.*

★ Icelandic Punk Museum

MUSEUM | This tinier-than-tiny museum is crammed into what used to be a set of public bathrooms at the bottom of a stairwell right off the sidewalk. Somehow it all seems fitting for a museum focused on punk rock. Photos, posters, handbills, equipment, and instruments line the walls and displays at this subterranean memorial to one of the country's favorite music genres. The museum opened in November 2016 with a performance by Sex Pistols frontman Johnny Rotten. ✉ *Bankastræti 2, Miðbær* ☎ *354/568–2003* ⊕ *www.facebook.com/Bankastraeti0* 🎫 *ISK 1000.*

Ingólfur Arnarson Statue

PUBLIC ART | **FAMILY** | Ingólfur Arnarson is renowned as the first Nordic settler in Iceland. Beyond this statue lies the city's architectural mélange: 18th-century stone houses, small 19th-century wooden houses, and office blocks from the 1930s and '40s. ✉ *Arnarhóll, Miðbær.*

Menntaskólinn í Reykjavík (*Reykjavík Junior College*)
COLLEGE | Many graduates from the country's oldest educational institution, established in 1846, have gone on to dominate political and social life in Iceland. Former president Vigdís Finnbogadóttir and numerous cabinet ministers, including Iceland's former prime minister, Gunnlaugsson Davíð Oddsson, are graduates, as are film producer Hrafn Gunnlaugsson and well-known author Þórarinn Eldjarn. ⊠ *Þingholtsstræti 12, corner of Amtmannsstígur and Lækjargata, Miðbær.*

Perlan
ARTS VENUE | FAMILY | Glittering like the upper hemisphere of a giant disco ball, Perlan (the Pearl) is a grand construction of steel and mirrored glass. Perched atop Öskjuhlíð, the hill overlooking Reykjavík Airport, it's also one of the first landmark buildings to greet visitors. Supported by six massive water tanks and illuminated by 1,900 light bulbs, this impressive building opened in 1991 as a monument to Iceland's invaluable geothermal water supplies. It has since become a major tourist attraction, offering guests a host of amenities beneath its shiny surface, including souvenir shops, a café, an ice cave, a massive exhibition space, and a viewing platform with telescopes. Its crowning glory, though, is the revolving restaurant—it's pricey, but the panoramic views of the city and beyond are second to none. ⊠ *Varmahlíð 1, Miðbær* ☎ *354/566–9000* ⊕ *www.perlan.is* ▤ *ISK 2690.*

Sun Voyager Sculpture
LOCAL INTEREST | This steel sculpture resembling a Viking ship is hard to miss as you drive along the water in Reykjavík. If you're driving along Sæbraut, you'll see it on the water right before you hit the Harpa Concert Hall (when traveling east to west). The Sun Voyager was created by local sculptor Jón Gunnar Árnason. The original intention was to create a dreamlike boat that appears to float off into the sun. If you visit during sunset, you'll feel immediately transported. ⊠ *Sæbraut, Miðbær* ☎ *354/551–5789* ⊕ *www.sunvoyager.is*

Stjórnarráðshúsið (*Government House*)
GOVERNMENT BUILDING | This low white building, constructed in the 18th century as a prison, today houses the office of the prime minister. ⊠ *Lækjartorg Plaza, Stjórnarráðshúsinu við Lækjartorg, Miðbær* ☎ *354/545–8400* ⊕ *www.for.is* ⊗ *Closed weekends.*

★ **National Museum of Iceland**
MUSEUM | Viking treasures and artifacts, silverwork, wood carvings, and some unusual whalebone carvings are on display here, as well as maritime objects, historical textiles, jewelry, and crafts. There is also a coffee shop. ⊠ *Suðurgata 41, Vesturbær* ☎ *354/530–2200* ⊕ *www.thjodminjasafn.is* ▤ *ISK 2000.*

The Culture House (*National Cultural House*)
ARTS VENUE | FAMILY | Crests on the facade of the impressive former Landsbókasafnið (Old National Library) name significant Icelandic literary figures; the renovated building now houses interesting cultural displays and art exhibits. Erected between 1906 and 1908, it was primarily a library for most of the 20th century, but its book collection has been moved to the Þjóðarbókhlaðan at the National and University Library of Iceland. A free guided tour in English is offered Tuesday through Sunday at 2 pm, September through May, and weekdays (except Wednesday) between June and August. ⊠ *Hverfisgata 15, Miðbær* ☎ *354/530–2200* ⊕ *www.culturehouse.is* ▤ *ISK 2000* ⊗ *Closed Mon. Sept. 16–Apr. 30.*

City Center East

0 ——————— 500 ft
0 ——————— 100 m

Sights ▼

1 The Culture House.......**C2**
2 Hallgrímskirkja **D6**
3 Höfði......................**I3**
4 Iceland Phallological Museum **H6**
5 Icelandic Punk Museum **B2**
6 Ingólfur Arnarson Statue **C2**
7 Menntaskólinn í Reykjavík................**A3**
8 National Museum of Iceland...............**A5**
9 Perlan **I9**
10 Sun Voyager Sculpture **F2**
11 Stjórnarráðshúsið **B2**

Restaurants ▼

1 Austur Indíafélagið **E4**
2 Ban Thai Restaurant **I6**
3 Block Burger.............**C3**
4 Brauð & Co. **E5**
5 Café Loki **D6**
6 Dill Restaurant **C2**
7 Gló.......................**D3**
8 Grái Kötturinn **C2**
9 Hlemmur Mathöll **H5**
10 Holt Restaurant **B5**
11 Íslenski Barinn **B2**
12 Jörgensen Kitchen & Bar.............**I6**
13 Kaffi Paris...............**A3**
14 Kaffibennslan **D3**
15 Kol Restaurant **D5**
16 Lækjarbrekka............**B2**
17 Le Bistro **C3**
18 The Lobsterhouse **A3**
19 MAT BAR **C3**
20 Ostabúðin................**C3**
21 Restó **H7**
22 Reykjavík Chips **F5**
23 ROK......................**D5**
24 SKÁL! **I5**
25 Snaps Bistro Bar and Restaurant......**C5**
26 Solon Bistro & Bar.......**C3**
27 Te Og Kaffi..............**D3**
28 Þrír Frakkar.............**B6**

Quick Bites ▼

1 Eldur og Ís **B3**
2 Emilie and the Cool Kids.................**G5**
3 Kaffi Mokka..............**C3**
4 Kaffifélagið **C3**
5 Kaffitár **B3**
6 Reykjavik Roasters **D5**
7 Svarta Kaffið **F4**

Hotels ▼

1 Alda Hotel **F5**
2 Hótel Holt **B5**
3 Hotel Leifur Eiríksson...**D6**
4 Hotel Óðinsvé **C4**
5 Ion City Hotel...........**D4**
6 Kex **G4**
7 Loft Hostel **B3**
8 101 hotel **B2**
9 Room with a View **C3**
10 Sand Hotel..............**D4**

🍽 Restaurants

Austur Indíafélagið

$$$ | INDIAN | The menu at Austur Indíafélagið is overwhelming, only because so many of the options sound delicious. Ask your server to craft the perfect table of food for your group. **Known for:** vegetarian options; fish curry; beautiful interiors. ⓢ *Average main: ISK 4495* ✉ *Hverfisgata 56, Miðbær* ☎ *354/552–1630* ⊕ *www.austurindia.is.*

Ban Thai Restaurant

$ | THAI | FAMILY | When you find yourself tired of Icelandic dishes, check out Ban Thai. Here you'll find traditional dishes from another side of the world, and with a bit more kick. **Known for:** massive menu; generous portions; quick service. ⓢ *Average main: ISK 2190* ✉ *Laugavegur 130, Miðbær* ☎ *354/552–2444* ⊕ *www.banthai.is.*

Block Burger

$ | BURGER | On a particularly beautiful day, the best thing to do is grab lunch from Block Burger and enjoy it alfresco in the nearby square. **Known for:** family value meals; vegetarian options; waffle fries. ⓢ *Average main: ISK 2390* ✉ *Skólavörðustígur 8, Miðbær* ☎ *354/511–0011* ⊕ *www.blockburger.is.*

★ Brauð & Co

$ | BAKERY | Ágúst Einþórsson is the baker behind this local favorite. Brauð & Co has displays full of simple yet perfect pastries and other baked goods. **Known for:** super-fresh cinnamon buns; buttery croissants; open early. ⓢ *Average main: ISK 990* ✉ *Frakkastígur 16, Miðbær* ☎ *354/456–7777* ⊕ *www.braudogco.is.*

★ Café Loki

$$ | SEAFOOD | Café Loki is a must-stop for many people around the world—just take a look at their guest book. Do yourself a favor and visit after taking in the views from the iconic Hallgrímskirkja; you'll feel like you're in the center of a Nordic movie set. **Known for:** location across from Hallgrímskirkja; delicious home-made dishes; friendly service. ⓢ *Average main: ISK 2950* ✉ *Lokastígur 28, Miðbær* ☎ *354/466–2828* ⊕ *www.loki.is.*

★ Dill Restaurant

$$$$ | SEAFOOD | There's only one option at Dill: a tasting menu with a modern spin on traditional Icelandic dishes. In 2017, Dill was the first restaurant in Iceland to be awarded a Michelin star, with Chef Gunnar Karl Gíslason at the helm. **Known for:** tasting menu; careful attention to detail with presentation; downright delicious takes on Icelandic dishes. ⓢ *Average main: ISK 13900* ✉ *Hverfisgata 12, Miðbær* ☎ *354/552–1522* ⊕ *www.dillrestaurant.is* ⊙ *Closed Sun.–Mon.*

Gló

$ | VEGETARIAN | The latest brainchild of Solla Eiríks, one of the pioneers of the raw-food movement in Iceland, Gló's menu changes daily, featuring imaginative and varied vegetarian dishes such as nut steaks, pies, and a delicious coconut curry. Takeout is also available. **Known for:** ample vegetarian and vegan options; the pulled Oumph burger; reasonably priced healthy meals. ⓢ *Average main: ISK 1390* ✉ *Laugavegur 20b, Miðbær* ☎ *354/553–1111* ⊕ *www.glo.is* ▭ *No credit cards.*

★ Grái Kötturinn

$ | CAFÉ | This plain and simple breakfast spot has won the hearts of many politicians who work nearby—as well as Björk—and it tends to get quite busy on weekends. Hot meals are your best bet. **Known for:** "The Truck" breakfast; frequented by local celebrities; lots of books to read while you wait. ⓢ *Average main: ISK 2200* ✉ *Hverfisgata 16a, Miðbær* ☎ *354/551–1544* ⊕ *www.graikotturinn.is.*

★ Hlemmur Mathöll

$ | SCANDINAVIAN | FAMILY | This food hall features 10 vendors loved by locals: Brauð & Co., Fuego, SKÁL!, Micro Roast Te & Kaffi, Flatey Pizza, Kröst, Til Sjávar & Til Sveita, Osteria Emiliana. Báhn Mí, and Jæja. **Known for:** local favorites;

wide variety of options; kid-friendly. $ *Average main: ISK 1900* ✉ *Laugavegur 107, Miðbær* ☎ *354/577–6200* ⊕ *www. hlemmurmatholl.is.*

★ Holt Restaurant

$$$$ | **FRENCH** | Icelandic art covers the walls of this restaurant in the Hótel Holt, within walking distance of downtown; the cocktail lounge and bar showcase drawings by Jóhannes Kjarval. It has long been in the forefront of Icelandic restaurants, with impeccable service and mouthwatering wild-game and seafood dishes—favorites include gravlax and reindeer. **Known for:** impressive reserve wine list; welcoming vibe; attentive service. $ *Average main: ISK 5590* ✉ *Hótel Holt, Bergstaðastræti 37, Miðbær* ☎ *354/552–5700* ⊕ *www.holt.is.*

Íslenski Barinn

$$ | **SEAFOOD** | From the traditional fish pie and meat soup to a spectacular waffle fry, Íslenski Barinn covers a lot of ground on its menu, but the focus is local at this restaurant and bar. And at the latter, you'll find only beers and spirits made in Iceland—don't come here looking for imports. **Known for:** fish pie; hyperlocal beer and spirit options; a place to mix with the locals. $ *Average main: ISK 2850* ✉ *Ingólfsstræti 1a, Miðbær* ☎ *354/517–6767* ⊕ *www.islenskibarinn. is.*

Jörgensen Kitchen & Bar

$$ | **SCANDINAVIAN** | Although Jörgensen Kitchen & Bar has a similar menu to other eateries around the city (burgers, fish and chips, cod, and catch of the day), what's really intriguing about this restaurant is the private garden area. Dining in this dreamy oasis in the middle of the city's main shopping street is a real pleasure. **Known for:** private garden dining area; Icelandic pancakes; central location. $ *Average main: ISK 3400* ✉ *Laugavegur 120, Miðbær* ☎ *354/595–8565* ⊕ *www. jorgensenkitchen.com.*

★ Kaffibrennslan

$ | **CAFÉ** | By day, Kaffibrennslan is a cozy café. The menu is full of sandwich and soup options and every coffee drink you could think of. **Known for:** friendly bartenders; cozy seating in the loft; substantial sandwiches. $ *Average main: ISK 1390* ✉ *Laugavegur, Miðbær* ☎ *354/511–5888* ⊕ *www.kaffibrennslan101.is.*

Kaffi París

$$ | **CAFÉ** | **FAMILY** | This is a popular spot for dining and people-watching. The menu is broad, covers all main meals with basic dishes, and there are daily specials. **Known for:** covering all meals on one menu; friendly service; fantastic breakfast options. $ *Average main: ISK 2695* ✉ *Austurstraeti 14, Miðbær* ☎ *354/551–1020* ⊕ *www.cafeparis.is* ⊙ *Closed Fri.–Sat.*

★ Kol Restaurant

$ | **SCANDINAVIAN** | Sipping on a refreshing "Donkey" cocktail will add a spicy warmth to your cheeks while you take in the sights, sounds, and aromas, which intensify the evening progresses. Each dish at this friendly restaurant is carefully paired with wine and delivered with a detailed narrative by well-informed staff. **Known for:** incredibly cozy interior; "Simply the Best" desserts; inviting and inspired cocktail list. $ *Average main: ISK 1565* ✉ *Skólavörðustíg 40, Miðbær* ☎ *354/517–7474* ⊕ *www.kolrestaurant.is.*

Lækjarbrekka

$$$$ | **ECLECTIC** | Set in one of the oldest houses in Reykjavík (built in 1834), this restaurant serves a wide range of dishes, from salads and soups to meat and fish options. Among the menu's treats are the Icelandic lobster and the mountain lamb. **Known for:** serving up a mean Icelandic lobster dish; beautifully plated dishes; small portions. $ *Average main: ISK 7650* ✉ *Lækjarbrekka Bankastræti 2, Miðbær* ☎ *354/551–4430* ⊕ *www. laekjarbrekka.is.*

Le Bistro

$$ | **FRENCH** | French food may not be the first thing you think of when you set foot in Reykjavík, but Le Bistro will challenge that. Although this restaurant serves up a few Icelandic favorites, diners rave about the beef bourguignon (and some say it's better than in France). **Known for:** prix fixe options; beef bourguignon perfection; cozy ambience. $ *Average main: ISK 3990* ✉ *Laugavegur 12, Miðbær* ☎ *354/551–5979* ⊕ *www.lebistro.is.*

The Lobsterhouse

$$$$ | **SEAFOOD** | Housed inside a classic 19th-century building, Torfan—a new restaurant with an old name—invites those with a fat billfold (or anyone up for a splurge) to dine on a luxurious menu of seasonal dishes made from locally sourced Icelandic ingredients like lamb or langoustine. Courses are paired with a well-curated selection of wine and served by knowledgeable staff. **Known for:** creative and delightful decor; impeccable langoustine soup; attentive service. $ *Average main: ISK 7,900* ✉ *Amtmannsstíg 1, Miðbær* ☎ *354/561–3303* ⊕ *www.thelobsterhouse.is.*

★ MAT BAR

$$ | **EUROPEAN** | This Nordic-Italian restaurant does the classics very well, but the owner, Guðjón Hauksson, sought out an Italian cheese-maker for the mozzarella. It's best with pickled tomatoes and basil in MAT BAR's take on the traditional caprese salad. **Known for:** next-level mozzarella; great cocktail menu; food that's meant to be shared. $ *Average main: ISK 3990* ✉ *Hverfisgata 26, Miðbær* ☎ *354/788–3900* ⊕ *www.matbar.is* ⊘ *Closed Sun.*

Ostabúðin

$$ | **SCANDINAVIAN** | This traditional Icelandic menu checks all of the boxes: seafood soup, cod, lamb, and skyr. **Known for:** arctic char; reasonable prices; central location. $ *Average main: ISK 3190* ✉ *Skólavörðustígur 8, Miðbær* ☎ *354/562–2772* ⊕ *www.ostabudin.is.*

Restó

$$ | **SEAFOOD** | The daily specials at Restó incorporate fresh seafood and always come out perfectly. Make a reservation, as the space isn't very big. **Known for:** unpretentious dishes; quick service; excellent catch of the day. $ *Average main: ISK 3600* ✉ *Rauðarárstígur 27–29, Hlíðar* ☎ *354/546–9550* ⊕ *www.resto.is.*

Reykjavík Chips

$ | **FAST FOOD** | The talented owners here (one of whom is a BAFTA Award–winning musician) are keen to prove that they can make a tasty meal out of the lowly potato. Cooked in the simple Belgian style and offered with a range of tasty sauces and beverages, the "chips" are surprisingly good and certainly worthy of the hype. **Known for:** affordable prices; delicious thick-cut fries; more sauces than you'll know what to do with. $ *Average main: ISK 1050* ✉ *Vitastígur 10, Miðbær* ☎ *552–2221* ⊕ *www.rvkchips.is* ⊘ *Closed Mon.*

★ ROK

$ | **SCANDINAVIAN** | The *plokkfiskur* (fish stew) at this local favorite is the perfect thing to warm you up on a cold night. The restaurant also hosts a Champagne happy hour that includes a bottle of bubbly, licorice, and cantaloupe every day between 4 and 7 pm. **Known for:** traditional dishes; Champagne happy hour; extensive cocktail list. $ *Average main: ISK 2390* ✉ *Frakkastígur 26a, Miðbær* ☎ *354/544–4443* ⊕ *www.rokrestaurant.is.*

★ SKÁL!

$ | **SCANDINAVIAN** | Located in the Hlemmur Mathöll food hall, SKÁL! offers elegant platings in a casual setting. The best part is that prices are much more reasonable than you'd see in most restaurants around the city, but you really aren't giving up any quality when it comes to the food. **Known for:** arctic char; reasonable portions; quick service. $ *Average main: ISK 2350* ✉ *Laugavegur 107, Hlíðar* ☎ *354/519–6515* ⊕ *www.skalrvk.com.*

★ Snaps Bistro Bar and Restaurant
$$ | FRENCH FUSION | Always bustling, this popular bistro bar is famous for its weekend brunch and attracts a lively bunch of locals, whose musical inflections mingle nicely with the chatter of out-of-towners. Tables are arranged around an elevated open kitchen and central bar. **Known for:** a full gin and tonic menu; delicious fish of the day specials; fresh oysters. $ Average main: ISK 3890 ⊠ Þórsgata 1, Miðbær ☎ 354/511–6677 ⊕ www.snaps. is.

Solon Bistro & Bar
$$$$ | INTERNATIONAL | At the artsy Solon Bistro & Bar you can view some modern art, have a meal (try the fish of the day), and enjoy some people-watching through the large windows. You'll find local ingredients alongside Italian staples and fresher-than-fresh seafood dishes on the menu. **Known for:** perfectly prepared seafood; reasonable lunch specials; generous portions. $ Average main: ISK 5000 ⊠ Bankastræti 7A, Miðbær ☎ 354/562–3232 ⊕ www.solon.is ⊟ No credit cards.

Te og Kaffi
$ | CAFÉ | Iceland's biggest coffee chain is run by the couple largely responsible for starting the modern Icelandic coffee revolution. Far from its humble beginnings in 1984, the company today boasts its own roastery and operates 12 shops. **Known for:** citron muffin; Iceland's biggest coffee chain; quick service. $ Average main: ISK 700 ⊠ Laugavegur 27, Miðbær ☎ 354/555–1910 ⊕ www.teogkaffi.is.

Þrír Frakkar
$$ | SEAFOOD | According to urban legend, it's traditional for Icelanders returning home from abroad to make their first stop at this beloved restaurant, and indulge in chef Úlfar's legendary plokkfiskur. Not just a favorite with the locals, Þrír Frakkar—a curious name that can be interpreted either as "the Three Overcoats" or "the Three Frenchies"—has a number of high-profile celebrity

fans, including chef Jamie Oliver, who reportedly dined on guillemot during his visit. **Known for:** great take on classic plokkfiskur; celebrity sightings; traditional dishes like smoked puffin and whale steak. $ Average main: ISK 3950 ⊠ Baldursgata 14, at Nönnugata, Miðbær ☎ 354/552–3939 ⊕ www.3frakkar.is ⊙ No lunch weekends.

☕ Coffee and Quick Bites

Eldur og Ís
$ | FRENCH | "Fire and Ice" does two things really well: ice cream and crepes. You can choose from the menu they've put together, or you can make up your own crepe creation. **Known for:** customizable crepes; quick service; great gelato. $ Average main: ISK 990 ⊠ Skólavörðustígur 2, Miðbær ☎ 354/571–2480 ⊕ www. facebook.com/eldurogis.

Emilie and the Cool Kids
$ | BAKERY | Pastries and baked goods here are inspired by the French at this popular coffee shop. There isn't a ton of seating, but you can take the items to go. **Known for:** French-inspired baked goods; warm service; cozy interior. $ Average main: ISK 999 ⊠ Hverfisgata 98, Reykjavík ☎ 354/571–5887 ⊕ www. emiliescookies.com.

Kaffi Mokka
$ | CAFÉ | FAMILY | In business since 1958, Iceland's oldest café is a wonderful place to mingle with locals of all kinds. Many consider the waffles at this Reykjavík institution to be the best in town. **Known for:** best waffles in town; Swiss mocha; retro vibe. $ Average main: ISK 1540 ⊠ Skólavörðustígur 3A, Miðbær ☎ 354/552–1174 ⊕ www.mokka.is ⊟ No credit cards.

Kaffifélagið
$ | CAFÉ | This tiny coffee shop has built itself a solid reputation for excellent Italian espresso. Its delightful brand has been dubbed the "best cup of joe to go," and customers gather on the sidewalk,

where they sip from paper cups and talk about politics and the weather. **Known for:** quality Italian espresso; friendly service; free Wi-Fi. ⓢ *Average main: ISK 1000* ✉ *Skólavörðustígur 10, Miðbær* ☎ *354/520–8420* ⊕ *www.kaffifelagid.is.*

Kaffitár

$ | **CAFÉ** | Kaffitár is a name you'll see all over Reykjavík—it's where Icelanders grab coffee on their way to work (think: Nordic Starbucks)—but this coffee shop chain is known for paying careful attention to where its beans come from. **Known for:** quick service; consistently good coffee; inventive coffee drinks. ⓢ *Average main: ISK 890* ✉ *Bankastræti 8, Miðbær* ☎ *354/420–2732* ⊕ *www. kaffitar.is.*

★ Reykjavík Roasters

$ | **CAFÉ** | If you're serious about the quality of your cup of joe, then you should feel right at home at Reykjavík Roasters. Its dedicated patrons seem to occupy its shabby-chic seating all day long, occasionally getting up for a refill or to play the other side of a vintage vinyl. **Known for:** carefully selected coffee beans; hip atmosphere; record player where guests are encouraged to play what they want. ⓢ *Average main: ISK 1000* ✉ *Kárastígur 1, Miðbær* ☎ *354/517–5535* ⊕ *www. reykjavikroasters.is.*

★ Svarta Kaffið

$ | **CAFÉ | FAMILY** | There are only two options on the menu at Svarta Kaffið: a vegetarian soup and a meat soup. Known locally as the soup spot, this restaurant really has more of a café atmosphere, with a small list of beers and wine on tap. **Known for:** fantastic soup; two-item menu; lively atmosphere. ⓢ *Average main: ISK 1300* ✉ *Laugavegur 54, Miðbær* ☎ *354/551-2999.*

 Hotels

★ 101 Hotel

$$$$ | **HOTEL** | The five-story, 38-room hotel was designed by owner Ingibjörg Pálmadóttir. **Pros:** intimate feel; good facilities; large rooms. **Cons:** spa and sauna area is small; located in a noisy part of town; lacks a cozy vibe. ⓢ *Rooms from: ISK 59900* ✉ *Hverfisgata 10, Miðbær* ☎ *354/580–0101* ⊕ *www.101hotel.is* ⤳ *38 rooms, 1 apartment suite* ❙❍❙ *No meals.*

Alda Hotel

$$$ | **HOTEL** | At this lovely hotel in the trendy Lighthouse Village area of downtown Reykjavík, guest rooms are decorated in a typical Scandinavian-chic style, with a combination of rich, earthy tones contrasted with fresh, crisp whites and the occasional splash of vibrant color. **Pros:** location in happening neighborhood; high-speed Wi-Fi; great amenities. **Cons:** some rooms do not have great views; communal areas can be quite busy and often loud; lack of storage space in rooms. ⓢ *Rooms from: ISK 34087* ✉ *Laugavegur 66–68, Miðbær* ☎ *354/553–9366* ⊕ *www.aldahotel.is* ⤳ *64 rooms* ❙❍❙ *Free Breakfast.*

★ Hótel Holt

$$$ | **HOTEL** | This quietly elegant member of the prestigious World Hotels group has impeccable service, an excellent restaurant (Gallery), and free Wi-Fi throughout, making it a favorite among business travelers. **Pros:** free access to gym and swimming pool; excellent restaurant and bar; professional service. **Cons:** bathrooms can be small; slightly formal atmosphere; small rooms. ⓢ *Rooms from: ISK 30087* ✉ *Bergstaðastræti 37, Reykjavík* ☎ *354/552–5700* ⊕ *www.holt. is* ⤳ *42 rooms* ❙❍❙ *Free Breakfast.*

Hotel Leifur Eiríksson

$ | **HOTEL | FAMILY** | Across the street from the hilltop church of Hallgrímskirkja, this hotel is a short walk from most of Reykjavík's major attractions. **Pros:** good location; quiet area; friendly staff. **Cons:** rooms and bathrooms can be small and charmless; no elevator; faded furnishings. ⓢ *Rooms from: ISK 19269* ✉ *Skólavörðustígur 45, Miðbær*

☎ *354/562–0800* 🌐 *www.hotelleifur.is* 🛏 *47 rooms* 🍴 *Free Breakfast.*

Hotel Óðinsvé

$$$ | HOTEL | Five buildings in a calm corner of an older part of town make up this hotel with cheery and efficient guest rooms, some with nice views over Reykjavík's colorful rooftops. **Pros:** central but quiet; good restaurant loved by locals; professional service. **Cons:** some rooms lack views; small showers; expensive breakfast options. [$] *Rooms from: ISK 28666* ✉ *Þórsgata 1, Miðbær* ☎ *354/511–6200* 🌐 *www.hotelodinsve.is* 🛏 *50 rooms* 🍴 *Free Breakfast.*

★ **Ion City Hotel**

$$$$ | HOTEL | The Ion City Hotel is the urban counterpart to the original Ion Hotel, near Þingvellir National Park. **Pros:** soundproof between rooms; luxurious boutique hotel vibe; great location. **Cons:** no a/c; small rooms. [$] *Rooms from: ISK 47685* ✉ *Laugavegur 28, Miðbær* ☎ *354/578–3730* 🌐 *www.ioniceland.is* 🛏 *18 rooms* 🍴 *No meals.*

★ **Kex**

$$ | HOTEL | There's a reason you'll find locals hanging out at this space near the harbor on nights and weekends: The bar is fantastic and the restaurant's menu rivals the best in the city. **Pros:** local hangout; great bar and restaurant; beautiful room decor. **Cons:** can get rowdy on weekends; breakfast not included in room rate; no elevator. [$] *Rooms from: ISK 25000* ✉ *Skúlagata 28, Miðbær* ☎ *354/561–6060* 🌐 *www.kexhostel.is* 🛏 *32 dorms and rooms* 🍴 *No meals.*

Loft Hostel

$$ | HOTEL | A hostel with private rooms available, Loft is located right off Reykjavík's main shopping streets. **Pros:** local hangout; frequent events; central location. **Cons:** tends to get noisy; small rooms; basic amenities. [$] *Rooms from: ISK 28000* ✉ *Bankastræti 7, Miðbær* ☎ *354/553–8140* 🌐 *www.lofthostel.is* 🛏 *18 rooms* 🍴 *No meals.*

Room with a View

$$$$ | RENTAL | FAMILY | Room with a View offers a number of self-catering apartments in the center of town for those who prefer to cook their own meals and would like extra space. **Pros:** well established; friendly staff; independent atmosphere. **Cons:** no on-call staff; no concierge; no lobby or communal waiting area. [$] *Rooms from: ISK 40875* ✉ *Laugavegur 18, Miðbær* ☎ *354/552–7262, 354/552–1485* 🌐 *www.roomwithaview.is* 🕒 *Closed Sun.* 🛏 *46 rooms* 🍴 *No meals.*

★ **Sand Hotel**

$$$$ | HOTEL | Located right in the center of Reykjavík, the Sand is one of the more luxurious hotels in the city. **Pros:** Sóley Organics amenities; beautiful art deco design details; fantastic bakery next door that serves breakfast for guests. **Cons:** rooms along Laugavegur are noisy; very little storage space in rooms; rooms on the small side. [$] *Rooms from: ISK 56774* ✉ *Laugavegur 34, Miðbær* ☎ *354/519–8090* 🌐 *www.sandhotel.is* 🛏 *67 rooms* 🍴 *No meals.*

Shopping

★ **Geysir**

CLOTHING | Geysir is loved around the country (there are other outposts in Akureyri) for its classic, minimalist vibe and quality clothing. This location specializes in menswear, but you will find options for women at other Geysir shops around Reykjavík. ✉ *Skólavörðustígur 16, Miðbær* 🌐 *www.geysir.com.*

★ **Húrra Reykjavík Women**

CLOTHING | Step inside and you'll be awash in the neutral color palette of this trendy women's wear shop. Take some time to dive a bit deeper into the designs on display: They're simple, timeless, and will remind you of your trip for years to come. ✉ *Hverfisgata 78, Miðbær* ☎ *354/571–7101* 🌐 *www.hurrareykjavik.is* 🕒 *Closed Sun.*

★ Icewear

CLOTHING | Primarily an outerwear and outdoor gear store, Icewear is a popular local chain that can be found in a number of places around Reykjavík. If you're looking to bring home a wool blanket, this is often the place to find the least expensive options. They may be one of the best deals in the store; prepare to spend the usual (expensive) prices for sweaters, jackets, socks, and shoes. ⊠ *Laugavegur 91, Miðbær* ☎ *354/585–0503* ⊕ *www.icewear.is.*

★ Reykjavik Raincoats

SPECIALTY STORES | If you ever wonder what kind of outerwear could handle the ever-changing weather patterns of Iceland, this raincoat shop has an answer for you. Aside from being completely functional, the jackets sold at Reykjavik Raincoats are undoubtedly Instagram-worthy—classic and minimal (thigh-length and hooded) putting bold colors front and center. ⊠ *Laugavegur 62, Miðbær* ☎ *354/571–1177* ⊕ *www.reykjavikraincoats.com* ⊙ *Closed Sun.*

★ Hrím Hönnunarhús

HOUSEHOLD ITEMS/FURNITURE | Hrím Hönnunarhús is a wonderland of home decor, trinkets, accessories, and locally made ceramics, with a few other delightful designs thrown in for good measure. Don't miss the display case of locally made jewelry to the left of the front door. ⊠ *Laugavegur 25, Miðbær* ☎ *354/553–3003* ⊕ *www.hrim.is.*

★ Litla Jólabúðin

SPECIALTY STORES | One look at Litla Jólabúðin and you'll know what it's all about: Christmas. The shop is open year-round despite its seasonality, selling ornaments and other wintertime trinkets. Chances are you'll learn a thing or two about Icelandic holiday culture while you're in there. ⊠ *Laugavegur 8, Miðbær* ☎ *354/552–2412* ⊕ *www.facebook.com/little.christmasshop.iceland.*

★ Handprjónasambandið

CRAFTS | The Handknitting Association of Iceland has its own outlet, selling (of course) only hand-knit items of various kinds. The back room is a wonderland of woolen knits and other handmade apparel. ⊠ *Skólavörðurstígur 19, Miðbær* ☎ *354/455–5544* ⊕ *www.handknit.is.*

★ Ísey

SPECIALTY STORES | You'll want to spend an entire afternoon in Ísey, with its friendly service and huge selection of woolen products. ⊠ *Laugavegur 23, Miðbær* ☎ *354/552–6970.*

Smekkleysa (*Bad Taste*)

MUSIC STORES | This record store with its own label doubles as a gift shop. Smekkleysa is known by locals for releasing music by the Icelandic alt-rock band Sugarcubes, of which Björk was a founding member. Unfortunately the group disbanded in 1992, but you can still buy their music at this shop. ⊠ *Skólavörðustígur 16, Miðbær* ☎ *354/551–3730* ⊕ *www.smekkleysa.net* ⊙ *Closed Sun.*

🅨 Nightlife

b5

BARS/PUBS | For a night of reckless glamour among a crowd of well-dressed and heavily perfumed party people, head to b5, a classy (at least before midnight) yet comfortable nightspot illuminated throughout with backlit rose-color panels. ⊠ *Bankastræti 5, Miðbær* ☎ *354/552–9600* ⊕ *www.b5.is.*

★ Kaffibarinn

BARS/PUBS | One of the city's most famous cafés and nightspots—thanks to its associations with local and international celebs, like Damon Albarn from Blur—Kaffibarinn is a relaxed café during the day but hopping on nights and weekends, when DJs show up and play until the wee hours. ⊠ *Bergstaðastræti 1, Miðbær* ☎ *354/551–1588* ⊕ *www.facebook.com/kaffibarinn.*

★ Kíkí Queer Bar

DANCE CLUBS | Unofficially Iceland's best gay bar, Kiki Queer Bar is a spirited mix of locals and travelers on any given night. Located in the heart of Reykjavík's nightlife hub, you can dance until the wee hours here. ⊠ *Laugavegur 22, Miðbær* ☎ *354/571–0194* ⊕ *www.kiki.is.*

Kofinn

BARS/PUBS | Kofinn is your basic, no-frills bar serving up drinks and cake beginning in the afternoon and hosting DJs into the early morning hours. It's located in the main shopping district, making it a great spot to grab a snack and libation in the late afternoon. ⊠ *Laugavegur 2, Miðbær* ☎ *354/551–1855* ⊕ *www.facebook.com/ kofinn.ktf.*

The Lebowski Bar

THEMED ENTERTAINMENT | Admittedly a tourist attraction, this bar and restaurant is themed after—you guessed it—the Cohen Brothers' cult classic *The Big Lebowski,* and has an entire menu dedicated to White Russians. The decor is full of references: The bar is lined with rugs, and the barstools look like bowling shoes, and "the Dude" himself can be found on the cocktail napkins. The neon sign out front provides quite the photo op. ⊠ *Laugavegur 20a, Miðbær* ☎ *354/552–2300* ⊕ *www.lebowskibar.is.*

★ Mikkeller and Friends

BREWPUBS/BEER GARDENS | The Reykjavík outpost of this Scandinavian string of bars is as trendy and well designed as its counterparts. The space is the work of local set designer Hálfdán Pedersen: walls of graphic prints, an arc of glassware over the bar, and cozy benches greet visitors. There are 20 Mikkeller beers available on tap. When you get hungry, head downstairs to Dill Restaurant. ⊠ *Hverfisgata 12, Miðbær* ☎ *354/437–0203* ⊕ *www.mikkeller.dk.*

Petersen Svítan

BARS/PUBS | If you don't feel like heading to the top of Hallgrímskirkja to take in 360-degree views of Reykjavík, check out Petersen Svítan. This rooftop lounge is on the third floor of Gamla Bíó, a historic cinema. In a previous life, the bar was the cinema owner's apartment; today, it's an open-air bar with a bilevel terrace. ⊠ *Ingólfsstræti 2a, Miðbær* ☎ *354/563–4000* ⊕ *www.gamlabio.is.*

★ Prikið

BARS/PUBS | The line of people waiting to get in to this bar stretches around the block on weekends. And it's totally worth the wait: inside, you'll find some of the city's best DJs, as well as a ton of locals relaxing and mingling with travelers. Prikið is open during the day too, when the crowds are much smaller. The burger is a sleeper hit, so make sure to stop by for lunch if you can. ⊠ *Bankastræti 12, Miðbær* ☎ *354/517–1743* ⊕ *www.prikid. is.*

★ Vedur

BARS/PUBS | This loud bar's open floor plan can accommodate groups easily. The best seats are the pillow-topped benches along the window—they were practically made for people-watching. All of the cocktails are great here, but the classics are treated with special care: You will never go wrong with an Old- Fashioned at Vedur. ⊠ *Klapparstígur 33, Miðbær* ⊕ *www.vedurbarinn.is.*

City Center West

⊙ Sights

Alþingishús (*Parliament House*)

GOVERNMENT BUILDING | Built in 1880–81, this structure is one of the country's oldest stone buildings. Iceland's Alþingi (parliament) held its first session in AD 930 and therefore can lay claim to being the oldest representative parliament in the world. You can view the parliament

Harpa Music Hall and Conference Center.

proceedings from the visitor's gallery here. Depending on the urgency of the agenda, any number of Iceland's 63 members of parliament, from five political parties, may be present. ⊠ *Austurvöllur Sq., Miðbær* ☎ *354/563–0500* ⊕ *www.althingi.is.*

Aðalstræti 10

MUSEUM | FAMILY | This museum and exhibition space was put together by the National Museum of Iceland and the Reykjavík City Museum to help celebrate the country's 100th anniversary as a sovereign state. Aðalstræti 10 is the beginning of a five-location museum that covers Icelandic life through the ages and includes turf houses. ⊠ *Aðalstræti 10, Miðbær* ☎ *354/411–6375* ⊕ *www.visitreykjavik.is* ⊡ *ISK 1700.*

Dómkirkjan (*Lutheran Cathedral*)

RELIGIOUS SITE | A place of worship has existed on this site since AD 1200. The small, charming church, built 1788–96, represents the state religion, Lutheranism. It was here that sovereignty and independence were first blessed and endorsed by the church. It's also where Iceland's national anthem, actually a hymn, was first sung in 1874. Since 1845, members and cabinet ministers of every Alþingi (parliament) have gathered here for a service before the annual session. Among the treasured items inside is a baptismal font carved and donated by the famous 19th-century master sculptor Bertel Thorvaldsen, who was half Icelandic. ⊠ *Austurvöllur Sq., Lækjargötu 14a, Miðbær* ☎ *354/520–9700* ⊕ *www.domkirkjan.is.*

★ Harpa Concert Hall and Conference Center

ARTS FESTIVALS | The shimmering queen of the performing arts scene and home of both the Iceland Symphony Orchestra and the Icelandic Opera, this venue is an amazing modern labyrinth of stunning concert halls, event spaces, and places to dine or purchase designer souvenirs. Many of the city's most popular annual events, such as Airwaves, Sónar, and the Reykjavík Fashion Festival, are now hosted inside these glorious glass-paneled walls. Tours include Eldborg, the main hall and a marvel of visual and acoustic design that wouldn't be out of place in a *Star Wars* movie. ⊠ *Austurbakka 2, Miðbær* ☎ *354/528–5000* ⊕ *www.harpa. is.*

i8 Gallery

ART GALLERIES—ARTS | Both Icelandic and international artists display their work at this gallery near the harbor. Exhibitions rotate constantly, and there are often events held at this location featuring local artists. ⊠ *Tryggvagata 16, Miðbær* ☎ *354/551–3666* ⊕ *www.i8.is.*

Icelandic Printmakers Association

ART GALLERIES—ARTS | Established in 1984, there are now more than 100 members creating work in the Icelandic Printmakers Association community. This is their gallery, studio, and event space, which has a bustling calendar of exhibitions, workshops, and studio hours. ⊠ *Tryggvagata 17, Miðbær* ☎ *354/552–2866* ⊕ *www.islenskgrafik.is* ☞ *Closed Mon.–Wed.*

Lækjartorg (*Brook Square*)

PLAZA | Now a focal point in Reykjavík's otherwise rambling city center, this square opens onto **Austurstræti,** a semi-pedestrian shopping street. A brook, now underground, drains Tjörnin Pond into the sea (hence the street's name). ⊠ *At Bankastræti and Lækjargata, Lækjartorg, Miðbær* ⊕ *www.visitreykja-vik.is* ☜ *Free.*

Listasafn—the Reykjavík Art Museum (*Reykjavík Art Museum*)

MARINA | Also known as Hafnarhús, this former warehouse of the Port of Reykjavík now houses the city's art museum. The six galleries occupy two floors, and there's a courtyard and "multipurpose" space. The museum's permanent collection includes a large number of works donated by the contemporary Icelandic artist Erró. There are also regular temporary exhibitions. Admission is free with the Reykjavík City Card. ⊠ *Tryggvagata*

17, Miðbær ☎ *354/411–6400* ⊕ *www. artmuseum.is* ☜ *ISK 1800.*

Ráðhús (*City Hall*)

GOVERNMENT BUILDING | Modern architecture and nature converge at this building overlooking Tjörnin Pond. Inside is a visitor information desk and coffee bar with Internet access. A three-dimensional model of Iceland, over 819 square feet in size, is usually on display in the gallery, which often hosts various temporary exhibitions. ⊠ *Bounded by Fríkirkjuvegur, Vonarstræti, and Tjarnargata, Tjarnargata 11, Miðbær* ☎ *354/411–1000* ⊕ *www. reykjavik.is.*

Reykjavík 871±2: The Settlement Exhibition

ARCHAEOLOGICAL SITE | **FAMILY** | The core exhibit features the remains of a Viking longhouse dating back to around the year 871. Unearthed in 2001 during the construction of Hotel Centrum, this remarkable find was preserved in situ and now occupies an oval-shape basement designed especially to frame the excavation site. A large, backlit panoramic image, showing how Reykjavík might have looked during the age of settlement, encircles the longhouse, and an illuminated strip installed in the surrounding walls marks the layer of tephra used to determine the approximate date of the remnants. Sounds and aromas add a multisensory dynamic to the experience, while high-tech media installations provide historic insight into life in Iceland's Saga Age. ⊠ *Aðalstræti 16, Miðbær* ☎ *354/411–6370* ⊕ *www. borgarsogusafn.is/en/the-settlement-exhibition* ☜ *ISK 1700.*

Reykjavík Museum of Photography

MUSEUM | At this museum you can explore thousands of photographs from both amateur and professional photographers, dating back as far as 1860. This is a unique opportunity to explore more than a hundred years of Reykjavík—and Iceland—through a variety of perspectives. ⊠ *Tryggvagata 15, Miðbær*

☎ *354/411–6390* 🌐 *www.borgarsogusafn.is* 🎫 *ISK 1000.*

Tjörnin Pond

BODY OF WATER | FAMILY | This natural pond by the City Hall is popular among ice-skaters in winter and attracts birds (and bird lovers) year-round. Visitors are discouraged from feeding the birds during nesting season, as it attracts seagulls who like to feast on young waterfowl. ✉ *Between Fríkirkjvegur and Tjarnagata, next to Raðhús (City Hall), Miðbær* 🎫 *Free.*

Tollhúsið

GOVERNMENT BUILDING | The Customs House—a bureaucratic necessity, especially for an island nation—is decorated with an impressive mosaic mural. The piece of art depicts scenes from the local harbor and was designed by Gerð Helgadóttir. There isn't a ton to see inside, but the mural is worth a visit in itself. ✉ *Tryggvagata 19, Miðbær* 🌐 *www.tollur.is.*

Volcano House

MUSEUM | FAMILY | Iceland has more than 200 volcanoes across 30 different systems. At this museum you can learn about the county's volcanic heritage through documentaries about past eruptions and a free hands-on exhibition of semiprecious stones and minerals. You can also take home gifts and clothing from the on-site boutique. ✉ *Tryggvagata 11, Miðbær* ☎ *354 /555–1900* 🌐 *www.volcanohouse.is* 🎫 *Documentary tickets ISK 1700.*

🍴 Restaurants

Apotek Restaurant

$$ | SCANDINAVIAN | The menu at Apotek is much as you'll see at other upscale spots in Reykjavík—tons of fish, some sort of take on a tasting menu of traditional dishes (often with whale and puffin), and a few turf additions here and there—but the care and attention to detail is obvious here. It's a great splurge for those looking to get in one last memorable meal before heading home. **Known for:** tasting menus; vegetarian friendly; stunning dessert presentation. [$] *Average main: ISK 3890* ✉ *Austurstræti 16, Miðbær* ☎ *354/551–0011* 🌐 *www.apotekrestaurant.is.*

Bæjarins Beztu

$ | FAST FOOD | FAMILY | In a parking lot facing the harbor, this tiny yet famous fast-food hut is known for serving the original Icelandic hot dog—and a single person serves about a thousand of them a day from the window. Ask for *eina með öllu* (pronounced " *ayn*-ah med *utl*-lou"), or "one with everything," which gets you mustard, tomato sauce, rémoulade (mayonnaise with finely chopped pickles), and chopped raw and fried onions. **Known for:** quick service; a wide variety of locally loved condiments; incredibly helpful hot dog holders on the nearby tables. [$] *Average main: ISK 400* ✉ *Tryggvagata and Pósthússtræti, Austurströnd 3, Miðbær* ☎ *354/511–1566* 🌐 *www.bbp.is.*

★ **Bergsson Mathús**

$ | CAFÉ | Most flights into Iceland from the United States get in early (we're talking 6 am and sometimes earlier), so if you have some time to kill in the wee hours, head here for breakfast—they're open early. Fill up on the Bergsson Brunch, which comes with yogurt and muesli, a boiled egg, prosciutto, cheese, salad, fruit, hummus, bacon, fried potatoes, fresh orange juice, sourdough bread, and baked beans. **Known for:** piled-high plates of breakfast food; delicious sourdough bread baked on-site; enviable interior design. [$] *Average main: ISK 2290* ✉ *Templarasund 3, Miðbær* ☎ *354/571–1822* 🌐 *www.bergsson.net.*

★ **Grillmarket** (*Grillmarkaðurinn*)

$$$ | EUROPEAN | A collaborative project by well-known culinary innovators Hrefna Rós Sætran (founder and owner of the Fish Market) and Guðlaugur P. Frímannsson, Grillmarkaðurinn serves seasonal, organic, locally grown ingredients in a beautifully designed interior that's heavy on natural materials such as wood and stone. **Known for:** creative dishes using tried-and-true local ingredients; traditional dishes served with a modern twist; noteworthy tasting menus. $ *Average main: ISK 4340* ✉ *Lækjargata 2A, Miðbær* ☎ *354/571–7777* ⊕ *www.grillmarkadurinn.is* ⊟ *No credit cards.*

Habibi Kebab

$ | **MIDDLE EASTERN** | The best place in Reykjavík for an affordable late-night bite, here you can satisfy a craving for a great-tasting kebab in less than five minutes—and No. 7 (chicken shawarma) might just be your lucky number. You can either take it to go or hang out for a while, read the local newspaper, or people-watch from its clean and bright, tangerine-colored interior. **Known for:** late-night eats; quick service; reasonable prices. $ *Average main: ISK 1300* ✉ *Hafnarstræti 18, Reykjavík* ☎ *354/578–5858* ⊕ *www.habibiiceland.is.*

Hornið

$$ | **ITALIAN** | **FAMILY** | This welcoming bistro is light and airy, with lots of natural wood, potted plants, and cast-iron bistro tables. The emphasis is on pizza and pasta, but there's also a selection of meat and fish dishes. **Known for:** large pizza menu; cozy interior; flavorful calzones. $ *Average main: ISK 3040* ✉ *Hafnarstræti 15, Miðbær* ☎ *354/551–3340* ⊕ *www.hornid.is.*

Hressó

$$ | **PIZZA** | Fire-baked sourdough pizzas are the thing to get at Hressó, where the atmosphere is casual and the toppings are truly local. If you've ever wanted to try a pizza with shrimp on top, this is the place to do it. **Known for:** sourdough pizza; shrimp pizza; relaxed atmosphere. $ *Average main: ISK 2590* ✉ *Austurstræti 20, Miðbær* ☎ *354/561–2240* ⊕ *www.hresso.is.*

Kolabrautin

$$$ | **EUROPEAN** | Located on the third floor of the Harpa Concert Hall, Kolabrautin offers harbor views in an upscale atmosphere. The lamb is always a great choice, but branch out and try the black bean steak for a pleasant surprise, and definitely save room for dessert. **Known for:** beautiful views of the harbor; modern takes on traditional favorites; upscale atmosphere. $ *Average main: ISK 4600* ✉ *Austurbakki 2, Miðbær* ☎ *354/519–9700* ⊕ *www.kolabrautin.is.*

Le Kock

$ | **AMERICAN** | This restaurant is clearly inspired by American cuisine, from chicken wings to burgers. The potato options are downright creative, especially the Greek potatoes with feta spread, ranch dressing, red grapes, peanuts, and spring onions. **Known for:** creative burger options; American-inspired cuisine; quick service. $ *Average main: ISK 2200* ✉ *Tryggvagata 14, Miðbær* ☎ *354/571–1555* ⊕ *www.lekock.is.*

Lobster Hut

$ | **SEAFOOD** | **FAMILY** | This food truck serves fresh lobster in sandwiches and salads. Fun flavors accompany each menu item (think: a savory garlic sauce for your salad) and the prices won't cause a double-take like they do elsewhere in Iceland. **Known for:** lobster sandwiches; quick service; views of the harbor. $ *Average main: ISK 2490* ✉ *Kalkofnsvegur and Lækjartorg, Miðbær* ☎ *354/772–1710* ⊘ *Closed Fri.–Sun.*

Matarkjallarinn

$$ | **SCANDINAVIAN** | The atmosphere is the real crowd-pleaser here—especially if you're looking for a romantic restaurant with low lighting for date night, or a sceney dinner with perfectly fine food. **Known for:** sceney vibe; friendly bartenders; group seatings. $ *Average main: ISK 3190* ✉ *Aðalstræti 2, Miðbær* ☎ *354/558–0000* ⊕ *www.matarkjallarinn.is.*

Messinn

$ | **SEAFOOD** | Fish pans are what Messinn is known for: the sizzling catch of the day accompanied by butter-fried potatoes and

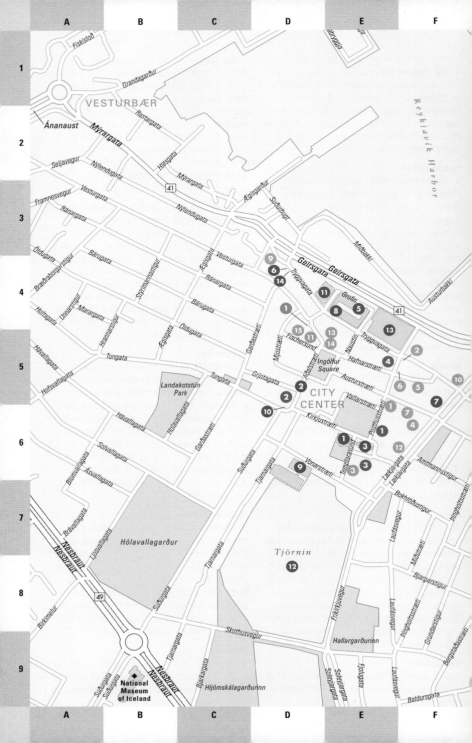

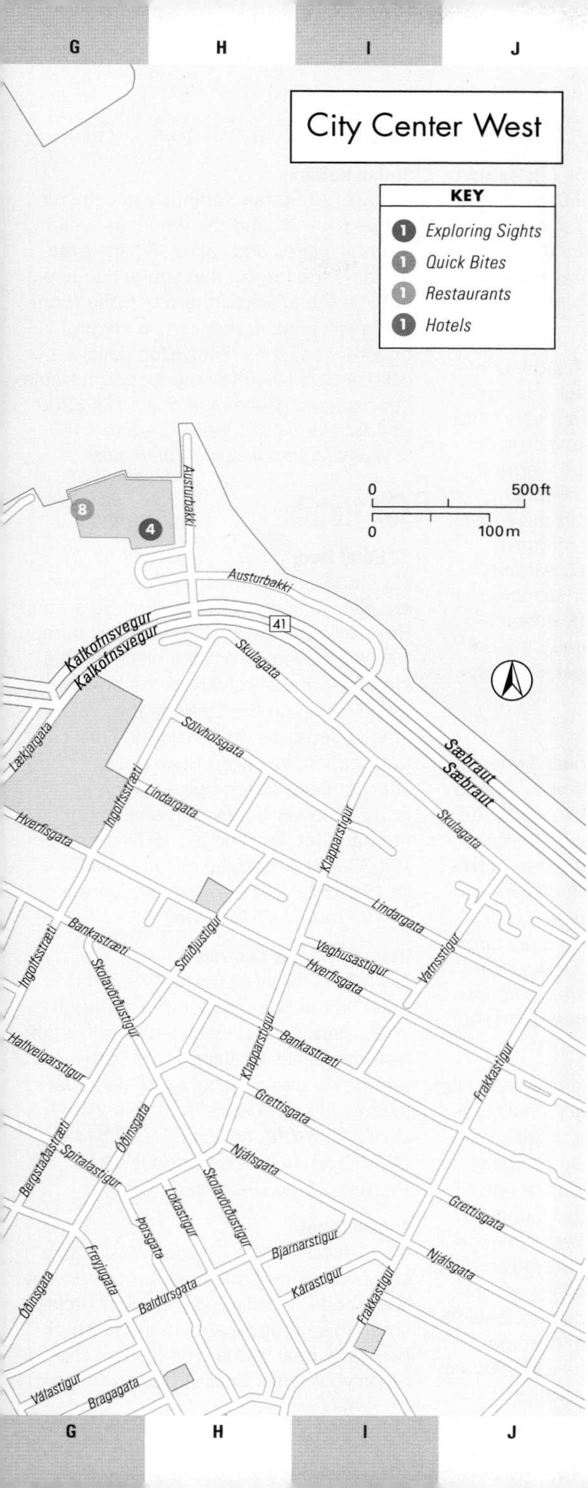

City Center West

KEY

1 Exploring Sights
1 Quick Bites
1 Restaurants
1 Hotels

0 _____ 500 ft
0 _____ 100 m

41

Sights ▼

1 Alþingishús............................E6
2 Aðalstræti 10.......................D5
3 Dómkirkjan..........................E6
4 Harpa Concert Hall and
  Conference Center................H4
5 Icelandic Printmakers
  Association..........................E4
6 i8 Gallery............................D4
7 Lækjartorg...........................F5
8 Listasafn—the Reykjavík
  Art Museum.........................E4
9 Ráðhús...............................D6
10 Reykjavík 871±2:
   The Settlement Exhibition........D6
11 Reykjavík Museum of
   Photography.......................D4
12 Tjörnin Pond.......................D8
13 Tollhúsið............................E5
14 Volcano House.....................D4

Restaurants ▼

1 Apotek Restaurant.................E5
2 Bæjarins Beztu.....................F5
3 Bergsson Mathús...................E6
4 Grillmarket..........................F6
5 Habibi Kebab.......................F5
6 Hornið...............................F5
7 Hressó...............................F6
8 Kolabrautin.........................G3
9 Le Kock.............................D4
10 Lobster Hut.........................F5
11 Matarkjallarinn.....................D5
12 Messinn..............................F6
13 Restaurant Reykjavík..............E5
14 Sæta Svínið Gastropub............E5
15 Tapas Barinn........................D5

Quick Bites ▼

1 Stofan Kaffihús.....................D4

Hotels ▼

1 Hótel Borg...........................E6
2 Hótel Reykjavík Centrum..........D5
3 Kvosin Hotel........................E6
4 Radisson Blu 1919 Hotel..........E5

for families; all rooms have kitchen facilities. **Cons:** thin walls; basic amenities; service can be less than stellar. [$] *Rooms from: ISK 45851* ✉ *Kirkjutorg, Miðbær* ☎ *354/415–2400* 🌐 *www.kvosinhotel.is* 🛏 *24 rooms* 🍴 *No meals.*

Radisson BLU 1919 Hotel

$$$ | **HOTEL** | Downtown in one of Reykjavík's oldest and most famous buildings, this hotel opened its doors in the summer of 2005. **Pros:** smart and modern atmosphere; good service; great location. **Cons:** slightly sterile atmosphere; excess street noise at night; some guests report less-than-clean rooms. [$] *Rooms from: ISK 34615* ✉ *Pósthússtræti 2, Miðbær* ☎ *354/599–1000* 🌐 *www.radissonblu.com* 🛏 *88 rooms* 🍴 *No meals.*

Nightlife

The Dubliner

BARS/PUBS | As one of the few bars in Reykjavík with more TVs than you can count on one hand, the Dubliner is often busiest during televised matches and games. For a pleasant surprise, ask the bartender to make you something special. ✉ *Hafnarstræti 1–3, Miðbær* ☎ *354/527–3232* 🌐 *www.dubliner.business.site.*

Icelandic Craft Bar

BARS/PUBS | You'll find both local and imported beers at the Icelandic Craft Bar. The bartenders are friendly, the beers are plentiful, and the food is great too. You can't go wrong stopping here to try some local brews. ✉ *Lækjargata 6a, Miðbær* ☎ *354/691–3350* 🌐 *www.icelandiccraftbar.com.*

★ **Klaustur Bar**

WINE BARS—NIGHTLIFE | At this elegant wine bar there are always crowds of people lounging on sumptuous upholstery, bathed in flattering lamplight. Located close to Alþingishús (Parliament House), not only is it the best place to mingle with the country's decision makers, it's also a place where you can sample a good deal of quality wine at reasonable prices (one serving amounts to a quarter bottle). ✉ *Kirkjutorg 4, Miðbær* ☎ *354/577–4421* 🌐 *www.klaustur.bar.*

Micro Bar

BREWPUBS/BEER GARDENS | The best time to visit Micro Bar is between the hours of 3 and 7 pm, when the bar has two beers on special for happy hour. You'll find a solid selection of Icelandic beers and an inviting atmosphere that's perfect for making new local friends. ✉ *Vesturgata 2, Miðbær* ☎ *354/865–8389.*

Pablo Discobar

DANCE CLUBS | Technically a nightclub, Pablo Discobar also serves food and some notable cocktails. Since the bar is open until 5 am on Friday and Saturday, you'll often find people making this their last stop after a night on the town. There is a bit of a dress code on weekends (think stylish over formal). You can also catch some great drag shows here, if you're lucky. ✉ *Veltusund 1, Miðbær* ☎ *354/552–7333* 🌐 *www.pablodiscobar.is.*

Skúli Craft Bar

BARS/PUBS | You can't go wrong with any of the 14 craft beers on tap here. This bar is certainly a bit more refined than other beer-focused watering holes in Reykjavík, and prices reflect that. If you're on a budget, opt for smaller pours. ✉ *Aðalstræti 9, Miðbær* ☎ *354/519–6455* 🌐 *www.facebook.com/skulicraft.*

Performing Arts

MUSIC

Íslenska Óperan

MUSIC | **FAMILY** | The Icelandic Opera, a resident company, performs during the winter at its home in the Harpa Concert Hall. ✉ *Harpa, Austurbakka 2, Miðbær* ☎ *354/528–5050* 🌐 *www.opera.is.*

Sinfóníuhljómsveit Íslands

MUSIC | **FAMILY** | The Iceland Symphony Orchestra has bloomed beautifully, winning fine reviews for its tour appearances

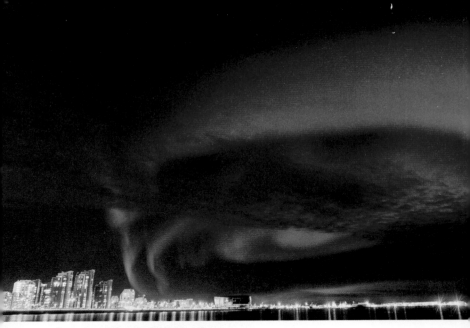

Aurora borealis over the Reykjavík skyline.

at Carnegie Hall and the Kennedy Center. Regular performances are held throughout the year at the eye-catching Harpa Concert Hall. ✉ *Harpa, Austurbakki 2, Miðbær* ☎ *354/545–2500* ⊕ *www. sinfonia.is.*

THEATER

Light Nights

THEATER | FAMILY | You can go to Light Nights to watch traditional folk performances (in English) based on Icelandic sagas and folktales; it takes place in July and August, and has been running for over 40 years. Tickets are sold at the door, starting one hour before the show, but reserving a ticket is recommended. ✉ *Baldursgata 37, Miðbær* ⊕ *www.light-nights.com* 🎟 *ISK 3,000.*

SHOPPING

★ Akkurat

CLOTHING | Since opening in May 2017, Akkurat has been stocking curated picks from the best local designers, as well as some Nordic and international names. There's a well-curated selection of clothes as well as home goods (think candles, art magazines, pillows, and the like). Search the racks for something from Döðlur, a local studio with a great handle on streetwear. ✉ *Aðalstræti 2, Miðbær* ☎ *354/895–4452* ⊕ *www. akkurat.is.*

★ Fischer

PERFUME/COSMETICS | Owned by Jónsi, vocalist for the Icelandic post-rock band Sigur Rós, this might be the most unique shopping experience in Reykjavík. Draped in a dark color palette, Fischer is a whole mood from the moment you walk through its doors from the alley. The experience begins with a taste of mint, which changes in your mouth as you sample the various fragrance placed in front of you. Every moment in Fischer is a kind of lesson, from the scents of the room sprays, candles, and perfumes to the story behind the few jewelry pieces. Take a moment to climb the ladder in the corner, as well—there's a special peephole at the top with a delightful little visual waiting to be seen. ✉ *Fischersund 3, Miðbær* ⊕ *www.fischersund.com.*

Old Harbor and Vesturbær

With its busy slipway and throng of multicolor boats, the **Reykjavík Old Harbor** is an important quarter of the City Center and a vibrant hub of industrial activity. Over the past few years, the area has also become a hotbed of cultural and culinary activity. It's home to the city's landmark building, the Harpa Concert Hall and Conference Center, which houses both the Iceland Symphony Orchestra and the Icelandic Opera. Old Harbor is where you'll find many of City Center's restaurants, cafés, and small businesses, offering everything from whale-watching tours to Segway rides—you just might discover the city's best lobster soup and crab cakes here, too. The cultural activity of the Old Harbor has thoroughly spilled over into the neighboring **Grandi Harbor** area, where you can now explore a new generation of trendy shops, cafés, and attractions, as well as some prime views of the bay.

Sights

★ Guido van Helten Murals

PUBLIC ART | The most impressive murals to be found in Reykjavík are the work of Australia-born artist Guido van Helten. He carried out a series of commissions in Iceland between 2013 and 2014, and his work can be found on a number of buildings around Iceland. Guido's most noted, however, are those painted on the walls of an old theater building in the hip Grandi Harbor area of the city, featuring characters from a 1961 staging of Sartre's *No Exit.*Guido frequently uses old photographs to guide his work: Those used for this epic mural were sourced from the Reykjavík Museum of Photography. ✉ *Seljavegur 2, Vesturbær* 🌐 *www.guidovanhelten.com.*

★ Omnom Chocolate Factory

SPECIAL-INTEREST | You can't walk into a store in Reykjavík without spotting the colorful and artfully designed packaging of an Omnom bar. The chocolate factory is located here in town and offers hour-long tours every weekday at 2 pm (make sure to book in advance). ✉ *Hólmaslóð 4, Vesturbær* ☎ *354/519–5959* 🌐 *www.omnomchocolate.com* 🎫 *ISK 3000.*

★ Saga Museum

MUSEUM | **FAMILY** | In addition to exhibits that explore important moments throughout Iceland's history, this museum also lets you try on clothing from Viking times. The wax models illustrating events of the Sagas are oddly endearing. ✉ *Grandagarður 2, Vesturbær* ☎ *354/511–1517* 🌐 *www.sagamuseum.is* 🎫 *ISK 2200.*

★ Stúdíó Ólafur Elíasson

ART GALLERIES—ARTS | Step into this world-renowned designer's studio in a secluded part of Reykjavík near the Old Harbor. Located inside the Marshall House, Stúdíó Ólafur Elíasson offers a focused look at Elíasson's portfolio of work. ✉ *Marshall House, Grandagarður 20, Vesturbær* ☎ *354/551–3666* 🌐 *www.i8.is.*

Restaurants

★ Bergsson RE

$ | **SEAFOOD** | The family who run Bergsson Mathús in the older part of Reykjavík also helm Bergsson RE. The vibe is relatively similar, but the focus here is seafood, which makes sense given its harborside location. **Known for:** fresh seafood; vegan and vegetarian options; great views of the water. [$] *Average main: ISK 2400* ✉ *Grandagarður 16, Vesturbær* ☎ *354/571–0822* 🌐 *www.bergsson.net* 🕑 *Closed weekends.*

★ Flatey Pizza

$ | **PIZZA** | **FAMILY** | Flatey Pizza serves up Neapolitan-style pies with slow-rising sourdough made on site. Most of the

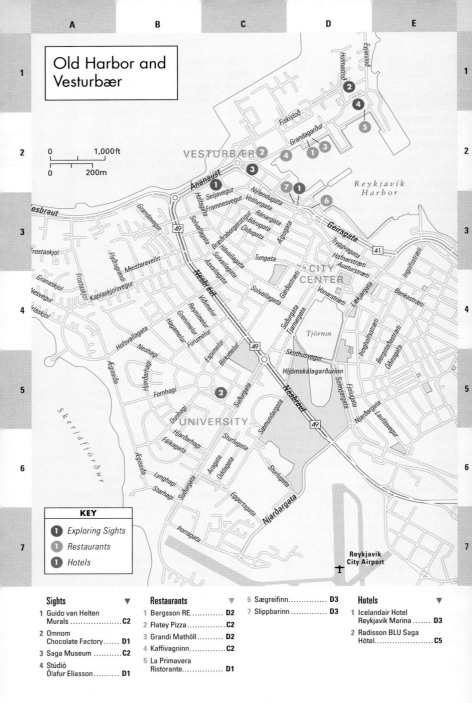

Old Harbor and Vesturbær

Reykjavík Harbor

VESTURBÆR

Ánanaust

CITY CENTER

Tjörnin

Skerjafjörður

UNIVERSITY

Reykjavik City Airport

0   1,000 ft
0   200m

KEY

1 Exploring Sights

1 Restaurants

1 Hotels

menu stays relatively traditional when it comes to toppings, but the Pizza of the Week tends to be a bit more creative. **Known for:** unusual toppings (like dates); home-fermented pizza dough; flavorful tomato sauce. [$] *Average main: ISK 2450* ✉ *Grandagarður 11, Vesturbær* ☎ *354/588–2666* ⊕ *www.flateypizza.is.*

★ Grandi Mathöll

$ | **FAST FOOD** | This beautifully designed food hall may not be that big, housing just nine food stations, but it brings together some of the most exciting spots to eat—including Fjárhúsið, Fusion Fish & Chips, Kore, Lax, the Gastro Truck, and a handful of rotating pop-up trucks. **Known for:** variety of options; design-forward space; some of Reykjavík's best vendors in one space. [$] *Average main: ISK 1400* ✉ *Grandagarður 16, Vesturbær* ☎ *354/787–6200* ⊕ *www.grandimatholl. is.*

★ Kaffivagninn

$ | **SCANDINAVIAN** | Way back before the Grandi area was cool, this value restaurant with exceptional harbor views served up good, old-fashioned hearty Icelandic food for a league of local fishermen. Although it's still mainly populated by marine-industry natives, there's an increasing number of tourists venturing through its humble doors, who come to enjoy the quality fish balls and other tasty dishes—recently made famous by Ainsley Harriott, who featured the restaurant on his latest TV travel-and-cooking series. **Known for:** fresh seafood stew; vegetarian friendly options; standout fish and chips. [$] *Average main: ISK 1890* ✉ *Grandagarði 10, Vesturbær* ☎ *354/551–5932* ⊕ *www. kaffivagninn.is* ▭ *No credit cards.*

★ La Primavera Ristorante

$$$ | **EUROPEAN** | Nestled in the first floor of the art-centric Marshall House, La Primavera's impressive interiors give you a taste of what's to come on the upper floors. If you never thought you'd find Italian dishes in Iceland to rival those

you'd find in Italy, think again. **Known for:** friendly service; impressive interior design; wine menu. [$] *Average main: ISK 4990* ✉ *Grandagarður 20, Vesturbær* ☎ *354/519–7766* ⊕ *www.laprimavera.is* ⊗ *No dinner Mon.*

★ Sægreifinn

$ | **SEAFOOD** | The old fish barrels used as seating in this humble harborside fishing shack are kept warm by an increasing number of tourists and the odd celebrity. The trademark lobster soup, previously featured on *Ainsley Harriott's Street Food,* is just as good as its well-traveled reputation. **Known for:** unforgettable lobster soup; the aptly named Moby Dick on a Stick; fresh seafood right on the harbor. [$] *Average main: ISK 1100* ✉ *Geirsgata 8, Vesturbær* ☎ *354/553–1500* ⊕ *www. saegreifinn.is.*

★ Slippbarinn

$$ | **BISTRO** | A port in all weather (especially for local professionals and tourists) this hotel bistro-bar—which also hosts the Reykjavík Bar Summit—has played a key role in reviving the heart of the Old Harbor. It's especially popular on weekends, when it pumps out a contagious flow of good vibes to go with its filling brunch, legendary cocktails, and highly addictive licorice-flavored popcorn. **Known for:** Omnom chocolate cake; addictive licorice popcorn; inventive cocktails. [$] *Average main: ISK 3490* ✉ *Geirsgata 8, Vesturbær* ☎ *354/553–1500* ⊕ *www. slippbarinn.is.*

🛏 Hotels

Icelandair Hotel Reykjavík Marina

$$$$ | **HOTEL** | Attention to service, detail, and atmosphere define this harborside hotel, which—thanks to its legendary cocktail bar and bistro—also serves as a popular dining and nightlife hot spot for locals. **Pros:** great conference facilities with a 26-seat cinema and presentation space; catering service available;

great harbor views from even-numbered rooms. **Cons:** excess noise from neighboring bars; rooms are on the small side; inconsistent room temperatures. ⓢ *Rooms from: ISK 46000* ✉ *Myrargata 2, Vesturbær* ☎ *354/560–8000* ⊕ *www. icelandairhotels.com* ⤴ *138 rooms* ❚◯❙ *No meals* ⊟ *No credit cards.*

Radisson BLU Saga Hótel

$$ | **HOTEL** | Just off the university campus, and close to the Þjóðminjasafn (National Museum), this hotel is a 15-minute walk from the city center. **Pros:** good service; clean and quiet rooms; good on-site facilities. **Cons:** 15-minute walk from center; breakfast not included in room rate; dated room decor. ⓢ *Rooms from: ISK 24689* ✉ *Hagatorg, Vesturbær* ☎ *354/525–9900* ⊕ *www. radissonblu.com/en/sagahotel-reykjavik* ⤴ *236 rooms* ❚◯❙ *No meals.*

🛍 Shopping

★ Steinunn

CLOTHING | Housed in an old fishnet repair shop, Steinunn is the studio of Icelandic fashion designer Steinunn Sigurðardóttir. She creates wearable art of various knits, which you can buy in this location. ✉ *Grandagarður 17, Vesturbær* ☎ *354/588–6649* ⊕ *www.steinunn.com* ⊗ *Closed Sun.*

🏃 Activities

Vesturbæjarlaug

SWIMMING | **FAMILY** | Vesturbæjarlaug is one of the most popular swimming pools in the city. It has outdoor geothermal swimming pools, a steam room, sauna, and hot tubs. There is also a pool for kids. ✉ *Hofsvallagata 107, Vesturbær* ☎ *354/411–5150* ⊕ *reykjavik.is/stadir/ vesturbaejarlaug.*

Greater Reykjavik

👁 Sights

★ Imagine Peace Tower

ARTS VENUE | **FAMILY** | The Imagine Peace Tower is a powerful light installation on Viðey Island by Yoko Ono. Dedicated to the vision of world peace she passionately shared with her late husband, John Lennon, the artwork features a large stone wishing well with the words "imagine peace" etched into its white, shiny surface in countless languages. Inside the well are 15 powerful beams that merge into a magnificent force of light when switched on. Yoko visits every year on John's birthday (October 9) to lead the lighting ceremony, where about 2,000 people gather to watch and sing along to Lennon's "Imagine." The impressive tower of light illuminates the skyline until the date of John Lennon's death on December 8th. Yoko provides a free ferry service for those who wish to attend the annual lighting ceremony. The ferry departs from Skarfabakki pier, less than a 10-minute drive from the city center. ✉ *Viðey Island, Reykjavík* ☎ *354/533–5055* ⊕ *www.imaginepeacetower.com.*

★ Laugardalur Park

NATIONAL/STATE PARK | Laugardalur Park is actually several parks in one large area. Aside from one of the best swimming pools in the city, the recreational expanse has picnic and barbecue areas. There's also a family park and a botanic garden with an extensive outdoor collection of native and exotic plants. ✉ *Laugardalur, Laugardalur* ⊹ *Take Bus S2, 5, 14, or 15 east* ☎ *354/411–8650* ⊕ *www.grasagardur.is* ⤳ *Free.*

🍽 Restaurants

★ Flóran Garden Bistro

$$ | **SCANDINAVIAN** | This bistro has a truly unique location: inside the botanic gardens of Reykjavík. Of course, much

of what you'll find on the menu is grown in the gardens, and guests can learn all about the sustainable practices of the kitchen. **Known for:** organic ingredients; truly unique atmosphere; beautiful dish presentation. $ *Average main: ISK 3400* ✉ *Grasagarðinum Laugarda, Laugardalur* ☎ *354/553–8872* ⊕ *www.floran.is.*

🛏 Hotels

★ Oddsson Hotel

$$ | HOTEL | The interior of this hotel, which moved from the harbor to a more central location in 2019, would look right at home in a Wes Anderson movie; there's a wide range of room styles to fit groups of different sizes—family suites even include private kitchenettes. **Pros:** beautiful interiors; affordable room options; breakfast included in room rate. **Cons:** can get noisy; self check-in; rooms tend to get stuffy. $ *Rooms from: ISK 21500* ✉ *Grensásvegur 16a, Háaleiti* ☎ *354/419–0200* ⊕ *www.oddsson.is* ⇆ *77 rooms* ⦿ *Free Breakfast.*

🛍 Shopping

★ Heilsuhúsið

SPECIALTY STORES | This health food store carries everything from natural remedies to organic snacks and skincare. One of the hidden gems: tea made with Icelandic moss. ✉ *Lágmúli 9, Háaleiti* ☎ *354/578–0300* ⊕ *www.heilsuhusid.is.*

🏃 Activities

Laxnes Horse Farm

HORSEBACK RIDING | FAMILY | Two-hour horseback-riding tours (11,900 ISK) include guides and transportation to and from Reykjavík. There are also combo tours that vary from spending a day learning about life at the Laxnes farm to riding around the Golden Circle. ✉ *271 Mosfellsdalur, Mosfellsbær* ☎ *354/566–6179* ⊕ *www.laxnes.is.*

Ísafjörður

544 km (338 miles) from Reykjavík

You'll find Ísafjörður nestled in a fjord—as its name suggests—in the northwest section of the Westfjords, south of and across the bay from the Hornstrandir Nature Reserve. From the moment you drive into town, you'll be wowed by the area's dramatic landscapes. The city's location alone, surrounded by the fjord, gives your time here a fairytale vibe. Ísafjörður is a town with a lot of history, which is palpable as you walk through the city's oldest section, with its wooden homes. This town has been and still is a fishing community, and you can learn all about its history at the Westfjords Heritage Museum, which houses a collection of old fishing boats and gear.

GETTING HERE AND AROUND

During the summer months, there are three Westfjords Adventures buses every week between Patreksfjörður and Ísafjörður. There are also two daily flights from Reykjavík into Ísafjörður on Air Iceland Connect. Once you're in town, you'll find it's quite walkable, but it's best to rent a car to take in the nearby natural sights.

TOURS

There are many tour companies based in Ísafjörður offering ATV, bus, and horseback-riding tours of the region.

VISITOR INFORMATION

There is one main information center, located inside of the Edinborg Cultural Center. Here you can find information on local tours and experiences, hiking trails, bus schedules, and events around town.

👁 Sights

★ Arctic Fox Center

NATURE PRESERVE | FAMILY | Iceland isn't known for its abundance of wildlife, but it is home to the adorable and elusive arctic fox. You can find these animals in the

Ísafjörður is a fishing town nestled into a fjord.

wild—and if you do, watch from afar and let them be—but you're sure to see them at the Arctic Fox Center in Súðavík, a quick drive from Ísafjörður. At this wildlife refuge and research center, guests are invited to learn all about these curious little mammals. The arctic fox population has been dwindling for years, and the center also puts forth efforts to maintain it. ✉ Eyrardalur, 420 Súðavík, Ísafjörður ☎ 354/456-4922 ⊕ www.arcticfoxcentre. com ⓣ ISK 1200 ⊙ Oct.-Apr. by appointment only.

★ Aurora Arktika

BOAT TOURS | FAMILY | Although custom itineraries are available, a handful of tours are designed to showcase the best of what the Westfjords have to offer. Experiences focus on multiday journeys to different parts of the Westfjords; all of the sailboat tours depart from the harbor in Ísafjörður. The six-day Iceland Sailboat Skiing tour will show you some of the best skiing the country has to offer by way of sailboat (available in March and May). The sailboat will be your home base for Running Fjord to Fjord, which features guided runs along some of the most stunning landscapes in the Westfjords. ✉ Ísafjörður harbor, Ísafjörður ☎ 354/899-3817 ⊕ www.aurora-arktika. com.

★ Hornstrandir Nature Reserve

NATURE PRESERVE | Ísafjörður is the place to catch a ferry to the Hornstrandir Nature Reserve. Two companies offer regular service to the area (in summer): Borea and Sjóferðir. Tickets can be pricey, but it's worth the investment. There is a wide range of hiking trails, and it's common to see arctic foxes, as this region boasts one of the largest communities of them in the country. Getting here in winter is nearly impossible due to severe weather. ✉ Aðalstræti 10, Ísafjörður ☎ 354/591-2000.

🍴 Restaurants

★ Gamla Bakaríið

$ | BAKERY | Look no further than Gamla Bakaríið to find out where locals get their coffee and baked goods. You'll be completely overwhelmed by choice when it comes to the latter, but you really can't go wrong. **Known for:** amazing selection of baked goods; chocolate-covered cinnamon rolls; reasonably priced sandwiches. [$] *Average main: ISK 999* ✉ *Aðalstræti, Ísafjörður* ☎ *354/456-3226* ⏲ *Closed Sun.*

★ **Tjöruhúsið**

$$$$ | SEAFOOD | FAMILY | You never know what the menu will bring at the family-owned Tjöruhúsið, and for good reason: it all depends on what the local fishermen catch. You have your pick of two dinner seatings, at 7 and 9 (so don't be late) and three menu options—soup only, fish only, or fish and soup. **Known for:** catch of the day; delicious soups; dinner seatings only at 7 and 9. [$] *Average main: ISK 6817* ✉ *Nedsti kaupstadur, Ísafjörður* ☎ *354/456–4419* 🌐 *www.tjoruhusid.is.*

Flateyri

21 km (13 miles) from Ísafjörður

Flateyri was in its prime in the 19th century, when it was a trading post and—somewhat unfortunately—a hub for whaling and shark hunting. Today, it's a popular spot for those looking to try their hand at sea angling. Plan on spending an afternoon here, as there are plenty of museums and historic spots, plus a beach to explore. (Fun fact: The area hosts what just may be the northernmost sandcastle-building competition in the world.) Flateyri has had its fair share of avalanches, and these days it's equipped with special protection, which you can see when you visit. The village bookshop has been transformed into a museum that goes over this tragic history.

GETTING HERE AND AROUND

Driving to Flateyri is certainly the easiest way to get there, but there are local buses that connect Þingeyri, Flateyri, and Ísafjörður. This bus route runs three to four times daily on weekdays (depending on weather). A ticket will cost you ISK 350. The nearest airport is in Ísafjörður, but many travelers rent a car and drive from Keflavík International Airport.

🍴 Restaurants

★ **Vagninn**

$$$ | SEAFOOD | The first thing to know about this small-town, middle-of-nowhere restaurant is that you can get an amazing lamb burger. The second thing to know is that the best time to go is on weekends, when there's live music playing late into the night. **Known for:** live music on weekends; delicious lamb burger; great view of the surrounding bay. [$] *Average main: ISK 3800* ✉ *Hafnarstræti 19, Flateyri* ☎ *354/456–7751.*

🛏 Hotels

Korpudalur

$ | HOTEL | The best part about Korpudalur may be how far removed you are from civilization and how close you are to Iceland's biggest attraction: nature. **Pros:** beautiful remote setting; incredibly quiet; private rooms for rent. **Cons:** few rooms; shared bathrooms; basic amenities. [$] *Rooms from: ISK 14000* ✉ *Kirkjubol Korpudal, Flateyri* ☎ *354/456-7808* 🌐 *www.hostel.is* ⏲ *Closed Sept. 16–May 19* 🛏 *6 rooms* 🍽 *No meals.*

🛍 Shopping

★ **The Old Bookstore**

BOOKS/STATIONERY | FAMILY | This is exactly what it sounds like: a historic spot to buy a new read. The Old Bookstore has been owned by the same family since 1914, and everything you find inside—aside from the books—has remained relatively unchanged since then. Beyond the books, however, you'll also find an exhibit that tells the history of the town. ✉ *Hafnarstraeti 3, Flateyri* ☎ *354/840-0600* 🌐 *www.flateyribookstore.com.*

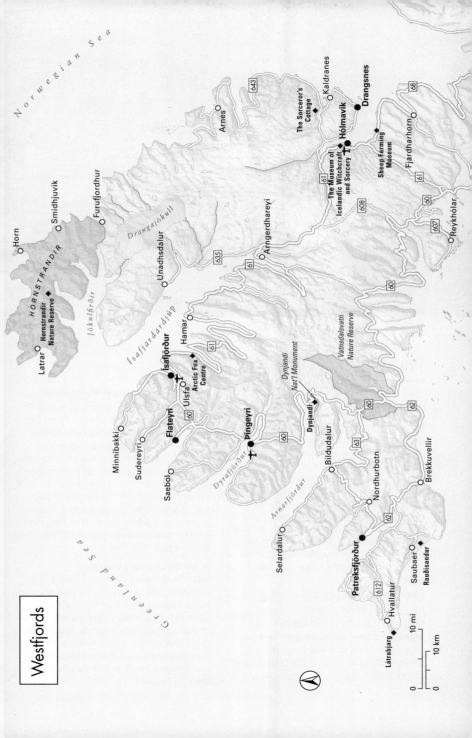

Westfjords

Norwegian Sea

Greenland Sea

Horn ○
Smidhjuvik ○
Latrar ○ **HORNSTRANDIR**
Hornstrandir Nature Reserve ◆
Jökulfirðir
Furufjorhur ○
Smidhjuvik
Drangajökull
Unadhsdalur ○

Arnes ○

643

The Sorceror's Cottage ◆
Kaldranes ◆
Drangsnes ●
68
Hólmavik ●
The Museum of Icelandic Witchcraft and Sorcery ◆
Sheep Farming Museum ◆
Fjardharhorn ○
61
60
607
Reykhólar ○

643
61
Arngerdhareyi ○
608
60

Ísafjardardjúp
Hamar ○
Ísafjörður ●
Arctic Fox Centre ◆
Ulsfa ○
61
635
61

Minnibakki ○
Sudereyri ○
Saebol ○
Flateyri ●
60
Þingeyri ●
Dýrafjörður
60

Vatnsdalsvatn Nature Reserve
Dynjandi
Dynjandi Nat'l Monument ◆
60
62

Bildudalur ○
Nordhurbotn ○
63
Brekkuvellir ○
Arnarfjörður

Selardalur ○
Patreksfjörður ●
62
Saubaer ◆
Raudisandur ◆

612
Hvallatur ○
Látrabjarg ○

10 mi
10 km
0

The village of Flateyri was a trading post in the 19th century.

Þingeyri

39km (24 miles) from Flateyri

Located on the stunning Dýrafjörður, Þingeyri is a small village and the home of the oldest functioning blacksmith workshop (now a museum) in the country. Small, random facts like this will keep you entertained on your visit to Þingeyri, since there isn't much in the way of nightlife, shopping, or dining. That's not necessarily a bad thing, however: here in Þingeyri, you get to experience a small fishing community as it's meant to be experienced—without distraction. This area is often referred to as "the Alps of the Westfjords."

GETTING HERE AND AROUND

It's possible to drive from Reykjavík to Þingeyri. The total trip is 408 km (253 miles), and the road is paved. There are local buses that connect Þingeyri and Flateyri *(Bus contacts at the beginning of this chapter).*

⊙ Sights

★ Dynjandi

BODY OF WATER | FAMILY | Dynjandi is one of the most famous waterfalls in the Westfjords, and it's located a 45-minute drive from Þingeyri. Some refer to this waterfall as "the bridal veil," given its stairwell formation. It actually comprises seven waterfalls in total, all feeding one another in the most graceful way. Expect a crowd if you go in the middle of the day; this waterfall draws a lot of visitors to the area. ⊠ *Þingeyri* ✛ *Take the gravel road toward the waterfall off of Vestfjarðavegur; then follow signs.*

★ Old Blacksmith's Workshop

MUSEUM | FAMILY | Opened in 1913, this blacksmith shop was run by Guðmundur J. Sigurðsson after learning the trade in Denmark. This living museum still has all of the old machines, and you can learn about blacksmithing as it was done more than 100 years ago. This is the perfect activity for a family with kids of various ages. ⊠ *Þingeyri.*

🍴 Restaurants

★ Simbahöllin
$$ | **CAFÉ** | Built in 1915, this former general store is now a restaurant loved by locals and visitors alike. Go for Belgian waffles in the morning or afternoon, and visit again at night for the local catch of the day and lamb tagine. **Known for:** Belgian waffles; soup of the day; service with a smile. [$] *Average main: ISK 1600* ✉ *Fjarðargata 5, Þingeyri* ☎ *354/899–6659* 🌐 *www.simbahollin.is.*

Patreksfjörður

130 km (81 miles) from Þingeyri

In the 20th century, Patreksfjörður was a major Icelandic fishing center, and it continues to play a large part in commercial fishing today. One of the larger cities you'll encounter in the Westfjords, it has plenty of lodging and dining options, as well as a community pool where you can mingle with the locals. Don't miss the biggest draw of this town: its proximity to Látrabjarg, a massive sea bird colony on the westernmost tip of the Westfjords.

GETTING HERE AND AROUND

There are six flights a week from Bíldudalur. You can also reach this city by bus, but it will be a journey: hop on Strætó in Reykjavík and ride it to Stykkishólmur, then take the ferry from Baldur to Brjánslækur, and finally a bus to Patreksfjörður. As you can imagine, it's easier to drive yourself. Keep in mind that many tourist-oriented businesses shut down in winter on account of the weather.

TOURS

There are a number of sightseeing tours that depart from Patreksfjörður. Westfjords Adventures and Umfar are two tour operators with a good number of offerings in the region.

VISITOR INFORMATION

For information about everything you can see in Patreksfjörður and beyond, head to the Patreksfjörður Tourist Information Center, where you can ask for recommendations for hiking trails, tours, and other experiences.

👁 Sights

★ Látrabjarg
NATURE PRESERVE | **FAMILY** | The cliffs at Látrabjarg are home to millions of birds—the main reason people from around the world flock to this region—and to answer your burning question: yes, you can see adorable puffins here. You'll also catch sight of razorbills, fulmars, and guillemot in the clouds of birds that surround this area; in fact, no fewer than 10 sea bird species call these cliffs home. Látrabjarg is actually just one of four sections: the Keflavíkurbjarg, Bæjarbjarg, Breiðavíkurbjarg and Látrabjarg cliffs. All have slightly different viewpoints with one thing in common: a whole lot of birds. There's also a scenic lighthouse on-site, which happens to be the westernmost lighthouse in Europe. To get here, drive along Route 612 until you can't anymore; this is the westernmost point of the Westfjords. ✉ *Patreksfjörður.*

🍴 Restaurants

★ Heimsendi
$$$ | **SEAFOOD** | This pub-style restaurant serves up some serious meals to some serious crowds—past guests have gone in groups of 10 to 12 and left completely satisfied with the service. As with many other restaurants in Iceland, a lot of thought and detail goes into the presentation, and luckily the quality of the dishes lives up to its appearance. **Known for:** good for groups; fish stew; vegetarian options. [$] *Average main: ISK 3800* ✉ *Eyrargata 5, Patreksfjörður* ☎ *354/456-5150* 🌐 *www.heimsendi.com.*

★ Stúkuhúsið

$$ | SEAFOOD | FAMILY | If you want to do yourself a favor, grab an outdoor table at Stúkuhúsið (assuming the weather is cooperating), order dinner, take in the views, and finish up with a slice of rhubarb pie. The food here is fresh and delicious, the service is friendly, and the desserts are the perfect ending to your day. **Known for:** catch of the day; friendly service; vegetarian options. $ *Average main: ISK 2400* ⊠ *Aðalstræti 50, Patreksfjörður* ☎ *354/456-1404* ⊕ *www. stukuhusid.is.*

🛏 Hotels

★ Radagerdi Guesthouse

$$ | B&B/INN | This is the very picture of a "Nordic guesthouse on the coast"—the design is minimalist and on point, breakfast is included, and there's a terrace area for taking in the scenery. **Pros:** free breakfast; beautiful terrace area; modern design. **Cons:** shared bathrooms in some rooms; small rooms; some guests report loud plumbing. $ *Rooms from: ISK 24600* ⊠ *Aðalstræti, Patreksfjörður* ☎ *354/456-1560* ⊕ *www.radagerdi.net* ⮐ *11 rooms* ⦿| *Free Breakfast.*

🏖 Beaches

★ Rauðasandur Beach

BEACH—SIGHT | FAMILY | Although black-sand beaches may get the most attention in Iceland, the red sand of Rauðasandur Beach is something that needs to be seen in person. What makes it that golden red color? Pulverized scallop shells. Depending on the day, the beach can appear more yellow, red, or black. To get here from Patreksfjörður, take Route 62 and follow the signs for Route 614, then take Route 612. Note that the road leading to this beach is not unpaved and often quite rough—it's a windy road, so take it slow. ⊠ *Patreksfjörður.*

🎭 Performing Arts

★ HÚSIÐ / creative space

ARTS CENTERS | Not only does HÚSIÐ host various music performances and art exhibitions, the creative organization also offers residencies for artists—all of which usually end in an event of some sort. It's a great place to stop and take in some local, as well as global, art. ⊠ *Eyrargata, Patreksfjörður* ☎ *354/695-7620* ⊕ *www. husid-workshop.com.*

🏃 Activities

★ Birkimelur Swimming Pool

HOT SPRINGS | FAMILY | Pools are central to Icelandic communities and the Birkimelur Swimming Pool is no exception. Relax among the locals in this man-made pool, which is heated with geothermal water. There are changing rooms on-site, as well as a sauna. ⊠ *Lauganes við Haga-vaðal, Patreksfjörður* ☎ *354/456–2040* ⊘ *Closed mid-Aug.–May.*

Hólmavík

220 km (137 miles) from Patreksfjörður

Hólmavík is the repository of Iceland's witchcraft and sorcery history, and not just because of its museum. In the 17th century, this shepherding and fishing community was also the country's center of witch-hunting. Today, Hólmavík offers essentials like restaurants, gas stations, a grocery store, and a few hotels.

GETTING HERE AND AROUND

There are two to four buses between Reykjavík and Hólmavík on Strætó routes every week. There is also a bus route to and from Ísafjörður two to three times a week, depending on weather.

Sights

★ The Sorceror's Cottage
MUSEUM | FAMILY | The Sorceror's Cottage is a sight to behold, even if you don't have time to enjoy the museum inside. Just a quick drive from the Museum of Icelandic Witchcraft and Sorcery, this cottage serves as the second part of the main museum. You'll learn all about how people lived in the 17th century and why sorcery became such a huge part of life here. ✉ *Strandavegur* ☎ *354/897–6525* ⊕ *www.galdrasyning.is* 🎟 *ISK 950.*

Restaurants

★ Café Riis
$$$ | SEAFOOD | This restaurant is often packed with locals and travelers, which is just a testament to how great it is. Café Riis serves up a mean fish soup, as well as pizza that some past guests have deemed "the best in Iceland." It's cozy interior feels a lot like a family holiday cabin. **Known for:** seafood soup; delicious pizza options; cozy interior. $ *Average main: ISK 3200* ✉ *Hafnarbraut 39* ☎ *354/451–3567* ⊕ *www.caferiis.is.*

Hotels

Finna Hotel
$ | B&B/INN | One of the very few options for lodging in Hólmavík, the Finna Hotel has basic amenities; if you're not looking for luxury, you'll find it perfectly suitable. **Pros:** breakfast included in room rate; affordable rates; beautiful surroundings. **Cons:** no storage in rooms; thin walls; can be hard to find. $ *Rooms from: ISK 13900* ✉ *Borgarbraut 4* ☎ *354/451–3136* ⊕ *www.finnahotel.is* 🛏 *17 rooms* ⦿ *Free Breakfast.*

Drangsnes

30 km (19 miles) from Hólmavík

Although it may be a simple fishing village without a ton of activities to fill your day, Drangsnes is well known as the access point for Grímsey Island—a fantastic destination for bird-watching, arctic snorkeling, and golfing. There are also plenty of hiking trails through Drangsnes, and the community swimming pool shouldn't be missed.

GETTING HERE AND AROUND
Weather permitting, visitors can drive from Hólmavík to Drangsnes on Route 61, which turns into Route 645. To the north is a winding road that takes you past dramatic views of the coast. From Drangsnes you can take a boat to Grímsey Island.

Sights

★ Kerling the Cliff
NATURE SITE | You have to know the story to truly appreciate this place: Kerling was a troll woman who, along with two other trolls, wanted to turn the Westfjords into an island. As they started digging, they realized they had nowhere to shelter from the sun as it rose. Kerling did not make it out of the sunlight in time, turned to stone, and sits here still in the form of this cliff. The troll women created many little islands behind them, one of which is known today as Grímsey. ✉ *Drangsnes.*

★ The Museum of Icelandic Witchcraft and Sorcery
MUSEUM | If you find the ancient world of Icelandic witchcraft intriguing, this museum is a must-visit. Inside you'll find artifacts with morbid histories, exhibits with terrifying stand-ins, and a pair of necropants with a background so chilling we'll leave you to discover it yourself. ✉ *Höfðagata 8–10* ☎ *354/897–6525* ⊕ *www.galdrasyning.is* 🎟 *ISK 950.*

Drangses Hot Tubs (or hot springs) overlooking the ocean are free to the public.

★ **Sheep Farming Museum**

MUSEUM | **FAMILY** | You only have to drive around the country for a few minutes to understand what an important role sheep play in the Icelandic economy. The Sheep Farming Museum has been a local and visitor favorite since it opened in 2002. If the season is right, after learning all about the industry (specifically the Strandir region), you can meet some of the farm's lambs and help feed them. ☎ *354/451–3324* 🌐 *www.strandir.is.*

Hotels

★ **Malarhorn**

$$ | **B&B/INN** | **FAMILY** | Although there's hardly any lodging in Dragsnes, Malarhorn really hits a home run when it comes to variety, as guests have a choice between three houses: House 1, with 10 double rooms that have private patios and bathrooms; House 2, with four double rooms that share a living room and kitchen; and House 3, with a family-size room, a two-bedroom apartment, four double rooms, and a superior double room with private entrance. **Pros:** cozy rooms; variety of room options; some rooms have patios. **Cons:** only option in the village; some rooms have shared bathrooms; restaurant closed during the wintertime. [$] *Rooms from: ISK 22400* ✉ *Grundargata 17, Drangsnes* ☎ *354/853-6520* 🌐 *www.malarhorn.is* 🛏 *21 rooms across 3 houses* 🍴 *No meals.*

Activities

★ **Drangses Hot Tubs**

HOT SPRINGS | Like most communities in Iceland, Drangses has a local hot spring. There are three different tubs on-site of varying temperatures, and they are fantastic—free to the public and each one with a beautiful view of the ocean. Just be sure to follow cultural protocol and shower before entering the water. You won't find large crowds at these hot pots. ✉ *Drangsensvegur, Drangsnes.*

★ Grímsey Island
GOLF COURSE | **FAMILY** | Take a 10-minute boat ride from the Drangses harbor to Grímsey for some serious bird-watching. You can even see puffins here if you come in the right season (usually the warmer, summer months). There's also a golf course, bike rentals, arctic snorkeling, sea fishing, and more. It's the perfect day trip from Drangses and the main reason why people find themselves in the area.

Akranes

48 km (30 miles) from Reykjavík

The trip between Akranes and Reykjavík is quick. Akranes is the largest community in the western corner of the country, and it's a great place to stock up on necessities. If you plan on camping in West Iceland or up in the Westfjords, take advantage of the grocery stores and outerwear shops you'll find here.

GETTING HERE AND AROUND
Akranes is less than an hour from Reykjavík, making it the perfect location for an afternoon trip out of the capital city. It's best to rent a car and explore on your own, but you can ride the local bus, Strætó, between Reykjavík and Akranes. Once you're there, the town is easily walkable.

Sights

★ Guðlaug Baths
HOT SPRINGS | On Langisandur Beach you'll be greeted by the Guðlaug Baths, a new addition as of December 2018. The manmade springs are located in a natural rock garden and have a stunning view of Reykjavík across the bay. These public hot springs are free to enjoy, but they can get quite crowded on especially sunny days (the pool itself isn't very large). ✉ *Langisandur, Arkanes.*

Beaches

★ Ytri Tunga Beach
BEACH—SIGHT | **FAMILY** | This area next to a farm of the same name is well known for nearby "Seal Beach," where harbor seals and grey seals spend the summer months basking in the near-constant sunlight on rocks just offshore. You're likely to see them in this area year-round, but you're more likely to catch the eye of a friendly seal swimming by in the warmer months. ✉ *Arnarstapi* ✣ *From Guesthouse Hof, drive a few minutes west on Snæfellsnesvegur before taking the first available right turn toward the beach.*

Restaurants

★ Lesbókin Café
$$ | **CAFÉ** | Exactly what you imagine a cozy, small-town coffee shop to be, Lesbókin Café is the perfect place to hole up and dig into your day's itinerary with a latte. If you're lucky, you'll find a special piece of milk-foam art waiting for you. **Known for:** cozy interiors; quality coffee; delicious waffles. [$] *Average main: ISK 1200* ✉ *Kirkjubraut 2, Arkanes* ☎ *354/863–5793.*

Borgarnes

47 miles from Reykjavík

Located right on the bay, Borgarnes is a scenic fishing town on the western coast. The Settlement Center is certainly worth a visit, and the local pool is a popular place for tourists and locals alike, if you're looking for a spot to relax after a long day of exploring. This is a great place to spend the night or grab a bite to eat, given its many restaurant and hotel options—far more than you'll find in other cities in West Iceland.

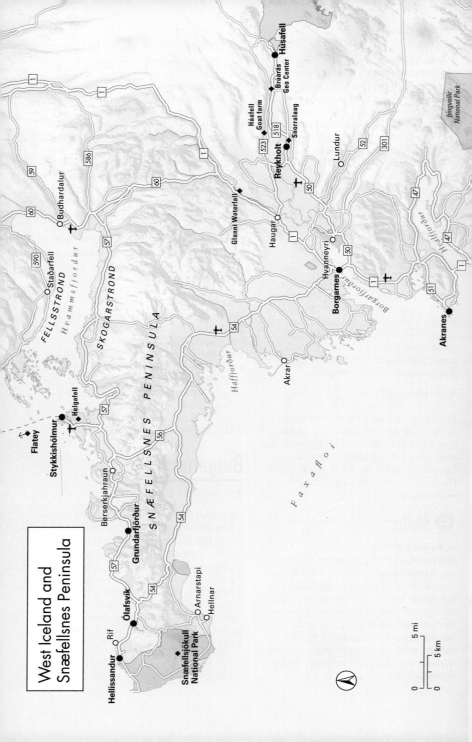

West Iceland and Snæfellsnes Peninsula

Húsafell

Brúarás Geo Center

Háafell Goat farm

518

523   Snorralaug

Reykholt

Lundur

52   301

47

þingvellir National Park

47

Glanni Waterfall

Haugar

50

Hvanneyri

50

Hvalfjörður

Borgarnes

51

Akranes

60   Búðardalur

59

60

586

590   Staðarfell

FELLSSTROND

Hvammsfjörður

SKOGARSTROND

57

Helgafell

Flatey

Stykkishólmur

Berserkjahraun

Grundarfjörður

S N Æ F E L L S N E S   P E N I N S U L A

Haffjörður

54

Akrar

Faxaflói

57

Ólafsvík

Rif

Hellissandur

Arnarstapi

Hellnar

Snæfellsjökull National Park

5 mi

5 km

0

GETTING HERE AND AROUND

If you don't rent a car, you can take the Strætó bus to Borgarnes. Bus 57 (Reykjavík Mjódd–Akranes–Borgarnes–Blönduós–Sauðakrókur–Akureyrir), Bus 58 (Borgarnes–Stykkishólmur), Bus 59 (Borgarnes–Búðardalur–Hólmavík), Bus 81 (Borgarnes–Reykholt), and Bus 82 (Stykkishólmur–Grundarfjörður–Ólafsvík–Hellissandur).

◉ Sights

★ Brúarás Geo Center

NATURE SITE | FAMILY | The Brúarás Geo Center is a strikingly modern building against a backdrop of lava fields and mountain ranges. Inside, you'll find information about the local area, a restaurant, and souvenirs. The sleeper hit here is the dining room windows—a meal with a panoramic view of the countryside should not be missed. ⊠ *Brúarás, Borgarnes* ✛ *Close to Hraunfossar* ☎ *354/435–1270* ⊕ *www.geocenter.is.*

🛏 Hotels

★ Englendingavík

$ | B&B/INN | FAMILY | The loudest noise you'll hear at this beautiful 1890 house is birdsong, and although it hasn't many luxury amenities, there's no substitute for the coziness of staying at this family's home. **Pros:** on-site restaurant; family-run with a very welcoming environment; prime location near Borgarnes. **Cons:** communal living is stressed over privacy; no luxury amenities. 🟰 *Rooms from: ISK 19373* ⊠ *Skúlagata 17, Borgarnes* ☎ *354/896–8926* ➴ *5 rooms* ◎ *No meals.*

🍽 Shopping

★ Ljómalind Local Market

LOCAL SPECIALTIES | FAMILY | Nearly 70 local artisans and farmers sell their goods at the Ljómalind Local Market. A group of women started the market in May 2013, and it has since become a local favorite for grabbing dinner ingredients, as well as a beloved stop for tourists looking for a souvenir. ⊠ *Brúartorg 4, Borgarnes* ☎ *354/437-1400.*

🏃 Activities

★ Bjössaróló Playground

PARK—SPORTS-OUTDOORS | FAMILY | Bjössaróló Playground is a brightly colored oasis for kids and adults alike looking to have a bit of fun. Getting here is an adventure in itself—intentionally so, as designed by the creator of this wonderland. Spend some time playing on the slides, teeter-totters, climbing dome, and swings. Everything in the playground was made from salvaged discarded materials, which somehow makes it all a little more delightful. ⊠ *Skúlagata 23, Borgarnes.*

Reykholt

108 km (67 miles) from Reykjavík

It's impossible to leave Reykholt without a history lesson of sorts. Sure, the city is surrounded by gorgeous sights and natural attractions, but it's also the home of Snorri Sturluson, who was responsible for two of Iceland's most important pieces of writing: the Prose Edda and the Heimskringla. It was in Reykholt that most of his writing was completed. Aside from reading up on our friend Snorri, you can visit glaciers, waterfalls, the strongest hot spring in Europe, and other natural wonders in this area.

GETTING HERE AND AROUND

Reykholt is located off of Route 518, about a 30-minute drive from Borgarnes. There is no direct public bus line between Reykjavík and Reykholt, but you can get to this area via bus from Borgarnes: take Strætó Bus 58 from Reykjavík to Borgarnes, and then hop on Bus 81 to Reykholt. If you rent a car, getting to and from the cities in West Iceland is simple and—more often than not—quick.

VISITOR INFORMATION

Snorrastofa
Part museum and part visitor center, Snorrastofa serves up everything you need to know about Reykholt and its storied history, focusing on the famed writer Snorri Sturluson. ✉ *Hálsasveitavegur, Reykholt* ☎ *354/433–8000* 🌐 *www.snorrastofa.is.*

Sights

★ **Háafell Goat Farm**
FARM/RANCH | FAMILY | The main goal here is to give locals and visitors a peek at the lives of a farmer and farm animals. Háafell mainly cares for Icelandic goats, which are endangered, but they also keep sheep, chickens, horses, dogs, and cats. You can visit the farm on a tour (ISK 1,500) or just browse the shop for products made on site. ✉ *Hvítársíðuvegur, 320 Borgarnes* ☎ *354/845–2331.*

★ **Snorralaug**
HOT SPRINGS | What may well be the oldest hot spring in Iceland was first mentioned in the writings of medieval Icelandic historian and poet Snorri Sturluson, who used to bathe here. The water is often far too hot for a dip, so visit the nearby Snorrastofa instead to learn about Sturluson himself. ✉ *On-site at Snorrastofa.*

Restaurants

★ **Friðheimar**
$$$ | VEGETARIAN | FAMILY | When you eat at Friðheimar, you're in for an experience. The restaurant is located in a tomato greenhouse and every single thing on the menu uses tomatoes in some shape or form. **Known for:** tomato soup; unique atmosphere; green-tomato-and-apple pie. [$] *Average main: ISK 2800* ✉ *Bláskógabyggð* ☎ *354/486–8894* 🌐 *www.fridheimar.is.*

Activities

★ **Krauma Geothermal Baths**
ECOTOURISM | FAMILY | This man-made hot spring gets its geothermal water from Deildartunguhver, the most powerful hot spring in Europe. Here you can re-center in any of six different baths (one cold, five hot), two steambaths, or the relaxation room. There is also a restaurant on-site. ✉ *Deildartunguhver, 320 Reykholt* ☎ *354/555–6066* 🌐 *www.krauma.is/en* 🎟 *ISK 3950.*

★ **Víðgelmir Cave Tour**
ADVENTURE TOURS | Although the rooftop of Víðgelmir, the country's mightiest cave, has collapsed, you can still experience its intriguing rock formations and incredible colors. Operators like Into the Glacier lead tours of the cave. They will pick you up in Húsafell and bring you straight to Víðgelmir—it's a quick 15-minute drive. You can explore the cave on your own, but a group tour is better; guides provide all necessary safety gear and tell you everything you need to know about what you're seeing. 🌐 *www.intotheglacier.is* 🎟 *ISK 6500.*

Húsafell

132 km (82 miles) from Reykjavík

First things first: Húsafell is tiny. But if you're looking to set up camp in a remote village in Iceland, this is the place to do it. Its relatively close proximity to Reykjavík makes it a good place to spend a night under the stars if you've got only a short time in the country. There are a handful of sights to see while you're here as well—including the mighty Húsafell Stone, which has been used to show off feats of strength for generations.

GETTING HERE AND AROUND

Húsafell is easiest to get to by car, but there is a bus to and from Reykjanesbær (Bus 88), if you're looking to take public transportation. Once you're in Húsafell, the town itself is walkable but some sights require a car.

Hotels

★ **Hotel Húsafell**

$$$ | HOTEL | There are few hotel options here, but Hotel Hísafell has everything you need for a solid home base while exploring the region. **Pros:** beautiful design; great location for outdoor activities; access to geothermal pools and float gear. **Cons:** past guests report that the rooms can get quite hot; lackluster buffet breakfast; basic amenities given room rate. [$] *Rooms from: ISK 35999* ✉ *Stórarjóður* ☎ *354/435–1551* 🌐 *www.hotelhusafell.com* 🛏 *48 rooms* 🍴 *No meals.*

Activities

★ **Sturlureykir Horse Farm**

GUIDED TOURS | Horseback riding is a popular activity all across Iceland, and the family-run Sturlureykir Horse Farm will let you take in the sights with help from one of their friendly steeds. The farm offers horse rentals, as well as guided tours. You can also pay a visit to the stable, where one of the family members will walk you through what it's like to work and live at a horse farm in Iceland's countryside. ✉ *Sturlureykir Horse Farm, 320 Reykholt* ☎ *354/691–0280* 🌐 *www.sturlureykirhorses.is.*

Snæfellsjökull National Park

209 km (130 miles) from Reykjavík

A national park since June 2001, Snæfellsjökull is a treasure chest of Icelandic natural attractions: jaw-dropping scenery you can't see many other places around the world. The national park can be seen in a single day—or even an afternoon if you really push it—but it's nice to spend a few days in the area so you can take full advantage of local hiking opportunities. The main draw of this national park is its namesake glacier, which you can summit with the help of local guides and tour operators. If you're looking for some added perspective, watch the original film adaptation of Jules Verne's *Journey to Center of the Earth*—some of this 1959 film takes place in the area, and the 2008 remake was filmed here.

GETTING HERE AND AROUND

Plenty of tour buses take people between Snæfellsjökull National Park and Reykjavík, but if you're looking to build your own itinerary, renting a car is your best bet. The drive from Reykjavík on a clear day is a real treat. Once you're inside the park, there are plenty of signs directing you to the area's most popular viewpoints and attractions. Roads are relatively well maintained, but do keep an eye on the weather as a heavy bout of rain can turn this area into a bit of a mud pit.

Sights

Snæfellsjökull

NATURE SITE | On a clear day, you can see this 700,000-year-old glacier from Reykjavík. Book with local tour outfitters to hike the glacier or even ride a special terrain-specific bike on it. This is the place that inspired Jules Verne's *Journey to the Center of the Earth*.

Hotels

★ **Hotel Búdir**

$$$$ | HOTEL | After you see the iconic Búðakirkja, you'll dream of nights of peaceful slumber under the stars surrounded by fields, and the Hotel Búdir is the closest you'll come. **Pros:** world-class restaurant; prime location in Snæfellsjökull National Park; the quietest hotel you'll ever stay in. **Cons:** expensive; breakfast not included with room rate; some past guests report cool service from staff. $ *Rooms from: ISK 41500* ✉ *356 Snæfellsbær* ☎ *354/435-6700* ⊕ *www. hotelbudir.is* ⇆ *28 rooms* ⦿ *No meals.*

Activities

⭐ Vatnshellir

GUIDED TOURS | This cave leads to close-up views of an ancient lava tube that last flowed 8,000 years ago. There's a small building at the cave opening in Snæfellsbær where you can buy tickets for the tour; hard hats are provided. ✉ *Gufuskalar, 360 Snaefellsbaer* ☎ *354/787–0001* ⊕ *www.vatnshellir.is* ✉ *ISK 3750.*

Hellissandur

203 km (126 miles) from Reykjavík

This village on the northwestern tip of Snæfellsnes Peninsula may be small— don't expect a bustling scene here—but there are some sights that make it worth a stop on your trip. Given the lack of hotels in the area, though, it's best to find another locale to lie your head and reserve Hellissandur for a stop on your tour of the west coast.

GETTING HERE AND AROUND

Driving here from Reykjavík is simple and obstacle-free (as long as the weather is fair) with beautiful scenery. Route 54 will take you along the coast all the way up from Borgarnes. If you're trying to get here by bus, it gets a bit trickier. Take Bus 57 from Reykjavík to Borgarnes, and then grab a seat on Bus 58 from Borgarnes to Stykkishólmur. From there, take Bus 82 to Hellissandur (the last stop on that route). Once you're in Hellissandur, the city is walkable, though you'll want a car to explore some of the more remote sights.

◉ Sights

⭐ Fishermen's Park and Maritime Museum

MUSEUM | FAMILY | What better place to visit in one of the oldest fishing villages in Iceland? The Fishermen's Park and Maritime Museum has a number of traditional turf houses you can explore while learning all about the industry that supported this community. Part of the museum is the back garden (free), where you'll find large whalebones from the nearby shore. If you're feeling strong, you can try to lift one of the Steintök, or lifting stones, that local people used to showcase their strength years ago. There are four total that range in weight from 50 to 339 pounds. ✉ *Utnesvegur, Hellissandur* ☎ *354/844–5969* ⊕ *hemaritimemuseum-hellissandi.business.site* ✉ *ISK 1300.*

🍴 Restaurants

⭐ Viðvík

$$$$ | SEAFOOD | If you want the best meal you can get in Hellissandur—and possibly the entire region—head to Viðvík. One peek at the menu, and you'll see how it earned its 2019 Certificate of Excellence. **Known for:** three-course tasting menu; next-level service; family-owned vibe. $ *Average main: ISK 5200* ✉ *360 Hellissandur, Hellissandur* ☎ *354/436–1026* ⊕ *www.facebook.com/vidvikrestaurant* ⊘ *Closed Mon.; closed Oct.–Apr.*

Ólafsvík

195 km (121 miles) from Reykjavík

Ólafsvík was once an important port between Denmark and Iceland in the 17th and 18th centuries. Today, it's a quiet fishing village with incredible curb appeal. Bird-watching and hiking are beloved activities in this area, and it's the perfect town to use as a base for exploring nearby Snæfellsjökull National Park.

GETTING HERE AND AROUND
Ólafsvík is located right on Route 54, making it an easy drive up along the western coast. If you're trying to get here via public transportation, you can do so by way of Stykkishólmur. Hop on Strætó Bus 57 from Reykjavík and get off at Borgarnes. From there, take Bus 58 to Stykkishólmur. You can get to Ólafsvík from Stykkishólmur on Bus 82 (it'll be the last stop). Getting around Ólafsvík is simple, and the city can be explored by foot. You'll need a car to see some of the more remote sights.

🍴 Restaurants

★ Hraun
$$$ | SEAFOOD | This picture-perfect Nordic restaurant on the water checks all of the boxes—quaint decor, cozy vibes, and great food—but it's the service that keeps people coming back again and again. Whether you're looking for menu advice or suggestions on what to do in the area, the friendly staff will help you out. **Known for:** fantastic service; locally sourced ingredients; surf and turf. $ *Average main: ISK 4300* ✉ *Grundarbraut 2, Ólafsvík* ☎ *354/431-1030* ⊕ *www.hraunrestaurant.com.*

★ Kaldilækur
$ | CAFÉ | Take a break from your tour of the west coast for a slice of cake at this quaint coffee shop. They have solid coffee and a great selection of baked goods—everything you need to keep you going while sightseeing. **Known for:** date cake; friendly service; really cold beer. $ *Average main: ISK 1000* ✉ *Mýrarholt 2, Ólafsvík* ☎ *354/846-6619* ⊕ *www.kaldilaekur.is.*

Grundarfjörður

175 km (109 miles) from Reykjavík

Grundarfjörður is known for being home to Kirkjufell, a mountain just outside of town with a strangely shaped peak. The town itself hasn't much to speak of, but it delivers the essentials: a grocery store, gas station, hostel, and a few restaurants. Don't miss the waterfalls just past the mountain—if you get there early enough, you'll have the entire area to yourself.

GETTING HERE AND AROUND
If you're driving, you can reach Grundarfjörður by continuing along Route 54 out of Ólafsvík. By bus, you can take Strætó Bus 57 from Reykjavík to Borgarnes, then Bus 58 to Stykkishólmur, and finally Bus 82 to Grundarfjörður. This is the same route to Ólafsvík, though you'll be getting off a stop sooner (if traveling from Reykjavík).

👁 Sights

Kirkjufell
NATURE SITE | FAMILY | It's possible to climb "Church Mountain," but you might want to enlist the help of a local guide to get to the top. At the peak, you'll find fossils and other remnants from years past. Don't miss the nearby waterfall, Kirkjufellsfoss, which is especially striking early in the morning. ✉ *Grundarfjörður.*

Stykkishólmur

171 km (106 miles) from Reykjavík

You can't really get a bad view from any of the towns in West Iceland, but Stykkishólmur harbor—surrounded by tiny islands—is truly special. Once you tire of the water views, take a walk through town. Stykkishólmur is known for its historic homes, which have been carefully renovated over time. There are plenty of museums, restaurants, and hotels that you can take an entire day (or two) in this area.

Aerial view of Grundarfjörður and Kirkjufell.

GETTING HERE AND AROUND

For drivers, take Route 54 out of Grundarfjörður until you hit the end in Stykkishólmur. You can also access this town by Strætó via Borgarnes. Take Bus 57 from Reykjavík to Borgarnes and then take a seat on Bus 58, which will bring you to Stykkishólmur. The city is walkable, but a car is recommended if you plan on exploring outside the city limits.

🍴 Restaurants

★ Narfeyrarstofa
$$$ | **SEAFOOD** | This restaurant is located in the oldest section of Stykkishólmur inside of a bright, airy building. The menu is full of local seafood, as well as lamb from the region. **Known for:** first-rate seafood; quaint interior design; blue mussels from the bay. [$] *Average main: ISK 4250* ✉ *Aðalgata 3, Stykkishólmur* ☎ *354/533-1119* 🌐 *www.narfeyrarstofa.is.*

★ Sjávarpakkhúsið
$$$ | **SEAFOOD** | The fresh catch of the day, sourced from local fishermen, is a crowd pleaser at Sjávarpakkhúsið. Come early for a meal at this popular spot; dinnertime can get crowded with locals enjoying the view of Stykkishólmur harbor. **Known for:** great harbor views; fresh catch of the day; local favorite. [$] *Average main: ISK 3250* ✉ *Hafnargata 2, Stykkishólmur* ☎ *354/438–1800* 🌐 *www.sjavarpakkhusid.is.*

Flatey

208 km (129 miles) from Reykjavík

Visit Flatey Island and you'll feel that you've been cast adrift in time. It was once a busy fishing community, but today only five residents live on the island year-round—which makes sense, given that it's really accessible only during the warm summer months. There's only one hotel on the island, so make sure to plan ahead for this truly unique experience; it might just be the quietest place in the country, with only occasional birdsong breaking the silence.

GETTING HERE AND AROUND

There's only one way on and off the island: by Seatours ferry, which runs less frequently in the winter. The island is small—a little over a mile long and about half a mile wide—and a good thing it is, since no cars are allowed on the island and you have to get around on foot. The hotel tends to fill up quickly during prime summer months.

TOURS

Seatours

BOAT TOURS | To get to Flatey, hop on the Seatours boat at Stykkishólmur; tickets cost ISK 3,060 in winter and ISK 3,920 in summer. Seatours have teamed up with the Hotel Flatey, which offers a discounted room rate with the purchase of a round-trip ferry ticket. The hotel is open only during the summer, so you can't spend the night any other time of year. ✉ *Smiðjustígur 3, Flatey* ☎ *354/433-2254* 🌐 *www.seatours.is.*

Hotels

★ **Hotel Flatey**

$$ | **B&B/INN** | Hotel Flatey is the only accommodation on the entire island, but luckily it's a beautiful property with a lot of charm. **Pros:** incredibly serene and quiet; very unique experience; cozy rooms and communal spaces. **Cons:** getting here is a commitment; not open during the winter months; no nearby nightlife. [$] *Rooms from: ISK 28500* ✉ *Flatey* ☎ *354/422–7610* 🌐 *www.hotelflatey.is/wordpress* 🛏 *11 rooms* 🍴 *Free Breakfast.*

Grindavík

About 52 km (32 miles) southeast of Reykajvík

Life in Grindavík has pretty much revolved around fishing for the past 10 centuries, but over the past few years it has seen remarkable growth as a tourist destination. It is, after all, the home of the world-famous Blue Lagoon.

GETTING HERE AND AROUND

On Route 41 to Reykjanesbær, take a left turn and take Route 43 to Grindavík. Bus 88 goes from Keflavík to Grindavík twice daily on weekdays; on weekends it only goes from Grindavík to the crossroads, where you must connect to Bus 55.

VISITOR INFORMATION

Saltfisksetur Information Desk

Here you can pick up maps of hiking trails and get insights into the many natural wonders of the region. There is also a small souvenir shop and a cafeteria. ✉ *Hafnargata 12a, Grindavík* ☎ *354/420-1190.*

Sights

★ **Blue Lagoon**

HOT SPRINGS | This world-renowned therapeutic pool is now a sheltered site where man-made structures blend with geologic formations. A reception area includes food concessions and boutiques where you can buy health products made from the lagoon's mineral-rich ingredients. Bathing suits are available to rent, and high-tech bracelets keep track of your locker code, any purchases, and the length of your visit. The lagoon is only 20 minutes from Keflavík Airport and 50 minutes from Reykjavík by car. Buses run from the BSÍ bus terminal in Reykjavík to the Blue Lagoon frequently. Booking in advance is essential. For a more personalized experience, you can also book a spa treatment at the lagoon's on-site Retreat Hotel, whether or not you're staying at the hotel. This is a little-known way to have your own private lagoon experience. ✉ *Bláa lónið, Norðurljósavegur 9, Grindavík* ☎ *354/420–8800* 🌐 *www.bluelagoon.com* 🎟 *ISK 6990.*

★ **Valhnúkur**

NATURE SITE | Valhnúkur mountain was formed in a single geologic event, and while exploring this magical stretch of

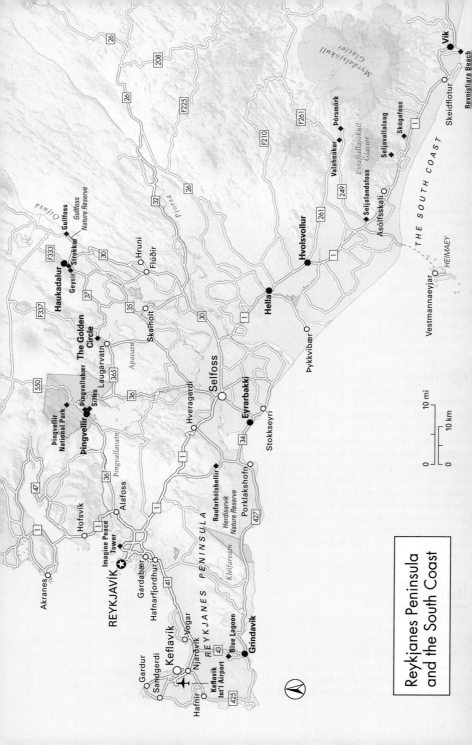

Reykjanes Peninsula
and the South Coast

The world-famous Blue Lagoon in Grindavík is a therapeutic geological wonder.

coastline, you can see evidence of the different phases of the eruption. Tuff forms during an explosive eruption, and pillow lava forms when lava flows underwater. Out on the sea you can see majestic black cliffs that serve as castles for birds. A bit farther out you can see the famous Eldey Island, where the great auk (a now-extinct species of bird) used to live. The auks survived the longest in Iceland, but the last great auk was killed on June 3, 1844, for a Danish natural history collector. Eldey is now a bird sanctuary. To reach Valhnúkur, take the road that leads off Route 425 through lava fields. Turn right (the turn is marked, "Reykjanesviti"), at the T-intersection and go 900 meters on an unpaved road, past the impressive Reykjanesviti lighthouse. On the way back, take the left branch at the T-intersection, and in 500 meters you'll reach Gunnuhver, Icleand's biggest mud pool. ✉ *Valahnúkur, Efstahraun 9, Grindavík.*

🍴 Restaurants

★ Moss Restaurant

$$$$ | SCANDINAVIAN | A stellar experience for the senses, the set menus at Moss Restaurant take diners on an Iceland-inspired food journey. Situated at the highest point of the Blue Lagoon, guests gaze through floor-to-ceiling windows upon the moonlike surroundings while enjoying delicious and diverse dishes made from seasonal produce gathered from the mountains, the rivers, the mossy fields, and the sea. **Known for:** recommended by the 2019 Michelin Guide; chef's table menu; outstanding vegetarian and vegan options. [$] *Average main: ISK 12100* ✉ *Norðurljósavegur 11, Grindavík* ☎ *354/420-8700* 🌐 *www.bluelagoon.is.*

A major site in the Golden Circle, the Geysir shoots boiling water and steam 100 feet in the air.

The Golden Circle

About 50 km (31 miles) northeast of Reykjavík. Take Ring Rd. about 11½ km (7 miles) just past the town of Mosfellsbær; turn right on Rte. 36, Þingvallavegur.

The Golden Circle is a famous tourist route comprising three famous natural sights: Þingvellir, Geysir, and Gullfoss. As a result of its popularity the route is often crowded with tourists, but few dare to skip it—seeing these natural wonders is a once-in-a-lifetime experience. The last stop along the Golden Circle route is the thundering 105-foot-high Gullfoss (Golden Falls), a double cascade in the river Hvítá that turns at right angles mid-drop into a dramatic chasm. It's the largest-volume falls in Europe and a majestic sight any time of year, but during the cold winter the outer layers of the waterfall can freeze, creating a dramatic effect. Watch your step and stick to the path. Þingvellir National Park has its own section in this chapter, and Geysir is listed under the town of Haukadalur.

TOURS

★ Arctic Adventures

ADVENTURE TOURS | Rafting in the canyon just below the majestic Gullfoss while being sprayed by the Hvítá River, which runs all the way from Langjökull glacier, is an incredible and exhilarating experience. For over 30 years Arctic Adventures have been offering whitewater rafting to people of all ages who crave some excitement while visiting Iceland. After the tour you'll be greeted by a hot sauna, with the option of a refreshing beer or barbecue dinner. You can arrange a pickup in Reykjavík or meet them on location in Drummboddstaðir. ✉ *Arctic Adventures, Drumbroddstaðir, Haukadalur* ☎ *354/562–7000* ⊕ *www.adventures. is* 🏷 *ISK 13900.*

👁 Sights

Gullfoss

BODY OF WATER | **FAMILY** | There used to be a modest visitor center named in memory of Sigríður Tómasdóttir, who fought against a hydroelectric reservoir scheme that would have flooded the falls in the early 20th century. Today it's a tour-booking center, a small shop, and a restaurant that prides itself on a warm and filling Icelandic meat soup. The center's bathrooms are free to use.

From the first stop in the Golden Circle, Þingvellir, continue east on Route 36, turn left on route 365, and turn left again on Route 37 at Laugarvatn. When Route 37 ends, turn left and take Route 35 northeast to Hótel Geysir, next to the hot springs; from there it's another 10 minutes on to the falls. Gullfoss can also be reached by private bus. Reykajvík Excursions' "Iceland On Your Own" service runs between Reykjavík and Akureyri, stopping at Geysir and Gullfoss en route. In summer, that bus leaves daily at 8 am from BSÍ Bus Terminal in Reykjavík. The trip takes about 2½ hours, since the bus stops at major sites for 30 minutes to give passengers time to explore. ✉ *Biskaupstungubraut, Selfoss* ☎ *354/486–6500* 🌐 *www.gullfoss.is.*

Hotels

Hótel Gullfoss

$$ | **HOTEL** | **FAMILY** | Family-run for over 20 years, this hotel sits in a valley just five minutes from the magnificent Gullfoss. **Pros:** great location; country-style cooking at the hotel restaurant; spacious and modern rooms. **Cons:** no hot tub; quite busy; no entertainment in the area. [$] *Rooms from: ISK 24600* ✉ *Brattholt* ☎ *354/486–8979* 🌐 *www.hotelgullfoss.is* 🛏 *35* 🍴 *Free Breakfast.*

Þingvellir

About 50 km (31 miles) northeast of Reykjavík

After not quite an hour's drive from Reykjavík along Route 36, across the Mosfellsheiði heath, the broad lava plain of Þingvellir suddenly opens up in front of you. This has been the nation's most hallowed place since AD 930, when the settler Grímur Geitskór chose it as the first site for what is often called the world's oldest parliament, the Icelandic Alþingi (General Assembly). In July of each year delegates from all over the country camp at Þingvellir for two weeks, meeting to pass laws and render judicial sentences. Iceland remained a nation-state ruled solely by the people without a central government until 1262, when it came under the Norwegian crown. Even then—and although it had lost its law-making powers—the Alþingi continued to meet at Þingvellir until 1798.

GETTING HERE AND AROUND

The easiest way to get to Þingvellir is with a rental car. Take Ring Road about 11½ km just past the town of Mosfellsbær; turn right on Route 36, Þingvallavegur. Parking per vehicle costs between ISK 300 and ISK 750. No buses currently stop here, but Þingvellir is a stop on almost every tour of the Golden Circle.

VISITOR INFORMATION

Þingvellir Visitor Centre

At the top of the Almannagjá rift is the Þingvellir Visitor Centre with information about the ecology and geology of the park, as well as information about its extensive history. There's also a small cafeteria, a souvenir shop, and an interactive exhibit about the park. In front of the center are parking lots (ISK 750) and toilets. ✉ *Þingvellir, Þingvellir* ☎ *354/482-3613* 🌐 *www.thingvellir.is.*

Sights

★ **Þingvallabær**

HOUSE | Across the plain from Lögberg stands the church and the gabled manor house of Þingvallabær, where the government of Iceland often hosts visiting heads of state. Þingvallarkirkja, the church of Þingvellir, is open daily to visitors over the summertime. Free one-hour tours of the area are offered every day in summer, leaving from the church at 10 am and 3 pm. Note that the house of Þingvallabær is the official summer residence of the prime minister of Iceland and can only be admired from the outside. ✉ *Þingvellir, Þingvellir* ☎ *354/482–2600* 🌐 *www.thingvellir.is* 🎫 *Free* ☞ *Contact the information center for winter hrs.*

★ **Þingvellir National Park**

NATIONAL/STATE PARK | **FAMILY** | Located at the northern end of Þingvallavatn—Iceland's largest lake—Þingvellir National Park is a powerful symbol of Icelandic heritage. Many national celebrations are held here, and it was named a UNESCO World Heritage Site in 2004. Besides its historical interest, Þingvellir holds a special appeal for naturalists: it is the geologic meeting point of two continents. At Almannagjá, on the west side of the plain, is the easternmost edge of the North American tectonic plate, otherwise submerged in the Atlantic Ocean. Over on the plain's east side, at the Heiðargjá Gorge, you are at the westernmost edge of the Eurasian plate.

A path down into Almannagjá from the top of the gorge overlooking Þingvellir leads straight to the high rock wall of **Lögberg** (Law Rock), where the person chosen as guardian of the laws would recite them from memory. At the far end of the gorge is the **Öxarárfoss** (Öxará Waterfall); beautiful, peaceful picnic spots sit just beyond it. Behind Lögberg the river cascades down and forms the forbidding **Drekkingarhylur** pool. ✉ *Þingvellir, Þingvellir* 🌐 *www.thingvellir.is* 🎫 *Free; fee for parking.*

★ **Silfra**

BODY OF WATER | Most people visit Þingvellir for its historical and geological significance, but in this same place another perspective awaits those who don't mind trading their walking boots and windbreaker for a dry suit and flippers. Named one of the top three freshwater dives on the planet, at Silfra you can snorkel on the surface of crystal clear water or dive to depths up to 30 meters. Exploring these underwater cracks is like entering another world: The silence is striking—a perfect companion to the vision of muted blues, bejeweled with silver globules of gas mushrooming to the surface from the divers below. An adventure in this underwater wonderland between the continents of North America and Europe leaves you with vivid images but no words. For tours with qualified instructors, book with DIVE.IS. ✉ *National Park Þingvellir, Þingvellir* ☎ *354/578–6200* 🌐 *www.dive.is.*

🛏 Hotels

★ **ION Luxury Adventure Hotel**

$$$$ | **HOTEL** | Clean, green, and emerging from the landscape, the ION Hotel is a striking sight in the primordial surrounds of Nesjavellir, a geothermal area close to Þingvellir National Park. **Pros:** well serviced by tour operators providing a range of outdoor activities; striking design in an unusual landscape; luxury spa with an oudoor hot tub and bar. **Cons:** culturally speaking, it's completely off-piste (no nearby shops, bars, or restaurants); proven difficult for some cars to reach in winter; breakfast not on par with the rest of the hotel. [$] *Rooms from: ISK 40500* ✉ *Nesjavöllum við Þingvallarvatn, Selfoss* ☎ *354/578–3720* 🌐 *www.ioniceland.is* 🛏 *46 rooms* 🍴 *No meals.*

Haukadalur

About 30 km (19 miles) northeast of Laugarvatn and about 108 km (67 miles) north east of Reykajvíkand

The geothermal field in Haukadalur is one of Iceland's classic tourist spots. The famous Geysir hot spring (the literal origin of the term *geyser*) erupts only a few times a year, but the more reliable Strokkur spouts boiling water as high as 100 feet at five-minute intervals. In the same area there are small natural vents from which steam rises, as well

Raufarhólshellir is the fourth-largest lava cave to be discovered in Iceland.

as beautiful exotic-color pools. Don't crowd Strokkur, and always be careful when approaching hot springs or mud pots—the ground may be treacherous, suddenly giving way beneath you. Stay on formal paths or established tracks.

GETTING HERE AND AROUND

From Þingvellir, continue east on Route 36, turn left on Route 365, and left again on Route 37; drive until you see Laugarvatn. Bus 73 runs to Laugarvatn from Selfoss daily and takes 1 hour 15 minutes. Reykajvík Excursions' "Iceland on Your Own" bus service stops at Laugarvatn en route between Reykjavík and Akureryri; in summer, it runs daily at 8 am from BSÍ Bus Terminal in Reykjavík.

From Laugarvatn, take Route 37 northeast for 30 km (18 miles) to the junction with Route 35, which you'll take 10 km (6 miles) northeast to get to Geysir. (From Lake Laugarvatn you can take the short spur Route 364 southwest to Route 37.)

TOURS

The Cave People

HISTORIC SITE | On this guided tour it feels like you've been transported back 100 years, to a time when certain Icelanders still lived in caves. Laugarvatnshellar are two man-made caves near Laugarvatn; no one has yet determined exactly when they were made or by whom. In the beginning of the 20th century two separate couples moved into the caves and lived there for a couple of years. Their "house" in the caves has now been redone, and these charismatic guides will lead you on a journey and tell you interesting stories of the cave people. Afterwards you are offered coffee or tea and some Icelandic pastries. ⊠ *Laugarvatnshellar, Háholt 2c, Haukadalur* ⊕ *Off main road between Þingvellir and Laugarvatn* ☎ *354/ 888-1922* ⊕ *www. thecavepeople.is.*

Geysir Hestar

HORSEBACK RIDING | FAMILY | This Icelandic horse farm is only 4 km (2½ miles) east of the famous Geysir. They manage over

You're likely to see a rainbow at Skógafoss, a waterfall that is 60 meters high.

100 horses and offer various riding experiences for the whole family—special rides around the farm for small children, day trips through the magnificent Hvítá River and up the canyon to Gullfoss, as well as week-long trips. ✉ *Kjóastaðir 2, Haukadalur* 📞 *354/847-1046* 🌐 *www. geysirhestar.com.*

👁 Sights

★ Geysir
NATURE SITE | The world famous Geysir (from which all other geysers get their name), shoots boiling water and steam 100 feet in the air. From Þingvellir, the first stop in the Golden Circle, continue east on Route 36, turn left on Route 365, and turn left again on Route 37 at Laugarvatn. At the end of Route 37, turn left and take Route 35 northeast to Hótel Geysir, which is next to the hot springs. Geysir can also be reached by bus. Reykajvík Excursions' "Iceland on Your Own" bus service between Reykjavík and Akureyri stops at Geysir and Gullfoss en route. In summer, it leaves daily at 8

am from BSÍ bus terminal in Reykjavík; the journey takes about two hours, since the bus stops at major sites and waits 30 minutes in order for people to explore. ✉ *Haukadalur.*

★ Strokkur
NATURE SITE | This highly popular activated geyser is located in the Geysir Geothermal area, and is also along the Golden Circle. Though not as powerful as the Great Geysir, it does erupt much more frequently. ✉ *Haukadalur.*

🍴 Restaurants

★ Efstidalur II
$$ | **BURGER** | This family farm, located 12 km (7½ miles) northeast of Laugarvatn, serves amazing farm-fresh dishes at their restaurant, Hlöðuloftið, like stuffed trout from the nearby lake and hamburgers from their own meat. But their downstairs ice cream bar truly takes farm-to-table to another level: enjoy their delicious homemade ice cream while watching the dairy cows through a big glass window.

Known for: freshly baked rye bread; the Skyburger; family-run. $ *Average main: ISK 2750* ✉ *Efstidalur, Haukadalur* ☎ *354/486-1186* ⊕ *www.efstidalur.is.*

Eyrarbakki

About 61 km (38 miles) southeast of Reykavík

Eyrarbakki and its neighbor fishing village Stokkseyri, 6 km (4 miles) apart, are often regarded as sibling towns because of their history and proximity. The two towns are built by the beautiful, black seaside, with colorful houses and friendly inhabitants. Since 1852 the children of the two towns have attended a joined school. They are both located between two glacial rivers, Ölfusár and Þjórsár.

GETTING HERE AND AROUND
From Selfoss, both Eyrarbakki and Stokkseyri can be reached in about 10 minutes by car. Stokkseyri and Eyrarbakki can also be accessed through the less traveled but beautiful South Coast Road. From Grindavík take Route 42 (the South Coast Road) that will lead you through the town of Þorlákshöfn. When you exit Þorlákshöfn, take Route 38 and take a right turn at Route 34.

◉ Sights

★ Raufarhólshellir
CAVE | At 1,360 meters, the Lava Tunnel is the fourth-longest lava cave discovered in Iceland. The cave is remarkably spacious—from 10 to 30 meters wide and up to 10 meters tall—making it quite easy and accessible for most. Walking along the lava's 5,200-year-old path is a humbling experience in itself, and the views of the geological formations and spectacular colors are extraordinary. In winter, big crystal-like ice sculptures form inside the cave entrance. The standard Lava Tunnel tour takes about an hour. ✉ *Þorlákshafnarvegur, Eyrarbakki* ☎ +

354/760-1000 ⊕ *www.thelavatunnel.is* ✉ *ISK 6,900.*

Hella and Hvolsvöllur

Hella is 94 km (58 miles) east of Reykjavík; Hvolsvöllur is 66 km (107 miles) east of Reykjavík.

Hella is a small agricultural community that sits on the banks of the river Ytri-Rangá. Home to the world's largest Icelandic horse show, it's one of Iceland's most important horse-breeding areas. On good weather days you can see the volcano Hekla watching over the town.

The Ring Road runs through the small town of Hvolsvölllur, east of Hella. The towns surrounding this area feature prominently in "Njálssaga," one of the most famous old Icelandic sagas. Today the town provides services for the surrounding farms and the area's ever-growing tourism.

GETTING HERE AND AROUND
The Ring Road passes through Hella on its way east. Frequent buses stop at the Olís Petrol Staion in Hella, including Reykjavík Excursions and Sterna. Strætó Bus 51 stops at Hella daily on its way from Reykjavík to Höfn, and Bus 52 as well.

VISITOR INFORMATION
Árhús Information Center Hella
Located right off the Ring Road, the staff here will provide you with maps, as well as information about the region and guided tours. The center is open only from 7 am to 9 am and from 3 pm to 10 pm. ✉ *Rangárbakkar 6, Hella* ☎ *354/487-5577* ⊕ *www.arhus.is.*

◉ Sights

★ Seljalandsfoss
BODY OF WATER | This waterfall is situated right off the ring road, East of Hvolsvöllur, so anyone who drives by can't help but marvel at its majesty. Seljalandsfoss is

The cliffs at this black sand beach are home to many puffins during summer.

65 meters tall and its special trade is that you can walk behind it. Be ready to be heavily drizzled by the fresh mountain water but be careful because the steps can be slippery. Bathroom facilities and a small coffee shop can be found by the parking lot. There are also lots of beautiful small walking paths all around that can easily add to the experience of this unique waterfall. ⊠ *Þórsmerkurvegur, Hvolsvöllur.*

★ Seljavallalaug

HOT SPRINGS | In a narrow valley beneath the now world-famous Eyjafjallajökull is one of the more authentic geothermal baths around with the hot springs from the mountain running straight into the pool. The 25-meter pool was built in 1923 and is considered semi-abandoned and therefore is free of charge. There are changing rooms next to the pool. ⊠ *Seljavallalaug, Hvolsvöllur ✛ From Rte. 1 take Rte. 242 to Seljavellir, and then it is a 15-minute walk from the parking lot.*

★ Skógafoss

BODY OF WATER | Farther east, about 25 minutes away from Seljalandsfoss, you will find another falling beauty, framed in by green hills in the summer and ice during winter. The waterfall Skógafoss is located at Skógar, a small Icelandic village, south of the glacier Eyjafjallajökull. Skógafoss is around 60 meters high, 25 meters wide and is square in shape. A steep staircase leads up to the top of the hill above the falls, and on the way up you will often see a rainbow. ⊠ *Hvolsvöllur.*

★ Þórsmörk

NATURE PRESERVE | Sheltered between three towering glaciers (Tindafjallajökull, Eyjafjallajökull, and Mýrdalsjökull), and surrounded by three rivers (Krossá, Þröngá, and Markarfljót), is the nature reserve Þórsmörk. Named after the hammer-wielding Norse god Þór, it is among the most popular hiking destination in Iceland. At Þórsmörk you will find snow-capped mountain ridges, twisted gorges, moss-covered caves, and hidden waterfalls. The area has scenic surprises around every corner making it a hiker's paradise. The views are especially dramatic in the fall when the whole valley turns into spectacle of colors, from oranges, yellows, and reds to the ever-present lava black of the rock beneath. It can be hard to get to, especially during winter, but it is truly worth the hassle in any season. Þórsmörk cannot be reached in a regular car or even regular 4WDs. You will need to take an amphibious bus or with a guide (*see: Tours at the beginning of the chapter*) in a Superjeep to cross the unpredictable and dangerous rivers that close off the valley to the south. ✉ *Hvolsvöllur* ✣ *158 km from Reykjavík.*

Hotels

Hotel Rangá

$$$$ | **HOTEL** | This rustic four-star hotel with uniquely decorated themed rooms and outdoor Jacuzzis is in the countryside just east of Hella. **Pros:** great honeymoon stay; excellent restaurant (modern Nordic cuisine with French and Italian influences); celebrity hot spot. **Cons:** very hyped; decor is more "country" than "luxury"; few entertainment options at night. [$] *Rooms from: ISK 45000* ✉ *Hella* ☎ *354/487–5700* 🌐 *www.hotelranga.is* 🛏 *51 rooms (including several suites in the World Pavilion and the Master Royal Suite)* 🍴 *Free Breakfast.*

★ **Skálakot Hotel**

$$$$ | **B&B/INN** | Right by the root of a mountain lies this horse farm that has been in the same family for seven generations, and their newly built, incredibly cozy yet luxurious manor. **Pros:** guided horseback rides to Seljalandsfoss from the hotel; luxurious guestrooms with cozy bathrobes and lovely selection of soaps; candlelit farm-to-table dinners in the dining room. **Cons:** standard breakfast; no hot tub; expensive. [$] *Rooms from: ISK 78700* ✉ *Skálakoti, Hvolsvöllur* ☎ *354/487-8953* 🌐 *skalakot.is* 🛏 *14 rooms* 🍴 *Free Breakfast.*

Vík

186 km (116 miles) from Reykjavík

A layer of mist seems clings to the little town of Vík all year long, giving it a bewitching atmosphere. This southernmost town in Iceland is known for its dramatic black sea stacks, Reynisdrangar, rising out of the ocean. Surrounded by some of the most scenic glacial views imaginable on the north side, and black sand, puffin-populated beaches on either side of the Ring Road, Vík is an excellent base of operations when exploring the south coast. You'll also find several restaurants, a liquor store, and a grocery store.

Sights

Reynisfjara

BEACH—SIGHT | Take route 215 for 5 km to reach the popular black sand beach, Reynisfjara, located on the western side of Reynisfjall. The surrounding cliffs are the home to thousands of puffins in the summer, as well as arctic terns and fulmars. The dramatic splattering of the explosive waves on the obsidian black beach is a thrill to watch, but for safety reasons visitors must stay far from the edge of the water. The waves off Reynisfjara can rise quickly, sweeping people up in seconds, which has resulted in many accidents and even deaths. Offshore are the towering basalt sea stacks, Reynisdrangar. Their silhouette is seen from both Vík and Reynisfara. ✉ *Route 215, Vík.*

486

Index

seasonal vegetables. It's a basic dish, but it can't be beat—and it's really, really good at this small restaurant in the heart of the city. **Known for:** fish pans; generous portions; sharable dishes. $ *Average main: ISK 2300* ✉ *Lækjargata 6, Miðbær* ☎ *354/546–0095* ⊕ *www.messinn.com.*

★ Restaurant Reykjavík

$$$$ | SEAFOOD | Housed in a 19th-century building (with a fascinating history printed in the menu) this beautifully designed, spacious, and clean restaurant offers the finest fish buffet in town, served by an attentive staff. Guests will be warmed throughout by its gentle atmospheric charm and will delight in both the elegant decor and the presentation of quality dishes. **Known for:** extensive seafood buffet; reasonable prices for an incredible meal; tourist hot spot. $ *Average main: ISK 6450* ✉ *Vesturgata 2, Miðbær* ☎ *354/552–3030* ⊕ *www.restaurantreykjavik.is.*

Sæta Svínið Gastropub

$$ | SCANDINAVIAN | If your ideal dinner consists of eating on a patio with a good beer in hand, you won't be disappointed by this lively pub. You can even mingle with the locals for a rousing game of bingo on Sunday night. **Known for:** flavorful grilled salmon; outdoor seating (great for people-watching in the square); lamb sandwich with waffle fries. $ *Average main: ISK 3990* ✉ *Hafnarstræti, Miðbær* ☎ *354/555–2900* ⊕ *www.saetasvinid.is.*

Tapas Barinn

$$$ | SCANDINAVIAN | If you're interested in trying some of the more traditional dishes of Iceland (think puffin or whale), pay Tapas Barinn a visit. Here you can pass small plates among your group or opt for the more substantial Icelandic Gourmet Feast, which includes smoked puffin, minke whale, and a shot of Brennivín. **Known for:** Icelandic Gourmet Feast tasting menu; lively crowd; traditional Iceland ingredients in tapas form. $ *Average main: ISK 4990* ✉ *Vesturgata 3b, Miðbær* ☎ *354/551–2344* ⊕ *www.tapas.is.*

☕ Coffee and Quick Bites

Stofan Kaffihús

$ | CAFÉ | At Stofan Kaffihús you can find coffee from around the world, as well as small plates and cakes. What's even better is the feeling that you're hanging out in a friend's apartment or living room while you drink it, thanks to a handful of comfy couches. **Known for:** delicious cake; a worldly coffee menu; comfortable atmosphere. $ *Average main: ISK 2200* ✉ *Aðalstræti, Miðbær* ☎ *354/546-1842* ⊕ *www.facebook.com/stofan.cafe.*

🛏 Hotels

★ Hótel Borg

$$$ | HOTEL | In contrast to the ultramodern glass-and-chrome architecture around Reykjavík, the city's oldest hotel is pure 1930s art deco—from the black marble statues in the entryway to the brass-and-wood railing on the stairs to the square little coffee cups in the rooms. **Pros:** central location; lovely art deco design; good service. **Cons:** street noise can be an issue on lower floors; some visitors find the beds too firm; no a/c. $ *Rooms from: ISK 33204* ✉ *Pósthússtræti 11, Miðbær* ☎ *354/551–1440* ⊕ *www.hotelborg.is* 🛏 *107 rooms* ⊙ *No meals.*

Hótel Reykjavík Centrum

$$ | HOTEL | Situated downtown, this hotel opened its doors in the spring of 2005. **Pros:** central location; friendly staff; historical building. **Cons:** small bathrooms; no free parking; room decor lacks personality. $ *Rooms from: ISK 27141* ✉ *Aðalstræti 16, Miðbær* ☎ *354/514–6000* ⊕ *www.hotelcentrum.is* 🛏 *89 rooms* ⊙ *Free Breakfast.*

Kvosin Hotel

$$$$ | HOTEL | FAMILY | If you want to stay somewhere that offers a bit more privacy and freedom (including your own kitchen area), this hotel, located in the heart of Reykjavík next to the Dómkirkjan, should be on your radar. **Pros:** large rooms; great

488

492

Photo Credits

Fodor's ESSENTIAL SCANDINAVIA

Publisher: Stephen Horowitz, *General Manager*

Editorial: Douglas Stallings, *Editorial Director*; Jill Fergus, Jacinta O'Halloran, Amanda Sadlowski, *Senior Editors*; Kayla Becker, Alexis Kelly, Rachael Roth, *Editors*

Design: Tina Malaney, *Director of Design and Production*; Jessica Gonzalez, *Graphic Designer*; Mariana Tabares, *Design and Production Intern*

Production: Jennifer DePrima, *Editorial Production Manager*; Carrie Parker, *Senior Production Editor*; Elyse Rozelle, *Production Editor*; Jackson Pranica, *Editorial Production Assistant*

Maps: Rebecca Baer, *Senior Map Editor*; Mark Stroud (Moon Street Cartography), *Cartographers*

Photography: Viviane Teles, *Senior Photo Editor*; Namrata Aggarwal, Ashok Kumar, Carl Yu, *Photo Editors*; Rebecca Rimmer, *Photo Intern*

Business and Operations: Chuck Hoover, *Chief Marketing Officer*; Robert Ames, *Group General Manager*; Devin Duckworth, *Director of Print Publishing*; Victor Bernal, *Business Analyst*

Public Relations and Marketing: Joe Ewaskiw, *Senior Director Communications and Public Relations*; Esther Su, *Senior Marketing Manager*

Fodors.com: Jeremy Tarr, *Editorial Director*; Rachael Levitt, *Managing Editor*; Teddy Minford, *Editor*

Technology: Jon Atkinson, *Director of Technology*; Rudresh Teotia, *Lead Developer*; Jacob Ashpis, *Content Operations Manager*

Writers: Michelle Arrouas, Tim Bird, Cecilie Hauge Eggen, Annika Hipple, Erika Owen, Alexandra Pereira, Megan Starr, Birna Stefánsdóttir, Lisa Stentvedt, Aram Vardanyan, and Barbara Woolsey

Editors: Jacinta O'Halloran (lead editor); Debbie Harmsen, Maggie Kelly, Rachael Roth, Mark Sullivan

Production Editor: Jennifer DePrima

2nd Edition

ISBN 978-1-64097-252-0

ISSN 1943–0078

All details in this book are based on information supplied to us at press time. Always confirm information when it matters, especially if you're making a detour to visit a specific place. Fodor's expressly disclaims any liability, loss, or risk, personal or otherwise, that is incurred as a consequence of the use of any of the contents of this book.

SPECIAL SALES

This book is available at special discounts for bulk purchases for sales promotions or premiums. For more information, e-mail SpecialMarkets@fodors.com.

PRINTED IN THE UNITED STATES OF AMERICA

10 9 8 7 6 5 4 3 2 1

About Our Writers

Michelle Arrouas is a Danish-French journalist based in Berlin and Copenhagen. She writes travel books about Berlin and Morocco, and her work has appeared in publications such as BBC, *Roads & Kingdoms, Explore Parts Unknown*, and Adventure.com. Michelle updated our Denmark chapter.

Tim Bird settled in Helsinki in 1982, having moved to Finland from his native England. A freelance journalist, travel writer, and award-winning photographer, he has written and photographed several books about the Baltic region and contributed to hundreds of publications in Finland, the UK, the USA, and elsewhere on diverse topics. Tim updated the Finland sections of the book.

Oslo-based **Cecilie Hauge Eggen** is a freelance journalist and yoga instructor. Since 2016 she has been freelancing, enjoying the freedom to travel, write, and teach yoga. Cecilie updated the Central Norway section of Norway.

Annika Hipple is a dual citizen of the United States and Sweden and has covered Sweden for publications such as *Time Out, Sierra Magazine, Travel Age West*, and British Airways' *The Club*, as well as for her own website, Real Scandinavia. For this edition she roamed the streets of Sweden's historic cities and explored its varied landscapes.

Erika Owen is a Brooklyn-based writer and professional Iceland enthusiast. Her work has appeared in *Vogue, Bon Appétit, Departures*, and *Travel + Leisure*, among other travel and lifestyle publications. She is also the author of *The Art of Flaneuring: How to Wander with Intention and Discover a Better Life*. Erika wrote the Reykjavík, Westfjords, and West Iceland and Snæfellsnses Peninsula sections of Iceland.

Alexandra Pereira is a Scandinavia-based writer originally from Worcester, England. She worked in film and television and has written about travel and the arts for *Condé Nast Traveler, Vanity Fair, Suitcase, Playboy, The Paris Review*, and a host of international inflight magazines. Alexandra updated the Oslo and Oslofjord sections of Norway.

Birna Stefánsdóttir is a political scientist and journalist based in Reykjavík, Iceland. Birna wrote the Reykjanes Peninsula and the South Coast sections of the Iceland chapter.

Lisa Stentvedt is a travel writer and blogger from the beautiful fjords of Norway. She shares her adventures from around the world, along with her best travel tips, on her blog called "Fjords and Beaches." She brought her knowledge to the Southern Norway and Western Fjords sections of Norway.

Aram Vardanyan and **Megan Starr** are travel writers and bloggers hailing from Armenia and the United States. Their websites and projects focus on developing tourism in Scandinavia, eastern Europe, the Caucasus, and central Asia. They wrote the Trondheim and the Lofoten Islands and the Northern Norway sections of Norway.

Barbara Woolsey is a Canadian journalist who has been to over 50 countries by plane, train, and motorbike. Her work has been published by Reuters, *The Guardian,*and *USA Today*. She updated the Travel Smart chapter.